W9-ATD-816

DOING RESEARCH
in the REAL WORLD

PRAISE FOR THE SECOND EDITION

An excellent resource for people who are undertaking research, or for increasing understanding of the research process – such as for students or practitioners undertaking CPD. It is attractively presented – the writing is confident and clear. It has clear signposts for reading and using. I liked the activities, and case studies, which enable the reader to test their understanding, and also make it a real world handbook. I also thought the 'top tips' – which I look forward to testing out – were really helpful.

Miss Sue Macdonald, Education Research & Practice Development, Royal College of Midwives

When a student recommends a book to the lecturer, it's worth taking a second look at a product in what is already a relatively well-served market. This book ticks so many boxes and I intend to make this required reading.

Dr Darrell Jackson, Nova Research Centre, Redcliffe College

The book offers comprehensive learning objectives and the students find the book easy to follow. Also, the web resources that can be found for the book are great.

Mr George Shaw, Jr., School of Journalism and Mass Communication, University of South Carolina

Gray's text is an excellent text for social work students, actually one of the best books on research methods.

Professor Johann Gleich, Abteilung Köln, Katholische Hochschule Nordrhein-Westfalen

Provides a sensible real world view of research. It dispels the myth that research is a tidy, very organised process and shows how things can and do happen.

Ms Maria Burton, Department of Health and Social Care, Sheffield Hallam University

This deals with the research process in a way that is accessible and enjoyable for students of all levels. The case studies, activities and 'top tips' provide context and help to bring the subject to life.

Mr Alex Gillett, Business School, University of Teesside

THIRD
EDITION

DOING RESEARCH
in the REAL WORLD

DAVID E. GRAY

Los Angeles | London | New Delhi
Singapore | Washington DC

Los Angeles | London | New Delhi
Singapore | Washington DC

SAGE Publications Ltd
1 Oliver's Yard
55 City Road
London EC1Y 1SP

SAGE Publications Inc.
2455 Teller Road
Thousand Oaks, California 91320

SAGE Publications India Pvt Ltd
B 1/I 1 Mohan Cooperative Industrial Area
Mathura Road
New Delhi 110 044

SAGE Publications Asia-Pacific Pte Ltd
3 Church Street
#10-04 Samsung Hub
Singapore 049483

Editor: Jai Seaman
Development editors: Amy Jarrold & Robin Lupton
Digital content assistant: Isabel Drury
Production editor: Ian Antcliff
Copyeditor: Christine Bitten
Proofreader: Jennifer Hinchliffe
Indexer: Silvia Benvenuto
Marketing manager: Ben Griffin-Sherwood
Cover design: Francis Kenney
Typeset by: C&M Digitals (P) Ltd, Chennai, India
Printed and bound in Great Britain by Ashford
Colour Press Ltd

© David E. Gray 2014

First edition published 2004. Second edition published
2009. This edition 2014

Apart from any fair dealing for the purposes of
research or private study, or criticism or review, as
permitted under the Copyright, Designs and Patents
Act, 1988, this publication may be reproduced, stored
or transmitted in any form, or by any means, only with
the prior permission in writing of the publishers, or in
the case of reprographic reproduction, in accordance
with the terms of licences issued by the Copyright
Licensing Agency. Enquiries concerning reproduction
outside those terms should be sent to the publishers.

Library of Congress Control Number: 2013938404

British Library Cataloguing in Publication data

A catalogue record for this book is available from
the British Library

ISBN 978-1-4462-6018-0
ISBN 978-1-4462-6019-7 (pbk)

MIX
Paper from
responsible sources
FSC
www.fsc.org   FSC® C011748

Contents

List of Case Studies   vi
List of Figures   viii
List of Tables   xii
Guided Tour   xvi
Companion Website   xviii
About the Author   xx
Acknowledgements   xxi

1   Introduction   1

PART A: PRINCIPLES AND PLANNING FOR RESEARCH   13
2   Theoretical Perspectives and Research Methodologies   15
3   Selecting and Planning Research Proposals and Projects   39
4   Research Ethics   67
5   Searching, Critically Reviewing and Using the Literature   97

PART B: RESEARCH METHODOLOGY   125
6   Research Design: Quantitative Methods   127
7   Research Design: Qualitative Methods   159
8   Research Design: Mixed Methods   189
9   Sampling Strategies   207
10   Designing Descriptive and Analytical Surveys   235
11   Designing Case Studies   265
12   Designing Evaluations   295
13   Action Research and Change   327

PART C: DATA COLLECTION METHODS   349
14   Questionnaires   351
15   Interviewing   381
16   Non-participant Observation   411
17   Ethnography and Participant Observation   437
18   Focus Groups   467
19   Unobtrusive Measures   497
20   Secondary Analysis   513

PART D: ANALYSIS AND REPORT WRITING   535
21   Getting Started Using SPSS   537
22   Analysing and Presenting Quantitative Data   553
23   Analysing and Presenting Qualitative Data   601
24   Writing up the Research   631
25   Preparing for Presentations and Vivas   659

Glossary   679
References   693
Name Index   714
Subject Index   719

List of Case Studies

2.1	The conflict of paradigms	22
2.2	Experimental research	30
2.3	Phenomenological research	31
2.4	Analytical surveys	32
2.5	Action research	32
2.6	Heuristic research	33
3.1	Identifying a theme for research	50
3.2	Developing a research theme into a proposal	62
4.1	Examples of ethically contentious practice	71
4.2	Examples of how different ethical codes of practice deal with observation	77
4.3	Getting approval through an institution's ethics committee	80
4.4	The negative results of not gaining ethical agreement	83
4.5	The importance of getting approval in field research	84
4.6	Ethical dilemmas in research	91
5.1	Using the literature to identify research methods	99
5.2	An illustration of the literature search process	111
6.1	Getting those research question right	133
6.2	A quasi-experimental design	139
7.1	Examples of observational data gathering techniques	172
7.2	The limits of generalization	184
8.1	Mixed methods: Qualitative then Quantitative	201
8.2	Mixed methods: Quantitative then Qualitative	202
8.3	Mixed methods: Quantitative and qualitative concurrently	203
9.1	Sampling under-represented groups	229
10.1	Survey lessons from US opinion polls	238
10.2	Conducting a survey through an email discussion group	249
11.1	The taxi-dance hall	272
11.2	A case study of team working	284
11.3	Time-series analysis	285
11.4	Japanese transplant companies in the UK	290

12.1	Programme evaluation through force-field analysis	300
12.2	Invalid evaluation – getting it wrong on a Friday afternoon	317
12.3	Short supply of ethics at the Stock Exchange	322
13.1	Improving children's health through action research	341
13.2	The real world – when an action research project goes wrong	345
14.1	Applying the Q-sort methodology	356
14.2	Questionnaire piloting to get it right	374
15.1	Interviewer bias – it can drive you to drink!	390
15.2	Secret boxes, soap operas and spiders	403
16.1	How smart is covert observation?	415
16.2	Using structured observation	424
16.3	The impact of gaudy colours	427
16.4	The role of observation in market research	433
17.1	Ethnography, reciprocity and getting too close?	446
17.2	Example of an ethnographic diary	450
17.3	Challenges in ethnographic research	454
17.4	The challenges of 'getting in'	456
17.5	'Getting close' – a cautionary tale	458
17.6	The challenges of abiding by ethical codes	460
18.1	Getting a focus group to focus	480
18.2	Getting a blend of professionals together	484
18.3	AIDS Media Research Project	492
19.1	Natural accretion measures – cold coffee!	499
20.1	Imaginative use of secondary data sources	524
20.2	Reusing qualitative data sets	526
20.3	Using secondary data to conduct a meta-analysis	530
20.4	Using secondary data in a mixed methods study	532
22.1	From survey instrument to data matrix	559
23.1	Developing grounded theory – open coding	613
23.2	Developing grounded theory – selective coding	618
23.3	Coding with NVivo	625
24.1	Typical structure for an academic journal article (abridged)	644
25.1	What happens when you don't rehearse and when you do	669
25.2	Surviving the viva	676

List of Figures

1.1	Overview of the (simplified) research process	5
1.2	An overview of the typical research process	7
2.1	An illustration of how the inductive and deductive methods can be combined	18
2.2	Relationship between epistemology, theoretical perspectives, methodology and research methods	19
2.3	The elements of the research process	35
3.1	Organizational sponsorship and support networks	44
3.2	Johari window showing choices between familiar and unfamiliar work experience and personal knowledge	45
3.3	Example of project planning using a Gantt chart	51
3.4	Linking the literature and methodology via research questions	55
3.5	Proposal development flowchart	63
5.1	Touring and camping to acquire, analyse and synthesize information	100
6.1	Stages in the planning and operation of an experimental and quasi-experimental research project	129
6.2	Illustration of the relationship between dependent, independent and intervening variables	136
6.3	Interpretable and uninterpretable patterns of results in a non-equivalent control group design with pre-test and post-test	144
6.4	A 2 x 2 factorial design showing all possible combinations of factors	145
6.5	Relationship between the population, sampling frame and sample	147
6.6	Relationship between research instrument and operationally defined subject areas and the issue of validity	151
7.1	Conceptual framework for a research project on drug liberalization and policing	169
7.2	Inductive and deductive approaches and research questions	171
7.3	Example of document sheet	178
8.1	Mixing or not mixing methods: purist, situationalist and pragmatist	193
8.2	A broad variety of mixed methods research	195
8.3	Four mixed methods models	200
9.1	Simple random sample	211
9.2	Systematic sampling taking every kth unit from the listed population	212
9.3	Stratified random sampling, randomly selecting three units from each strata	213
9.4	Cluster sampling	214

| 9.5 | A taxonomy of non-probability sampling schemes | 216 |
| 9.6 | Two-dimensional mixed methods sampling model | 226 |

10.1	Stages in the survey planning process	241
10.2	Types of questionnaire	245
10.3	Google consumer survey website	248
10.4	Survey-response hierarchy-of-effects model	260

11.1	A comparison of two case study positions: inductive and deductive	269
11.2	Multiple case study method	270
11.3	Main types of case study design	275
11.4	Replication through use of multiple cases	277
11.5	Pattern matching of case study data	283
11.6	Four written forms of case study	288
11.7	Alternative written report structures	289

12.1	Cost-benefit analysis of a proposed training event	298
12.2	Force-field analysis of organizational change programme	301
12.3	The European TQM model	302
12.4	Model of schools of thought in evaluation	304
12.5	Sample opinionnaire	313
12.6	Repertory grid showing an individual's constructs of an appraisal	314
12.7	Communication methods for a variety of audiences	320
12.8	Format for an evaluation report	321
12.9	A framework for ethical evaluation	324

| 13.1 | The action research model | 334 |
| 13.2 | The data gathering process: concept mapping of team conflict within a workplace | 337 |

14.1	Example questionnaire	359
14.2	An ordinal scale	364
14.3	A continuum scale	364
14.4	Flowchart for planning of question sequences	365
14.5	Example of a questionnaire cover page	368
14.6	Uses of typography and emphasis to aid the functionality of skip instruction	369
14.7	The uses of spacing to help identify groups of elements	370

15.1	Pre-interview timeline	392
15.2	The 'pacing' of quotations from interviews in the final report	399
15.3	Example of an informed consent form	407

16.1	Observation research roles	414
16.2	The data gathering process	418
16.3	Field notes and reflective comments of researcher	420
16.4	Analysis of dialogue between manager and subordinate using the Flanders interaction analysis system	424
16.5	Alternative ways of event coding	424

17.1 Example of an ethnographic diary   450

18.1 Steps in the design and running of a focus group   472
18.2 Questioning framework from the general to the specific   478
18.3 Research design for product or programme development   485
18.4 Single-category design   486
18.5 Multiple-category design   487
18.6 Double-layer design   487
18.7 Broad spectrum design   488

20.1 Sources of personal records   518
20.2 Criteria for evaluating the use of secondary qualitative data   529

21.1 The SPSS interface – Data Editor window in Data View   539
21.2 The File menu in Data View   540
21.3 The Edit menu in Data View   540
21.4 The View menu in Data View   541
21.5 The Analyze menu in Data View   542
21.6 The Graphs menu in Data View   542
21.7 The Variable View window   543
21.8 Changing the variable Type   545
21.9 The Value Labels box after '1' has been added to Value and 'Male' to Label   546
21.10 Output in the Viewer window   548

22.1 Types of categorical and quantifiable data   555
22.2 Types of questions that yield nominal data   556
22.3 Types of questions that yield ordinal data   557
22.4 Section of questionnaire compromising an age profile   561
22.5 Bar chart for the nominal data in Table 22.2   562
22.6 Pie chart of the nominal data in Figure 22.2   563
22.7 Histogram illustrating interval data in Table 22.10   564
22.8 Bar chart for nominal data with comparison between groups   565
22.9 Stacked bar chart for nominal data with comparison between groups   565
22.10 Frequency polygons for two sets of continuous data showing test scores 566
22.11 Solid polygon showing data for two variables: department and age   567
22.12 The theoretical 'normal' distribution with mean = 0   569
22.13 Areas of acceptance and rejection in a standard normal distribution with $\alpha = 0.05$ 572
22.14 Example of a portion of a survey on skin care products   580
22.15 Perfect positive correlation (left) and perfect negative relationship (right)   585
22.16 Example of a highly positive correlation with cigar-shaped envelope   586
22.17 Scatterplot illustrating relationship between rainfall and face creams 589
22.18 A linear regression scatterplot   592
22.19 Moving the independent variables food quality and service quality into
       the Independent variable box   593

23.1 The process of analytic induction   603
23.2 Qualitative analysis as a circular process   608
23.3 Development of a thematic map   610

23.4 Making connections between categories and sub-categories by examining a
      phenomenon in terms of its properties, dimensions and causal conditions   615
23.5 Making connections between categories and sub-categories: the impact of
      intervening conditions   616
23.6 The impact of outcomes and consequences on the original causal conditions   619
23.7 Twitter posts imported into NVivo 10   627

24.1 Pyramid of evidence model for report design   640
24.2 The Manuscript Central site for the journal *Management Learning*   646

25.1 The team presentation preparation process   668

List of Tables

1.1   Basic and applied research   3
1.2   Examples of real world research topics   4

2.1   Summary of the deductive process within an organizational context   17
2.2   Summary of positivist and phenomenological paradigms   25
2.3   Distinctions between phenomenological research and ethnography   25

3.1   Techniques for generating and refining research ideas   46
3.2   Typical structure for an academic proposal   52
3.3   Examples of descriptive, explanatory, exploratory and interpretive questions   57
3.4   Typical research methodologies associated with quantitative and qualitative approaches   59

4.1   A summary of ethical stances   69
4.2   Summary of the ten points of the Nuremberg Code on human experimentation   70
4.3   Research organizations and their websites dealing with ethics and codes of practice   78
4.4   A typical university proposal structure   82
4.5   Example of a participant consent form   86
4.6   Metaphors and how Internet subjects should be treated by researchers   89
4.7   A checklist of ethical issues   91
4.8   Best practice guidelines for researcher safety   93

5.1   An overview of literature sources   103
5.2   Examples of online public and private bibliographic databases   105
5.3   Examples of screening criteria for a study of mentoring women managers in organizations   113
5.4   Evaluating the quality of sources   114
5.5   Skills for critical engagement with the literature   115
5.6   Positive and negative judgements by two reviewers on a set of articles   115
5.7   Criteria for undertaking a critical literature review   119
5.8   Research method and uses of the literature   120
5.9   Summary of sources and information required using the Harvard System   121
5.10   Examples of sources and references using the Harvard system   122

6.1   Examples of statements of dilemmas formulated as research questions   131
6.2   Types of applied research questions with examples   132
6.3   Differences between experimental, quasi-experimental and non-experimental research   138
6.4   Non-experimental design with intact group   140

6.5	Post-test only with non-equivalent control groups	140
6.6	One group pre-test/post-test design	140
6.7	Experimental group with control	142
6.8	Quasi-experimental design with non-equivalent control	142
6.9	A three digit random numbers table of numbers between 0 and 999 (from Black, 1993)	148
7.1	Some typical criticisms of quantitative research by qualitative researchers	161
7.2	An overview of qualitative paradigms, strategies and methods	164
7.3	Orientation of research questions	170
7.4	Types of data, their characteristics and collection approaches	173
7.5	Checklist of ethical commitments and responsibilities during qualitative research	181
7.6	Techniques for demonstrating validity in qualitative design	183
7.7	Comparison of criteria for judging the trustworthiness of quantitative and qualitative research	186
7.8	Types of research question	188
8.1	Some differences between quantitative and qualitative methods	191
8.2	Examples of how quantitative and qualitative methods are mixed in mixed methods research	196
8.3	Purposes of mixed methods evaluation design	198
9.1	Example of sampling table	220
9.2	Characteristics of mixed methods sampling	225
9.3	Levels of confidence and associated z values	230
9.4	Mean and standard deviation of set of pilot data	231
9.5	Table for determining minimum returned sample size for a given size for continuous and categorical data	232
10.1	Methods for increasing response rates with postal questionnaires	259
10.2	Research questions, constructs, data collection methods and developing valid instruments	262
11.1	Selection criteria for different research strategies	267
11.2	The process of case study construction	274
11.3	Six sources of evidence and their strengths and weaknesses	278
11.4	Personnel and production practices in the case study plants	291
12.1	Five levels of evaluation	299
12.2	Types of evaluation and their defining question or approach	303
12.3	An evaluation schema based on the systems approach	306
12.4	Type of evaluation and data collected	326
13.1	Differences between outsider and insider questions	330
13.2	Sectors where action research projects have been used	332
13.3	Elements that contribute to community relationships in action research	339
14.1	The frequency of staff behaviour/attitude and reliability statements (acceptable statements appear with an asterisk)	357

14.2   Approaches to asking the embarrassing question: 'Did you sabotage the intranet?'   360
14.3   The advantages and disadvantages of open and closed questions   365
14.4   Common response category quantifiers   366
14.5   Likely timing of responses for postal survey   377

15.1   Comparison of interviews and self-administered questionnaires   384
15.2   Characteristics of structured, semi-structured and unstructured interviews   387
15.3   Checklist of dos and don'ts of interviewing   401
15.4   Temporary non-response and non-response to telephone interviews   404
15.5   Example of explanations given by telephone interviewers   405
15.6   Action that can be taken for conducting an ethical interview   406

16.1   Features of social situations as a basis for observational data sources   416
16.2   Flanders interaction analysis system   423
16.3   Chronology of activities   425
16.4   Mail record   425
16.5   Contact record   425
16.6   Examples of what to observe when entering field settings   428

17.1   Positioning the presence of the researcher   464

18.1   Summary of strengths and weaknesses of the focus group approach   471
18.2   Ground rules established by the moderator   475
18.3   Questions posed in focus group using funnelling approach   479
18.4   Possible difficult behaviours in a focus group   481
18.5   Grid to facilitate comparison of data across focus groups   486
18.6   Methodological tensions between constructionist and realist perspectives   491

20.1   Sites for large scale survey data   522

21.1   Examples of full and abbreviated variable names   544

22.1   Measurement scales and their uses   555
22.2   Number of employees per department (nominal scale)   556
22.3   Frequency table showing number of responses on attitude questionnaire (ordinal)   557
22.4   Frequency table showing number of employees scoring within various
       ranges on IQ test   558
22.5   Frequency distribution of employee scores on an in-house work-related test   558
22.6   Data matrix from survey showing data coding for each variable   559
22.7   Distinguishing between different types of non-response   561
22.8   Appropriate use of charts and graphs for frequency data   562
22.9   Age profile of e-commerce development company   564
22.10 Frequency table for age range (interval) data   564
22.11 Percentage of respondents answering for each attitude category over a
       two-year period   567
22.12 Method of scoring each response category in order to calculate the mean score   568
22.13 Calculation of mean scores for attitude categories to discover attitude
       trends over a two-year period   568

22.14	Potential errors in hypothesis testing	571
22.15	Guide to selection of statistical tests	573
22.16	Contingency table of data for analysis	574
22.17	Analysis of data in Table 22.16	574
22.18	Example of a one-sample chi-square test with uneven expected frequency	575
22.19	Summary of statistical tests available for measuring association between two variables	582
22.20	Observed values for coach–coachee matching by gender	583
22.21	Strength of association based upon the value of a coefficient	586
22.22	Three simplified sample sets of data illustrating Spearman's rho (r_s)	586
23.1	Open coding: definition of terms	613
23.2	The properties and dimensions of the category 'information seeking'	615
23.3	Selective coding: definition of terms	617
23.4	Techniques for demonstrating validity at the analysis and presentation stages	623
24.1	Example of heading hierarchy	638
24.2	Proportion of words in a typical piece of academic dissertation writing	643
24.3	Unethical reporting of results	650
24.4	Examples of wordiness and how to avoid it	653
25.1	From negative to positive thoughts	662
25.2	Typical structures for 10 and 20 minute presentations	664
25.3	Some of the 'deadly sins' when using visual aids: design	666
25.4	Some of the 'deadly sins' when using visual aids: delivery	666
25.5	Criteria for choosing an external examiner	672
25.6	Examples of questions posed at a viva	675

Guided Tour

Doing Research in the Real World offers a range of learning resources in the text and online including the following:

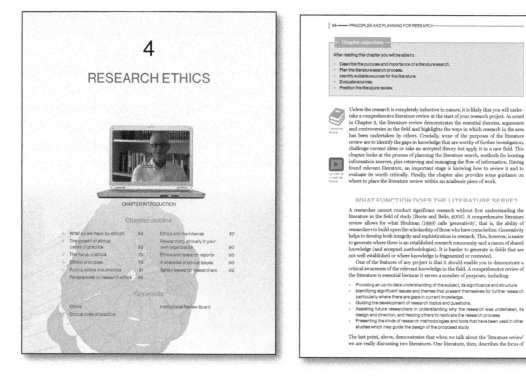

Chapter Introduction author videos explain what will be covered in each chapter and its relevance to the real world.

Chapter Outlines list what is covered in each chapter at a glance.

Keywords highlight the key terms introduced. In the eBook, hover over the word in the chapter with your mouse to reveal the definition.

Chapter Objectives detail what you will learn in each chapter.

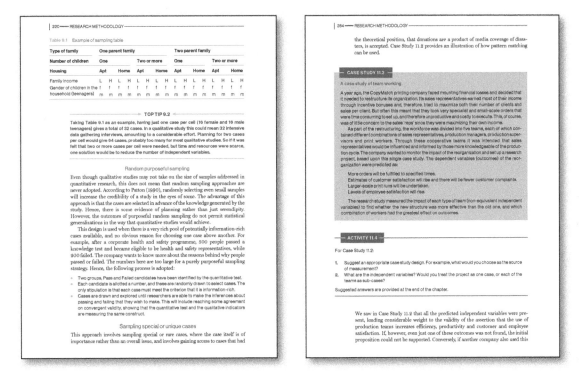

Figures and Tables simplify and illustrate key concepts.

Top Tips give expert advice on how to avoid common research pitfalls. Trickier concepts are supported by top tip videos from the author available on the companion website.

Activities allow you to check your understanding. Answers are provided at the end of the chapter.

Case Studies give a real world look at actual research.

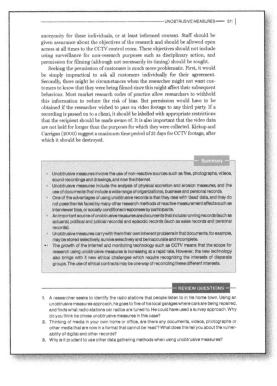

Summaries recap what the chapter covers and are ideal for revision.

Review Questions give you one more chance to make sure you have mastered the key concepts covered.

Companion Website

Learning isn't static, so why should your book be?

When you are doing research in the real world, you never know where your research will take you, not to mention if you will have your textbook to hand.

Not to worry. If you purchased *Doing Research in the Real World* with 12 months **FREE** access to the interactive eBook, you now have the flexibility to learn how, when and where you want.

To access your interactive eBook follow the instructions on the access code, on the sticker in the back cover of this book. You will then be able to read your textbook and engage with the book's online resources on your PC, smart phone or tablet.

What makes it interactive?

Click on the icons in the margins to access a wealth of additional resources such as:

 Video content including **chapter introductions and top tips from the author** along with tried and tested open access videos on YouTube, introduce you to key chapter concepts.

 Further Reading linking you to a range of resources including Encyclopaedia entries, book chapters, journal articles and real world examples to help you deepen your understanding of key concepts.

 Data sets allowing you to play around with real data in SPSS giving you an opportunity to put your statistics knowledge into practice.

 Weblinks to useful websites direct you to real world examples to broaden your knowledge.

 Checklists supporting selected chapters to help guide you through a specific research process such as focus groups and interviewing.

Glossary terms in the text are emboldened. Hover over them to view the definition.

If you prefer to engage with your textbook in a more traditional manner, you can still read the book and access all the interactive resources and much more at **www.sagepub.co.uk/gray3e**. To find out more about how you can get the most out of your textbook and its companion website see the guided tour.

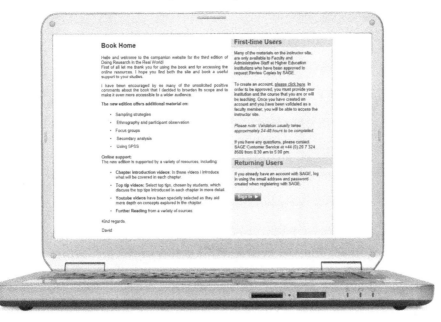

Visit **www.sagepub.co.uk/gray3e** to access:

- **Author videos** introducing each chapter and its key concepts.

- **Top tip videos** from the author explaining some of the trickier research method processes.

- **YouTube videos** that have been vetted by Research Methods experts, to aid revision or in class discussion.

- **Journal articles** provide real world examples of research in action.

- **Encyclopaedia entries** give a more in depth definition of research principles.

- **Methodspace** is an online research method community for students and lecturers. Ask questions. Get answers.

- **Real world data** allows you to practise statistics principles in your own time.

- **Checklists** help you plan challenging research activities like interviews and focus groups.

- **PowerPoints** for instructors aid lecturers.

- **Weblinks** give you access to useful online resource to inform you study.

About the Author

 David Gray studied economics and history at the London School of Economics before commencing on a teaching career in further education. He then spent three years as a training manager at the London Stock Exchange before joining the University of Surrey as a lecturer. David is now Professor of Leadership and Organisational Behaviour at the University of Greenwich. His research interests, and publication record, include research methods, management learning (particularly coaching and mentoring), action learning, reflective learning, and learning in small and medium sized enterprises (SMEs). He has been involved in many empirical research studies over the last 20 years including projects across the European Union and more recently a national study into the triggers for SME success. Apart from research methods David has also written books and published articles on work-based learning, teacher education and coaching and mentoring. When not leading research projects he tries to play golf.

Acknowledgements

I would like to thank the team at SAGE for asking me to write this 3rd edition of *Doing Research in the Real World* and particularly Jai Seaman and Amy Jarrold for their encouragement, and constructive comments on the text, and Ian Antcliff, my meticulous production editor. Thanks also go to the six anonymous reviewers who evaluated many of the chapters and who gave me such detailed and helpful feedback. Finally, my thanks to Professor Yuksel Ekinci at Oxford Brookes University and Jenna Brown of the University of Greenwich for their comments and contributions to Chapter 22. Of course, it goes without saying, that any errors or omissions in this 3rd edition of the book are entirely my own.

David E Gray
Business School
University of Greenwich
January 2014

With thanks to the following people for their feedback on the third edition

Edward Groenland	Nyenrode Business Universiteit
Barbara Read	University of Glasgow
Susan Skipper	University Centre at Blackburn College
Keith Donne	University of Gloucestershire
Michelle Rogerson	Applied Criminology Centre, University of Huddersfield
Theo Papadopoulos	University of Bath
Karen Corteen	University of Chester
Clive Sealey	University of Worcester
Alex Gillett	The York Management School, University of York
Hazel Brown	University of Southampton
Eva Draborg	University of Southern Denmark
Darrell Jackson	Morling College
Jamie Harding	Northumbria University
Christine Little	Bournemouth University
Carole Murphy	St. Mary's University College
Sabina Siebert	University of Glasgow
Shaun Best	University of Manchester
Gwen Urey	California State Polytechnic University, Pomona
Luke Sloan	Cardiff University
Douglas Chalmers	Glasgow Caledonian University
Hanna Yakavenka	University of Greenwich Business School
Morag Gray	Edinburgh Napier University
Kay Peggs	University of Portsmouth
Carlos Oya	SOAS, University of London
Rob Monks	Uinversity of Central Lancashire
William Graham	Glasgow Caledonian University
Teresa Carmichael	Wits Business School, University of the Witwatersrand, Johannesburg, South Africa
Alex Seago	Richmond, The American International University in London
Sharon Wray	University of Huddersfield
Graham Taylor	University of the West of England, Bristol
Paul Fenton	Oasis College of Higher Education
Martin Dempster	Queen's University Belfast
Fiona Bloomer	University of Ulster
Lucy Land	Birmingham City University
Mehmetali Dikerdem	Institute for Work Based Learning, Middlesex University
Jason Schaub	Buckinghamshire New University
Nancy Harding	University of Bradford School of Management
David McGuinness	Northumbria University

1

INTRODUCTION

CHAPTER INTRODUCTION

Chapter outline

Research in the real world   3

The nature of theories   5

An overview of the research process   6

The organization of the book   7

How to use this book   10

Keywords

Methodology

Theory

Basic research

Applied research

Research topics

Research process

Chapter objectives

After reading this chapter you will be able to:

- Describe why research in the real world is of increasing importance.
- Explain the nature of theories.
- Outline the stages in the research process.
- Use this book effectively by making use of its features such as Activities and Top Tips.

This book is designed to introduce you to some of the essential methodologies, approaches and tools of research. In doing so, we will explore some of the philosophies and theoretical perspectives behind the many different ways of conducting research, as well as providing practical examples and guidance as to how research should be planned and implemented. Later in this chapter we will look at the structure of the book, but first we need to examine the nature of the research process and why research is being seen as increasingly important in a growing number of organizations, communities and contexts.

GLOBALIZATION The term 'globalization' is often used to describe a world that is becoming increasingly integrated and interdependent and where large, international organizations dominate. Within this globalized world, change in business and working environments has become rapid and pervasive. Organizations have adapted to this uncertainty in a number of ways. One approach has been to understand (often through research) and develop relationships with both markets and supply chains. Most forward-looking organizations have also recognized the need for a multi-skilled and occupationally agile workforce. It has also required that organizations understand what motivates their workforce and how people embrace change. All this has had an enormous impact on the way organizations operate and interact with the 'real world', and how they communicate and work. Small and medium-sized enterprises (SMEs) have also had to modernize their organizational practices and to understand their working environment, as have public sector organizations (including hospitals,

EVIDENCE-
BASED PRACTICE schools, colleges and universities) and voluntary organizations. Indeed, in terms of research in the health sector and in education, it is common to now talk of evidence-based practice. Furthermore, governments and other sponsors of research, have shown a desire to see 'value for money' when funding research projects, based, at least in part, on projects providing evidence of sound and robust research methodologies.

Faced with a more competitive, dynamic and uncertain world, knowledge of research **methods** is important because it helps people in organizations to understand, predict and control their internal and external environments (Sekaran, 2007). It also means that those involved in commissioning or sponsoring organizational research are better placed to understand and manage the work of researchers and to objectively evaluate and interpret the outcomes of research. Hence, it becomes possible to calculate the potential risks and benefits in implementing research projects.

Research is also of value in itself. Completing a research project (such as a dissertation or thesis) can provide you with lifelong skills (writing research proposals, planning the research, designing data gathering instruments, collecting data and abiding by a code of research ethics, to name but a few). These and other skills from research are really important for the world of work and so may prove of real value for your future. Sometimes employers will show a genuine interest in the kinds of research you have undertaken because the subject may link with the job you are applying for. But what do we mean by the term 'research'? Let's look at this in more detail.

RESEARCH IN THE REAL WORLD

Research in this context is a 'systematic and organized effort to investigate a specific problem that needs a solution' (Sekaran, 2007: 4). Hence, research is often about how (process) to solve real problems (content) (Gill and Johnson, 2002). This may have a very practical focus (applied research), with an emphasis on achieving measurable outputs that are specific to a particular society or organization. The results of such research may be of significance to a specific context, but difficult to generalize elsewhere. On the other hand, research may also be concerned with clarifying, validating or building a theory (basic research). Its importance to society or to organizations may be determined by the extent to which this theory is translatable into a specific context. However, most organizations will only see research as valid if it is seen to lead to practical outcomes (Easterby-Smith et al., 2002). Then there are forms of research comprising collaboration between the researcher and professional practitioners (often an element of **action research**). Table 1.1 provides a summary illustrating a continuum between basic and applied research.

BASIC &
APPLIED
RESEARCH

Research in the real world brings with it many challenges. First, it needs to draw upon broad fields of inquiry such as sociology, psychology, anthropology, philosophy, communication and economics. This often means having to adopt an inter-disciplinary approach, incorporating ideas and approaches from a diverse range of subject backgrounds. Secondly, research in the real world means the researcher has to gain access to social settings or working environments where key research sponsors, gatekeepers or stakeholders may have their own agendas that are not necessarily the same as those of the researcher. Thirdly, research may be influenced by the fact that research sponsors such as governments or businesses are working in a world of competition, market influences and financial

Table 1.1   Basic and applied research

Basic research	Applied research
Purpose	*Purpose*
Expand knowledge of social or organizational processes	Improve understanding of specific social or organizational problems
Develop universal principles	Create solutions to social or organizational problems
Produce findings of significance and value to society	Develop findings of practical relevance to public and organizational stakeholders

Source: Adapted from Saunders et al., 2012

Table 1.2   Examples of real world research topics

Women firefighters – breaking down barriers to recruitment

Disability awareness training – does it change attitudes?

Project management in virtual organizations

Identifying the factors that influence youth club membership and attendance

Why don't people buy recycled paper?

The feasibility of transferring advanced horticultural practices to a poor developing country. A case study of three Romanian villages

Does targeted neighbourhood policing work?

Housing association accommodation and services – an evaluation of tenant attitudes

How can call centre response times and the quality of feedback to customer queries be improved?

The impact of intensive 'exam culture' on pupil sickness and medical referral

An evaluation of government 'special measures' on pupil attainment and teacher retention

Working trajectories – getting disaffected youths from ethnic communities into the jobs market

Measuring and improving customer satisfaction in a library

constraints. Research projects may have to be modified or cancelled. Research sponsors may criticize what they read in research reports, especially when these reveal inadequacies or inefficiencies in the systems they manage.

But what do we mean by the 'real world'? For many, it means businesses, hospitals, schools, colleges or other organizations, and certainly these are important sites for, and sponsors of, research. The real world, however, can also include communities where people live, including residential areas, parks, shops, local amenities or areas where people congregate. It could also mean networks such as community groups, educationalists, professional associations, management associations or trades unions. Increasingly it could also include virtual communities where people communicate with each other through the Internet. In other words, the real world comprises any setting where human beings come together for communication, relationships or discourse.

The real world, of course, contains a myriad of subjects that lend themselves to research. Table 1.2 provides just a general 'feel' for the kinds of areas that this book will explore. You will, of course, be thinking about or developing a research topic of your own.

But how do we go about addressing these kinds of research areas? One way to solve any problem in the real world is to do so *systematically*. While Figure 1.1 presents a very simplified version of such an approach (which will be modified in later chapters), it does at least offer a starting point. Gill and Johnson (2002) rightly caution that the wise researcher is one who gives equal attention to each of these phases. Many naïve researchers are tempted to rush into the 'collect information' stage without first very clearly defining the research topic, and its objectives. The results of this fuzziness only become transparent later on, with the effect that the researcher has to cycle back to an earlier stage in the research process, or to start again.

Figure 1.1 shows that it is possible, in principle, to move from the identification of the research focus right through to the presentation of the findings in a neat sequence of steps. This, however, is an idealized model and is not necessarily the norm. The complexities of researching in the real world mean that the researcher may often have to revisit previous stages in the research process. For example, at the analysis stage it might emerge that the collection of important **data** has been overlooked. New plans will have to be formulated and the data collected before the researcher is able to return to the analysis and presentation of the findings. Indeed, as we shall see in later chapters, it is also valid for the researcher to enter 'the field' to gather data, with only the most general of notions of what she/he is looking for, and for the data to help in the generation of concepts and theories.

Figure 1.1 implies that the research process is a highly practical one. You identify a problem, decide on how to tackle it, collect data (which often involves discussions with other people), analyse and present findings and take action. But research, as was mentioned above, is more than a mere pragmatic activity; behind it lies the foundations of academic theories that have emerged through the process of scientific enquiry and investigation over many decades and even centuries. To theories we now turn.

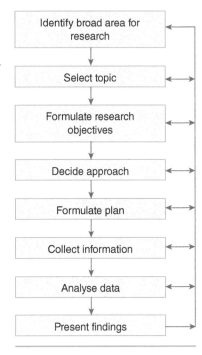

Figure 1.1 Overview of the (simplified) research process

Source: Adapted from Gill and Johnson, 2002

THE NATURE OF THEORIES

A theory has been defined as:

> A set of interrelated constructs (concepts), definitions, and propositions that present a systematic view of phenomena by specifying relations among variables, with the purpose of explaining and predicting phenomena. (Kerlinger and Lee, 2000: 9)

One might, for example, have a theory of business failure in a business start-up company such as a new online retailer for folding bicycles. The factors that might explain this could be: poor Web design, faults in product design, insufficient sales staff training, or a lack of investment. The actual failure of the business has to be explained by examining and understanding the interrelationship between these factors. Such understanding may take the form of a theory that is predictive or explanatory in nature. Indeed, a theory is only worthy of the term if it has some predictive qualities. As we shall see, if a theory is no longer predictive, a crisis ensues and the theory will, over time, be challenged and replaced by a new one.

There is no reason, however, to denigrate research activity that is not theory-orientated. In research it may be quite valid to undertake an investigation that merely seeks to find the immediate goal of a relationship between two **variables** (a characteristic that is measurable such as income, attitude, action, policy, etc.) Taking our online bicycle retailer above the variables might be profit levels and management skills (related to Web design, product design, etc.).

But as Kerlinger and Lee (2000) point out, the most satisfying and usable relationships are those that can be *generalized*, that is, applied from the specific instance of the research findings to many phenomena and to many people. This is the nature of theory.

ACTIVITY 1.1

Examine each of the following statements and decide whether you agree with them. A theory:

- Is an accumulated body of knowledge, written by acknowledged experts.
- Informs 'state-of-the-art' concepts and innovations.
- Is a body of work where inconsequential or misleading ideas can be filtered out.
- Represents knowledge that should be viewed critically and rejected when incompatible with practice.
- Adds interest and intellectual stimulation to a project.
- Acts as a model against which 'live' business processes can be evaluated.
- Guides the execution of research **methodology**.

Suggested answers are provided at the end of the chapter.

Source: Adapted from Gill and Johnson, 2002

AN OVERVIEW OF THE RESEARCH PROCESS

We saw above that research often comprises an investigation into the relationship between two (or more) variables. However, before we undertake a research study, we need to know more about these variables and what studies, if any, have been conducted into their relationship. Hence, we undertake a literature review (see Figure 1.1). In doing this, we will be interested in the literature on the dependent variable (the variable that forms the focus of the research) and the independent variable (the variable that acts on or predicts the dependent variable). So, for example, we might investigate public attitudes to healthy eating (the dependent variable) following a local campaign (independent variable). But there is a third source of literature we also need to investigate and that is where studies have already been completed that have explored the relationships between healthy eating and campaigns designed to improve eating patterns (see dependent/independent variable in Figure 1.2). As we

DEPENDENT VS
INDEPENDENT
VARIABLES

will see when looking at inductive and qualitative methods, this sequential, literature first approach, is not always followed, but it is typical of many studies.

The literature review has another important purpose. It helps to define the focus and scope of the research project about to be undertaken. Above all, it leads to one

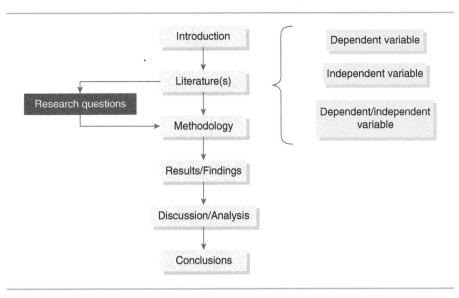

Figure 1.2   An overview of the typical research process

or more research questions which give direction and frame the study. As we will see later, research questions, providing they are written accurately and concisely, provide an essential bridge between the literature review (the subject) and methodology (how the subject is going to be investigated and researched). It is difficult to exaggerate how important it is to formulate a set of clear research questions.

THE ORGANIZATION OF THE BOOK

The book is divided into four parts. Part A prepares the way by looking at the underpinning philosophy of research and the selection of suitable research topics. In Chapter 2 the nature and significance of theory is justified and the epistemological (philosophical) basis of theory explored. The chapter also describes how different epistemological perspectives provide the basis for research methodologies like **experimental research, surveys, grounded theory** and action research, all of which are discussed in detail in later chapters. If you have little or no previous experience of philosophy you may find this chapter rather daunting, but you are encouraged to tackle it, as it will help you to understand the approaches taken in later chapters.

Having provided an overarching view of research philosophy, methodologies and methods, Chapter 3 gets down to the practical issue of selecting and planning a research project. Advice is offered on how to identify research topics that meet your personal needs and experience and how to write a successful research proposal.

Chapter 4 on **ethics** in research is important given the fact that students and professional researchers now usually have to abide by the ethical frameworks devised by their educational institutions or professional associations – often referred to as Institutional Review Boards. This chapter shows you how to construct research designs that follow these important principles. Note that the discussion of ethics is not confined to this chapter but appears often throughout the book.

Chapter 5 looks at some of the many ways in which you can begin to locate, search and use the literature on your chosen subject. It shows you how to plan your search, store data and undertake a critical review of your literature sources.

Part B deals with research methodology, beginning with quantitative research designs, including experimental and **quasi-experimental design** (Chapter 6). This is an appropriate place to begin our discussion of methodology since this is one of the oldest and, in a sense, the classical approach to research design. The chapter not only describes and justifies alternative experimental designs, but introduces concepts (such as validity and reliability) that are appropriate for, or at least addressed by, many other research methodologies. Chapter 7 provides a description of various qualitative designs, while Chapter 8 takes you a step further by introducing the notion of combining quantitative and qualitative designs to produce a mixed methods approach. Mixed methods can help you by combining some of the best elements of quantitative and qualitative approaches. Of course, none of these approaches will work if the sampling design is not right. In this 3rd edition, a new, complete chapter (Chapter 9) is now devoted to this key theme.

In Chapter 10 we take another, and increasingly popular, research methodology, surveys, and describe different types of survey and the process of survey design. A distinction is made between self-administered and interview-administered surveys and the merits of each are discussed. Partly because of their scale, surveys can be prone to sources of error such as sampling error, data collection error and interviewer error. Some practical advice is provided on how to cope with these.

Another widely used research methodology is the **case study** (Chapter 11). For many years, the case study approach has been wrongfully denigrated by some researchers as lacking in rigour, partly because it is often based upon a small number of cases. However, as this chapter shows, case studies, if carefully planned, can provide a powerful means of exploring situations where there is uncertainty or ambiguity about phenomena or events.

While some research methodologies attempt to uncover new knowledge, **evaluation** (Chapter 12) involves exploring how existing knowledge is used to inform and guide practical action. Hence, evaluation might be used to gauge whether a teaching or training programme has been successful. But evaluation can also be used to report on much larger units of analysis such as national policies or government-sponsored intervention programmes.

Chapter 13 completes Part B by exploring the purposes and methods behind action research. In this chapter and, indeed, throughout the book, we look at real world issues and problems. Action research is about addressing and, in some cases, solving these problems. The key focus is not research for the sake of expanding knowledge but on achieving change (often in a company, school, college or community setting).

Of course, whichever research methodology (or combination of methodologies) we use, none can be successful without the use of sound and reliable data collection tools (Part C). We start here with a look at, perhaps, one of the most commonly used research instruments, the questionnaire (Chapter 14). This chapter shows how designing valid and reliable questionnaires requires adherence to a large number of design considerations that range from the writing of individual questions to the layout of the questionnaire itself.

Questionnaires are often used as the data gathering instrument for structured or semi-structured interviews. But interviews (Chapter 15) also necessitate that the researcher acquires a wide range of other skills associated with actually conducting the interview. This chapter, then, provides some practical advice on planning and conducting a variety of interview approaches.

But how do we know that interviewees tell the truth? It may be that they do not know the answer to a question or that they want to hide something from us. Another data gathering method, then, is observation (Chapters 16 and 17). Chapter 16 discusses non-participant observation, while Chapter 17 (new to this 3rd edition) looks at observation through participant observation, and particularly through ethnographic approaches. Ethnography is a research method that seeks to understand cultural phenomena that reflect the knowledge and meanings that guide the life of cultural groups within their own environment. In both participant and non-participant observation, the observation may be conducted overtly, where the subjects of the research know that they are being observed or covertly where the role of the researcher is disguised.

Chapter 18 on focus groups is also a new chapter. **Focus groups** in recent years have become an increasingly popular data gathering method among researchers in part because they stimulate dialogue and debate among participants, often eliciting a rich array of views and perspectives.

One of the problems in using questionnaires, interviews and observations is that they are potentially reactive – that is, the data may become contaminated because of, say, the bias of the research instruments or the way data are interpreted by the researcher. An often neglected but equally powerful data gathering method is what is termed 'unobtrusive measures' (Chapter 19), which offer the benefit of being non-reactive. Unobtrusive measures include physical evidence, documentary evidence and archival analysis, including documents held on the World Wide Web. **Unobtrusive measures** can offer flexible, creative and imaginative ways of collecting data, often to verify findings from the use of other data collection methods.

Chapter 20 (a new chapter in this 3rd edition) looks at the analysis of secondary sources. Secondary analysis involves the use of existing data, collected for the purpose of a prior study, in order to pursue a research interest which is distinct from the original work. This may comprise a new research question or an alternative perspective on the original question. Sometimes researchers will make use of secondary sources because it becomes possible to make use of longitudinal data; other researchers (often student researchers) will use secondary sources in situations where access to primary data is problematic.

Having collected data, they have to be analysed and the results presented (Part D). Of course, plans and designs for analysis should have been completed long before this stage.

Chapter 21 is another new chapter for the 3rd edition, helping you to get started in using IBM SPSS Statistics. Researchers who are new to statistics find the additional challenge of getting to grips with a new software program like SPSS somewhat daunting. This new chapter introduces you to some of the basic functions of SPSS so you are up and running for Chapter 22 which looks at techniques for presenting and analysing quantitative data, including ways of categorizing quantitative data and cleaning and coding data. This chapter also examines ways of analysing data using descriptive statistics and the use of some elementary inferential statistical techniques.

In contrast, Chapter 23 looks at approaches to how qualitative data can be analysed. It looks particularly at **content analysis** and grounded theory methods and also includes approaches such as the use of **narratives, conversational analysis** and **discourse analysis**. You will probably notice in reading Chapters 22 and 23 how some of the philosophical issues raised in Chapter 2 are given substance in terms of what is researched, and how the research is conducted.

After you have collected your data, you now want to present them in a way that enhances their credibility and impact. Chapter 24 looks at different types of research report including organizational and technical reports, and studies written up as part of an academic dissertation or thesis. Advice is given on key features, such as the use of appropriate language and writing style for the intended audience, and the structure of the report. Finally, Chapter 25 explores the 'art' of giving a presentation (often required at the end of an academic programme) and passing a viva.

HOW TO USE THE BOOK

How is the book best used as an aid to research? You could think of it as a research manual that also explains the theoretical underpinnings of research methods and provides guidance on where to find further information. It is recommended that you read through the book, focusing on the objectives listed at the beginning of each chapter. Try to get a feel for which aspects will be of particular interest to you, noting any ideas or topics, approaches and practices that strike you as relevant to your research. During the research process revisit these parts and if you need further guidance, check with the Further readings lists at the end of each chapter, which include brief details of the nature of the sources mentioned. Note also any associated Case Studies (which are designed to illustrate key research methodologies or approaches) and Activities (designed to promote thinking, reflection and skills development and, in the case of websites, a guide to additional information or resources). It is not expected that you attempt to complete all Activities – tackle those that you think would be most useful. Where it is felt appropriate, suggested answers are given for some Activities at the end of the relevant chapter. 'On the Web' encourages you to visit useful websites that often provide valuable additional information.

→ **TOP TIP 1.1** ◄

Finally, take time to read the Top Tips. These are specifically designed to focus and give constructive, practical advice on those topics that students often struggle with. These include help with overcoming popular misunderstandings and misconceptions.

Summary

- The growing complexity of the world means that research in the real world is of growing importance. An understanding of the world is underpinned by theory.
- Basic research seeks to develop universal principles and to produce findings that are of value to society; applied research seeks to create practical solutions to organizational problems.
- Organizational and social research draw upon fields of inquiry such as sociology, anthropology, philosophy, communication, economics and statistics, often adopting an inter-disciplinary approach.
- A theory consists of a set of interrelated concepts, definitions and propositions that demonstrate relationships between variables.
- In using this book, do take the time to read the Case Studies, undertake the Activities and to visit the 'On the Web' sites.

JOURNAL RESOURCES

Tavallaei, M. and Abu Talib, M. (2010) 'A general perspective on role of theory in qualitative research', *Journal of International Social Research*, 3 (11): 570–577. Discusses the positioning of theory in qualitative research.

Calvert, J. (2006) 'What's special about basic research?', *Science, Technology & Human Values*, 31(2): 199–220. Argues that 'basic research' is a flexible and ambiguous concept that is drawn on by scientists to acquire prestige and resources. Also shows that it is used for boundary work.

Lehtinen, U., Öhlén, J. and Asplund, K. (2005) 'Some remarks on the relevance of basic research in nursing inquiry', *Nursing Philosophy*, 6 (1): 43–50. Explains why basic research may be an important precursor for applied research in nursing.

Suggested answers for Activity 1.1

Actually, it is all of them!

PART A

Principles and Planning for Research

Contents

2. Theoretical Perspectives and
   Research Methodologies   15
   Inductive and deductive
   reasoning   16
   Epistemological and ontological
   perspectives   19
   Theoretical perspectives   21
   Research methodologies   29
   Selecting research approaches
   and strategies   34

3. Selecting and Planning Research
   Proposals and Projects   39
   Selecting a research topic   40
   Topics to avoid   48
   Planning the project   50
   Writing academic proposals   50
   Writing organizational proposals   63
   The final stages for academic
   and organizational proposals   64

4. Research Ethics   67
   What do we mean by ethics?   68
   The growth of ethical codes
   of practice   69
   The focus of ethics   73
   Ethical principles   73

   Putting ethics into practice   81
   Perspectives on research ethics   85
   Ethics and the Internet   87
   Researching ethically in your own
   organization   90
   Ethics and research reports   90
   A checklist of ethical issues   90
   Safety issues for researchers   92

5. Searching, Critically Reviewing
   and Using the Literature   97
   What function does
   the literature serve?   98
   The literature search journey   99
   The literature search process   101
   Searching source materials   102
   The process of critically
   evaluating sources   112
   Managing information   115
   Synthesizing and integrating
   search results   116
   Structure and content of
   the literature review   117
   Positioning the literature review   118
   Doing a critical literature review   118
   Referencing sources   120

2

THEORETICAL PERSPECTIVES AND RESEARCH METHODOLOGIES

CHAPTER INTRODUCTION

Chapter outline

Inductive and deductive reasoning   16

Epistemological and ontological
perspectives   19

Theoretical perspectives   21

Research methodologies   29

Selecting research approaches
and strategies   34

Keywords

Inductive

Deductive

Epistemology

Ontology

Theory

Objectivism

Constructivism

Subjectivism

Research methodology

Chapter objectives

After reading this chapter you will be able to:

- Distinguish between ontology and epistemology in research.
- Distinguish between inductive and deductive methods.
- Explain the different perspectives taken by positivism and interpretivism.
- Describe the different research methodologies and the conditions for their selection.
- Distinguish between exploratory, descriptive, explanatory and interpretative research studies.

We saw in Chapter 1 that the research process requires us to engage at some stage with theoretical perspectives. Sometimes this will occur before undertaking the research (the **deductive approach**) and at other times after it (**inductive**). But the question remains: which theories? The purpose of this chapter is to examine the range of theoretical perspectives available, and also to provide some guidance as to which ones are most appropriate to the research project or task you are undertaking.

This is far from being a simple process. If you are relatively new to the study of philosophical perspectives, the nature of theories and their significance to research methodologies may not be instantly obvious. Furthermore, the nature and meaning of some philosophical perspectives is still contested and debated.

➤ **TOP TIP 2.1** ◄ ————————————

At this stage it is suggested that you read this chapter without dwelling too much on individual sections. If some of the discussion seems rather abstract do not worry – keep going. It is suggested that you return to this chapter at a later stage when its relevance will, hopefully, be clearer and more easily absorbed.

INDUCTIVE AND DEDUCTIVE REASONING

INDUCTIVE & DEDUCTIVE REASONING

We have briefly examined the nature and uses of theory – but in research should we begin with theory, or should theory itself result from the research? Dewey (1933) outlines a general paradigm of enquiry that underpins the scientific approach, consisting of inductive discovery (**induction**) and deductive proof (**deduction**). Deduction begins with a universal view of a situation and works back to the particulars; in contrast, induction moves from fragmentary details to a connected view of a situation.

The deductive process

EXAMPLE OF DEDUCTIVE REASONING

The deductive approach moves towards **hypothesis** testing, after which the principle is confirmed, refuted or modified. These hypotheses present an assertion about two or more concepts that attempts to explain the relationship between them. Concepts themselves are abstract ideas that form the building blocks of hypotheses and theories. The first stage, therefore, is the elaboration of a set of principles or allied ideas that are then tested through **empirical** observation or experimentation.

Table 2.1   Summary of the deductive process within an organizational context

Stages in the deduction process	Actions taken	Example: media campaign to increase public awareness of AIDS
Organizational mission	Read and take into account.	We would start by looking at the aims of government health policy in respect to sexually transmitted diseases.
Theory	Select a theory or set of theories most appropriate to the subject under investigation.	Theoretical models might include aspects of communication theory, as well as public attitudes to risk.
Hypothesis	Produce a hypothesis (a testable proposition about the relationship between two or more concepts).	The hypothesis might state a relationship between a social media publicity campaign and heightened public awareness.
Operationalize	Specify what the researcher must do to measure a concept.	We would define and state how 'awareness' would be measured. Also, by 'public' do we mean everyone, or specifically targeted groups?
Testing by corroboration or attempted falsification	Compare observable data with the theory. If corroborated, the theory is assumed to have been established.	The hypothesis would suggest a relationship (for example a 6 month media campaign) and, say, a 20 per cent improvement in awareness among 'at risk' groups.
Examine outcomes	Accept or reject the hypothesis from the outcomes.	The statistical analysis would reveal whether the intended outcomes had been reached.
Modify theory (if necessary)	Modify theory if the hypothesis is rejected.	The results would also help determine if campaigns of this type actually work. The results would be compared to those achieved in previous, similar studies.

But before such experimentation can take place, underlying concepts must be operationalized (made measurable) in such a way that they can be observed to confirm that they have occurred. Hence, measures and indicators are created. For example, if research is to be conducted into doctor–patient communication and its impact on patient well-being, we would first have to establish an operational definition of 'communication' within the context of the doctor–patient relationship. Through the creation of operational indicators, there is a tendency to measure and collect data only on what can actually be observed; hence, subjective and intangible evidence is usually ruled out. Table 2.1 provides a summary of this process.

The inductive process

Through the inductive approach, plans are made for data collection, after which the data are analysed to see if any patterns emerge that suggest relationships between variables. From these observations it may be possible to construct generalizations, relationships and even theories. Through induction, the researcher moves towards discovering a binding principle, taking care not to jump to hasty **inferences** or

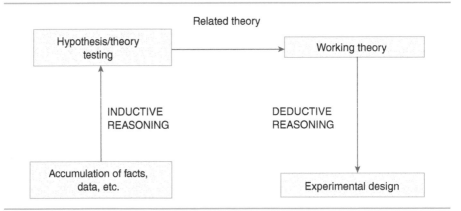

Figure 2.1   An illustration of how the inductive and deductive methods can be combined

conclusions on the basis of the data. To ensure a degree of reliability, the researcher often takes multiple cases or instances, through, for example, multiplying observations rather than basing conclusions on one case (see Figure 11.4, Chapter 11).

EXAMPLE OF
INDUCTIVE
RESEARCH

It would not be true to say that the inductive process takes absolutely no note of pre-existing theories or ideas when approaching a problem. The very fact that an issue has been selected for research implies judgements about what is an important subject for research, and these choices are dependent on values and concepts. This may help to formulate the overall purpose of the research. But the inductive approach does not set out to corroborate or falsify a theory. Instead, through a process of gathering data, it attempts to establish patterns, consistencies and meanings.

Combining the inductive and deductive methods

Inductive and deductive processes, however, are not mutually exclusive. Adapting Dewey's (1933) formulation to a modern problem, let us say a researcher has been asked to investigate the problem of staff absenteeism. Taking a selection of facts (absentee rates over time, in different departments and across staff grades), the researcher is able to formulate a theory (inductive approach) that absenteeism is related to working patterns (see Figure 2.1). It is particularly rife among lower grade workers who are the objects of quite rigorous supervision and control. The researcher then becomes interested in what other impact this form of control may have on working practices (deductive approach). A working hypothesis becomes formulated that over-zealous supervision has produced low morale and therefore low productivity levels among sections of the workforce. This hypothesis is tested by the introduction of new working methods in some sections, but not others (an experimental approach using a control group), to compare productivity levels between traditionally supervised sections and those using the new supervision methods. Figure 2.1 provides a summary of this process.

___

ACTIVITY 2.1

For your own research project, consider whether you intend to adopt an inductive approach, a deductive approach, or a combination of the two. List three reasons for your choice.

EPISTEMOLOGICAL AND
ONTOLOGICAL PERSPECTIVES

We looked in Chapter 1 at the nature of theories and their relationship to practice. We now need to explore the range of theories available to us as researchers, and how we can select between them. As Crotty (1998) demonstrates, one of the problems here is not only the bewildering array of theoretical perspectives and methodologies, but the fact that the terminology applied to them is often inconsistent (or even contradictory). Crotty suggests that an interrelationship exists between the theoretical stance adopted by the researcher, the methodology and methods used, and the researcher's view of the **epistemology** (see Figure 2.2).

Despite the natural tendency for the researcher (and especially the novice researcher!) to select a data gathering method and get on with the job, the choice of methods will be influenced by the **research methodology** chosen. This method- ology, in turn, will be influenced by the theoretical perspectives adopted by the researcher, and, in turn, by the researcher's epistemological stance. For example, researchers who decide at an early stage that they intend to use a structured questionnaire as part of a survey and to investigate associations between respondents' perspectives and the type of respondent (e.g. age, gender, etc.) are, whether they are aware of it or not, adopting an objectivist approach.

METHODOLOGY: WHO NEEDS IT?

Ontology is the study of being, that is, the nature of existence and what constitutes reality. So, for example, for positivists the world is independent of our knowledge of it – it exists 'out there' while for relativists and others, there are multiple realities and ways of accessing them. While ontology embodies understanding *what is*, epistemology tries to understand *what it means to know*. Epistemology provides a philosophical background for deciding what kinds of knowledge are legitimate and adequate. As Easterby-Smith et al. (2002) point out, having an epistemological

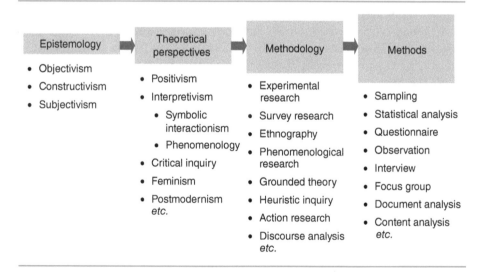

Figure 2.2   Relationship between epistemology, theoretical perspectives, methodology and research methods

Source: Adapted from Crotty, 1998

perspective is important for several reasons. First, it can help to clarify issues of research design. This means more than just the design of research tools. It means the overarching structure of the research including the kind of evidence that is being gathered, from where, and how it is going to be interpreted. Secondly, a knowledge of research philosophy will help the researcher to recognize which designs will work (for a given set of objectives) and which will not.

EPISTEMOLOGY & ONTOLOGY

Western thought remains divided by two opposing ontological traditions. Heraclitus (*c*.535–*c*.475BC), who lived in Ephesus in ancient Greece, placed an emphasis on a changing and emergent world. Parmenides (*c*.515–*c*.445BC), who succeeded him, placed quite a different emphasis on a permanent and unchanging reality. Between a Heraclitean ontology of *becoming* and a Parmenidean ontology of *being*, it is the latter that has held sway in Western philosophy. Hence, reality is seen as being composed of clearly formed entities with identifiable properties (in contrast to a Heraclitean emphasis on formlessness, chaos, interpenetration and absence). Once entities are held to be stable they can become represented by symbols, words and concepts. Thus a representationalist epistemology results in which signs and language are taken to be accurate representations of the external world. This representationalist epistemology orientates our thinking towards outcomes and end-states rather than processes of change. According to Chia (2002), only relatively recently has postmodern epistemology challenged traditional *being* ontology with notions of a *becoming* orientation and the limitations of truth-seeking.

It would be a mistake, however, to view *being* ontology as leading to epistemological positions that are unitary and holistic. As Figure 2.2 shows, at least three positions have emerged. Objectivist epistemology, for example, holds that reality exists independently of consciousness – in other words, there is an objective reality 'out there'. So, research is about discovering this objective truth. In doing this, researchers should strive not to include their own feelings and values. Objectivism, however, does not entail the rejection of subjectivity: we can study peoples' subjective views (their values, attitudes and beliefs) but we must do so objectively (Bunge, 1993).

A theoretical perspective closely linked to objectivism is **positivism** which argues that reality exists external to the researcher and must be investigated through the rigorous process of scientific inquiry. In contrast, **constructivism** rejects this view of human knowledge. Truth and meaning do not exist in some external world, but are created by the subject's interactions with the world. Meaning is *constructed* not discovered, so subjects construct their own meaning in different ways, even in relation to the same phenomenon. Hence, multiple, contradictory but equally valid accounts of the world can exist. A theoretical perspective linked to constructivism is interpretivism. Yet, while interpretivism and objectivism hold different epistemological positions, both are still based upon a *being* ontology (Chia, 2002).

PARADIGMS & META CRITERIA

In contrast to constructivism, for subjectivism, meaning does not emerge from the interplay between the subject and the outside world, but is imposed on the object by the subject. Subjects do construct meaning, but do so from within collective unconsciousness, from dreams, from religious beliefs, etc. Despite Crotty's assertion that this is 'the most slippery of terms' (1998: 183), postmodernism can be taken as an example of a theoretical perspective linked to subjectivism (and *becoming* ontology).

THEORETICAL PERSPECTIVES

Of the different theoretical perspectives available, positivism and various strands of interpretivism are, or have been (arguably) among the most influential. These, and a number of other stances such as critical inquiry, postmodernism and feminism, will be used here to illustrate the value of adopting theoretical perspectives that are congruent with the researcher's epistemology and demonstrate the kinds of research methodologies that emerge from them.

Positivism

Positivism was the dominant epistemological paradigm in social science from the 1930s through to the 1960s, its core argument being that the social world exists externally to the researcher, and that its properties can be measured directly through observation. In essence, positivism argues that:

POSITIVISM

- Reality consists of what is available to the senses – that is, what can be seen, smelt, touched, etc.
- Inquiry should be based upon scientific observation (as opposed to philosophical speculation), and therefore on empirical inquiry.
- The natural and human sciences share common logical and methodological principles, dealing with facts and not with values.

Hence, ideas only deserve their incorporation into knowledge if they can be put to the test of empirical experience. Positivists saw the natural sciences as progressing through the patient accumulation of facts about the world in order to produce generalizations known as scientific laws. To achieve this, the act of scientific inquiry was taken to be the accumulation of 'brute data' such as shape, size, motion, etc. For positivists, then, both the natural and social worlds operated within a strict set of laws, which science had to discover through empirical inquiry. This is a brief summary of positivism, but, as Bryman (2007a) notes, there have been many different versions of positivism which overlap, and which rarely agreed precisely on its essential components.

The case against positivism

Positivism has been described as 'one of the heroic failures of modern philosophy' (Williams and May, 1996: 27). As Hughes and Sharrock (1997) show, one of the fundamental mistakes of positivism is some of the assumptions it made about scientific inquiry. Science is, certainly, interested in producing theoretical explanations but not just on the basis of what can be observed. Indeed, some branches of science consist almost entirely of mathematical formulations. Black holes and sub-atomic particles, for example, have been reasoned from only the most indirect of evidence. Typically, science does not begin from observation, but from theory, to make observations intelligible. Thus, even observations are 'theory laden' (Williams and May, 1996).

Adopting a positivistic stance is not only about adopting certain approaches to the design of research studies. As Crotty (1998) points out, it implies that the results of research will tend to be presented as objective facts and established truths. Popper (1968), however, suggests that no theory can ever be proved simply by multiple observations, since only one instance that refutes the theory would demonstrate it as false. According to Popper, theories cannot be proved to be true – they can only be proved to be false. Hence, with the deductive approach, theories are tested through observation, leading either to the falsification and discarding of the theory, or to the creation of, as yet, unfalsified laws.

Normal science consists of extending the knowledge of the facts that a **paradigm** suggests are especially important, by extending the match between those facts and the paradigm's predictions, and by further articulation of the paradigm itself. But normal science is a puzzle-solver and if it persistently fails to solve problems, then the failure of existing rules will lead to a search for new ones. This is part of what Kuhn (1996) has called a paradigm crisis. It is a crisis which may turn into a revolution if anomalies continue and new people enter the field, such as researchers who are not committed to the traditional rules of normal science and who are able to conceive of a new set of rules.

Case Study 2.1 provides an illustration of how stubbornly existing paradigms resist change – even in the face of emerging evidence that strongly contradicts their fundamental underpinning principles.

┤ CASE STUDY 2.1 ├

The conflict of paradigms

On 22 June 1633, Galileo Galilei was put on trial by the Inquisition in Rome. Charged with heresy, this old man of 69 was threatened with torture, imprisonment and even burning at the stake unless he renounced his claim that the Sun and not the Earth was the centre of the universe, and that the Earth moved around the Sun, and not vice versa.

The idea of an Earth-centred universe was first promulgated by Ptolemy of Alexandria in AD 150. The beauty of the Ptolemaic system was that it worked with some accuracy, enabling astronomers to predict, through complex geometry, the movements of the heavenly bodies. Later, these geocentric (Earth-centred) ideas became entrenched into the teachings of the Church, largely because they fitted neatly with the Christian notion of the centrality of mankind (Hellman, 1998). Hence, Ptolemaic theory became a combination of science, philosophy and religious ideas. Note the long-standing relationship between science and philosophy!

In 1543 Nicolaus Copernicus, a canon in the Polish Catholic Church, challenged the accepted Ptolemaic paradigm with a heliocentric (Sun-centred) system, but, as was traditional, his book was written in Latin and thus was not widely read. A century later, Galileo's repetition of these ideas in *Dialogue on the Great World Systems, Ptolemaic and Copernican* (1632) was written in Italian. As such it was widely accessible and seen by the Pope, Urban VIII, as a direct threat to the teachings of the Church.

Under the Inquisition's threats, Galileo recanted. These threats, after all, were not idle. A friend, Bruno, who had advocated the idea of an infinite universe, was tried by the Inquisition, refused to recant and was burned at the stake in 1600. Of course, the Church could not completely suppress the *Dialogue*. In fact, it was published in England before Galileo's death in 1642. But the trial before the Inquisition is an interesting example of the bitterness that can be generated when far-reaching new ideas come into open conflict with the vested interests of long-accepted paradigms – and the entrenched nature of these paradigms.

— ACTIVITY 2.2 —

What kind of crisis would Kuhn call the events in Case Study 2.1? How were vested interests threatened by Galileo's ideas? Has this crisis been resolved?

We have seen that, at least in the social sciences, many of positivism's avowed certainties about the nature and results of scientific inquiry have been strongly challenged. It should be noted, however, that some of the approaches to research developed under positivism, such as an insistence on empirical inquiry, the use of experimental designs and inductive generalization (to name but three), are still with us (as we shall see in later chapters) in one form or other. In general, however, we now inhabit a **post-positivist** world in which a number of alternative perspectives (for example, anti-positivist, post-positivist and naturalistic) have emerged. Indeed, as Onwuegbuzie, Johnson and Collins (2009) make clear, today's practising quantitative researchers would regard themselves as post-positivists, holding that there is an independent reality to be studied, but that all observation is inherently fallible – we can only approximate the truth, never explaining it perfectly or completely. Hence, given the fallibility of observations, post-positivist research lays emphasis on inferential statistics with its emphasis on assigning *probabilities* that observed findings are correct (not certainties).

Interpretivism

A major anti-positivist stance is **interpretivism**, which looks for 'culturally derived and historically situated interpretations of the social life-world' (Crotty, 1998: 67). There is no, direct, one-to-one relationship between ourselves (subjects) and the world (object). The world is interpreted through the classification schemas of the mind (Williams and May, 1996). In terms of epistemology, interpretivism is closely linked to constructivism. Interpretivism asserts that natural reality (and the laws of science) and social reality are different and therefore require different kinds of method. While the natural sciences are looking for consistencies in the data in order to deduce 'laws' (**nomothetic**), the social sciences often deal with the actions of the individual (**ideographic**).

> Our interest in the social world tends to focus on exactly those aspects that are unique, individual and qualitative, whereas our interest in the natural world focuses on more abstract phenomena, that is, those exhibiting quantifiable, empirical regularities. (Crotty, 1998: 68)

Let us now look at five examples of the interpretivist approach: **symbolic interactionism, phenomenology, realism, hermeneutics** and naturalistic inquiry.

Symbolic interactionism

Symbolic interactionism grew in the 1930s out of the work of the American pragmatist philosophers, including John Dewey and the social psychologist George Herbert Mead. These philosophers shared a disenchantment with what they saw as

SYMBOLIC
INTERACTIONISM

the irrelevance of contemporary philosophy and social science. Instead, they wanted to develop a way of conceptualizing human behaviour that focused on people's practices and lived realities. Central to social behaviour is the notion of meaning. Human interaction with the world is mediated through the process of meaning-making and interpretation. The essential tenets of symbolic interactionism are that:

- People interpret the meaning of objects and actions in the world and then act upon those interpretations.
- Meanings arise from the process of social interaction.
- Meanings are handled in, and are modified by, an interactive process used by people in dealing with the phenomena that are encountered.

Thus, meanings are not fixed or stable but are revised on the basis of experience. This includes the definition of 'self' and of who we are. For example, if someone is promoted from supervisor to manager their perception of themselves and the company may change, which in turn leads to changes in the meaning of objects, and thereby to changes in behaviour.

In order to understand this process, researchers have to study a subject's actions, objects and society from the perspective of the subject themselves. In practice, this can mean entering the field setting and observing at first-hand what is happening. The kinds of research methodologies that are often associated with symbolic interactionism include ethnography and the use of participative observation methods (Chapter 17) and grounded theory (Chapter 7).

Phenomenology

PHENOMENOLOGY

Phenomenology holds that any attempt to understand social reality has to be grounded in people's experiences of that social reality. Hence, phenomenology insists that we must lay aside our prevailing understanding of phenomena and revisit our immediate experience of them in order that new meanings may emerge. Current understandings have to be 'bracketed' to the best of our ability to allow phenomena to 'speak for themselves', unadulterated by our preconceptions. The result will be new meaning, fuller meaning or renewed meaning. Attempts are made to avoid ways in which the prejudices of researchers bias the data. The key is gaining the subjective experience of the subject, sometimes by trying to put oneself in the place of the subject. Hence, phenomenology becomes an exploration, via personal experience, of prevailing cultural understandings. Value is ascribed not only to the interpretations of researchers, but also to the subjects of the research themselves. Far from using a theoretical model that imposes an external logic on a phenomenon, this inductive approach seeks to find the internal logic of the subject. Table 2.2 provides a summary of some of the major distinctions between positivism and phenomenology.

Tesch (1994) distinguishes between phenomenological research and **ethnography**. While both are based upon description and interpretation, ethnographic research is focused more on culture and phenomenology, on human experience of the 'life-world'. So, while the **unit of analysis** of phenomenology is often individuals, ethnographers make use of 'sites'. Phenomenology makes use almost exclusively

Table 2.2   Summary of positivist and phenomenological paradigms

	Positivist paradigm	Phenomenological paradigm
Basic beliefs	The world is external and objective.	The world is socially constructed and subjective.
	The observer is independent.	The observer is a party to what is being observed.
	Science is value-free.	Science is driven by human interests.
The researcher should	Focus on facts	Focus on meanings
	Locate causality between variables	Try to understand what is happening
	Formulate and test hypotheses (deductive approach)	Construct theories and models from the data (inductive approach)
Methods include	Operationalizing concepts so that they can be measured	Using multiple methods to establish different views of a phenomenon
	Using large samples from which to generalize to the population	Using small samples researched in depth or over time
	Quantitative methods	Qualitative methods

Source: Adapted from Easterby-Smith et al., 2002

Table 2.3   Distinctions between phenomenological research and ethnography

Ethnography	Phenomenological research
Study of culture	Study of the 'lifeworld' human experience
Discovering the relationship between culture and behaviour	Exploring the personal construction of the individual's world
Studying 'sites'	Studying individuals
As many informants as possible	Between 5 and 15 'participants'
Use of observation, and some interviewing	Use of in-depth, unstructured interviews
Unit of analysis: event	Unit of analysis: meaning unit
Reliability: triangulation	Reliability: confirmation by participants

Source: Adapted from Tesch, 1994

of interviews, while ethnography's prime mode of data collection is observation (as a participant or outside observer), which is sometimes supplemented by interview data for clarification. Ethnographers pay particular attention to language and the ways in which terms are used in certain cultures. A summary of the distinctions between phenomenological research and ethnography is given in Table 2.3.

Realism

Realism begins from the position that the picture that science paints of the world is a true and accurate one (Chia, 2002). So for the realist researcher, objects of research such as 'culture', 'the organization', 'corporate planning' exist and act quite independently of the observer. They are therefore as available for systematic

REALISM

analysis as natural phenomena. Hence, knowledge is advanced through the process of theory-building in which discoveries add to what is already known. But although reality comprises entities, structures and events, realism holds that some observable 'facts' may be merely illusions. Conversely, there may be phenomena that cannot be observed but which exist none the less. In general, realism holds that there is an external reality 'out there' that can be measured – but achieving this can be difficult.

Madill, Jordan and Shirley (2000) distinguish between three realist epistemologies: naïve, scientific and critical. Naïve realism asserts a rather simplistic correspondence theory of truth in which the world is largely knowable and is, just as it appears to be – provided research methods and instruments are adequately crafted (Niiniluoto, 1999). Scientific realism considers that the scientific method can tap true representations of the world, although this may sometimes be fallible. Critical realism, however, contends that the way we perceive the world depends, in part, on our beliefs and expectations, one outcome being that the complete truth may be hard to come by (Bunge, 1993). Critical realism admits an inherent subjectivity in the production of knowledge and has much in common with constructionist positions (Madill et al., 2000).

In terms of methodology, pluralism is the 'gold standard' of realist research (Pawson and Tilley, 2001: 323). This means that nothing is ruled out, with methods being used according to opportunity and need. Hence, in a comparison of blood donation processes between market and non-market suppliers, Titmuss (1970) used a national survey of 3,800 blood donors, unstructured interviews, meta-analysis of previous studies, document analysis and statistics.

Hermeneutics

HERMENEUTICS

The hermeneutic tradition is associated largely with nineteenth-century German philosophy, but also has connections with phenomenology and the psychoanalysis of Freud. According to a hermeneutic perspective, social reality is seen as socially constructed, rather than being rooted in objective fact. Hence, hermeneutics argues that interpretation should be given more standing than explanation and description. Social reality is too complex to be understood through the process of observation. The scientist must interpret in order to achieve deeper levels of knowledge and also self-understanding.

Naturalistic inquiry

NATURALISTIC INQUIRY

According to Lincoln and Guba (1994), in the **naturalistic paradigm** there are multiple constructed realities that can only be studied holistically. Inquiry into these multiple realities raises more questions than it answers, so that prediction and control of outcomes is a largely futile expectation, although some level of understanding can be achieved (Guba, 1985). Inquiry itself cannot be detached but is value-bounded by the perspectives of the researcher. Rather than aiming to generalize, inquiry develops an ideographic body of knowledge that describes individual cases. Within these cases, plausible inferences on events and processes are made, but this falls short of claiming causality. Phenomena can only be understood within their environment or setting; they cannot be isolated or held constant while others are manipulated. The real world is too complex, diverse and interdependent for this (Lincoln, 1985).

Research designs cannot be pre-specified, but 'emerge, unroll, cascade, or unfold during the research process' (Lincoln, 1985: 142). Because naturalists believe in the concept of multiple, constructed realities, it would be incongruent to specify these designs in advance. However, the types of research methods usually selected by naturalistic inquirers involve those most closely associated with a human component: interviewing, participant observation, document and content analysis (and other forms of unobtrusive measures).

Critical inquiry

It is worth having a brief overview of **critical inquiry** because it offers quite a different perspective to positivism and interpretivism. This critical form of research is a meta-process of investigation, which questions currently held values and assumptions and challenges conventional social structures. It invites both researchers and participants to discard what they term 'false consciousness' in order to develop new ways of understanding as a guide to effective action, confronting unjust social systems. In a Marxist sense, the critical inquiry perspective is not content to interpret the world but also seeks to change it. The assumptions that lie beneath critical inquiry are that:

- Ideas are mediated by power relations in society.
- Certain groups in society are privileged over others and exert an oppressive force on subordinate groups.
- What are presented as 'facts' cannot be disentangled from ideology and the self-interest of dominant groups.
- Mainstream research practices are implicated, even if unconsciously, in the reproduction of the systems of class, race and gender oppression.

Those adhering to the critical inquiry perspective accuse interpretivists of adopting an uncritical stance towards the culture they are exploring, whereas the task of researchers is to call the structures and values of society into question.

Feminism

Like Marxism and critical inquiry, feminist epistemologies take the view that what a person knows is largely determined by their social position. But whereas Marxism defines social class in terms of a person's relationship to the means of production, feminism regards women themselves as an oppressed social class. Because men come from a position of dominance, their knowledge of the world is distorted. In contrast, women, being subject to domination, have a less distorted social experience that has the potential to produce less distorted knowledge claims (Williams and May, 1996). But what counts as knowledge is also challenged. Attempts at rational or objective approaches to research are seen as the remit of male researchers, reflecting and prioritizing male values. In contrast, women have access to a deeper reality through their personal experiences (of oppression), and through their feelings and emotions.

FEMINIST
RESEARCH

As we will see in Chapter 17 on ethnography, there are some research methodologies that have become to be seen as particularly appropriate by feminist researchers. According to Huisman (2008) what makes ethnography feminist is its concern with the social positioning of the researcher in relation to research subjects, particularly the notion of reflexivity. Hence, the researcher seeks to make her assumptions and values (biased or otherwise) as explicit as possible. Just as important as self-examination is the idea of reciprocity – researchers and participants are equal and both should benefit from the research (McNamara, 2009).

Postmodernism

Postmodernism is far from being a unified system of thought and is sometimes used interchangeably with concepts such as deconstructionism and post-structuralism. Emerging from the disillusionment of French intellectuals with Marxism after the events of 1968, postmodernism was not just an attack on positivism, but on the entire historical agenda of modernity – and particularly Marxism (Delanty, 1997). Postmodernism rejects any notion of social 'emancipation', emphasizing instead multiplicity, ambiguity, ambivalence and fragmentation. Whereas philosophers such as Habermas had seen fragmentation in negative terms and as a threat to communication, postmodernism views it quite positively as an opportunity for choice. Hence postmodern analysis often focuses on themes within advertising, lifestyles, fashion, sub-cultures and gender.

In terms of research, the primary task becomes the deconstruction of texts to expose how values and interests are embedded within them (Williams and May, 1996). The focus becomes not one of how these texts describe the 'reality' of the world, but how the social world becomes represented, and how meanings are produced. Texts are therefore seen as social practices, embedded with multiple values and vested interests, not the reporting of independent, objective judgements. As we have seen, in contrast to other epistemologies, postmodernism stresses a *becoming* ontology.

Pragmatism

Pragmatism is presented here because it is a relatively old philosophy but one that has seen a recent revival. Pragmatism was founded by American philosophers Charles Pierce (1839–1914), William James (1842–1910) and John Dewey (1859–1952) at the beginning of the twentieth century in an attempt to help American society face the many problems it was confronting at the time. Pierce is often referred to as the first spokesman of pragmatism, James as its translator to a wider audience, and Dewey as its most well-known advocate, due to his influence on pedagogical methods and educational systems (Sundin and Johannisson, 2006). For pragmatism, an ideology is true only if it works (particularly in promoting equity, freedom and justice) and generates practical consequences for society. Hence, pragmatists focus not on whether a proposition fits a particular ontology, but whether it suits a purpose and is capable of creating action (Rorty, 1998). A belief is true if that belief opens opportunities for better ways of democratic, purposeful living. However, pragmatism struggled to maintain its influence beyond the first three decades of the twentieth century (Kelemen and Rumens, 2012).

Since the 1970s, however, pragmatism has regained some of its popularity, largely because of the insights it has provided for research into management and organizations and also because it is seen by some to provide an epistemological justification for mixing approaches and methods (Onwuegbuzie et al., 2009). While in pragmatist research, research paradigms can remain separate, they can also be mixed or combined into another research design. Hence, pragmatism views the mixing of quantitative and qualitative data in a single study not only as legitimate, but in some cases necessary. We will look at mixed methods in detail in Chapter 8.

RESEARCH METHODOLOGIES

We have examined, briefly, the significance of both epistemology and theoretical perspectives in research design. Let us now look at applying these in practice by exploring some of the alternative research methodologies. The choice of research methodology is determined by a combination of several factors – for example, whether the researcher believes that there is some sort of external 'truth' out there that needs discovering, or whether the task of research is to explore and unpick people's multiple perspectives in natural, field settings. It is influenced, then, by whether the research is inclined towards a positivist, interpretivist, or other perspective. It will also be influenced, for example, by the researcher's attitude towards the ways in which she or he thinks theory should be used – whether research should begin with a theoretical model or perspective (deductive approach) or whether such models should emerge from the data itself (inductively).

RESEARCH
METHODS
INTERVIEW

In examining each of the following research methodologies (selected to illustrate a range of approaches), pause each time to consider whether you think each is inclined towards a more 'being' or 'becoming' ontology. A Case Study is provided for each methodology to help you.

Experimental and quasi-experimental research

In classical, scientific experiments, subjects are randomly assigned to either an experimental or a control group. The experimental group receives the 'treatment' and the results are compared with the control group that does not receive the treatment. Hence, the researcher manipulates the **independent variable** (the variable that the researcher has some control over) to see its effect on the **dependent variable** (the response that is measured). For example, an experiment could measure the effect on test scores (dependent variable) of a new computer-assisted teaching system (independent variable). In the real world, however, it is often not possible to conduct truly experimental research because it is difficult to find experimental and control groups that are closely matched in terms of key variables (such as age, gender, income, work grade, etc.). Instead, a quasi-experimental design is used where the researcher, for example, has to take existing groups rather than drawing on random samples. Instead of trying to manipulate an independent variable the researcher will often attempt to find groups of people who have experienced it in their own natural setting. An attempt is then made to compare the behaviour of this group with that of a similar group that has not experienced the event or phenomenon. In experimental and quasi-experimental research there is also the tendency to make use of hypotheses which the experiment seeks either to support or to refute. In other words, experimental research is usually deductive.

EXPERIMENTAL
RESEARCH

QUASI-
EXPERIMENTAL
RESEARCH

Experimental and quasi-experimental research, then, places an emphasis on:

- Reproducing the techniques of the laboratory experiment with highly structured methods.
- The generation of initial hypotheses.
- The control of variables.
- Accurate (quantitative) measurement of outcomes.
- Generalization from samples to similar populations.

CASE STUDY 2.2

Experimental research

A global organization selling Internet hardware, software and services, has an extensive set of internal training programmes, each of which is formally assessed. The company wants to reduce the size of the overall training budget through the use of e-learning, but is concerned as to whether learning through this mechanism is more effective, less effective or makes no difference. It is believed by the research team that e-learning will be marginally more effective – thus they have a working hypothesis.

All 200 members of a representative sample are given a pre-test of their understanding of a selected subject. Then the subject is taught to 100 participants through traditional, classroom learning (the control group) and to the other 100 participants through a specially designed e-learning program (the experimental group). All employees are given a post-test, and the gain-scores (the differences between the pre-test and post-test score) compared between the two groups.

Experimental and quasi-experimental research designs will be considered in more detail in Chapter 6.

Phenomenological research

Phenomenology is a theoretical perspective that uses relatively unstructured methods of data collection. One of the advantages of phenomenology is that, because of its emphasis on the inductive collection of large amounts of data, it is more likely to pick up factors that were not part of the original research focus. For example, Groenewald (2004) describes a study in which he sought to investigate the phenomenon of the growing of talent and the role of cooperative education in this process. In carrying out the study he conducted long, unstructured interviews with 10 school managers, created field notes including reflective 'memos' on his experience of the process, and got programme students to write essays about their experiences, with the aim of getting to understand the participants' world. He was not 'looking for answers', but allowing the data to emerge.

Phenomenological research is about producing **'thick descriptions'** of people's experiences and perspectives within their natural settings. But it is often based upon quite small case studies giving rise to concerns about its generalizability to other situations. Also, because it is generally unstructured, phenomenological research may be difficult to replicate. Phenomenological research, then:

- Emphasizes inductive logic.
- Seeks the opinions and subjective accounts and interpretations of participants.
- Relies on qualitative analysis of data.
- Is not so much concerned with generalizations to larger populations, but with contextual description and analysis.

Phenomenological research

A city police authority has spent three years conducting a 'war' on street soliciting in one of the city's poorest areas. Since the legal crackdown has not had the desired result, the police authority decides that the problem needs to be understood before new solutions are tried. A research study is commissioned to find out why these women turn to prostitution, the attitudes of the local community to their activities, and what sort of clients seek the women's services and where they come from.

Three female researchers rent a flat in the area for six months. They do not try to hide who they are or what they are doing, but nevertheless, manage to build up a rapport and trust with 10 of the women. Sometimes this is through visiting their 'pitches' where they are working, at other times it is through chance meetings while shopping, in bars or at the launderette. The researchers also take time to talk to local people about the issue, including local police officers, through casual conversations, rather than formal interviews. The team gathers data sets consisting of detailed personal biographies of the women, their own attitudes towards their work, and the range of problems and issues raised by members of the local community. Having written these biographies, the researchers revisit the women to have the transcripts checked for accuracy.

Phenomenological research will be considered in greater detail in Chapter 7.

Analytical surveys

These attempt to test a theory in the field through exploring the association between variables. **Analytical surveys** are highly structured and place an emphasis on the careful random selection of samples, so that the results can be generalized to other situations or contexts. On the other hand, the very tightness of the survey structure may hinder the ability of respondents to provide illuminating information in a way that they would like.

Like the truly experimental approach, analytic surveys emphasize:

- A deductive approach.
- The identification of the research population.
- The drawing of a representative sample from the population.
- Control of variables.
- The generation of both qualitative and quantitative data.
- Generalizability of results.

Action research

Action research involves close collaboration between researcher and practitioners, and places an emphasis on promoting change within organizations such as offices, hospitals, schools and prisons. While the emphasis is on seeking information on the attitudes and perspectives of practitioners in the field, the way in which data are collected may involve both quantitative and qualitative methods. The main action research medium, however, is the case study, or multiple case studies. In some

— CASE STUDY 2.4 —

Analytical surveys

A government department is becoming increasingly concerned that the level of waste recycling by domestic households is not increasing despite a major publicity campaign and the provision of local amenities for recycling. The department commissions a nationally based survey to explore for each household contacted:

- The level of recycling.
- Attitudes to the environment.
- Attitudes to recycling specific waste products.
- The size and location of the household.
- The convenience of recycling facilities available.
- The household income level.
- The number of adults and children per house.

The survey is constructed so that **correlation** levels (strength of relationships) between levels of recycling and the other variables can be calculated and analysed. The hypothesis being tested is that levels of recycling are strongly positively correlated with attitudes to the environment (determined through the collection of qualitative data) and moderately positively correlated with access to local recycling amenities. Hence, if the hypothesis is confirmed, government policy will focus on changing attitudes towards recycling rather than on the provision of more amenities.

Analytical surveys will be considered in more detail in Chapter 10.

ACTION
RESEARCH

research designs, both an experimental and a control case study may be used, so emulating the experimental approach. Action research then:

- Involves both researchers and practitioners (or practitioners as researchers within their own organization).
- Can be highly structured and involve the use of experimental and control groups used to test a hypothesis.
- Can also be quite unstructured and used inductively (and qualitatively).

— CASE STUDY 2.5 —

Action research

A group of 20 teachers provide intensive educational support to children with special educational, emotional and physical needs in four community schools. The educational attainment of the special needs children in these schools has remained depressingly low over time. The special needs teachers decide to undertake an action research study using their four schools as the experimental cohort and four other schools in the district as the control. Working collaboratively with their other teaching colleagues in the school, a series of ten 'mould-breaking' workshops are run in which issues are explored and new solutions formulated. These are prioritized and a number of solutions implemented in the second semester. The educational attainment and other indicators are then calculated for the children from the four schools involved in the action research project, and compared to those of children in the other district schools (the control).

Action research methods will be considered in more detail in Chapter 13.

Heuristic inquiry

Heuristic inquiry is a process that begins with a question or a problem which the researcher tries to illuminate or find an answer to. The question itself is usually focused on an issue that has posed a *personal* problem and to which answers are required. It seeks, through open-ended inquiry, self-directed search and immersion in active experience, to 'get inside' the question by becoming one with it.

According to Moustakas (1990), one of the primary processes of heuristic research is self-dialogue in which the researcher enters into a conversation with the phenomenon and is questioned by it. It is hoped that the process will lead to self-discoveries, awareness and enhanced understanding. Through this, the researcher is able to develop the skills and ability to understand the problem itself and, in turn, to develop the understanding of others.

Philosophically, heuristic inquiry does not start from the premise that there is an external 'objective' truth to be discovered. In contrast, it starts phenomenologically from the belief that understanding grows out of direct human experience and can only be discovered initially through self-inquiry. Heuristic research, then, is autobiographical, providing for a deep, personal analysis. It is richly descriptive, but also strongly subjective, and weak in terms of generalizability.

HEURISTIC
INQUIRY

Heuristic research, then, involves the researcher in:

- A deep personal questioning of what it is they wish to research.
- Living, sleeping and merging with the research question.
- Allowing inner workings of intuition to extend understanding of the question.
- Reviewing all the data from personal experiences to identify tacit meanings.
- Forming a creative synthesis, including ideas for and against a proposition.

— CASE STUDY 2.6 —

Heuristic research

The Operations Director of a company finds that he is passed over for promotion to Chief Executive for the third time. In an attempt to understand why this has occurred, he approaches the Chairperson, who has been largely responsible for this decision and asks if she will join him in a heuristic research project to uncover the reasons behind the decision. At first, the Chairperson is reluctant because she thinks (rightly) that the process will reveal some of her confidential thoughts. But she eventually agrees because she realizes that the process of working together might articulate for her the personal qualities she is seeking in a Chief Executive.

The Operations Director, who acts as the researcher, begins with a deep personal reflection on what he wants to achieve in the research. Then, through a series of open and frank discussions with the Chairperson, he works through his feelings towards his current role, his successes and failures in numerous projects, his expectations of the Chairperson and her expectations of him. Over a period of five meetings he begins to understand that the blockage is not based upon prejudice, but on a feeling (shared by other members of the Board) that he is an excellent Operations Director, but lacks the *strategic* vision to be the Chief Executive. Through a process of explication (the full examination of awakened consciousness), he begins to realize that this analysis is probably correct.

Examine the range of research methodologies outlined above. Select one methodology that you think could be valid for your own research uses and one that is inappropriate. Justify your choices.

SELECTING RESEARCH APPROACHES AND STRATEGIES

In this chapter we have examined some of the philosophies of research, two approaches to research (inductive and deductive) and, within the context of truth and perspective-seeking objectives, some research methodologies (experimental, survey, phenomenological, etc.). We now need to put these together within a coherent framework (or as near to one as we can get) and to add a time horizon and data collection methods. Notice that data collection methods are being discussed last (see Figure 2.3). Novice researchers may be tempted to begin with the design, say, of a questionnaire, so that data can be gathered without delay, but Figure 2.3 shows that other stages must be considered first.

Connecting the research elements

As we saw earlier, it is wise to start by considering epistemology. At first sight, this might seem rather irrelevant. But your approach to research and the research methods that you use will be influenced by whether you think it is possible (or desirable) to try to measure an objective 'truth', or whether you think that the real world cannot be measured in this way. As we have seen, the theoretical perspective of interpretivism sees the world as too complex to be reduced to a set of observable 'laws'. Generalizability is less important than understanding the real workings behind 'reality'. With your research topic in mind, you will probably have a view as to whether you want to measure and generalize to a larger population or to seek 'thick descriptions', through the collection of qualitative data. Alternatively, your approach might include elements of both. Hence, Figure 2.3 does not illustrate a dividing wall between epistemologies and perspectives, but a gradual shading of one into the other.

We also have access to a range of research methodologies. Figure 2.3 deliberately shows the experimental methodology beneath the deductive/positivism side of the diagram. Conversely, action research has been placed more towards inductive/interpretivism. But it is dangerous to categorize research methodologies against specific approaches and philosophies. Action research, for example, can incorporate a qualitative, inductive approach with an emphasis on seeking the views and perspectives of participants. Equally, it can use, say, a series of case studies involving an intervention with a number of groups, with others used as a control – in other words, an experimental methodology. Figure 2.3, then, illustrates some broad tendencies that should not be interpreted as concrete relationships. What is important, is that whatever philosophy, approach and methodology you adopt for your research, you should be able to justify your mix in relation to your research philosophy and research question(s).

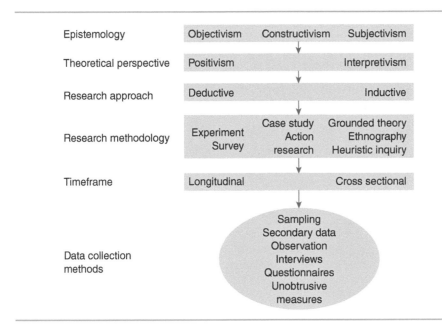

Figure 2.3   The elements of the research process

Source: Adapted from Saunders et al., 2012

→ **TOP TIP 2.2** ←

In planning a research project, never begin by deciding on what data gathering tool or approach to use. Begin by identifying what it is you are actually trying to research. Link this issue to your appreciation and commitment to one or more of the epistemological stances discussed above. If you come to the selection of data gathering tools towards the end of your planning process, you should be on the right lines.

GRAY ON
PLANNING A
RESEARCH
PROJECT

Timeframes for research

In planning your research you will usually have some sort of idea as to the time-scales you have available to you. If these are short-term, then you will probably have to adopt a **cross-sectional study** using a 'snapshot' approach where the data are collected at one point in time. Cross-sectional studies often use a survey methodology. For example, they might seek to measure staff attitudes towards the introduction of new working practices, or to compare crime rates for particular types of crime between different cities. Most research studies are cross-sectional, mainly because of the pressure of time and resources.

CROSS-
SECTIONAL
STUDY

If your timescales are more generous, it may be possible to undertake a **longitudinal study**, to study change and development over time. Taking our example above, a longitudinal study of working practices might examine changes in staff attitudes over time, looking at attitudes before the introduction of new working practices, and then at various periods afterwards. Similarly, crime rates can be studied to identify where rates are falling and rising. This might allow researchers to begin to identify explanatory factors such as demographic changes, social conditions and policing methods.

LONGITUDINAL
STUDIES

Exploratory, descriptive, explanatory and interpretive studies

While we have so far classified studies by their research methodology, they can also be classified according to their purpose. As Robson (2002) explains, there are three possible forms of study: exploratory, descriptive and explanatory. To these Maxwell (1996) adds a fourth, interpretive studies. Punch (2005) maintains that where a research area is relatively new or unexplored, descriptive studies may be adequate. However, for well worked research areas, where there is already a plethora of descriptive information, a more exploratory approach is advisable.

Exploratory studies

As the name suggests, exploratory studies seek to explore what is happening and to ask questions about it. They are particularly useful when not enough is known about a phenomenon. An exploratory study, then, may help to decide whether it is worth researching the issue or not. As Saunders et al. (2007) suggest, exploratory studies can be conducted by:

- A search of the literature.
- Talking to experts in the field.
- Conducting focus group interviews.

Having established the main constructs or focus of a study, it may then be possible to conduct explanatory or interpretive research.

Descriptive studies

According to Hedrick et al. (1993), the purpose of a descriptive study is to provide a picture of a phenomenon as it naturally occurs. This may, indeed, by purely descriptive (for example, the level and nature of crime among 16–21-year-olds). But it may also comprise a normative study, comparing the data against some standard (for example, comparing drug use against legal standards of drug classification to gauge the seriousness of crime). Descriptive studies seek to 'draw a picture' of a situation, person or event or show how things are related to each other. As Blumberg, Cooper and Schindler (2005) point out one of the weaknesses of descriptive studies is that they cannot explain why an event has occurred.

Explanatory studies

An explanatory study sets out to explain and account for the descriptive information. So, while descriptive studies may ask 'what' kinds of questions, explanatory studies seek to ask 'why' and 'how' questions. This distinction between descriptive and explanatory research applies equally to both quantitative and qualitative research.

Some studies can also be correlative in nature, with the emphasis on discovering causal relationships between variables. So we could determine the relationship between drug use and other variables such as social class, employment, attitudes to drugs, etc.

Interpretive studies

Interpretive studies seek to explore peoples' experiences and their views or perspectives of these experiences. Interpretive studies are, typically, inductive in nature and often associated with qualitative approaches to data gathering and analysis.

Using multiple methods

Much of the discussion so far has tended to offer a dichotomy of approaches – inductive or deductive, experimental or case study, cross-sectional or longitudinal. In practice, however, it is often the case that multiple methods will be used. One reason is that research projects usually include a number of different research questions, so a research method appropriate for one question may be inappropriate for another. The second reason for using multiple methods is that it enables **triangulation** to be used. Easterby-Smith et al. (2002) refer to data triangulation as the collecting of data over different times or from different sources. This approach is typical of cross-sectional designs. Methodological triangulation is also possible, with the use of a combination of methods such as case studies, interviews and surveys. All methods have their strengths and weaknesses. So not only does the use of multiple methods assist in data triangulation, it helps to balance out any of the potential weaknesses in each data collection method. But whichever methods are used, in the final analysis Oakley's argument is sound: '*all* methods must be open, consistently applied and replicable by others' (1999: 252, original emphasis). These multiple methods approaches to research are discussed in more detail in Chapter 8: Research Design: Mixed Methods.

TRIANGULATION

Summary

- The dominant research paradigm for much of the twentieth century was positivism, but, today, at least in the social sciences, this has been largely replaced by anti-positivist or post-positivist stances such as interpretivism.
- Through the inductive approach, data are accumulated and analysed to see if relationships emerge between variables. The deductive approach uses a theory to generate a working hypothesis concerning relationships between variables. The hypothesis is operationalized and tested and is either accepted or rejected on the basis of the evidence.
- The inductive and deductive methods are not mutually exclusive. A researcher may turn a collection of data into a set of concepts, models or even theories (inductive approach) which are then tested through experimentation (deductive).
- Approaches to research include both truth-seeking and perspective-seeking methods. Truth-seeking methods tend to adopt more experimental or quasi-experimental approaches. Perspective-seeking methods tend to be more interpretivist (for example, phenomenological) and to generate qualitative data. These relationships should be treated as tendencies rather than as laws.
- Selecting approaches to research involves adopting a research philosophy, and an appropriate research approach and methodology. In practice, research often necessitates the use of multiple methods to achieve triangulation.

REVIEW QUESTIONS

1. Can we ever conduct research without having first established our epistemological position?
2. Positivism has been described as 'one of the heroic failures of modern philosophy.' Do you agree with this statement?
3. Why is reflexivity often associated with feminist theoretical perspectives? Should it be associated with all perspectives?
4. We can mix data collection methods in the same study (for example, surveys plus interviews), but is it ever acceptable to mix epistemological positions?

FURTHER READING

Paul, J. (2004) *Introduction to the Philosophies of Research and Criticism in Education and the Social Sciences.* London: Prentice Hall. A comprehensive book that deals with nine alternative philosophies of research including postmodernism, constructivism, interpretivism and post-structuralism.

Cohen, L., Manion, L. and Morrison, K. (2011) *Research Methods in Education*, 7th edn. London: Routledge. See especially Chapter 1 on Paradigms of Social Research.

Crotty, M. (1998) *The Foundation of Social Research: Meaning and Perspectives in the Research Process.* London: Sage. Provides a very readable description and explanation of the major epistemological stances and how they originated.

Scheurich, J.J. (1997) *Research Methods in the Postmodern.* London: Falmer. Provides an introduction to how postmodernism can be applied to critiquing a wide range of approaches to research, and describes the implications of postmodernism for practice.

Reinharz, S. (1992) *Feminist Methods in Social Research.* New York: Oxford University Press. Covers approaches such as ethnography, survey research, experimental research, case studies and action research, all from a feminist perspective.

JOURNAL RESOURCES

Wynn, Jr. D. and Williams, C.K. (2012) 'Principles for conducting critical realist case study research in information systems', *MIS Quarterly*, 36(3): 787–810. Shows how critical realism can be applied to research methodologies. Although the focus is information systems, the analysis is of general applicability.

Chen, Y.Y., Shek, D.T. and Bu, F.F. (2011) 'Applications of interpretive and constructionist research methods in adolescent research: Philosophy, principles and examples', *International Journal of Adolescent Medicine and Health*, 23(2): 129–139. Gives a brief introduction to interpretivism, constructionism and constructivism, showing similarities and differences between interpretivism and constructionism in terms of their histories, ontological and epistemological stances, and research applications.

JUSTIFYING
KNOWLEDGE

Carter, S.M. and Little, M. (2007) 'Justifying knowledge, justifying method, taking action: Epistemologies, methodologies, and methods in qualitative research', *Qualitative Health Research*, 17(10): 1316–1328. An article that demonstrates some of the relationships between knowledge, epistemology, methodology and methods from a qualitative research perspective.

METHODS
MATTER

Schmierback, M. (2005) 'Method matters: The influence of methodology on journalists' assessments of social science research', *Science Communication*, 26(3): 269–287. Describes a study of journalists to determine whether the use of a quantitative or qualitative approach to research influences their judgement as to the quality of a study. It does!

Johnson, M. (1999) 'Observations on positivism and pseudoscience in qualitative nursing research', *Journal of Advanced Nursing*, 30(1): 67–73. Examines the boundaries between positivism, interpretivism, and what the author refers to as pseudoscience.

3

SELECTING AND PLANNING RESEARCH PROPOSALS AND PROJECTS

CHAPTER INTRODUCTION

Chapter outline

Selecting a research topic	40
Topics to avoid	48
Planning the project	50

Writing academic proposals	50
Writing organizational proposals	63
The final stages for academic and organizational proposals	64

Keywords

Research topics

Academic proposals

Organizational proposals

Chapter objectives

After reading this chapter you will be able to:

- Generate new ideas for research topics.
- Identify a good research topic using selected criteria.
- Identify which kinds of topics to avoid.
- Write an academic proposal for a research project.
- Write an organizational proposal.

Having read Chapters 1 and 2, you should now have a clearer idea about the methodologies, approaches and tools that are essential for the design and implementation of a good research topic. The question remains, of course, what *is* a good research topic? Generally, research projects can be designed as part of an academic programme of study, or as a result of a business or organizational need. While the former will probably require a stronger element of theoretical underpinning, both will need a sharp, practical focus or application. The outputs from research projects not only have potential benefits for organizations and their management, they can also be a vital element in personal learning and development. Clearly, the best approach is to select a research topic that interests you, and one that is likely to maintain your interest. The research process can be a long and arduous one, so you need to be committed to your subject. Winkler and McCuen (2007) suggest that you also need to select a subject area that has sufficient scope to generate several research projects. So, for example, investigating how a particular brand of laptops is produced and shipped to a local retail outlet may not prove particularly illuminating. On the other hand, a study of laptop component international supply logistics may offer greater scope for the research process (including products, processes and regions), the range of literature to be consulted and the value of the research outcomes.

If you find you have difficulty finding a research subject, then talk to colleagues to see what sort of issues concern them. Discuss the matter with your academic supervisor or line manager. Think back over your course about which topics really interested you and how the themes here could be developed. Other useful sources are professional journals and magazines that often contain articles on issues that are currently engaging the minds of business, commerce, public sector and voluntary organizations. You might also browse through the relevant sections of your local bookshop to see what kinds of titles are being published in your areas of interest. Some more practical suggestions for generating ideas are given in this chapter. Advice is also given on how to select a research topic and on how to write a successful proposal for your research. It also suggests how you can plan a schedule for conducting your research and how you should carry out the project, not only efficiently, but ethically.

SELECTING A RESEARCH TOPIC

You may already have a research topic in mind and hence want to use this section as a means of checking its validity. Alternatively, you may have been commissioned by your organization to undertake a specific piece of research. In the latter case, do not feel that you should be a passive recipient of such projects. Make use of the criteria in this section to evaluate and renegotiate the focus of your project if you feel that this is necessary.

GETTING STARTED IN RESEARCH

When to select a research topic

Obviously, this is going to be a matter of individual choice. Some researchers have a very clear idea and focus at an early stage. Indeed, they may have embarked on a programme of study precisely because they want to tackle a specific end project. For others, and probably the majority, a research topic emerges only towards the end of the study programme, or as a result of an emerging problem in the workplace. For some, the problem may be making a choice between a number of potential topics; for others, there may be only one focus.

Sources of research topics

There are, essentially, two ways of identifying a research topic. One is through the literature – books and academic and professional journals – which may raise interesting themes and topics that can be related to your own interests. The other route is directly from the workplace or community setting. Line managers, supervisors or project teams may all require assistance, and this can often be a fruitful source of research focus. In effect, the researcher then acts as a kind of internal consultant to a project team.

What is a good research topic?

Whatever topic you choose, it is likely that you will begin to develop or enhance a range of personal skills. A good topic, then, is one that gives you free rein to maximize this self-development. Jankowicz (2004) argues that such personal development might include:

WHAT MAKES GOOD RESEARCH

- Improving personal time management.
- Gaining access to respondents.
- Interviewing respondents.
- Speaking to an audience.
- Persuading people to cooperate.
- Dealing with uncertainty about data.

But it must also be a subject that interests you. Since research may involve many hours of planning, execution, data analysis and report writing, you will quickly tire of any topic that you thought was only moderately interesting at the outset. It is also a good idea to choose a subject that allows you to demonstrate your skills and abilities. Hence, if, say, you are undertaking a project at the end of an academic programme, you will need to select a subject that gives you scope for showing the integration of various fields of knowledge and analysis. For example, if you are researching in a health context and want to evaluate the effectiveness of a programme given to newly qualified nurses for counselling the next of kin of patients who have died, this provides you with an opportunity to integrate a knowledge of programme evaluation, counselling techniques and ethics. Conversely, researching the attainment levels between boy and girl Year 5 pupils in one state primary school would be too narrow, partly because the sample size used is so small and unlikely to yield results of any (statistical) significance.

Within the workplace, being able to demonstrate the skills of planning, data analysis and report writing can enhance your prestige and even promotional opportunities.

Meeting academic requirements

You must ensure that the research subject is capable of meeting academic requirements if you are undertaking a programme of study – for example, it is capable of generating a dissertation, thesis or report of sufficient length. As Raimond (1993) suggests, also be sure that your topic is capable of being linked to the appropriate academic theory. Management theory, for example, tends to evolve and change quite quickly – for example, there are countless theories of leadership with new ones being coined each year. It is bad practice to rely entirely on textbooks, since they can take years to write and are often out of date by the time they are published. Your research should also incorporate the use of academic journals (many of which are now online), which tend to be more topical. Academic journals also include reports on empirical studies from which you can glean a greater understanding of research methodologies and tools.

➤ TOP TIP 3.1 ◄

Before writing an academic dissertation or thesis, check out the university's guidelines. Look in particular at requirements for length. Also pay close attention to marking schemes and how marks are distributed for different elements such as descriptions of the literature, methodology and analysis.

Gaining access

You will need access to relevant information, material and data. If you select an issue where these are lacking, you have little chance of completing the project.

- Can you gain access? Remember that some issues in organizations, communities or networks are sensitive or confidential, for example, some financial data (such as pay scales), redundancy plans, legal records (for example, sex offenders records), health records, etc. Indeed, Flick (2009) warns that a research project is an intrusion into the life of an institution and is inherently unsettling for it.
- Can you minimize disruption? Apart from written or Web-based information, one of the essential elements of research is access to people. Who will you need to meet (perhaps to interview) and how busy are they? A classic contradiction is that the more important your project (to the organization), the more likely it is that the people you need to see are senior in the organization, and too busy to spare the time to be interviewed. The challenge is to gain access to these people despite this by being flexible and offering a range of interview dates/times.

In community settings, the researcher may be seen as an intruder or outsider. Gaining access will be facilitated if you can use someone who is respected by the community who can act as a gatekeeper.

Thankfully, new phenomena such as social media (and particularly LinkedIn) can help here. If you do not have your own direct access into an organization, many businesses have their own LinkedIn website. You can locate people (and their job titles) and contact them using what LinkedIn call 'InMail'. However, you will have to join one of the Premium Accounts and pay a fee for this. The protocols for doing this are just as important (indeed, more important) as when you are using your own contacts – see Top Tip 3.2 below.

➤ TOP TIP 3.2 ◀

Gaining access will be made easier if you:

- Get sponsorship/support as high up the organization or community setting as possible.
- Be clear and transparent about the aims and focus of the research.
- Keep the aims of the research coherent and bounded. Do not give the impression that you are about to 'hunt around' for any interesting fact that might emerge.
- Be clear about the research methodology (e.g., number of interviews and with whom) so the potential level of disruption is known.
- Make clear what the organization might gain from allowing you access. Typically, this might be a copy of your research or a summary.
- Demonstrate how confidentiality is going to be kept.
- Above all, make sure that any communication you send is accurate and contains no errors of grammar or fact. Even the slightest mistake creates a very bad impression and will almost certainly reduce your chances of gaining sponsorship.

GRAY ON
GAINING
ACCESS TO
ORGANIZATIONS

Getting sponsorship and using networks

It helps if you have a sponsor or client who can give you either financial backing, or at least moral or practical support. The latter might involve 'opening doors' in the organization and facilitating your access to people with information. Figure 3.1 shows the kind of networks that may exist, or which you may request are established, to provide you with assistance. Note that not all elements of this network are necessarily connected. They all perform different roles, so you need to understand or negotiate what each can offer you.

➤ ON THE WEB 3.1 ◀

Make a list of the support networks available to you. These might include online social networks such as LinkedIn. See the following Web link for a list of social networks available: http://en.wikipedia.org/wiki/List_of_social_networking_websites.

Are they readily accessible? Are they sufficient?

Using the time available

Be sure that the research can be completed within the time available. There is always a tendency to underestimate the time needed for a project. However, note that there are texts on time management and project planning that can help you here. Further difficulties may arise if the topic chosen is dependent upon the

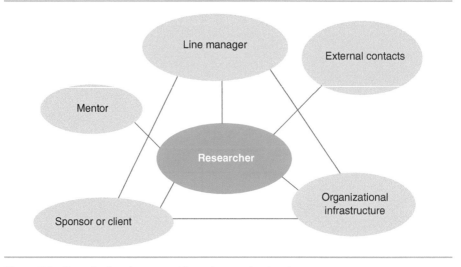

Figure 3.1   Organizational sponsorship and support networks

implementation of another project within the organization. If this project becomes delayed (which is often the case), or abandoned, then your research project may quickly reach an impasse. For example, IT projects (particularly large ones) are notorious for going 'over time' as well as over budget. The best approach is to draw up a research plan before starting the project, with clear indications of dependencies and potential bottlenecks.

Considering your capabilities and experience

This may seem obvious, but selecting an issue that is within your capabilities is essential. Your skills will, hopefully, develop during the course of the research process, but, say, choosing a topic that requires robust statistical skills when you are comfortable with only basic mathematics may be a recipe for disaster. Experience may be a different matter. As the Johari window in Figure 3.2 shows, you can choose projects that are congruent with both your work area and experience (the safe approach), or, moving towards the top-right side of the diagram, beyond both your work and current knowledge set. This poses greater risks, but also enhances opportunities for personal development. Moving the project into an unfamiliar work area may also provide opportunities for networking amongst new groups of people which can be advantageous for both the project and your own professional future (including your future as a researcher).

ACTIVITY 3.1

Take the project that you intend to do, or one or more projects that you are considering. Locate the position of the project(s) within the Johari window. How risky is the project, and are the risks worth taking? How 'stretching' is the project and is such development a personal objective?

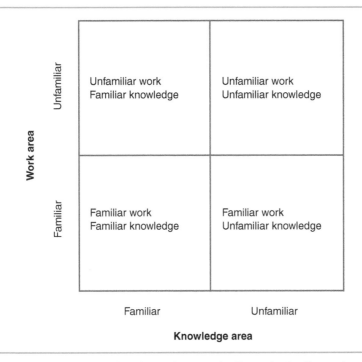

Figure 3.2   Johari window showing choices between familiar and unfamiliar work experience and personal knowledge

THE JOHARI
WINDOW

Reflecting on the value of the project

Projects that have value to the organization (say, in terms of identifying cost savings, new marketing opportunities, IT strategies, etc.) will have a much greater chance of success than those that merely re-plough old ground. Innovative, provoking and original projects have a better chance of sponsorship and support from within the organization (at the appropriate level), of opening new networks for meeting and interviewing people, and of eventual implementation. Of course, innovative projects also bring with them the potential added bonus of higher academic grades. A high value project is also more likely to motivate both you and your line manager or sponsor. But ambitious projects may be more difficult to manage and complete. Sometimes, a more modest project may be both more feasible and achievable.

Achieving a symmetry of potential outcomes

Gill and Johnson (2002) suggest that one way of reducing the risks involved in a project is to achieve symmetry of potential outcomes. This means that, no matter what the results are, they will be useful. For example, a project to examine whether a company's e-commerce website produced any increase in overall sales would be significant whatever the outcome. Conversely, a project that examined the relationship between levels of stress and output levels amongst line workers would be interesting if strong correlations were found, but would be of little value if they were not.

Table 3.1   Techniques for generating and refining research ideas

Rational thinking	Creative thinking
Examining your own strengths and weaknesses	Brainstorming
Looking at past projects	Exploring personal preferences using past projects
Searching the literature	Relevance trees
Gaining ideas through discussion	Keeping a notebook of ideas
	SWOT analysis

Source: Adapted from Saunders et al., 2012

Thinking of career goals

You may consider whether the research topic may be of value to you in the future in terms of your personal career development. The research may make you an 'expert' in a particular subject or area, and enhance your value as an internal consultant or help you in applying for a particular post. For example, completing a research project in performance-related pay can make you attractive to a human resource department. Research can also be cumulative. A good undergraduate dissertation can lead on to a Master's degree; in turn, a Master's dissertation can form the basis for a future PhD. Academic qualifications can enhance employability, particularly if the research is seen as having some practical application to employers.

Generating research ideas

FREAKANOMICS:
PICKING A
RESEARCH TOPIC

If you are devoid of ideas for a topic, how can you create some imaginative ones? Table 3.1 suggests that new ideas can be generated either through rational or creative processes. Let us look at each of these in turn.

Examining your own strengths and weaknesses

You will benefit from choosing a topic that you enjoy and for which you have probably received good marks for previous assignments and other course assessments, or positive feedback from a work-based project. Why not make a list of your strengths and weaknesses. Get a friend or colleague to critique the list (prepare yourself for a shock!), then amend it as necessary.

Looking at past projects

This is often a useful way of generating new ideas. A glance towards the end of some projects may reveal a section entitled 'Suggestions for future research' that may be helpful. There may also be a bibliography which could prove a useful starting point for your own research – although take care that the references are not too dated. Also note that some universities and colleges place *all* theses and dissertations in the library. Their presence there, then, is not a necessary guide to their quality.

Searching the literature

The literature includes articles in the academic journals, reports, books and websites (although be wary of the authenticity and quality of the latter). Becoming aware

Image 3.1   A group brainstorming using a flipchart

through the literature of the significance of some issues, or new angles on old ones, can be a stimulus to undertake research in how these ideas can affect your own organization. More detail on reviewing the literature is provided later in this chapter.

Gaining ideas through discussion

Ideas might be generated by talking to fellow students, work colleagues, line managers, university tutors, practitioners and professional networks (the latter, possibly, through online discussion groups).

Brainstorming

This is a well-known problem-solving technique for generating and refining ideas. Jarvis (1995) suggests that the quantity of ideas produced by the brainstorming group is more important than the quality. All points made by participants are recorded (for example, on a flipchart) over a mutually agreed period of time. No member of the group may criticize the ideas of another, irrespective of how ridiculous some ideas may sound, since this would inhibit discussion. At the end of the agreed time period, the group discusses and selects from the points raised.

Exploring personal preferences using past projects

Here, you simply take a look at the subjects you have chosen for previous modules, programmes or work projects, and identify the kinds of topic areas you have selected. This may be a guide to what you are generally interested in.

Relevance trees

This is similar to mind mapping, where you start with a broad concept from which you generate more specific topics. From each of these branches, new sub-branches

RELEVANCE
TREES

can be generated. Do this quickly (say, in no more than 10 minutes) with an emphasis on generating ideas rather than evaluating them for quality. Once the process is finished, look over your material and evaluate the results.

Keeping a notebook of ideas

This simply involves noting down any new ideas as and when they occur. It is best to keep the notebook with you at all times. This could be a section in a research log book (see Managing information, Chapter 5, p. 115).

SWOT analysis

GRAY ON SWOT
ANALYSIS
FRAMEWORK

SWOT stands for Strengths, Weaknesses, Opportunities and Threats. Using this well-known method, you could make a list of ideas under each of these categories. For example, if you work in a school, a strength of this position might be that you have access to the school as a case study. A weakness might that the school is small, representing only a single case (when you might need more). The opportunity might be the potential for using the results of the study to implement practical improvements in the school. The threat might be bias, because you are researching a site about which you are committed and passionate. Can you stand back and act objectively as a researcher? Undertaking this kind of SWOT analysis usually works best, however, when undertaken by a group since good ideas tend to generate others.

ACTIVITY 3.2

Go to Google Scholar at

http://scholar.google.co.uk/

Type in a theme that might be of interest to you, for example, 'health promotion'. If you also add the letters 'pdf' the hits will include documents such as research articles and reports, some of which can be downloaded immediately. Even if you can't always download the documents directly, the hits will indicate what articles are available and in which academic journals. Providing you have access to the appropriate electronic database, you can then access the article. If you also click on 'Any Time' in Google Scholar and the current date (year), you will see what kinds of subjects are 'current' in terms of what is being researched. This can generate new ideas for your own research.

TOPICS TO AVOID

It is often only possible in retrospect to recognize the topic you should not even have attempted! However, here are a few hints that may help you to avoid the research disaster. The topics to avoid are those that are:

- *Too big.* For example, 'Human resource management – innovative international perspectives'. Some very large projects can be worthy and valuable to an organization, but you need to ask yourself whether you have the time, experience and resources to complete them. The human resource management theme, for example, would be more feasible if, instead of 'international perspectives' which imply a global focus, you contrasted, say, two countries. Even this would be an enormous task involving national surveys and large samples. More feasible would be to contrast human resource management perspectives between two groups of companies, each group being representative of a different approach. Winkler and McCuen (2007) also warn that the big topic is also the most difficult to write about: it is difficult knowing where to begin, and omissions and oversights are more crudely exposed.

- *Too trivial.* This may seem rather subjective, but you should use your common sense to evaluate the kinds of projects that are worth doing and those that are not. As a general rule of thumb try using the 'So what?' test. Ask yourself, after completing the research, whether the results have any meaning or significance (to others not just to yourself). For example, a research project that surveyed how to reduce the use of paper in a marketing department of 10 people would yield very little of value. On the other hand, a project that took the issue of recycling (paper, printer cartridges, furniture, computers, etc.) across an organization could have considerable scope and link into the broader environmental debate.
- *Lacking in resource materials and people.* Look out for warning signs – very few references to the topic in the main textbooks, practitioner journals or other refereed journals or websites. If the project is going to rely on access to in-house knowledge experts, make sure that they are both available and willing to cooperate with you. This, of course, needs to be planned well in advance. If undertaking an academic thesis or dissertation it may be particularly important that human as well as text based resources are accessible. Often it is necessary to gain access to an organization as part of a case study or to gain access to respondents. Here it is vital to get the commitment or sponsorship of key people such as directors, senior managers or the leaders of networks or groups at an early stage.

➤ TOP TIP 3.3 ◄

When focusing an academic dissertation on one or a limited number of organizations, conduct the negotiations for access in parallel with your literature search; don't leave it until the literature search is finished. If access becomes problematic, this still gives you time to find another organization, which may want you to focus on a different subject area.

- *Too technical.* Some projects are more concerned with solving highly technical problems rather than organizational or social research. Leave these to the technical gurus. Often these kinds of highly technical projects also turn out to be intractable. You may be offered a problem that nobody else has been able to solve. Be highly suspicious of this kind of gift! Ask yourself: 'Why me?' It may be an offer you need to refuse.
- *Dependent on the completion of another project.* Even if you are 'guaranteed' that projects you hope to use as data sources will be completed in time for your use, you are strongly advised not to make your own project dependent on them. If slippage occurs, your own research will be held up or even scrapped. This is particularly the case when negotiating access to an external organization. If you get the slightest hint that your research will be dependent on the completion of, say, an ongoing study, pull out. As an outsider you have no influence or control over the organization's timescales, in circumstances when your own timescales (for completing your dissertation) may be tight.
- *Unethical.* Avoid taking on projects that can damage other people physically, emotionally or intellectually. Refuse to take on a project that forces you to breach confidentiality or trust. When using interviews, observation or surveys, you will need to pay particular attention to politically sensitive issues such as power relationships, race, gender and the disclosure of personal information. Ethics are discussed in more detail at the end of this chapter, in Chapter 4 and elsewhere in this book.

— CASE STUDY 3.1 —

Identifying a theme for research

Marion has reached the final stage of her part-time MSc programme and has decided that she wants to do her dissertation on 'leadership'. She meets with her academic supervisor and tells her that this is going to be her topic, but is surprised by her supervisor's reaction – laughter. Her supervisor advises her that the subject of 'leadership' is somewhat large and unwieldy. She should try to identify more of a focus. Marion goes away and talks to her line manager at work – she is a project manager in the police force – and to some of her fellow students. She has always been concerned by what she perceives to be a lack of promotion of women into leadership positions in the police. She therefore conceives of her research project as: 'Women and leadership: are there glass ceilings in the modern police force?' This subject has the double bonus of not only being relevant to her academic institution but also to her organization and the development of its equal opportunities policy. (For how this theme is converted into a Proposal, see Case Study 3.2.)

— ACTIVITY 3.3 ———

Consider each of the following 'big' topics and formulate a more focused, narrower research project from each of them:

- Communication in the workplace.
- Mergers and acquisitions.
- Health and safety.
- Teenage pregnancies.
- Equal employment legislation.

PLANNING THE PROJECT

It may seem obvious that all research projects should be carefully planned, but it is surprising how many researchers rush forward into data collection without a plan of campaign. Disaster is the inevitable result. Planning also helps with time management, one of the greatest problems when work and research commitments compete. There are many ways of planning a project and presenting the plan. One technique is to make use of a table, which sets out the tasks and the planned dates for their completion. A better approach is through the use of a Gantt chart (see Figure 3.3) through which you not only specify tasks but whether they are going to be completed in sequence or in parallel. Project management software such as *Microsoft Project* not only generates various graphics such as Gantt charts, but also allows you to specify timescales for the completion of each task. However, it is probably only worth the investment in time learning the program if your project is a large and complex one.

WRITING ACADEMIC PROPOSALS

A research proposal is described by Punch (2000) as a document that deals with issues such as:

	WEEK									
Research Project Plan	1	2	3	4	5	6	7	8	9	10
Literature review	▓	▓	▓							
Methodology				▓						
Findings and Analysis						▓	▓			
Conclusions and recommendations								▓		
Review and editing									▓	
Final draft										▓

Figure 3.3   Example of project planning using a Gantt chart

- The proposed subject of the research.
- What the research intends to achieve.
- The methods by which the research will be conducted.
- What will be learned from the research and why it is worth doing.

Since a research proposal can only be constructed through a detailed process of planning and design, it almost goes without saying that a proposal has to be developed through a process of research. Indeed, Punch (2000) contends that the research proposal is just as important as the research project that comes after it. Even if the boundaries of the intended research are blurred and the research inductive and emergent, the proposal should still be distinct and concise in terms of what is intended and how the research is to be carried out.

WRITING A
RESEARCH
PROPOSAL

Before you even think about writing a proposal, you need to identify an appropriate academic institution in which to study and a supervisor from that institution. Locating a suitable institution may be simply a matter of applying to one that is most convenient to where you live or work. But it pays to be more discriminating than this, because you will be needing somewhere with good resources (particularly in your subject area) and a supervisor who is an expert in your field of study (if you know what that subject area is at this stage) and who is actively publishing in this field. Also find out whether the institution has an active research community of both academics and postgraduate students. Possession of such a community means that the institution sees research as one of its priorities. It is also more likely to recruit some of the better research academics. Being a member of an active research community will help you to discuss academic and research issues with your fellow researchers. As Locke et al. (2013) put it, working knowledge is not in college

Table 3.2   Typical structure for an academic proposal

Section	Contents
Working title	Describes the breadth and depth of the topic and gives an indication of the methodology to be used (e.g. case study, evaluation, etc.).
Introduction (abstract)	A summary of the research topic, describing the core problems or issues, the gaps in the current research and how this research will address them.
Aims	General statements on intent and direction of the research.
Objectives	Clear and measurable statements of intended outcomes.
Justification	Rationale for the research with reference to gaps in current knowledge, and potential application of results.
Review of the literature	Describes the history of the topic and key literature sources; illustrates major issues and refines focus to indicate research questions (qualitative research) or hypotheses (quantitative research).
Research questions and hypotheses	Describes the key research questions, expressed in measurable terms, plus hypotheses (if needed).
Methodology	Justifies methodological approach, including data collection and analytical techniques; use of quantitative or qualitative methods; choice of research approach and paradigm; anticipation of ethical issues; how the data will be analysed.
Work schedule	A timetable for completing the research indicating tasks and timescales.
References	Bibliography of works cited in the proposal.
Limitations	An acknowledgement of the potential limitations of the research, including the quality and representativeness of samples.
Related material	For example, letters of support for the research, agreement to collaborate from interested institutions.

libraries; it takes the form of unpublished academic papers, conference speeches, seminars and email communications.

LECTURE ON WRITING A GOOD RESEARCH PROPOSAL

The structure of proposals is normally set out by the academic institution in which you will be studying, so it is important that you follow the specifications you are given. However, the following sections provide you with a typical structure and guidance on what to write. In writing a proposal it is important not to use unnecessarily technical or obscure language and to write in a style that is fluent, clear and accessible. The use of extensive quotes should be avoided and, as a general rule, the first paragraph should be completely free of citations. An example of a typical structure for an academic proposal is given in Table 3.2. The themes presented in the table are discussed below.

Working title

This is a 'working' title because you may decide to change it once you come to write your final thesis or dissertation. The title describes the breadth and depth of the topic and can often give an indication of the methodology to be used. For example: 'Employee commitment during organizational change – a case study in the public sector', or 'Reducing the level of drug prescriptions in general practice – an action research study'. Ensure that the working title is phrased grammatically and would provide a non-expert with a clear notion of what your research is about. If you are unsure, get your title reviewed by your supervisor or by a friend or colleague.

Introduction

The Introduction provides a summary of the research topic, describing the core problems or **constructs**, and how the research will address them. One of the most common weaknesses in introducing research is to make a series of sweeping generalizations without coming to the central point. It is usually simpler to write the Introduction once you have finished composing the remainder of the proposal, and you know the direction the research is taking. Avoid making the Introduction too long and detailed. It should not, for example, contain a comprehensive description or analysis of models or theories, as these should be discussed in the Review of the Literature.

Aims

The aims are general statements on the intent and direction of the research. So, for example, the aim of a project might be to: 'Identify the factors that influence the decisions of shoppers to buy online'. Aims describe the purpose of the research. They do not describe research outputs (such as reports, documents or policy statements) or research questions which are more focused.

Objectives

While the aims are general statements, the objectives are clear statements of intended outcomes, all of which can be measured in some way.

Justification

This is a rationale for the research with reference to the current gaps in knowledge, and potential application of the results. The justification attempts to persuade the reader that, not only does the investigation merit attention, but that the nature of the problem has been correctly identified. This is not the place to launch into a lengthy and detailed analysis of the problem, a description of core theories or models, or to discuss the methodology of how the issue will be researched as this comes later in the proposal. At this stage, the justification needs to be direct and succinct.

Review of the literature

According to Boote and Beile (2005) a substantive and thorough **literature review** is a precondition for doing substantive and thorough, sophisticated research. In order to advance our collective knowledge, a researcher has to understand what has gone before. The literature review, therefore, describes the history of the topic and key literature sources, illustrating major issues and refining the focus of the research in a way that can ultimately lead to one or more research questions. We will explore the purpose and outputs from a literature review in more detail in Chapter 5. Suffice it to say here, the literature review must cover the main sources in the field, or closely related fields of study. One of the simplest ways of ensuring that your coverage is comprehensive is to make use of your supervisor who should

LITERATURE REVIEWS

be able to point you to what sources and theories are essential. However, this is only a research proposal. You would not be expected to have completed an entire literature review at this stage, as this is what you will do when you are actually working on your thesis or dissertation. The purpose of the proposal literature review is to explain the choices of literature made for the study, and this can be successfully done in a succinct manner. The purpose of the literature review, then, is to:

- Demonstrate the key theories, arguments and controversies in the field.
- Highlight the ways in which the research area has been investigated to date.
- Identify inconsistencies and gaps in knowledge that are worthy of further investigation.

Punch (2000) suggests three guiding questions for identifying the appropriate literature for a research study.

What literature is relevant to the project?

In answering this it is important to remember:

- For some subject areas, the volume of literature will be extensive, but for others, relatively limited.
- One subject area may have more than one body of literature associated with it (including both theoretical literature and empirical studies).
- Some literature will be central to a study and other literature quite peripheral (but the latter might still be worth discussing).

What is the relationship of the proposed study to its research literature?

In particular, this means showing how the proposed study moves beyond what is already known. This might mean taking some main trends in the literature but extending them; confirming or challenging current findings; or researching an accepted theory but in a new field. Figure 3.4 illustrates a common (and erroneous) way of approaching this, represented by a). Here the researcher presents a chunk of literature and then a methodology chapter but with little, if any, relationship between the two. A far better approach is adopted in b). Here the literature review leads, logically and clearly to a set of research questions that are set out clearly (see Research questions and hypotheses, below). However, these questions should not appear 'out of the blue'. Far better is to signpost the themes and issues from the literature that are relevant to the proposed research study, as the literature is described. By the time the reader comes to the actual research questions, they should be able to say to themselves: 'Yes, this is what I expected the focus of the research to be'. The Methodology chapter then sets out the research design for tackling the research questions. Of course, this approach should not just be contained in the proposal, but also in writing up the research study itself.

Let us take an example. Suppose you were researching the subjective experiences of first year teachers, including their levels of confidence, motivation and intention to continue in the profession. In describing the literature and various research studies already completed in this field, at the end of, say, a section on new teacher confidence, you might explicitly state: 'So, as we have seen, levels of initial teacher confidence are subject to varying levels of doubt and uncertainty, often linked to critical incidents in

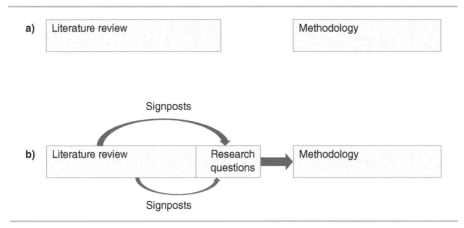

Figure 3.4   Linking the literature and methodology via research questions

the classroom. Measuring the linkages between teacher confidence and such critical incidents will be a focus of the current study. In doing this, use will be made of a survey of regional secondary schools, followed by ten in-depth case studies'.

How will the proposed study use the literature?

As far as the proposal is concerned, there are a range of approaches that might be adopted, including:

- A review of the entire relevant literature (probably the least likely option given the scale of work involved).
- A clear statement and justification for not reviewing the literature at this stage, since the study is inductive. The relevant literature will be reviewed as and when the data are collected and analysed.
- A review that includes a sample of the literature or the main themes in the review, supported by the relevant literature.

The literature search needs to be much more than merely a series of descriptions of what the major 'authorities' in the field have said. Above all, it must avoid what Boote and Beile claim is often merely 'disjointed summaries of a haphazard collection of literature' (2005: 9). There must, at the very heart of the review, be the development of a research problem or series of problems worthy and capable of being researched. It is the statement of the research problem that can then be converted into a specific research question (see next section).

→ **TOP TIP 3.4** ←

Students often say, 'I know what my research subject is, but I don't think that there is a body of literature associated with it!' This is never true. There is always a body of literature associated either directly or indirectly with a subject, the challenge is identifying it. If your topic is quite specialized, or one where there have been few, if any, studies, you may need to locate a body of literature that relates to it at a more abstract or theoretical level.

Research questions and hypotheses

As we have just seen, the literature review should lead the reader to one or more **research questions**. Hence, there needs to be a tight connection between the literature reviewed and the research study that follows. The connection between the two is the formulation of research questions and/or hypotheses.

Research questions

All proposals must contain a formal statement of questions which must be researchable and explicit. As O'Leary (2014) points out, research questions help to:

- Define an investigation i.e., whether its purpose is to discover, explore, explain or compare, and the kinds of relationship foreseen between concepts (such as correlations or one concept causing another).
- Establish boundaries for the research. In studying peripheral topics, it then becomes possible to ask: 'Does this answer my research question?' If the answer is: 'No, but I now see it as being important,' then it will become necessary to modify or completely rewrite the research question. Thus, we see that research questions are not 'set in stone' but are often modified during the research process.
- Provide direction, pointing to the theories that are pertinent, the literature that is relevant to the study and the kinds of research methodologies required. At least for deductive approaches it is impossible to select a research methodology without first having a clearly articulated research question.

One of the challenges researchers face is that topics are broad but research questions definitive and narrow. How do we move from the general to the specific? O'Leary (2014) suggests finding an 'angle' on the topic. For example, taking a topic but looking at what contemporary commentators are saying about it, or what 'hot issues' are generating argument and debate. Another obvious angle is if you identify a gap in the literature where a theme has been ignored or where a researcher has recommended further themes worthy of research at the end of an article.

The next stage is to write a research question that is concise and unambiguous. This, however, is easier said than done. It is astonishing how difficult most students find the formulation of research questions. Even when they have identified a focus for their research, locating one or more researchable questions seems to pose a Herculean task. Just as problematic are those novice researchers who write a set of vague aims or intentions then claim they have written their research questions!

━━━━━━━━━━━━━━━━━━━━━━━━▸ **TOP TIP 3.5** ◂━━━━━━━━━━━━━━━━━━

Consider the question: 'Is alcohol abuse a problem?' This question needs a considerable amount of reworking and clarification. What is meant by 'abuse'? A problem for whom? It is also prudent to avoid questions that you have an emotional connection with. In the case of the alcohol abuse question, a researcher who grew up in a family where the parents had a serious alcohol dependency, may have difficulty in formulating a neutral, unbiased question. Questions also need to be achievable in terms of the time you have available, and your potential access to respondents. They also need to be ethical (see Chapter 4).

Table 3.3   Examples of descriptive, explanatory, exploratory and interpretive questions

Question	Type of question	Comments
What changes in alcohol consumption have taken place over the last 10 years?	Descriptive	The research could explore changes in aggregate alcohol consumption levels and/or changing levels across different age groups, social classes or between the sexes.
Do high levels of alcohol consumption lead to absenteeism at work?	Explanatory	Seeks to explore a relationship between two variables (alcohol consumption and absenteeism). It also suggests a direction for the relationship – that high levels of alcohol consumption lead to higher levels of absenteeism. It is relatively easy to convert this question into a hypothesis.
Why is alcohol consumption on the increase?	Explanatory	A question that seeks to identify the factors behind a phenomenon.
What is the scale and cause of alcohol abuse amongst the under 16s?	Exploratory	A question which seeks to identify themes when little is currently known about the subject.
What is the impact of rising alcohol consumption on family life?	Interpretive	Seeks to uncover people's views and perspectives. A valid question for exploratory, largely qualitative studies.

As we saw in Chapter 2, approaches to research include exploratory, descriptive, explanatory and interpretive studies. Given their distinctive approaches to research, it follows that the kinds of research questions asked will be quite different. Table 3.3 provides some examples of specific questions using the subject of alcohol consumption as a focus.

It is worth noting that not all researchers would accept that the formulation of research questions is actually necessary. Some qualitative researchers argue that their approach is so inductive and emergent that the application of research questions is not only superfluous but inappropriate. Most qualitative researchers, however, are prepared to formulate research questions, even if they regard these as tentative and subject to change during the research process.

Hypotheses

Locke et al. (2013) point out that when the research is largely exploratory or for qualitative studies, it may be sufficient to formulate a question rather than a hypothesis. Indeed, for purely qualitative research a hypothesis would not be appropriate. In all other cases, however, and particularly in quantitative studies, hypotheses are necessary. Hypotheses are used when existing knowledge and theory allows for predictions to be made about a relationship between variables.

CHOOSING A METHOD

A hypothesis describes a research question in a testable format which predicts the nature of the answer. A hypothesis can also be written as a null statement such as 'There is no difference between x and y', or as a directional statement such as, 'When this happens, then that happens' (positive), or 'When this, then not that' (negative). As Locke et al. (2013) suggest, the use of directionality in hypotheses allows for the use of more powerful statistical tests. Punch (2000) suggests that, in determining whether a hypothesis is appropriate, a researcher needs to reflect on the following questions:

- For each research question, is it possible to predict, in advance of the research, what findings will emerge?
- Is the basis for this prediction a rationale, a set of propositions, or a 'theory' which explains the hypothesis?

If the answer to both these questions is, 'Yes' then Punch (2000) argues that a hypothesis should be formulated. Otherwise, he advises that it is perfectly acceptable to work from a set of research questions. Researchers should not adopt a hypothesis just for the sake of it. For a more detailed description of hypotheses see Chapter 6.

GRAY ON
WRITING A
HYPOTHESIS

━━━━━━━━━━━━━━━━━━━━━ ➤ **TOP TIP 3.6** ◀ ━━━━━━━━━━━━━━━

Avoid the mistake often made by inexperienced researchers of making the hypothesis statement too long and complex. Several short, testable hypotheses are infinitely prefer-able to one, long, rambling one.

Methodology

The methodology section of the proposal sets out and justifies the methodological approach and must be tightly related to the research question identified above. It is likely that it is this section that will receive the most attention from academics who will be scrutinizing and evaluating your proposal, hence it is this section that requires the greatest attention to detail and accuracy. You will need to follow the guidelines of your own academic institution, but it is likely that in most cases the methodology section will require a description of:

- The research methodology.
- The target population and sampling methods chosen.
- The data gathering instruments and techniques and the procedures for the collection and recording of data (for example, paper-based questionnaires, tape recorders, video recorders or digital cameras, etc.).
- The data analysis procedures to be used.
- How ethical issues are to be catered for.

One important issue the methodology section will need to address, is whether the study is to be primarily quantitative, qualitative or both. If, for example, some kind of intervention or experimental design is planned, then it is likely that quantitative methods will be adopted. On the other hand, if the project seeks to conduct an ethnographic study which focuses on the meanings and interpretations participants give within a particular cultural setting, then the data are likely to be qualitative. In each of these examples, once the decision is made to adopt a quantitative, qualitative or mixed methods approach, then this will have a significant influence on the choice of data gathering methods and approaches to data analysis. Punch

Table 3.4   Typical research methodologies associated with quantitative and qualitative approaches

Quantitative approaches	Qualitative approaches
Experiment	Case study
Quasi-experiment	Ethnographic study
Correlational survey	Phenomenological study
Longitudinal study	Grounded theory
Action research	Action research
Evaluation	Evaluation
	Heuristic inquiry

(2000) insists that it is therefore very important to revisit the research questions and the way in which they are phrased, and to ask oneself about what implications this has for research design.

Research methodology

Once a decision is made on whether to use quantitative, qualitative or a mixed approach, then this influences the research methodology to be adopted. Table 3.4 suggests some common methodologies that are associated with each of these approaches. It needs to be stressed, however, that these are influences and not rules. Note, for example, that action research and evaluation appear in both columns, implying that these kinds of projects can adopt a largely quantitative or qualitative approach – or, indeed, a combination of the two. Recall some of the descriptions of these methodologies in Chapter 2.

Sampling strategies

But once an appropriate strategy has been adopted, it is then necessary to convert this into a research design. This means stating in clear terms exactly how and with whom the research is to be conducted. This, then, brings us onto sampling. Since it is rarely practical to involve data collection from everyone, it is necessary to select a **sample**. Sampling strategies for quantitative designs are discussed in detail in Chapter 6 and for qualitative designs in Chapter 7 and a complete chapter devoted to the principles and approaches to sampling in Chapter 9. The point to be made here, is that sampling should not be considered merely as an afterthought, but should be planned as an integral part of the overall research design. The sampling strategy should include details on:

- The size of the sample.
- The composition of the sample.
- How the sample will actually be chosen (e.g. randomly, through volunteers, etc.).

In some qualitative projects there will be no initial, pre-determined sample size – successive samples are accessed depending on what trends are emerging from the data analysis. But if this is the case, the choice of this strategy should be made explicit at the outset.

————————————————————→ **TOP TIP 3.7** ←————————————————

In quantitative studies, it is common for students to falsely claim (largely without thinking) that they have adopted a random, probability sampling approach. In other words, they hope that their chosen sample is representative of the entire population under study. **Random probability sampling** means adopting a selection approach whereby each member of the population has an equal chance of being selected for the sample. Yet, in the case of many student projects, an organization is chosen because it is convenient (for example, local) or the student knows someone who works there. Or an online survey is launched, in which case there is no control over who responds. So, look at the research methods literature (including this book!) on the various kinds of sampling techniques to identify the one you are using. Using **non-probability sampling** is not a sin – as long as you acknowledge the limitations that this sampling imposes on the claims you can make for your results.

Data collection instruments

For quantitative approaches, data collection instruments include questionnaires, standardized measuring instruments (such as psychometric tests) and the kinds of observation schedules that involve counting the number of times an event or activity occurs. As Punch (2000) points out, an important decision here (which requires discussion and rationalization in the proposal), is whether to use existing standardized collection instruments or to design them specifically for the research. For pre-existing instruments details need to be provided of how and when they were developed, their use in other research projects (especially ones that are similar to your own, if possible) and how they have been validated. If developing new instruments, detailed descriptions need to be provided of how they have been piloted and validated.

Qualitative data gathering instruments could include questionnaires for a qualitative survey where the questions are open-ended and qualitative interview or observation schedules. While it may be possible to make use of instruments that have already been developed, it is more likely that qualitative researchers will construct their own data collection instruments. Just like quantitative data collection instruments, it is important to describe how the instrument was constructed and validated. Apart from questionnaires, qualitative data gathering approaches also include the use of interview and observational schedules, documents, journals and diaries and non-written materials such as photographs and video recordings.

Whatever the data collection instrument (quantitative or qualitative), it is essential to describe in detail how it is going to be used. For example, if using a questionnaire, describe whether it is to be used face-to-face, distributed by post, or delivered online via the Internet. If using an interview schedule, describe where the interviews will take place and whether the interview is to be tape-recorded. In all cases where people are being asked to volunteer their views, a Participants Consent form (see Chapter 4, p. 86) should be signed and a copy of the form provided as an appendix to the proposal. In other words, imagine that a reader knows nothing about your study, and take them through what you plan to do, step by step. Apart from collecting data, you also need to provide details on how they will be securely stored.

Data analysis

If dealing with quantitative data, then the analysis will involve the use of appropriate statistical techniques. The proposal should indicate which statistical tests will be applied. In the case of qualitative research, there are many more analytical approaches available, including grounded theory, template analysis, content analysis and discourse analysis. Again, even at this early stage, the research proposal should be able to state the choice of analytical approach.

Having chosen an analytical approach, it is not necessarily the case that the researcher would be expected to demonstrate in-depth knowledge and mastery of applying one of these approaches to data analysis. This will come later at the actual data analysis stage. What is important here is that you show how the analytical approach chosen is consistent with the general logic of the study and the kinds of research questions chosen.

Ethical considerations

The important issue of ethics will be discussed in detail in Chapter 4 so will only be covered briefly here. The proposal should always seek to demonstrate how the study will abide by ethical principles. For example, it should show that respondents are giving their views voluntarily, that their privacy will be safeguarded and that the information they provide will be treated confidentially. The proposal should also make clear how the data are going to be stored securely so that the anonymity of respondents can be protected.

Work schedule

This is a timetable for completing the research, indicating the tasks to be undertaken and their dates for completion. Note that students frequently underestimate the amount of time it takes to complete these tasks, so be as realistic as you can when calculating how long each task will take you.

References

It is best to get into good habits in using references at this early stage. You may want to invest some time in learning to use one of the bibliographic software packages such as Endnote or Reference Manager to store and organize your references. Find out which reference system is used by your academic institution (for example, the Harvard system) and keep to it. Note the distinction between References and Bibliography. The Reference section lists all the sources that you have cited in your study. A Bibliography lists all the main sources in the subject area under study, some of which you may not have read. In most cases, it is a Reference section that is needed in a proposal.

Limitations

No research is perfect, and it is important that researchers themselves identify and are honest about the weaknesses and limitations of their own research (otherwise readers such as supervisors and examiners will be critical for them!). Typical limitations, at least for quantitative studies, include an inability to control factors in the study design such as the assignment of members to experimental and control groups. All studies may suffer from low sample sizes or problems in gaining access to key respondents. What is important is that the implications of these weaknesses are acknowledged (and not avoided or 'skated over'), particularly on the validity and generalizability of the results. If, for example, statistical analysis does not reach significance, this itself is a finding. Of course, if the sample size was only 30 then this might be the prime cause. So here again, it would be prudent to acknowledge the limited size of the sample contributing to the result. However, if, say, the study design also included a qualitative element such as interviews, the results from these might add some weight to answering the project's research questions. In the final analysis, it is not always necessary to produce results that put you in line for a Nobel Prize! Modest studies that nudge forward the boundaries of knowledge are acceptable.

Related material

These could include

- Letters of support for the research.
- An agreement to collaborate from interested institutions or sponsors.
- Instructions to subjects or participants.
- Participant consent forms (see Chapter 4).
- Questionnaires for surveys or interviews.
- Supplementary bibliographies.
- Approval letters from ethics committees.

CASE STUDY 3.2

Developing a research theme into a proposal

As we saw in Case Study 3.1, Marion's dissertation title is: 'Women and leadership: are there glass ceilings in the modern police force?' In her proposal, she readily identifies a number of literatures she wishes to access and discuss. One, of course, is the general literature on leadership itself. Within this, she identifies three important models, namely: transactional, transformational and situational leadership. A sub-set of leadership theory, is the literature that deals with women and leadership which contains not only conceptual but also empirical articles based on field research. There is also a much smaller, but, for Marion's purposes, wonderfully focused literature on women and leadership in the public services (which includes a small number of articles on women, leadership and the police).

Marion reflects on her attitude towards epistemology. She believes that knowledge is not absolute but contextual and relative. She does not, therefore, see her role as producing 'the truth' about women leaders in the police. Instead, she wants to highlight the experiences of women who have 'made it to the top'. Her main research question is: What are the key skills, competencies and behaviours that contribute to the promotion of women into leadership positions in the police? She sees her epistemological stance as interpretivist, and a series of case studies (of successful women) as central to her research design. The use of qualitative interviews fits comfortably with case study design. In terms of sampling, she decides to begin with ten face-to-face interviews with purposively selected women leaders, and to analyse the data before deciding on whether additional interviews are necessary to validate existing themes or to pursue new ones.

If Marion had adopted a more objectivist epistemological stance, what difference would this have made to her proposal in terms of the kinds of research questions she asked, and the research design adopted?

WRITING ORGANIZATIONAL PROPOSALS

There are two main types of organizational proposal, comprising those that are written:

- In response to a request for proposals or 'invitations to bid' from, say, government agencies or companies.
- For submission to an internal organization or department, often in response to a request for help with a problem or a need to improve a product or service.

Whichever kind is written, White suggests that a proposal is a 'sophisticated advertisement of approaches and abilities' (1997: 218) and not just a description of how a project could be tackled.

To bid or not to bid?

Many proposals are written within tight timescales and in the knowledge that other individuals, teams or organizations are competing for the project. In deciding whether to respond to any request for proposals (RFPs), you will need to take a view of:

- Whether you and/or your team possess the necessary expertise to respond.
- The number of bids you are competing against and the likely strength of opposing bids.
- The number of bids that will be funded.
- Whether all bids are to be fairly evaluated, or whether the process is possibly biased.

These criteria will help you to undertake a risk assessment, weighing up the probability of success and the potential size of the funding if successful, against the time it will take to write the bid.

Preparing to write the proposal

Figure 3.5 illustrates a series of steps that should be observed in writing any organizational proposal. We will look in detail at each stage.

- *Review the request for proposal specifications.* Take another, careful, look at the request for proposals (RFPs) and make sure that they are complete, consistent and clear. The RFP document should contain a description of the background of the proposed project, why it is needed, the intended outcomes and budget.

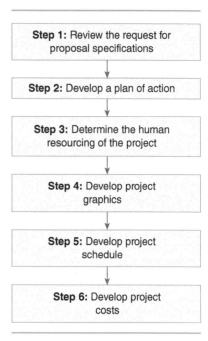

Step 1: Review the request for proposal specifications

Step 2: Develop a plan of action

Step 3: Determine the human resourcing of the project

Step 4: Develop project graphics

Step 5: Develop project schedule

Step 6: Develop project costs

Figure 3.5   Proposal development flowchart

Source: Adapted from White, 1997

Some RFPs may contain information on how responses to each of the specifications will be scored – for example, some requirements may be more important to the project than others and receive a higher weighting. If anything in the RFP is unclear, then it is legitimate to contact the creators of the RFP (preferably in writing) and ask for clarification.

- *Develop a plan of action.* This should include a rationale for the project, the key research objectives and a plan of how these are to be met, that is to say, the research methodology. Take care to show that the project has value. To do this apply the invaluable 'so what?' test. This means looking at your proposed project outcomes and asking yourself to evaluate honestly whether they have any real worth in terms of practical application or contribution to knowledge.
- *Determine the human resourcing of the project.* Those who commissioned the proposal will be keen to evaluate not only the number of people committed to the project, but also their experience and qualifications. If any element of the project is going to be outsourced to a third party, then again, evidence should be provided of their 'fitness for purpose'.
- *Develop the project graphics.* This will be particularly important for more technical projects, but should always be considered for research projects of any kind. Graphics, particularly flow diagrams showing how different elements of a project relate to one another, can be easy to read and understand. Ensure that if graphics are used, there is a clear description provided in the text (such as the way in which the text is describing Figure 3.5).
- *Develop a project schedule.* A project schedule such as a Gantt chart (see p. 51) provides a list of the main project tasks and the dates for their completion. These tasks could include arrangements for seeking permissions from an ethics committee, preliminary arrangements for getting research subjects, a timetable for constructing research tools, analysing data and writing the research report.
- *Develop project costs.* White (1997) warns that this is more an art than a science because there are so many variables to take into account. Particular care needs to be taken when estimating labour costs since these often eat up the bulk of a research project's budget. Since the research process is rarely linear and smooth, it is prudent to add in some contingency costs in case unexpected results emerge that require further research. The less experienced the research team, or riskier the project, the higher the contingency costs should be. Given that commissioning organizations are highly unlikely to pay for contingency costs, these will have to be built into (i.e. hidden!) in general costs. Of course, the higher your overall costs, the less competitive your bid.

THE FINAL STAGES FOR ACADEMIC AND ORGANIZATIONAL PROPOSALS

Preparing the final document

In writing the final project or academic proposal, try to ensure that the document is internally consistent, and that there are no gaps or contradictions between objectives and research processes. Remember that once the proposal is submitted you are committed to it, so you need to ensure that all errors have been eliminated. It helps, then, to elicit the assistance of some experienced reviewers who should be asked to answer the following questions:

- Is the proposal clear and understandable?
- Is the proposal realistic – are the aims attainable?
- Is the proposal consistent with the specifications against which it was written?

Also, in the case of organizational proposals, get an appropriate person to review the budget. White (1997) makes the useful suggestion that you should do a hand calculation of all columns and rows of financial data, even if they were calculated by computer (in case a decimal point has slipped!). When you have finished the proposal, print it off and read it one more time.

Success or failure?

It is worth having a strategy in place for whether the proposal is approved or rejected. If the latter, Williams (2002) offers the advice that you should try to get feedback on the proposal from those who have evaluated it. This may allow you to improve the proposal if there are later opportunities for resubmitting it. In the case of organizational proposals, if the bid is successful, you may be offered less funding than you asked for. At this point you need to decide whether to accept this funding, or, if possible, renegotiate the outputs of the project at a lower level.

Summary

- A good research topic must have the potential for demonstrating theoretical credibility. Allow for access to the relevant data, provide a symmetry of potential outcomes, and be congruent with your own interests, capabilities and career aspirations.
- To generate ideas for a research topic you could look at examples of projects completed by others, or ideas could emerge from your reading of the literature or by a brainstorming process.
- Before starting the project, produce a plan to show when and how you intend to conduct your research including data collection, analysis and the writing-up process.
- For any academic research proposal, pay particular attention to the methodology section including sampling procedures, and the choices made for research strategy and data collection tools.
- In writing any proposal, make sure that your bid matches the specifications accurately. Get your proposal evaluated by others before submission.

REVIEW QUESTIONS

1. Make a list of all the potential sources available to you for getting ideas on the subject matter or focus for your research. Which of these is most readily available to you? Which is less available but important?
2. Consider your familiarity with the knowledge area for your research and allocate a number for your familiarity with this area, with 1 being totally unfamiliar and 10 very familiar. What number have you chosen? How comfortable are you with this number? Does it suggest that you should aim for a higher or lower level of familiarity?
3. Imagine that you are working in an organization and are contacted by a student as a potential sponsor of a research project. What kind of reassurances would you want to receive before agreeing to sponsorship? What kind of payback would you want for your organization?

FURTHER READING

Locke, L.F., Spirduso, W.W. and Silverman, S.J. (2013) *Proposals that Work: A Guide to Planning Disserta-tions and Grant Proposals*, 6th edn. Thousand Oaks, CA: Sage. The fact that this is now in its 5th edition speaks for itself. A detailed book that provides valuable guidance on the structure and content of propos-als as well as the often forgotten issue of ethics in proposal writing.

Punch, K.F. (2006) *Developing Effective Research Proposals,* 2nd edn. London: Sage. A useful book that deals with both quantitative and qualitative approaches to research. It includes examples of successful research proposals and a checklist of 32 questions to guide proposal development.

JOURNAL RESOURCES

Kim, Y., Hahn, D. and Coursey, D. (2012) 'Decisions in research review boards', *Public Integrity*, 14(2): 173–192. By researching the decision making processes of Institutional Review Boards, the kinds of criteria that make for a successful bid are revealed.

Heath, M.T.P. and Tynan, C. (2010) 'Crafting a research proposal', *Marketing Review*, 10(2): 147–168. As well as guidelines, discusses the criteria against which proposals are assessed.

Klopper, H. (2008) 'The qualitative research proposal', *Curationis*, 31(4): 62–72. Deals with the process of writing a qualitative research proposal with regards to the most important questions that need to be answered.

Vivar, C.G., McQueen, A., Whyte, D.A. and Armayor, N.C. (2007) 'Getting started with qualitative research: Developing a research proposal', *Nurse Researcher*, 14(3): 60–73. Some basic but very practical guidelines.

Sandelowski, M. and Barroso, J. (2003) 'Writing the proposal for a qualitative research meth-odology project', *Qualitative Health Research*, 13(6): 781–820. Argues that writing a proposal for research using qualitative approaches is a particular challenge due to the emergent nature of qualitative designs. Shows, through an annotated commentary, how the authors con-structed such a qualitative proposal.

PROMPTING
INNOVATION
IN THE
WORKFORCE

Reave, L. (2002) 'Promoting innovation in the workplace: The internal proposal', *Business Communication Quarterly*, (4): 8–18. Guidelines for producing a work-based proposal includ-ing a suggested structure.

SUMMARY OF WEB LINKS

http://en.wikipedia.org/wiki/List_of_social_networking_websites

http://scholar.google.co.uk/

4

RESEARCH ETHICS

CHAPTER INTRODUCTION

Chapter outline

What do we mean by ethics?	68
The growth of ethical codes of practice	69
The focus of ethics	73
Ethical principles	73
Putting ethics into practice	81
Perspectives on research ethics	85

Ethics and the Internet	87
Researching ethically in your own organization	90
Ethics and research reports	90
A checklist of ethical issues	90
Safety issues for researchers	92

Keywords

Ethics

Ethical code of practice

Institutional Review Board

— **Chapter objectives** —

After reading this chapter you will be able to:

- Define what we mean by ethics.
- Explain why ethics are now so important to organizations and individuals undertaking research.
- Describe why adopting an ethical approach to research is important.
- Describe how ethical principles are of benefit to sound research design.
- Apply an ethical framework to your own research design and practice.

We will deal with a wide range of ethical issues that are particular to specific research methods in later chapters. Here, we will examine some of the ethical considerations of more general significance. Ethics is a philosophical term derived from the Greek word *ethos*, which means character or custom. The ethics of research concern the appropriateness of the researcher's behaviour in relation to the subjects of the research or those who are affected by it. Since research in the real world inevitably deals with people and the things that affect them, ethical issues can arise at the planning, implementation and reporting stages of research. Some ethical issues, at first sight, appear a matter of courtesy and common sense. However, as we shall see, ethical issues often give rise to complexity. As Korac-Kakabadse et al. (2002) suggest, one of the challenges of ethical behaviour is that it lies in a 'grey zone' where clear-cut dichotomies between what is right and wrong may not exist.

WHAT DO WE MEAN BY ETHICS?

RESEARCH
ETHICS

Research ethics refers to the moral principles guiding research (Economic and Social Research Council (ESRC), 2004) or as Homan (1991: 1) puts it, the 'science of morality'. It means conducting research in a way that goes beyond merely adopting the most appropriate research methodology, but conducting research in a responsible and morally defensible way. Ethics, then, are sets of moral principles or norms that are used to guide moral choices of behaviour and relationships with others (Blumberg et al., 2005). This makes it sound, however, that such principles are easily constructed and simply applied, when this is very far from the case, in part because research ethics involve ontological, epistemological and theoretical assumptions (Payne, 2000).

This chapter does not seek to offer a full and comprehensive review of ethical theories (for these see Miller et al., 2012, and Israel and Hay, 2006), but rather focuses on those models that relate to research practice. It is because of this that we will be looking primarily at normative rather than meta-ethics (which is about the form or foundation of ethics and asks questions such as: 'does good exist?' and 'if there are moral facts, how do we know them?'). Normative ethics includes the deontological perspective (from the Greek, *deon* meaning duty or obligation) which argues that the ends never justify the means, so ethical principles should never be compromised (see Table 4.1). The deontological perspective focuses on the rights of research participants, such as the right to privacy, the right to respect or the right to self-determination (Murphy and Dingwall, 2001). However, there are two views on this perspective. The universalistic argues that these rules or principles should

Table 4.1 A summary of ethical stances

	Universalistic	Contingent/relativistic
Deontological/non-consequentialist	Ethical principles should never be broken. Breaking these principles is both morally wrong and damaging to social research, e.g. Kantianism.	Duties to particular countries, communities, professional groups and clients, etc., e.g. forms of communitarianism.
Teleological/consequentialist	Means do not overlap with ends, but following a universal set of rules or practices can often be relied on to pursue those ends, e.g., *rule* utilitarianism, where keeping promises and recognizing human rights are usually best to produce the greatest happiness for the greatest number.	Acts should be judged purely on their possible outcomes – the ends justify the means. 'Morally questionable acts' (by universalistic standards, e.g. lying, treating some people inhumanely) are justified if they produce 'good' consequences, e.g. *act* utilitarianism.

never be broken; the contingent or relativistic position, though, sees that these rules or duties may vary across different countries, communities or professional groups.

An alternative position within normative ethics is the teleological (or consequentialist approach), which states that the morality of the means can only be judged in the context of what is achieved. The universalistic view of teleological perspectives argues that following a universal set of rules is legitimate if it leads to the desired ends (*rule* utilitarianism). The contingent view of teleological perspectives, however, holds that acts should be judged purely on their outcomes – the ends always justify the means, e.g., *act* utilitarianism. So, for example, using forms of deception are justified if the research outcomes are of tangible benefit to the research participants or another group. The problem here, however, is that not only might the benefits be morally questionable, but the research participants and so-called beneficiaries might be different groups of people. For example, putting participants into induced stressful situations in a laboratory controlled experiment might yield information on how people can cope better with stress. However, the experiment might leave the participants themselves with long-term symptoms of stress with no benefits.

As Murphy and Dingwall (2001) point out, most of the controversy around ethics has arisen at the level of practice, rather than principle.

THE GROWTH OF ETHICAL CODES OF PRACTICE

Concern about conducting ethical research became more acute after World War II when evidence about Nazi experiments on concentration camp victims became widely known. One result was the Nuremberg Code 1947, following on from the war crimes tribunal, which set out ten standards to which those conducting human experiments must adhere, including the voluntary and informed consent of research **subjects** (see Table 4.2).

NUREMBERG
CODE

This was later superseded by the Declaration of Helsinki which sought to balance the interests of research subjects with the need for scientific research. Compared to the medical sciences, the social sciences have not been as persistent and diligent in the way they have developed ethical standards (Schneider, 2006b). This is partly because the diversity of social sciences has meant that each discipline

Table 4.2   Summary of the ten points of the Nuremberg Code on human experimentation

1. The voluntary consent of the human subject is absolutely essential.
2. The experiment should be such as to yield fruitful results for the good of society, unprocurable by other methods or means of study, and not random and unnecessary in nature.
3. The experiment should be so designed and based on a knowledge of the problem under study that the anticipated results will justify the performance of the experiment.
4. The experiment should be so conducted as to avoid all unnecessary physical and mental suffering and injury.
5. No experiment should be conducted where there is an a priori reason to believe that death or disabling injury will occur.
6. The degree of risk to be taken should never exceed that determined by the humanitarian importance of the problem to be solved by the experiment.
7. Proper preparations should be made and adequate facilities provided to protect the experimental subject against even remote possibilities of injury, disability, or death.
8. The experiment should be conducted only by scientifically qualified persons.
9. During the course of the experiment the human subject should be at liberty to bring the experiment to an end if he has reached the physical or mental state where continuation of the experiment seems to him to be impossible.
10. During the course of the experiment the researcher must be prepared to terminate the experiment at any stage, if he has probable cause to believe that a continuation of the experiment is likely to result in injury, disability or death to the experimental subject.

Source: National Institutes of Health, 2008

Image 4.1   Photo of Nuremberg trials

has addressed ethics within its own context. It is now recognized that, like the natural and medical sciences, the social sciences are also capable of producing risk-generating endeavours (Haggerty, 2004). While the scale of risk generated by social science research is usually less, a number of prominent studies have alerted researchers to potential ethical dangers (see Case Study 4.1)

CASE STUDY 4.1

Examples of ethically contentious practice

One of the most infamous experiments to raise important ethical questions was that conducted by Milgram (1974) which explored the process of obedience to authority. In this case, an 'experimenter' oversaw an experiment in which two participants are informed that they are part of a study into the effects of punishment on memory retention. One participant took the part of the 'learner' with the other taking on the role of 'teacher'. The teacher was the actual research participant, but the 'experimenter' and 'learner' were, in fact, both undercover researchers. The 'learner' was taken to a separate room and hooked up to electrodes. The teacher then asked the learner a series of questions. Each time the learner got a question wrong, the teacher (research participant) was asked to administer an electric shock. Although, in practice, the equipment was fake and no shocks were administered, the teacher was asked to increase the voltage with each wrong answer. As the voltage increased, the learner started to grunt, then ask to be released, scream and then eventually went ominously silent. Approximately 60 per cent of participants punished the learner to the point where they 'passed out'. Milgram believed he was demonstrating the extent to which people will conform to authority when asked to perform a task, no matter how distasteful. Critics, however, have condemned the experiment on a whole range of counts, including doing psychological harm to participants, using deception and ignoring the need for informed consent. According to Cassell (1982: 21) what was unethical about Milgram's study was that he exposed the participants to 'unasked for self-knowledge'.

MILGRAM
OBSERVATION
STUDY

Image 4.2
The Milgram
experiment

—— ACTIVITY 4.1 ——————————————————————————————————

Was the Milgram experiment justified? Think about this in terms of the duties of researchers, human rights, outcomes and understandings of vulnerability and autonomy.

Over the past 20 or 30 years the ethics of research has emerged as an issue of increasing prominence, partly because in both business and the professions, people are having to cope with increasingly complex problems, many of them containing ethical dimensions (Nicholson, 1994). There are probably a number of reasons for this. Certainly most of the professional associations and educational institutions that involve themselves in research, have produced their own Code of Ethics partly to reduce the risk of legal action against any of their members who are accused of acting unethically. But on a more positive note, it is also because these institutions want to promote a more professional approach to research and to promote optimal behaviour, and the adherence to ethical conduct can only help here. Indeed, far from being seen as a hurdle, planning a project that adheres to ethical principles can only help the project – even if the plan never has to be presented to an ethics committee. Hopefully, the justification for this statement will emerge as you read this chapter.

Apart from professional researchers, the other large research grouping is students undertaking a qualification in subject areas such as the social sciences and business. As part of the dissertation stage of their studies, students usually have to conduct some primary research which will often involve data collection through, for example, surveys, interviews or focus groups. Awarding bodies such as universities have become increasingly concerned about the risks of litigation from research participants, or the organizations in which they work, should some of these studies go wrong. Most institutes of higher education and colleges, then, have established their own ethics committees, which evaluate research against a set of carefully formulated ethical guidelines. In cases where, say, a student's supervisor is concerned that ethical problems might arise, the student will be required to submit their research proposal to the institution's ethics committee for approval. If this is denied, then the research cannot go ahead.

———————————————— ➤ ON THE WEB 4.1 ◄ ————————————————

Take a look at ethical guidelines at some of the following academic institutions:

http://www.gre.ac.uk/research/rec/rep

http://www2.surrey.ac.uk/fahs/staffandstudents/ethicalprocedures/#A0

http://www2.warwick.ac.uk/services/rss/researchgovernance_ethics/research_code_ of_practice/researchethicscommittees/

If you are a student, undertaking a formal course of study, take a look at the ethical code of conduct for your institution. This is usually found as a published document (often in your course handbook), on the institution's website, or both. Is this code of practice based on universalistic or contingent approaches, as in Table 4.1?

Whether you are a professional researcher, student or anyone else involved in research, make sure that you are aware of, and attempt to abide by, any ethical code that governs your research.

THE FOCUS OF ETHICS

Potentially, any research that involves data gathering or contact with human (or animal) populations involves ethical considerations. According to the ESRC in the UK (2004) issues that involve a normally larger element of ethical risk include:

- Research involving vulnerable groups – for example children and young people, those with learning disabilities or special needs or individuals in an unequal or dependent relationship.
- Research involving sensitive topics – for example, sexual or illegal activities, or people's experience of abuse or violence.
- Research where subjects can only be accessed via a **gatekeeper** – for example, some ethnic or cultural groups.
- Research involving an element of deception such as covert observation (see Chapter 16) used without a participant's full or informed consent.
- Research involving access to confidential records or information.
- Research that would lead to stress, anxiety or humiliation among target groups.
- Research involving intrusive strategies that people would not normally meet in their everyday lives – for example, the administration of drugs or getting people to undertake extreme physical exercise.

What is common to many of these situations is that forms of deception are used, the privacy of respondents is invaded or participants run the risk of coming to some emotional or physical harm.

ETHICAL PRINCIPLES

Ethical principles, then, fall into four main areas, namely, the need to:

- Avoid harm to participants.
- Ensure informed consent of participants.
- Respect the privacy of participants.
- Avoid the use of deception.

RESEARCH
ETHICS
FRAMEWORK

Let us look at each of these in more detail.

Avoiding harm to participants

As you can, no doubt, tell, the term 'harm' can embrace a very wide range of issues, ranging from physical to mental and emotional harm. Research will be considered harmful, for example, if it causes a participant to be embarrassed, ridiculed, belittled or generally subject to mental distress (Sudman, 1998), or if it produces anxiety or stress to participants or produces negative emotional reactions. For example, comparing the emotional development of special needs pupils with those from the mainstream might highlight for the special needs pupils that they are different, a diagnosis they were originally unaware of (and are not thankful for).

Workplace research often requires respondents to express their views and opinions on work-related issues, some of which might include criticisms of the organization and its management. If individuals can be identified, then in extreme cases this could cause not just embarrassment, but even discipline or dismissal. If confidentiality is requested, it must be adhered to. However, even though attempts might be made to preserve the **anonymity** of individuals, it is by no means always impossible for people to be identified, especially those who are known to hold certain strong beliefs. So there can be a difference between (good) intentions and practice. If it is known in advance that confidentiality might be breached, the research must not go ahead. The situation is similar with organizations. If the research, say, has focused on a large hospital in a particular city, it might not require the skills of a detective to guess the organization's name. If there are any dangers that anonymity might be breached, individuals and organizations must be informed of this so that they can withdraw from the research if they wish – adhering to the principle of 'informed consent' (see below).

AVOIDING
HARM

What does avoiding harm mean in practice? Clearly, at one extreme, it means ensuring that no physical harm comes to respondents. In contrast to some medical research, most social or business research does not run this risk, although there can be exceptions. For example, an ethnographic study into drug gangs (to learn about illegal drug distribution) might highlight both their activities and location, resulting in a police crackdown and arrests. This in turn might threaten the safety of future researchers particularly if they are acting covertly and their 'cover' is blown.

However, there may be dangers of causing participants psychological damage, or causing anxiety, stress, embarrassment or loss of self-esteem. Sudman (1998) argues that avoiding harm could include seemingly trivial acts such as scheduling interviews to avoid disruption to the respondent. Moreno (1999), for example, argues that ethically acceptable research should abide by the principle of respect for persons. This means that a study should not be so poorly designed that it has little chance of achieving meaningful results. Even though a research project may not actually cause injury, the fact that its results are meagre is nonetheless disrespectful. Similarly, abiding by the principle of justice means that a study's research design should not cause a burden to any particular social group unless there are some compensating gains.

Indeed, it could be argued that researchers need to go beyond avoiding harm to participants and should aim, instead, for positive benefits. One potential benefit from research is adding to the stock of human knowledge. Acting ethically, therefore, means designing studies in such a way that they are capable of yielding accurate and valid results. It also means conducting studies, the results of which have relevance beyond the vested interests for the researcher. Even if the research falls short of being 'ground breaking', participants can benefit if the researcher provides them with a summary of the results of the study, or the results of any assessments (for example, psychometric tests or attitude scales) they have taken as part of the research. This at least may provide participants with better self-knowledge.

Ensuring informed consent

The principle of informed consent means that research participants are provided with sufficient and accessible information about a project so that they can make an informed decision as to whether to become involved, or not (Crow et al., 2006). The word 'sufficient' is important here. Sudman (1998) suggests that the amount of information given to respondents should reflect the degree of risk involved in the research study. Most survey research, for example, involves only low levels of risk to respondents, so the amount of time spent explaining the purpose of the study would be relatively small. Typically, for a survey questionnaire, for example, an introductory section would provide the following information:

INFORMED
CONSENT

- The aims of the research.
- Who will be undertaking it.
- Who is being asked to participate.
- What kind of information is being sought.
- How much of the participant's time is required.
- That participation in the study is voluntary.
- That responding to all questions is voluntary.
- Who will have access to the data once it is collected.
- How anonymity of respondents will be preserved.
- Who should it be returned to and by when.

→ **TOP TIP 4.1** ←

When composing the introductory section of a survey, be as accurate and succinct as possible, avoiding waffle and ambiguity. Get the description checked and critiqued by others such as friends, fellow students or a supervisor, so that the final version is 'polished'.

SURVEY
INTRODUCTION
EXAMPLE

Informed consent is particularly important where groups are considered 'vulnerable', because they may be more open to coercion, exploitation or harm than others (for example, victims of crime, children, refugees, people with special educational needs). Gaining informed consent can yield important positive spin-offs for research projects (Crow et al., 2006):

- Research participants are likely to have more confidence in the research and so be more open and frank in their responses.
- Greater confidence in the research should also improve participation rates.
- Researchers are forced to sharpen and clarify the purposes of their research which helps participants but also the researchers themselves.

It is essential, however, that participants are provided with information that is meaningful to them (avoiding complex, theoretical language and jargon), succinct and timely. Of course, there may be circumstances when gaining informed consent is simply impractical – for example, when researching illegal activities such as the observation of drug or people-trafficking gangs. But at least in the case of research being undertaken by students, such research is unlikely to obtain ethical approval from their supervisor or their institution's ethics committee.

REFUSAL

In practice, it is important to distinguish between different approaches to gaining consent. In surveys, for example, how much effort should be put into persuading someone to participate? Sudman (1998) distinguishes between 'hard' and 'soft' refusals. A soft refusal is if someone says 'No, I'm too busy at the moment', or 'This is not a convenient time for me'. A hard refusal is when someone says, 'No, I'm really not interested'. Hard refusals should not be followed up, but soft ones may be. But even in the case of soft refusals, there should not usually be more than one follow up. Similarly, with mail surveys, respondents who return a questionnaire saying that they do not wish to participate should not be followed up, but those who do not return it immediately, can be followed up with one reminder.

A common data gathering method in social and business research is covert observation (see Chapter 16) where the researcher does not reveal his or her identity. Where, for example, the researcher works alongside a group of workers observing and perhaps taking secret notes, people being observed without their consent. For example, a researcher conducting an ethnographic study on the quality of patient care in hospital wards might pose as an auxiliary worker and would be observing and taking notes without the knowledge or consent of nursing staff around her.

In a classic article, Erikson (1967) argues that there are a number of serious objections to disguised observation:

- The researcher can harm those being observed in the social scene in ways that cannot be anticipated.
- Deception is likely to damage the reputation of the subject upon which the research is being conducted.
- The very act of entering a social field in order to study it, changes or disrupts that scene, no matter what precautions are taken.

— ACTIVITY 4.3 —

To read Erikson's article go to:

http://www.sfu.ca/~decaste/deCastell_867/867pdfs2010/erikson_disguised.pdf

Goode (1996), however, challenges these notions, contending that there should be no absolute prohibition to covert research methods. He insists that the ethics of disguised observation be evaluated on a situational, case-by-case basis. Deception is only undesirable in the abstract, but if no harm befalls respondents and some benefit comes from the study in the form of new knowledge, then a study does more good than harm (Goode, 1996). Yet protecting respondents from harm needs to be the researcher's primary interest. This being the case, most ethics committees will seek to review any proposed covert observation studies in great detail.

Even in research designs involving overt observation or data gathering approaches such as interviewing, it is often quite difficult to give participants absolutely every piece of information that they might need. For example, for an online questionnaire, the estimated amount of time respondents need to complete it might be omitted so that respondents are not put off from completing it. Similarly, in ethnographic research, it may be simply impractical to inform the many people in a workplace or community setting. However, even where it is impossible or impractical to elicit the informed consent of participants before the research takes place, consent should be obtained after the event. Ethical approaches to observation may be influenced by the subject discipline the researcher belongs to – see Case Study 4.2.

CASE STUDY 4.2

Examples of how different ethical codes of practice deal with observation

British Psychological Society

Studies based upon observation must respect the privacy and psychological well-being of the individuals studied. Unless those observed give their consent to being observed, observational research is only acceptable in situations where those observed would expect to be observed by strangers. Additionally, particular account should be taken of local cultural values and of the possibility of intruding upon the privacy of individuals who, even while in a nominally public space, may believe they are unobserved.

Social Research Association

In observation studies where behaviour patterns are observed without the subject's knowledge, social researchers must take care not to infringe what may be referred to as the 'private space' of an individual or group. This will vary from culture to culture. Where practicable, social researchers should attempt to obtain consent post hoc. In any event, they should interpret behaviour patterns that appear to deliberately make observation difficult as a tacit refusal of permission to be observed.

Academy of Management

Confidentiality is not required with respect to observations in public places, activities conducted in public, or other settings where no rules of privacy are provided by law or by custom.

ACTIVITY 4.4

In what ways might the study of individuals in public places be conducted differently when adopting each of these ethical codes?

➤ **ON THE WEB 4.2** ◄

Compare and contrast some of the websites in Table 4.3 from some of the major research communities and sponsoring organizations for their ethical codes of practice:

Table 4.3   Research organizations and their websites dealing with ethics and codes of practice

Organization	Ethics website
Academy of Management (AoM)	www.aomonline.org/aom.asp?ID=268
Social Research Association (SRA)	www.the-sra.org.uk/ethical.htm
Economic and Social Research Council (ESRC)	http://www.esrc.ac.uk/ESRCInfoCentre/index.aspx
American Psychological Association	http://www.apa.org/ethics/code.html
British Educational Research Association	http://www.bera.ac.uk/guidelines.html
Central Office for Research Ethics Committees	http://www.corec.org.uk/
Institute of Management Consultants (see Ethics and Discipline under 'Our Standards')	http://www.imc.co.uk/index3.html

Respecting privacy of participants

The right to privacy is one of the basic tenets of living in a democratic society. As law abiding citizens, we do not expect our communications with other people (whether letters, emails or discussions) to be monitored by, say, agents of the state. Nor would we expect to have to provide personal information to government or other agencies, unless a very good rationale was provided first. Similarly, researchers do not have any right to intrude into a respondent's personal affairs. The overarching principle here is that respondents must always have to give their *informed consent* in giving information. This not only means giving such consent before, say, an interview starts, but during the interview itself. Hence, respondents have the right to withdraw from an interview at any time, or refuse to answer any question they find intrusive. Researchers have to make it transparently clear to respondents that their participation in the research is entirely voluntary and that they have the right to withdraw at any time. So, this right to withdraw needs to be stated in any preamble before an interview, or in the introduction to a questionnaire.

➤ **TOP TIP 4.2** ◄

STOPPING AN
INTERVIEW

AGITATED
INTERVIEWEE

If, during an interview, you observe a respondent becoming agitated, stressed or withdrawn, do not ignore these warning signs and plough on regardless. Ask them if they are comfortable. If they state they are not, ask if they would like to terminate the interview. If this gets a 'Yes', switch off any recording equipment and thank them for their participation. If researching vulnerable groups, you may be required by your institution's code of ethics at this point to offer additional psychological support such as counselling or other forms of help.

As we have seen, covert observation or, indeed, any kind of covert method is, almost by definition, an invasion of the individual's privacy, largely on the basis that people are not given an opportunity to refuse to participate. A researcher, for example, covertly working alongside a group of postal workers in order to observe their work practices (or even malpractices) would potentially be party to hearing personal information, gossip about other people and sometimes, clandestine activities. In this situation, none of the workers involved is aware of the role of the researcher, and, while unwittingly providing information, none has been given the opportunity to remain anonymous.

Issues of anonymity and confidentiality are compounded when it comes to ways in which data collected by a researcher are stored and what kind of controls are in place to prevent the data being accessed and used by others (both researchers and non-researchers). In the UK the Data Protection Act, 1998 relates to personal data (including both facts and opinions) held on a living individual who can be identified either from the data or from other information held by the data holder. The Act is designed to impose restrictions on the processing of data including how the data are obtained, recorded and stored and also the analysis conducted on them. The key points to note are that:

CONFIDENTIALITY

- The Act relates to both facts and opinions.
- Personal data must be obtained fairly and lawfully. Respondents should be provided with the name of the data holder (the institution); the purpose for which the data are being collected and processed; to whom the data will be disclosed.
- Personal data relates to data that are held in both electronic form and manual form (e.g., paper files, card indices).
- Personal data must be accurate and kept up to date and shall not be kept longer than necessary.
- Appropriate security measures must be taken against accidental loss or destruction of data and against unlawful or unauthorized processing of personal data.
- Personal data shall not be transferred to a country outside the European Economic Area unless those countries can offer adequate data protection.

In practice, this means that information on names, telephone numbers, email and postal addresses and any other identifying features should be restricted. If other researchers wish to gain access to the data, they must be required to sign non-disclosure confidentiality forms. (See Top Tip 4.3, overleaf.)

MEETING DPA
REQUIREMENTS

Privacy laws, of course, vary internationally, and, according to the Organization of American States (OAS, 2013), are stricter in Europe than in many other parts of the world. According to the OAS, the European view on privacy covers every aspect of the individual's life, with legislation covering both the processing of personal data by the government and private organizations. The situation is different in the USA with industries mostly self-regulated, including most private corporations, data-mining businesses, personal data repositories and internet-based social-networking sites.

Avoiding deception

Deception means researchers representing their research as something which it is not. A classic case of its kind is the now notorious Stanford prison experiment. Here a young researcher, Philip Zimbardo, recruited a group of people to take part in a study, with some randomly assigned as guards and some as prisoners, to show how each group would slip into predefined roles and behaviours rather than using their

STANFORD
PRISON
EXPERIMENT

own judgements. The experiment degenerated quickly, with those acting as guards imposing an array of punishments on the 'prisoners'. Prisoners suffered physical and mental punishment as well as sexual abuse. So this study suffered from both deception and the fact that some participants were harmed.

———————————————————→ **TOP TIP 4.3** ◄——————————————————

Survey and interview forms used to collect the data should be made inaccessible to everyone except the researcher and those inputting the data. It is also advisable to weaken the link between the raw data and information stored in any database. For example, when input to the database, respondents could be assigned a code number identifier instead of their names. Data files that allow a researcher to reconstruct the link between an identifier number and the respondent's name should be kept under locked storage.

There are particularly stringent requirements laid down for sensitive data which includes data about racial or ethnic origin, physical or mental health or condition, and sexual life. For these kinds of data it is necessary that data subjects give their explicit consent. There are certain exceptions made for data which are collected for the purposes of research. These data can be kept indefinitely, and are exempt from the rights of data subjects to gain access, as long as the results of the work are not made available in a form in which individual data subjects can be identified. However, researchers are still obliged to give data subjects information about the intended uses of the research.

———————————————————→ **ON THE WEB 4.3** ◄——————————————————

For further details of the Stanford prison experiment, see Philip Zimbardo's website at:

http://www.prisonexp.org/

While most researchers would automatically condemn deception as wrong, in practice, many researchers are guilty of it, largely because they avoid being completely candid with participants in order to elicit the most natural of responses. A typical and common example would be not telling participants that an interview they have agreed to will take an hour to complete. Being against deception is not merely a matter of infringing human rights, it is also a practical matter of avoiding building a negative reputation that might in the long term reduce levels of participant cooperation. In practice, however, it is difficult to draw a line between outright deception and being less than honest about the truth.

DECEPTION

— **CASE STUDY 4.3** —

Getting approval through an institution's ethics committee

A team of university researchers has won a project grant to investigate the impact of executive coaching on a cohort of unemployed managers. The unemployed managers are going to be offered up to 10 hours of one-to-one, face-to-face coaching, through which, it is hoped, they will gain greater personal confidence, motivation and skills in job seeking and thus increase their chances of gaining full-time employment. Before the coaching intervention and research approach can be implemented, however, the research team meets to discuss the ethical implications of what they are doing. They have decided that their primary research aims will include measuring the impact the coaching has on the self-confidence and self-efficacy of respondents. However, the researchers understand that for the person being coached, the process can often open up deep-seated issues. Given that the target beneficiaries are also unemployed, they can be viewed as a potentially 'vulnerable' group.

The research team therefore put together a research protocol in which they make the aims of the project explicit, as well as how the coaching and research is to be conducted. Vitally, they also show how the interests of the beneficiary group are to be protected. All of the group will be volunteers; no one will coerce them onto the programme. A letter is written to all participants setting out the objectives of the research and guaranteeing them confidentiality in terms of their responses. The protocol, letter and additional documentation are submitted to the university research ethics committee and three weeks later the research team get their answer – 'reject'! The ethics committee is concerned that no steps have been taken to protect any participants who may have psychological problems related to their current unemployed state. The problem, however, is quickly rectified. The research team recruits a member of the psychology department who is an accredited clinical psychologist to act as a referral point, should problems be identified either through the battery of psychometric instruments used in the research or through the coaching. On second application, the research protocol is accepted and the research commences.

— ACTIVITY 4.5 —

The above study also includes a control group of unemployed managers who are asked to complete the battery of psychological tests but who do not receive the coaching. Is this ethical? What benefits, if any, do they receive for taking part?

PUTTING ETHICS INTO PRACTICE

So much for the principles of ethics. How do researchers actually abide by these principles in practice? Next, we look at the various stages involved.

Writing proposals

As we have seen in Chapter 3, when commencing an academic dissertation or thesis, or when embarking on a piece of consultancy, it is often necessary to compose a proposal or research protocol. The proposal will then be evaluated by the Research Ethics Committee (sometimes referred to as an Institutional Review Board) of the researcher's institution – as in Case Study 4.3. In the past, the proposal usually constituted a description of the purpose, objectives, methodology and approaches to data analysis for the research. Today, however, with the growth of ethical considerations, proposals may need an additional range of criteria, as outlined in Table 4.4. Hence, the review committee or board acts as a protective barrier between researchers and potential participants; they act to raise awareness about the importance of ethics; and they check to see if the research is actually worth doing (that is, if the benefits outweigh the costs) and whether the research duplicates previous work and whether the methods proposed are likely to answer the

PROTOCOL

Table 4.4   A typical university proposal structure

Title of project:

Names of principal investigators:	Qualifications:	Department/ Institution:
Names of co-investigators:	Qualifications:	Department/ Institution:
Details of other collaborators:	Qualifications:	Department/ Institution:

Details of sponsors (if any):

Aims of the research:

Background and rationale:

Methodology (including research objectives, study design, sampling strategy, etc.):

Size and composition of the sample. How the sample is to be obtained. Identification of any vulnerable groups:

Description of where the project is to be carried out (e.g., in the University, shopping areas, schools, homes, etc.):

Details of risk assessment carried out in respect of the research, either for potential participants or the researchers. If completed, please attach a summary document of the issues considered. If not completed, please explain why it has not been done:

What are the potential adverse effects, risks or hazards for (a) research participants?
(b) researchers?

Potential benefits for research participants, or third parties:

Detailed arrangements for the collection, retention, use and disposal of research data:

Measures taken to ensure confidentiality, privacy and data protection (e.g., the storage of data):

Procedures for gaining and documenting initial and continuing informed consent:

Has a Criminal Records Bureau (CRB) check been carried out in relation to this research? (This will be required for research activity which will bring staff and/or students into contact with children or vulnerable adults). If yes, please attach copies of the relevant documentation:

Expected outcomes of the research:

Identification of how feedback to participants is to be handled:

Signature of supervisor (where appropriate) to indicate that (s)he has read and approved the protocol submission:

Signature of researcher:

Date:

Source: Adapted from University of Surrey ethical guidelines

research questions (Alderson and Morrow, 2006). There are usually three potential outcomes: the proposal is accepted without amendment and the research goes ahead; problems are identified and the proposal has to be amended in line with the board's recommendations and resubmitted; the proposal is rejected, without the right to resubmit. Note that if you are a student, it is your supervisor who may have to be named as the principal investigator.

— CASE STUDY 4.4 —

The negative results of not gaining ethical agreement

Jacqueline Schneider (2006b), a researcher in criminology, relates how a failure to agree on a research protocol can lead to major problems. Her research project involved conducting qualitative interviews with known offenders, in collaboration with a local police division. Relations between the researcher and the police force quickly deteriorated, however, when the police insisted that she hand over interview tapes so that the data could be used either as evidence to prosecute specific individuals or as part of general intelligence-gathering. Schneider refused to hand over any tapes and was warned by the police that she could be prosecuted for perverting the course of justice. Therefore, for her next project, the researcher constructed a research protocol through which the police agreed that they would not ask for the data from specific interviews, waiting instead for a general pattern to emerge from the research. Information, however, was to be released by the researcher when or if people were identified in an interview as being about to suffer harm.

—ACTIVITY 4.6 —

Case Study 4.4 shows that confidentiality can never be total. Identify some circumstances in one of your own research projects when research confidentiality might have to be breached.

Getting written approval from research sites

Researching in organizations, or even using shopping-mall intercept surveys (where you stop passers-by to ask them questions) needs prior approval from the organization that owns the premises or property. It is essential that this is written approval which will often have to be obtained from the organization's 'head-office'. Approval may require long lead times, so this needs to be planned into research schedules. In asking for approval, researchers will need to use their own organization's headed letter paper so that the request looks as official as possible. The purpose of the research and the possible benefits to the organization should be outlined.

➤ TOP TIP 4.4 ◄

In attempting to gain approval from external organizations, make sure that any letter you write identifies at least one significant benefit the organization might gain from granting you access. Organizations are much more likely to cooperate with you if they think that they have something to gain – for example, a better knowledge of customers, improvements in internal communications, etc. In other words your research should identify some tangible outcomes.

— **CASE STUDY 4.5** —

The importance of getting approval in field research

This is a true story. An MSc student whose dissertation project was focused on 'the retail experience' of shoppers, decided that he would collect data, not just by intercepting shoppers in the street, but by entering a major UK department store with his video camera. He had not told his dissertation supervisor what he was going to do, and he had not approached the store to ask for permission for his activities. The first two minutes of his 'ethnographic' data gathering went well. He filmed a number of shoppers browsing through the ladies clothes section. What he didn't realize, of course, was that the store security system was also filming him! As he peered through his lens, he noticed two very large security guards approaching him at speed. Still trying to mutter an explanation, he found himself grabbed by the guards and frog-marched rather unceremoniously to the store exit and to the pavement outside. End of data gathering. His supervisor later required him to write a letter of explanation to the store manager, with an apology.

— **ACTIVITY 4.7** —

Set out a plan for how this student should have set about ensuring consent for his project. Which stakeholders should he speak to and in what order?

Communicating with sponsors and participants

It will often be necessary to communicate with sponsors and/or participants in order to explain the purposes of the research and to elicit their cooperation. When doing this, letters or participant information sheets should include all of the following:

- A brief description of the project, in a form and language that can be easily understood by participants.
- The use of the study and any potential benefits to participants (including benefits to participants in control groups, if any).
- The obligations and commitments of the participants during the study particularly in terms of their time commitment.
- The right of participants to withdraw from the study without having to give a reason and an assurance of confidentiality of all identifiable information and data.
- The name and address of who participants can contact if they have a complaint or concerns about the study, or just a need for more information. This might include the researcher's supervisor and/or contact details of the relevant ethics committee.

For surveys, the fact that a questionnaire is returned, is usually taken as an indication of consent, but this fact should be clearly stated on the information sheet provided. Note that even when an organization has given permission for the research to go ahead, it is still essential that all participants are fully informed about the aims of the project and their role within it. They may also be required to sign consent forms – see the following section.

➤ **TOP TIP 4.5** ◄

In order to give the information sheet or letter the necessary credibility, it is usual to print the content on your institution's letter headed paper. If you are a student, it often helps if you can get your tutor or research supervisor to also add their signature to the letter.

Issuing consent forms

These are used when participants are involved in focus groups, interviews or similar forms of data gathering. Typically, the information given in such forms will include: how the information is going to be collected (e.g. through tape-recording), how the data are going to be stored, and whether participants are going to be directly quoted. It is essential that consent forms are clear about the right of participants to withdraw at any time. An example of such a form is given in Table 4.5.

Practical steps for avoiding harm

There are various ways in which a researcher can cause physical, psychological or emotional harm, or even just embarrassment. It is essential, then, that the researcher identifies any potential for harm and takes steps to alleviate the situation. For example, if the research project is focused on bullying in the workplace, it would be prudent to identify counselling or other support services, should respondents show signs of distress and need to be referred for help.

PERSPECTIVES ON RESEARCH ETHICS

As we have seen, ethical principles and processes are of increasing concern for Institutional Review Boards (IRBs) and that all research should strive to avoid harm to participants, gain informed consent, respect the privacy of individuals and avoid the use of deception. This is an example of what Guillemin and Gillam (2004) call *procedural ethics*. We also saw how challenging it can be to apply these principles to research practice. However, a different approach, *situational ethics* (Guillemin and Gillam, 2004) are concerned with the often subtle and sometimes complex ways in which ethics must be applied to practice. To these, Ellis (2007) adds *relational ethics*, closely related to the ethics of care and feminist ethics where the researcher attempts to be true to one's character and responsible for one's actions and their consequences on others. Relational ethics are based on the values of mutual respect, dignity and connectedness between the researcher and the researched, recognizing that these relationships constantly change over time.

LESSONS ON RESEARCH ETHICS

In recent years, a division has emerged between those who support mainstream codes of ethics (traditionalists) and those who offer counter-arguments to this stance (radicals) (Ferdinand, Pearson, Rowe, and Worthington, 2007). The radical perspective, for example, rejects the authority of codes of ethics on the basis that being ethical is not something that can be measured against the kind of checklist favoured by IRBs. Ethics requires self-regulation mediated through self-reflexivity (Alvesson and Deetz, 2000). This does not mean that researchers can do anything they like, but that they assess the actual situation their research is embedded in. In contrast, however, Bryman and Bell (2007) call for caution, arguing that it assumes that researchers are aware of what constitutes an ethical issue and that they are

Table 4.5   Example of a participant consent form

PARTICIPANT CONSENT FORM

Title of Research Project:

- I have read the Participant Information Sheet describing the nature and purpose of the research project and agree to take part.
- I understand the purpose of the research project and the nature of my involvement in it.
- I understand that I may withdraw from the research project at any stage and that this will not affect my status within the project, either now or in the future.
- I understand that while information gained during the study may be published, I will not be identified and my personal results will remain confidential.
- I understand that I may be audio taped during any interview and that I reserve the right to terminate the recording at any point of time during the interview.
- I understand that data will be held confidentially, in a secure place and in a password-protected computer in the form of hard and electronic copies of transcripts and audiotapes. These data will be accessible to the researcher only.
- I understand that I may contact the Research Director if I require further information about the research, and that I may contact the Research Ethics Coordinator of the [Name of Institution] if I wish to make a complaint relating to my involvement in the research.

Signed _____
(Research participant)

Print name _____

Date _____

Signed _____
(Research Director)

Print name _____

Date _____

Contact details
Research Director: [Name and contact details]
Research Ethics Coordinator: [Name and contact details]

---

prepared to regulate their own behaviour. They further suggest that in the case of management research, for example, ethical frameworks have been adopted that were originally developed by social researchers in related disciplines such as psychology or sociology or by organizations such as the Market Research Society. This is despite the fact that management researchers often face different types of ethical situations from other social researchers. Whether ethical frameworks enhance the reputation of management researchers, or act as limiters on the individual researcher's professional autonomy, is also likely to be an ongoing source of argument and debate. However, whatever the arguments for and against these propositions, what is less contentious is that most undergraduate and postgraduate researchers are inadequately prepared for integrating ethical norms into their research.

That said, Bell and Bryman (2007) raise some important concerns about the value of many current ethical frameworks to management research. Although, undoubtedly they can be important, for example, when students use their fellow students in their research sample, when investigating the world outside the university, researchers are often at a disadvantage. This is because, although gaining 'informed consent' is laudable in principle, in practice it fails to recognize the power imbalance between researchers and organizations (Bell and Bryman, 2007). When managers, for example, are the subject of a research project, they tend to exert more power and possess higher status than the researchers themselves. For example, the views of a chief executive on the legitimacy or accuracy of the research outcomes into, say, the leadership style in their organization, would probably count for more in the public eye than those of the researcher.

Organizations can also determine what they will allow to be considered as a legitimate focus for a study and what they regard as 'out of bounds'. Hence, researchers can be required to sign confidentiality agreements before conducting the research, restricting what information they can later disclose about the organization, including ways in which the identity of the organization is hidden. Yet the meaning of a case is often only understood with reference to key details which can include the geographical location of the organization, its history and brand image (Bell and Bryman, 2007). It is also not always clear from ethical frameworks whether confidentiality alludes to individual participants or their organizations.

MANAGEMENT RESEARCH

ETHICS AND THE INTERNET

The Internet can be a valuable tool for gathering data, either through the use of online questionnaires, or through the facilitation of online discussion or focus groups. However, some serious ethical issues can arise. One problem is sampling – certain social or racial groups being under-represented in terms of Internet usage, means that samples may be skewed or unrepresentative. Another problem is that interviewers can never be absolutely sure that the comments given by respondents are not accessed and viewed by prying computer hackers. There is also the danger that some respondents might fake or alter their identities, personalities or roles during online interactions. For example, respondents may be less embarrassed about giving deliberately false information when completing an online survey than when, say, facing an interviewer face-to-face. Furthermore, there is less opportunity for determining the accuracy of responses. When using live interviews, the interviewer has an opportunity to observe the body language and hear the vocal tones of respondents, allowing for some corroboration of the honesty of the responses given. This, however, is clearly more limited with online interactions – although Skype with its video content can help here. The researcher–informant relationship is inevitably modified by the electronic environment (DeLorme et al., 2001).

INTERNET RESEARCH ETHICS

An important and growing source of interpersonal communication is through Internet chatrooms (for real time discussions) and forums (where discussions are posted as threads), so it is no surprise that the content and interactions within such facilities have become of increasing interest to researchers. However, as Hudson and Bruckman (2004) point out, a wide range of ethical dilemmas present themselves, including:

- Is it ethical to enter a chatroom and record its contents for research purposes?
- Is it necessary to obtain informed consent before entering?
- Is it sufficient merely to announce the researchers' presence and invite participants to opt out?
- How should data collected in chatrooms be protected?

———————————————————→ ON THE WEB 4.4 ←———————————————————

The following provides an example of an Internet discussion forum for which Hudson and Bruckman's (2004) concerns about online ethics still apply.

http://www.methodspace.com/forum/topics/using-online-discussion-forums

This page is taken from Sage's Methodspace site, which provides a wealth of information and discussions about research methods and the views of experienced researchers.

In attempting to determine the appropriate ethical approach, Hudson and Bruckman (2004) adopt a number of different metaphors to describe the Internet, each of which leads to a different conclusion about how human subjects in chatrooms should be treated (see Table 4.6). In some Internet spaces, the comments of authors clearly show that they regard their conversations as private, so the usual ethical conventions that apply to human subject research would come into play. The situation becomes more complicated when within the same forum one set of participants are promoting a political cause, whilst others are using it as a private space.

In a research study by Hudson and Bruckman (2004) (approved by the Institutional Review Board (ethics committee) of their workplace), the researchers entered a total of 525 chatrooms to measure how participants react to online studies. They found an overwhelmingly negative reaction to being studied without prior consent. When given the option to 'opt in' to the study only 4 out of 766 individuals did so, implying that attempting to gain consent for studying online chatrooms is simply impractical. Hence, researching online chatrooms is only practical when the research is covert.

Since this is potentially unethical, the researchers conclude that the only ethical step is to attempt to gain prior ethical approval for a covert study from the relevant ethics committee. In doing this, the researcher cannot claim that respondents will be anonymous, even if they are using pseudonyms (which is often the case) since Internet Protocol addresses can always be traced back to individual computers. Another concern that an ethics committee would have to take into account would be the danger of minors becoming research subjects. In chatrooms, it is virtually impossible to ascertain the age of those taking part. Given the growing number of children using the Internet, it is likely that some minors will be caught in the net of chatroom research. Since research that involves minors requires more stringent subject protection, the ethics committee might wish to discuss the implications of this in detail. Hudson and Bruckman (2004) argue that an ethics committee will waive informed consent only when four criteria have been met, namely:

- The research involves no more than minimal risk to participants.
- Any waiver of informed consent will not adversely affect the rights or welfare of the subjects.

Table 4.6   Metaphors and how Internet subjects should be treated by researchers

Metaphor	Implications for the treatment of subjects
Public square	Researcher is free to observe behaviour and write about aggregated results.
Private living room	Researcher is required to gain permission from participants.
Town hall meeting	Researcher is free to observe behaviour but must attribute any direct quotations.
Newspaper letters column	Researcher does not need permission but has to cite his/her references.

Source: Adapted from Hudson and Bruckman, 2004

Image 4.3   Using the web as a research tool

- The research could not be practically carried out without the waiver.
- Whenever appropriate, subjects will be provided with additional pertinent information after participation.

So, in the case of their own research, Hudson and Bruckman pointed chatroom participants to a website where the purpose and methodology of the study was explained. We will return to ethical issues and the Internet later in Chapter 16.

— ACTIVITY 4.8 —

Go to the website of the Association of Internet Research (http://aoir.org/) and look for the link to Ethics Working Group where you will find the Association's 33-page ethics report, endorsed by the AoIR executive committee in 2012. What guidelines provided by the report might be valid for your own project? Also take a look at the extensive bibliography for sources that might be useful.

RESEARCHING ETHICALLY IN
YOUR OWN ORGANIZATION

If you are a part-time student or someone acting in an internal consultancy capacity, you may need or want to undertake research in your own organization. Being internal to an organization means that you often have a clearer understanding of the issues requiring research, or you may have a sponsor that has asked you to work on a particular project. In either case, working internally is often beneficial because you have easier access to resources, including human resources. However, familiarity with an organization can also lead to problems, particularly protecting the anonymity of respondents, many of whom may be known to the researcher. The fact that the researcher may be known to participants can also lead some to not answer as honestly as they otherwise would, or even to withdraw from participation. Note that even though you may have obtained organizational permission to conduct the research, this does not mean that employees are required to participate. Ideally, the organization should be able to identify the most suitable participants for the project, but after that, participation should be entirely voluntary. If you detect the slightest whiff of coercion, then the research should not proceed.

➤ **TOP TIP 4.6** ◄

GRAY ON
MAXIMISING
SURVEY RETURN
RATES

There are a number of approaches to ensure that the rights of individuals within organizations you are familiar with are not breached. Polonsky (1998) suggests:

- **Getting others in the organization to collect the data anonymously.**
- **Having another member of the research team (if there is one), but not involved in the firm, collect the data.**
- **Using reply-paid envelopes and drop off boxes for responses in the case of surveys.**

It needs to be stressed that not only should responses be anonymous they must be *seen* to be anonymous by participants. If this is not the case, then it is more than likely that return rates on surveys will be lower than otherwise, and refusal rates for interviews will be higher.

ETHICS AND RESEARCH REPORTS

Even if research has been conducted using sound designs and carefully constructed data gathering tools, it is still possible for researchers to damage their efforts 'at the last fence' by producing a research report, or dissertation, that contains errors or is misleading. Ethics, then, also plays an important role at this stage of the research process. The ethics of report writing is discussed in greater detail at the end of Chapter 24.

A CHECKLIST OF ETHICAL ISSUES

Table 4.7 provides a brief checklist of some of the issues we have explored so far. The Case Study and Activity which follows provides you with an opportunity to apply some of these principles, and illustrates some of the complexities of trying to adopt an ethical stance in 'real world' situations.

Table 4.7   A checklist of ethical issues

Ethical issue	Description
Privacy	The right not to participate. The right to be contacted at reasonable times and to withdraw at any time.
Promises and reciprocity	What do participants gain from cooperating with the research? If promises are made (such as a copy of the final report) keep them.
Risk assessment	In what ways will the research put people under psychological stress, legal liabilities, ostracism by peers or others? Will there be political repercussions? How will you plan to deal with these risks?
Confidentiality	What constitutes the kinds of reasonable promises of confidentiality that can be honoured in practice? Do not make promises that cannot be kept.
Informed consent	What kind of formal consent is necessary and how will it be obtained?
Data access and ownership	Who will have access to the data and who owns it? Make sure that this is specified in any research contract.
Researcher mental health	How will the researcher be affected by conducting the research? What will they see or hear that may require debriefing or counselling?
Advice	Who will the researcher use as a confidente or counsellor on issues of ethics during the research?

Source: Adapted from Patton, 2002

CASE STUDY 4.6

Ethical dilemmas in research

A financial services company implements a new information technology system that gives email capability to all employees, irrespective of grade. After 12 months, company directors are anxious to know if the investment is providing a financial payback. One indicator is whether the email facility is improving inter-employee communication and general productivity. Hence, they want an analysis of email traffic. An external researcher is commissioned to conduct the study.

She decides to use a blend of **quantitative** and **qualitative methods.** On the quantitative side, negotiating access to the information poses no problems, since all she has to do is contact the head of information services. Given that this is a legitimate company project, commissioned by the executive board, he is obliged to give the researcher free access to whatever information she requests.

For the qualitative side of the research she wants to interview a sample of 40 employees. Believing that imposing herself on these people would be unethical, she writes to all of them individually requesting access, and provides details of the purpose of the research, how the information is being collected, and who will read the final report. She had made a request to the executive board that she should be allowed to provide a summary of the final report to all respondents but this was refused. Despite her reassurances, only 12 of the original sample agree to being interviewed, most excusing themselves on the basis that they are too busy. One option would be to obtain an instruction from the managing director, ordering everyone to cooperate. She decides, however, that, not only would this be counter-productive, it would be unethical on a number of grounds not least because the responses would no longer be voluntary. Eventually, she decides that these 12 in-depth interviews will be sufficient to yield high quality data.

(Continued)

(Continued)

Having set up the interviews, the researcher first turns to the quantitative analysis of the emails, which she intends to place into a number of categories. However, as the research progresses, she discovers a significant number of personal emails, including jokes, a betting syndicate, plans for illicit liaisons and inflammatory comments about senior managers and the executive board!

The researcher now faces a difficult ethical dilemma. She decides to include general descriptions of the personal emails in her report but not to reveal the names of individuals (although it will not be difficult for the company to trace them given that it now has an email audit trail). She also decides that she will ask some questions about personal emails in her interviews to gain an employee perspective. Before doing this, she takes another look at her letter to the interviewees and the description of her research. She decides that the description, 'To investigate the purpose of email traffic' is still valid and an additional letter flagging the new 'personal email' probe is not necessary. Participants will still be given the assurance that they can refuse to answer any question and that their responses will be anonymous.

— ACTIVITY 4.9 — ————————————————————————————————————

Examine Case Study 4.6 and consider the following questions:

- Is the research conducted by a researcher or a consultant? Does it make any difference to the ethical issues involved?
- Have sufficient steps been taken to safeguard ethical principles? Are there any additional steps that you would take?
- Should the research be abandoned before the qualitative stage?

Suggested answers are provided at the end of the chapter.

SAFETY ISSUES FOR RESEARCHERS

RESEARCHER
SAFETY

Safety is probably not an issue that is uppermost in the minds of most researchers as they plan their research. Often, respondents are known to the researcher, or if using interviews to collect data, these are conducted over the telephone or in a public place. Occasionally, however, a study may require that interviews are conducted in someone's home or isolated work location in circumstances where the respondent is not known to the researcher. Kenyon and Hawker (1999) raised this issue in an email discussion with fellow researchers (see Case Study 10.2 in Chapter 10, p. 249). While most researchers (thankfully) have never experienced any problem, a minority had, and as the authors comment: 'once would be enough'. Their email survey helped them to compile a list of 'best practice' guidelines for researcher safety, presented in Table 4.8. Once again, it must be emphasized that the majority of interviewers face no significant problems in conducting their research. But as these guidelines make clear, it is better to be safe than sorry – so adhere to the checklist in Table 4.8 as well as the section on Ethical principles, above.

Table 4.8   Best practice guidelines for researcher safety

Equipment	Carry a mobile phone. This helps researchers to check 'in and out' of interviews and provides a means of summoning help if needed.
	Use official stationery to arrange and confirm interviews and show an identity card if you possess one, as these can help to confirm a professional identity and show that you are affiliated to an institution.
Personal demeanour	Develop an awareness of body language (both your own and that of your respondents).
	Be honest, but not over friendly, dress in an appropriate manner and avoid carrying or wearing valuables.
Knowledge and accountability	Have a good knowledge of the working environment both in terms of the research venue and the geographical area in which it is situated.
	Record and report any doubts or incidents, however trivial they may seem.
	Advise others (particularly friends or relatives) of your whereabouts and movements at all times during fieldwork.
Avoidance strategies	Use daylight hours for interviews if possible.
	If interviewing someone in their home, take along a second interviewer as a 'minder'.
	Avoid potentially dangerous areas such as unlit stairwells, lifts and empty buildings.
	Try to use informants that are 'known' in some way, for example, through a third party or through a network. Male respondents should be accessed through female friends or partners.
	Avoid pressurizing anyone to become involved in the research.

Source: Adapted from Kenyon and Hawker, 1999

— Summary —

- Research ethics refers to the moral principles guiding research, conducting research in a responsible and morally defensible way.
- In recent years there has been a substantial growth in ethical frameworks, constructed by professional associations and other institutions such as universities. This is to promote higher professional standards but also out of a concern for avoiding legal action by respondents.
- Any research involving the study of human populations can involve ethical considerations, but particularly research that deals with vulnerable groups involves sensitive topics that could cause distress or anxiety, or involves any element of deception.
- Central to the principles of research are that it should: avoid harm to participants; ensure informed consent; respect the privacy of participants; and avoid deception.
- In most cases, institutions will expect researchers to complete a proposal or ethical protocol which an institutional review board will then evaluate.
- In gaining participants' cooperation, consent forms should be used which describe the purpose of the study and what is being asked of respondents.
- The Internet is a relatively new source of data with no governing body to set down ethical standards. Researchers should adopt the ethical framework of their institution or professional association, noting that ethical approaches to data gathering on the Internet are still emerging.
- Researching your own organization raises particular challenges about ensuring informed consent and genuine anonymity of respondents.
- Safety issues apply just as much to researchers as they do to respondents. You must ensure that you always take the necessary precautions to ensure your own safety when conducting research.

REVIEW QUESTIONS

1. To what extent would you agree with the view that research should rely on a relativist ethical position – rules or duties may vary across different communities and professional groups. What examples could you suggest to support your view?
2. If research should go beyond not causing harm and instead aim to create positive benefits for participants, what benefits could you claim for your own research?
3. If researchers should be self-regulating rather than under the jurisdiction of Institutional Review Boards, should this also apply to student researchers?
4. Is it more difficult to abide to ethical standards when researching one's own organization or one with which one has a personal or professional connection?

FURTHER READING

Miller, T., Birch, M., Mauthner, M. and Jessop, J. (2012) *Ethics in Qualitative Research*. London: Sage. This book explores key ethical dilemmas – including research boundaries, access (including the role of gatekeepers), gaining informed consent, participation, rapport and analysis – within the context of a rapidly changing research environment.

Oliver, P. (2010) *The Student's Guide to Research Ethics*, 2nd edn. Maidenhead: OUP. A clearly written and comprehensive look at ethics both in terms of the overall research process and then by individual ethical themes. A series of imagined dialogues between two researchers gives the reader an insight into the ethical complexities we face in research.

Israel, M. and Hay, I. (2006) *Research Ethics for Social Scientists*. London: Sage. Explores ethical codes in a wide range of different countries, and the tensions that have emerged between researchers and regulators. Particularly useful for those for whom ethics itself is a focus of their research.

Sales, B.D. and Folkman, S. (2000) (eds) *Ethics in Research with Human Participants*. Washington DC: American Psychological Association. All the essentials including ethical ways of recruiting participants, gaining informed consent, privacy and confidentiality issues, written by experts in the field.

JOURNAL RESOURCES

Greaney, A.M., Sheehy, A., Heffernan, C., Murphy, J., Mhaolrúnaigh, S.N., Heffernan, E. and Brown, G. (2012) 'Research ethics application: A guide for the novice researcher', *British Journal of Nursing*, 21(1): 38–42. As the title suggests, an article aimed at those submitting research proposals for the first time. Addresses the ethical principles of respect for persons, beneficence and justice.

Rivière, D. (2011) 'Looking from the outside/in: Re-thinking research ethics Review', *Journal of Academic Ethics*, 9(3): 193–204. The author shares her reflections on the research ethics review process, from the point of view of both a qualitative researcher and as a member of an institutional research ethics review board.

Chenhall, R., Senior, K. and Belton, S. (2011) 'Negotiating human research ethics: Case notes from anthropologists in the field', *Anthropology Today*, 27(5): 13–17. Examines three case studies of qualitative researchers working with Indigenous Australian communities, focusing on the researchers' experiences with ethics committees and how they approached a range of ethical issues arising in the course of their research.

http://www.gre.ac.uk/research/rec/rep

http://www2.surrey.ac.uk/fahs/staffandstudents/ethicalprocedures/#A0

http://www2.warwick.ac.uk/services/rss/researchgovernance_ethics/research_code_of_practice/researchethicscommittees/

http://www.sfu.ca/~decaste/deCastell_867/867pdfs2010/erikson_disguised.pdf

http://www.aomonline.org/aom.asp?ID=268

http://www.the-sra.org.uk/ethical.htm

http://www.esrc.ac.uk/ESRCInfoCentre/index.aspx

http://www.aapor.org/aaporcodeofethics?s=ethics

http://www.apa.org/ethics/code.html

http://www.bera.ac.uk/guidelines.html

http://www.corec.org.uk/

http://www.imc.co.uk/index3.html

http://aoir.org/

http://www.prisonexp.org/

http://www.methodspace.com/forum/topics/using-online-discussion-forums

— Suggested answers for Activity 4.8 —

1. Since the researcher is hired from outside the organization, it is probably fair to call her a consultant. Does this make a difference to the ethical stance adopted? Well, possibly, yes. Researchers, for example, may be measured against the code of conduct of their relevant professional association. Consultants may also have a professional association, but also have to answer to the research sponsor or manager who will tend to be more concerned with 'results'.
2. The consultant has adopted a number of ethical safeguards, including asking for participation and providing information about the purposes of the research.
3. If this project was being conducted in an academic research context it would probably have to be abandoned. But for the consultant, while needing to give due weight to stakeholders' interests, the interests of the client come first.

5

SEARCHING, CRITICALLY REVIEWING AND USING THE LITERATURE

CHAPTER INTRODUCTION

Chapter outline

What function does the
literature serve?   98

The literature search journey   99

The literature search process   101

Searching source materials   102

The process of critically
evaluating sources   112

Managing information   115

Synthesizing and integrating
search results   116

Structure and content of
the literature review   117

Positioning the literature review   118

Doing a critical literature review   118

Referencing sources   120

Keywords

Literature review

Search terms

Bibliographic databases

Google Scholar

Evaluating sources

Kappa score

Chapter objectives

After reading this chapter you will be able to:

- Describe the purpose and importance of a literature search.
- Plan the literature search process.
- Identify suitable sources for the literature.
- Evaluate sources.
- Position the literature review.

LITERATURE REVIEW

LECTURE ON LITERATURE REVIEW

Unless the research is completely inductive in nature, it is likely that you will undertake a comprehensive literature review at the start of your research project. As noted in Chapter 3, the literature review demonstrates the essential theories, arguments and controversies in the field and highlights the ways in which research in the area has been undertaken by others. Crucially, some of the purposes of the literature review are to identify the gaps in knowledge that are worthy of further investigation, challenge current ideas or take an accepted theory but apply it in a new field. This chapter looks at the process of planning the literature search, methods for locating information sources, plus retrieving and managing the flow of information. Having found relevant literature, an important stage is knowing how to review it and to evaluate its worth critically. Finally, the chapter also provides some guidance on where to place the literature review within an academic piece of work.

WHAT FUNCTION DOES THE LITERATURE SERVE?

A researcher cannot conduct significant research without first understanding the literature in the field of study (Boote and Beile, 2005). A comprehensive literature review allows for what Shulman (1999) calls 'generativity', that is, the ability of researchers to build upon the scholarship of those who have come before. Generativity helps to develop both integrity and sophistication in research. This, however, is easier to generate where there is an established research community and a canon of shared knowledge (and accepted methodologies). It is harder to generate in fields that are not well established or where knowledge is fragmented or contested.

One of the features of any project is that it should enable you to demonstrate a critical awareness of the relevant knowledge in the field. A comprehensive review of the literature is essential because it serves a number of purposes, including:

- Providing an up-to-date understanding of the subject, its significance and structure.
- Identifying significant issues and themes that present themselves for further research particularly where there are gaps in current knowledge.
- Guiding the development of research topics and questions.
- Assisting future researchers in understanding why the research was undertaken, its design and direction, and helping others to replicate the research process.
- Presenting the kinds of research methodologies and tools that have been used in other studies which may guide the design of the proposed study.

The last point, above, demonstrates that when we talk about the 'literature review' we are really discussing two literatures. One literature, then, describes the focus of the study, but another vitally important literature is that concerned with research methods. This means that the methodology chapter in particular has to engage with this literature, not just discussing which research designs, approaches and tools have been used, but the academic sources that describe and justify them.

The literature review is not something you complete early in the project and then put to one side. It is likely to continue almost to the writing up stage, especially since your own research may generate new issues and ideas that you will want to investigate through the literature. As we saw in Chapter 2, if you are adopting a deductive approach to your study, your literature review will help to provide a source for the focus of your research, including aims, objectives and, in some cases, hypotheses. Conversely, if you favour a more inductive approach, you may begin with the collection and analysis of data, a process that leads to questions that are then addressed through engagement with the literature.

PURPOSE OF
LITERATURE
REVIEW

— CASE STUDY 5.1 —

Using the literature to identify research methods

The alcohol consumption of people aged 65 and over is of growing concern to doctors and other health professionals. Even if average consumption per head stays the same, the ageing population means that in gross terms, the problem will get worse. Most surveys have focused on the alcohol consumption habits of the young, but few have looked at the problem among the older population.

A group of public health workers therefore conducted a literature review to find the kinds of methods health workers can use to identify older persons who are at risk of alcohol abuse. In undertaking this review, the health workers first of all approached a group of experts in the field of geriatric medicine and alcohol abuse research and asked for a list of studies they felt to be significant. The reviewers then examined these studies as well as the references they contained. They then performed an online search of two major medical bibliographic databases to ensure that they had not omitted any vital studies.

This literature review revealed that the study into the alcohol problems of older people was under-researched. The review showed that more research was needed to identify methods for detecting risks associated with alcohol misuse.

Source: Adapted from Fink, 2005

— ACTIVITY 5.1 —

For your own study, make a list of experts in the field. If you are unsure as to who these might be, identify which names appear most frequently in the reference section of key academic articles. Show the list to your supervisor to elicit feedback.

THE LITERATURE SEARCH JOURNEY

At the outset you may have only a general notion of your research theme (for example, performance management in an organization, the effectiveness of mixed ability teaching, public attitudes to the integration of schizophrenic

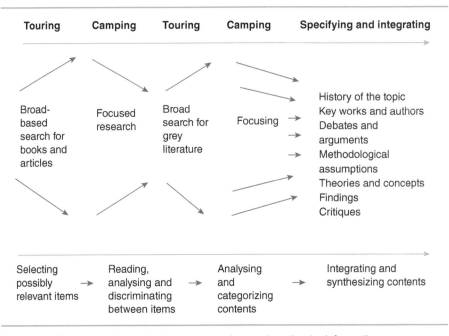

Figure 5.1   Touring and camping to acquire, analyse and synthesize information

Source: Adapted from Hart, 2001

patients into society, etc.). This is obviously where you will start. It may happen, however, that your reading takes you down some unanticipated paths. This is acceptable, as long as it results in a coherent topic for your research. Alternatively, your initial theme may appear too wide (for example, brands in marketing), and through reading the relevant literature you may be able to focus on a specific area of the topic which is actually feasible to implement (for example, getting a new brand image accepted and promoted by an organization).

Planning the literature search is not like getting on a train and travelling from A to B. You may have a general intention of getting to B, but your route may involve several modes of transport (sources) and you may find yourself travelling sideways or sometimes backwards! Indeed, you may even decide when on your journey that you intend to travel to C instead! Planning, then, means aiming for a destination (even though this goal may change) and knowing where the modes of transport and timetables are. To modify Hart's (2001) analogy of trawling and mining, the research process is about touring (looking around) and camping (stopping to explore in more depth), as Figure 5.1 shows. Notice that the travelling process involves an enticing journey around the literature. But camping involves a more discriminating approach, selecting, synthesizing and analysing in more detail. By the end of the literature search journey, you will be familiar with the history of the subject, the key sources and authors, and methodological approaches, theories and findings. Above all, you will be familiar with the problems, debates, arguments and uncertainties within the territory, and these should begin to clarify your own concerns, objectives and research focus.

THE LITERATURE SEARCH PROCESS

A literature search is defined by Fink as 'a systematic, explicit, and reproducible method for identifying, evaluating, and synthesizing the existing body of completed and recorded work produced by researchers, scholars, and practitioners' (2005: 3). To achieve this, it is necessary to focus on high-quality research rather than rely on the second-hand interpretations of others. Note that the kinds of sources that can be used are discussed later on in the chapter.

SEARCHING FOR NURSING LITERATURE

Selecting the research focus and questions

In identifying your research focus you will have developed an 'angle' (as discussed in the previous section) which hopefully serves to define and narrow the subject area. After this, you may decide to focus on one sub-theme more than another. Whether research questions are formulated at the start of the research, or during it, will depend on the attitude of the researcher to inductive or deductive methods. Clearly, the literature search is made easier if the research questions have been formulated, if only because they provide a focus and key terms for conducting the research. In many cases, however, it is more than likely that sets of coherent research questions will flow *from* the literature review.

IDENTIFYING RESEARCH AREAS

Choosing search terms

Provided that research questions, or at least the research focus, have been clearly formulated, it then becomes possible to choose appropriate search terms – usually because they are contained in the research question or theme itself. Take, for example, the research question, 'What is the relationship between having a mentor and a woman manager's career development?' We have three concepts: mentoring, women managers and career development. These terms, often called identifiers, are the key words that will be searched on. A search in the EBSCO bibliographic database on the term 'mentor' yielded 5,924 'hits', clearly an unmanageable number. Before inputting the term 'career development' a check was made that it was contained in the bibliographic site's thesaurus (database of terms). It was found that this was the case. A search using the term 'career development' produced an even more daunting 6,607 hits. Putting the terms 'mentors' and 'career development' together, however, came up with 327 hits, suggesting articles that probably have greater relevance to the proposed study. Adding a further term, 'women' narrowed the search down to a mere 55 hits, and changing 'women' into 'women managers' reduced the total down to a mere 4. However, narrowing down the search too far can run the risk of missing some vital studies. In this case it would be fruitful to scroll through, say, the 'mentors/career development/women' hits as these studies might reveal themes and issues that are of relevance to women managers but have not been considered by the researcher.

EFFECTIVE LITERATURE SEARCHING

PICO SEARCH STRUCTURE

Searches are often conducted using Boolean operators such as AND, OR, or NOT. Hence, in the example above, a search was made for mentors AND career development. If it is certain that the main focus should be on mentoring but not on its near cousin, coaching, then the search could include the operator NOT coaching in one of the search fields. Using Boolean operators provides much greater control over the searching process. If the number of hits is still excessively large, some researchers refine the search using the same search terms but on abstracts rather than full articles.

➤ TOP TIP 5.1 ◄

Conducting a search using key terms can often be frustrating, especially when it reveals either no or very few hits of any relevance. If this happens, check in the database's thesaurus that the term is used by the database. Then try modifying the terms you are searching under. If you still have no luck, consider inputting your terms into a different database.

Sequencing the search

There is no strict order in which you have to locate source materials. Creswell (2009), however, suggests that the following order is helpful:

- *Journal articles.* But ensure that you concentrate on peer-reviewed journals. This is not to say that you should always avoid, say, professional magazines or periodicals. Articles in credible, peer-reviewed journals, however, are scrutinized for their relevance, originality and validity by other academic researchers. Hence, the quality and reliability of such articles, while not guaranteed, is more assured.
- *Books.* Begin with research monographs that are summaries of the academic literature on a particular subject. Then look at complete books on a single topic or ones that contain chapters written by different authors. Note, however, that textbooks quickly become dated, so it is best to use them in conjunction with other sources.
- *Conference papers.* These often contain the most up-to-date information and developments in research. Recall Chapter 3 in which it was argued that working knowledge is not in books but in conference papers, seminars and unpublished academic papers.

In contrast, Hart (2001) advises that the best start is delving into a library's quick reference section, where you can find sources such as guides to the literature, dictionaries, directories and encyclopaedias. After this, the focus becomes one of using books and bibliographies in more detail. Clearly, there are alternative approaches! Try dipping into the reference sources and see what you find the most rewarding.

Having conducted the literature search, it is important to check that no essential articles have been overlooked. One way to do this is by asking a subject matter expert in the field, or to examine one of the reference sections of a key high-quality article or literature source. It is not always necessary to download or print off such an article, because the bibliographic database often provides a list of the references cited by articles.

SEARCHING SOURCE MATERIALS

SELECTION OF
DATABASES

We have looked at the literature search process, including defining the research focus or questions and establishing search criteria. We now explore a wide variety of potential research sources. These are not offered in any particular order of priority, although as we have just seen, Creswell (2002) suggests using academic articles first, followed by books and then conference papers. Perhaps the best advice is that you should be flexible and above all, persistent in your searches. Table 5.1 offers a brief overview of some of the sources.

Table 5.1   An overview of literature sources

Sources where research and information is published	Sources and organizations providing publications	Tools for searching published works and data
Textbooks	Academic libraries	Library catalogues
Articles	Public libraries	Subject indexes
Theses	National libraries	Subject abstracts
Government publications	Specialist libraries	Bibliographies
Legal and professional publications	Museums	Encyclopaedias
	Archives	Guides to the literature
Trade literature	Special collections	Internet directories
Conference papers	Political parties	Internet search engines
Monographs	Commercial organizations	
Statistics	Trusts	
	Internet	

Source: Adapted from Hart, 2001

Articles

There are, essentially, two types of journal article: academic articles written in peer-reviewed journals and articles published in professional journals (that are not usually peer-reviewed). How do you tell the difference? There are no strict rules here, but typical features of peer-reviewed articles include:

PEER REVIEW

- The journal features a page with a list of reviewers, most of whom emanate from international universities.
- Details are provided on how to submit an article for consideration by the journal; these will include the kinds of academic fields the journal is interested in.

If you only have access to an article rather than the full journal, its quality will usually be evident by the academic rigour of its contents, including its description of methodology and/or concepts and the use of formal language, as well as the number of sources in the reference section. Articles in non-peer-reviewed publications (such as professional journals or magazines) come with few, if any, references and are more informal in tone. Both kinds of article can be accessed through bibliographic and abstracting databases.

Searching bibliographic databases

A bibliographic database is an electronic (usually online) source that provides an index to articles and other materials, plus abstracts, citations and either the full article itself or links to where the article can be accessed. Most academic institutions provide students with free access to a number of bibliographic databases. Unfortunately, no single database is sufficient to cover all articles or materials in existence, so it is usually a case of having to use more than one database to access the articles required. There are five main bibliographic sources:

- Online public bibliographic databases (e.g., ERIC, EconLit, PsychINFO).
- Private bibliographic databases (e.g., EMBASE, PubMed).

- Specialized bibliographic databases (e.g., government reports, collections maintained by environmental, business and legal bodies).
- Manual and hand searches based upon references in articles.
- Using experts and authors.

Table 5.2 provides some examples of both public and private bibliographic databases, with Web addresses and a brief description of each.

Clearly, choosing between all the bibliographic database sites presented in Table 5.2 is not completely straightforward. If you are researching, say, the impact of new technology on the social behaviour of young people, do you search in the information technology or the social science databases? The answer is probably both, since each might contain relevant articles but approaching the issue from different perspectives. Success in locating the right article(s) depends in large part on how well search terms are specified and your own determination. Another problem is that the same journal may be referenced in 20 different databases. This is further complicated by the fact that these databases might cover journal issues dating back to different dates. Thus, no single database can be relied on to give comprehensive coverage – what we have is a 'tangled maze' (Dochartaigh, 2007: 27). Hart (2001) advises that it is best to search the multi-subject indexes and abstracts first, and subject-specific abstracts (if there are any) last.

USING
GOOGLE
SCHOLAR

Some bibliographic databases are now allowing their contents to be searched via one of the popular search engines such as Yahoo or Google – especially Google Scholar, with its focus on academic articles. Google Scholar is a very useful way of performing a speedy search and offers a way of identifying a wide array of books, book chapters and articles. Sometimes these will be immediately available as a link to a website or as a pdf file. Even if these sources are not available, it may be possible to find, say, the article on a bibliographic database. Note that if you are accessing articles through a database your institution subscribes to, then downloading the article from this private site will be free of charge. If, however, your institution does not have a subscription and the bibliographic database is private (commercial) then you will usually have to pay for each article.

━━━━━━━━━━━━━➤ **ON THE WEB 5.1** ◄━━━━━━━━━━━━━

Take a look at Google Scholar at:

http://scholar.google.co.uk/

Note that like most online search facilities you are able to perform an Advanced search, giving you more control over what you are looking for. A search on any topic will yield a list of sources, many of which will comprise the abstracts of books or book chapters or sample previews of the sources themselves. Before you get too excited, you will find that there will be vital missing pages from the book or article, meaning that you will eventually have to access the source itself. When scrolling down the Google Scholar list, look out for pdf files. Sometimes these are academic articles, but more often they are reports written by practitioners or professional associations. Using practitioner sources like these can provide a valuable complement to the use of scholarly articles.

Table 5.2   Examples of online public and private bibliographic databases

Title of bibliographic database	Web address	Comments
GENERAL		
WorldCat	www. worldcat.org	The world's largest bibliographic database, which itemizes the collections in more than 10,000 libraries. You can locate the nearest library that holds the book you need.
The British Library	http://www. bl.uk/	Retains copies of every book published in Britain and Ireland.
EBSCO	http://www. ebscohost.com/	A database covering a wide variety of disciplines including business, IT, history, media, general science, health and medicine, law and psychology.
OVID	http://www. ovid.com/	Provides links to a wide range of databases, particularly in medical and health research.
Web of Science	http://scientific. thomson. com/ products/wos/	Provides access to databases covering about 8,700 leading journals in science, technology, social sciences, the arts and humanities.
Zetoc	http://zetoc. mimas.ac.uk/	Offers access to the British Library's electronic table of contents for over 20,000 journals and 16,000 conference proceedings published per year. The database covers 1993 to the present day.
CSA (formally Cambridge Scientific Abstracts)	http://www.csa.com/	Provides access to over 100 databases in the arts and humanities, natural sciences, social sciences and technology.
SOCIAL SCIENCES		
Educational Resources Information Center (ERIC)	http://www.eric.ed.gov/	Contains records of 1.2 million articles indexed since 1966, including books, journal articles and conference papers.
Social Science Research Network	http://ssrn.com/mrn/index	Main focus is on economics, accounting, law and management.
MEDICINE		
PubMed	http://www. ncbi.nlm.nih. gov/ sites/ entrez/	A free search engine for accessing the PubMed database of articles in medicine, health and nursing. Contains over 16 million citations from MEDLINE and other life science databases.
EMBASE (Excerpta Medica Database)	Search for EMBASE in: http:// www.elsevier.com/	A biomedical and pharmacological database containing over 11 million records from 1974 to the present, fully indexed and covering over 5,000 biomedical journals.

→ **TOP TIP 5.2** ←

If you have difficulty finding the full text of an article, do a Google search (www.google. com) or use one of the other search engines to find a link to the author's home page. You may find not only the article, but other, more recent examples of the author's work you were unaware of.

Indexing and abstracting databases

Articles can be accessed through using either an indexing or abstracting tool. These provide citation details such as author, title of article, journal and year and place of publication. Abstracting services, however, also give a brief synthesis and summary of what the article is about, which can be helpful. Since indexing services are not concerned with whether a journal provides full text articles or not, they are much more comprehensive in coverage than full text services. However, many abstracting services are now also providing links to full text articles. Hence, the distinction between abstracting and full text services is breaking down.

WEB OF
KNOWLEDGE

One citation database is the ISI Web of Science which provides information on who is citing who among academic scholars. It is possible, then, to see how important a particular article has become, by seeing how many times it has been cited in the reference section of other articles. It also provides an audit trail through long-term academic debates through the references that academics are making to previous works.

→ **ON THE WEB 5.2** ←

Take a look at the following websites:

ISI Web of Science site at: http://apps.isiknowledge.com which provides a citation index for the social sciences, and the arts and humanities.

Also see ComAbstracts at: http://www.cios.org/ which deals with article abstracts, books and Internet materials on communication.

Books

Library sources

One of the main sources for locating relevant books is the Online Public Access Catalogue (OPAC) of a library. These can usually be searched by subject, author, title and key words. They also often offer access to other online catalogues, and gateways. Using the Internet, you can access libraries across the world. For example, take a look at the BUBL Link public access catalogues, and locate the online public catalogues in your own country at: http://link.bubl.ac.uk/library opacs/.

When browsing in a library or bookshop, a useful evaluation procedure for deciding on whether a book is worth borrowing or purchasing is to look at a number of features, including the:

- Title and subtitle – are they relevant?
- Preface – does it cover your subject area or at least an element of it, and is it at the right level?
- Contents list – does it offer material on your topic?
- Publisher – is the organization respected for publishing quality texts in your field?
- Bibliography – is there one, and do the references look familiar, at the appropriate level and 'on topic'?

Online bookshops

These provide a valuable supplement to library catalogues in that they often provide a detailed description of the book, including its contents and sometimes some sample pages. Amazon, for example, provides reviews by other readers as well as 'Customers who bought this item also bought', offering, at least potentially, a guide towards sources you were unaware of.

➤ ON THE WEB 5.3 ◄

See www.amazon.com or www.amazon.co.uk. Note that the amazon.com site is more comprehensive.

Theses and dissertations

It is often a concern to researchers that the study they are about to embark upon has been done before. An important early 'port of call' is therefore the library of your own institution to see what has been researched and published through theses and dissertations. After this you can then go online and use the *Index to Theses* site. If you are able, for example, to locate a thesis on a subject related to your own, you then have access to a comprehensive list of references at the end of the thesis.

Grey literature

This is the sort of published and unpublished material that cannot be identified through the usual bibliographic methods. A growing and significant example here are websites, but grey literature also includes academic theses and dissertations (as above), newspaper and magazine articles, editorials, materials produced by business and trade journals, reports, and publications by clubs and societies. Many of these can be accessed through libraries or the websites of professional associations and business.

➤ ON THE WEB 5.4 ◄

See the Grey Literature Network Service at: http://www.greynet.org/

The site provides Web links to a host of other grey literature sites, as well as archives on the subject of grey literature itself.

Reference sources

When you are new to a subject, it is best to gain an overview of the key arguments, authors and sources. Reference sources such as dictionaries and encyclopaedias are often a good place to start. Specialist encyclopaedias such as the *International Encyclopaedia of the Social and Behavioural Sciences* are particularly useful. See the section in Chapter 20 on *Academic sources* for more on reference books, almanacs and yearbooks.

Conference papers

EXAMPLE OF
CONFERENCE
ABSTRACT

Conference proceedings (papers given at a conference and subsequently published) are a valuable source of contemporary discussions in the field. A disadvantage of using conference papers is that although papers submitted to conferences are usually peer reviewed, this is rarely performed with the same level of rigour as happens with academic journals. Conference papers also often represent 'work-in-progress' rather than final, definitive findings. Nevertheless, researchers can sometimes find them to be a source of new ideas.

ON THE WEB 5.5

The Scopus site provides proceedings for 500 conferences in the life, health, physical and social sciences:

http://www.scopus.com/scopus/home.url

You can also receive email alerts about forthcoming conferences in your subject area, see:

http://www.conferencealerts.com/

Not only will this enable you to identify a conference you might wish to attend (or even give a paper at), but some conference websites provide links to the proceedings of previous years' conferences.

Official publications, statistics and archives

These can be of enormous value to the researcher, but it will depend, of course, on the extent to which a government collects these kinds of data, and the level of access provided to the public. Of the kind of material that is available, an increasing amount is finding its way onto the Web. Sites that offer official statistics data are discussed in some depth in Chapter 20 on the use of secondary data sources.

Online resources

Search engines

Dochartaigh (2007) recommends that researchers search the academic literature before making use of search engines. This is because search engines can yield a fairly diverse and scattered set of sources which may be difficult to evaluate. Looking at the academic literature first will give you a greater critical understanding of their context and what is worth using. Search engines include:

- www.google.com
- www.yahoo.com
- www.Ask.com
- www.MSNSearch.com

Although Google currently enjoys the largest market share in terms of usage, it should be remembered that all search engines perform their searching using slightly different sets of criteria. This means that they are all likely to yield broadly similar but also a number of different results. Hence, it is worth using more than one of these search engines when looking for articles or data.

Wikipedia

Of course, no discussion of reference sources would be complete without mention of Wikipedia. Most academic institutions take a very negative view of students using Wikipedia as an academic source. So if you use Wikipedia to give you a 'feel' of the subject, you should then progress to using more academic and scholarly sources. Never, under any circumstances, use Wikipedia as your main source.

You can explore Wikipedia at: http://www.wikipedia.org/

Access to reading lists

Especially if you are new to a subject and simply do not know where to start, try using a course reading list that links to your subject area. This might be a course at your own institution. Today, however, thousands of course syllabi are being put onto the Web and this is often a useful place to find comprehensive reading lists.

➤ **ON THE WEB 5.6** ◄

Take a look through some of the millions of course syllabi at: http://chnm. gmu.edu/tools/syllabi/index.php

The site provides a search engine for searching on specific subjects. It also offers a wide range of other tools such as Survey Builder that allows you to create online surveys.

Publishers' websites

Some publishers are now starting to offer resources on their websites. Sage, for example, has a very useful site (Methodspace) devoted to articles and other sources on research methods, all of which are free of charge. See: http://www.methodology. co.uk/

Social and other networks

So far we have focused on getting information from libraries and other sources. In this section we look at how researchers can become more proactive, communicating with individuals, organizations and through networks.

Today a lot of debate and discussion between academics and scholars takes place via the Internet, often through informal groups using various online communication tools. One of the benefits of using these kinds of e-communities is gaining access to up-to-date thinking and ideas in your field of interest. There are many kinds of email lists often run by and for academics, covering a huge range of subjects. Most of these lists are unmoderated, that is, the list owner does not review every posting before allowing it onto the site. There is, however, a basic standard of etiquette (netetiquette) that members need to adhere to, avoiding postings that might be offensive or inflammatory to other members or the outside community.

One of the largest online communities is LinkedIn which proclaims itself as the world's largest professional network. Hence, it is possible to link to friends, colleagues or others of similar professional standing to yourself. But it is also possible to use LinkedIn for research purposes. For example, you can set up a closed group (only those you invite are permitted to join) or open group on a research topic and host a discussion. The discussion itself could comprise part of your data set for later analysis. Alternatively, if your aim is to construct a questionnaire on a theme for which little has been published, getting the comments of a professional or experienced group via LinkedIn might help to identify key constructs.

ON THE WEB 5.7

Take a look at Google Groups, one of the most comprehensive Usenet archives, where you can search for discussions on any research topic that interests you. See http:// groups.google.com/. Using Google Groups you can also create a site of your own (say on your research subject) and attract members (fellow researchers or respondents) to it.

One of the most popular mailing lists is JISCmail (the Joint Academic Mailing List service). You can search for a topic by category (for example, social studies, humanities, business studies and computing) which will give you a list of all the mailing lists in that category. A search under business studies, revealed subjects such as 'Total quality', 'Marketing' and 'Finance', each of which contained around 20 separate mailing lists. 'Tourism', for example, contained 22 mailing lists for areas including 'Heritage', 'Hospitality industries' and 'Maritime Leisure Research'. Once you have joined a mailing list, you will find that you start to receive emails from other members of the list (directed, of course, not just to you but to all members of the list). These might include questions, requests for advice or help, or useful information on forthcoming workshops, seminars or conferences. See JISCmail at: http://www.jiscmail.ac.uk/index.htm

Last, and certainly not least, there is Facebook, which, given its global reach, has a diverse and highly international audience. Used by many as a recreational site, Facebook also has a serious side which includes its use by businesses, organizations, governments and, of course, researchers. Hence, inputting a search word or phrase into the search bar can yield a surprising number of groups and individuals who may also be interested in your research topic. For example, using the search string 'qualitative research groups' offers a vast array of both open and closed groups through which you can, say, elicit advice on literature sources. You can, of course, gauge the popularity and activity level of most groups by the number of members. If you don't see a research group that meets your needs you can always start your own!

Joining professional associations

You can join relevant professional associations, many of which publish their own professional journal, and hold conferences or seminars. Some even have their own libraries that can provide a rich source of material in the field. You can usually gain access to an association through its website.

Using organizations

Do not forget that you can also make use of organizations as an important source of data, particularly if they are the focus of your research, for example, if you are using them as case studies. But note that the academic literature should underpin the theoretical elements of the project. Using grey literature such as institutional or company documents is valid for providing background information and supporting detail, but they should not carry the main burden of the theoretical argument. Another important source of organizational information is an organization's website. Unfortunately, of course, such websites change fairly constantly. All is not lost, however. You can track the changes that have occurred over time by using the Internet Archive (see: http://www.archive.org/web). A drawback of the site is that the owners of Web domains can block materials being made available to the public (Dochartaigh, 2007).

Using authors

If you have been impressed with a particular author's work, why not try contacting them? These days, many people are quite easy to locate through their organization's website – particularly if they are an academic. You can ask them if they have published anything else in your field of interest, or if they are writing something new at the moment. You may be lucky enough to receive copies of articles, drafts of work in progress, or at least new references. On the other hand, they may be too busy to reply to you, so if there is no response do not be disappointed!

CASE STUDY 5.2

An illustration of the literature search process

Kate works in a special school for severely autistic children. Two years ago she enrolled on a part-time MSc programme at a local university and is now at the dissertation stage. Not surprisingly, her topic is going to be on autism in children. She is particularly interested in why the phenomenon seems to be on the increase, particularly in boys, and what teaching strategies are most appropriate for helping them. In undertaking her literature review, she starts with the OPAC database in her university library. Using the search words 'autism in children' yields 77 hits. She focuses on books published after 2000, selecting Rebecca Moye's (2006) *Addressing the Challenging Behaviour of Children with High Functioning Autism*, and Uta Frith's (2003) work *Autism: Explaining the Enigma*. She then searches Amazon.com but finds that many recent publications are of the 'self help for parents' type, whereas she is looking for a more academic and practitioner focus. She does, however, find a publication by the National Research Council titled *Educating Children with Autism*. She is confident that it is worth buying this book, because the Amazon site provides a detailed description of it and there are 9 highly positive reviews, including one that states it is 'essential reading!'

Kate now turns to a source for academic articles and again searches OPAC by inputting the search word 'autism' under Periodicals. She is delighted to find that there is a *Journal of Autism and Developmental Disorders* held in the library. She locates the journal and searches through the issues from 2000 to the current issue, finding 6 articles that seem highly relevant to her interests. On reading the articles during the next week, she notices a number of authors and studies that are frequently cited and decides that she needs to locate and read them.

For the next stage she searches through the online psychology bibliographic database provided by her university, using the search terms 'autism' and 'children'. This yields a massive 2,804 hits.

(Continued)

(Continued)

Kate then adds a third search term, 'teaching' which brings the total down to a manageable 174. She spends the next two hours looking at the description of each article, and adding those articles she needs to a folder facility on the website. At the end of the search she views the contents of the folder. Some of the articles are PDF full text, so she prints these off immediately. Others she has to order through her library. Next, she searches Wikipedia which provides an extensive article at the end of which there are 120 references, many of which provide links to journal or online articles.

Finally, Kate inputs the search terms 'Autism conferences' into Google and finds quite a vast array of conferences all over the world. She notices that many of the speakers match the names she has come across in her literature searches. Three months later, Kate attends an autism conference and finds she is able to talk to not only autism teachers, but to practitioners like herself who are also undertaking research. This is very useful because she notices that many of the problems and challenges in research that she is facing, are being experienced by all the people she meets! Kate manages to have a discussion with several of the keynote speakers, some of whom are academic researchers in the field. Through these conversations she is able to 'try out' some of her preliminary thoughts on her possible research focus and get feedback from these experienced researchers in the field. Kate comes to realize that her literature searching and interactions with fellow researchers have provided her with the opportunity to shape and give some focus to her own research project.

— ACTIVITY 5.2 —

Compare the actions of Kate in Case Study 5.2 with the potential array of sources discussed in the section Searching source materials. Are there any important steps she may have missed out?

THE PROCESS OF CRITICALLY EVALUATING SOURCES

EVALUATING
SECONDARY
SOURCES

We have now explored ways in which a fairly vast array of articles, books and other sources can be accessed. But how do we know if they are worth using? This is where the use of robust evaluation techniques becomes essential. There are, basically, two steps in this process. The first is establishing a set of screening criteria. This will narrow down your search considerably. The next step is reading abstracts or full-text articles and making critical judgements about their worth. This, of course, is a skill that is acquired over time and with experience.

Devising practical screening criteria

Fink (2005) recommends that this should be done in two screening stages. The first screening is practical, setting out, including, and in some cases, excluding criteria. Table 5.3 provides a summary of these criteria, for the mentoring study discussed on p. 101.

The second screening stage examines the methodological quality of sources, looking at how well a study has been designed and implemented to achieve its

Table 5.3 Examples of screening criteria for a study of mentoring women managers in organizations

Criteria	Example (choice)
Publication language	Include only studies in English.
Journal	Include human resource and organizational studies journals published in UK or USA. Exclude psychology journals.
Author	Include all articles by Kathy Kram.
Setting	Include all studies that take place inside organizations. Exclude studies in social settings or local communities.
Participants or subjects	Include women managers and exclude male managers.
Research design	Include only studies that use experimental designs with control groups.
Sampling	Include only studies that use randomized samples.
Date of publication	Include only studies published from 2000 onwards.
Content (topics, variables)	Include only studies that focus on mentoring of women; exclude studies on mentoring of men. Exclude coaching studies.

Source: Adapted from Fink, 2005

objectives. Hart (1998) warns that, in evaluating a piece of research, the researcher must be aware of the methodological tradition from which it emanates – even if the researcher is not sympathetic to that tradition. For example, it is not enough to criticize a quasi-experimental research study for taking a quantitative approach to data collection, since this is what one would expect. A more valid argument would be that the research design was not matched to the research objectives, or that assertions made for the study were insufficiently supported by the data or analysis.

Making critical judgements

If conducting a literature review as the sole researcher, you will need to develop the kinds of criteria outlined in Table 5.3 and apply them to the articles or sources under review. However, it is necessary to go beyond the application of selection criteria, to making value judgements about what constitutes an authentic source and what does not (see Table 5.4).

Even when applying the kind of evaluation methods suggested in Table 5.4, it is worth noting that a person's judgements can change from day to day, as Activity 5.3 may demonstrate. It is therefore worth examining a source more than once, especially if its value or worth is unclear the first time.

ACTIVITY 5.3

To evaluate the extent to which judgements are stable over time, take a small sample of articles and review them, deciding which are 'high quality' to be included and which are not. Return to the same articles, say, two weeks later and perform the same exercise. Are your judgements broadly the same? Did you include and exclude articles for the same reasons?

Table 5.4 Evaluating the quality of sources

Quality concept	Questions to ask about the source
Authority	Does it emanate from an unknown individual, or from an institution such as a university, government or public agency? If the source is an individual, is it possible to link to their home pages and check what else they have published and with what publisher? Have they published in high quality peer-reviewed journals?
Accuracy	Is the source from a peer-reviewed journal (in which case it will have been reviewed by experts before being accepted for publication)? Does the source make reference to other well-known sources or texts? If a website, when was it last updated?
Bias and objectivity	Is the language calm and logical or aggressive and strident? Does it present opposing viewpoints to provide a sense of balance? Does it provide references to unbiased sources? How is validity addressed? How are ethical issues handled?
Coverage	Does the source come from a 'boutique' site, that is, one that is highly specialized and lacking in breadth?

Source: Adapted from Anderson and Kanuka, 2003 and Hart, 1998

Operationalizing the issues listed above means using sets of tools to analyse and evaluate the literature. This means developing a complex set of critical skills, acquired through practice. Table 5.5 provides a brief overview of the types of skill involved. Note that this is hierarchical, with higher order skills at the top.

If conducting the review as part of a research team, the question of achieving inter-judge reliability of measurement comes into play. Let us take an example of two researchers who both will have to agree on which articles are going to be included in the literature review, and which are to be excluded. They will first of all have to agree a set of selection criteria similar to those in Table 5.3. The next stage is to conduct the review itself. But how do we know if the researchers are applying the criteria in a similar way? How reliable is this process? A useful way of calculating this is using the Kappa statistic, which compares the level of agreement between two people against what might have been predicted just by chance. The Kappa score itself ranges from +1 (perfect agreement) to 0 (no agreement above what would have been predicted by chance) to -1 (perfect disagreement), and is calculated as follows:

$$K = \frac{0 - C \text{ (Agreement beyond chance)}}{1 - C \text{ (Agreement possible beyond chance)}}$$

According to Fink (2005) a literature review should aim for a Kappa score of between 0.6 and 1.0. Scores of 0.0–0.2 are regarded as slight; 0.2–0.4 = fair; 0.4–0.6 = moderate; 0.6–0.8 = substantial; 0.8–1.0 = almost perfect.

Assume that two reviewers are conducting a literature review on the research question: 'What is the relationship between having a mentor and a woman manager's career development' and are judging whether the studies they are reviewing

Table 5.5 Skills for critical engagement with the literature

Skill	Actions	Description
Analysis	Select, differentiate, break up	Dissecting data into their constituent parts in order to determine the relationship between them.
Synthesis	Integrate, combine, formulate, reorganize	Rearranging the elements derived from analysis to identify relationships.
Comprehension	Understand, distinguish, explain	Interpreting and distinguishing between different types of data, theory and argument to describe the substance of an idea.
Knowledge	Define, classify, describe, name	Describing the principles, uses and function of rules, methods and events.

Source: Adapted from Hart, 1998

Table 5.6 Positive and negative judgements by two reviewers on a set of articles

REVIEWER 1	REVIEWER 2		
	Negative	Positive	Total
Negative	11	8	**19**
Positive	9	28	**37**
Total	**20**	**36**	

express positive or negative findings on the impact of mentoring. Table 5.6 illustrates the number of articles that each reviewer (acting independently) considers to be positive or negative. The Kappa score then calculates the extent to which these sets of scores are in agreement.

———— **ACTIVITY 5.4** ————

To calculate a Kappa score for these data, input the figures into the Kappa value calculator at: http://www.dmi.columbia.edu/homepages/chuangj/kappa/ What score do you get? Is the result slight, fair, moderate, substantial or almost perfect?

Suggested answer at the end of the chapter.

MANAGING INFORMATION

It is all too easy to be enthusiastic and motivated in searching the literature, but sloppy in storing your findings. Without an accurate, consistent and searchable means of storing your literature search data, your efforts will lack the rewards that they deserve. The key is the maintenance of a research log. This can be paper-based or a computer file, depending on which you are most comfortable with. The research log could contain sections on:

- Search parameters – details of your main subject focus and the keywords that describe it.
- Search logs – information on what you have searched, when, how and with what results.
- Contact details of people, organizations, Internet newsgroups, online discussion groups, etc.
- Inter-library loans, including what you ordered and when.
- CD ROM and Internet sources.
- Bibliography.

Maintaining an accurate and searchable bibliography is important for a number of reasons. First, it means that you have a printable bibliographical record at the end of your research project. Secondly, keeping a searchable record allows you to locate all your references on specific issues (topics, authors, dates of publication, etc.) when you are writing up your research. This is much easier to carry out if you maintain computerized records. There are a number of bibliographic software products on the market that allow you to store records in a database, create bibliographies and even conduct Internet searches of online and Web databases.

ON THE WEB 5.8

You can download trial versions of two bibliographic software products from the Adeptscience website at:

http://www.adeptscience.co.uk

Look for Reference Manager and EndNote.

For a tutorial on using Reference Manager see:

http://www.ion.ucl.ac.uk/library/rm.htm

For a tutorial on using EndNote see:

http://www.library.uq.edu.au/endnote/how_use.html

TOP TIP 5.3

Because of the danger of plagiarism when making notes, it is usually safest to construct them in your own words, so reducing the chance of unwittingly copying someone else's words by mistake.

SYNTHESIZING AND INTEGRATING SEARCH RESULTS

The final stage in the literature review process is to bring the results together, providing an answer to some of the original questions that were posed and which may include areas where the current state of knowledge is weak. Taking our example of mentoring women managers and their career development, the literature review could comprise answers to at least the following questions:

- How is mentoring defined and how does it differ from other interventions such as coaching or counselling?

- How widespread is mentoring among managers in general and women managers in particular?
- What impact does mentoring have on women who receive it compared to women who do not?

The last question implies that studies will be examined that have conducted empirical research involving an experimental group of women who have received mentoring and a control group that have not. Such studies will then measure the career progression of each group and make statistical comparisons.

As is often the case, the literature review might reveal equivocal results in the empirical studies, some showing a statistically significant improvement in career progression for those women who have engaged with mentoring, but others perhaps showing slight and non-significant differences. Researchers may have suggested a number of potential reasons as to why mentoring has not been as effective as predicted and have recommended further research. It is these recommendations that can then be taken forward as the basis for a new study. Given that all reviews should adopt a *critical* stance to the literature, this is also an opportunity to highlight the weaknesses of some of the studies described, particularly in terms of the validity and reliability of their results. The literature review hence becomes the basis for showing how the future research study will avoid these mistakes and produce more robust findings.

Note the important difference here between what could be termed an annotated bibliography and an integrated literature review. An annotated bibliography is often what students produce (thinking it is a literature review!), presenting a 'laundry list' of sources with a brief description or summary of each. So, it might read: 'Smith (2013) comments that .... Shah (2010) describes .... Rosenberg (2012) talk about ....' This, however, is not a critical review of the literature (as described above), in which sources are discussed *critically*, strengths and weaknesses identified, and gaps in the research and research questions emerge.

ANNOTATED
BIBLIOGRAPHY

> **TOP TIP 5.4** ◄

A good way of checking whether you have written a descriptive summary of the literature (the wrong approach!) as opposed to a critical review is to see if you have also identified some research questions in this section. If no research questions have emerged and been made explicit, you have probably written an annotated bibliography.

GRAY ON
WRITING A
LITERATURE
REVIEW

STRUCTURE AND CONTENT OF THE LITERATURE REVIEW

In terms of structure, Creswell (2002) suggests that a literature review should comprise five components:

- An Introduction, informing the reader about how the review is to be organized and structured.
- Review of Topic 1, addressing the literature on the independent variable or variables (the influences on the dependent variable or subject, upon which the research is focused). Note: we will explore descriptions of dependent and independent variables in more detail in Chapter 6.

- Review of Topic 2, the literature on the dependent variable. If there are multiple dependent variables, devote a sub-section to each one, or focus on a single important dependent variable.
- Review of Topic 3, the literature that relates the independent variable to the dependent variable. Creswell (2002) warns that this section should be relatively short and should focus on studies that are extremely close in topic to the proposed study. If nothing specific has been written on the topic, then review studies that address it at a general level.
- Provide a summary of the review, highlighting the most significant studies and the key themes that have emerged.

LITERATURE
REVIEW
EXAMPLE

This last point is vitally important. It is not enough to simply read around a subject or theme. You must produce a synthesis of subjects or related subjects in the form of an increasingly *focused* argument or set of concerns. The key word here is 'refinement'. Recall Figure 5.1, touring the literature. Pausing to focus on areas that have emerged as important, means that the discussion is gradually refined down to a set of core issues and arguments. These, then, provide the basis for the formulation of research questions and the focus of the research.

A comprehensive and critical literature review, then, should cover the kinds of criteria outlined in Table 5.7. Creating a literature review based upon this checklist will allow you to establish the boundaries of your research, the gaps in current knowledge, the methodologies applied to researching the subject and how the proposed study contributes to knowledge.

POSITIONING THE LITERATURE REVIEW

Should your review of the literature come at the beginning of your thesis or dissertation, in the middle or at the end? Creswell (2002) offers three possible locations: in the *Introduction,* as a *separate section* and as a *final section* in the study. Table 5.8 provides a brief summary. For some qualitative studies, for example, the literature can be discussed in the *Introduction* to 'frame' the subject being studied. However, using a separate literature review section towards the beginning of a study is more typical of a quantitative approach. The purpose of this section becomes to provide a basis on which questions and hypotheses can be generated, and can influence the design and direction of the research. In contrast, in some types of qualitative research, such as the use of grounded theory, theoretical perspectives are developed inductively from the data itself. Any literature review is created towards the end of the research, providing a benchmark against which the results can be compared. Literature reviews within qualitative approaches are discussed in more detail in Chapter 7.

DOING A CRITICAL LITERATURE REVIEW

CRITICAL
LITERATURE
REVIEW
EXAMPLE

So far we have assumed that the literature review has been linked in some way to an empirical study. However, it is legitimate to conduct a literature review (especially if it is a *critical* literature review), as a study in its own right. The word 'critical' has many meanings. Mingers (2000) identifies four aspects of the critical approach:

- Critique of rhetoric. Evaluating a problem with the use of effective language and making reasoned judgements.
- Critique of tradition. Challenging conventional wisdom.

Table 5.7   Criteria for undertaking a critical literature review

Category	Criterion	Comments
1. Coverage	A Justifies criteria for inclusion and exclusion from review.	Justifies what is 'nearly in' the research but actually excluded. This helps to establish the boundaries of the research.
2. Synthesis	B Distinguishes what has been done in the field from what needs to be done.	Identifies the gaps in current knowledge and therefore the role and value of the current study.
	C Places the topic or problem in the broader scholarly literature.	Shows that the topic or problem is linked to wider issues that have already merited research.
	D Places the research in the historical context of the field.	Critically explores the background and history of the topic to contextualize current themes.
	E Acquires and enhances the subject vocabulary.	Demonstrates that is able to link into and build upon the discourse through which the subject is studied and understood.
	F Articulates important variables and phenomena relevant to the topic.	Distinguishes between what is central to the argument/problem and what is peripheral or unimportant. Provides focus.
	G Synthesizes and gains a new perspective on the literature.	Moves beyond a mere synopsis of the literature by providing a focus to reveal what is significant. Clarifies tensions and inconsistencies in the literature.
3. Methodology	H Identifies the main methodological and research techniques that have been used in the field, and their advantages and disadvantages.	Critically evaluates how the topic has been researched to date to justify own choice of methodology.
	I Relates ideas and theories in the field to research methodologies.	Recognizes the methodological weaknesses of previous research and shows how they can be improved in the proposed study.
4. Significance	J Rationalizes the practical significance of the research problem.	Shows how the research contributes to practical solutions.
	K Rationalizes the scholarly significance of the research problem.	Shows how the research contributes to knowledge.
5. Rhetoric	L Writes with a coherent, clear structure that supports the review.	Moves beyond mere description to a set of logical, refined arguments.

Source: Adapted from Boote and Beile, 2005

Table 5.8   Research method and uses of the literature

Research method	Use of the literature	Comments
Qualitative studies: all types	Used in Introduction to 'frame' the problem.	Some literature must be available.
Quantitative	Located as separate 'review of the literature' section at beginning of study.	Helps to generate research questions and hypotheses; also used at end of study against which results compared.
Qualitative: grounded theory	To compare and contrast theories generated from the data with theories in the literature.	The literature does not guide or direct the study, but becomes an aid once patterns emerge from the data.

Source: Adapted from Creswell, 2002

- Critique of authority. Challenging dominant views.
- Critique of objectivity. Recognizing that the information being discussed is not value free.
- Conducting a critical literature review therefore means combining knowledge and understanding of what has been written, with evaluation and judgement skills, and an ability to structure these into a clear and logical argument (Saunders and Rojon, 2011).

In terms of content, critical reviews need to cover the key academic theories within the chosen field of research. Clearly, it is impossible to review every single source. What is essential, however, is that the most relevant and significant sources are covered. Identifying these is often a matter of reading some of the most recent works on the subject and seeing which authors or 'authorities' are referenced and in what depth. Critical reviews also need to be more than just an annotated bibliography, noting what each author has written. The review must compare and contrast the views presented by different authors to provide a holistic perspective on the subject, and do so in a way that differentiates between fact and opinion.

───────────────────────────── ➤ **TOP TIP 5.5** ◄ ─────────────────────────────

If you are conducting research as part of an academic programme check on the programme regulations as to whether they allow for this type of structure. If they do, consider undertaking a critical review of the literature, particularly if your access to organizations or respondents for empirical research is limited.

REFERENCING SOURCES

So far in this chapter we have focused on locating and making use of literature sources. But how do we make reference to these sources in what we write? Students make a lot of mistakes in this area either because they have failed to read their academic institution's rules on doing this, or they do not think it is important. However, it is important. Let's look at a typical approach that some students use:

Table 5.9 Summary of sources and information required using the Harvard System

Source	Author and initial*	Year of publication	Title of article/chapter/programme	Title of publication	Issue information (volume, issue no.)	Place of publication (city)	Publisher	Edition (if available)	Page numbers	Full web address	Date accessed
Book	✓	✓		✓		✓	✓	✓			
Chapter in book	✓**	✓	✓	✓		✓	✓	✓	✓		
Journal article	✓	✓	✓	✓	✓				✓		
Electronic journal article	✓	✓	✓	✓	✓				✓	✓	✓
Website	✓	✓	✓	✓ (title of website)						✓	✓
Television programme	✓	✓	✓		✓ (day and month)		✓				

* This will normally be a person but may also be an organization (for example, the National Health Service)

* The initial is required in the list of References, but is omitted for 'in-text' references

** Both the author(s) of the chapter and the editor(s) of the publication (i.e. book) are required.

Source: Adapted from Gould, 2007

Table 5.10   Examples of sources and references using the Harvard system

Source	Example	Comments
Book	Bloggs, M. (2013) *The Importance of Referencing*, 2nd edn. Darlington: Black and White Press.	Note the full stop after 'M'. Also note the colon after the place name. Title of the publication is in *italics*. As this is a 2nd edition, this is indicated after the title.
Chapter in book	Bloggs, M. (2013) 'More on Referencing', in J. Pink (ed.), *All you need to know about Referencing but were afraid to ask*. Darlington: Black and White Press.	The chapter title is in quotation marks. The book editor's initial comes before, not after the name – hence, J. Pink and not Pink, J. As she is the editor, this is indicated (ed.) The book title is in *italics*.
Journal article	Bloggs, M. (2012) 'An approach to getting those references right: a biographical study', *The Journal of Pedantic but Important Things*, 6(1): 20–32.	Title of the article is in quotation marks. The title of the journal is in *italics*. The volume number (and issue number) is followed by the page numbers.
Electronic journal article	Bloggs, M. (2012) 'An approach to getting those references right: a biographical study', *The Journal of Pedantic but Important Things*, 6(1): 20–32. Available at: www.cheappublishing.co.uk (Accessed: 8 November 2014).	The same article as above, but how it would be referenced if it was *only* published online. Note, this does not include many of the journals in electronic databases such as Emerald or Ebsco (or others) since, while these are accessed electronically, most are published in paper-based versions and hence do not count as electronic journals. So, you reference these as in Journal article, not Electronic journal article.
Website	The Good Referencing Society of Australia (2011) Referencing for Idiots Available at: www.idiots.co.au (Accessed: 1 April 2014).	Name of the author organization, date of publication. Title of the website, address and when accessed.
Television programme	*Referencing – the hidden truth.* (2010) BBC 2, 5th March.	The title of the programme, year, television channel and date.

'Mike Bloggs in *How to Be Careless in Referencing*, shows us that....' This approach is wrong on three counts. Firstly, in referencing you should not make use of any-one's first name or even their initial. Hence, M. Bloggs is not an improvement. Secondly, it is incorrect to make reference here to the source itself – this should be left to the References section of the thesis or dissertation (more of this below). Finally, there is no mention of the date of publication. The correct referencing in the text should therefore read: 'Bloggs (2013) shows us that....' In other words, the second name of the author and the correct date (year). It's as simple as that.

In the References section you will make use of one of the main referencing systems, the most common one being the Harvard system. Table 5.9 provides a summary of the kinds of information used in the Harvard system for some commonly used sources, while Table 5.10 offers some practical examples. However, before using this you should check on what referencing system is recommended by your own academic institution.

— Summary —

- A literature review provides an up-to-date understanding of a subject and helps to identify significant issues and themes for research – particularly where there is a gap in current knowledge.
- When writing a thesis or dissertation there are two literatures that have to be covered – the subject matter itself but also the research methods literature.
- Adopt a systematic approach to retrieving information, including the use of people (e.g., supervisors, subject librarians), and the use of research logs and bibliographic software.
- In retrieving information, keep in mind that reports on some of the most contemporary research are likely to be at conferences and seminars rather than in books or even academic research articles.
- Ensure that the literature review contains an emphasis on peer-reviewed articles and books rather than non-peer-reviewed sources.
- Reviewing the literature requires the adoption of an 'angle' to achieve more of a focus. The review should also adopt a critical stance.
- Devise practical evaluation criteria including the use of screening criteria and search terms.
- In traditional, quantitative studies, the literature review is normally positioned after the Introduction. However, in some, particularly qualitative, studies, the literature review could come later or even at the end of the report or dissertation.
- A critical literature review can be a study in its own right, covering and critiquing the key academic theories within the chosen field of research.
- Ensure that you are accurate and consistent in using references in your text and in the References section at the end of your thesis or dissertation.

— REVIEW QUESTIONS —

1. Name 5 functions served by a literature review.
2. When the research approach is inductive, the literature review is likely to be conducted iteratively. Discuss.
3. Which of the following are more likely to be 'up to date' in terms of their topicality: conference papers, books, journal articles, dissertations.
4. What role can a social media site like Facebook play in conducting a literature research?

— FURTHER READING —

Machi, L.A. and McEvoy, B.T. (2009) *The Literature Review: Six Steps to Success*. Thousand Oaks, CA: Sage. The six steps comprise: selecting the topic, searching the literature, developing the argument, surveying the literature, critiquing the literature and writing the review. Practical and easy to read.

Dochartaigh, N.O. (2007) *Internet Research Skills: How To Do Your Literature Search and Find Research Information Online.* London: Sage. Given the value and growing importance of the Web as a research source, this book provides some excellent search strategies, as well as guidance on evaluating sources.

Anderson, T. and Kanuka, H. (2003) *e-Research: Methods, Strategies, and Issues.* Boston, MA: Allyn & Bacon. Contains a chapter devoted to the conduct of an online literature review, as well as chapters on ethics in e-research and dissemination of e-research results.

Hart, C. (2001) *Doing a Literature Search*. London: Sage. An essential guide that includes plenty of practical advice and also a host of useful online resources.

Hart, C. (1998) *Doing a Literature Review*. London: Sage. Another essential source that justifies the importance of the literature review and demonstrates the review process.

JOURNAL RESOURCES

Fry, M. (2011) 'Literature review of the impact of nurse practitioners in critical care services', *Nursing in Critical Care*, 16(2): 58–66. An example of a comprehensive review examining the impact of Critical Care Nurse Practitioner models, roles, activities and outcomes.

Khoo, C.S.G., Na, J.-C. and Jaidka, K. (2011) 'Analysis of the macro-level discourse structure of literature reviews', *Online Information Review*, 35(2): 255–271. Distinguishes between descriptive literature reviews which summarize papers and integrative literature reviews which focus on ideas and results extracted from academic papers.

Rowley, J. and Slack, F. (2004) 'Conducting a literature review', *Management Research News*, 27(6): 31–39. Outlines some of the basics for conducting a literature review and offers some useful tips.

SUMMARY OF WEB LINKS

http://www.adeptscience.co.uk

www.amazon.com

http://apps.isiknowledge.com

http://www.archive.org/web/

www.Ask.com

http://assda.anu.edu.au/

http://chnm.gmu.edu/tools/syllabi/index.php

http://www.cios.org/

http://www.conferencealerts.com/

http://www.dmi.columbia.edu/homepages/chuangj/kappa/

http://www.europa.eu.int/comm/eurostat/

www.google.com

http://www.greynet.org/

http://groups.google.com/

http://www.ion.ucl.ac.uk/library/rm.htm

http://www.jiscmail.ac.uk/index.htm

http://www.library.uq.edu.au/endnote/how_use.html

http://link.bubl.ac.uk/libraryopacs/

http://www.methodology.co.uk/

www.MSNSearch.com

http://www.psr.keele.ac.uk/data.htm

http://scholar.google.co.uk/

http://www.scopus.com/scopus/home.url

http://www.statistics.gov.uk/

http://www.wikipedia.org/

www.yahoo.com

Suggested answer to Activity 5.4

The Kappa score is 0.696 making this a substantial level of agreement.

PART B
Research Methodology

— Contents —

6. Research Design: Quantitative
    Methods   127
    The structure of experimental
    research   129
    Experimental and quasi-
    experimental research design   137
    Generalizing from samples to
    populations   145
    Designing valid and reliable
    research instruments   150

7. Research Design: Qualitative
    Methods   159
    Some criticisms of quantitative
    research   160
    Characteristics of qualitative
    research   161
    Paradigms and strategies for
    qualitative research   162
    Approaches to qualitative design   168
    The role of the researcher   175
    Using the literature in
    qualitative research   175
    Collecting qualitative data   177
    Ethics and qualitative research   180
    Ensuring rigour in qualitative
    research   181

8. Research Design: Mixed Methods   189
    Differences between quantitative
    and qualitative research   190
    What do we mean by mixed
    methods research?   194
    The benefits of mixed methods
    designs   196
    Looking at mixed methods
    research critically   198
    Types of mixed methods design   199

9. Sampling Strategies   207
    Probability sampling   209
    Non-probability sampling   215
    Mixed methods sampling   225
    Sampling hard to reach
    populations   228
    Sample size – how much
    is enough?   230

10. Designing Descriptive and
    Analytical Surveys   235
    What is a survey?   236
    Types of survey   237
    Stages in the survey process   240
    Selecting a survey method   245
    Conducting a staff opinion survey   252
    Reducing sources of error   256
    Ethics and good practice
    in survey design   262

11. Designing Case Studies   265
    When should we use
    case studies?   267
    The case study design process   268
    Types of case study design   274
    Data collection sources   277
    Quality in case studies:
    validity and reliability   279
    Analysing the evidence   282
    Composing case study
    reports   286

12. Designing Evaluations   295
    The focus of evaluation   297
    Schools of evaluation   304
    Data collection sources   309
    Data collection tools   311
    Quality issues in evaluation   316

Planning the evaluation report 318
Enhancing the impact of
evaluation 319
The ethics of evaluation 322

13. Action Research and Change 327
What is action research? 329
The action research process 332

The role of researchers and
participants 338
Methods of data gathering 339
Validating action research 342
Ethics and action research
projects 343
Some of the limitations
of action research 345

6

RESEARCH DESIGN: QUANTITATIVE METHODS

CHAPTER INTRODUCTION

Chapter outline

The structure of experimental research 129

Experimental and quasi-experimental research design 137

Generalizing from samples to populations 145

Designing valid and reliable research instruments 150

Keywords

Experimental research
Research questions
Hypotheses
Dependent variables
Independent variables
Descriptive statistics

Inferential statistics
Experimental design
Quasi-experimental design
Sampling
Validity
Reliability

Chapter objectives

After reading this chapter you will be able to:

- Describe the experimental and quasi-experimental research approaches.
- Formulate appropriate questions and hypotheses.
- Identify **populations** and samples.
- Describe the principles of research tool design.

A **research design** is the overarching plan for the collection, measurement and analysis of data. Typically, a research design will describe the purpose of the study and the kinds of questions being addressed, the techniques to be used for collecting data, approaches to selecting samples and how the data are going to be analysed.

We saw in Chapter 2 that experimental research methodology usually involves truth-seeking (as opposed to perspective- or opinion-seeking) and may often involve the use of quantitative methods for analysis. It tends, therefore, to utilize a deductive approach to research design, that is, the use of **a priori** questions or hypotheses that the research will test. These often flow from sets of issues and questions arising from the researcher's engagement with a relevant body of litera-ture, such as marketing (in business research), youth crime (in sociological research), trends in the uptake of herbal medicine (in health research) or school absenteeism (in education). The intention of experimental research is the produc-tion of results that are objective, valid and replicable (by the original researcher, or by others). In terms of epistemology, then, experimental research falls firmly into the objectivist camp, and is influenced by positivistic theoretical perspectives. It takes, for example, some of the principles of research design (such as the use of experimental and control groups) from the natural sciences. However, given the discredited status of positivism, advocates of the experimental approach are now likely to make more cautious and modest claims for the veracity and status of their research results.

A PRIORI

In an organizational context, research might stem not from issues prompted by a body of literature, but from a real, live problem the researcher is asked to solve. The initial focus, then, is the problem itself (rising absenteeism, communication bottlenecks, data security, etc.), but the researcher will probably soon have to access both the academic literature (including technical and institutional sources) and also grey literature such as internal organizational documents and reports. Chapter 3 showed how the researcher journeys through a process of refinement, whereby the territory covered by the research literature becomes increasingly focused. But this is not just a question of narrowing the research. The core issues that emerge from the literature gradually build into significant sets of themes, or concerns that link to, and help to specify, the research questions and the research design for solving them.

Note that many of the issues discussed in this chapter (for example, the gen-eration of research questions, the identification of samples from populations and issues of **validity** and **reliability**) are also discussed in many of the chapters that follow – even those associated with more qualitative designs.

THE STRUCTURE OF EXPERIMENTAL RESEARCH

The experimental research design process, put simply, comprises two steps: the planning stage and the operational stage (see Figure 6.1). At the planning stage, the main issue or research question may be posed and the relevant literature and theories investigated. From these it should be possible (if the issue is capable of being researched) to formulate research hypotheses. The dependent variables (the subject of the research) and independent variables (variables that effect the dependent variable) are identified and made explicit after which we move into the operational stage. After the experiment has been conducted, the analysis stage may involve the use of both **descriptive** and **inferential statistics** (described in Chapter 22). From the analysis it then becomes possible to either accept or reject the hypothesis. A formal document or presentation is then prepared to report the results. Let us look at each of these stages in more detail.

EXPERIMENTAL
RESEARCH
DESIGN

Identifying the issue or questions of interest

We saw in Chapter 3 that some of the criteria that make up a 'good' research topic include the availability of resources and access to sponsors and other people who may be able to help in the research. Sometimes a research issue may arise from your reading of a body of literature. In a workplace setting, issues or questions spring up as a result of real problems that require a solution, or as a result of a pilot study prior to the implementation of a research project.

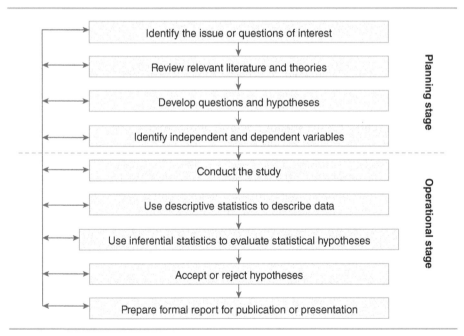

Figure 6.1   Stages in the planning and operation of an experimental and quasi-experimental research project

Source: Adapted from Keppel et al., 1992

Reviewing relevant literature and theories

As we saw in Chapter 2, the experimental approach to research is often deductive, so once an area or issue has been chosen for research, the next stage is to identify and delve into a relevant body of literature. Chapter 5 illustrated some of the sources where you might find the literature you need. Early on in your research, you should try to identify the theories that are relevant to addressing your topic, and also what kinds of research methods have been used to address the subject. The literature search will also identify who are the dominant and influential writers in the field. Having looked at the literature, you may decide that the scale of the subject is too large (particularly in terms of your own tight timescales), or that the investigation you were considering has already been done. However, you may also see that previous investigations have been flawed, or that there are gaps in the research that are worth filling. For example, you may become aware of emerging technology-based learning theories, but notice that there have been few studies of their application within the realm of social media (in which you have personal experience). This could be your niche, your experience in the area giving you a head start.

Developing questions and hypotheses

HOW TO PICK A
QUESTION

Research questions and hypotheses are merely the configuration of issues into a transparent and measurable formulation. The way in which research questions are stated, their focus and the kinds of data they seek, are strongly connected to the philosophy and research paradigm of the researcher (recall Chapter 2). As Wield (2002) also cautions, writing questions and hypotheses is not necessarily a linear process. Even after they have been formulated, either further reading of the literature, or surprises at the piloting or data gathering stages, can force the researcher to amend or even rewrite them. Let us look at research questions and hypotheses in more detail.

Constructing research questions

RESEARCH
QUESTIONS

The ways in which we formulate key questions can sometimes drive us down unfruitful paths, even when the underlying concerns that motivate our questions are genuine and important. It might help if we reflect for a moment on the genuine concerns that drive us to ask the questions we ask (Sarasvathy, 2004). As Alford (1998) points out, research questions are not the same as problems. Problems, themes and concerns may be allocated to you by a sponsor, or may emerge from your engagement with a relevant body of literature. Alford, however, asserts that, in contrast to a problem, a research question comprises two elements: first, a connection to a theoretical framework; secondly, a sentence in which every word counts and which ends (not surprisingly) with a question mark. Questions also describe potential relationships between and among variables that are to be tested. Blumberg et al. (2005) similarly distinguish between what they call dilemmas and research questions. A dilemma is a signal that all is not well – for example, falling sales, higher incidents of crime, poor examination results. The key is knowing how to turn statements of dilemmas into tight research questions. Table 6.1 offers some examples.

Table 6.1   Examples of statements of dilemmas formulated as research questions

Statement of dilemma	Research question	Comments
Rising incidence of drug possession in secondary schools	What is the medium-term change in drug possession in secondary schools?	Medium-term needs defining.
	What factors have influenced detection rates for drug possession in schools?	It may be the case that the rising incidence may be due to better detection rather than more drug use itself.
	How have social attitudes towards drug use changed among school students?	
Increase in 'fly-tipping', i.e. the anti-social dumping of waste in non-designated areas	How has the volume of fly-tipping changed over time?	Fly-tipping needs to be operationally defined.
	Is there a connection between charges for waste disposal at public amenity sites and changes in fly-tipping?	
	What kinds of anti fly-tipping campaigns have been successful in reducing the problem?	Seeks to examine and evaluate initiatives to inform policy
Whether to invest in social media campaigns for product marketing	What kinds of social media are available for product marketing?	Helps to define and describe what is meant by social media.
	How have businesses made successful use of social media?	Establishes how social media is actually used in business.
	If a social media campaign was initiated, what about the business would need to change to support this new approach?	Starts from the realization that engaging with this approach will have implications for how the organization does its business

It is clear from Table 6.1 that each dilemma is addressed by at least one question that explores the relationships between two variables. Kerlinger and Lee (2000) argue that a good research question:

- Expresses a relationship between variables (for example, company image and sales levels).
- Is stated in unambiguous terms in a question format.

But, as Black (1993) states, a question could meet both of Kerlinger and Lee's criteria and still be invalid, because it may be virtually impossible to operationally define some of its variables. What, for example, do we mean by 'image' (in the above example), and how would we define it in ways that could be measured? As Hedrick et al. (1993) argue, researchers may have to receive sets of questions from research sponsors, and these may be posed by non-technical people in non-technical language. The researcher's first step, then, is to re-phrase the questions into a form

Table 6.2   Types of applied research questions with examples

Type of research question	Example
Descriptive	How common is drug use among university students?
	What is the frequency of e-learning to classroom learning in large companies?
	What proportion of medium-sized organizations has human resource directors?
Normative	How serious is drug abuse among university students?
	How well run is the local transport system?
	To what extent are engineering companies complying with health and safety legislation?
Correlative	What is the relationship between gender, academic performance and university drug use?
	Is there an association between personality type and seniority in companies?
	What is the relationship between obesity and heart disease?
Impact	Has a drug awareness programme had any effect on the level of drug use among university students?
	Do increased computer literacy skills have any impact on the probability of future employment?
	Have new forms of supervision reduced errors in production?

Source: Adapted from Hedrick et al., 1993

that is both researchable and acceptable to the client. Research questions can be classified into four major categories:

- Descriptive ('What is happening?', 'Which methods are being used?').
- Normative ('What is happening compared to what should happen?'). The standards against which the outcomes are evaluated could include legal requirements, professional standards or programme objectives.
- Correlative ('What is the relationship, and the strength of this relationship, between variable X and Y?'). Note that this establishes a relationship, but it does not imply a cause.
- Impact ('What impact does a change in X have on Y?'). In contrast to correlation studies, impact questions do try to establish a causal relationship between variables.

Table 6.2 provides some examples of research questions for each of these categories

It is often useful to take a research question and to break it down into subordinate questions. These are highly specific and assist in answering the question to which they are attached. Taking the first question in Table 6.2, we might devise a set of subordinate questions such as:

- How common is drug use among male and female students?
- How does drug use compare across different universities?
- How has drug use increased or decreased over the past five years?

This is also a useful exercise because subordinate questions can provide a stage between the original objective and the kinds of detailed questions needed for research tools such as questionnaires and interview or observation schedules. Case Study 6.1 provides an illustration of how research questions often have to be revised and refined before they become sufficiently focused and usable.

CASE STUDY 6.1

Getting those research questions right

A researcher, working for a voluntary association giving advice to the public, is concerned that most of those seeking the bureau's help are white, with very few clients coming from the ethnic minority population. She receives a small grant from the bureau's trustees to carry out a research project. She formulates her research questions as follows:

Research questions

1. To produce a report detailing the research. To check if the bureau is conforming to its organizational aims and objectives and if not how it can improve the delivery of services.
2. To increase awareness of the needs of ethnic minority clients and potential clients of the bureau among staff and to inform the organization of staff training needs.
3. To use this as a starting point for further work to be carried out by volunteers at the bureau.

Take a look at these research questions. What is wrong with them? Well, to be honest, quite a lot. Question 1 is not really a question but an output. This is what will be produced *through* the research. Questions 2 and 3 are aims or ambitions. What are listed as research questions do not deserve the description. They may result from the research but are not objectives, since there is nothing here that can be *measured*.

After some thought, the researcher arrives at the following list of questions.

1. What are the needs of ethnic minority groups in the district?
2. What access to information about the bureau do they have?
3. Do those that access the information, implement its contents effectively?
4. Is there a relationship between the quality of information given, and ethnic minority trust in the bureau?
5. What degree of awareness should bureau staff have (in relation to their organizational service levels) about the needs of ethnic minority groups?

ACTIVITY 6.1

Examine the final set of questions in Case Study 6.1. Which of these research questions belongs to the descriptive, normative, correlative or impact categories?

Suggested answers are provided at the end of the chapter.

FORMULATING
A RESEARCH
QUESTION

Research questions are formulated as part of many research studies, whether perspective-seeking or truth-seeking, although not necessarily at the same stage of the research. In perspective-seeking studies, for example, questions may emerge as part of the data-gathering exercise. For truth-seeking research, including experimental and quasi-experimental research, they are usually formulated at the beginning of the research process. But while perspective-seeking research usually relies just on research questions, truth-seeking approaches usually go further and require the formulation of a hypothesis.

Constructing hypotheses

Research questions are usually broad in nature, and may lend themselves to a number of answers, but a hypothesis is capable of being tested and is predictive. For example, the statement 'Why is street crime more common in inner-city areas?' is a research question and not a hypothesis. To convert the question into a hypothesis we might conjecture that: 'High street crime in inner-city areas is a product of liberal policing policies'. Kerlinger and Lee (2000) suggest that a hypothesis is a speculative statement of the relation between two or more variables. Good hypotheses, then, should contain a statement containing two or more variables that are capable of measurement. Measurement, however, can only occur if the variables contained in the hypothesis can be operationally defined (see next section). Certainly, in the above hypothesis, the two variables 'street crime' and 'liberal policing policies', can each be operationally defined, compared through a research study, and the statement either accepted or rejected.

HYPOTHESES

In formulating a hypothesis, care should be taken to avoid what Kerlinger and Lee (2000) describe as value questions, for example, those that contain words such as 'should', 'ought' or 'better than'. Similarly, the statement 'The implementation of the new information technology system has led to poor results' is also a value statement because of the use of the word 'poor' – what, exactly, is meant by this? A better approach would be to state the results in measurable terms such as 'reduced output', 'lower staff satisfaction', or 'computer error'. It is useful to reflect that negative findings are sometimes just as important as positive ones since they can highlight new lines of investigation.

— ACTIVITY 6.2 —

Examine each of the following statements and decide which (if any) make valid hypotheses.

1. Mixed ability teaching leads to disappointing levels of student attainment.
2. What are the major causes of car theft in inner-city areas?
3. The 'Total Quality Care' system will increase levels of patient satisfaction.

Suggested answers are provided at the end of the chapter.

Operationally defining variables

One of the problems in formulating research questions and hypotheses is that they tend to be somewhat generalized and vague. Before research tools can be drawn up, it is important to operationally define key variables so it is quite clear *what* is being measured. Kerlinger and Lee (2000) define an **operational definition** as something that gives meaning to a construct or a variable by setting out the activities or 'operations' that are necessary to measure it. Classifying operational definitions can sometimes be quite challenging. For example, our research question might be: What factors provide the key drivers for ensuring business success in the medium term? As it stands, the question is far too vague to provide a basis for measurement. Returning to the question, we need to operationally define what we mean by 'business success': is it output, profitability, cost control or perhaps a combination of all of these? Similarly, what is meant by 'medium term'? Is it one year, two years, 10 years? Going through the process of producing operational definitions allows us the opportunity to rethink some of our assumptions and may even encourage us to rewrite our original research question or questions. Note the loops back to previous stages in Figure 6.1.

Identifying independent and dependent variables

Scientific research aims to identify why conditions or events occur. These causes are called *independent variables* and the resulting effects, *dependent variables*. A variable is a property that can take different values. Thus, the focus of research might be the introduction of a new performance-related pay system (independent variable) which is designed to lead to greater output (dependent variable). But as Black (1993) warns, relationships between variables may be ones of **association**, but this does not necessarily imply causality, that is, that changes in one variable lead to changes in another. For example, after the introduction of performance-related pay, output may rise, but this increase may have been caused by completely different factors (for example, better weather or victory by the local football team, each of which might boost morale and hence output).

INDEPENDENT & DEPENDENT VARIABLES

Indeed, independent variables may act upon dependent variables only indirectly via **intervening variables**. Thus, someone may undertake high calibre professional training hoping that this will eventually lead to a higher income level. But in practice, the professional training (independent variable) acts upon income level (dependent variable) via its effects on the person's job prospects (intervening variable, as illustrated in Figure 6.2). In addition to this Figure 6.2 also shows other relationships. For example, it is conceivable that, having achieved a higher level of income, some people may then want to (and be able to afford) more professional training.

VARIABLES FOR RESEARCH DESIGN

In experiments, it is the independent variable that is manipulated to see the effect. So, using the above example of performance-related pay, we might introduce such a scheme into a company and observe the effect on output. But, as has already been suggested, there may be other factors at work that might influence such changes in output. These are termed **extraneous variables** and must be 'controlled for', that is, the study designed in such a way that the impact of extraneous variables does not enter the calculations.

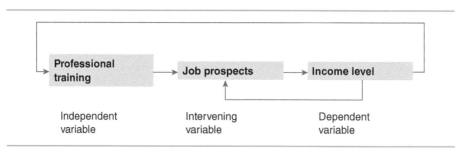

Figure 6.2   Illustration of the relationship between dependent, independent and intervening variables

There are various ways of controlling for extraneous variables. One is through *elimination*. So, using our example of performance-related pay, if the study was concerned about the possible influence of current status or grade, we would only choose people from a certain grade for the study. Another way of controlling extraneous variables is through *randomization*. If randomization is achieved, then it is probable that the experimental groups are equal in terms of all variables. It should be noted, of course, that complete randomization is difficult to achieve in practice. Say, for example, that we know that male and female workers are exactly equally represented in the workforce. If we were to take a random sample of 100 workers, we might expect to finish with 50 men and 50 women. In practice, we often end up with slight variations such as 48 men and 52 women. If gender constitutes the independent variable of interest to the study, we might want to ensure that the groups are equally represented, and randomly select male workers until the numbers reached 50 and likewise for female workers (see **stratified random sampling**, p. 210).

Conducting the study

Here begins the operational stage of the research, the success of which depends, not only on how the data are gathered, but on how well the study has been planned. While the research strategy (experimental) has been selected, there are still a variety of research designs at the researcher's disposal (see experimental and quasi-experimental research design, next) and these have to be selected with care.

Using descriptive and inferential statistics

The data are analysed using a variety of statistical methods, all of which should have been selected at the planning stage. Descriptive statistics are used to describe or summarize a set of data, while inferential statistics are used to make inferences from the sample chosen to a larger population (see Chapter 22).

Accepting or rejecting hypotheses

As we saw in Chapter 2, it is impossible to 'prove' that any theory is right. All theories are provisional and tentative (until disproved). However, the weight of evidence must be sufficient that a hypothesis can be accepted as proved. As we will see in Chapter 22, experimental design makes use of inferential statistics and probability to calculate the risk involved in accepting the hypothesis as true (when it is in fact false) and rejecting the hypothesis as false (when it is in fact true).

Preparing the formal report

Particularly when a study has been sponsored or commissioned, the researcher will need to prepare and deliver some kind of formal presentation of the findings. At this stage the focus will be on:

- Why the study was conducted.
- What research questions and hypotheses were evaluated.
- How these were turned into a research design (with sufficient detail that the experiment could be replicated).
- What differences were observed between the hypotheses and the results.
- What conclusions can be drawn and whether they support or contradict the hypothesis and existing theories.

In a more organizational and less academic setting, the formal report will tend to focus on the rationale for the study, the kinds of questions being posed, the results, and what findings, if any, can be implemented. Writing the research report is covered in detail in Chapter 24. For projects that have received research funding, sponsors usually want to go beyond the report and to be provided with information on how the results of the project will be disseminated.

EXPERIMENTAL AND QUASI-EXPERIMENTAL RESEARCH DESIGN

The basis of true experimental design is that the researcher has control over the experiment, that is, who, what, when, where and how the experiment is to be conducted. This particularly includes control over the 'who' of the experiment – that is, subjects are assigned to conditions randomly. So, for example, a health authority might seek to measure whether a health promotion programme was effective, or not. Hence, it might run the campaign in several randomly selected areas, but not in others. Where any of the elements of control is either weak or lacking, the study is said to be a quasi-experiment. Often, in organizational settings, for example, for practical purposes it is only possible to use pre-existing groups. Hence, it is only possible to select subjects from these groups rather than randomly assign them (as in a true experimental study). Another important difference is that while in experiments we can *manipulate* variables, in quasi-experimental studies we can only *observe* categories of subjects. So, we could consider the differences between two groups to be the independent variable but we would not be manipulating this variable. So, taking our health issue mentioned above, we would collect data on health indicators across the health authority, and then seek to discover what independent

EXPERIMENTAL
DESIGN

QUASI-
EXPERIMEN-
TATION

variables might impact on different health rates – for example, social class, ethnic group, etc.

One of the strengths of experimental design is that randomization improves the control over threats to **internal validity**. In other words, if the experimental intervention (treatment) does lead to a change in the dependent variable, there is some justification for believing that this has been caused by the treatment itself, and not just by the effect of some extraneous variable. Yet it should not be assumed that random assignment is the goal of all experimental studies. As Hedrick et al. (1993) point out, using an **experimental group** also means using a **control group** who do not receive the intervention. Even if the treatment does not prove to be effective, it usually comes with more resources. The control group will be denied these, and for a long period if it is a longitudinal study. For example, in the health promotion example, above, those in the control group would not receive any potential benefits of the health promotion campaign. This of course can be rectified if they are presented with the campaign but after the study is over. However, this would still be after any benefits enjoyed by those in the experimental group – an institutional review board might not approve such a study because of these time lags.

EXPERIMENTAL DESIGN

One of the strengths of a quasi-experimental design is that it is about as near as one can get to an experimental design, so it can support causal inferences. In the words of Hedrick et al. (1993), it provides 'a mechanism for chipping away at the uncertainty surrounding the existence of a specific causal relationship' (1993: 62). Quasi-experimental designs are best used when:

QUASI-EXPERIMENTAL DESIGNS

- Randomization is too expensive, unfeasible to attempt or impossible to monitor closely.
- There are difficulties, including ethical considerations, in withholding the treatment.
- The study is retrospective and the programme being studied is already underway.

According to McBurney and White (2009), generally, experimental designs are usually considered superior to quasi-experimental (and quasi-experimental to non-experimental). However, it may not always be possible to replicate social, organizational or behavioural conditions in a laboratory setting. Therefore, observation in a field setting, say, might be preferable to an experiment because the advantage of realism outweighs the loss of control. The broad differences between experimental, quasi-experimental and non-experimental studies are summarized in Table 6.3, and an example of a quasi-experimental design provided in Case Study 6.2.

Table 6.3 Differences between experimental, quasi-experimental and non-experimental research

Research type	Selection of research sample	Manipulation of variables
Experimental	Random	Yes
Quasi-experimental	Intact	Yes
Non-experimental	Intact	No

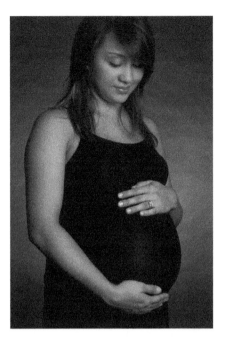

Image 6.1   Teenage pregnancy
and negative economic effects

CASE STUDY 6.2

A quasi-experimental design

Research has suggested that teenage pregnancy has significant effects on girls in terms of their later income level, educational attainment and general welfare – putting them on a lower rung of the economic ladder. But it is also acknowledged that teenage pregnancy is more common among lower income families, a potentially confounding factor.

It is not possible to randomly assign teenage girls to become or not to become pregnant! In the research quoted by Hedrick et al. (1993) this problem was overcome by using as a non-equivalent group the sisters of girls who became pregnant in their teens, but who themselves did not become pregnant until at least the age of 20. This allowed the researchers to control for the family economic disadvantage variable. When the data were analysed, it was found that the previously negative effects associated with teenage pregnancy were not as pronounced as expected.

ACTIVITY 6.3

Taking Case Study 6.2, explain:

1. Why this is a quasi-experimental rather than an experimental study.
2. Why the greater incidence of teenage pregnancy among lower income groups is a confounding factor for this particular study.

Suggested answers are provided at the end of the chapter.

Let us take a look at a number of research designs, starting with frequently used (but faulty designs) and then some sound designs.

Table 6.4   Non-experimental design with intact group

Group	Allocation of subjects	Treatment	Test
Single	No – intact	No	No

Table 6.5   Post-test only with non-equivalent control groups

Group	Allocation of subjects	Treatment	Test
1	No	Yes	Yes
2	No	No	Yes

Table 6.6   One group pre-test/post-test design

Group	Allocation of subjects	Treatment	Test
Single	No – intact	Yes	Yes

Faulty designs to avoid

Design 1: Non-experimental with intact group

In this design, an intact group is taken, and attempts made to discover why changes in an independent variable occurred. There is no attempt made here to manipulate any independent variables – hence the design is non-experimental (see Table 6.4). Say that a voluntary organization analyses its charitable donation patterns over the past three years by geographic region. The dependent variable is the level of charitable donations for each region. The independent variable is not manipulated but is imagined. In other words, researchers would conduct a study that would try to find explanations for any regional differences, perhaps using documentary evidence. Clearly, the problem here is providing convincing evidence of causation – that a particular independent variable caused the changes in the dependent variable.

In their influential work, Campbell and Stanley (1963) describe designs that are devoid of a control group as being of almost no scientific value. This is not to say that they are completely worthless. Each design might reveal some interesting evidence of value to an organization, but they are worthless in the sense that it would be a mistake to draw firm conclusions from them.

Design 2: Post-test only with non-equivalent control groups

In this type of design, a treatment is given to one group (the experimental group), but not to another (the control). Both groups are then given a **post-test** to see if the treatment has been effective (see Table 6.5). Unfortunately, subjects have not been randomly allocated between the experimental and control groups, so that it is impossible to say that the two groups are equivalent. If, say, the experimental group performs better in the test, it is not possible to rule out the possibility that this was because the subjects in this group were more able or better motivated. Say, for example, that in an educational setting, one group of students is given additional French lessons to improve their linguistic skills, but a control group does not receive the extra tuition. Both take a post-test but the control group does better! This may be because there was no random allocation of subjects (both groups were taken intact) and it so happens that there are more able students in the control group (or some had actually lived for a time in France).

Design 3: One group, pre-test/post-test

In Design 3, a group is measured on the dependent variable by a **pre-test**, an independent variable is introduced, and the dependent variable measured by a post-test. So, an organization could measure staff attitudes towards racial tolerance, introduce a race-awareness programme, and measure staff attitudes once the programme was completed. Any change in attitudes would be measured by changes in scores between the two tests.

This design is an improvement on Design 1 as it appears that any changes in attitude could be attributed to the impact of the treatment – the attitude training. Unfortunately, as Campbell and Stanley (1963) point out, there are other factors that could have affected the post-test score. These can impact on the experiment's internal validity, that is, the extent to which we can be sure that experimental treatments did make a difference to the independent variable(s). Such factors include:

- **Maturation** effects: people learn over time, which might affect scores on both mental ability and attitude, or they may grow more fatigued over time, which may also affect their post-test scores.
- *Measurement procedures*: the pre-test itself might have made the subjects more sensitive to race issues and influenced their responses on the post-test. Both controversial and memory issues are prone to be influenced in this way.
- *Instrumentation*: in which changes, say, in the observers or scorers used to assess the test results may affect the scores obtained.
- *Experimental* **mortality**: or the differential loss of respondents from one group compared to the other, for example, through absence, sickness or resignations.
- *Extraneous variables* might influence the results, particularly if there is a large time gap between the pre-test and post-test.

Some sound designs

McBurney and White (2009) state that there is no such thing as a perfect experiment. Nevertheless, there are two elements of design that provide some control over threats to validity and which form the basis of all sound experimental designs: (a) the existence of a control group or a control condition; (b) the random allocation of subjects to groups. Some of the principles of random assignment are explained in the following Web link.

→ **ON THE WEB 6.1** ←

View the short video clip at:

http://www.youtube.com/watch?v=V_GIjFw6RZE

Image 6.2   An experimental group receiving training and a control group

Design 4: Experimental group with control

In this design, subjects are randomly assigned to each of the experimental and control groups, which means that, at least theoretically, all independent variables are controlled. Hence, again using our racial tolerance example, the study would randomly assign groups of people to both the experimental and control groups.

The experimental group would receive the treatment (the race-awareness training) while the control group would not receive the training. Notice that any extraneous variables, such as the effects of the pre-test on attitudes, would be controlled for, since the impact should be the same on both the experimental and control groups. If the training has been genuinely successful, then the improvements in test scores for the experimental group should exceed those for the control.

Table 6.7   Experimental group with control

Group	Allocation of subjects	Treatment	Pre-test	Post-test
1	Random	Yes	Yes	Yes
2	Random	No	Yes	Yes

Table 6.8   Quasi-experimental design with non-equivalent control

Group	Allocation of subjects	Treatment	Pre-test	Post-test
1	No – intact	Yes	Yes	Yes
2	No – intact	No	Yes	Yes

Design 5: Quasi-experimental design with non-equivalent control

Recall that one of the features of quasi-experimental designs is that it is not possible for the researcher to control the assignment of subjects to conditions, and he/she will often have to take groups that are intact. For example, studies in education will often have to use classes that already exist. A typical feature of quasi-experiments is where we have an experimental and a control group, but subjects have not been randomly allocated to either of the two groups.

NON-EQUIVALENT CONTROL

The use of a control group makes this design superior to Designs 1, 2 and 3, since at least the impact of extraneous variables is controlled for, but not as reliable as Design 4. If steps can be taken to improve the equivalence between the two groups then this will improve the validity of the study. Matching, for example, will help in this direction. Here, steps are taken to match subjects between groups against significant variables such as age, sex, income, etc. If matching is not possible, then at least both groups should be chosen from the same population. So, for example, if we are investigating whether electronic tagging helps to reduce reoffending rates, we would want to match the experimental (tagging) and control (non-tagging) groups against key variables such as age, type of crime committed, number of crimes and lengths of time in prison. Obviously, it would not make sense to place young, first-time offenders in the tagging group but have reoffending 'old lags' in the control group since the tagged group would appear to have a greater chance of demonstrating lower reoffending rates, irrespective of the intervention.

One of the challenges of using a non-equivalent control group design is in the analysis of the results. McBurney and White (2009) distinguish between desired result patterns and those that it is impossible to interpret. In pattern A (Figure 6.3), for example, both the experimental and control groups exhibit the same performance in a pre-test, but only the experimental group improves its performance in the post-test. Although the experimental and control groups are not equivalent, their performances can be compared because their behaviour was the same at the beginning. A similar situation pertains for pattern B – the experimental group performed worse than the control group in the pre-test but improved in the post-test, with the control showing no improvement. It would be difficult to find a reason as to why this process had occurred by chance alone.

Pattern C, however, is much harder to interpret. Although it is true that the performance of the experimental group has improved, the lack of improvement by the control group may be due to the ceiling effect – they began by being better than the experimental group and it may not be possible to improve on this level of performance. Hence, it cannot be deduced that the improvement in the experimental group was due to the treatment. In pattern D the performance of both the experimental and control groups has improved, with the experimental group improving to a higher level. At first sight this might appear to be a significant result but a claim for this would be mistaken since both groups have improved their performance by the same proportion.

Design 6: Developmental designs

Like interrupted **time-series** designs, developmental designs involve measurement across time and, again, do not involve the use of control groups. One kind of

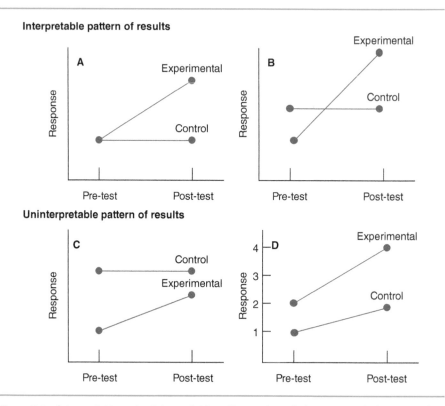

Interpretable pattern of results

Uninterpretable pattern of results

Figure 6.3   Interpretable and uninterpretable patterns of results in a non-equivalent control group design with pre-test and post-test

Source: Adapted from McBurney and White, 2009

developmental design is the use of a *cross-sectional study*, which looks at a phenomenon at a particular period of time. For example, a cross-sectional design might study the determinants of accidents in an organization. A survey might be used to calculate an average number of days lost in accidents per employee. The next stage of the survey might examine accident rates by age group, gender, occupational role and seniority. One of the advantages of cross-sectional design is that it can reveal associations among variables (age, gender, etc.). But what it cannot do is reveal causation. To achieve this, we would have to turn to a *longitudinal study*, taking a series of samples over time. The problem here, however, is that it may be difficult to gain access to the same set of people over a long period. Indeed, even different sets of researchers may have to be employed.

Design 7: Factorial designs

The designs we have considered so far have involved **manipulation** or change in one independent variable. Sometimes, however, it becomes necessary to investigate the impact of changes in two or more variables. One reason for this could be that there is more than one alternative hypothesis to confirm or reject. Another reason

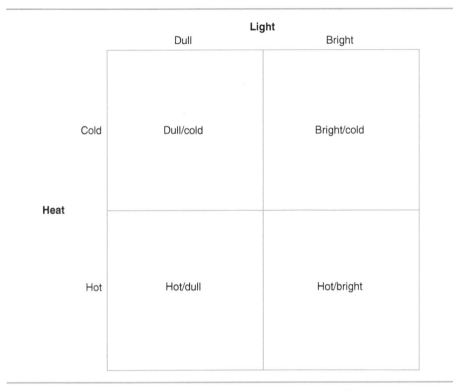

Figure 6.4 A 2 x 2 factorial design showing all possible combinations of factors

might be to explore relationships and interactions between variables. Here we use a factorial design which allows us to look at all possible combinations of selected values.

The simplest form is where we have two variables, each of which has two values or levels. Hence, it is known as a two-by-two (2 x 2) factorial design. In Figure 6.4, for example, the two variables are light and heat, each of which has two levels (cold/ hot and dull/bright). Hence, we have four possible combinations, as illustrated. We could conduct an experiment to see which combination of factors gives rise to the most attentiveness (measured, say, by production levels, or on a self-assessment questionnaire) in a workplace. We might find, for example, that dull light combined with both heat and cold leads to low levels of attentiveness, as do bright/hot conditions; but the interaction of brightness with cold temperatures keeps all workers 'on their toes'!

GENERALIZING FROM SAMPLES TO POPULATIONS

A typical human trait is to make generalizations from limited experience or information. For example, we may ask a member of staff what they think of the new company environmentally friendly transport policy. We may infer that this could be the opinion throughout the organization, the entire workforce constituting what in research terms is known as the population. A population can be defined as the total

POPULATIONS

Image 6.3 'A good sample is a miniature of the population – just like it, only smaller' (Fink, 2002)

number of possible units or elements that are included in the study. If it is not possible to evaluate the entire population (because of its large size or a lack of research resources), then we might select a *sample* of employees for evaluation. According to Fink, 'A good sample is a miniature of the population – just like it, only smaller' (2002a: 1).

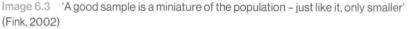

→ **TOP TIP 6.1** ←

The word population can often cause some confusion. When we use this word in research methods we do not usually mean the population of a country. In research, a population refers to a group that have something in common – for example, Glasgow NHS human resource managers, Berlin bar owners or Parisian cyclists.

The process of selecting samples

REPRESENTATIVE SAMPLE

A sample will be chosen by a researcher on the basis that it is a **representative sample** of the population as a whole, that is, the sample's main characteristics are similar or identical to those of the population. Samples are selected from a **sampling frame**, that is, a list of the population elements (see Figure 6.5). Notice that, while every attempt will be made to select a sampling frame that provides details of the entire population, practical circumstances may make the sampling frame incomplete. For example, the population may comprise all people working in a hospital Accident and Emergency ward over a weekend, but the personnel records may have missed out some staff by mistake, whilst new starters have not even been

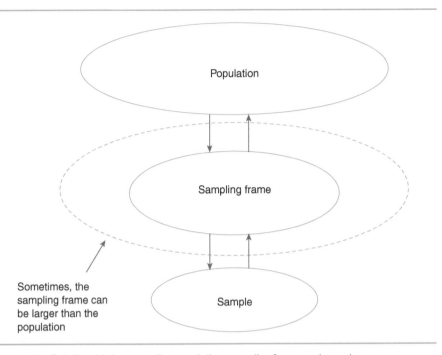

Sometimes, the
sampling frame can
be larger than the
population

Figure 6.5   Relationship between the population, sampling frame and sample

entered onto the database yet. The research sample itself might be less than the sampling frame just because using all sampling frame records is too expensive. But having established the sampling frame and how many people we are going to use, how do we choose them?

Most methods utilized to achieve representative samples depend, in some way, on the process of random assignment. Random probability sampling is the selecting of a random sample such that each member of the population has an equal chance of being selected. Clearly, this can present practical problems. Can we, for example, acquire a full list of company employees from which to draw the sample (the sampling frame)? But as Black (1993) warns, even after taking a random sample, there remains a finite possibility that it may not be representative of the population after all. The chances of this happening are reduced if the study can be replicated, that is, other random samples are used and studied. Nevertheless, the chances of a sample being representative are higher through *random* selection than if the sample is purposive (specifically selected by the researcher).

Of course, we may not always want to attain completely random samples. Again using the simple example of gender, a factory workforce of 100 people might comprise 90 women and 10 men. A random sample of 25 people might give us 23 women and 2 men. Clearly, if gender is the independent variable, a sample of 2 men would probably be of little value to the study. In this case, we might use stratified random sampling by deciding to randomly sample female workers until 15 are picked and follow the same strategy but oversample for men until we have a sample of 10. Let us look at some of the approaches to achieving representativeness in samples.

What size sample should we use?

CONFIDENCE
INTERVAL

The first stage is to determine the actual size of the sample needed. Before doing this, we need to decide on the size of the **confidence interval**. This is the range of figures between which the population **parameter** is expected to lie. Say we set the confidence interval at 4 per cent, and 45 per cent of the population pick a particular answer. This means that we are saying that we are confident that between 41 per cent (45–4) and 49 per cent (45+4) of the entire population would have picked that answer. We also decide on a *confidence level*, usually of either 95 per cent or 99 per cent. This states the probability of including the population **mean** within the confidence interval. This is chosen before working out the confidence interval. In many studies, a confidence level of 95 per cent is often deemed sufficient. In medical research, a level of 99 per cent is usually taken because of the need to be highly confident of estimates. Experimenting with the next Activity should make this clearer.

→ **ON THE WEB 6.2** ←

To calculate the size of sample you need from a given size of population, point your Web browser to:

http://www.surveysystem.com/sscalc.htm

Selecting random samples

Having estimated the size of sample you need, you can now go about randomly selecting it. As we have seen, randomization is the process of assigning subjects to experimental and control groups such that the subjects have an equal chance of being assigned to either group. The process of random selection can be accomplished either by using the appropriate statistical table (see Table 6.9) or using a special computer program (see Activity 6.4).

Say you have acquired a list of 1,000 of the company's staff from which you want to randomly select 50 as your research sample. First, ascribe a number to each staff member on the list. Then, using a pencil, close your eyes and point to part of the

Table 6.9   A three digit random numbers table of numbers between 0 and 999 (from Black, 1993)

777	841	707	655	297	947	945	734	697	633
297	522	872	029	710	687	064	660	555	489
672	573	065	306	207	112	703	768	377	178
465	436	070	187	267	566	640	669	291	071
914	487	548	262	860	675	846	300	171	191
820	042	451	108	905	340	437	347	999	997
731	819	473	811	795	591	393	769	678	858
937	434	506	749	268	237	997	343	587	922
248	627	730	055	348	711	204	425	046	655
762	805	801	329	005	671	799	372	427	699

table. If you happen to select, say, 707, the top number of the third column (Table 6.9), take the first two numbers, 70, and work down your list of random numbers in the table to the 70th. Hence, your first number is 799. Then, using the last digit from 707 and the first digit of the next three digit figure, 872, you get 78. Select the 78th position down the list which gives you 343. Go back to the number 872 and choose the last two digits of that number, 72, and take the 72nd number from the table, etc. Repeat this process until 50 names have been selected. Now take a look at the Web randomizer (Activity 6.4) – you may find it easier!

ACTIVITY 6.4

Your sample comprises 100 people from whom you want to randomly select 10 as your sample. All people are allocated a number from 1 to 100. You now want to produce a set of 10 random numbers ranging from 1 to 100. In your Web browser, go the following address:

http://www.randomizer.org/

Click on [Randomizer] then respond as follows to the questions presented:

- How many sets of numbers do you want to generate? = 1
- How many numbers per set? = 10
- Number range = 1 to 100
- Do you wish each number in a set to remain unique? = Yes
- Do you wish to sort your outputted numbers (from least to greatest?) = Yes
- Click on [Randomize Now!]
- You should see a set of 10 random numbers arranged in a row.

Types of random sample

In an ideal world, you would have sufficient time and resources to choose completely random samples. In the real world, due to practical constraints, you may have to choose other types of sampling techniques. In quantitative research, random samples are usually preferable to non-random. Given the importance of sampling in research design (both quantitative and qualitative designs), Chapter 9 *Sampling Strategies*, is entirely devoted to this theme.

TOP TIP 6.2

Research students often agonize about the need to select a random sample. Indeed, even when using non-random samples, they can become tempted to make claims that the sample was somehow randomly selected. This is misguided for a number of reasons. Firstly, these kinds of studies (especially when undertaken for the purpose of writing a thesis or dissertation), for practical purposes, often work with fairly modest sample sizes, meaning that the ability to generalize is limited. Secondly, when working with such modest samples, it is the quality of the sample that becomes more important rather than the size.

Generalizing from samples to populations

One of the objectives of experimental research is to achieve a situation where the results of a study using a sample can be generalized. According to Kerlinger and

Lee (2000), generalizing means that the results of a study can be applied to other subjects, groups or conditions. Generalizing means that the fruits of research can have a broader application than merely being limited to a small group. For example, say that researchers evaluated a hospital staff development programme in which nursing and other clinical staff were taught to adopt new hygiene practices to reduce the spread of infection. If the study showed that scores for the trained group were significantly better than for a control group, then the results might be of relevance to other hospitals and health policy makers. On the other hand, just because a study does not find results that are capable of generalization does not mean they have no relevance. A small case study, for example, may produce findings that are interesting and possibly indicative of trends worthy of replication by further research. And from a perspective-seeking view they may be seen as valid in their own right. The important point is that you should not make firm or exaggerated claims on the basis of small, unrepresentative samples.

DESIGNING VALID AND RELIABLE RESEARCH INSTRUMENTS

We have looked, so far, at some of the general principles of research design, including the use of experimental and control groups and the selection of representative samples so that results can be generalized to a larger population. However, for defensible **statistical inferences** to be made on the basis of the data, any research tools used (such as questionnaires, interview schedules and observation schedules) must be internally valid and reliable. To achieve external validity, such instruments must be designed in such a way that generalizations can be made from the analysis of the sample data to the population as a whole.

This section deals with some of the general principles of validity and reliability, but these important issues are taken up in more detail when describing the design of specific data collection tools in later chapters.

Principles of validity

To ensure validity, a research **instrument** must measure what it was intended to measure. This may sound like an obvious statement, but many novice researchers make the mistake of asking spurious questions in a misguided attempt to collect as much data as possible – just in case some of it may be needed at the analysis stage! For example, a school-sponsored study might explore the attitudes of parents of special needs children towards the integration of their children into mainstream schools. The central theme is the integration of special needs children, but the data gathering instrument might (erroneously) stray into asking about parental attitudes towards government inspection policies or the use of additional teaching resources. Both of these are important, but not relevant to the study itself. In discussing validity, McBurney and White (2009) pose the interesting analogy of using a measurement of hat size to determine intelligence. You could measure someone's hat size, say, every hour and always come up with the same result. The test, then, is reliable. However, it is not valid, because hat size has nothing to do with what is being measured.

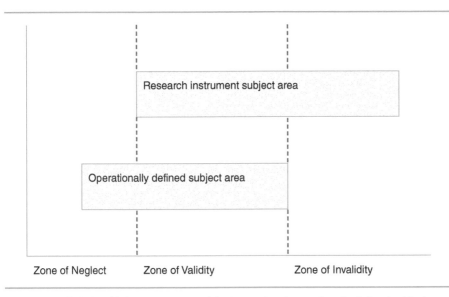

Zone of Neglect   Zone of Validity   Zone of Invalidity

Figure 6.6   Relationship between research instrument and operationally defined subject areas and the issue of validity

In Figure 6.6 we can see that only part of the research instrument covers the subject areas that have been operationally defined. Some operationally defined subjects have not been addressed by the instrument (Zone of Neglect), while other parts of the instrument cover issues of no direct relevance to the research study at all (Zone of Invalidity). To achieve validity, the research instrument subject area and operationally defined subject areas must exactly match (Zone of Validity).

The issue of validity, however, is much more complex than this. The central question around validity is whether a measure of a concept really measures that concept – does it measure what it *claims* to measure? So, for example, do IQ tests really measure intelligence? Do formal examinations measure academic ability? At a basic level, validity can be defined as eight types: **face, internal, external, criterion, construct, content, predictive** and **statistical validity**. We will look at each in turn.

Face validity

When developing a new research instrument (such as a questionnaire), it is vital that it is able to demonstrate at least face validity otherwise all is lost. Face validity means that the instrument at least appears to measure what it was designed to measure. But how do we demonstrate such face validity? For a start, it is up to the researcher to study their own instrument and critically evaluate what they have produced. Because they are so 'close' to their own work, the next step is to get other people to comment particularly if they are subject experts in relation to the concept being measured. However, as McBurney and White (2009) warn, face validity is not an end in itself. A test may have a high or low degree of validity regardless of whether it has face validity or not.

FACE VALIDITY

➤ **TOP TIP 6.3** ◄

In the event that you do not have ready access to relevant subject matter experts, the next best step is to ask friends or colleagues to evaluate the instrument. Make it clear to them what the instrument is meant to measure and that you want a *critical* appraisal.

Internal validity

INTERNAL
VALIDITY

Internal validity refers to correlation questions (cause and effect) and to the extent to which causal conclusions can be drawn. If we take, for example, an evaluation of the impact of a health education campaign, one group receives the educational material (the experimental group) while one does not (the control group). Possible **confounding variables** are controlled for, by trying to make sure that participants in each group are of similar ages and educational attainment. Internal validity (the impact of the campaign) may be helped by testing only those who are willing to participate in the experiment. But this reduces the completely random nature of the experimental group and hence the external validity of the study (see next).

External validity

EXTERNAL
VALIDITY

This is the extent to which it is possible to generalize from the relationships found in the data within the samples' experimental subjects to a larger population or setting (Cook and Campbell, 1979). Clearly, this is important in experimental and quasi-experimental studies where sampling is required and where the potential for generalizing findings is often an issue. As Robson (2002) points out, the argument for generalization can be made by either direct *demonstration* or by *making a case*. The problem of generalizing from a study is that cynics can argue that its results are of relevance only to its particular setting. Direct demonstration, then, involves carrying out further studies involving different participants and in different settings. If the findings can be replicated (often through a series of demonstrations), then the argument for generalizing becomes stronger. Making a case simply involves the construction of a reasoned argument that the findings can be generalized. So, this would set out to show that the group(s) being studied, or the setting or period, share certain essential characteristics with other groups, settings or periods (Campbell and Stanley, 1963).

Criterion validity

CRITERION
VALIDITY

This is where we compare how people have answered a new measure of a concept, with existing, widely accepted measures of a concept. If answers on the new and established measures are highly correlated, then it is usually assumed that the new measure possesses criterion validity. However, as de Vaus (2002) suggests, a low correlation may simply mean that the old measure was invalid. Furthermore, many concepts have no well-established measures against which to check the new measure. Hence, Oppenheim (1992) is probably correct to state that good criterion measures are notoriously hard to find.

Construct validity

Construct validity is concerned with the measurement of abstract concepts and traits, such as ability, anxiety, attitude, knowledge, etc. and is concerned with whether the indicators capture the expected relationships among the concepts being researched (Cook and Campbell, 1979). As we saw above, each of these traits has to be operationally defined before it can be measured. Taking each trait, the researcher proceeds to elaborate on all of the characteristics that make up that trait. For example, if we use the construct 'confidence' within a particular research context this might be defined as:

CONSTRUCT VALIDITY

- The ability to make quick decisions.
- Sticking with personal decisions once these are made.
- Strong interpersonal skills.

You might reflect here that, in fleshing out traits to this level of detail, it is only a relatively short step to the creation of a research instrument like a questionnaire. While a test that has construct validity should measure what it intends to measure, it is equally important that it should not measure theoretically unrelated constructs (McBurney and White, 2009). So, for example, a test designed to measure attitudes to change should not contain items that seek to measure, say, extraversion.

Content validity

Content validity is associated with validating the content of a test or examination. Since it is important to create a match between what is taught and what is tested, this might include comparing the content and cognitive level of an achievement test with the original specifications in a syllabus. Let us take the case of a computer company that provides a training programme in fault finding and rectification for those retail companies that sell its products. After a two-day training programme, participants are given a 50-question multiple-choice test. The computer company will want to ensure that the content of the test is matched with the content of the training programme so that the entire syllabus is covered, and only issues that have been taught are assessed. Equally, it will want to assure itself that it has delivered the training programme at a level so that attendees learn the skills of problem-solving. The assessment, then, will also have to be at this problem-solving level (rather than, say, merely applying rules, or recalling facts) for the test to be valid.

CONTENT VALIDITY

Predictive validity

This shows how well a test can forecast a future trait such as job performance or attainment. It is no use if a test for identifying 'talent' in an organization has both construct and content validity but fails to identify, say, those who are likely to be 'high performers' in a key work role.

PREDICTIVE VALIDITY

Statistical validity

This is the extent to which a study has made use of the appropriate design and statistical methods that will allow it to detect the effects that are present.

Principles of reliability

According to Black (1999) reliability is an indication of consistency between two measures of the same thing. These measures could be:

- Two separate instruments.
- Two similar halves of an instrument (for example, two halves of a questionnaire).
- The same instrument applied on two occasions.
- The same instrument administered by two different people.

If we were to take another sort of measuring device, a ruler, how sure can we be that it is always a reliable measure? If it is made of metal, does it expand in extreme heat and therefore give different readings on hot and cold days? Alternatively, we might use it on two different days with similar temperatures, but do we mark off the measurement of a line on a piece of paper with the same degree of care and accuracy? For a research tool to be reliable we would expect it to give us the same results when something was measured yesterday and today (providing the underlying trait(s) being measured has not changed). Similarly, any differences found in traits between two different people we would expect to be based on real differences between the individuals and not be due to inconsistencies in the measuring instrument. Reliability is never perfect and so is measured as a **correlation coefficient**. In the social and business sciences it is rarely above 0.90. If a research instrument is unreliable, it cannot be valid. Like validity, there are several ways of measuring reliability. Black (1993) describes five of them.

Stability

STABILITY
COEFFICIENT

This measures the scores achieved on the same test on two different occasions. Any difference is called **subject error**. For example, a survey of employee attitudes towards their workplace may yield different results if taken on a Monday than on a Friday. To avoid this, the survey should be taken at a more neutral time of the week.

Equivalence

Another way of testing the reliability of an instrument is by comparing the responses of a set of subjects with responses made by the same set of subjects on another instrument (preferably on the same day). This procedure is useful for evaluating the equivalence of a new test compared to an existing one.

Internal reliability

This measures the extent to which a test or questionnaire is homogenous. In other words, it seeks to measure the extent to which the items on the instrument 'hang together' (Pallant, 2007; Sekaran, 2007). Are the individual scale items measuring the same construct? Internal reliability is measured by Cronback's alpha test which calculates the average of all split-half reliability coefficients. An alpha coefficient varies between 1 (perfect internal reliability) to 0 (no internal reliability). As a rule of thumb a figure of .7 or above is deemed acceptable. However, as Pallant (2007) warns, Cronback alpha results are quite sensitive to the number of items on a scale. For short scales (with items fewer than 10) it can be quite common to find Cronbach values as low as .5.

Inter-judge reliability

Inter-judge reliability compares the consistency of observations when more than one person is judging. An example would be where two people judge the performance of a member of an organization's marketing staff in selling a product over the telephone to the public. The reliability of the observation is provided by the degree to which the views (scores) of each judge correlate. *Observer error* can be reduced by using a high degree of structure to the research through the use of a structured observation schedule or questionnaire.

➤ **TOP TIP 6.4** ◄

A useful way of measuring inter-judge reliability is through use of the Kappa score (recall the calculation in Chapter 5) which compares the level of agreement between two people against what might have been predicted by chance.

Intra-judge reliability

Where a large amount of data have been collected by a researcher over time the consistency of observations or scores can be checked by taking a sample set of observations or scores and repeating them. A further problem, and often a significant one, is **bias** on the part of respondents. It is quite common, for example, for respondents to provide a response they think the researcher is seeking. Particularly if the researcher is seen to be representing 'management', respondents may be reluctant to provide honest answers if these are critical of the organization. Even assurances of confidentiality may not be enough to encourage complete honesty.

ACTIVITY 6.5

A district police force plans to conduct a survey to discover the attitudes of recent victims of crime to the way police officers have handled their cases. The aims of the survey are to: (a) measure public perceptions of the speed of police responses to reports of the crime; (b) reveal whether victims believe police are collecting appropriate information on the case; (c) evaluate whether victims feel they are receiving appropriate and sufficient help/support from the police; and (d) establish whether, as a result of the case, victims feel more or less confident in the police.

There are insufficient financial resources to send the questionnaire to *all* the district's victims of crime so you must select a sample that comprises no more than 10 per cent of all crime victims in the district over the past 12 months.

1. What is the population for this research?
2. What is the sampling frame?
3. What kind of sample will you select? Justify your choice.
4. Identify dependent and independent variables.
5. Produce an appropriate research design.
6. Using the aims outlined above, construct a valid and reliable research instrument.

Suggested answers are provided at the end of the chapter.

Summary

- The structure of experimental research generally comprises two stages: the planning stage and the operational stage.
- Experimental research begins from a priori questions or hypotheses that the research is designed to test. Research questions should express a relationship between variables. A hypothesis is predictive and capable of being tested.
- Dependent variables are what experimental research designs are meant to affect through the manipulation of one or more independent variables.
- In a true experimental design the researcher has control over the experiment: who, what, when, where and how the experiment is to be conducted. This includes control over the who of the experiment – that is, subjects are assigned to conditions randomly.
- Where any of these elements of control is either weak or lacking, the study is said to be a quasi-experiment.
- In true experiments, it is possible to assign subjects to conditions, whereas in quasi-experiments subjects are selected from previously existing groups.
- Research instruments need to be both valid and reliable. Validity means that an instrument measures what it is intended to measure. Reliability means that an instrument is consistent in this measurement.

REVIEW QUESTIONS

1. The use of control groups is essential in quantitative research designs. Do you agree with this view?
2. Studies that make use of descriptive (but not inferential) statistics are of limited value. Discuss.
3. Pre-test/post-test quantitative designs have been criticized. What practical steps can be taken to address the limitations of such a design if it is the only one available?
4. Should generalization *always* be the goal of quantitative research?

FURTHER READING

Creswell, J.W. (2009) *Research Design: Qualitative, Quantitative, and Mixed Methods Approaches*, 3rd edn. Thousand Oaks, CA: Sage. Although written with a broad spectrum of research designs in mind, the book provides useful guidelines on writing research questions and hypotheses and on quantitative methods design.

McBurney, D.H. and White, T.L. (2009) *Research Methods*, 8th edn. Belmont, CA: Wadsworth. Written from a psychology perspective, this book provides a useful, largely, quantitative approach to some of the principles of research design.

Kerlinger, F.N. and Lee, H.B. (2000) *Foundations of Behavioural Research*, 4th edn. Fort Worth, TX: Harcourt College Publishers. Excellent on the pros and cons of various experimental designs and on quantitative research design in general.

JOURNAL RESOURCES

Hartung, D.M. and Touchette, D. (2009) 'Overview of clinical research design', *American Journal of Health-System Pharmacy*, 66(4): 398–408. Although this has 'clinical research' in the title it deals well with many of the basics of quantitative research design.

Mun, W-K., Hew, K-F. and Cheung, W-S. (2009) 'The impact of the use of a response pad system on the learning of secondary school physics concepts: A Singapore quasi-experiment study', *British Journal of Educational Technology*, 40(5): 848–860. Describes a pre-post test quasi-experimental study, with a control group.

Harris, A.D., Lautenbach, E. and Perencevich, E. (2005) 'A systematic review of quasi-experimental study designs in the fields of infection control and antibiotic resistance', *Clinical Infectious Diseases*, 41(1): 77–82. Discusses a range of quasi-experimental designs and makes recommendations for how these designs can be improved.

SUMMARY OF WEB LINKS

http://www.youtube.com/watch?v=V_GIjFw6RZE

http://www.randomizer.org/

http://www.surveysystem.com/sscalc.htm

Suggested answers for Activity 6.1

1. Descriptive.
2. Descriptive.
3. Impact.
4. Correlation.
5. Normative.

Suggested answers for Activity 6.2

1. Not a good hypothesis, since it contains the subjective word 'disappointing'. The statement should contain a parameter capable of measurement.
2. This is a research question (to which there could be a variety of answers) not a hypothesis, capable of being tested.
3. A good hypothesis since it is testable. Levels of patient satisfaction can be measured and we can see whether levels increase, decrease or stay the same.

Suggested answers for Activity 6.3

1. This is a quasi-experimental study because there was no opportunity to randomly assign subjects to the condition (pregnancy!).

2. The objective of the research is to examine the impact of teenage pregnancy on later income levels, educational attainment and general welfare. If teenage pregnancy was evenly spread across all income groups the independent variable of income level would be controlled for. Unfortunately, as we are told, this is not the case. Lower income families tend to have higher incidences of teenage pregnancy – which could confound the results.

Suggested answers for Activity 6.5

1. The population comprises all the victims of crime within the police district.
2. The sampling frame consists of 10 per cent of the district's population who were victims of crime during the past 12 months.
3. One approach would be to take a completely random sample by allotting a number to each crime victim and selecting a series of numbers randomly. However, it might be hypothesized that certain groups, for example, the elderly, are highly anxious about crime. Hence, an alternative approach would be to take a purposive sample which focuses more heavily on the older age groups. The results might highlight the perceptions of these groups, but could not be claimed to be representative of crime victims as a whole.
4. The dependent variable is the attitude of crime victims to police handling of their cases. There are many potential independent variables but some might include those identified for study by the research – the speed of police responses to the crime, whether police are seen to be collecting appropriate evidence, the extent of police help and support, etc.

7

RESEARCH DESIGN: QUALITATIVE METHODS

CHAPTER INTRODUCTION

Chapter outline

Some criticisms of quantitative
research   160

Characteristics of qualitative
research   161

Paradigms and strategies for
qualitative research   162

Approaches to qualitative design   168

The role of the researcher   175

Using the literature in qualitative
research   175

Collecting qualitative data   177

Ethics and qualitative research   180

Ensuring rigour in qualitative
research   181

Keywords

Field settings

Ethnography

Ethnomethodology

Phenomenology

Grounded theory

Participatory action research

Narrative analysis

Cultural studies

Gender studies

Sampling

Transferability

Dependability

Credibility

> ### Chapter objectives
>
> After reading this chapter you will be able to:
>
> - Identify the characteristics of qualitative data.
> - Formulate qualitative research questions.
> - Develop a robust qualitative design, including an appropriate sampling strategy.
> - Select and apply the criteria that make for a rigorous qualitative research study.

We saw in the previous chapter that there are well established and generally accepted approaches to quantitative design. As we shall see in this chapter, however, qualitative design is different in a number of ways. Firstly, within qualitative research, the role of the researcher is to gain a deep, intense and 'holistic' overview of the context under study, often involving interacting within the everyday lives of individuals, groups, communities and organizations. It is a naturalistic approach that seeks to understand phenomena within their own context-specific settings. Capturing data on the perceptions of actors in the field of study, means being attentive, suspending (often called 'bracketing') preconceptions about a subject and being empathetic to those being studied. The focus of study becomes not just the field setting, but also the researcher's role within it.

Secondly, qualitative researchers often differ in the kinds of claims they make for their research. Some seek to emulate 'traditional science' in attempting, for example, to make generalizations from their results. Others, however, reject this approach, selecting instead to conduct a study which is 'authentic', and providing results that are dependable and trustworthy within a specific context – for example, within an individual school, hospital, community or business. The types of data gathering tools and resources used by qualitative researchers also tend to be different, including the use of semi-structured interviews, observation, focus groups and the analysis of materials such as documents, photographs, video recordings and other media. This chapter deals primarily, with the **design** of qualitative studies. Principles and processes in the analysis of qualitative data are covered later in Chapter 23.

SOME CRITICISMS OF QUANTITATIVE RESEARCH

Before we look in detail at qualitative research design, let us pause for a moment to examine some of the most common criticisms of quantitative research often made by qualitative researchers. Exploring these criticisms helps us to understand the kinds of concerns held by qualitative researchers and how they view the world. As the list in Table 7.1 suggests, quantitative research can often involve designs that disengage the researcher from the people and field they are researching. While quantitative researchers would regard this positively (as a means of generating objectivity and detachment), qualitative researchers would see it as failing to gain access to people's social and cultural constructions of their 'reality' (Guba and Lincoln, 1994; Silverman, 2000). According to qualitative critics, quantitative researchers claim objectivity, but end up arbitrarily defining the variables in their research, or trying to explain away correlations using common-sense reasoning.

COMPARISON
LECTURE

Table 7.1   Some typical criticisms of quantitative research by qualitative researchers

1. Quantitative research can involve little or no contact with people or field settings.
2. Statistical correlations may be based upon 'variables' that are arbitrarily defined by the researchers themselves.
3. After-the-fact analysis about the meaning of correlations may involve some very common-sense reasoning or even speculation that science claims to avoid.
4. The pursuit of 'measurable' phenomena means that difficult concepts such as 'criminality' or 'intelligence' are treated unproblematically.

All research is selective and depends on collecting particular sorts of evidence through the prism of particular methods (Mays, 1995). For example, in a quantitative survey, the categories and questions selected by the researcher may not be shared or understood by respondents. Similarly, even if two respondents give the same reply, their interpretation of the response may have different meanings. As Flick (2009) also points out, despite methodological controls in quantitative research, the researcher's personal interests, and the influence of their social and cultural backgrounds are difficult to avoid.

Beyond these practical complaints, quantitative research has also come under attack from critical epistemological positions. As Snape and Spencer (2003) relate, postmodern arguments have questioned the very notion of objectivity, and also maintain that the notions of meaning and reality are problematic. There can be no overarching meanings, because meanings are a product of time and context. Other criticism has come from neo-Marxism, feminism and race researchers who have called for a greater equality between the researcher and those they research. Wallerstein (1999) for example, points to the danger of power (of the researcher) when undertaking community-based evaluation projects, particularly if they research on the community rather than with the community. Indeed, for some, research should be a collaborative process involving the subjects of the study in formulating the focus of research and the ways in which it is conducted (Reason, 1994). A logical extension of this belief has been the development of action research methods (see Chapter 13), involving the active engagement of participants in the research process.

CHARACTERISTICS OF QUALITATIVE RESEARCH

Qualitative research is not built upon a unified theory or methodological approach (Flick, 2009) and can adopt various theoretical stances and methods, the latter including the use of observations, interviews, questionnaires and document analysis. While, even today, qualitative research is often regarded in some quarters as less valid and reliable than its quantitative cousin, qualitative data can be a powerful source for analysis. First, qualitative research is highly contextual, being collected in a natural 'real life' setting, often over long periods of time. Hence, it goes beyond giving a mere snapshot or cross-section of events and can show how and why things happen – also incorporating people's own motivation, emotions, prejudices and incidents of interpersonal cooperation and conflict (Charmaz, 1995). Far from

QUALITATIVE
RESEARCH

lacking scientific rigour, qualitative research can (in certain circumstances) even be used for testing hypotheses to see if theoretical **propositions** can be supported by the evidence. Qualitative studies can be used in circumstances where relatively little is known about the phenomenon, or to gain new perspectives on issues where much is already known (Strauss and Corbin, 1990). Qualitative research can also be used to identify the kinds of concepts or variables that might later be tested quantitatively (as in a mixed methods research design – see Chapter 8).

As Miles, Huberman and Saldana (2013) show, most qualitative research involves a number of characteristics:

- It is conducted through intense contact within a 'field' or real life setting.
- The researcher's role is to gain a 'holistic' or integrated overview of the study, including the perceptions of participants.
- Themes that emerge from the data are often reviewed with informants for **verification**.
- The main focus of research is to understand the ways in which people act and account for their actions.

Qualitative data are open to multiple interpretations (but some are more compelling than others either on theoretical grounds or because of internal consistency). As Flick (2009) points out, these interpretations can include the voices of those being studied as well as that of the researcher. Indeed, **reflexivity** – the researchers' own reflections on their actions and observations in the field and their feelings – become part of the data themselves. We will see what kinds of factors influence these interpretations in Chapter 23.

PARADIGMS AND STRATEGIES FOR QUALITATIVE RESEARCH

Qualitative research comes with a confusing array of different categories and descriptive headings, which tend to be used interchangeably by different scholars. So, for example, grounded theory can be seen as both a 'school of thought' but also as a particular research design or strategy. Qualitative research is also influenced by the kind of research paradigm adopted by the researcher. At the outset, however, it needs to be stressed that in qualitative research the adoption of strategies and data collection methods tends to be highly flexible. Indeed, it is not a case of adopting one strategy rather than another, but often the combining of several strategies and methods within a research design. Taking strategies of enquiry in Table 7.2, for example, it is both feasible and legitimate (depending on the kinds of research questions asked), to adopt a case study strategy, which also includes the use of **participatory action research** within a case site (for example, a workplace). In using these combined strategies, the researcher may select interviews, focus groups and observations as the prime data collection methods. However, how this is done will partly depend on the research paradigm adopted. For example, if the researcher holds to a naturalistic tradition, the research design will probably require the collection of data from representative, multiple case sites using a variety of sources to achieve substantiation of the findings. So, in investigating the quality of leadership development in higher education, the researcher would use, say, 12 universities, ensuring that some were older, traditional institutions and others new universities; within these categories, the researcher would ensure that there were a range of sizes. Substantiation would be gained by minimal interference and bias by the researcher through objective coding of verbatim accounts of participants in the leadership development programmes and non-participant observation by the researcher (sitting in on some programmes but as unobtrusively as possible). If committed to a progressive paradigm, the researcher will be less concerned with replicating findings (across sites) than with achieving deep engagement with participants to achieve authentic accounts of how they construct their social reality. Taking the leadership example above, it might include detailed interviews with leaders which would delve into the context (complex and evolving higher education environment) in which their development is taking place. The account would also include how the researcher constructs social reality through their interpretation of their findings. Hence, the views and feelings of the researcher (including critical self-reflections) themselves become part of the research data. Table 7.2 provides an overview of paradigms, strategies and methods.

PROCESSES OF QUALITATIVE RESEARCH

— ACTIVITY 7.1 —

Examine the naturalistic and progressive paradigms outlined in Table 7.2. What major differences do you see between them?

Now let us examine the strategies of enquiry described in Table 7.2 in more detail, noting that a qualitative research design may utilize a number of them at the same time.

Case studies

The term case study is strongly associated with qualitative research (indeed, the two are sometimes used synonymously), partly because case studies allow for the generation of multiple perspectives either through multiple data collection methods, or through the creation of multiple accounts from a single method (Lewis, 2003). The integration and contrasting of different perspectives can build up rich and detailed understanding of a context. As Punch (2005) asserts, a case is not easy to define since almost anything can serve as a case. But typical examples include: individuals, a role or occupation, organizations, a community or even a country. It could even be a policy, process, crisis or event.

CASE STUDY

　　Case study designs are generally flexible, but at the design stage, a number of issues arise that require addressing.

- What is the 'unit of analysis' for the case, e.g. individuals, organizations, local communities, etc.?
- What criteria are to be used in selecting cases for study?
- Who are the key participants?
- How many cases are there and how many participants within each case?

The design of case studies is discussed in more detail in Chapter 11.

Table 7.2   An overview of qualitative paradigms, strategies and methods

Paradigms and perspectives	Strategies of enquiry	Data collection methods
All items usable by all items in other columns		
NATURALISTIC	**Case study**: studies a specific 'bounded system', e.g., a person or institution (Stake, 1994).	Interviewing
Postpositivism		Observation
Realism	**Ethnography**: explores the nature of a specific social phenomenon, often using a small number of cases (Atkinson and Hammersley, 2004).	Focus groups
Reality is 'out there'.		Documents
Deeper social reality needs qualitative enquiry.	**Ethnomethodology**: investigates people's everyday procedures for creating, and managing a sense of objective reality (Holstein and Gubrium, 2008).	Video and photographs
Truth is supported by extensive recording in real settings.		Unobtrusive measures
	Phenomenology: explores how people's taken-for-granted world is experienced and how structures of consciousness apprehend the world (Holstein and Gubrium, 1994).	Research diary
Researchers must remain detached from real settings.		
PROGRESSIVE	**Grounded theory**: uses the interplay between analysis and data collection to produce theory (Strauss and Corbin, 1994).	
Critical theory		
Constructivism		
Postmodernism	**Participatory action research**: implies an effort on the part of people to understand the role of knowledge as a significant instrument of power and control (Reason, 1994).	
Feminism		
Reality and science are socially constructed.		
Researchers are part of the research setting.	**Narrative analysis**: the analysis of a chronologically told story, exploring how various elements are sequenced.	
Research must engage in reflexive and self-critical dialogue.	**Cultural studies**: the study of a complex web of social customs, values and expectations that affect our ways of working (Frow and Morris, 2003).	
Purpose of research is to problematize, reveal hidden realities.	**Gender studies**: explores the process of constructing and differentiating gender and particularly gender inequalities (Cranny-Francis et al., 2003).	

Source: Adapted from Holliday (2002)

Ethnography

Although first associated with anthropological studies, around the 1970s the term ethnography came to be used for describing participant observation studies in social and organizational settings. Ethnography seeks to understand social processes less by making reports of these events (for example, through using an interview), than by participating within them, often for long periods of time. Overt or **covert participant** observation, then, would be a typical approach to data collection in ethnographic research (see Chapter 17). While ethnography generally involves 'immersion' in the field for long periods, micro-ethnography adopts a more

ETHNOGRAPHY

Image 7.1   Conducting observational field research

focused approach on, say, one aspect or element of a work or social setting, allowing for observation over a few weeks or months.

Ethnomethodology

Ethnomethodology, founded in the 1960s by the American sociologist Harold Garfinkel, studies the ways in which people make sense of their social world, and accomplish their daily lives. Ethnomethodologists start with the assumption that social order is an illusion. While social life appears ordered, it is, in fact, chaotic. Social order is constructed in the minds of actors as a series of impressions which they seek to organize into a coherent pattern. While ethnography seeks to answer questions about *what* is happening, ethnomethodology seeks answers on *how* realities in everyday life are accomplished (Seale, 1999). So, by carefully observing and analysing the processes used in actors' actions, researchers will uncover the processes by which these actors constantly interpret social reality (Coulon, 1995).

ETHNO-
METHODOLOGY

Phenomenology

Phenomenologists argue that the relation between perception and objects is not passive – human consciousness actively constructs the world as well as perceiving it. Phenomenological ideas were first applied to social science research by the German philosopher Alfred Schutz (1899–1959), who argued that social reality has a specific meaning and relevance structure for people who are living, thinking and experiencing it. And it is these thought structures (objects) that determine their behaviour by motivating it. It also follows that the thought objects constructed by researchers who are trying to grasp reality, have to be founded upon the thought objects of ordinary men and women living their daily lives in the social world. It is necessary, then, for researchers to gain access to people's common-sense thinking in order to interpret and understand their actions. In other words, phenomenology seeks to understand the world from the participant's point of view. This can only be achieved if the researcher 'brackets out' their own preconceptions.

PHENOM-
ENOLOGY

Grounded theory

GROUNDED
THEORY

First developed by Glaser and Strauss (1967), grounded theory has been highly influential in qualitative research in terms of its inductive but systematic approach to design and data analysis, and the important principle that qualitative research is capable of generating theory. Theories are not applied to the subject being studied, but emerge or are discovered from the empirical data themselves. Unlike quantitative approaches which seek simplicity by breaking down constructs into variables, grounded theory seeks to build complexity by including context (Flick, 2009). Grounded theory is discussed in greater detail in Chapter 23.

Participatory Action Research

PARTICIPATORY
ACTION
RESEARCH

Participatory Action Research (PAR) builds upon the action research model first developed by Lewin (1946) particularly incorporating an understanding of the power of group dynamics and the relationships between individuals, groups and communities. Some approaches to PAR have also adopted a critical pedagogy espoused by Freire (2000), which seeks to empower learners to take responsibility for their learning. In essence, PAR follows the cyclical processes of planning, taking action, observing and reflecting. But PAR distinguishes itself from other action research approaches in that participants will also critically reflect on the political and cultural context in which the action is taking place.

Narrative analysis and biographical research

NARRATIVE
ANALYSIS

Narrative analysis is the analysis of a chronologically told story, with a focus on how the various elements of the story are sequenced. Key elements in narrative analysis include 'scripts', predictive frames that people use to interpret events, and stories that expand on scripts, adding evaluative elements that reveal the narrator's viewpoints. Narrative analysis tends to use the narrative interview as the primary method of data collection, with a focus on the biographical experiences of the respondent. The research focus of narrative analysis often includes issues that deal with ethical, moral and cultural ambiguities. An important focus of feminism is the study of lives from the narrator's experience, emphasizing the role of these narratives in empowering persons through a more subtle understanding of their life situation. Using a small number of stories, narrative analysis can be used to cast a light on the culture, complexities and contradictions in organizations.

Cultural studies

For nineteenth century social theorists, culture was regarded as merely a by-product of wider social, economic and political forces underpinning society. The everyday life of individuals was seen as a product of the structural forces acting beyond the consciousness of social actors. From the late nineteenth century, however, new theoretical perspectives began to emerge which started to take into account the individual's capacity for agency (self-motivated action) in their everyday lives. During the late twentieth and early twenty-first centuries, social and cultural theorists have begun to conceptualize the 'everyday' as dynamic, pluralistic and contested (Bennett, 2005). At the root of this transformation are several interrelated factors. Firstly, there is the

Image 7.2 A focus of cultural studies – blogging

rupturing of modernity and the decreasing importance of modernist notions such as social class, gender, race and occupation. Secondly, witness the increasing prevalence of media and cultural industries which have helped to form new kinds of social identity based around patterns of consumption and leisure.

Cultural studies has often been concerned with focusing on those who are marginalized and at the edges of modern culture, using sources drawn from anthropology, textual analysis, social and cultural history and psychoanalysis. Studies are centred on analysis of texts, images, observational notes or transcripts of everyday talk.

➤ ON THE WEB 7.1 ◄

For examples of research in this area look at the *International Journal of Cultural Studies* at:

http://ics.sagepub.com/

Gender studies

Gender studies explore the processes of constructing and differentiating gender and gender inequalities, particularly in areas such as literary theory, film studies, drama, anthropology, sociology, psychology and psychoanalysis. Gender is not simply what one is, but rather a set of meanings that sexes assume in particular societies. Gender, then, is seen as a social construct (Cranny-Francis et al., 2003). The school is, not surprisingly, strongly influenced by feminist theory. Gender studies have been associated with qualitative methods, largely because such methods allow the voices of women to be 'heard', in contrast to quantitative methods, which feminists have criticized for being value-neutral and turning women into objects rather than the subjects of research.

— ACTIVITY 7.2 —

Taking each of the qualitative strategies above, what similarities can you identify among them? What important differences do you notice?

APPROACHES TO QUALITATIVE DESIGN

Research design sits between a set of research questions and the data, and shows how the research questions will be addressed (Punch, 2005). It is strongly influenced by the epistemological stance adopted by the researcher (recall Chapter 2). A further, and connected, influence will occur if the researcher is an adherent of any of the qualitative strategies discussed above. For example, adherents of the ethnographic school will, obviously, adopt ethnographic design methods, usually involving observation and participation. It is important, however, to distinguish between qualitative data gathering methods (such as observation or focus groups) and the holistic framework of a research design. Data gathering methods are incorporated, and are sometimes intrinsically associated, with a particular design. Observation, for example, is often associated with ethnographic research design. For other qualitative research designs, such as case studies or grounded theory, a wide variety of data gathering instruments are valid.

An important feature of qualitative design is that it is 'emergent'. Although a researcher may set off with some provisional ideas about design, these may change during the research process – often as a result of the analysis of data providing new directions (Patton, 2002). Qualitative research design, then, should be seen less as a linear, sequential pathway, but rather as a series of iterations involving design, data collection, preliminary analysis and re-design.

➤ **TOP TIP 7.1** ◄

COMPONENTS
OF QUALITY
FRAMEWORK

Student researchers who adopt a qualitative approach sometimes confine themselves to describing a set of research questions, a sampling strategy and one or more data gathering methods and leave it at that. It is important, however, that these are positioned within an overarching qualitative design strategy, discussed in this section. An overarching design provides a framework through which both the practical but also the theoretical and philosophical traditions of the design can be presented.

According to Eisner (1991: 169) there is a 'paucity of methodological prescriptions' as to how to formulate a qualitative design. However, bringing together recommendations from a range of scholars provides a quite detailed design outline, the main elements of which are discussed next.

Determining the focus of the inquiry

The purpose of making clear, unambiguous statements about the focus of the study helps to establish a boundary for the research. Above all, it makes clear what is 'in' and what is 'out' and the kinds of criteria for judging the inclusion/exclusion criteria for new information. These boundaries, however, are not fixed and may alter during the research process. Miles et al. (2013) provide an approach which helps in formulating this focus by constructing what they refer to as a conceptual framework. This describes in narrative, and often in graphical format, the key factors, constructs and variables being studied – and the presumed relationship between them. Of course, whether this relationship really exists is one of the elements of the study.

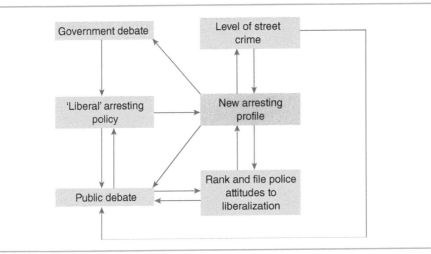

Figure 7.1   Conceptual framework for a research project on drug liberalization and policing

Miles et al. (2013) conceive of this conceptual framework as a series of intellectual 'bins' containing key events and behaviours. Hence, Figure 7.1 shows a study of new 'liberal' policing policies which have de-criminalized possession of 'soft' drugs, and a hypothesized conceptual framework containing interrelated bins. For example, it is believed that the new policy will change the profile of arrests, with fewer people being arrested for possession of soft drugs (that is, if the policy is being effectively implemented by officers on the street) and that this will reduce the level of street crime. Producing a conceptual framework forces the researcher to specify what it is that is going to be studied and what is going to be omitted, and hypothesized relationships between key variables. This, of course, is not a hypothesis in the positivistic sense, but a way of alerting the researcher to the possible relationships that exist and which can be explored through the formulation of research questions.

ACTIVITY 7.3

Examine Figure 7.1. Do you agree with its hypotheses? Draw an alternative conceptual framework adding new bins and relationships.

Formulating research questions

We saw in Chapter 1 that qualitative research is often associated with inductive research designs. If the research design is entirely inductive, there may be no formulation of a priori questions for study. But it would be wrong to assume that qualitative researchers always enter a field of study with no prior theoretical assumptions or research questions. For highly ethnographic studies this may be the

Table 7.3   Orientation of research questions

Orientation	Resulting questions
States	Which type of object, event or behaviour is this?
	How often does this event occur?
	What caused it?
	How is it maintained?
Processes	How is the object, event or behaviour changing over time?
	What are the consequences of this process?
	What strategies are being used?

case, but, often, qualitative researchers will wish to impose at least some structure on the study in terms of the kinds of questions that are being asked, the focus of the research and the selection of field sites. The amount of structure required will depend on factors such as the time available and how much is already known about the phenomenon. Other decisions then have to be made about what is going to be researched (including the units of analysis and the sampling frame). Again using Figure 7.1 as an illustration, we might ask about the actual impact of policy changes on practice (the number and profile of drug-related arrests), and how rank and file police attitudes have mediated between policy and practice. Like the conceptual framework, research questions allow the researcher to see where the boundaries of the study lie. Of course, having established the research questions, the researcher still has to remain open to new and perhaps unexpected results (Flick, 2009). Research questions can be orientated towards describing states or describing processes, as Table 7.3 shows.

As Flick (2009) notes, the less clearly research questions are formulated, the greater the chance that researchers will find themselves confronted with mountains of data. As Figure 7.2 shows, starting with a purely inductive approach (which implies relatively little focus and no research questions) usually leads to the accumulation of large volumes of data, which then have to be analysed.

— ACTIVITY 7.4 —

Return to Table 3.3 in Chapter 3 and review the types of research question that can be formulated. Do any of these lend themselves more naturally to qualitative research?

Suggested answer at end of chapter.

Determining the units of analysis

As in any research approach, in qualitative research decisions have to be taken at the design stage on the unit of analysis to be used. Typically, this might include: individuals, groups, organizations or communities. Using healthcare as an example, the research might focus on individuals (patients, doctors, nurses and other healthcare

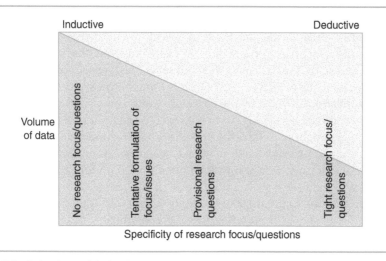

Figure 7.2   Inductive and deductive approaches and research questions

professionals), groups (the hospital management board), organizations (hospitals or professional bodies) and communities (a town and its hospitals and local surgeries). Alternatively, the unit of analysis might be the government's policy on, say, reducing HIV infection. As Mason (2002) points out, identifying the unit of analysis is important, especially when it comes to analysing the data. Using the healthcare example, we might study the level of care given by nurses. The data gathered are for individual nurses (in which case, the unit of analysis is the individual). If, however, we wanted to compare the level of care given across a group of hospital wards (say, to identify inefficiencies), results for individuals would be aggregated for each ward – hence the unit of analysis is the ward rather than the individual.

Image 7.3   Determining the unit of analysis: the individual nurse, the ward or the hospital?

Determining the types of qualitative data

In quantitative research the purpose is to collect quantitative data in the form of numbers measuring occurrences and to fragment or delimit phenomena into measurable categories. In qualitative research, however, the types of data to be collected are much more diverse. While, generally, most qualitative studies tend to depend on the assimilation of data in the form of words (interview transcripts, diary entries, observational notes), qualitative design is quite flexible in terms of the variety of data types applicable. Table 7.4 provides a brief summary of the types of data collected, their characteristics and how they are collected, including an imaginary example for illustration. It is also worth noting that, even though plans may have been made at the outset to collect one type of data, these plans may change at any time due to the evolving nature of qualitative research. Gathering data using a variety of these types will contribute to the construction of the kind of 'thick descriptions' upon which qualitative research depends.

CASE STUDY 7.1

Examples of observational data gathering techniques

A qualitative researcher is conducting a study on power relationships within the health service. One data gathering process in the study is a two-day non-participation observation, involving the 'shadowing' of a hospital consultant. Table 7.4 provides an outline of the types of data collected, their characteristics, data collection methods and some examples from each data type. The Case Study illustrates the use of observational data gathering techniques, but also the use of a reflective diary, documentary evidence and video recordings.

ACTIVITY 7.5

Review Case Study 7.1. What does this tell you about the richness of data collected in a qualitative study? What does it tell you about the time and resources needed?

Deciding on a sampling strategy

We saw in Chapter 6 that experimental and quasi-experimental research designs are concerned to use samples that are as representative as possible of the population under study – hence the use of random **probability sampling**. In qualitative research this approach is usually impractical or rejected by researchers on epistemological grounds. However, as Mays (1995) argues, there are no a priori reasons for supposing that qualitative research will never use random sampling. For example, in a study investigating the quality of health and safety training in sports centres, a random sample of such centres could be taken to discover its prevalence and impact. Onwuegbuzie and Leech (2007) refer to this as external statistical generalization and compare it to external statistical sampling in quantitative research. If this is the preferred route, then the authors recommend the use of simple random sampling, stratified random sampling, cluster sampling or systematic random sampling.

PURPOSEFUL
SAMPLING

Table 7.4   Types of data, their characteristics and collection approaches

Type	Characteristics	Collection method	Examples
Description of behaviour	What people are doing or saying	Observation notes, research diary, etc.	The consultant moved closer to the patient's bed, but continued talking to the nurse in a low voice (observational notes).
Description of event	Behaviour within an event – e.g., meeting, car journey, argument, training session	Observation notes, research diary, maps, etc.	The consultant's 'bleeper' went off. He looked at it, frowned, and rushed from the ward, muttering the word, 'Problem'. The doctors and nurses around the bed looked surprised and unsure as to what to do (observational notes).
Description of institution	How the organization 'works' in terms of its rules, rituals, culture, etc.	Observation notes, research diary, maps, etc.	As a private hospital, the use of every resource (drugs, bandages, even meals) is logged and added to the patient's bill. This looks very much to me like a profit-led culture (extract from researcher's diary).
Description of appearance	What the setting and/or people look like (e.g., buildings, spaces, clothing, arrangement of office furniture, etc.)	Observation notes, research diary, photographs, drawings, diagrams, maps, etc.	The consultant's office was larger than those of lower rank doctors, but its walls were painted the same faded, pale green. On his desk was a laptop computer, a photograph of his family, and a half finished cup of coffee. A set of golf clubs stood in a corner (observational notes).
Description of research event	What people say or do in interview or focus group, etc.	Observation notes, research diary, etc.	I noticed that the consultant looked nervous during the interview. He shuffled about in his seat, particularly when talking about the recent complaint made against him (extract from researcher's diary).
Account	What people say or write to the researcher – verbatim	Interview, audio recording, questionnaire, participant's diary, transcription, verbatim notes	The whole thing was a complete misunderstanding. My words were taken out of context (transcript from interview with consultant).
Talk	The actual words that people are heard saying	Audio recording, transcription, verbatim notes	Mr Giles is one of the politest people I know. I've never seen him lose his temper (verbatim notes from overheard conversation between two nurses).
Behaviour in setting	What is seen happening	Film, video recording	Digital recordings of 'life on the ward' taken by two nurses and one hospital manager using a camcorder
Document	Piece of writing belonging or relevant to the setting	Photocopy	I absolutely refute the accusations made against me. I wish you to note that I have already taken legal advice (letter from consultant to hospital board).

Source: Adapted from Holliday, 2002

However, qualitative research usually works with purposive non-probability samples because it seeks to obtain insights into particular practices that exist within a specific location, context and time. Informants are therefore identified because they are known to enable the exploration of a particular behaviour or characteristic relevant to the research. Purposive sampling seeks to identify information-rich cases which can then be studied in depth (Patton, 2002). Qualitative research, then, often works with small samples of people, cases or phenomena nested in particular contexts. Again, in contrast to more quantitative approaches, samples may not always be pre-planned in advance, but may evolve once **fieldwork** has begun. So an initial choice of informants may lead to a decision to select a more contrasting set of deviant subjects (cases) as a comparison (Lincoln and Guba, 1994).

Very often it is not a case of selecting between the various approaches but combining some of them into multiple case sampling. By using a number of cases that yield similar findings we can show replication (see Figure 11.4 in Chapter 11) hence strengthening claims for the validity of findings and the grounds for their generalizability. What is needed, however, is an explicit sampling frame where, between them, the cases cover the various issues and variables detailed in the study's research questions. For example, in a study of inner-city gangs, where the research is interested in exploring links between the growth of gangs and family breakups, sampling would explicitly target those inner-city areas of high social deprivation and disproportionately large numbers of single-parent families. Miles et al. (2013) advise that the best strategy is to initially target those cases that are most likely to yield the richest data, leaving more peripheral cases until later. But peripheral sampling is still important because it may often yield negative or exceptional cases (those that contradict the initial case findings or the findings of previous empirical studies). Similarly, Lincoln and Guba (1994) recommend maximum variation sampling as a way of identifying common themes that cut across samples that vary when measured across key criteria. More can be found on sample selection in qualitative research in Chapter 9 on sampling strategies, particularly in the section on non-probability sampling.

An important but often neglected consideration in qualitative sampling is selecting the size of the sample. Onwuegbuzie and Leech (2007) suggest that sample sizes in qualitative research should not be so large that it becomes difficult to extract thick, rich data. At the same time, the sample should not be too small so that it becomes difficult to achieve data saturation (Flick, 2009), theoretical saturation (Strauss and Corbin, 1990) or information redundancy (Lincoln and Guba, 1994). As will be suggested in Chapter 11, in case study research Eisenhardt (1989) suggests that between 4 and 10 cases usually works well.

Plan data analysis processes

The data analysis processes should be planned for at the design stage, not as an afterthought just before the data analysis process is due to start. Approaches to the analysis of qualitative data are discussed in Chapter 23.

GRAY ON
COMMON
MISTAKES IN
QUALITATIVE
METHODS

→ TOP TIP 7.2 ←

One of the classic mistakes made by novice qualitative researchers is to think about approaches to data analysis far too late. By knowing in advance what analytical approach you are going to take, you will also know how this approach influences your approach to sampling and other issues. For example, are your analytical codes going to be a priori codes (from the literature – in which case you will influence your choice of samples) or in vivo (emerging from the data), or a mixture of both?

THE ROLE OF THE RESEARCHER

As we saw in Chapter 6, in quantitative research the role of the researcher is to try to maintain objectivity and detachment from the research process. In qualitative research, the researcher's role is very different. According to Glaser and Strauss (1967) and Strauss and Corbin (1990), researchers need to adopt a stance of **'theoretical sensitivity'**, which means being 'insightful', demonstrating the capacity to understand and the ability to differentiate between what is important and what is not. They must be able to perceive of situations holistically and be responsive to environmental cues in the field. For example, they need to be sensitive to situations where they risk biasing the responses of people they are interviewing. In addition, they usually adopt a reflexive stance, reflecting on the subtle ways in which bias might creep into their research practice through the influence of their personal background and belief systems.

USING THE LITERATURE IN QUALITATIVE RESEARCH

We saw, briefly, in Chapter 3, that qualitative research differs from quantitative research in its approach to positioning the literature review. While in quantitative studies the literature review normally comes at the beginning of the research process, in qualitative research the issue of where to position the literature is less pre-determined. This issue has been heavily influenced by Glaser and Strauss (1967) who, in their description of grounded theory, argued that research should start with data collection without any reference to the literature, which should come later. Strauss later modified this position, but some qualitative researchers have stubbornly retained this approach. Flick (2009) suggests that, in qualitative research, there are several types of literature that play a part in the development of a qualitative study, namely:

- the theoretical literature
- the literature from empirical studies
- the methodological literature on how the study is to be conducted.

The theoretical literature

The purpose of exploring the theoretical literature around a research topic is to gain an insight and contextual knowledge about the subject in order to raise questions such as:

- What is already known about the subject?
- Which theories or models are accepted or influential?
- Which concepts or theories are disputed?
- What can be said critically about what is already known?
- What are the main theoretical or methodological debates in the field?
- What new research is worth doing?

The theoretical literature, then, provides a detailed description and critical analysis of the current state of knowledge.

The empirical literature

Previous empirical studies in the field illustrate what has been studied and help in providing concrete evidence in support of, or in opposition to, an argument. They also provide evidence on the kinds of methodological approaches or traditions used in studying the field. A critical evaluation of these studies might suggest the adoption of similar methodological approaches, or, indeed, the need to adopt alternative ones. Empirical studies might also highlight contradictory findings or ambiguities that are worthy of further research. Both the empirical and theoretical literature can be used to identify current gaps in knowledge, and therefore in the formulation of research questions.

The methodological literature

Reviewing the methodological literature allows the researcher to identify the kinds of methodological approaches that have, typically, been used to address the subject they are interested in. This includes issues of qualitative research design and also the choices made for approaches to qualitative data analysis. Having reviewed the methodological literature it will also be necessary to study qualitative research methods textbooks and academic articles in order to gain a deeper understanding of the kinds of issues involved (Silverman, 2000).

> **TOP TIP 7.3**

Inexperienced researchers often believe that conducting a literature review on qualitative methodology means developing an unfocused discourse on qualitative methods in general. Nothing could be further from the truth. As this chapter suggests, qualitative methods comprise a wide and diverse set of approaches. So, you should try to give some focus to the qualitative methodology you are actually using. For example, if using grounded theory, do not waste time telling the reader about the wonders of content or framework analysis. Describe, briefly, the history of grounded theory, some of the changes in the views of its originators and discuss the grounded theory stages in data collection and analysis (for details of grounded theory analysis see Chapter 23). Also, take a look at the work of experienced researchers and how they have conducted a study using the relevant qualitative method. For an example of grounded theory see Ellis and Chen (2013) in Journal resources section, below.

COLLECTING QUALITATIVE DATA

Qualitative data emerge from a wide spectrum of sources. One of the most common is field studies where the researcher enters a selected setting to gather data, often through the use of observations or interviews. While observation is likely to elicit qualitative data (such as **field notes** and analysis), interviews may be used to collect both qualitative and quantitative information. Similarly, case studies might involve the use of research instruments such as questionnaires, interview schedules and observations, all of which might yield data that is qualitative in nature.

Conducting interviews

Qualitative interviews can be used as either the main instrument of data collection, or in conjunction with observation, document analysis or some other type of data gathering technique. Qualitative interviews utilize open-ended questions using either informal, conversational interviews, semi-structured interviews (where additional probing questions can be used) or standardized interviews, where they are not. Chapter 15 discusses approaches to interviewing in more detail.

Observations

Observations are one of the prime data collection methods for naturalistic or fieldwork settings. Observational data is primarily descriptive of settings, people, events and the meanings that participants ascribe to them. As we will see in Chapter 16, observation may be conducted with the knowledge of those being observed (overt) or without their knowledge (covert). Researchers may also remain detached from the field setting as a non-participant or become a member of a group or setting.

Field notes remain one of the mainstays of qualitative data collection methods through observations. Accurate, detailed and extensive field notes are difficult to write, especially when the researcher is busy observing in the field (and particularly if that research has to be covert).

➤ TOP TIP 7.4 ◄

It is always important that field notes are written up on the same day as the observation and not after this point. Field notes can be supplemented by diaries written by researchers, and also by participants, so that triangulation can be performed. Photographs, drawings, maps and other visual material can also be added (see next section). Remember, that under ethical protocols, field notes, just like all data, should be stored safely.

Lofland and Lofland (1995) recommend that if field notes are supplemented by tape recordings, these should be transcribed as quickly as possible, and that at least as much time should be spent studying and analysing the materials as spent in the interview itself. Flick (2009) also recommends the use of documentation sheets that provide useful summary information on the context within which the data were collected (see Figure 7.3). Document sheets allow for an overview of the data and can provide a guide as to which files and transcripts to consult at the analysis stage.

Interviewee data summary

Date of interview _____

Place of interview _____

Duration of interview _____

Interviewer _____

Identifier number for interviewee _____

Gender of interviewee _____

Age of interviewee _____

Job role of interviewee _____

Qualifications of interviewee _____

Professional training of interviewee
undertaken in the past 3 years _____

Figure 7.3   Example of document sheet

Using photographs and other sources

PHOTO
INTERVIEWS

In addition to text, photographs or other visual data such as video or film recordings are also sources of qualitative data. Photographs in particular have a long history in ethnography and anthropology (Flick, 2009). Photographs allow the detailed recording of facts, including the presentation of lifestyles and living and working conditions. They can also capture processes that are too rapid for the human eye. Sometimes, the subjects of research can be encouraged to take on the role of the photographer, documenting either a subject of their choice, or a theme that the researcher wants them to record. If desired, these photographs can subsequently be used to stimulate an interview or encourage a participant to produce a narrative to accompany and expand upon the photographic evidence. This can be seen as a concretization of the focused interview (Flick, 2009). But do photographs tell the truth? Of course, what the camera focuses on, and what it leaves out, is selective.

There may also be problems of **reactivity**, with the subjects altering their behaviour in the presence of the photographer (note the natural versus the staged poses in the photographs above). Hence, there are always dangers of bias, and questions about the extent to which photographs help in the social construction of reality. It may be best to use visual data alongside other sources such as observational and interview data and documents.

Using unobtrusive data

As we shall see in Chapter 19 organizations contain a rich array of unobtrusive data in the form of documents such as company reports, business plans, written

Image 7.4   Example of natural versus staged photograph

statements by members of staff, accounts and contracts. Most medium-sized and large organizations also have dedicated websites that present a 'public' image to the world. Analysis of such a site may reveal not only the organization's perception of itself and the image it wants to present, but also what it does not wish to reveal. The organization's intranet site and evidence from email interactions may also prove of interest (if accessible as part of a study).

Atkinson and Coffey (2004) warn that it is not only the content of documents that should be of concern to researchers, but also the way in which they are produced, circulated, read, stored and used for a variety of purposes. This means that they are not necessarily a description of 'reality' nor are they necessarily 'transparent representations of organizational routines, decision making processes or professional diagnoses' (Atkinson and Coffey, 2004: 47). Although they should be treated seriously, documents should not be taken as factual evidence of what they report. Rather, they should be examined for their place within the organizational setting, and the cultural values attached to them. But conversely, the temptation should be avoided to use only observational or oral data as the primary source and downgrade documentary evidence to a validating role. Atkinson and Coffey (2004) urge that documents should be regarded as valid sources in their own right.

Keeping a research diary

Given that, particularly in progressive qualitative research, the researcher is considered a valid part of the research setting, then the ideas, feelings and perceptions of the researcher become part of the data. But there is a danger in qualitative research that the reader is presented with what Silverman (2000: 193) calls a 'seamless web' of ideas that conceals the researcher's complex experience of the research process including false leads, inspirational hunches, triumphs and disappointments. Keeping a diary maintains a proper record of the researcher's thinking and helps to develop a reflexive stance (Miles et al., 2013). For example, there is a tendency in qualitative research to present the 'voices' of respondents as

THE RESEARCH
JOURNAL

though these voices speak on their own. Yet it is the researcher who makes choices about how to interpret these voices and which quotations to use as evidence (Mauthner and Doucet, 2003).

Hence, the kinds of issues noted in a research diary could include:

- The processes involved in approaching the field and making contact (in the terms often used by participatory action research – 'getting in').
- Experiences (positive and negative) in getting access to respondents and in using data gathering instruments.
- Details of literature sources read (and ordered).
- Reflections on the interpretation and presentation of results, including important changes in direction.

As Silverman (2000) points out, there is no single correct method for keeping a diary. What is important is that researchers are meticulous in record keeping and reflective about their data.

ETHICS AND QUALITATIVE RESEARCH

ETHICS IN
QUALITATIVE
RESEARCH

As we saw in Chapter 4, all researchers need to take into account ethical principles when conducting their research. Ethics, however, can pose a particular problem for qualitative researchers who often work so closely and for longer periods of time with research participants, and deal with the most sensitive and intimate matters in people's lives (Punch, 2005). Indeed, with some qualitative research methods such as, say, ethnography using **participant observation**, the researcher may develop close relationships with those they are studying. This has important implications for issues such as respecting the privacy of participants and avoiding deception (especially if the observation is covert). Furthermore, as we have seen earlier, the flexibility of qualitative research design means that questions and focus may change during the research process. Since this may mean that the samples used and the kinds of question asked may have to change, this implies that, in qualitative studies, ethical consent may have to be renegotiated on an ongoing basis. For example, once initial findings are presented, new research questions may emerge (and even new samples) which might raise new ethical issues or challenges.

Mason (2002) agrees that, for qualitative research, the issue of informed consent needs to be revisited regularly. Some research methods, for example interviews, can promote a high degree of trust among research subjects, which imposes a special responsibility on researchers to avoid reneging on commitments, acting deceitfully or producing explanations that in some way cause harm to the interests of those subjects. For example, the use of visual data such as photographs can make confidentiality impossible to maintain. Table 7.5 provides a brief checklist of issues qualitative researchers would do well to reflect on during the research process.

According to Bell and Bryman (2007), many ethical frameworks are based upon a model of research processes that is insensitive to the kinds of open-ended research strategies associated with qualitative methods. Lincoln and Tierney

Table 7.5 Checklist of ethical commitments and responsibilities during qualitative research

- Have I honoured my commitments about confidentiality and privacy?
- Have I acted in the spirit of informed consent?
- Have I used my research effectively and morally?
- Have I generalized appropriately?
- Do I have a responsibility to anticipate how others might use my research and explanations?

Source: Adapted from Mason, 2002

(2004: 222), for example, note that some institutional review boards (IRBs) have rejected qualitative research projects on the grounds that they are 'unscientific' and incapable of generalization – a judgement based upon a 'realist' ontology and 'objectivist' epistemology that underpins conventional science (Lincoln and Guba, 1989). One result is a series of endless revisions as IRBs seek to make such projects appear more conventional.

One approach to qualitative research, ethnography, has difficulties in meeting ethical protocols because the research questions can rarely be specified in advance and it can be difficult to specify when projects start and when they end (Bosk, 2004). Similarly, grounded theory promotes an open-ended approach that allows new lines of enquiry to emerge during the research process, making it difficult to determine an exact set of research questions in advance of the project. In these circumstances, the best approach is probably to recognize that informed consent is a fluid process requiring constant monitoring rather than a pre-research agreement which precludes further thought.

— ACTIVITY 7.6 —

Given the fluid nature of qualitative research, what kinds of processes should researchers put in place to ensure that ethical principles are followed throughout the project? For example, how often should ethical protocols be reviewed?

ENSURING RIGOUR IN QUALITATIVE RESEARCH

One of the criticisms levelled at qualitative research is that it is 'unscientific', anecdotal and based upon subjective impressions. It is also claimed that qualitative research lacks reproducibility – the research is so based in or confined to one context that it lacks **generalizability**. In addition, it is argued that the research is so personal to the researcher that another researcher might use the same data to come to radically different conclusions (Mays, 1995). These contentions are countered by qualitative researchers who seek to show, through a range of strategies, how qualitative research can, indeed, demonstrate rigour. We will look at how rigour is preserved in the analysis of qualitative data in Chapter 23, confining ourselves here largely to the issue of rigour in qualitative design and data collection.

RELIABILITY & VALIDITY

In discussing the issue of quality in qualitative research, some commentators resist the temptation to even address such matters as validity and reliability, because, they argue, these concepts were originally developed in a quantitative tradition and are rooted in a positivist paradigm (Bryman, 1988; Golafshani, 2003). Lincoln (1985) also asserts that naturalistic researchers, for example, tend anyway to be more modest and reluctant about making generalizations from their findings. Issues of external validity, then, are not high on their agendas. However, as we shall see, even some of the most enthusiastic adherents to the qualitative approach see the need to address validity and reliability as inescapable, although some do suggest additional quality criteria, some of which they see as having more importance.

Designing for validity in qualitative research

Validity has traditionally been a concept used in quantitative research (Campbell and Stanley, 1963). The word, however, has been adopted in qualitative research, resulting in 17 different terms associated with it, with no generally agreed definition (Dellinger and Leech, 2007). Despite this caution, we will explore validity in qualitative research from two perspectives – internal validity and external validity.

Internal validity

The issue of internal validity revolves around the question of how far the constructions of the researcher are grounded in the constructions of those being researched (Flick, 2009). Hall and Callery (2001) criticize grounded theory in particular for assuming that the data collected reflect reality, and are independent of, and not influenced by, the subjective interpretations of researchers. What is needed, they argue, is for researchers to adopt a reflexive stance, through which they critically reflect on their influence on the research process. Self-reflective criticality is strengthened through repetitive checks of the researcher's interpretations (Whittemore et al., 2001). Of course, another approach is to involve those being researched in checking the data for accuracy and in the analysis for the faithfulness of interpretation.

Data can be fabricated, discounted or misinterpreted. One way of avoiding such problems is where research can be validated through replication, but as Dey (1993) cautions, qualitative research is notoriously difficult to replicate. In place of external validation, 'internal' replication may be adopted, whereby other researchers can inspect the procedures through which the research has been conducted. This is much easier, of course, where two researchers collaborate on the same project. Another approach might be to split the data and analyse them in two stages to see if the results are similar.

Establishing principles for validity is all very well, but how do researchers plan to achieve them in practice? McMillan and Schumacher (1997) present a useful checklist (see Table 7.6). Note, however that selection depends upon contextual factors and the purpose of the research.

External validity

One important aspect of external validity is the extent to which it is possible to generalize from the data to other cases or situations. Generalizations can be defined as

Table 7.6   Techniques for demonstrating validity in qualitative design

Prolonged and persistent field work	Allows interim data analysis and corroboration to ensure the match between findings and participant reality
Low-inference descriptors	Record precise, almost literal, and detailed descriptions of people and situations
Multiple researchers	Agreement on descriptive data collected by a research team
Mechanically recorded data	Use of tape recorders, photographs and videotapes
Participant researcher	Use of participant recorded perceptions in diaries or anecdotal records for corroboration
Member checking	Check informally with participants for accuracy during data collection; frequently done in participant observation studies
Participant review	Ask each participant to review researcher's synthesis of all interviews with the person for accuracy of representation; frequently done in interview studies
Negative cases or discrepant data	Actively search for, record, analyse, and report negative cases of discrepant data that are an exception to patterns

Source: Adapted from McMillan and Schumacher (1997)

assertions of enduring value that are context-free (Lincoln and Guba, 1994). Since sampling in qualitative research tends to be purposive rather than random, and data gathered from a limited number of cases (sometimes one), can we generalize? Lincoln and Guba (1994) distinguish between two kinds of generalization. The first is nomothetic, based upon a rationalistic, law-like stance, as in the positivist paradigm. The second they term 'naturalistic generalization', which is a more intuitive, ideographic but none the less, an empirical approach based upon personal, direct experience. The authors then dismiss the notion of nomothetic generalizations that are truly universal to all times and situations. Local conditions, they contend, make it impossible to generalize. 'If there is a "true" generalization, it is that there can be no generalization' (Lincoln and Guba, 1994: 124). At best, the results from individual cases allow us to build working hypotheses that can be tested in subsequent cases. As Miles et al. (2013) point out, through the use of multiple case studies, attempts are made to match on the basis of underlying theories. As more similar or contrasting cases are used, we can justify, through replication, the stability of the findings. Even then, as Dey (1993) asserts, as a basis for generalization, qualitative analysis is more likely to be suggestive than conclusive. At best, rather than generalize, we can see if the findings from Context A can be transferred to Context B.

If qualitative researchers decide that generalizing is essential, then this entails treating it as an integral element of the research design. In particular, it means taking extra care over sample selection (of both people and sites). Efforts then need to be made to demonstrate the similarities between the sample and the target population or research sites to which generalization is to be made. Hence, if generalization is an aim of the research, care with sample selection has to be built into the research design, and not considered as an afterthought. Payne and Williams (2005) suggest that in attempting to formulate generalizations, qualitative researchers will achieve more **plausibility** if they are:

- Cautious, moderating the range of generalizing conclusions. Being too ambitious in conclusions merely undermines the credibility of otherwise competent research. If the sample is specialized in some way, be clear that the results may only be applicable to a limited type of site or categories of person – and say what they are.
- Careful in recognizing the limitations of time periods. So, claims are more believable if made for current conditions than about some period in the future.
- Meticulous in demonstrating clear linkages between generalizing conclusions and the specific data that provide its foundation.
- Honest and transparent about findings from sub-groups, the views or behaviours of which differ or are similar to those of the population being reported.
- Modest by making claims for basic patterns or tendencies, so that other studies may find similar but not identical findings.
- Diligent in reporting alternative explanations or the constraints on generalizations. The constraints on generalizations need to become a standard element of the analysis.

CASE STUDY 7.2

The limits of generalization

A group of researchers are conducting an observational study of an international supermarket chain based in the UK, France and Germany. To what extent should they attempt to generalize their findings to other supermarkets in Europe? They decide that this will depend on the features being explored. As far as products or brands are concerned, generalization is quite feasible because many products and brands are sold all over Europe. Similarly, features such as management structures may be quite similar across many countries, particularly in Western Europe. However, the researchers decide that they would be unwise to generalize to Eastern European supermarkets, because forms of management structure and culture are still emerging from a post-communist society and still tend to be hierarchical. The ability to generalize, then, is influenced by arguments about the similarities or otherwise between the research (sending) site and sites to which generalizations are being made (receiving site).

──────────────────────────────── ➡ **TOP TIP 7.5** ◄ ─────────────────────────

GRAY ON
GENERALIZATIONS
IN QUALITATIVE
RESEARCH

Decide at the research planning stage on your attitude towards generalization. If rejecting the necessity of generalizing, explore the qualitative research methods literature for what alternative measures of rigour you may use to justify the quality of your research. If generalizing, follow the advice of Payne and Williams (2005) to acknowledge the modesty of your findings.

Designing for reliability in qualitative research

Reliability refers to the stability of findings. A reliable observation, for example, is one that could have been made by any similarly situated observer (Denzin, 1989). For most qualitative approaches, reliability is improved, if not guaranteed, by triangulation, gathering information, for example, from multiple sources or by using multiple data gathering tools. Denzin (1989) offers four kinds of triangulation:

- *Data triangulation* – where data are gathered using multiple sampling strategies. This can include: time triangulation, when data are collected on the same phenomenon over a period of time; space triangulation, when data are collected from multiple sites and; person triangulation, where data are collected at three levels in an organization – for example, individuals, groups and departments.

- *Investigator triangulation* – using more than one observer in field situations so that observer bias can be reduced (and inter-judge reliability improved). Thus, a training programme would teach observers to keep an 'open mind' and not to become obsessed with their hypothesis (if they start with one). They should not jump towards 'solutions' to a problem as this will tend to make them ignore facts that do not confirm their expectations. In making a study, they are trained to notice all aspects of a situation and to deliberately search for unexpected facts, and to seek alternative interpretations. The data will then be checked by other trained colleagues (and even informants) who will, if possible, repeat the observation to see if they get the same results.
- *Multiple triangulation* – in which a combination of multiple methods, data types, observers and theories are combined in the same investigation. While it is often a practical difficulty to achieve a combination of all of these, it is more common to at least use multiple data levels and methods.
- *Methodological triangulation* – of which there are two kinds: within-method, where the researcher employs varieties of data gathering techniques within the same method; and between method, where a variety of different methods are used – for example, quantitative data from a survey, with qualitative data from observations (see Chapter 8 on using mixed methods).

It should be noted, however, that the significance of reliability is not universally accepted. Glaser (1992), for example, asserts that verification has no place in grounded theory, the task of which is to generate hypotheses, not to test them. This is in sharp contrast to the views of Strauss and Corbin (1994), who suggest that within the data collection and analysis process there is an in-built mandate to strive towards the verification of any resulting hypotheses. For interview data, reliability can be increased through the training of interviewers and through the use of standardized interview schedules. For observations, researchers also need to be trained before they enter the field. Reliability can also be improved through the use of pre-designed observation schedules.

Other approaches to rigour

Some researchers, particularly those from the naturalistic tradition, argue that *trustworthiness* is more important than concerns over the validity or reliability checks that have just been outlined. Skrtic (1985), for example, suggests that this is addressed through a focus on:

- Transferability, with purposive sampling to illustrate pertinent issues and factors when comparing two contexts for similarity, and thick descriptions to provide evidence for making judgements about similarities between cases.
- Dependability, through the use of **audit trails** through the data.
- Confirmability, with the audit showing the connections between data and the researcher's interpretations.
- **Credibility**, the use of persistent observations; triangulation (of data, methods, theories and investigations); and member checks (where data and interpretations are tested with research participants).

Lincoln and Guba (1994) argue that credibility can be strengthened through the researcher making a conscious effort to establish confidence in the accuracy of interpretation, and the fit between description and explanation.

To these we can add *authenticity*, which relates analysis and interpretation to the meanings and experiences that are lived and perceived by the subjects of the research. This means the research being aware of the multiple voices contained within the data, and the subtle, sometimes conflicting realities within it. Do the interpretations ring true? Have rival explanations been considered? Davies and Dodd (2002) also suggest that just as important are practices that are honest, open, empathetic, sensitive, respectful and engaging. Perhaps these concepts should also be seen as essential ingredients of research quality. Table 7.7 offers a brief comparison of criteria used by quantitative and qualitative approaches, and the measures suggested by Lincoln and Guba (1994) for developing the trustworthiness of qualitative data.

TRUST-
WORTHINESS

However, as Johnson and Harris (2002) comment, one problem with qualitative research is that a standard practice for achieving validity, reliability or any other quality indicator has yet to be established. This is because of the variable nature of qualitative research and the relative novelty of many research studies.

Table 7.7 Comparison of criteria for judging the trustworthiness of quantitative and qualitative research

Conventional terms	Naturalistic terms	Naturalistic terms developed through...
Internal validity	Credibility	Examining the study design and methods used to derive findings.
External validity	Transferability	Exploring the degree to which findings are context bound, so assessed by examining the characteristics of sample.
Reliability	Dependability	Evaluating reliability of the study's conclusions.
Objectivity	Confirmability	Addressing the degree to which the steps of the study can be audited, confirmed or replicated.

Source: Adapted from Hoepfl, 1997 and Lincoln and Guba, 1994

Summary

- Qualitative research has advantages over quantitative research in that researchers are closer to the fields or settings they are trying to research – it is highly contextual.
- Qualitative research is not built upon a unified theory or methodological approach – hence its variety and flexibility.
- In qualitative research, data analysis does not necessarily follow data gathering – there can be a number of iterations between the two.
- Even though there are various schools of qualitative research including grounded theory, ethnomethodology, narrative analysis and ethnography, they all have one element in common – generally, an inductive approach (although deduction or prior questions cannot be ruled out).
- Methods of collecting qualitative data include interview transcripts, field notes from observations, photographs, video and unobtrusive data.
- Decisions on whether to attempt generalization need to be built into the research design paying particular attention to sampling strategies.
- Qualitative approaches to achieving rigour include building trustworthiness, authenticity, credibility, transferability, dependability and confirmability.

REVIEW QUESTIONS

1. The wide number of approaches to qualitative research designs constitutes one of its strengths and its weaknesses. Discuss.
2. Should qualitative research designs attempt to address the issues of validity and reliability? Present arguments both for and against.
3. One of the most fundamental differences between qualitative and quantitative research designs is the position of the researcher. To what extent do you agree or disagree with this statement?
4. Ethical dilemmas occur more frequently and deeply in qualitative than in quantitative research because in the former, the researcher is closer to those being researched. Discuss.

FURTHER READING

Maxwell, J.A. (2013) *Qualitative Research Design: An Interactive Approach*. Thousand Oaks, CA: Sage. Presents what the author describes as an interactive model, showing that research questions are at the centre of research design, that are linked to goals which are grounded in theoretical models. The operational side of the model includes methods and checks for validity.

Denzin, N.K. and Lincoln, Y.S. (2011) *The Sage Handbook of Qualitative Research*, 4th edn. Thousand Oaks, CA: Sage. Includes 14 topics not touched by previous editions, including institutional review boards, critical and performance ethnography, narrative enquiry and strategies of online research. Previous authors have all updated their chapters.

Berg, B.L. and Lune, H. (2011) *Qualitative Research Methods for the Social Sciences*, 8th edn. Needham Heights, MA: Allyn & Bacon. Shows inexperienced researchers how to design, collect and analyse data. Discusses seven different qualitative data collecting strategies in detail, including a guide to conducting focus groups.

Flick, U. (2009) *An Introduction to Qualitative Research*, 4th edn. London: Sage. Provides a systematic framework for doing qualitative research, as well as a guide to research design. Each chapter concludes with a helpful overview.

JOURNAL RESOURCES

Ellis, L.M and Chen, E.C. (2013) 'Negotiating identity development among undocumented immigrant college students: A grounded theory study', *Journal of Counseling Psychology*. Advance online publication. doi: 10.1037/a0031350. Provides an example of how grounded theory should be conducted.

Smith, J., Bekker, H. and Cheater, F. (2011) 'Theoretical versus pragmatic design in qualitative research', *Nurse Researcher*, 18(2): 39–51. Discusses some of the challenges of qualitative research design and offers some approaches for matching the design with research questions.

Tomkins, L. and Eatough, V. (2010) 'Towards an integrative reflexivity in organisational research', *Qualitative Research in Organizations and Management: An International Journal*, 5(2): 162–181. Offers an alternative model of reflexivity and some practical guidelines of value to researchers working across a range of different qualitative methodologies.

Johansson, E.E., Risberg, G. and Hamberg, K. (2003) 'Is qualitative research scientific, or merely relevant?', *Scandinavian Journal of Primary Health Care*, 21(1): 10–14. An empirical study that shows that qualitative research is valued for its relevance, but seen as less scientifically accurate.

There might tend to be more confidence in the validity of results from a comprehensive sample since this covers every case in a given population. Similarly, intensity samples focus on cases that are typical of the population rather than outliers or atypical examples. Deviant case sampling, which looks at extreme cases, may be accused of producing invalid results, but may, in fact, yield illuminating and unexpected data that allow new avenues of exploration. Critical case sampling, with its focus on one case or site, can only provide a strong case for validity if evidence is provided that the case is, indeed, typical of the trait, characteristic or phenomenon under investigation.

Table 7.8   Types of research question

Question	Type of question	Comments
What changes in alcohol consumption have taken place over the last 10 years?	Descriptive	A question that deals with national aggregates – a quantitative question.
Do high levels of alcohol consumption lead to absenteeism at work?	Explanatory	At one level this is a quantitative question exploring a relationship between two variables. But if a relationship is identified, a follow-up qualitative study could seek to understand why.
Why is alcohol consumption on the increase?	Explanatory	A quantitative study would attempt to identify variables (such as demographic changes, income levels, etc.) that might explain the increase. But a qualitative study could delve into people's attitudes to alcohol and explore changing personal and cultural values.
What is the scale and cause of alcohol abuse among the under 16s?	Exploratory	The scale of alcohol consumption is a quantitative question, but the cause could adopt a qualitative approach to establish reasons for this change, including changing social attitudes.
What is the impact of rising alcohol consumption on family life?	Interpretive	Seeks to uncover people's views and perspectives. A valid question for exploratory, largely qualitative studies.

8

RESEARCH DESIGN: MIXED METHODS

CHAPTER INTRODUCTION

Chapter outline

Differences between quantitative and qualitative research 190

What do we mean by mixed methods research? 194

The benefits of mixed methods designs 196

Looking at mixed methods research critically 198

Types of mixed methods design 199

Keywords

Epistemological positions

Between-methods triangulation

Sequential research designs

Concurrent research designs

Chapter objectives

After reading this chapter you will be able to:

- Distinguish between quantitative, qualitative and mixed research designs.
- Identify when quantitative and qualitative approaches can complement each other.
- Select from a range of mixed methods designs.
- Explain when mixed methods designs may not be appropriate.

MIXED
METHODS
DESIGN

The social and behavioural sciences have been dominated by positivist schools of thought on the one hand and interpretivists on the other, generating a 'great divide' between what have become often hostile, antagonistic camps. One negative result of this has been that academics and researchers have often felt it necessary to pledge their allegiance to one camp or another, and to accept the notion that the quantitative and qualitative research approaches are mutually incompatible. The purpose of this chapter, however, is to illustrate how two, seemingly opposite approaches to research can in fact support and complement each other. But since this statement is not without controversy some of the arguments against the mixing of research methods will also be explored.

Mixed method designs are those that include at least one quantitative method and one qualitative, where neither type of method is inherently linked to any particular inquiry paradigm (Greene et al., 1989). This implies, for example, that an ethnographic study that incorporates not only qualitative data from participant observation (the classic ethnographic data gathering method), but also quantitative data from a survey would be considered inappropriate. This is because ethnographers would deem the use of quantitative data as incompatible with the epistemology of ethnography. The quantitative and qualitative approaches typically embrace incompatible assumptions about the nature of the world. However, as we shall see later in this chapter, this hard divide between the two has broken down in recent years, some researchers at least being prepared to combine methods without any qualms about mixing epistemologies. 'No longer do we ask, "Is this the right method?" Instead, we ask, "What is the quality of knowing within the practice of this person or community?"' (Reason and Torbert, 2001: 7). Some researchers are now referring to mixed methods as a 'third methodological movement' with quantitative methods being seen as the first movement and qualitative the second (Tashakkori and Teddlie, 2009: ix).

DIFFERENCES BETWEEN QUANTITATIVE AND QUALITATIVE RESEARCH

CONDUCTING
MIXED METHODS

Before exploring approaches to mixed methods research, it is useful to describe some of the well-known arguments about the differences between quantitative and qualitative methods – if only to show why so many researchers do not subscribe to mixed methods research. Table 8.1 illustrates a number of areas in which quantitative and qualitative methods differ, demonstrating a divide both in terms of epistemology and use of methods. These important differences are discussed below.

Table 8.1 Some differences between quantitative and qualitative methods

	Quantitative methods	Qualitative methods
Epistemological positions	Objectivist	Constructivist
Relationship between researcher and subject	Distant /outsider	Close/insider
Research focus	'Facts'	Meanings
Relationship between theory/concepts and research	Deduction/confirmation	Induction/emergent
Scope of findings	Nomothetic	Ideographic
The nature of data	Data based upon numbers	Data based upon text

Source: Adapted from Bryman, 1999

Epistemological positions

In terms of the scale of the quantitative and qualitative 'divide', it is the epistemological arguments that are the most serious, seeing the two approaches as philosophically irreconcilable. Indeed, those who hold to epistemological distinctiveness, regard the two approaches as constituting different paradigms. It is argued, for example, that quantitative research emanates from an objectivist position which holds that reality exists independently of the researcher – the truth is 'out there'. In contrast, qualitative research is more closely linked to a constructivist paradigm, which sees truth and meaning as constructed and interpreted by individuals.

PAPER ON
EPISTEMOLOGICAL
POSITIONS

Relationship between researcher and subjects

Another difference is the way in which quantitative and qualitative methods demonstrate different approaches to the relationship between researchers and their study. In quantitative research, for example, researchers aim to keep themselves at a distance from those they are researching. This distance could be either emotional (maintaining detachment from the issues being researched) or physical (using data gathering tools which do not require direct contact with respondents, or both). In large projects using structured interviews, for example, contact with respondents may be through the use of hired interviewers rather than with the researcher, an approach often seen in market research where the emphasis is on using large samples. Here there is often an emphasis on training the interviewers so as to avoid the manipulation of responses. Qualitative research, however, usually involves direct contact between researcher and those they are researching, sometimes for long periods of time. Indeed, with some forms of observation, the researcher may become a member of the social group or community she/he is researching.

NURSE
RESEARCH

Quantitative research sees social reality as static, typically exploring the relationship between variables over a restricted time period. Qualitative researchers argue that quantitative researchers rarely examine the processes that link these variables and the flow of events in which they are located. In contrast, qualitative researchers argue that they are better positioned to examine the linkages between events and activities, especially since, as researchers, they are more personally immersed in these events.

Research focus

In line with an objectivist philosophical position, quantitative research concentrates on the gathering of 'facts', in order that 'truth claims' can be established. Such facts are less likely to be tainted by the biases of the researcher if he or she maintains a distance from those they are studying (see previous section). Qualitative researchers, however, contend that truth and meaning do not exist in some external world, but are constructed through peoples' interactions with the world. Hence, for the same phenomenon, two people could construct two quite different meanings. For example, taking the concept 'justice' you would expect a police officer and a criminal to hold quite different interpretations of the term.

Relationship to theory

Another important difference between quantitative and qualitative methods is in their approach to the relationship between theory and research. Quantitative studies usually commence deductively with a theory which will subsequently be tested through the process of research, while qualitative approaches inductively build theory. Hence, quantitative research seeks to verify theory, while qualitative research seeks to establish it. This formulation, however, is too simplistic. As Brennan (1992) points out, deduction and induction are involved in all types of research. Rather than build theory, many surveys are largely descriptive, and some quantitative research is concerned with theory generation rather than confirmation. Some qualitative studies also commence with at least some notion of a theoretical framework. So, the contrast between quantitative and qualitative research is not as clear cut as is sometimes implied (Bryman, 1999).

Scope of findings

Another commonly conceived difference between the two methods is in terms of their scope. Quantitative methods, for example, are regarded as nomothetic whilst qualitative studies are seen as ideographic. Nomothetic research attempts to establish law-like findings that hold irrespective of time or place. One implication is the care often taken to select representative samples for the research and the attempt to generalize to wider populations. Ideographic research, however, locates its findings in specific time periods and localities and is much more concerned with the depth and intensity of findings rather than breadth (generalizability). However, as Bryman (1999) warns, qualitative researchers sometimes exhibit some unease over this point, seeking to illustrate in some way how their findings can be applied beyond the confines of a specific case. And even quantitative studies can struggle to make nomothetic claims if they are not based upon random samples, or if they refer to highly restricted populations. The consistency of findings over time is also rarely given much consideration.

The nature of data

The kind of data collected by quantitative and qualitative researchers is also seen as different. Quantitative studies generate data in the form of numbers, often depicted positively as reliable and rigorous, probably because of their association with 'science'. In contrast, qualitative research generates what is claimed to be 'rich' or 'deep' data, usually in the form of text but sometimes in photographs, maps or other visual media. Quantitative surveys, however, also frequently collect qualitative comments, while in qualitative analysis, the number of times a word or phrase occurs may be measured through a **frequency count**, yielding numerical data.

We have seen, then, that various authors have highlighted both differences and similarities between quantitative and qualitative research. However, Rossman and Wilson (1985) suggest that these views fall into three alternative schools of thought, namely: the *purists*, the *situationalists* and the *pragmatists* (see Figure 8.1). These camps can be considered as lying on a continuum, with the purists and pragmatists at opposite ends and the situationalists positioned somewhere in the middle. Purists argue that quantitative and qualitative methods are mutually exclusive, because they stem from different ontological and epistemological positions about the nature of research. Hence, their ways of looking at the world and determining what is important to know are very different. Situationalists maintain that both methods have value but that certain research questions lend themselves more to quantitative approaches and others to qualitative. Situationalists, then, see the two approaches as potentially complementary, but representing fundamentally different epistemological traditions. Pragmatists, however, see the whole debate between the two approaches as a false dichotomy, arguing that, for example, quantitative methods are not necessarily positivist and qualitative methods not necessarily hermeneutic (socially constructed). Bryman (2007a), for example, argues that the epistemological differences between quantitative and qualitative methods have been exaggerated. Pragmatists, then, recommend integrating the two methods within a single study, utilizing the

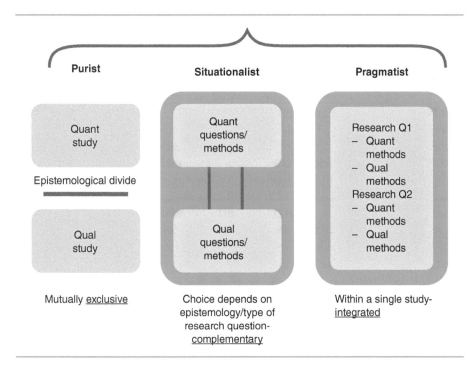

Figure 8.1 Mixing or not mixing methods: purist, situationalist and pragmatist. Adapted from Rossman and Wilson (1985).

strengths of both. Rather than come at a research problem from a position of epistemological purity, researchers should begin with their research questions and select
the most appropriate method(s) (Tashakkori and Teddlie, 2009).

WHAT DO WE MEAN BY MIXED METHODS RESEARCH?

Mixed methods research is becoming increasingly recognized as the third major
research approach or paradigm (Johnson et al., 2007). But if this confident statement is correct, what do we understand mixed methods to mean? It should be
acknowledged straightaway that this is not an easy question to answer, partly
because the paradigm (if that is what it is) is relatively new, and so its philosophy,
approaches to design, methodology and approaches to analysis, still promote argument and controversy. A study of the definitions provided by 19 mixed methods
research scholars, found that three definitions considered that the mixing occurred
at the data collection stage, two definitions suggested that mixing occurred at both
the data collection and data analysis stages, while four assumed that mixing can
occur at all stages of the research process (Johnson et al., 2007). Furthermore, as
Bryman (2007b) points out, there is currently an absence of well-known exemplars
of mixed methods research. A number of scholars, however, are engaging in a productive dialogue that is beginning to create at least the beginnings of consensus.

MIXED
METHODS
RESEARCH

Mixed methods have been defined as 'the collection or analysis of both quantitative and qualitative data in a single study in which the data are collected concurrently or sequentially, are given a priority, and involve the integration of data at one
or more stages in the process of research' (Creswell et al., 2003: 212). Yin (2006),
however, argues that there are many different mixes or combinations of methods –
for example, using a combination of experimentation and survey, both being commonly recognized as quantitative methods. Hence, according to Yin, mixed methods
do not necessarily include qualitative approaches. Similarly, he argues that a study
could combine two qualitative methods without the use of quantitative methods.
According to Yin (2006) a mixed methods study can exist when it includes methods
between (or to a lesser extent within) the items illustrated in Figure 8.2.

However, most researchers conceptualize mixed methods research as a mixture
of quantitative and qualitative methods. As Hanson et al. (2005) suggest, using
mixed methods allows researchers to simultaneously generalize from a sample to a
population and to gain a richer, contextual understanding of the phenomenon
being researched. Quantitative research, then, allows us to identify relationships
between variables and to make generalizations. Qualitative research, on the other
hand, is appropriate because it is capable of analysing concrete cases in their 'temporal and local particularity' (Flick, 2009 13) and starting from peoples' expressions and actions embedded within a local context.

MIXED
METHODS
QUALITATIVE
RESEARCH

> ... the careful measurement, generalizable samples, experimental control,
> and statistical tools of good quantitative studies are precious assets. When
> they are combined with up-close, deep, credible understanding of complex
> real-world contexts that characterize good qualitative studies, we have a very
> powerful mix. (Miles and Huberman, 1994: 42)

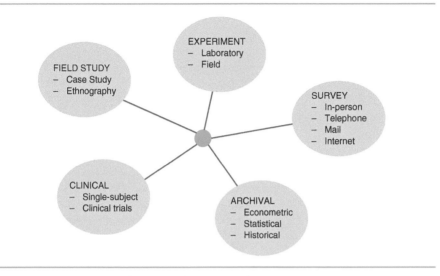

Figure 8.2   A broad variety of mixed methods research

Source: Adapted from Yin, R.K. (2006) 'Mixed methods research: are the methods genuinely integrated or merely parallel,' *Research in the Schools* 13(1): 41–47. Reprinted with permission of the original copyright holder.

Philosophically, mixed methods research adopts a *pragmatic* method and system, based on a view of knowledge as being both socially constructed *and* based upon the reality of the world we experience and live in (Johnson et al., 2007). Its mode of inquiry then makes use of induction (to identify patterns), deduction (testing theories and hypotheses) and abduction (uncovering and relying on the best explanations for understanding one's results) (Johnson and Onwuegbuzie, 2004). Research methods are not determined dogmatically according to a set of assumptions that flow from one paradigm or another, but flow from the nature of the research questions being asked in a way that offers the best chance of obtaining useful and workable answers. Table 8.2 offers an overview of how the 'mix' in mixed methods research manifests itself in actual studies.

Mixed research has its recent history in the social and behavioural sciences, particularly in the work of cultural anthropologists and especially fieldwork sociologists. However, the term mixed methods was not coined until many years later. Johnson et al. (2007) describe how Campbell and Fiske's (1959) article on 'multiple operationalism', introducing the idea of triangulation, is sometimes viewed as pioneering the use of mixed methods. But it was Webb et al. (2000) who actually coined the term triangulation, arguing that two or more independent measurement processes greatly reduced the uncertainty in interpreting data. Denzin (1978) later defined how these triangulation methods should be put into practice, distinguishing between *within-methods* triangulation using either multiple quantitative or multiple qualitative methods, and *between-methods* triangulation which involves both quantitative and qualitative methods. Denzin (1978) argued that it was between-methods triangulation that was potentially the most powerful because the bias of methods from one paradigm could be counterbalanced by the methods from the other.

Table 8.2   Examples of how quantitative and qualitative methods are mixed in mixed methods research

Types of mixing	Comments
Two types of research question	One fitting a quantitative approach and the other qualitative
The manner in which the research questions are developed	Preplanned (quantitative) versus participatory/emergent (qualitative)
Two types of sampling procedure	Probability versus purposive
Two types of data collection procedures	Surveys (quantitative) versus focus groups (qualitative)
Two types of data analysis	Numerical versus textual (or visual)
Two types of data analysis	Statistical versus thematic
Two types of conclusions	Objective versus subjective interpretations

Source: Adapted from Tashakkori and Creswell, 2007

Many subsequent ideas on mixed methods design, data gathering methods and other elements are reflected in the content presented in the rest of this chapter. It is worth noting, however, that much work still needs to be done in the area of mixed methods research in terms of its philosophical position, designs, data analysis, validity strategies, mixing and integrating procedures (Johnson and Onwuegbuzie, 2004).

➔ ON THE WEB 8.1 ◅

Take a look at this video clip in which John Creswell describes how quantitative and qualitative approaches can be integrated into a mixed methods research design.

http://www.youtube.com/watch?v=1OaNiTlpyX8

THE BENEFITS OF MIXED METHODS DESIGNS

Greene et al. (1989) in a review of 57 evaluation studies, identify five main purposes of using a combination of methods, namely: triangulation; complementarity; development; initiation; and expansion (see Table 8.3). Of these studies, 80 per cent of the primary purposes were either complementarity or expansion. Many studies, however, make use of triangulation because the application of multiple methods ensures that the inherent bias of one measure is counterbalanced by the strengths of the other. Hence, using multiple methods, the results converge or corroborate one another, strengthening the validity of the findings (Greene et al., 1989).

Triangulation

JOURNAL OF
TRIANGULATION

Triangulation means combining several qualitative methods or combining quantitative and qualitative methods. Combining methods allows for one method compensating for the weaknesses or blind spots of the other, but the different methods remain autonomous, operating side by side (Flick, 2006). Triangulation which combines quantitative and qualitative methods can focus on a single case, in which the same people complete a questionnaire and are also interviewed. The answers from both data sets are combined and compared.

Complementarity

In a complementarity mixed methods study, quantitative and qualitative methods are combined to measure overlapping but also different elements of a phenomenon. This contrasts with triangulation which is using different methods to assess the same conceptual phenomenon. So, for example, in an educational study, a qualitative interview could be used to measure a group of students' educational aspirations and the influences on these aspirations; a quantitative questionnaire could then be used to explore the nature, level and perceived ranking of participants' aspirations. Hence, the two measures are assessing similar as well as different aspects of the aspirations concept.

COMPLEMEN-
TARITY IN
HEALTH
RESEARCH

Development

Here the results of one method are used to inform the development of the second. For instance, taking the example in the section above, a quantitative survey could be used to identify groups of respondents with contrasting educational aspirations. These purposive samples could then be followed up for in-depth qualitative interviews.

Initiation

In contrast to triangulation which seeks to combine methods towards convergence, initiation uses mixed methods to uncover paradoxes, new perspectives and contradictions. The focus of initiation, then, is the generation of new insights which may lead to the reframing of research questions. In the words of Rossman and Wilson 'a feeling of a creative leap' (1985: 637).

Expansion

Expansion uses mixed methods to broaden and widen the range of a study. In the evaluation of a training programme, for example, quantitative methods could be used to assess programme outcomes, but qualitative interviews to explore the perspectives of participants and the group processes taking place within the programme.

ON THE WEB 8.2

Take a look at the following website that offers a glossary of mixed methods research concepts as well as links to Web resources, training programmes and conferences:

http://www.fiu.edu/~bridges/

Table 8.3   Purposes of mixed methods evaluation design

Purpose	Rationale
Triangulation: Seeks convergence, corroboration, correspondence of results from different methods.	To increase the validity of constructs by counteracting or maximizing the heterogeneity of irrelevant sources of variance attributable to inherent method bias, inquirer bias or biases in inquiry context.
Complementarity: Seeks elaboration, enhancement, illustration, clarification of results of one method with the results from the other method.	To increase the meaningfulness and validity of constructs by capitalizing on inherent method strengths and counteracting inherent method biases.
Development: Seeks to use the results of one method to help or inform the other method.	To increase the validity of constructs and inquiry results by capitalizing on inherent method strengths.
Initiation: Seeks the discovery of paradox and contradiction, new perspectives, the recasting of questions or the results from one method with questions or results from the other method.	To increase the breadth and depth of inquiry results and interpretations by analysing them from the different perspectives of different methods and paradigms.
Expansion: Seeks to extend the breadth and range of inquiry by using different methods from different inquiry components.	To increase the scope of inquiry by selecting the methods most appropriate for multiple inquiry components.

Source: Adapted from Greene et al., 1989

LOOKING AT MIXED METHODS RESEARCH CRITICALLY

Fielding and Fielding (1986) call attention to the fact that researchers should not always assume that mixed methods are of benefit. What is important is that at the end of a mixed methods project, the end product should be more than the sum of the individual quantitative and qualitative parts (Bryman, 2007b). This, however, may not always be the case. Researchers, for example, may misinterpret commonalities and differences when data sets are collected using incompatible methods. The mere convergence of research results from quantitative and qualitative methods does not necessarily assure validity (Bryman, 2007a). Another source of discrepancy is related to measurement. Quantitative studies may rely on pre-existing standardized measurement scales. Although these may have been satisfactorily tested by researchers in previous studies for reliability, they may not correspond sufficiently with the constructs being measured. As a result, between group differences can emerge in the qualitative study, but not be found in the quantitative.

From a merely practical perspective, collecting both quantitative and qualitative data can be expensive (Krahn et al., 1995). Adding, say, interviews or participant observation to a quantitative study increases the time required for both participants and the researcher. Problems can also arise in trying to synthesize the findings and interpretations from the two approaches (see Case Study 8.3). Sometimes, for example, puzzling and quite discrepant findings can emerge, adding more complexity rather than validation and congruence. One reason that such discrepancies may arise is the wording of questions. Qualitative research uses more open-ended questions, whereas quantitative research tries to elicit numerical responses. It is quite possible, then, that each type of question elicits different perceptions on the part of respondents and therefore different recollections. 'Obtained responses then address related but different issues and are not easily blended to form a single, well-integrated interpretation' (Krahn et al., 1995: 208).

It is perhaps because of these kinds of difficulties that Bryman (2006) in an analysis of mixed methods articles, found that in many cases the quantitative and qualitative elements had barely been integrated at all. In another study involving interviews with mixed methods researchers, Bryman (2007b) found a host of reasons why many admitted problems in achieving integration of their findings. Some researchers, for example, tended to emphasize one set of findings rather than another, usually because of a bias towards one methodological position. Others admitted that there was a lack of integration because of variations in time-lines, with the qualitative phase often lagging behind the quantitative. Bryman (2007b) concludes that there is still considerable confusion concerning how mixed methods findings can be integrated. Giddings (2006) takes this further, arguing that mixed methods are nothing more than 'positivism dressed in drag' (2006: 198). Rather than offering the 'best of both worlds', mixed methods finds itself located within the thinking of positivism because it rarely reflects a constructionist or subjectivist view of the world. Thinking is planned in advance, designs are set in place and protocols followed. Qualitative methodological designs that focus on meaning, symbolism and the power of words are marginalized. In the next section we look at how quantitative and qualitative methods can be genuinely integrated.

TOP TIP 8.1

If you are undertaking a dissertation as part of a Masters level programme, think very carefully before you embark on a mixed methods design. Often the timescales for completion of dissertations are very tight and using a mixed methods approach might add to your time problems, particularly if your design uses methods sequentially rather than concurrently. Consult with your supervisor for advice. For those undertaking doctoral or post-doctoral studies, these kinds of issues are less relevant since more time is usually available.

GRAY ON
USING MIXED
METHODS

TYPES OF MIXED METHODS DESIGN

Quantitative and qualitative methods can be used interdependently (and in a range of different sequences) or independently, focusing either on the same research question or different questions. Whatever design is chosen will depend on the kinds of research questions asked, and how the combination of methods can bring added dimensions to the research.

Design 1 (see Figure 8.3) begins with an exploratory, qualitative framework which helps towards the identification and classification of themes and concepts.

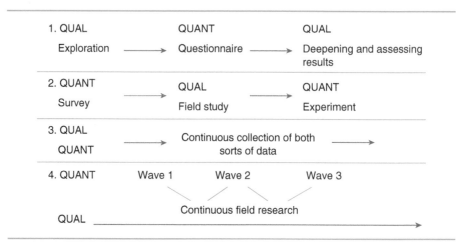

Figure 8.3 Four mixed methods models

These in turn help towards the development of a quantitative questionnaire. The questionnaire findings are then deepened and tested by the next round of qualitative research. Design 2 begins with an initial survey which helps to point the fieldworker to phenomena of importance. A qualitative stage then helps to establish and deepen understanding of the phenomenon. A quantitative experiment is then designed to test some resulting, perhaps competing, hypotheses. In Design 3 both quantitative and qualitative methods are used in an integrated fashion, as needed to generate an understanding of the case, while Design 4 demonstrates what Miles and Huberman (1994) call a multiwave survey. The first survey draws attention to what the qualitative fieldworker must look for, the findings of which inform and modify the next wave of quantitative research. We will now examine a number of designs in depth, some being illustrated by a Case Study.

Qualitative then quantitative

This is a common approach to mixed methods design, and occurs when the results of a qualitative study are used to inform the quantitative research phase. This design is used in circumstances where relatively little or nothing is known about the research setting or research problems. In such a situation, it would be unfeasible and impractical to design a questionnaire, since the constructs being measured are either unknown or not sufficiently understood. The qualitative study, then, explores, identifies and can provide clarity about the kinds of variables requiring further investigation.

As Darlington and Scott (2002) comment, this qualitative and quantitative design has sometimes led to the perception among some researchers that the qualitative phase is somehow inferior to the quantitative, but this should not be seen as the case. Instead, the qualitative stage should be seen as having a developmental purpose (see Table 8.3). Although one method might be more prominent than the other, it is still the case that both methods have a specific purpose and therefore value.

CASE STUDY 8.1

Mixed methods: Qualitative then quantitative

A study reported by Laurie (1992) illustrates some of the benefits but also some of the challenges of using qualitative followed by quantitative methods. She describes the Household Allocative Systems Project (HASP) which formed part of the preliminary work for the British Household Panel Study (BHPS) which sought to identify the allocative systems that exist within UK households through studying the values, attitudes, beliefs and behaviours of household members. The second objective was to pre-test a short questionnaire that was to be incorporated into a larger BHPS questionnaire schedule.

Qualitative techniques were used by HASP to identify the key indicators and to clarify concepts to be used in the more extensive quantitative study. The quantitative research was to provide data, showing how changes in income, labour market behaviour, housing conditions, education and health, etc. influence patterns of consumer spending. Because the data sets are longitudinal, they were to show how events can have an effect on 'outcomes', that is, changing patterns of consumption. However, while the analysis was to show the direction of change and causality, it would say little about the process through which the change occurred. Shifts in motivation and perception often occur in quite a subtle manner rather than being shifted decisively by just one event. These processes are more easily accessed through qualitative research – 'the subjective interpretation of events and social processes ... are not easily measured in the context of a structured questionnaire' (Laurie, 1992: 148).

Hence, the qualitative element of the research was conducted in two main stages. The first stage consisted of unstructured qualitative interviews, group discussions and the pre-test of the structured questionnaire with a sample of 19 married or cohabiting couples. The second stage consisted of further unstructured interviews and group discussions with members of a sample of multi-adult households.

The qualitative data revealed that each member of a household legitimates their claim to household funds on the basis of the use to which they are put. For women, this is strongly linked to their labour market status. For example, women who are dependent upon a sole main earner, feel that they have the least legitimate claim to spend money other than on what was defined as 'household expenditure'. For example, if they spent money on a new dress, they would hide it in a wardrobe for a few weeks before saying, truthfully, that they bought it a few weeks ago. Alternatively, they would admit to a price lower than what they actually paid. Where women were earning and contributing to the household budget, these feelings of guilt were much less pronounced.

It was found that the qualitative research greatly aided conceptual clarification, particularly through the negative cases which revealed the shortcomings of the emerging conceptual framework. In addition, the qualitative data provided the researchers with greater insights into the types of household arrangements, helping them to analyse the quantitative data with greater understanding.

Source: Adapted from Laurie, 1992

ACTIVITY 8.1

Case Study 8.1 identifies some of the very real benefits of combining a qualitative and quantitative design. What else does it tell us about the kinds of monetary and time resources needed in this type of design?

Quantitative then qualitative

This occurs when the findings of a quantitative study are used to develop the qualitative stage. As noted in Design 2 above, a quantitative study could be used to identify important themes that qualitative fieldwork could then deepen. However, as Bryman (1992) points out, it is more usual that a quantitative survey is used to identify groups of respondents with strongly contrasting views about a subject. These polarized groups can then be used for follow-up qualitative interviews to gain an in-depth understanding of why these differences exist.

— CASE STUDY 8.2 —

Mixed methods: Quantitative then qualitative

In a study of the social and sexual relationships of American couples, Blumstein and Schwartz (1983) collected postal questionnaires from 12,000 individuals. The researchers, however, wanted more detailed data and conducted in-depth interviews with 300 couples. For the qualitative research four types of group were selected: married couples, heterosexual couples who lived together (called cohabiting), gay males or gay females. As Bryman (1992) comments, this approach to selection allowed for a range of contrasting groups to be identified. From the 300 interviews, 20 were presented as detailed case studies, with five cases from each of the four group types, providing rich ethnographic data. The qualitative research explored how these couples dealt with a broad range of issues including managing money, dividing housework and dealing with sexual jealousy.

— ACTIVITY 8.2 —

In Case Study 8.2 the detailed case studies were selected through stratified sampling (five cases from each group type (married, cohabiting, etc.)). What other approach could have been taken to selecting the sample for the presentation of detailed cases?

Quantitative and qualitative concurrently

COMBINED
STUDY

Mixed designs do not always have to be interdependent. Sometimes quantitative and qualitative elements can be conducted quite independently and not in any particular order – hence, they could be carried out concurrently, sequentially, with qualitative before quantitative or vice versa. Different methods could be used to address the same research question or focus on different aspects of the research. The following example shows a research project in which the qualitative data did not neatly 'mesh' with the quantitative information, but extended it and provided a context for trying to make sense of it.

Krahn et al. (1995) describe a longitudinal study of parents' adjustment to the handicap of their firstborn child, with particular reference to parental perception of and satisfaction with the initial informing process. In gathering the data, parents participated in a lengthy structured interview, usually conducted in their home, which included open questions about the diagnostic experience and quantitative ratings about the professional who informed the parents about the diagnosis of their child. These ratings were based upon variables such as: 'warmth', 'rapport', 'patience' and 'ability to listen' the elements being measured on a 5-point **Likert scale**.

As part of the data analysis, grounded theory was applied using the **constant comparison method** of Glaser and Strauss (1967) – see Chapter 23. As a result, nine main themes emerged from the data, including: 'communication and information', 'characteristics of the informing professional', 'pacing the informa- tion process', and 'when told'. Parents' quantitative ratings of the professionals were generally highly positive. Based upon a maximum rating of 45, mothers gave a mean rating of 36.4 and fathers a rating of 35.3. The quantitative ratings, then, suggested that parents rated the professionals positively, with most rating them very positively. However, analysis of the qualitative data told a slightly different story. In the qualitative data, parents expressed both praise and criticism. More puzzling, some parents were highly critical of some of the professionals but still gave high quantitative ratings. For example, one mother gave the informing profes- sional a rating of 43 (out of 45), but when asked what she liked about the informing process replied: 'Nothing. He was organized, but not good about explaining detail'.

It seems that both quantitative and qualitative methods were useful here in exploring parental experiences of the diagnostic informing process. The opportu- nity for parents to tell their own stories revealed a depth and complexity of expe- rience that would have been difficult to capture using quantitative ratings alone. The discrepancy between the quantitative ratings and qualitative data suggests that the process of asking them about their likes and dislikes prompted a more careful scrutiny of their remembered experiences. Case Study 8.3 provides another illustration which shows how quantitative and qualitative studies can be used so that one method can deepen and validate the other.

CONSTANT
COMPARISON

━ CASE STUDY 8.3 ━

Mixed methods: Quantitative and qualitative concurrently

Qualitative research can provide an alternative methodology to quantitative. Bartunek and Myeong-Gu (2002) describe a Finnish study by Kinnunen et al. (2000) which addressed two primary research questions: (1) What are the organizational factors that influence employees' perceived job insecurity; and (2) What is the effect of the perceived job insecurity on employees' well-being at the organizational level? The Finnish researchers investigated these questions in three locations, reflecting different economic conditions in three major sectors of Finnish indus- try, namely: a factory in the export industry, a domestic bank, and a healthcare department in the public sector. In conducting the study, the researchers constructed a quantitative questionnaire based upon constructs well known in the literature, comprising antecedents of job insecurity (organizational communication and a restorative strategy), three indices of perceived job inse- curity (powerlessness, importance of changes and the likelihood of changes) and four outcomes of perceived job insecurity (organizational commitment, colleague relations, superior relations and organizational efficiency). The variables were measured using combinations of questionnaire items that formed reliable scales. The findings included: (1) perceived job insecurity varies with gender and organizations but not with time; (2) managers' use of restorative strategies decreases perceived job insecurity; (3) perceived job insecurity negatively affects colleague relationships, employees' relationships with their line managers, and perceived organizational efficiency.

(Continued)

(Continued)

Bartunek and Myeong-Gu (2002), however, argue that a potential weakness of quantitative studies like this, is the assumption that the predefined variables used have the same meanings for actors across multiple settings. Kinnunen et al. (2000) pre-selected their variables, based upon previously developed theories and scales. But what if local meanings differ from researchers' meanings (particularly if a scale developed on one continent is used to assess experiences on another continent)? And what if different respondents' meanings differ from each other? Even in the literature there is no unanimous agreement as to the precise definition of job insecurity. Bartunek and Myeong-Gu discuss how this same study could have been explored using a qualitative methodology, arguing that such an approach allows researchers to attend to the depth of local actors' understandings of job insecurity.

They do not argue that academic definitions of constructs should be replaced by those of local organizational members. What is important is that these constructs are explored in a local context in order to validate them. This process can also lead to the discovery of new dimensions that have not been used in previously developed scales. Even if local validation only indicates consensus with researchers' definitions, this helps to 'flesh out the phenomenological experience of the construct in the local setting' (Bartunek and Myeong-Gu, 2002: 239). This is because questionnaire studies leave out the dynamics of sense-making in a local context. Qualitative approaches can help to provide an understanding of the underlying dynamics of meaning-making, and how constructs evolve. Finally, rather than aggregate data across sites, qualitative researchers are more likely to take each site as an individual case, seeing each organization as having its own unique environment and dynamic history. Hence, a qualitative study would seek to compare the similarities and differences in patterns of interactions between the organizations, the meanings associated with key variables and their influences on organizational outcomes. Hence, the qualitative methodology would validate but potentially widen and deepen the findings of the quantitative study.

Source: Bartunek and Myeong-Gu, 2002

ACTIVITY 8.3

Consider what should be done when the quantitative and qualitative data produce different or even conflicting results. Should one set of data be relied upon more than the other? Should one set of data be discarded? Should further data be gathered and if so, how?

▷ **TOP TIP 8.2** ◁

INTERVIEWS
ABOUT
RESEARCH
METHODS

Many researchers are trained in, or come to adopt, either the quantitative or qualitative paradigm. Hence, they often lack experience and in-depth understanding in the paradigm that is new to them. New skills have to be learned and old habits put in check. Miles and Huberman (1994) recommend that those who are attempting to use mixed methods for the first time should make use of a 'friendly stranger' (1994: 43). A more modern phrase would probably be a 'critical friend', defined by Costa and Kallick as: 'a trusted person who asks provocative questions, provides data to be examined through another lens, and offers critiques of a person's work as a friend' (1993: 50). The critical friend should, ideally, be someone who has both theoretical and working experience of using mixed methods research. So, for example, this might be your academic supervisor, another academic in your department, or a fellow researcher who has undertaken a mixed methods study. Also, try typing 'mixed methods conference' into a search engine to identify where mixed methods research is being showcased and debated.

Summary

- Quantitative and qualitative research methods have traditionally been associated with conflicting research paradigms based upon quite different epistemological positions.
- Many modern researchers, however, recognize that quantitative and qualitative approaches can be combined into a mixed methods design.
- Mixed methods approaches can be based upon different types of research question, sampling procedures, data collection methods or approaches to data analysis.
- Mixed methods designs are flexible and can include sequential designs with quantitative methods preceding qualitative, or vice versa, or concurrent designs.
- Mixed methods designs should be based upon the kinds of questions being addressed and how the design can aid in the answering of these questions.

FURTHER READING

Creswell, J.W. and Clark, V.P. (2011) *Designing and Conducting Mixed Methods Research*, 2nd edn. Thousand Oaks, CA: Sage. Aimed mainly at graduates and researchers, this book usefully contains four complete published articles that exemplify different mixed methods approaches.

Tashakkori, A. and Teddlie, C. (2009) (eds) *Handbook of Mixed Methods in Social and Behavioral Research*, 3rd edn. Thousand Oaks, CA: Sage. A lively mix of contributors offering a diverse range of perspectives from a variety of disciplines.

Tashakkori, A. and Creswell, J.W. (eds) *Journal of Mixed Methods Research*. First published in January 2007, this journal contains contributions from some of the scholars who have molded mixed methods research into the 'third methodological movement'. A mixture of conceptual articles that tackle the philosophy, methodology and methods in mixed research, and reports on empirical studies applying mixed methods.

JOURNAL RESOURCES

Lund, T. (2012) 'Combining qualitative and quantitative approaches: Some arguments for mixed methods research', *Scandinavian Journal of Educational Research*, 56(2): 155–165. Elaborates four general advantages of the mixed methods approach and proposes a five-phase evaluation design that demonstrates the usefulness of mixed methods research.

Malina, M.A., Nørreklit, H.S.O. and Selto, F.H. (2011) 'Lessons learned: Advantages and disadvantages of mixed method research', *Qualitative Research in Accounting & Management*, 8(1): 59–71. Describes the methodological lessons learned while conducting a series of mixed methods longitudinal studies.

Ihantola, E-M. and Kihn, L-A. (2011) 'Threats to validity and reliability in mixed methods accounting research', *Qualitative Research in Accounting & Management*, 8 (1): 39–58. Addresses the specific threats to quality that come to the fore when inferences from the quantitative and qualitative components of the study are combined to form meta-inferences. A comprehensive list provided of threats to internal and contextual validity.

Vandenberg, H. and Hall, W. (2011) 'Critical ethnography: Extending attention to bias and reinforcement of dominant power relations', *Nurse Researcher*, 18(3): 25–30. In this article, which explores qualitative, ethnographic research, the concern is to address potential power

Billiet, J. and Loosveldt, G. (1988) 'Improvement of the quality of responses to factual survey questions by interview training', *Public Opinion Quarterly*, 52(2) 190–211. Here, in quantitative research, the emphasis is on discovering whether training interviewers minimizes the ways in which their use of questions biases responses between the researcher and the researched.

SUMMARY OF WEB LINKS

http://www.fiu.edu/~bridges/

9

SAMPLING STRATEGIES

CHAPTER INTRODUCTION

Chapter outline

Probability sampling   209

Non-probability sampling   215

Mixed methods sampling   225

Sampling hard to reach
populations   228

Sample size – how much is
enough?   230

Keywords

Sampling strategies

Probability sampling

Non-probability sampling

Mixed methods sampling

Sampling hard to reach populations

Sample size

— **Chapter objectives** —

After reading this chapter you will be able to:

- Distinguish between probability and non-probability approaches to sampling.
- Describe the implications of using non-probability sampling for external validity.
- Select from a taxonomy of quantitative and qualitative sampling schemes.
- Integrate quantitative and qualitative sampling approaches into a mixed methods sampling design.
- Sample hard to reach populations.
- Know when to continue sampling and when to stop.

In this chapter we will discuss the process of selecting samples from a population, a population being any group that shares a common set of traits (Black, 1999). So a population could be all the history teachers in a country, all female cyclists in a town, or pupils in a specific city under the age of 12 who have special needs. In Chapter 6 we explored sampling in the context of quantitative methods and also ways of actually selecting random samples using either random numbers tables or Web tools. In this chapter we will broaden the discussion and explore a wide range of sampling strategies available in both quantitative and qualitative methods. The careful sampling of participants and data sources is a key component of any research study. Indeed, in research 'sampling is destiny' (Kemper, Stringfield and Teddlie, 2003: 275). In quantitative research (as discussed in Chapter 6) this primarily involves the use of probability sampling techniques which involve the selection of a relatively large number of units from the population, or from specific sub-groups (strata), in a random manner where each unit has an equal chance of being selected. Random selection helps to achieve (but does not always guarantee) a sample that is representative of the population being researched. One of the primary aims of quantitative designs is producing results which can be generalized to a larger population. In qualitative research the primary aim is not usually generalization, but the need to select respondents and data that are likely to generate robust, rich and deep levels of understanding (Thompson, 1999), that is, people who possess the characteristics or who live in circumstances relevant to the phenomenon being studied (Mays and Pope, 1996).

SAMPLING

In qualitative research, sample selection will have a profound impact on the ultimate quality of the research, one reason why a considerable amount of this chapter is devoted to this theme. Sampling design in qualitative research varies according to the paradigm and research epistemologies adopted (Creswell, 2002). Phenomenological research, for example, tends to involve purposively selected individuals who tend to share common experiences so that detailed patterns of meaning and relationships can be identified (Moustakas, 1994). Ethnographic researchers use layers of sampling decisions to achieve rich and thick descriptions of cultures, community or social context (Lofland and Lofland, 2006). In case study research, the researcher makes the vital decision on which cases to select, and may use any number of probability and non-probability sampling approaches. However, while these qualitative research approaches encompass a range of

Image 9.1   A population – in research terms, a group that shares common characteristics

research traditions, there are a number of discernible common threads across the approaches in that qualitative sampling is:

- Naturalistic, that is, it takes place in ordinary settings where people live and work
- Unified, in that there are common threads between the questions, goals and purpose of the research
- Emergent, in that sampling strategies and the goals of the research are based on ongoing reflections, data analysis, provisional hypotheses and often further sampling
- Serial, that is, choices about sampling are based upon data collected from previous samples

As we will see, just as there are many qualitative methods, there are also many types of qualitative sampling strategies. In contrast, approaches to quantitative sampling are less diverse, but no less important.

PROBABILITY SAMPLING

As we have just seen, probability sampling is one of the defining features of quantitative research. Chapter 6 discussed probability sampling which involves selecting random samples of subjects from a given population, a population being the total number of possible units or elements that are part of the study. Samples are chosen on the basis that they are representative of the population as a whole, in terms of key characteristics. Confidence in the representative nature of a sample makes it possible to make inferences from the results to the larger population. For example, in undertaking clinical trials of a 'super drug' to cure dementia, the sample would comprise older people rather than teenagers, as it is the former who tend to suffer from the disease. Probability sampling includes random sampling, stratified sampling, cluster sampling and stage sampling.

Random sampling

SIMPLE
RANDOM
SAMPLING

This relies on taking a completely random sample of the population (as in Activity 6.4 in Chapter 6) and is used when it is believed that the population is relatively homogenous with respect to the research questions of interest. It relies, however, on having access to a complete list of the population (the sampling frame is equal to the population) so this may not always be practicable. With simple random sampling (SRS), as was demonstrated in Chapter 6, we can use either a random numbers table or (as in Activity 6.4) an online number generating tool to generate numbers which are then applied to numbers assigned to the elements in a sampling frame. Let's say that we want to interview 40 out of the 400 students in a school. Each square in Figure 9.1 represents one of the students, with each square being numbered from 1, top left, to 400 bottom right. Simple random sampling might lead to the sort of selection as represented in Figure 9.1. However, even a casual glance shows that the distribution of units is uneven. Say that the larger squares in Figure 9.1 (each with 25 small squares) represent a class. We can see that random sampling has led to five pupils being selected in one class and only one pupil in three classes. To avoid this over-sampling and under-sampling, we might adopt systemic sampling (next) or stratified random sampling (below).

Systematic sampling

In systematic sampling every kth element of a sampling frame is chosen for the sample. So, if the intention was to select a sample of 40 from a list of 400, every tenth element would be chosen. K is called the sampling interval, with the first element being chosen randomly. So, if the first randomly selected number was 3, we would then take this and then the 13th unit from the list, then the 23rd, etc. until we have our 40 randomly selected elements from the list (as in Figure 9.2).

Stratified random sampling

STRATIFIED
SAMPLING

Stratified random sampling represents a modification of simple random sampling and systematic sampling (Dattalo, 2010). However, stratified random sampling is a method for achieving a greater degree of representativeness and for reducing the degree of sampling error (recall Chapter 6). Recall that sampling error is reduced by increasing the size of the sample and by increasing the homogeneity of elements within the sample. Stratified random sampling, then, consists of taking a random sample from various strata. Taking our school example again, each of the 16 classes in the school represents a stratum and we randomly select three pupils from each strata (class) as in Figure 9.3.

An advantage of stratified random sampling is that it increases the likelihood of key groups being in the sample while still ensuring an element of random selection. The disadvantage is that very often the researcher will not have sufficient information on which to base the strata (Fife-Schaw, 2000). For example, if conducting research using income levels to create the strata sub-groups, organizations and individuals are often reluctant to reveal this kind of data as it felt to be confidential.

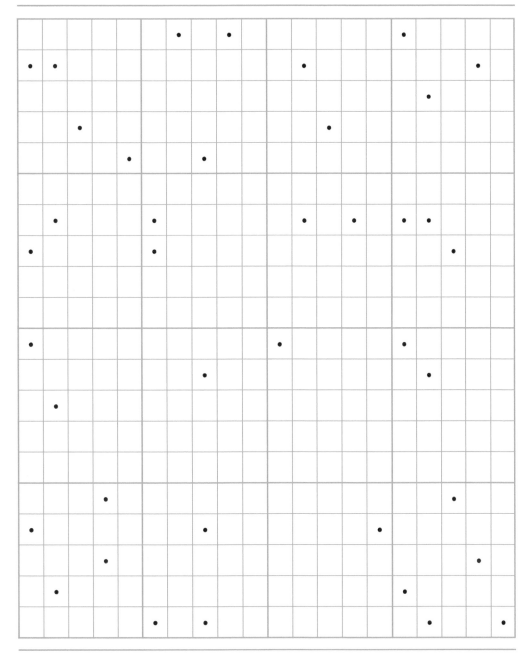

Figure 9.1 Simple random sample

Cluster sampling

CLUSTER
SAMPLING

Cluster sampling acknowledges the difficulty in sampling a population as a whole, especially when convenient sampling frames are not available. For example, in an educational study, you might not be granted access to a college's enrolment list. Instead, you could obtain a list of all the classes in the college and randomly select

Start

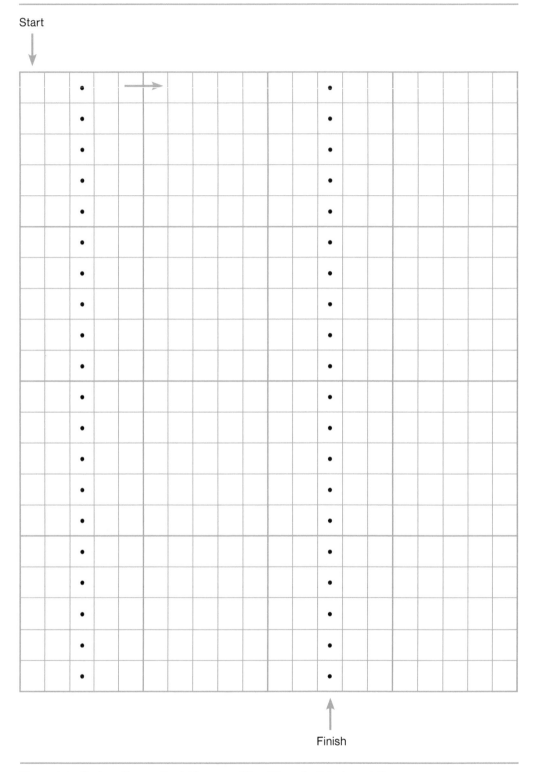

Finish

Figure 9.2 Systematic sampling taking every *k*th unit from the listed population

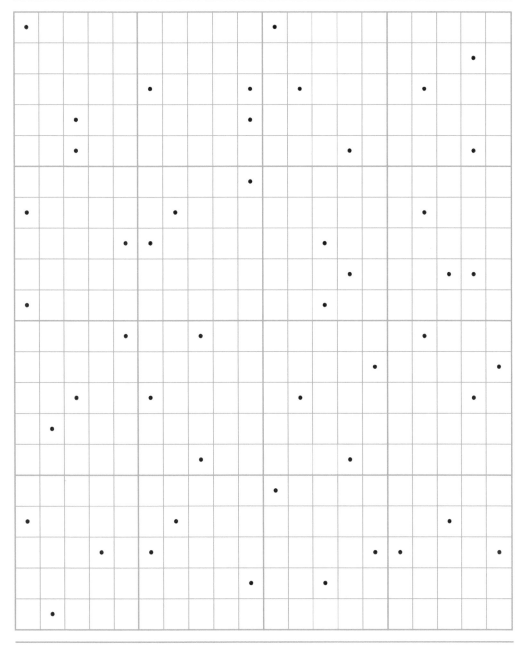

Figure 9.3   Stratified random sampling, randomly selecting three units from each strata

a percentage of them. You would use all the students from these classes as your sample (this is the cluster element of cluster sampling). Hence, in Figure 9.4, three classes have been randomly selected from the 16 classes in the college and all the students from these three classes used for the study. For the purposes of increasing accuracy, it is better to have a large number of small clustering units than a small

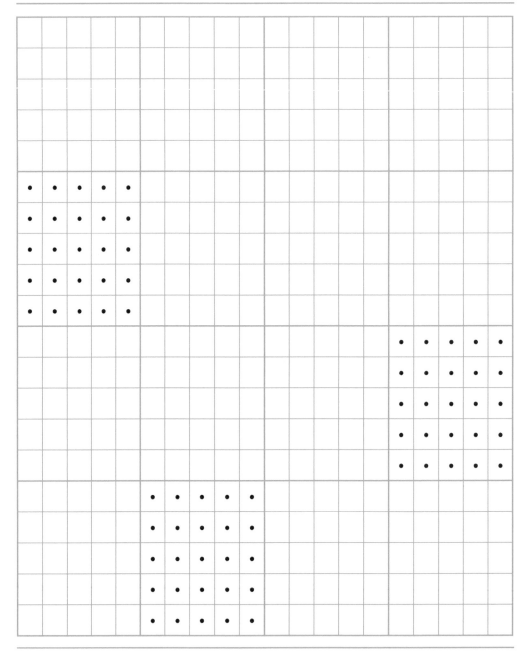

Figure 9.4   Cluster sampling

number of large units (Fife-Schaw, 2000). So, in the college example, it would be better to cluster on the basis of individual colleges than, say, clustering on the basis of the educational authorities that oversee the colleges. A form of cluster sampling, geographical clustering, is common in many large scale surveys. So, rather than randomly sampling every household in a city, a number of streets are randomly selected and all households in those streets used for the study. Although this runs the risk that some of the streets might not be representative of the city, it is usually a more cost-effective approach.

Cluster sampling is useful because it is not always possible to get access to a comprehensive sampling frame. One of the disadvantages of cluster sampling is that it is possible to inadvertently select clusters that contain very few people. As Dattalo (2010) also points out, whereas simple stratified sampling is subject to a single sampling error, two-stage cluster sampling is prone to two sampling errors. First, the initial sample of clusters will represent the population of clusters only within a range of sampling error; secondly, the sample of elements within a cluster will represent all the elements in that cluster within a range of sampling error. So, in our college example, the researcher runs the risk of selecting a disproportionate number of classes where overall performance is below the norm, and then selecting within those classes a disproportionate number of disruptive and poorly performing students. As with random sampling, sampling error is reduced by increasing the size of each cluster and by increasing the homogeneity within each cluster.

CLUSTER
ANALYSIS
EXAMPLE PAPER

Multi-stage sampling

Multi-stage sampling is an extension of cluster sampling that involves successive random selections at more than one stage. The population represents the primary stage beneath which there lies the second and third stages, etc. So, for example, a researcher wants to select 1,000 schools within a country using multi-stage sampling. Firstly, within a country of 50 states (the primary stage), 5 states are randomly selected. At the second stage, within these 5 states, 10 districts are selected. At the third stage, 5 cities within each of the 10 districts are randomly selected. Finally, at the fourth stage, 4 schools within each city are selected, making a total of 1,000 schools. Typically, multi-stage sampling is used for large-scale studies that may address large geographical areas (Kothari, 2004).

MULTI-STAGE
SAMPLING

NON-PROBABILITY SAMPLING

Patton (1990) suggests 15 different purposive strategies, each dependent on the purpose of the study. Teddlie and Yu (2007) have taken these and organized them into three broader purposive categories, namely, sampling to achieve representativeness or comparability, sampling special or unique cases, and sequential sampling. To purposive sampling, Teddlie and Yu (2007) add two more approaches, convenience and mixed methods sampling which are added to Figure 9.5. Sekaran and Bougie (2013) argue that non-probability sampling can be divided into purposive and quota sampling – hence quota sampling is added to the taxonomy in Figure 9.5. Each scheme is then discussed below in detail.

Quota sampling

Quota sampling is similar to random stratified sampling in that both select units from the strata chosen. However, in the case of random stratified sampling this is done (as the name suggests) randomly. In quota sampling researchers use

QUOTA
SAMPLING

1. **Non-probability sampling: Quota**

2. **Non-probability sampling: Purposive**

   a. Sampling to achieve representativeness or comparability

      i. Typical case sampling

      ii. Extreme or deviant case sampling (outlier sampling)

      iii. Intensity sampling

      iv. Maximum variation sampling

      v. Homogenous sampling

      vi. Stratified purposeful sampling

      vii. Random purposeful sampling

   b. Sampling special or unique cases

      i. Critical case sampling

      ii. Sampling politically important cases

      iii. Criterion sampling

   c. Sequential sampling

      i. Theoretical sampling

      ii. Confirming or disconfirming case sampling

      iii. Opportunistic sampling

      iv. Snowball sampling

   d. Sampling using multiple purposive techniques

3. **Non-probability sampling: Convenience**

4. **Mixed methods sampling**

   a. Basic mixed methods sampling

   b. Sequential mixed methods sampling

   c. Concurrent mixed methods sampling

   d. Multilevel mixed methods sampling

   e. Combination of mixed methods sampling strategies

Figure 9.5   A taxonomy of non-probability sampling schemes

Source: Adapted from Patton. 1990, Teddlie and Yu, 2007 and Sekaran, 2010

non-random sampling methods to gather data from a stratum until the required quota, fixed in advance by the researcher, is fulfilled. So, the researcher may choose to stratify the study according to social class, and go on selecting subjects until each of the strata is filled to a chosen level. An advantage of quota sampling is that each group is of equal size which can be important for certain inferential statistical tests (see Chapter 22). The disadvantage is that the size of certain strata may not accurately reflect their proportion in the overall population. For example, production workers outnumber managers in most industrial organizations. Lempp and Seale (2004) describe the use of random and quota sampling when investigating the attitudes of undergraduate medical students to the teaching they received. The researchers stratified by sex and ethnicity, with the whole school population in a UK medical school as a sampling frame. Recruitment was stopped when saturation was reached for the key study themes, attitudes towards the hidden curriculum.

→ **TOP TIP 9.1** ←

It is not always possible to know who is representative of the key criteria in a study and who is not. Hence, having chosen the key criteria in advance, go on contacting respondents. If, after the interview or survey, you find they are eligible for the study, count them into the relevant sub-group. If they are not eligible, discard the data or put it to one side. Go on sampling until the sub-groups are full to the pre-determined size.

Purposive sampling

As Patton (1990) comments, the approach to sampling is perhaps one of the most distinguishing features between quantitative and qualitative research. While quantitative research, typically, relies on large samples, qualitative research uses small samples or even single cases (N = 1), selected *purposefully* on the basis that they are information-rich cases. Purposive samples, then, are used when particular people, events or settings are chosen because they are known to provide important information that could not be gained from other sampling designs (Maxwell, 1997). In this kind of approach, the researcher exercises a degree of judgement about who will provide the best perspectives on the phenomenon of interest and then invites these participants into the study. However, a disadvantage of purposive sampling is that the researcher may inadvertently omit a vital characteristic on which to select the sample, or may be subconsciously biased in selecting the sample. For example, in conducting a study on gender bias in the recruitment of senior managers, a researcher selects a disproportionate number of women who feel they have been discriminated against (with whom the researcher feels empathy) rather than women who have 'made it' to the top.

PURPOSIVE
SAMPLING

Sampling to achieve representativeness or comparability

Sampling to achieve representativeness tries to identify cases that are typical or representative of a dimension of interest or seeks to achieve comparability across different types of cases on a dimension of interest. Typical case sampling would seek to identify cases that are typical (that is, representative) of the dimension being investigated. But qualitative researchers are also interested in extreme or deviant cases – hence, extreme or deviant case sampling – because these extreme cases generate interesting contrasts with other cases, thereby allowing for comparability across cases (Teddlie and Yu, 2007).

PURPOSIVE
SAMPLING
TYPES

Typical case sampling

Typical cases are chosen because they are not in any way extreme or deviant or unusual – they represent and are 'typical' of key aspects of a phenomenon. The researcher, of course, may have to get confirmation from others (for example, gatekeepers or other key informants) that a case is, indeed, typical of a category of cases. For example, within a teaching institution, researchers could study 'typical' successful students in order to understand what factors make for success, successful, say, being taken to mean those in the top quartile of examination results. Note that since the focus is on 'typically' successful students, the study might not include those who are on the extreme end of the successful scale, that is, those who are performing exceptionally well (say, the top decile). These might constitute part of an extreme sample (see next).

Extreme or deviant case sampling (outlier sampling)

Extreme or deviant cases are selected because they are unusual or special in some way. For example, a study might be interested in hospital waiting lists and identify those hospitals where waiting lists are particularly long and compare these to hospitals where the waiting lists are very short. The point of extreme cases is that they help to identify the conditions or features that might explain the differences in outcomes. In the hospital case, the variables that make for shorter waiting times might include better use of computer systems, higher levels of motivation among staff, and a hospital leadership that stresses the significance of shorter waiting times. Often, qualitative schemes will be combined in a study; so, for example, a study might explore typical cases and then contrast them with extreme or deviant cases.

Intensity sampling

An intensity sample consists of information-rich cases that can provide detailed information. They are not, however, extreme or deviant cases. To be able to undertake intensity sampling, prior investigations may be needed to identify such cases. For example, in investigating the challenges of leadership, information-rich cases might include:

- Directors of start-up companies (that often struggle to survive the first few years of trading)
- The Chief Executives of large global corporations (that operate in complex, global markets)
- Leaders of not-for-profit organizations (that struggle to raise money in recessionary times)

Intensity sampling may be used with other sampling methods; for example, typical case sampling could be used with 20 cases, before conducting intensity sampling with five information-rich cases. Heuristic research (recall Chapter 2) exemplifies intensity sampling because the heuristic researcher draws intensely on his or her own personal experiences as part of the data gathering process.

Maximum variation sampling

In maximum variation sampling the researcher selects a diverse range of cases so that common patterns that emerge from this variation can be identified. One of the potential weaknesses of qualitative research is that with small samples comes a lot of heterogeneity, which can be a problem if all the cases are different to each other. However, maximum variation sampling turns this problem into a virtue. Any common patterns that emerge from a maximum variation sample are of particular interest in capturing core values and experiences. For example, when studying crime statistics, the researcher could explore crime rates across inner-city, suburban, and rural areas to identify shared patterns that cut across these quite different cases. The aim of maximum variable sampling, then, is not to highlight differences or extremes (as in extreme case sampling), but to describe central themes across diverse cases.

Homogenous sampling

The purpose of homogenous sampling is to describe a small, homogenous group in depth (Patton, 1990). As we will see in Chapter 18, some researchers prefer homogeneity when selecting participants for focus groups (see Krueger, 1994) because the commonalities within the participant group (for example, age, occupation, social class) help to generate positive group dynamics and discussion. Phenomenological approaches tend to favour the use of homogenous groups or communities who share common experiences and purposes so that patterns and meanings can be identified. For example, in researching the views of those who believe in the paranormal, researchers might join some of their online communities to understand how they perceive and construct their world view.

Stratified purposeful sampling

Each of the strata constitutes a fairly homogenous sample, the purpose being to capture the major variations between the strata. As Patton (1990) warns, this is not the same as stratified sampling in quantitative methods, described above, in that the sample sizes are going to be much smaller and hence less capable of producing generalizations. Trost (1986) offers a stepwise process for developing a stratified purposeful sampling design as follows:

- List a number of independent variables for the purpose of the study.
- Eliminate those variables which are less visible or discernible and keep those that are easily used.
- Decide on the borderlines between variables. For example in a study of 'older workers' what age should be designated 'old' – 50, 55, 60?
- Combine the variables into a sampling table (see Table 9.1). If it becomes clear that there are too many cells (and hence too large a sample for the resources at hand), then reduce some of the variables.
- Recognize that some cells will be empty. For example in a table dealing with women and their children, for women in the 50 to 59 age group, the cell for at least one toddler, although not logically empty, would most likely be empirically empty – researchers should not bother themselves too much in trying to fill it.
- Fill the cells with one or more subjects.

Trost (1986) then offers an example of how a researcher can construct a sampling table (see Table 9.1) for studying the relationship between teenagers and their parents – the so-called 'generation gap' – by studying a variety of relationships and variables. Hence, the table shows a combination of cells for variables such as size of family (single parent/two parent), number of children (one/more than one), housing (apartment/home), family income (high/low) and gender of the teenager (male/female). These variables yield a total of 32 cells. Producing a sampling table adds clarity to sampling design, gets the researcher to think carefully about the number of independent variables, and illustrates clearly the minimum number of cases the study will require.

Table 9.1 Example of sampling table

Type of family	One parent family				Two parent family			
Number of children	One		Two or more		One		Two or more	
Housing	Apt	Home	Apt	Home	Apt	Home	Apt	Home
Family income	L H	L H	L H	L H	L H	L H	L H	L H
Gender of children in the household (teenagers)	f f m m	f f m m	f f m m	f f m m	f f m m	f f m m	f f m m	f f m m

---

→ **TOP TIP 9.2** ←

Taking Table 9.1 as an example, having just one case per cell (16 female and 16 male teenagers) gives a total of 32 cases. In a qualitative study this could mean 32 intensive data gathering interviews, amounting to a considerable effort. Planning for two cases per cell would give 64 cases, probably too many for most qualitative studies. So if it was felt that two or more cases per cell were needed, but time and resources were scarce, one solution would be to reduce the number of independent variables.

Random purposeful sampling

Even though qualitative studies may not take on the size of samples addressed in quantitative research, this does not mean that random sampling approaches are never adopted. According to Patton (1990), randomly selecting even small samples will increase the credibility of a study in the eyes of some. The advantage of this approach is that the cases are selected in advance of the knowledge generated by the study. Hence, there is some evidence of planning rather than just serendipity. However, the outcomes of purposeful random sampling do not permit statistical generalizations in the way that quantitative studies would achieve.

This design is used when there is a very rich pool of potentially information-rich cases available, and no obvious reason for choosing one case above another. For example, after a corporate health and safety programme, 500 people passed a knowledge test and became eligible to be health and safety representatives, while 200 failed. The company wants to know more about the reasons behind why people passed or failed. The numbers here are too large for a purely purposeful sampling strategy. Hence, the following process is adopted:

- Two groups, Pass and Failed candidates have been identified by the quantitative test.
- Each candidate is allotted a number, and these are randomly drawn to select cases. The only stipulation is that each case must meet the criterion that it is information-rich.
- Cases are drawn and explored until researchers are able to make the inferences about passing and failing that they wish to make. This will include reaching some agreement on convergent validity, showing that the quantitative test and the qualitative indicators are measuring the same construct.

Sampling special or unique cases

This approach involves sampling special or rare cases, where the case itself is of importance rather than an overall issue, and involves gaining access to cases that had previously been inaccessible to investigators. For example, in a study of serious crime, researchers might gain access to a convicted murderer who, after many years of proclaiming his innocence, is nearing the end of his life, and decides to 'come clean'.

Critical case sampling

Critical cases are those that can make a point dramatically or are, for whatever reason, particularly important (Patton, 1990). They can sometimes be identified by key informants. A critical case approach might be adopted when the researcher's resources are limited, and it is only possible to select one or a few cases. For example, in investigating 'failing' schools, researchers might choose those that are actually facing closure, rather than ones that are merely delivering poor pupil results.

Sampling politically important cases

Sampling sites or organizations where there are political sensitivities might mean deliberately choosing such samples or deliberately avoiding them. Politically important cases are a variation of critical case sampling. A sociologist, for example, might wish to identify and interview people involved in inner-city riots, a subject that some would see as politically sensitive (particularly if conducted shortly after the events). However, exploring politically sensitive cases offers the potential advantage of providing valuable information for policy makers.

Criterion sampling

In criterion sampling all the cases meet some pre-determined criterion – for example, people with a certain type of disease, or those who have had a particular life experience (such as bereavement). Sometimes, quantitative instruments such as survey questionnaires might identify a set of criteria which are then followed up with a study of cases that meet these criteria. Cases may be chosen because they typify average scores on the quantitative instrument, an approach that would be an example of typical case sampling. But cases can also be chosen that typify extreme scores; these would be examples of extreme or deviant case sampling. Or cases may be identified through the quantitative instrument that show a variable intensity but not extremely, an example of what Patton (2002) terms intensity sampling (Sandelowski, 2000). Participants will be sampled in each scoring category until the point of information redundancy is reached.

Critical incidents can often be a source of criterion sampling, a critical incident being an emotional event that represents a period of intense feelings both at the time and during subsequent reflective interpretation. Cope and Watts (2000), for example, describes a phenomenological study of six business cases in which the entrepreneurs all experienced different kinds and levels of emotional trauma. However, one of the challenges of using critical incidents in a planned, sampling process is that their existence may only become known during the data gathering phase and not before. Key informants may again be necessary to identify suitable cases.

Sequential sampling

Sequential sampling involves a process of gradual sample selection, and is used when the goal of research is to generate theory (theoretical sampling) or the sample evolves as data are being collected. Sequential sampling is one element of mixed methodology sampling discussed later.

SEQUENTIAL
SAMPLING

Theoretical sampling

Here, the researcher samples people, organizations, events or incidents on the basis that they may help to develop theoretical constructs. As we will see in Chapter 23, theoretical sampling is a central tenet of grounded theory and it is difficult to discuss one without the other. Theoretical sampling was first developed by Glaser and Strauss (1967) as a rigorous way of analysing qualitative data to generate theory. According to Glaser (1992) the researcher jointly collects data, analyses and codes the data and decides on which data to collect next in order to develop the theory. Hence, sampling is controlled by the emerging theory, not as in most methods where it is the other way round. At an early stage, theoretical sampling may involve some purposeful sampling undertaken because the researcher will not have yet established any guiding concepts or theoretical constructs. After this, however, sampling is done to test, elaborate and refine a category, and further sampling to develop categories and their relationships and interrelationships (Chenitz and Swanson, 1986). As Coyne (1997) makes clear, this could even include sampling in different locations to increase the breadth of the category. Theoretical sampling includes studying documents, conducting observations or participating in real events as well as interviewing or re-interviewing with a reference to emerging categories (Charmaz, 2006).

➤ TOP TIP 9.3 ◄

A note of caution needs sounding when planning to use a theoretical sampling approach. Institutional Review Boards (IRBs) may be reluctant to give ethical approval to studies where specific subjects for the research have not been identified in advance – obviously because IRBs will want to be certain that participants are not members of vulnerable groups or may be at risk from the research. Within theoretical sampling design, it is necessary to start with initial sampling where sampling criteria (for example, age, gender, race, occupation, etc.) are defined. This includes whether you are sampling people or settings or institutions. Initial sampling, then, precedes theoretical sampling.

Confirming or disconfirming case sampling

The early stages of research are often exploratory as new patterns and concepts emerge from the data. However, later stages become confirmatory as themes and ideas are tested to ensure their viability and robustness. At this stage, the research may look for confirming cases that add strength to the analysis and disconfirming cases that challenge it. The latter are often very important because they provide a source of alternative interpretations, or may help to construct boundaries around emerging themes (Patton, 1990).

Opportunistic sampling

Qualitative research is often emergent in the sense that once fieldwork has begun, new samples may become evident or offer themselves during the study. Being open to wherever the data lead is one of the primary strengths of qualitative research (Patton, 1990). However, there is a downside to this. As with theoretical sampling, Institutional Review Boards (IRBs) may be cautious about this type of approach because it suggests a haphazard and probably unplanned approach to sampling. As we have seen, IRBs like to judge the suitability of the sample and whether access to particular groups meets the ethical principles of the institution.

Snowball sampling

With this approach, the researcher identifies a small number of subjects, who, in turn, identify others in the population. Snowball sampling is particularly suited to situations where the focus of a study is a sensitive issue and therefore requires the knowledge of insiders to locate respondents for the study (Biernacki and Waldorf, 1981). It is also useful for research into 'hidden populations', where there are difficulties in locating, gaining access to and recruiting participants because no useable sampling frame is available (Eland-Goossensen, van de Goor, Vollemans, Hendriks and Garretsen 1997). Although it is self-contained, this does not mean that it is self-propelled and proceeds according to its own 'magical' process. As Biernacki and Waldorf (1981) make clear, snowball sampling requires the researcher to be actively involved in developing and controlling the sample's initiation, progress and termination. Some populations are easy to locate because the researcher knows where they work or live, for example, police officers, dentists, school teachers etc. Other populations, however, because of their low visibility are harder to locate and contact – for example, corrupt accountants, untreated ex-heroin addicts and people who have injured others in motor accidents.

SNOWBALL
SAMPLING

In terms of finding respondents, certain people may have great knowledge of a field and its members and should be recruited as locators of study participants. However, care must be taken that locators can explain the purposes of the research in an acceptable and serious way to others (Biernacki and Waldorf, 1981). Knowledge about a project can easily become distorted and inaccurate rumours can quickly develop. Once respondents' accounts are known, it is then prudent, if possible, to get independent verification through third parties, particularly from people who know respondents and can validate the critical aspects of their accounts. Eland-Goossensen et al. (1997) recommend that the first stage group of respondents (zero-stage) are selected randomly if researchers wish the sample to represent a random sample as closely as possible.

Sampling using multiple purposive techniques

Sampling using multiple purposive techniques involves using more than one purposive method in combination, an approach used in many qualitative studies (Teddlie and Yu, 2007). Hence, a study might use theoretical sampling to identify cases that it is hoped will help develop theory about a phenomenon, but then use extreme or deviant case sampling to locate outlier cases that may challenge or contradict the emerging theory as part of the process of testing it. Given that the deviant cases might, say, involve individuals involved in anti-social or illegal activities, snowball sampling might also be used.

Convenience sampling

Convenience sampling is one of the most common sampling strategies, and involves gaining access to the most easily accessible subjects such as fellow students, neighbours or people responding to a newspaper or internet invitation to complete a survey. So, for example, in determining the attitudes of shoppers, the researcher

CONVENIENCE
SAMPLING

could interview the first 500 people who enter the shopping mall; or the researcher could knock on doors of houses that are nearby, or at the flats that are on the first floor (rather than higher and more difficult to get to). Hence, as Bajpai (2010) points out, here it is the convenience of the researcher that takes precedence. While it is an approach that is least costly to the researcher in terms of time, effort and money, the downside is that convenience sampling is neither purposeful nor strategic, and therefore has the lowest credibility of all the qualitative sampling designs. However, as Blumberg et al. (2005) suggest, convenience sampling may prove useful to test out ideas about a subject during the exploratory stages of a research project. If the results are overwhelming, it may prove unnecessary to proceed with more sophisticated sampling techniques.

→ **TOP TIP 9.4** ←

When conducting research as part of an academic programme, researchers may often use samples from organizations to which they know useful contacts (for example, friends or family members – acting as link gatekeepers). While this is an example of convenience sampling, efforts can still be made to link the sampling approach to one of the probability or non-probability schemes. For example, departments, sections or individuals in the organization could be randomly selected. Or each department could be considered as a stratum and individuals randomly selected within each department (stratified random sampling). Or, if it was felt that certain departments, locations or individuals offered information-rich data, then cases could be purposively selected on the basis of one of the schemes offered in Figure 9.1. So, for example, the link gatekeepers could nominate key informants (snowball sampling) whose responses allow for the generation of emerging constructs or themes on which new samples are chosen (theoretical sampling). Later, some outlier views (extreme case sampling) are sought to challenge the orthodoxy of the mainstream views to gain a more rounded and holistic picture of what is happening in the organization.

━ ACTIVITY 9.1 ━

A large multinational computer manufacturing company has two factories in the UK, one in Eire, five in Japan and three in the USA. In total it employs 25,000 people worldwide. The Board of Directors wishes to sponsor a survey of staff attitudes towards a proposed branding change in the company's name, logo and marketing profile. It does not wish to poll the entire workforce since this would resemble a plebiscite that the company might, then, find itself morally obliged to implement. To aid decision making flexibility, it decides to use a sample of 2,500 employees. Examine each of the following scenarios and decide which constitutes (a) stratified random sampling; (b) random sampling; (c) stage sampling; (d) purposive sampling; (e) convenience sampling.

1. Five of the company's 11 factories are randomly selected. A random selection is then made that selects five departments in each factory and 100 people are interviewed in these departments in each of the factories chosen.
2. Ten per cent of staff are chosen from each individual grade of staff in each factory in the organization.
3. A sample is chosen to ensure an even distribution between males and females in the sample, and a balance in terms of grade, age, seniority and years of service in the organization.

4. A central computer holds details of all employees in the organization across the globe. A computer program is written that randomly selects 2,500 names.
5. A Web-based questionnaire is designed for the company intranet, and an email sent to each employee inviting them to complete it. Once 2,500 responses have been received, the website is shut down.

Suggested answers are provided at the end of the chapter.

MIXED METHODS SAMPLING

One of the most important differences between quantitative and qualitative methods is the kind of sampling used (Sandelowski, 2000). As we have seen, quantitative research typically involves the use of some kind of probabilistic sampling with the aim of making statistical inferences, while qualitative research is oriented towards more purposeful sampling to enhance understanding of information-rich cases (Patton, 2002). However, as we saw in Chapter 8, quantitative and qualitative methods can be combined in a mixed methods study to generate data that have both breadth and depth (Teddlie and Yu, 2007). Although this combination can be at the level of sampling, collection or analysis (or all of them in a single study) here we will focus at just the sampling level. Table 9.2 offers a summary of the characteristics of a mixed methods sampling approach.

But how might quantitative and qualitative sampling approaches be combined? Collins, Onwuegbuzie and Jiao (2006) offer what they call a two-dimensional mixed methods sampling model (see Figure 9.6). In the model, quantitative and qualitative methods are used either at the same time (concurrent) or one after the

Table 9.2   Characteristics of mixed methods sampling

Dimension	Mixed methods sampling
Overall purpose of sampling	To generate a sample that will address *all* research questions
Intended outcomes	For some strands/research questions intended outcome is external validity; for other strands intended outcome is transferability
Rationale for selecting cases/units	For some strands the focus is on representativeness; for other strands, the focus is on information-rich cases
Sample size	For some strands there will be a large number of cases/units; for other strands, there may be one case or a few cases
Depth/breadth of information per case/unit	Focus on both breadth and depth of information across all research strands
When the sample is selected	For quantitative-type strands, the sample is selected prior to the study; for more qualitative strands, sampling can occur both before and during the study
Sampling frame	Both formal and informal are used
Form of data generated	Both numeric and narrative data are generated

Source: Adapted from Teddlie and Yu, 2007

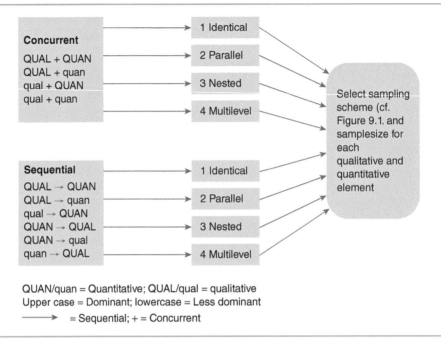

QUAN/quan = Quantitative; QUAL/qual = qualitative
Upper case = Dominant; lowercase = Less dominant
———→ = Sequential; + = Concurrent

Figure 9.6   Two-dimensional mixed methods sampling model

Source: Adapted from Collins et al., 2006

other (sequentially). In a sequential design, quantitative methods can precede qualitative or vice versa and one phase informs the other. However, in concurrent designs, the two phases are conducted separately, the integration of data only occurring at the data analysis stage. According to Collins et al. (2006) another difference is that with both concurrent and sequential approaches, the relationships can either be identical, parallel, nested or multilevel (see Figure 9.6). We will look at these in more detail below.

Design 1: Identical

In identical designs, exactly the same members of the population take part in the study at both the quantitative and qualitative stages. The stages are conducted concurrently or sequentially. If concurrently, participants might be interviewed through which rich and detailed data are generated; at the same time, a quantitative survey is used to investigate these same themes with the same sample members. Using both quantitative and qualitative methods would help to validate the findings of whichever method was given precedence. As Figure 9.6 shows, the emphasis could be placed on quantitative methods, or qualitative methods. In sequential designs, either the quantitative or qualitative stages come first. So, for example, if QUAN is dominant, a quantitative survey could be used to identify themes and constructs for further qualitative investigation. But, whatever the approach, the same sample is used for both stages.

Design 2: Parallel

In a parallel design, the samples for the quantitative and qualitative elements of the study are different but are drawn from the same underlying population. Parallel designs facilitate the comparison between two or more cases (pairwise sampling design) or sub-group sampling design (Onwuegbuzie and Leech, 2007). In pairwise designs, all the selected cases are treated as a set, and their 'voice' is compared to all other cases, one at a time in order to understand the underlying phenomena. Pairwise sampling can arise in any of the qualitative sampling schemes outlined in Figure 9.1. In contrast, in sub-group sampling designs, comparisons are made between sub-groups (for example, girls vs. boys) that are extracted from the same level of study (for example, primary school pupils). According to Onwuegbuzie and Leech (2007) comparing the voices of sub-groups can help prevent researchers from assuming that their findings apply to all groups in the sample. The commitment to generalize across all groups is often too dominant in the researcher's focus. Collins et al. (2006) describe research by Scherer and Lane (1997) who conducted a sequential study using parallel samples to examine the needs of disabled people towards assistive technologies. First of all, a quantitative survey was used to identify the assistive products that they perceived to need improvement. In the qualitative phase, another group of consumers participated in focus groups to further assess the quality of products identified in the quantitative phase.

Design 3: Nested

In a nested design, the sample members used in one phase of the study represent a sub-set of those chosen for the other part component of the study – for example, key informants of the full sample. The sub-sampling often takes the form of theoretical sampling, which involves sampling additional people, events, documents and incidents in order to develop emerging themes and to identify conceptual boundaries (Charmaz, 2013). The idea is to refine ideas not to increase the size of the sample. Hence, a nested design is a hallmark of grounded theory (Glaser and Strauss, 1967) and a popular approach used by grounded theorists. Collins et al. (2006) refer to a study by Hayter (1999) who implemented a concurrent design using nested samples. The study aimed to describe the prevalence and nature of clinical burnout among nurses working in HIV/AIDs care. In the quantitative phase, 32 nurses completed three quantitative instruments designed to measure burnout and the psychological impact of working with people with HIV/AIDS. In the qualitative part of the study, five nurses were randomly selected from the 32 for semi-structured interviews. Although one phase followed another, this is still a concurrent design since one phase did not *inform* the other.

Design 4: Multilevel

In a multilevel design, two or more sets of samples are obtained from different levels, or populations, for the study. For example, a researcher might be interested in the perception of students regarding a new type of standardized test to those of their teachers (Onwuegbuzie and Leech, 2007). Although, in principle, these students and teachers could be selected from different schools, in practice it is more usual conditionally related, that is, once a group of students is selected, the other level (their teachers) is chosen. Similarly, Collins et al. (2006) describe a study by Savaya, Monnickedam and Waysman (2000) which sought to evaluate a decision support system (DSS) designed to help youth probation officers in the process of making court recommendations. In the quantitative phase of this concurrent design, the probation officers were surveyed to determine their utilization of the DSS; in the qualitative phase, analysis of documents and senior administrators took place.

SAMPLING HARD TO REACH POPULATIONS

A growing number of hard to reach populations has emerged, often due to the threatening nature of the specific trait that characterizes their members (Faugier and Sargeant, 1997). Such populations include marginalized groups including homeless people, prostitutes, drug addicts and individuals who are incarcerated, institutionalized or cognitively impaired. As Lee (1993) comments, the less visible the activity, the harder it is to sample. This lack of visibility often has a number of implications for any thought a researcher might have of using random sampling. Firstly, the potential legal sanctions faced by respondents can make them reluctant to cooperate; secondly, a very large sample is needed to elicit sufficient data (a 1 per cent prevalence rate would require a sample of 10,000 subjects to yield 100 subjects who possess the trait being studied); thirdly, some populations might be missed because they are not living in stable communities. Quantitative studies may also yield limited understanding when exploring new fields or phenomena. Conversely, as we have seen, snowball sampling can be particularly effective in locating hidden or hard to find populations. As Faugier and Sargeant (1997) point out, in accessing hard to reach populations, fieldworkers often concentrate on the difficulties faced rather than the ways in which this kind of ethnographic research can offer special advantages. For example, in her work with street prostitutes, Faugier (1996) was able to develop a close rapport as a 'wise person', probably because she was a trained nurse and was able to respond to questions about sexual health issues.

ACCESSING
HARD TO REACH
POPULATIONS

From a practical perspective, researchers accessing hard to reach populations often have to do so via gatekeepers such as institutions or agencies. Once access is granted, institutional rules may limit access to participants in unexpected ways. For example, as Abrams (2010) points out, courts may not grant researchers access to certain types of prisoner. For some populations that are deemed to be vulnerable, many Institutional Review Boards (IRBs) do not permit direct recruitment or snowball sampling. Researchers are therefore required to post recruitment flyers or make group presentations, with participants contacting the researchers if they are interested in taking part. Hence, participants have to volunteer to take part in the study, if they are prisoners, by making a phone call. Abrams (2010) also raises some pertinent questions when it comes to screening within hard to reach populations. IRBs may require researchers to implement standard screening consent scripts, where potential participants respond to a set of screening questions. The kinds of questions posed might not be understood by some vulnerable groups or might be found offensive – particularly if questions include reporting on criminal or anti-social behaviour.

HARD TO REACH
POPULATIONS

While ethical considerations are important for all types of research they may raise particular concerns when dealing with hard to reach populations, given that sometimes these populations may constitute deviant or marginalized groups where the researcher may witness illegal activities. Also the vulnerability of some groups may make the power differential between them and the researcher all the greater – for example, the researcher's greater knowledge and the group's lack of insight into how the research may affect them (Faugier and Sargeant, 1997). Hence, they may be less able to judge the purpose of the study and anticipate the risks they might be taking in participating in it. Confidentiality is paramount. In her study of drug taking prostitutes, Faugier (1996) describes how issues of confidentiality were tested every day as the women in her study's referral chain met each other on the streets, in court or in prison; any disclosure which was seen to emanate from the researcher would have been disastrous for the study and for further recruitment of participants.

CASE STUDY 9.1

Sampling under-represented groups

Relatively little is known about the psychological health and the quality of life of older gay men and lesbian women in the UK, in part because of the difficulties of identifying a sufficiently large and representative sample for the research. Warner, Wright, Blanchard and King (2003) report on how they used a snowball sampling approach to gain access to this hard to reach population. Probabilistic sampling methods might be ineffective here because a relatively small proportion of the sample will be gay and individuals may be unwilling to reveal their sexuality using these approaches. As we saw in the section on snowballing above, this approach is useful when there is no adequate sampling frame available.

In an attempt to recruit a heterogeneous and representative pre-snowballing (Level 1) sample, Warner et al. (2003) used the following methods to advertise the study: newspaper advertisements, notices to societies for older gay men and lesbians, posters in bookshops, pubs, and cafes and a newspaper article. Each person making Level 1 contact was sent five recruitment packs, one for their own use and four to distribute to friends. These recruitment packs contained a fact-sheet about the study, a screening questionnaire seeking information about their socio-demographic details and their involvement in gay venues and to define their sexual orientation as gay, lesbian or heterosexual. All contacts who returned a screening questionnaire were sent the General Health Questionnaire to complete and further recruitment packs for distribution. Participants were encouraged to also recruit heterosexuals of a similar age (within five years) to act as a control group.

Of the 365 questionnaires distributed, 126 were returned (85 gay men, 26 lesbians and 14 heterosexuals). Newspaper advertisements and articles were the most effective means of attracting respondents. The researchers concluded that snowball sampling was a useful method for recruiting hard to access individuals, but there were drawbacks. Firstly, few heterosexuals were recruited, possibly because gay men and lesbians were reluctant to approach heterosexual friends or colleagues for fear of 'outing' themselves, or they simply did not have many heterosexual contacts. Or heterosexuals who were approached may not have felt that the research was relevant to them. Participants, then, tend to recruit others through their social networks, which might limit the representative nature of the sample.

Source: Adapted from Warner et al., 2003

> **TOP TIP 9.5**
>
> Ensure that the sampling strategy adopted, including its limitations, is fully described in research proposals and the outputs emanating from the research. Be clear about whose perspectives may have been excluded from the research, based on the sampling decisions taken. Also include information on the barriers and problems encountered during sampling and how these were addressed.

SAMPLE SIZE – HOW MUCH IS ENOUGH?

SAMPLE SIZE

There is no simple answer to this question since it depends on a number of considerations, not least of which are time and cost. All we can say with any certainty is that increasing the size of the sample usually increases its precision (note we did not say it guaranteed precision), since larger samples are more likely to be representative of the underlying population they are seeking to measure. As sampling size increases, sampling error decreases. Certainly, precision gains are noticeable when increasing sample size from 50 to 100 or from 100 to 150. However, after a certain point, often around 1,000, while precision rates increase, they do so at a much smaller rate. But how do we calculate the sample size for a particular research study? The formula below offers a solution where:

N = the minimum sample size

z = degree of confidence required

SD = the standard deviation, and

E = acceptable amount of sample error

$$N = \frac{z^2 \times SD^2}{E}$$

We can make some decisions about some of these elements. For example, we could choose a level of confidence (that the estimate is accurate) required for the research, ranging, typically, from being 90 to 99 per cent certain – see Table 9.3. Next, we could factor in the acceptable amount of sample error that can be tolerated, plus or minus the true percentage – say, 5 or 10 per cent.

But this still does not give us the standard deviation. We could get this either by using the results of previous surveys (assuming that these were available), by guessing or by conducting a small pilot study. Given that previous surveys may not be readily available and that guessing is nearly always a bad idea, this leaves us with a pilot study.

Table 9.3   Levels of confidence and associated z values

Level of confidence	z value
90% certain	1.65
95% certain	1.96
99% certain	2.57

Table 9.4   Mean and standard deviation of set of pilot data

Descriptive Statistics

	N	Mean	Std. Deviation	Variance
total	10	116.5000	15.86926	251.833
Valid N (listwise)	10			

WORKED EXAMPLE 9.1

Let us say that we are conducting a survey among a population of 2,000 nurses in a large, local hospital. What is the minimum size of sample we need to achieve? We will assume that we want a confidence level of 95 per cent certainty, with 5 per cent as an acceptable amount of sample error. We conduct a small pilot study among 10 respondents which yields a set of data as presented in Table 9.4.

Conducting the calculation we get:

$$N = \frac{1.96^2 \times 15.86^2}{25} = 38.65$$

However, if you find the use of formulas difficult, Bartlett, Kotrlik and Higgins (2001) offer a generalized table for calculating sample size which is presented in Table 9.5. We can see that as the population increased, so does the required sample, but at a diminishing rate. For categorical data a 5 per cent margin of error is acceptable, while the continuous data the figure is 3 per cent (Krejcie and Morgan, 1970). For studies where the margin of error is different to these, the appropriate sample size must be calculated as in the formula above. Bartlett et al. (2001) suggest that an alpha of .05 is acceptable for most research studies.

Roscoe (1975) recommends that most behavioural research statistical analyses should work with samples of not less than 30. However, in experimental research with tight controls (such as matched-pair designs), samples may be as small as 10 or 20. But in most ex post facto research (where variables are not manipulated) and experimental research (where variables are manipulated) samples of 30 or more are recommended. Roscoe (1975) also maintains that where samples contain sub-samples then the above rules for sample size should also apply to these sub-samples. So, for example, if the sample is divided into males and females for an experimental design, then both groups should contain a minimum sample of 30. For other kinds of research, for example, multiple regression, the sample size should be at least 10 times larger than the number of variables being considered. In descriptive research the sample should be 10 per cent of the population (Gay and Diehl, 1992). However, in pilot or exploratory studies, a sample size of 10 to 30 is usually sufficient (Isaac and Michael, 1995).

A common fallacy in qualitative research is that numbers are unimportant in ensuring the adequacy of a sampling strategy (Sandelowski, 1995). In practice, sample sizes should be not too large so that it is difficult to extract thick, rich descriptions

Table 9.5   Table for determining minimum returned sample size for a given size for continuous and categorical data

	Sample size					
	Continuous data (margin of error = .03)			Categorical data (margin of error = .05)		
Population size	alpha = .10 t = 1.65	alpha = .05 t = 1.96	alpha = .01 t = 2.58	alpha = .50 t = 1.65	alpha = .50 t = 1.96	alpha = .50 t = 2.58
100	46	55	68	74	80	87
200	59	75	102	116	132	154
300	65	85	123	143	169	207
400	69	92	137	162	196	250
500	72	96	147	176	218	286
600	73	100	155	187	235	316
700	75	102	161	196	249	341
800	76	104	166	203	260	363
900	76	105	170	209	270	382
1,000	77	106	173	213	278	399
1,500	79	110	183	230	306	461
2,000	83	112	189	239	323	499
4,000	83	119	198	254	351	570
6,000	83	119	209	259	362	598
8,000	83	119	209	262	367	613
10,000	83	119	209	264	370	623

and not too small that it becomes difficult to achieve data saturation (Flick, 2009 Morse, 1991), theoretical saturation (Strauss and Corbin, 1990) or informational redundancy (Lincoln and Guba, 1994). Yet as Neergaard (2007) comments sampling often stops prematurely due to the inexperience of the researcher, or lack of time or resources. However, saying that a sample should not be too large and not too small gives us less than a total solution. Part of the answer comes at the sampling planning stage. We saw in the discussion on stratified purposive sampling above that sample size increases with the number of independent variables used in the study. Table 9.1, for example, shows that with variables such as size of family, number of children, housing types, size of family income, and gender of the teenager gives 32 cells in the sampling table. Of course, we know that in any sampling table some cells may be either theoretically or empirically difficult or impossible to fill, or both. However, the basic lesson is there – increasing the number of independent variables used in a study will increase the sample size needed. Figure 9.1 is also based on only one case per cell. Onwuegbuzie and Leech (2007) caution that using even two cases per cell may not be enough, as it may be difficult to reach data saturation if at least one of the cases is atypical. Onwuegbuzie and Leech (2007) recommend that researchers avoid comparing more than four sub-groups for phenomenological studies, and more than seven sub-groups (using Creswell's 2002 criteria) for grounded studies.

→ **TOP TIP 9.6** ←

A common mistake made by novice researchers is the claims they make for their research when using small samples. In many studies it is simply not possible or practical to make use of random samples. So be honest about the kinds of claims you can make for your findings based on the size of sample you have gained access to. Instead of spurious claims to generalization, it is often better to highlight some of the positive features of your sample (if they exist) such as the range of people included, the good response rate and the high level of collaboration received from respondents. This might, for example, include comments from respondents on how much they enjoyed completing the questionnaire or taking part in the interview.

GRAY ON
USING SMALL
SAMPLES

Summary

- The sampling of participants and sources is one of the key components of any research study
- In quantitative research sampling primarily involves the use of probability sampling techniques which involve the selection of a relatively large number of units from the population
- Probability sampling includes random, stratified, cluster sampling and sampling using multiple probability techniques
- In qualitative research sampling primarily involves non-probability samples, the aim of which is to select respondents and data that are likely to generate robust, rich and deep levels of understanding
- Non-probability sampling includes purposive, convenience and mixed-methods sampling approaches
- Hard to reach populations are often accessed using snowball sampling approaches often adopted via gatekeepers such as institutions or agencies
- The sample size should be not too large so that it is difficult to extract thick, rich descriptions and not too small that it becomes difficult to achieve data saturation
- The limitations of the sampling strategy adopted should be acknowledged in research proposals and outputs emanating from the research, including whose perspectives may have been excluded from the research

REVIEW QUESTIONS

1. Under what circumstances would you recommend (a) a probability sample; (b) a non-probability sample?
2. Why do Institutional Review Boards tend to favour proposals that specify their intended sampling frame in advance? What implications does this have for theoretical sampling?
3. Why is convenience sampling both frequently used yet is also one of the least strategic or purposeful qualitative sampling methods?
4. What benefits do mixed-methods sampling offer researchers? What are the potential drawbacks?
5. If you were to adopt one method for sampling hard to reach populations such as drug-users, criminals or social deviants, what would it be? Explain your reasons.

FURTHER READING

Emmel, N. (2013) *Sampling and Choosing Cases in Qualitative Research.* London: Sage. Using a realist approach, this book critically evaluates widely used sampling strategies. Drawing on international case studies from across the social sciences the author explains why it is not the size of a sample that matters, it is how cases are used to interpret and explain that is important.

Daniel, J. (2010) *Sampling Essentials: Practical Guidelines for Making Sampling Choices*. Thousand Oaks, CA: Sage. Designed for the non-technical researcher, this quite comprehensive text includes details on selecting sample size and type.

Lohr, S.L. (2010) *Sampling: Design and Analysis*, 2nd edn. Boston, MA: Brookes/Cole. Starts with the basics of sampling design including simple probability sampling, stratified and cluster sampling, before exploring complex surveys and discussing strategies for non-response.

Henry, G.T. (1990) *Practical Sampling*. Newbury Park, CA: Sage. A short but very accessible book that deals with both probability and non-probability sampling and presents some useful case studies as illustration.

JOURNAL RESOURCES

Carlsen, B. and Glenton, C. (2011) 'What about N? A methodological study of sample-size reporting in focus group studies', *BMC Medical Research Methodology*, 11(1): 26–35. Describes the current status in the reporting of sample size in focus group studies in health journals. Points to the lack of clarity in this reporting.

Kelly, B.C. (2010) 'Sampling and recruitment issues in qualitative drugs research: Reflections on the study of club drug users in Metro New York', *Substance Use & Misuse*, 45(5): 671–683. Describes the role and implications of sampling and recruitment in qualitative drugs research, and describes experiences utilizing theoretical sampling and time–space sampling to study club drug users.

Higginbottom, G.M.A. (2004) 'Sampling issues in qualitative research', *Nurse Researcher*, 12(1): 7–19. Provides an overview of the complexity of sampling in qualitative research, and offers insights into the various philosophical underpinnings and sampling techniques in qualitative research.

Suggested answer for Activity 9.1

1. Stage sampling. But note that if the factories vary in size, taking 100 people might constitute a different proportion of each factory. The employees in very large plants, for example, might hold different views to those in the smaller ones. Hence, you might want to weight the results.
2. Stratified random sampling.
3. Purposive sampling.
4. Random sampling.
5. Convenience sampling.

10

DESIGNING DESCRIPTIVE AND ANALYTICAL SURVEYS

CHAPTER INTRODUCTION

Chapter outline

What is a survey?	236	Conducting a staff opinion survey	252
Types of survey	237	Reducing sources of error	256
Stages in the survey process	240	Ethics and good practice in	
Selecting a survey method	245	survey design	262

Keywords

Descriptive surveys

Analytical surveys

Survey design

Postal questionnaires

Online questionnaires

Telephone surveys

Staff opinion surveys

Sampling error

Ethics

Chapter objectives

After reading this chapter you will be able to:

- Distinguish between descriptive and analytical surveys.
- Describe and apply different approaches to both analytical and descriptive surveys.
- Select alternative survey data collection methods.
- Implement special approaches to maximize response rates to organizational surveys.
- Take steps to counteract some of the limitations of survey design.

SURVEY
RESEARCH

In this chapter we examine surveys, today one of the most popular methodologies and widely used in the business and commercial worlds. Surveys are described by Fink (2002b) as a system for collecting information to describe, compare or explain knowledge, attitudes and behaviour. They are a common methodology in research because they allow for the collection of significant amounts of data from a sizeable population. But many surveys go further than this, looking for associations between social, economic and psychological variables and behaviour. Market researchers, for example, may be interested in how changes in income level and status affect people's spending patterns. The results of surveys, whether commissioned by organizations, companies or the government, are frequently quoted in the media. Most surveys are conducted using a questionnaire, but structured observation and structured interviews may also be used. Unlike many other research methodologies, surveys are often a team effort, involving a division of labour between survey designers, interviewers and those who capture the data onto computer files prior to analysis.

Surveys fall into two main categories: *analytical* and *descriptive*. Analytical surveys take many of the features of experimental, deductive research and so place an emphasis on reliability of data and statistical control of variables, sample size, etc. It is hoped that the rigour of these controls will allow for the generalization of the results. In contrast, descriptive surveys tend to use an inductive approach, often using open-ended questions to explore perspectives. Descriptive surveys may be quite ethnographic in character. If a theory does emerge, it may be tested, subsequently, using more structured research instruments. This chapter, then, looks at how surveys are planned, the types of designs available, some of the special features of organizational surveys, as well as some limitations of survey methodology.

WHAT IS A SURVEY?

According to Sapsford (2006), a survey is a detailed and quantified description of a population – a precise map or a precise measurement of potential. Surveys involve the *systematic* collecting of data, whether this is by interview, questionnaire or observation methods, so at the very heart of surveys lies the importance of standardization. Precise samples are selected for surveying, and attempts are made to standardize and eliminate errors from survey data gathering tools. The very first survey, the Doomsday Book of 1085, was largely an exercise in counting (people, ownership of land and livestock, etc.) but modern surveys are usually exercises in measurement (often of attitudes). They attempt to identify something about a population, that is, a set of objects about which we wish to make generalizations. A population is frequently a set of people, but organizations, institutions or even countries can comprise the unit of analysis. Since populations often tend to be fairly large, and therefore time-consuming and expensive to survey, we tend to collect data from samples, as we saw in Chapter 9, a portion or subset of the population.

SURVEY
RESEARCH

Conducting surveys is now a thriving business, and being on the receiving end of surveys is often a component of modern life. Companies make use of surveys to measure customer attitudes towards their products and services. Educational establishments survey (evaluate) student opinions about courses and programmes as part of their quality assurance processes. Governments and politicians pay close attention to surveys of public opinion to gauge the mood of the populace on issues such as transport, education, health, the environment, and, of course, voting intentions. For example, in 1982 the Policy Study Institute obtained UK government funding for a national survey of ethnic minorities, using a sample of 5,000 adults (Hakim, 2000). The survey considered the extent and causes of 'racial disadvantage' in relation to residential segregation, housing, education, employment and healthcare.

A particular form of survey, a **census**, is a study of every member of a given population and *the* Census is an official survey of a country's entire population – in the case of the UK, one that is carried out every 10 years. A census provides essential data for government policy makers and planners, but is also useful, for example, to businesses that want to know about trends in consumer behaviour – such as ownership of durable goods, and demand for services.

WHAT IS A
CENSUS?

An increasingly common focus of surveys is employees' attitudes. Hartley (2001) reports research showing that in the USA employee surveys are becoming an integral part of human resources strategy. In the UK, in large firms employing over 5,000 people, nearly half have reported using employee surveys. Surveys, then, have moved from being used as barometers of attitudes and opinions, to constituting essential links to business strategy and organizational change.

TYPES OF SURVEY

As we have seen, surveys fall into two broad categories: descriptive and analytical.

Descriptive surveys

Descriptive surveys are designed to measure the characteristics of a particular population, either at a fixed point in time, or comparatively over time. They are designed to measure *what* occurred, rather than *why*. Descriptive surveys are used in a wide range of areas such as market research, public opinion polling, voting intention surveys and media research (ratings surveys). Surveys of this kind have often been used to identify the scale and nature of social problems, including poverty, crime and health-related issues. Hence, descriptive surveys can be the source and stimulus for policy changes and social action.

DESCRIPTIVE
SURVEY?

Characteristics of descriptive surveys

While, generally, inductive in approach, it would be entirely wrong to assume that descriptive surveys are devoid of theory. Indeed, reference to relevant theories may be necessary before the research can be formulated. De Vaus (2002) goes further, arguing that good description is the basis of sound theory. Unless something is described accurately and thoroughly, it cannot be explained. Illuminating descriptions can highlight puzzles that need to be solved, and thus provide the inspiration for the construction of theories. Furthermore, the identification of problems can provide the cornerstone for action.

Descriptive surveys are often undertaken to ascertain attitudes, values and opinions. For example, a survey might examine staff views about whether the organization's customers *seem* content with the service they are receiving. Indeed, the working practices of organizations would be a typical subject for descriptive surveys. But as Black (1993) notes, there may be differences between the opinions found through a survey, which is a description of people's *perceptions*, and the actual reality of practice. In other words, people may articulate a particular view, but in practice behave differently. Hence, caution needs to be exercised in drawing conclusions from such surveys.

Mass descriptive surveys: the opinion poll

In modern, democratic societies, one particular type of descriptive survey, the opinion poll, has become an essential arm of the government policy-making process. Sometimes large corporations also commission their own surveys to check on shifting public priorities and attitudes that could influence government initiatives (Ferguson, 2000). The following Case Study, however, shows how difficult it is for opinion polls to make accurate predictions.

— CASE STUDY 10.1 —

Survey lessons from US opinion polls

Should we trust opinion polls? The track record is patchy because signs that the methods used are failing can be ignored until disaster strikes – like calling the wrong winner in an election! This happened to the *Literary Digest* in 1936. The magazine had been polling since 1916 and getting its predictions acceptably close. In 1932, for example, it predicted Roosevelt's victory within a fraction of a percentage point. But in 1936 it predicted a victory for Alfred Landon when Roosevelt won again. So what went wrong?

The problem was that the *Literary Digest* accessed its sample by using telephone directories and car registrations. But Roosevelt's New Deal coalition had brought minority groups, such as Southern farmers and organized labour, towards his Democratic Party. But these were precisely the kinds of groups under-represented in terms of telephone and car ownership.

The next major polling crisis came in 1948 when they failed to predict the victory of Harry Truman. Statisticians later found that the polls had stopped asking questions too soon. Many people switched their votes at the last minute, largely due to Truman's effective campaigning. After this, the polls stayed in the field longer. They also replaced quota sampling with probability sampling, meaning that respondents were chosen purely on chance. Polling accuracy improved dramatically, and was further improved in the 1970s with the introduction of telephone polling. This was cheaper and therefore allowed for much greater sample sizes (and therefore purer samples).

But in the 1990s the average error (the difference between the final pre-election poll and the winner's vote) rose to over 3 per cent. Why the rise? Well, a major factor must be the problem of public resistance to telephone interviewing, probably as a result of being burdened with too many junk phone calls. People are wary of strangers calling at inconvenient times.

One result of this has been a growing interest in Net polling. The problem here, of course, is that not everyone is linked to the Internet. The polls try to get around this by giving more weight in the survey to those Internet users who are most like (in key variables such as social groups) non-Internet users. In the 2000 US presidential election some of these Net polls were predicting a win for Gore when the election was won by Bush. Back to the drawing board!

Source: Adapted from Meyer, 2000

→ ON THE WEB 10.1 ←

Go to Qb: Survey Questionnaires at:

http://qb.soc.surrey.ac.uk/docs/surveys.htm

Explore the wide range of surveys including:

- British Election Surveys
- Family Expenditure Surveys
- Labour Force Surveys

Pay particular attention to the Overview section for each survey, explaining the aims and methodology of the survey.

Now take a look at:

http://www.yougov.com

Pay particular attention to the sampling methods. To what extent do you think they could be justified as representative?

From descriptive to analytical surveys

Often, descriptive surveys might only be the precursor to more detailed analytical studies. For instance, a descriptive survey of UK management attitudes towards sterling currency integration with Europe might reveal the strength of feelings one way or another. But we might quickly come face-to-face with the 'so what?' question. If a trend or attitude has been described, what caused it? As Saunders et al. (2012) make clear, descriptive studies in business and management research have their place, but they are generally a means to an end rather than an end in themselves.

In practice, what determines whether a survey is analytical or descriptive is often the size of the sample. If the sample is relatively small, and the research deals with relationships between multiple variables, it is unlikely that any associations found will be statistically significant. In these circumstances, an analytical survey would be of little value so the survey will be largely descriptive.

─────────────── ► **TOP TIP 10.1** ◄ ───────────────

If you are about to undertake a survey, say as part of a dissertation or project, go to your research questions. Is your focus mainly on 'What' is happening? If so, ask yourself (or your supervisor!) whether you should also be asking 'How' or 'Why' type questions. For example, if you have designed a survey dealing with employee attitudes towards an organization's policy for promoting diversity in management grades, this might tell you what people think. But also delving into why people hold certain views adds a layer of analysis.

Analytical surveys

As has been pointed out, analytical surveys attempt to test a theory in the field, their main purpose being to explore and test associations between variables. As Oppenheim (1992) shows, analytical surveys take on typical characteristics of experimental research when it comes to dealing with these variables. As was shown in Chapter 6, the survey will have to distinguish between:

- *Dependent* variables – the subject of the research, the gains or losses produced by the impact of the research study.
- *Independent* variables – the 'causes' of the changes in the dependent variables that will be manipulated or observed, then measured by the analytical survey.
- *Uncontrolled* variables – including error variables that may confound the results of the study. It is hoped that such variables are randomly distributed so any confounding effects are limited.

Controlling extraneous variables can be achieved in a number of ways through careful planning of the survey. They can be controlled, for example, through *exclusion* (such as only using females in the study so as to eliminate the possible confounding effects of gender). Variables can also be controlled by *holding them constant* (for example, by interviewing respondents on the same day so as to eliminate the effects of time). Randomizing can also assist in controlling extraneous variables, since, if the sample is truly random, any extraneous variables should, in all probability, be represented in the sample in the same proportions as in the population being studied.

─────────────── ► **ON THE WEB 10.2** ◄ ───────────────

Take a look at the website for the NOP Research Group at:

http://www.nop.org.uk

Examine some of the surveys conducted. Pay special attention to the size of some of the samples used. Can you pick out any particular designs such as longitudinal or cross-sectional?

STAGES IN THE SURVEY PROCESS

Before conducting a survey it is essential to understand the phases and steps involved. Conducting a survey is much more than just a process of designing a questionnaire and collecting data. Czaja and Blair (2005) suggest a five-stage process (see Figure 10.1).

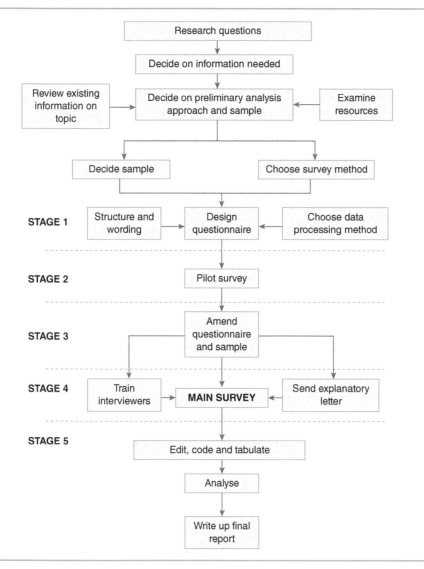

Figure 10.1 Stages in the survey planning process

Source: Adapted from Czaja and Blair, 2005

Stage 1: Survey design and preliminary planning

As with most research strategies, the first step involves the specification of the central research questions that the survey needs to address. These might be articulated in a number of different ways, for example:

- A *hypothesis*: Industrial workers are more likely to favour 'blood sports' than service-sector workers.
- A *causal hypothesis*: People who like classical music are more likely to visit art galleries.
- A *description*: What proportion of people believe that all first-time offenders should be jailed?

Some research questions may focus on the views or actions of individuals, others on groups, organizations, networks or businesses. In formulating research questions it is important that they achieve a sense of specificity and focus. De Vaus (2002) suggests that this can be achieved by asking the following questions:

- What is the *time frame* for the survey? Do we need to know about the issue now, in the past, or do we need to project trends into the future?
- What is the geographical *location* of the research? Is it local, regional, national or international?
- Is the focus of the research broad and general, or does it need to *compare* and *specify* patterns among sub-groups? For example, in looking at absentee levels in a country, are we also interested in a breakdown of data by region, sector, industry or gender?
- What *aspect* of the topic is of interest? If, for example, the research issue is e-commerce, are we interested in trends in its growth, companies who do (and who do not) use e-commerce and why, or what kinds of software platform firms are building their e-commerce Web system on?
- How *abstract* is the research interest? Is the main focus of the research on the gathering of raw data, say, the sale of expensive consumer durables, or what this might reveal about general consumer confidence and standards of living?

In writing research questions for surveys, it is important to establish the research's frame of reference. Hence, if we find that in a customer satisfaction survey, 56 per cent of customers expressed themselves as 'broadly satisfied' with the service they were receiving, what are we to make of this figure? Furthermore, whatever the figure, individuals may interpret it differently. It would be helpful to know before we start the survey, the benchmark criteria for 'good', 'bad' and 'indifferent' performance. One way of achieving this is by benchmarking against other companies in the field. If we found, for example, that no industry competitor had achieved a satisfaction rate above 40 per cent, then any figure above 50 per cent would look relatively good.

Collecting benchmark data, of course, is not always a simple exercise. If we need data on competitors they are unlikely to give it to someone working in a rival organization. There are a number of possible solutions, including the use of:

- Overseas organizations. Concentrate on overseas organizations who are in the same business or service but not in direct competition (due to geographical distance). Sometimes organizations might have websites that offer data on their mission, structure, products and services, etc. There may be articles about the organization in trade or professional magazines or journals.
- Organizations in different industries that share similar problems or have business activities in common. A researcher, for example, working for an airport might research customer satisfaction data for bus or train companies. The challenge here is to show how the lessons from a related but different industry can be transferred to the target area for the research.

Whatever the focus of the study, one of the key issues is the selection of the *sample*. For example, in surveying attitudes of residents towards a city transport system, do we contact those who live in the city centre, in the suburbs, or also include people who commute into the city from outlying towns? What age groups do we use? Do we only count people who are 18 years old and above? What about young adolescents, say, above the age of 14 who also use the transport system? There needs to be an age cut-off point somewhere, so it is sensible to limit the sample to those people who are capable of providing accurate information.

Another important issue is the selection of the *sampling frame*, that is, the source or sources that include the population members from which the sample is to be selected. For general population surveys, the most common source for the sampling frame is telephone directories. If we were to conduct a survey of teaching staff in a university, the sampling frame would be the names held on the human resources department's records. As we saw in Chapter 6, of central importance is the question of how much the sampling frame is representative of the eligible population. If we take the example of telephone directories, obviously not everyone has a telephone. Telephone ownership tends to be lower for poorer social groups and in certain localities, and these people may hold different views from those of telephone-owning households. How much bias does this generate in a survey? Czaja and Blair (2005) suggest that most researchers are not too concerned by this threat because non-telephone households are proportionately so small (at least in most industrialized countries).

SAMPLING
FRAME

At this preliminary design stage other factors that need to be considered are the budget for the study and the time available. In general, the cheapest form of survey is through using mail, then telephone surveys. Face-to-face surveys are the most expensive, particularly for large-scale studies, when interviewers will have to be recruited and trained. This is also the stage at which careful thought needs to be given to how the data are to be collected, captured and analysed.

Now we come to instrument design. Here, if you are fortunate, there may already be validated scales available. For example, if you were investigating the relationship between job satisfaction and a dependent variable such as work performance, you might consider using the Warr, Cook and Wall (1979) scale for measuring job satisfaction. This scale has been used in many studies and has a coefficient alpha of 0.85–0.88 and test–retest correlation coefficient of 0.63 for a 6-month period (Warr et al., 1979). There are often, however, a number of scales available some of which might be more relevant for your own study.

JOB
SATISFACTION

→ **TOP TIP 10.2** ←

You need to select a scale that most closely matches what you are trying to measure. You then need to show evidence, from either the developers of the scale, or subsequent studies, of the scale's validity and reliability. If a pre-developed scale or instrument is not available, you will need to develop one yourself. This will mean following as closely as possible, the guidance given on instrument design in other chapters of this book.

Stage 2: Pre-testing

This stage involves the testing or piloting of elements such as the sampling frame (is it representative of the target population?), survey questions (especially if you have designed them yourself rather than using validated scales) and data collection

PRE-TESTING
EXAMPLE

tools. It is likely that several drafts of the research tool will have to be tested before a satisfactory version is reached. If resources permit, focus groups can be used to discuss the validity of individual questions, or to evaluate the overall design of the survey. If interviewers are going to be used, they will require training and debriefing to ascertain whether the training has been successful.

➤ TOP TIP 10.3 ◄

In running a pilot survey, respondents will be helped if you provide them with written instructions on what you want them to do. You could indicate, for example, that you want them to comment on:

- The instructions for completing the questionnaire.
- The validity of each question, asking respondents whether they want an individual question deleted or modified – and if the latter, how.
- The overall length of the questionnaire.

Stage 3: Final survey design and planning

The pre-testing will inform planners as to what changes need to be made to the various elements, such as the choice and size of sampling frame, the questionnaire itself, interviewer training, data coding and plans for data analysis. A common occurrence at this stage is to find problems with the representativeness of the sampling frame. For example, it might be found that the responses of a particular sub-group (say, male nurses) were quite different to the main group (female nurses). A decision would have to be made (within the constraint of time and budgets) on whether to increase the size of this sub-group sample. Of course, if the budget is fixed, this implies that the size of the other sub-group (female nurses) will have to be reduced. Researchers, then, need to consider what impact this may have on the reliability of the results.

Stage 4: Data collection

Apart from the data collection and coding process itself, at this stage one of the most important activities is to monitor the rate of completed interviews and the rate of non-response. The latter should be measured by specific category, each of which has different implications for the research, namely:

- Non-contacts (try to re-contact).
- Refusals (try to ascertain reasons for refusal).
- Ineligibles (replace by eligible respondents).

If interviews are being conducted, the performance of individual interviewers needs to be checked for their success rate at achieving interviewee cooperation and the quality of the interview data. For example, are there some interviewers who consistently fail to get all questions in the questionnaire completed? Is this accidental or does it point to a problem? The importance of reducing sources of error will be explored in more depth later in the chapter.

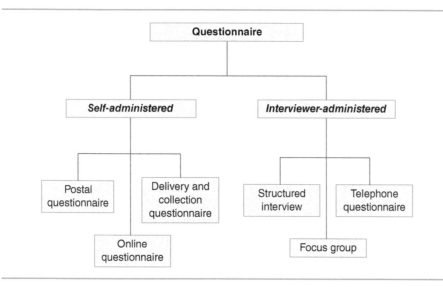

Figure 10.2   Types of questionnaire

Source: Adapted from Saunders et al., 2012

Stage 5: Data coding, analysis and reporting

At the coding stage, a number is assigned to the responses to each survey question, and these are then entered into a data record that includes all the responses from one respondent. Each respondent is then given a unique identity number. Before data analysis can begin the data have to be 'cleaned', that is, checked for obvious errors. If, for example, a question has only two possible responses, 'Yes' (= 1), or 'No' (= 2), but the data file contains the number 3, then clearly an error has been made and must be corrected.

━━ ACTIVITY 10.1 ━━

Take a survey that you have conducted or intend to carry out. Are there any steps in Figure 10.1 that you would omit? If so, justify your decision.

SELECTING A SURVEY METHOD

Saunders et al. (2012) comment that the design of a survey questionnaire will depend on how it is to be administered, that is, whether it is to be self-administered, or interviewer-administered. Within these categories, they distinguish between six different types of questionnaire (see Figure 10.2). Of these, the most commonly used are postal questionnaires, structured (face-to-face) interviews and telephone questionnaires, although the use of the online questionnaire is becoming increasingly popular. The starting point for selecting between them is the purpose of the survey and the kinds of questions that the research intends to ask. Resources such as time and budgets are also part of the decision making equation.

QUESTIONNAIRE
DESIGN GUIDE

Self-administered questionnaires

Postal questionnaires

Mangione (1995) suggests that **postal surveys** are best considered when:

- The research sample is widely distributed geographically.
- Research subjects need to be given time to reflect on their answers.
- The research subjects have a moderate to high interest in the subject.
- The questions are mostly written in a close-ended style.

POSTAL
QUESTION-
NAIRES

Certainly, postal questionnaires are most suited to situations where the questions are not over-elaborate and require relatively straightforward answers. They also allow respondents time to consult documents and to complete the questionnaire in their own time. Respondents may also be more amenable to answering personal and delicate questions through this more anonymous medium. It is possible that answers may be more honest than when faced by an interviewer, whom they may be tempted to impress by exaggerated responses or a socially desirable response (SDR). Postal questionnaires are normally one of the cheapest methods to use and can achieve relatively high response rates when the topic is relevant to the audience.

Kerlinger and Lee (2000), however, warn that the postal questionnaire has serious drawbacks unless it is used with other techniques. Problems include a low return rate and an inability to check the responses that have been given. They caution that response rates as low as 40 or 50 per cent are common, which means that the researcher has to be careful about making strong generalizations on the basis of the data. Czaja and Blair (2005) also caution that postal surveys are prone to response bias because of lower returns from people with low levels of literacy and education. This group are more compliant with, say, interviews, because no demands are made on their reading abilities. If response rates are low, those responding may be doing so on the basis of some interest or commitment to the subject, making them a volunteer rather than a genuinely random sample. Kerlinger and Lee (2000) argue that with postal questionnaires only a response rate of 80 or 90 per cent is acceptable, and every effort should be made to achieve this. Ways of improving response rates are explored later.

Delivery and collection questionnaires

Delivery and collection questionnaires are simply delivered by hand to each respondent and collected later. This has the advantage over postal questionnaires in that there is some direct contact with potential respondents that might in turn induce a greater proportion of people to complete the questionnaire. But like all questionnaires, this will largely be determined by how interesting the audience finds the survey. One of the considerable disadvantages of this approach, obviously, is the time and effort involved in delivering and collecting the questionnaires. For student researchers the use of this approach is quite common when undertaking research which requires responses from other students on their academic programme. So, for example, questionnaires might be distributed before a lecture with the request that they are dropped into a box as students leave.

Image 10.1   A traditional survey approach – a postal questionnaire

Online questionnaires

Online questionnaires are a relatively new, but an increasingly popular way of conducting surveys. Essentially, there are two ways in which an online questionnaire
can be delivered – as a word-processed document attached to an email, or via a
website (see Figure 10.3). With emails, the researcher will have to know the email
addresses of respondents so that the sample can be targeted. With Web-based surveys, if the site is not password-protected, there is no control over who completes
the survey form. This means that respondents will comprise a volunteer rather than
a random sample, with corresponding threats to the validity of the data. Conversely,
if the site is password-protected, this presents a further barrier to respondents and
could tend to push the response rate down. The problem of security is partially
solved if the research is focused on just one organization that possesses an intranet,
with firewalls to block access from external visitors. But again, the researcher may
find it difficult to control who responds. There is conflicting evidence as to whether
making use of Web-based surveys increases response rates, leads to lower response
rates or makes no difference. Certainly, response rates are likely to be higher for
groups who have Internet access, are experienced in using computers and have
some motivation to complete the survey. For an example of a web-based market
research survey tool see Figure 10.3.

INTERNET
SURVEYS

Sampling error is by far the greatest threat to the validity of online questionnaires (Ray and Tabor, 2003), mainly because certain demographic segments of the
population may be under-represented or simply not represented at all. Those
households who do not have access to the Internet probably differ to those who do
in terms of socio-economic status and education, for example. It becomes necessary, therefore, to provide evidence or arguments that the non-online population

Figure 10.3   Google consumer survey website

does not differ significantly in terms of its choices or decision making compared to online respondents.

Being more impersonal, it might be assumed that online surveys are less prone to elicit socially desirable responses (SDRs) that might bias the results. Hancock and Flowers (2001), however, report that while some studies have suggested that computer responses are more candid and less influenced by social desirability than responses provided on paper (such as postal questionnaires and structured interviews), their own research did not support these findings. At best, online responses were no worse. Online surveys, then, should probably be chosen more on the basis of lower costs, than for the reduction in response bias.

REPRESEN-
TATIVENESS
IN ONLINE
SURVEYS

ON THE WEB 10.3

For an example of software tools that you can use to build an online survey, see each of the following:

http://www.surveymonkey.com/

http://www.surveywriter.com/

http://www.sogosurvey.com

Use the Tutorial or Demo for each site to get the 'feel' of each tool.

In addition to constructing online questionnaires, Web-based surveys can also be carried out via a Web discussion group. Here a question, or set of questions, can be posted to the group in the form of a simple email. Since discussion groups (such as listservs) are set up around specific discussions, you need to be sure that the research subject is of relevance and interest to the group. The next Case Study provides an example of how a discussion group was used to conduct a research study.

— CASE STUDY 10.2 —

Conducting a survey through an email discussion group

Two researchers were interested in the views of fellow researchers on the safety procedures necessary in being a lone researcher. To gather data, they chose six email discussion groups. Initially they sent an email requesting only basic information, but after an encouraging response, they sent a more structured set of questions in a second email. This requested details on respondents': gender; age; occupation; area of work; country of fieldwork; whether they had been given safety guidelines; whether they had experienced incidents while conducting research; and recommendations for 'best practice' when researching alone.

A total of 46 responses were received, of which 13 were from males and 33 from females, with ages ranging from the late 20s to the early 60s. Thirty-one were from the UK (possibly resulting from the UK bias of four of the discussion lists). Four were from Australia, six from the USA, and one from each of Finland, Norway, Sweden, Italy and Canada. Some of the replies were quite detailed.

While the sample could not be regarded as representative, this survey method proved to be cheap, speedy at gathering data, and illuminative in terms of the quality of data it elicited. Also note its international character.

Source: Adapted from Kenyon and Hawker, 1999

→ **ON THE WEB 10.4** ←

Take a look at some of the email discussion groups available at:

http://www.jiscmail.ac.uk/

In the Find List, type in one of your research topics to see if a discussion list already exists. Alternatively, click on alphabetical indexes to browse the lists.

Interviewer-administered questionnaires

Structured interviews

Structured, face-to-face interviews are probably the most expensive survey method because they require large amounts of interviewer time, a significant proportion of which is often spent travelling to and from interviews. The questionnaires on which the interviews are based can be difficult, time-consuming and costly to produce. However, response rates are usually slightly higher than for methods such as telephone interviews, particularly if a letter can be sent in advance, explaining the purposes of the structured interview. Response bias is also fairly low because refusals are usually equally spread across all types of respondent. Structured interviews are the most effective method for asking **open questions** and for eliciting more detailed responses. Like telephone interviews but unlike postal questionnaires, structured interviews allow for the use of probing questions in response to unclear or incomplete answers.

Interview schedules may begin with factual information: the respondent's sex, marital status, education, income, etc. This is often referred to as the 'face sheet' and is vital for two reasons; first, it allows for the later studying of relationships between variables – for example, an attitude towards an organization's product or service and respondents' educational background, or income level. Secondly, it

Image 10.2
Interviews as a
survey method

allows for some rapport to be built with the interviewee at the start of the interview. The personal interview helps in ascertaining a respondent's reasons for doing something or holding a personal belief. Of course, there may be differences between what people believe and what they do, and between what they say they do and their real actions in practice. There is also the problem that respondents are more likely to over-report socially desirable behaviour than when answering through postal interviews.

Focus group interviews

The use of **focus groups** allows for a sample of respondents to be interviewed and then re-interviewed so that attitudes and behaviours can be studied over a period of time (a longitudinal survey). An advantage of focus groups is that they allow for a variety of views to emerge, while group dynamics can often allow for the stimulation of new perspectives. Indeed, sometimes these new perspectives may provide the basis for a survey.

Focus groups are increasingly used in the political arena and are also a common tool in market research. Within a business or organization, they can be useful in engaging the commitment of people, especially in circumstances where there is cynicism or hostility towards the research theme.

⟶ ON THE WEB 10.5 ⟵

There are now brokering organizations that provide a service by recruiting people to take part in focus groups and selling these services to external organizations that want to use a focus group. See such a brokering organization at:

http://www.focusforce.net/

Telephone surveys

The telephone survey is the most widely used of all the survey methods. One factor in its favour is the growth of household telephone ownership, reaching over 90 per cent in some countries. Indeed, with the spread of mobile phones many households are now multiple telephone owners. Most surveys are currently conducted through home telephones, but it is likely that cellphone surveys will spread, especially when researchers want access to younger age groups, for whom the cellphone is now a social accessory.

TELEPHONE INTERVIEWS

Response rates for telephone surveys are relatively high (60–90 per cent when repeated callbacks are made) because most people are willing to be interviewed by telephone (although recall the resistance to junk calls noted in Case Study 10.1). In contrast to postal surveys, it becomes possible for interviewers to convince people of the significance of the research or to reschedule the interview for a more convenient time. If people prove difficult to contact, Czaja and Blair (2005) recommend five to nine callbacks on different days of the week and at different times of day. With some groups, for example, older adults, making contact through either an interview or postal questionnaire prior to a telephone follow-up can boost the response rate (Wilson and Roe, 1998).

One of the limitations of telephone interviews is the type of questions that can be asked. Questions need to be short and fairly simple, and the kinds of response choices few and short. Sentences should be limited to 20 words or less and language kept as simple as possible. If calling groups who are not conversant with a country's first language, then it is prudent to use interviewers who can speak the respondent's language.

Image 10.3　Market research is often conducted through a call centre

—— ACTIVITY 10.2 ——

In deciding between the various survey methods, make a list of the advantages and disadvantages of each. Which, on balance, is the best for your own survey? Justify your choice.

CONDUCTING A STAFF OPINION SURVEY

STAFF
SURVEYS
GUIDE

Perhaps the most common survey in business is the staff opinion survey, which can provide valuable insights into many elements of an organization's operations, including working practices, communications, management structures, leadership, general organization and customer relations. Companies of all sizes and in many kinds of industries have used such surveys to gauge the feelings of employees. For example, a staff survey might be invoked to assess attitudes towards proposed changes to a company's redundancy scheme (with reduced benefits), or to predict problems before they occur, or to ascertain what actions need to be taken to improve staff morale, confidence and loyalty. Their value can be greater if a survey can be compared with a similar one conducted in the past (a longitudinal design), or with surveys conducted in similar organizations, or with other sources of benchmarking data. Whatever the subject of the staff opinion survey, it is essential that the results are fed back to all staff, particularly those who provided information, otherwise the response rates to future surveys is likely to be low.

As Figure 10.1 showed, all surveys must be conducted according to a carefully devised plan, and staff opinion surveys are no exception. Indeed, because they involve contacting many people within an organization, it is essential that, if 'political fallout' is to be avoided, they must be seen to be professionally designed and conducted. This is also essential in assisting a high return rate – vital if the organization's policy is to be influenced by the results. We will look in turn at the typical stages involved in a staff opinion survey, many of which should, by now, be familiar.

Identifying aims and objectives

An organization or researcher must have a sound reason for wanting to conduct the survey in the first place, since money and resources are going to be used in its planning and implementation. The anticipated results need to outweigh the costs of the survey. Once the organization is satisfied that this is the case, a concise set of aims and objectives should be drawn up. If, for example, a company has just taken over a rival firm, it might want to conduct a survey among the new set of employees on how they have reacted to the take-over and their perceptions of their new employers (including their fears and anxieties). A well-defined set of aims and objectives provide a basis for also determining the scope and structure of the survey and for evaluating its effectiveness.

As a student researcher, you might have an opportunity to become involved in a staff survey. While this would be an ideal opportunity to conduct a large-scale study and enhance your skills, there are also dangers. Firstly, does the opportunity come with an appropriate amount of financial resources to cover your expenses (such as the purchase of any survey software and administrative support)? Secondly, do you have sufficient time to negotiate, plan and execute the survey? Thirdly, do you have an appropriate amount of access to respondents? Finally, do you have sufficient experience and expertise?

The author once worked for a large London-based organization in which one of the human resources consultants decided to undertake an attitude survey of the middle and senior management team. However, he was relatively inexperienced in survey design and some of the questions were not well worded (at least to some of those who received the questionnaire). As a result, many senior managers phoned the human resources department to ask: What's this survey all about? I don't understand why I've got it or what it's for!' A week later the consultant was sacked! The moral of this story: employee surveys are high profile – you can't afford any mistakes! So take advice and pilot the survey thoroughly before release.

Planning the survey

Establishing the scope

Assessing the scope of the survey is important. It is relatively easy to construct long surveys that attack a range of themes, none of which fits comfortably together. The reports that result from surveys of this kind will have difficulty in providing coherent, focused recommendations for implementation. One approach is to start with a broad but shallow survey that addresses a range of topics, but not in significant depth, to highlight key themes. This could be followed with a detailed survey on prime concerns. If one of these problems was, say, the emergence of a key competitor, the survey could focus on corporate direction, customer focus and innovation. If, on the other hand, the problem was the emergence of a high staff turnover rate, the scope of the survey could be confined to employee appraisal systems, motivation, pay and benefits, and training and development.

Considering the audience

We saw in Chapter 6 that, often for practical reasons, representative samples must be chosen from the population. In designing a survey for a specific audience, it is necessary to consider their traits and attributes. For example, their educational and literacy levels (including first language), qualifications, experience in the sector or business, technical knowledge and national culture. A survey, say, that asked respondents to provide information on their 'Christian' name, would be offensive to people of non-Christian religions, or of no religious persuasion. No matter what the social or ethnic composition of an organization, survey designers need to be aware of multi-cultural sensitivities.

Getting the timing right

Even short-term changes in an organization can have an effect on staff morale and hence the chances of people being willing to complete a survey. This can also include rumours, whether substantiated or not, of changes about to occur. It is important to conduct staff opinion surveys during periods when the organization is not affected by these one-off developments. This is particularly important when the results are going to be compared with those from a previous survey. It will almost certainly help to pilot the survey first to make sure that there are no embarrassing misunderstandings. Staff opinion surveys are high profile!

Creating publicity

Taking Dillman's (2007) advice, advance notice of the survey is important for assisting the return rate. Employees need to know why the survey is being carried out and what will be done with the results. A guarantee of confidentiality is, of course, essential. Publicity for the survey and its credibility will be most effective if this comes from the highest level of the organization, particularly if this is the organization's chief executive or managing director. For many organizations, this publicity will be delivered via its intranet, or staff newsletter.

Selecting research tools

As we have seen earlier, there are a number of alternative survey methods, and any staff opinion survey will benefit from the use of a variety of approaches. Hence, a typical survey may use not only paper-based questionnaires, but questionnaires delivered via email and the intranet. Interviewer-administered questionnaires are less likely to be used for staff opinion surveys due to the time and costs involved as well as the lack of confidentiality.

Analysing the results

The impact of a survey is enhanced if comparisons can be drawn between different categories of respondent in the organization. Hence, for the analysis to have much significance, the survey should be aimed at capturing the opinions of staff in different departments or business units, functions, locations, age groups, levels of seniority, length of service, etc. It is also useful to compare the results with those of other, similar organizations (similar in terms of size and sector), in order to benchmark the organization against others. This of course, will be dependent on the extent to which such data is available.

Care should be taken, however, to ensure that the use of respondent demographic categories is accurate. In the modern world, organizations change quickly. Departments get renamed, moved or closed down. New departments or sections open up but news of this may not be generally shared throughout the organization, especially large ones. People get promoted or leave the organization. You need to ensure that you are working from the latest records (sampling frame) of organizational information. The analysis will be considerably strengthened if you are able to compare like with like – there is a consistency over time in terms of what is being explored.

Using the results

Reporting results to management

Many staff opinion surveys may require two different kinds of report. If the organization is a large company, a Corporate Report might be needed at top management level. The Corporate Report should include:

- An overview of the results for the whole organization.
- A comparison, if possible, between the current survey and previous surveys to illustrate trends over time.
- An Executive Summary that features key points, conclusions and recommendations.

Corporate Reports may also sometimes include the results of similar surveys conducted in other companies to establish benchmarks. An essential feature of a Corporate Report is that it should be easy to read, and so presenting data in tabular and graphical form is very important.

Another kind of document, a Management Report, is needed by the managers of individual business units, divisions, departments or locations. The Management Report might include a comparison between:

- Different business units, departments or locations within the organization.
- The views of people of different grades or levels.
- The views of people of different age ranges or length of service.

For very large surveys in complex organizations there can be quite a significant time gap between the collection of the data and the publication of the report. In this case the publication of a short one- or two-page Flash Report, summarizing the findings, could be useful, particularly if these could be broken down, by department or section. In some cases this could comprise a small set of Web pages that are linked from the 'What's New?' section of an organization's main Web home page. As a student reporting results, you might consider offering to give a short presentation of the findings to the management team or person that commissioned the research.

Reporting the results to employees

Staff opinion surveys create expectations among employees, hence, it is essential that results are disseminated as soon as possible. This should include those cases where the results of the survey are not in line with management hopes or expectations. Not to publish a report will only fuel resentment and make any future staff opinion survey difficult to implement. The best approach is for management to show that they are willing to acknowledge the results and to take action. Reporting results to staff could be through staff newsletters, bulletin boards, emails or team meetings – or all of these.

Implementing the results

For the results of a staff opinion survey to have any lasting impact it is necessary that a planned and coherent series of actions be conducted. These could include:

- The appointment of a director or senior manager responsible for coordinating follow-up actions across the organization.
- The appointment of a senior manager responsible for coordinating follow-up actions in each division or department.
- Agreement on a timetable and process for implementation.
- Agreement on a system for monitoring the implementation of recommendations stemming from the survey and for communicating the effectiveness of the implementation.

REDUCING SOURCES OF ERROR

TOTAL
SURVEY
ERROR

Total survey error (TSE) is the accumulation of all errors that may arise in the design, collection, processing and analysis of survey data (Biemer, 2010). It is the deviation of a survey response from its true value. In an ideal world, the selected sample exactly mirrors all facets of the target population. Each question in the survey is clear and precise and captures the sphere of interest exactly. Every person selected for the sample agrees to cooperate; they understand every question and know all the requested information and answer truthfully and completely. Their responses are accurately recorded and entered without error into a computer file and accurately analysed. If only real world surveys were like this! In the real world, gaps and distortions in the data become sources of error.

The two main sources of error are *variance* and *bias*. **Variance** results from different measures occurring in repeated trials of a procedure. One of the most common sources of this is sampling error (see next section). Variance can also refer to the variability of the dependent variables in a study that cannot be associated with changes in the independent variable. McBurney and White (2009) suggest that changes in the dependent variable associated with changes in independent variables is fine, but variance is an example of 'bad' variability because it distorts the data and should be controlled. Other sources of variance are the percentage of respondents who can be contacted for an interview, or the number of refusals to answer a particular question.

Bias occurs when a measurement tends to be consistently higher or lower than the true population value. If, say, we conducted a survey of income levels in a community, there might be a tendency for those on lower incomes to report that they earn more due to social embarrassment. Conversely there might also be a tendency for wealthier social groups to report lower income levels than they earn, perhaps because they subconsciously fear the listening ear of the tax authorities! More often, these kinds of groups will simply not complete the part of the survey that asks for data on income level – another source of error, non-response. Biemer (2010) suggests that the setting or environment within which a survey is conducted may also contribute to measurement error. For example, when collecting data on sensitive subjects like drug use, sexual behaviour or fertility, this is best done in a private and confidential setting if accurate responses are going to be obtained.

Sampling error

SAMPLING
ERROR

Sampling error, as we have seen, is one of the sources of variance. If the population for the study is split between males and females, even a random sample can finish up with, say, 52 per cent females and 48 per cent males. A common source of sampling error, however, lies with sampling frames. We would like the frame to list all members of the population that have been identified, and to exclude all others. Unfortunately, this is often not the case. One problem is that of *under-coverage*, where people are missing from the sampling frame. For example, if telephone directories are used as sources of the sampling frame, some groups of people may have their numbers excluded from the directory. This is not a problem if the under-coverage is random, but poses problems if the exclusion is more prone among some groups than others.

Furthermore, the sampling frame may not include people who have just moved house. This is not problematic if such people are typical of the population as a whole, but, again, becomes an issue if they are different in terms of key characteristics.

A reverse problem is that of *over-coverage* where the sampling frame contains people who are not members of the target population. This occurs, for example, when quite generalized sampling frames are available (such as telephone directories, or membership lists of clubs or associations) but specific groups are required for the sample. For example, a study of attitudes towards the recycling of domestic waste in a seaside town might use a directory of local residents, only to find that many of the homes are used for holiday lettings and are either empty or occupied by people not relevant to the research.

This difficulty can be overcome in several ways. One is to contact members of the sampling frame and ascertain whether they belong to the required sample. Another is to design the questionnaire or interview schedule in such a way that ineligible respondents are identified early and screened out.

➤ **ON THE WEB 10.6** ◄

To calculate sampling error for a given size of sample, population and confidence interval, visit the DSS Research site at:

http://www.dssresearch.com/toolkit/default.asp

Click on Sample Error calculator. Note that the site also contains a tool for calculating sample size.

Data collection error

One of the simple solutions to reducing error at the data collection stage is maintaining a robust record-keeping system so that the amount of missing data can be minimized. At the unit level (person or household), records will include details of all those who have responded, non-respondents and follow-up mailing or interview details, and the number and timings of re-attempted telephone calls.

SOURCES
OF ERROR

➤ **TOP TIP 10.5** ◄

Non-response can be reduced by making questionnaires easy to answer. Hence response rates can be improved by careful and meticulous questionnaire design. In the case of interviews, non-respondents can be re-contacted by more experienced and persuasive interviewers. Or rethink your approach to providing incentives for people to agree to be interviewed.

GRAY ON
REDUCING
QUESTION-
NAIRES NON-
RESPONSE
RATES

In addition to non-response, missing data is also a problem. In postal surveys there are several ways of coping with missing data:

- Ignoring the items and code as 'missing' in the data set.
- Trying to determine what the answer should be.
- Re-contacting the respondent.

The choice of steps taken partly depends on the value of the missing data. If it is of central importance to the study, then rather than ignoring it, or guessing what it might have been, the best step is to try to contact the respondent. Copas and Farewell (1998) discuss some of the statistical methods for dealing with non-response when these gaps in the data cannot be ignored. If the level of data loss is small, however, and of relatively low importance, then it may be safe to ignore the problem.

Improving response rates

A meta-survey based on 45 surveys (including Web surveys, telephone surveys, direct mailing and face-to-face interviews) showed that response rates for Web surveys averaged 6–15 per cent, that is, 11 per cent lower than for the other methods (Lozar Manfreda, Bosnjak, Berzelak, Hass and Vehovar, 2008). Web surveys also suffer because respondents often fail to answer all the questions, particularly when the survey is long (see item non-response next). To improve survey low response rates it is often necessary to locate their causes. Dillman (2007) suggests that low response rates may result from:

- Difficulties in defining the organizational entity. Does the survey deal with individual 'units' of the organization or the organization as a whole?
- Problems in getting to the targeted correspondent. In large organizations, for example, senior managers may have their post opened by administrative staff and personal assistants who may make the decision on whether the survey is passed on for completion.
- Organizations having a policy of not responding to surveys.
- Data sources needing to be consulted, taking up time, even if records are available and not confidential.

In general, response rates will be higher if the respondent has the authority to respond, the capacity to respond (access to the information) and the motivation to respond (it is in his or her interests to do so). Dillman (2007) suggests that a number of factors are critical to achieving a high return rate from organizational surveys.

- Identifying the most appropriate respondents and developing multiple ways of contacting them. This is particularly helped if names and job titles are known in advance. Prior telephone calls can help here, and can also assist in identifying where in the organization the survey should be sent.
- Planning for a mixed-mode design, using not only a questionnaire but other forms of contact such as emails or the telephone. While surveys targeted at individuals may require about five contacts, organizational surveys may require more.
- Developing an easy-to-complete questionnaire with embedded instructions on how to complete the questions (see Chapter 14).
- Conducting on-site interviews to help tailor the questionnaire to the knowledge and cognitive capabilities of the audience. This may also help identify questions that are too sensitive.
- Targeting organizational surveys on gatekeepers if possible.
- Being cautious about the use of financial incentives (unlike individual surveys), as this may not be ethically acceptable in some organizations.

Table 10.1   Methods for increasing response rates with postal questionnaires

Treatment	Response increase over control (percentage points)
Prior telephone calls	19
Monetary incentives	
10 cents (US)	17
25 cents (US)	19
$1 (US)	26
20p (UK)	15
Non-monetary incentives	
Pen	12
Pocket knife	15
Stamp business reply	7
Anonymity (in-company)	20
Anonymity (external)	10
Follow-ups	12

Source: Adapted from Jobber and O'Reilly, 1996

➤ **TOP TIP 10.6** ◀

It is worth spending additional time getting the 'look and feel' of the questionnaire right. Survey instruments that are professionally presented and easy to complete will, generally, get higher response rates.

Jobber and O'Reilly (1996), however, do suggest the use of direct incentives for responding. Table 10.1 illustrates data on monetary incentives taken from the authors' analysis of 12 studies. Even though the sums are relatively modest, the act of 'giving' helps to build an obligation to respond on the part of the recipient. Non-monetary incentives include the use of gifts such as pens or pocket-knives (the latter would definitely need ethical approval!), and even high quality, foil-wrapped milk chocolate (Brennan and Charbonneau, 2009) but various studies suggest that these are slightly less effective than direct monetary incentives. When using pre-paid envelopes for the return of questionnaires, evidence suggests that stamped rather than business reply envelopes elicit the larger response. Assurances of anonymity can also have an impact, whether the survey is organized from within the organization or from the outside. Finally, it makes sense to follow up any non-respondents with a letter and questionnaire.

Research by Helgeson (2002) led them to develop a model for improving response rates for mail surveys based on a five-stage process: attention, intention, completion, return and interest in results (see Figure 10.4).

- Attention. The amount of time survey recipients spent reading and reviewing their mail is an important factor influencing attention to the survey (they will tend to open the envelope and scrutinize the contents). Also important is that recipients have a general interest in research. Attention will be helped by a pre-notification that the survey is on its way.

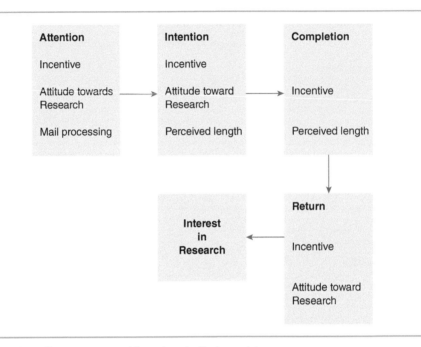

Figure 10.4 Survey-response hierarchy-of-effects model

Source: Helgeson et al., 2002

- Intention to complete the survey is influenced by the perceived length of the survey – the shorter the survey, the greater the intention will be to complete it.
- Completion and return. Once a survey is completed it is likely to be returned because of curiosity regarding the results.

What is important in the findings is that Helgeson et al. (2002) find that each phase has a significant relationship on subsequent phases. Indeed, the strength of these relationships becomes greater as the process progresses. So researchers need to give respondents encouragement to move between phases. Designing the survey so that it gains the potential respondent's attention and provides some rewards for its completion enhances the chances that the respondent will move on to completion and return.

Reducing item non-response

At the item (question) level, missing data may be far from random and pose a threat of bias to the study. For example, people may refuse to answer questions that are seen as intrusive or sensitive, or they simply may not know the answer. In interviews it is essential that interviewers are skilled in handling non-response to individual questions. This is helped by interviewers being able to remind respondents about the confidentiality of their answers (if they believe that the problem is one of sensitivity). Mangione (1995) argues that, for postal surveys, any problem of non-response should have been picked up at the piloting stage where it should have been clear which questions were giving respondents a problem. This is particularly the case with attitude surveys where subjects do not feel that their views have been represented in the questions or they dislike the way in which potential responses are phrased.

Reducing interviewer error

Unskilled, untrained or inexperienced interviewers can also be a source of error due to the way in which they handle the interview. The key is that the respondent should answer against the categories that are presented, and no other. So if these categories are 'Strongly agree', 'Agree', 'Disagree' and 'Strongly disagree', or 'No response', these are what are marked down and coded on the interview schedule. If such responses are not forthcoming, the interviewer responds with a **probe**, a question designed to elicit an acceptable response. So, say a respondent answered: 'Yeh, you're absolutely right!' the correct probe is: 'Would that be ... [read the categories again]?' The incorrect probe would be: 'So, would that be "Strongly agree", then?', as this, obviously, would be biasing the response.

Improving construct validity

Another source of error is invalidity. Particularly if you are designing your own survey instrument such as a questionnaire, it is easy to construct questions that do not match what you are trying to discover. The way around this is to develop a table like the one presented at Table 10.2. List your research questions down the left hand column. In the next column, outline the kinds of constructs being measured. So, if you have a research question that states: 'Does greater job satisfaction lead to improved performance?', then the two constructs, clearly, are 'job satisfaction' and 'performance'. This all may appear too obvious, but it helps you focus on what you are seeking to measure. In the next column, choose how you are going to collect data that addresses each research question and construct. As indicated in *Stages in the Survey Process*, above, there may be validated scales already available, so it is sensible to make use of them. In the case of job satisfaction, the scale by Warr et al. (1979) is often used, but there are others. If the scale is short, you might choose to include it in under 'Instrument questions' in the right hand column; if it is too long, include it in an Appendix and make reference to where it is. If a validated scale is unavailable, then you will construct one of your own, indicating in the table that the instrument is designed as part of 'This study'. In the right hand column, write out the questions so they can be checked against the construct being measured.

Of course, a survey questionnaire may be one option for measuring constructs but there are others. Indeed, you may want to show that, for the purposes of enhancing reliability, you are going to triangulate data gathering methods. So for Research Question 2, you not only measure intention to leave through three questions on your survey questionnaire, but you also conduct a number of qualitative interviews on the same theme. Here, you may use questions similar to the survey but you will add new ones in order to probe deeper.

Table 10.2 Research questions, constructs, data collection methods and developing valid instruments

Research question	Constructs being measured	Data collection method	Instrument	Instrument questions
RQ1 – stated here	Job satisfaction	Questionnaire	Validated instrument (Source, date)	See Appendix x
	Performance		This study	Q1 here
				Q2 here
				Q3 here
				Q4 here
RQ2 – stated here	Intention to leave	Questionnaire	This study	Q1 here
				Q2 here
				Q3 here
		Interview	This study	See interview schedule Appendix y

ETHICS AND GOOD PRACTICE IN SURVEY DESIGN

SURVEY
ETHICS

As we saw in Chapter 4, two of the essential principles of ethical conduct are informed consent and the protection of confidentiality, and these apply to the use of surveys as to any other research method. This means that respondents must be told about the nature and purposes of the survey, who is sponsoring it and how much of their time will be required in answering it. They should also know about the purposes to which the survey data will be put. Subjects should take part purely voluntarily and not as a result of pressure being imposed on them. In protecting confidentiality, care must be taken to ensure that data sets or the results of the study do not allow individuals to be identified. Sampling frame lists should not be passed on to third parties, including other researchers, without the consent of survey participants. Even if consent is given, care must be taken to remove all identifying features that could link specific data to individuals. When research is being conducted by professional survey researchers, these kinds of principles are usually codified into a set of ethical guidelines or rules. To compare and contrast the ethical codes of a number of professional research bodies, return to On the Web 4.1 in Chapter 4.

Summary

- Surveys are a common research tool because they allow for the collection of large amounts of data from large samples.
- Stages in survey design include the definition of research objectives, questionnaire design, piloting, survey distribution, and coding and analysis.
- There are, essentially, two kinds of survey: analytical and descriptive. Descriptive surveys can provide illuminating data which may provide the basis for more detailed analytical investigations. Analytical surveys are capable of finding associations between dependent and independent variables and between the independent variables themselves.
- Survey methods include self-administered questionnaires (postal, delivery and collection, and online) and interviewer-administered questionnaires (structured, focus groups and telephone). Postal and online questionnaires are usually the cheapest to use, but interviewer-administered questionnaires allow interviewers to explore issues of non-response and to follow-up with probes.
- Sources of error include variance and bias. To reduce sources of error, steps must be taken to minimize under-coverage and over-coverage in sampling frames, and to minimize the amount of missing data, including non-response to the survey and to individual items.
- In encouraging high response rates, care must be taken to abide by research ethics in not pressurizing people to participate or to answer questions that they find intrusive.

REVIEW QUESTIONS

1. Why is the use of surveys such 'big business' today?
2. Response rates for Web-based surveys are generally lower than for other methods. How can you explain this?
3. Piloting of surveys is usually strongly recommended. But *what* should you seek to pilot?
4. Name five practical incentives to respondents (other than money) to help maximize response rates.

SURVEY
CHECKLIST

FURTHER READING

Fowler, F.J. (2009) *Survey Research Methods*, 4th edn. Thousand Oaks, CA: Sage. The 4th edition pays more attention to the use of the Internet in survey research, discusses the sharp drop in response rates to telephone surveys and provides advice on reducing error in surveys.

Rea, L.M. and Parker, R.A. (2005) *Designing and Conducting Survey Research,* 3rd edn. San Francisco, CA: Jossey-Bass. First published in 1992, this is a comprehensive and accessible book that covers the field, including the construction of survey instruments, survey administration and data analysis.

Czaja, R. and Blair, J. (2005) *Designing Surveys: A Guide to Decisions and Procedures,* 2nd edn. Thousand Oaks, CA: Sage. An excellent introduction to the various survey methods, plus practical advice on survey design and writing questionnaires.

De Vaus, D.A. (2002) *Surveys in Social Research,* 5th edn. London: George Allen & Unwin. One of the most comprehensive texts available, it includes useful advice on constructing and administering questionnaires for surveys and details of statistical tests used in survey analysis. An added bonus is the presentation of many useful websites.

JOURNAL RESOURCES

Olsen, F., Abelsen, B. and Abel Olsen, J. (2012) 'Improving response rate and quality of survey data with a scratch lottery ticket incentive', *BMC Medical Research Methodology*, 12(1): 52–57. Shows how the use of scratch lottery tickets as an incentive may improve response rates and survey representativeness.

Martínez-Tur, V., Peiró, J.M. and Ramos, J. (2005) 'Linking situational constraints to customer satisfaction in a service environment', *Applied Psychology: An International Review*, 54(1): 25–36. Example of a customer satisfaction survey.

Cunningham, J., Connor, D.F., Miller, K. and Melloni Jr.,and Richard.H. (2003) 'Staff survey results and characteristics that predict assault and injury to personnel working in mental health facilities', *Aggressive Behavior*, 29(1): 31–40. Demonstrates the implementation of a staff opinion survey from sampling strategy to data analysis.

SUMMARY OF WEB LINKS

http://www.dssresearch.com/toolkit/default.asp

http://www.jiscmail.ac.uk/

http://www.nop.org.uk

http://qb.soc.surrey.ac.uk/docs/surveys.htm

http://www.surveymonkey.com/

http://www.surveywriter.com/HomePage.html

http://www.yougov.com

11

DESIGNING CASE STUDIES

CHAPTER INTRODUCTION

Chapter outline

When should we use case studies?	267
The case study design process	268
Types of case study design	274
Data collection sources	277
Quality in case studies: validity and reliability	279
Analysing the evidence	282
Composing case study reports	286

Keywords

Case study design

Causal relationships

Multiple data sources

Unit of analysis

Converging evidence

Cross-case comparisons

Chapter objectives

After reading this chapter you will be able to:

- Describe the purpose of case studies.
- Plan a systematic approach to case study design.
- Recognize the strengths and limitations of case studies as a research method.
- Compose a case study report that is appropriately structured and presented.

We saw in Chapter 10 that surveys are used where large amounts of data have to be collected, often from a large, diverse and widely distributed population. In contrast, case studies tend to be much more specific in focus. Indeed, according to Eisenhardt (1989) the case study is a research strategy which focuses on gaining an understanding of the dynamics present within single settings. While surveys tend to collect data on a limited range of topics but from many people, case studies can explore many themes and subjects, but from a much more focused range of people, organizations or contexts. As Tight (2010) makes clear, case study research involves a detailed examination of a small sample of interest, and typically also from a particular perspective. A case may be an individual, an organization, a role, a community or a nation (Punch, 2005). For many student projects, an organization they can get access to, becomes their case study.

Case studies typically combine data collection methods from a wide variety of sources including archives, interviews, surveys and participant observation (Dooley, 2002). The case study method can be used for a wide variety of issues, including the evaluation of training programmes (a common subject), organizational performance, project design and implementation, policy analysis, and relationships between different sectors of an organization or between organizations. In terms of disciplines, case study research has been used extensively in health services research, political science, social work, architecture, operations research and business management (Taylor, Dossick and Garvin, 2011). According to Stake (2000), case studies can prove invaluable in adding to understanding, extending experience and increasing conviction about a subject. The case study approach can be used as both a qualitative *and* quantitative method (Dooley, 2002). However, just a brief look at case studies shows why they are more often used qualitatively. Yin (2009) defines the case study as

> ... an empirical inquiry that
>
> - investigates a contemporary phenomenon within its real-life context, especially when
> - the boundaries between phenomenon and context are not clearly evident. (Yin, 2009: 13)

Case studies, then, explore subjects and issues where relationships may be ambiguous or uncertain. But, in contrast to methods such as descriptive surveys, case studies are also trying to attribute *causal* relationships and are not just describing a situation. The approach is particularly useful when the researcher is trying to uncover a relationship between a phenomenon and the context in which it is occurring. For example, a business might want to evaluate the factors that have made a recent merger a success (to prepare the ground for future mergers). The problem here, as with all case studies, is that the contextual variables (timing, global economic circumstances, cultures of the merging organizations, etc.) are so numerous that a purely experimental approach revealing causal associations would simply be unfeasible.

The case study approach requires the collection of multiple sources of data but, if the researcher is not to be overwhelmed, these need to become focused in some way. Therefore case studies benefit from the prior development of a theoretical position to help direct the data collection and analysis process, and the creation of a defined focus through an initial definition of a research question (Eisenhardt, 1989). Note, then, that the case study method tends to be deductive rather than inductive in character (although, as we shall see, this is not always the case). It is also, contrary to popular opinion, often a demanding and difficult approach, because there are no particular standardized techniques as one would find, say, with experimental design. Yin (2009, 2012), one of the authorities on case study research, who we will refer to extensively in this chapter, also stresses the wide range of skills and flexibility required by case study investigators.

LECTURE:
CASE STUDY

WHEN SHOULD WE USE CASE STUDIES?

The case study method is ideal when a 'how' or 'why' question is being asked about a contemporary set of events over which the researcher has no control. As Table 11.1 shows, 'what', 'who' and 'where' questions are likely to favour a survey approach, or the use of archival records (unobtrusive measures – see Chapter 19), where it is important to show the incidence of a factor. So, an education authority that needs to identify how many of its workforce are aged 55 or more, will either turn to its human resource records, or, if these are so fragmented as not to contain this kind of information, conduct a survey among its schools and colleges. This would reveal *who* and *where* these older workers were located. If, however, the organization wanted to know *how* an ageing workforce affected its teaching and staff retention, a case study would be able to deal with this more explanatory issue and to illuminate key features.

Table 11.1   Selection criteria for different research strategies

Strategy	Form of research question	Requires control over behavioural events?	Focuses on contemporary events?
Experiment	How, why	Yes	Yes
Survey	Who, what, where, how many, how much	No	Yes
Unobtrusive measures	Who, what, where, how many, how much	No	Yes/No
Case study	How, why	No	Yes

Source: Adapted from COSMOS Corporation, in Yin, 2009

Examine the following social policy problem and, using Table 11.1, suggest which research strategy or strategies could be used to address it.

Government statistics reveal a disturbing rise in inner-city drug addiction and substance abuse over the past five years. Increased policing and greater legal penalties have had no effect. Drug rehabilitation experts have recommended the provision of 'safe housing' for persistent offenders where their drug intake can be monitored, regulated and reduced over time. Apart from the threat of political 'backlash', the government wants to understand more about the effectiveness of such a programme before deciding whether to support it.

CASE STUDY
RESEARCH
MISUNDER-
STANDINGS

You probably decided that the safe houses approach could be used as a case study to explore *how* the drug intake methods affected addiction. The case study approach is not dissimilar to the use of unobtrusive measures such as documents, archives and the use of historical evidence – in each case no attempt is made to manipulate behaviours. But while unobtrusive measures can only rely on the use of existing documentation (historical or contemporary), case studies tend to focus on collecting up-to-date information. For this reason, data collection may involve the use of not only contemporary documentation, but also direct observation and systematic interviewing.

Nevertheless, as Yin (2009) makes clear, the case study approach has not been universally accepted by researchers as reliable, objective and legitimate. One problem is that it is often difficult (indeed, dangerous) to generalize from a specific case. But, in defence of case studies, Yin points out that most scientific inquiries have to be replicated by multiple examples of the experiment, and case studies too can be based upon multiple cases of the same issue or phenomenon. Gummesson (2000) supports this view, asserting that, even in medicine, doctors' skills are often built up from a knowledge of many individual cases.

Another criticism of case studies is the amount of time they take and the volume of documentation they generate. But Yin argues that this is to confuse case studies with one particular type, the use of ethnographic or participant observation studies where the amount of data collected can be vast. The one argument that Yin (2009) does concede is that conducting case studies successfully is an uncommon skill.

THE CASE STUDY DESIGN PROCESS

PLANNING
CASE
STUDIES

Before embarking on the design process itself, Yin (2009) recommends that the investigator is thoroughly prepared for the case study process. This includes being able to formulate and ask good research questions and to interpret the answers. This means turning off his or her own interpretative 'filters' and actually noting what is being said, or done (recall the discussion of phenomenology in Chapter 2). The investigator must be able to respond quickly to the flow of answers and to pose new questions or issues. Having a firm grasp of the theoretical principles involved will obviously help because issues will be thrown into sharp relief if the data contradict what was expected. This, again, reinforces the importance of the deductive approach. But the case study approach can also generate data that help towards the development of theory – and is, hence, inductive. So which is most important?

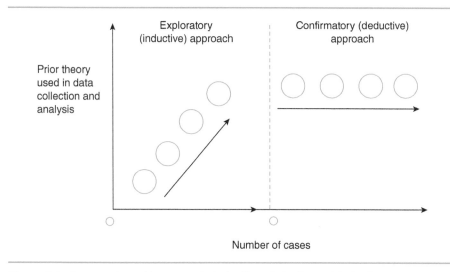

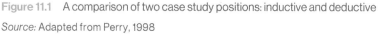

Number of cases

Figure 11.1 A comparison of two case study positions: inductive and deductive

Source: Adapted from Perry, 1998

Should we use inductive or deductive approaches?

A possible relationship between induction and deduction in case study research is illustrated by Perry (1998). In the left side of Figure 11.1, the first (extreme left-hand) case study is purely inductive or exploratory, starting from no theoretical position (pure grounded theory – see Chapter 23). Data collection and analysis in the next case study are informed by some of the concepts found in the first study. But it is difficult to draw inferences through this approach because, as new findings are generated with each study, the focus of subsequent studies (and the kinds of questions that are asked) begins to shift. Hence, data from each study cannot be compared, because we would not be comparing like with like.

This problem is overcome by the more deductive, or at least confirmatory, approach on the right side of Figure 11.1. Here, the first case study could constitute a pilot case, which establishes the theoretical boundaries and then the data gathering protocol and tools for all the remaining studies. The initial theory is then confirmed or rejected by cross-case data analysis across all the main case studies.

This approach is confirmed by Yin (2009), who also argues that, after adopting a particularly theoretical position, the research proceeds through a series of case studies, allowing for cross-case comparisons to be taken. In essence, Yin suggests that the research should progress through a series of stages (see Figure 11.2), each of which is described in more detail in the next section.

A case study process

Developing a theoretical stance

Building theory from case study research is most appropriate when the topic is relatively new, or when there is a need to inject some fresh perspectives into a theme that is well known (Eisenhardt, 1989). A provisional hypothesis or set of questions is developed – provisional in the sense that they are open to further improvement

CASE STUDY
THEORY

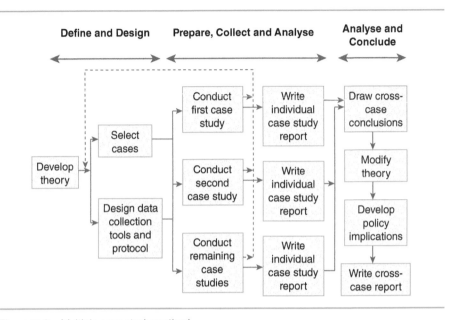

Figure 11.2 Multiple case study method

Source: Adapted from Yin, 2009

or modification during the process of the study. Hypotheses or questions should be linked, where possible, with previous research – hence, the first stage of the case study process is usually a thorough literature review to discover what past research has been done (Dooley, 2002). This is also an opportunity to identify rival hypotheses and theories, both of which will help in the analysis of the results. However, given that case study research is flexible and may follow leads into new areas, the theoretical framework that is adopted at the beginning of a study may not be the one that survives to the end (Hartley, 1994).

Let us take the example of a case study that seeks to evaluate the software development process for the building of an organization's intranet Web portal. The hypothesis is that: for Web portal design, the traditional principles of the software development 'life cycle' lead to project failure. Then, using what Yin (2012) calls *analytic generalization*, we are able to compare and contrast the results of the case study with an accepted set of principles or theory. If two or more cases are shown to support the theory, then it becomes possible to make a claim that the theory has been replicated. Yin warns, however, that while analytical generalization is appropriate, statistical generalization is certainly not. It should not be assumed, for example, that the results of a case study can be generalized to a larger population as one would do in an experimental or quasi-experimental design.

Selecting cases

The selection of cases is important in case study research especially where the intention is to build theory from the cases (Eisenhardt, 1989). While the cases may be chosen randomly, this is neither necessary nor preferable. Given that the number of cases studied is usually quite limited, it makes sense to choose those that are polar or extreme types. This helps to ensure that the entity under investigation is transparently observable. Once cases are selected, the main and subordinate units of analysis are provisionally defined. For example, the organization itself might be the main unit of analysis, with departments or geographically dispersed sites the subordinate units. Note that the main and subordinate units of analysis may require different research tools. While there is no ideal number of cases, Eisenhardt (1989) suggests that between four and ten cases usually works well. With fewer than four cases it is often difficult to generate theory with much complexity and the empirical underpinning is likely to be unconvincing unless there are several sub-cases within them. With more than ten cases the volume of data can quickly become overwhelming.

Designing and piloting research tools, protocols and field procedures

In the design process, care should be taken to ensure that all tools match the original hypothesis and research objectives. Protocols involve the design of a structured set of processes or procedures, often linked to how the research tool is to be administered. For example, a protocol might be used to specify to an interviewer exactly how the interview is to be conducted, and how the interview schedule is to be used.

CASE STUDY
METHODOLOGY

One of the key design issues in the case study method is the definition of the *unit of analysis,* and then ensuring that this unit of analysis fits with the research objectives of the study. Taking our Web portal development example, it is this *process* that is the unit of analysis and not the look or functionality of the portal itself (although this could be the subject of a different case study). The conceptual framework here is the software development process, including design, prototyping, development, testing and implementation. The study could also explore the group dynamics (another process) between the Web development team involved in building the portal, to understand how their efforts can be improved in future Web projects.

Conducting a case study or multiple studies

The data are collected, analysed and synthesized into individual case study reports. This is unlikely to occur in a sequential process. So there may be circumstances when analysis raises new questions for which new units of analysis may have to be formulated and additional data collected. Each of the case studies is regarded as a study in its own right, so one of the key steps is to conduct within-case analysis, with a detailed write-up for each case study site (Eisenhardt, 1989) so that the researcher can identify unique patterns within each case. But the findings of each case need to produce *converging evidence,* so that the data from one case replicate the data from another. Think in terms of the police detective at the scene of a crime looking for multiple pieces of evidence that, together, add up to a clear 'picture' or solution.

However, while much of the data may serve to 'prove' or illustrate an issue or phenomenon, negative instances may also make a vital contribution to the analysis. Kidder (1981), for example, shows how an initial hypothesis can be continually revised (on the basis of negative or contradictory data) until it can be validated by the data. Case studies can also sometimes be illuminated by key events. The routine of office, hospital or school life, for example, may serve to obscure phenomena or trends whereas a key event such as a staff 'away day' or a new computer system going 'live' may throw up revealing tensions and social dynamics.

In terms of data collection, the case study method requires the use of *multiple sources of evidence*. This might include the use of structured, semi-structured or open interviews, field observations or document analysis. As we saw in Chapter 6, multiple sources of data also help address the issue of construct validity because the multiple sources of evidence should provide multiple measures of the same construct. Case Study 11.1 provides an example of how rich data can be collected from multiple sources in order to develop a case study.

→ **TOP TIP 11.1** ←

GRAY ON
GAINING
ACCESS:
CASE STUDIES

Consider using a case study only when you are certain that you can gain the levels and intensity of access you need to the case study persons or site. Ensure that it is practical and feasible to make use of the kinds of multiple data sources an effective case study requires. Also make enquiries early in the project, or well before you commence it, so you know whether you have access, or not.

CASE STUDY 11.1

The taxi-dance hall

In 1932, a group of researchers from Chicago carried out an ethnographic study of an institution called the taxi-dance hall. These halls had developed in the nineteenth century during a period of mass immigration to the USA and were clubs where men could pay for dances with young women. The city social services department were concerned that these dance halls were dens of vice and prostitution.

Four research assistants were employed to collect data by attending dances as participant observers and later to interview taxi-dancers, their clients and the businessmen who ran the halls. The study is vague on precise methodological details, such as the length of the project or ethical or practical issues, but the study is rich in description, as the following passage shows:

> Before long the patrons and taxi-dancers began to arrive. Some patrons come in automobiles, though many more alight from street cars. Still others seem to come from the immediate neighbourhood. For the most part they are alone, though occasionally groups of two or three appear. The patrons are a motley crowd. Some are uncouth, noisy youths, busied chiefly with their cigarettes. Others are sleekly groomed and suave young men, who come alone and remain aloof. Others are middle-aged men whose stooped shoulders and shambling gait speak eloquently of a life of manual toil. Sometimes they speak English fluently. More often their broken English reveals them as European immigrants, on the way towards being Americanized. Still others are dapperly [sic] little Filipinos who come together, sometimes even in squads of six or eight, and slip quietly into the entrance. Altogether the patrons make up a polyglot aggregation from many corners of the world. (Cressey, 1932: 4–5)

Analysis of the data reveals that many of the girls see dancing as a glamorous and well-paid alternative to an early marriage, or to factory or office work. The backgrounds and motivation of the clients are revealed, and show them as isolated and lonely people. There is discussion of the language used by the dancers and their descriptions of clients as 'suckers', 'fruit' and 'fish'. As Travers points out, the result of the study is 'a revealing and intimate portrait of this social world, built up through a careful study of different group and individual perspectives' (2001: 28).

Source: Cressey, 1932, in Travers, 2001

Look back at Case Study 11.1.

1. Identify the implicit working hypothesis of the study.
2. What are the multiple sources of evidence?
3. On the basis of the evidence presented in the study, should the original hypothesis be accepted or rejected?

Suggested answers are provided at the end of the chapter.

Creating a case study database (optional)

This process is to ensure that information is collected systematically and that it is logically ordered in the database as well as being easily accessible. One factor that distinguishes the case study approach from other research methods is that the case study data and the case study report are often one and the same. But all case studies should contain a presentable database so that other researchers and interested parties can review the data as well as final written reports. Allowing other researchers to evaluate the data or to replicate it increases the *reliability* of the case study. Case study databases can take a variety of formats, including the use of:

CASE STUDY:
DATABASE

●   *Case study notes* resulting from observations, interviews or document analysis, and may take the form of computer files (word processed or an actual database), diary entries or index cards. Whatever form they take, it is essential that they are put into categories and that these can be accessed quickly and easily. Obviously, computer-based files are more efficient in terms of both storage space and search facilities.
●   *Case study documents*, which need to be carefully stored and an annotated bibliography produced for ease of later analysis and retrieval.
●   *Tabular materials* of quantitative data.

Drawing cross-case conclusions

After within-case analysis (see above), researchers will then look for patterns across cases by searching for similarities and differences. The dimensions measured can be those that emerged from previous literature searches, or can be chosen by the researcher (Eisenhardt, 1989). Another approach is to select pairs of cases and then list the similarities or differences between each pair. An alternative strategy is to analyse the cases by data source, that is, the researcher scours the interview data for cross-case comparisons, then examines survey data across the cases, etc. From within-case comparisons and cross-case analysis, tentative themes, concepts and even relationships between variables may emerge (Eisenhardt, 1989) with the researcher constantly comparing theory and data, iteratively moving towards a close fit between the two.

Writing the case study report

One of the problems with case studies is that they tend to produce large volumes of data, held in a case study database. The report writing stage, then, can sometimes

Table 11.2   The process of case study construction

Stage	Process	
Step 1	Assemble raw case data.	
	Consists of all the information collected about an organization, person(s) or event	Chain of evidence
Step 2 (optional)	Construct case record.	
	Organize, classify and edit raw data to condense it	
Step 3	Write case study narrative.	

Source: Adapted from Patton, 1990

appear quite daunting. Patton (2002) suggests that a useful intermediary step between this database and the writing of the case study report (which he terms a narrative) is the construction of a case record (see Table 11.2). Each record contains an edited and more condensed version of each case.

The case study report is conceptually linked back to the case study records and raw case data through a 'chain of evidence', including tables, reproduced documents, vignettes, etc. These allow the reader (such as another researcher, or the case study's sponsor) to question and even re-interpret the data if necessary. The evidence in the database should also be consistent with the questions and procedures cited in the case study protocol. Allowing a researcher to successfully check the chain of evidence increases the *reliability* of the case study if more than one researcher uses the data to come to similar conclusions (inter-judge reliability).

The task of report writing is much easier, and the results are likely to be more coherent, if the previous stages have been observed carefully; for example, if a case study protocol has been drawn up and implemented, and if individual case study reports have been written up and conclusions drawn. (See Composing case study reports, p. 286, for details of report types and structures.)

TYPES OF CASE STUDY DESIGN

TYPES OF
CASE STUDIES

Whatever the precise case study design chosen, it is essential that the case study takes the reader into the case situation. This means that descriptions should be holistic and comprehensive and should include 'myriad dimensions, factors, variables, and categories woven together into an idiographic framework' (Patton, 1990: 387). The design process for case studies involves deciding whether the unit of analysis for the study will be an individual case (for example, a person or organization) or multiple cases. Stake (2005) identifies three types of case study:

- Intrinsic, to better understand a particular case
- Instrumental, to provide insight into an issue or to create a generalization
- Multiple or collective, when a number of cases are studied jointly to investigate a phenomenon, population or general condition

Yin (2009) proposes four main types of case study design, as represented in Figure 11.3, each of which needs to be selected on the basis of particular sets of conditions.

	Single case designs	Multiple case designs
Holistic (single unit of analysis)	**Type 1** Single/holistic	**Type 3** Multiple/holistic
Embedded (multiple units of analysis)	**Type 2** Single/embedded	**Type 4** Multiple/embedded

Figure 11.3 Main types of case study design

This shows that case studies can be based upon single or multiple case designs and on single or multiple units of analysis.

Type 1: Single case study, holistic

In this type of study, only a single case is examined, and at a holistic level, for example, an entire educational programme, not individual elements (modules) within it. The single case study should be chosen when it can play a significant role in testing a hypothesis or theory. Another reason is when the case study represents a unique or extreme case, or a revelatory case, where, for example, a researcher is allowed into a previously sensitive or secretive organization to carry out research (for example, an organization fulfilling contracts for the military). There may be other times when a single case study is merely the precursor to further studies and may perhaps be a pilot for a later multiple study.

Type 2: Single case, embedded

Within a single case study, there may be a number of different units of analysis. For example, let us take a case study looking at the implementation of a mentoring programme. This is a single case (the mentoring programme) but the multiple units of analysis here might comprise:

- The official mentoring processes as laid down by the company's mentoring handbook.
- The perspectives of mentors.

- The perspectives of mentees.
- Tangible evidence that the mentoring system improves company collaboration, networking and morale.

Type 3: Multiple case, holistic

Where the multiple case study approach is needed (say, to improve the reliability or generalizability of the study) but it is not possible to identify multiple units of analysis, then a more holistic approach can be taken. Let us use the example of a region comprising several hospitals that is attempting to improve its communication processes through the implementation of a specially designed training programme. A researcher might use this communications training programme as a single, holistic unit of analysis, but look at the operation of the programme in all of the hospitals (multiple cases) and over a number of months. The aim here is not to increase the size of the hospital 'sample', but to *replicate* the findings of one case across a number of cases. In this sense, the approach is not very dissimilar to that of experimentation, where an attempt is made to replicate the findings of one experiment over a number of instances, to lend compelling support for an initial set of propositions. Figure 11.4 illustrates this.

Yin (2009), however, warns that a very serious danger of holistic designs is that the nature of the study may begin to shift under the very nose of the researcher. Hence, the researcher may have begun the investigation on the basis of one set of questions, but the evidence from the case study may begin to address a very different set of questions (recall the left-hand side of Figure 11.1). This is such a threat to the validity of the study that Yin (2009) argues that the only recourse is to begin the study again with a new research design.

Type 4: Multiple case, embedded

The problems faced by holistic case studies can be reduced if multiple units of analysis are used which allow for more sensitivity and for any slippage between research questions and the direction of the study to be identified at a much earlier stage. So, taking our example of the mentoring programme in Type 2: Single case embedded above, the evidence from this one organization might not produce convincing evidence. But addressing the various units of analysis across, say, ten organizations, would offer an opportunity to produce a compelling argument. But one of the dangers of embedded designs is that the sub-units of analysis may become the focus of the study itself (for example, the experiences of mentees), diverting attention away from the larger elements of analysis (does the programme work?).

Nevertheless, one of the advantages of multiple case studies is replication (see Figure 11.4, above). But how many case studies are sufficient for multiple case design? As we saw earlier, Eisenhardt (1989) suggests that between four and ten is often sufficient. If external validity (the generalizability of the results – see

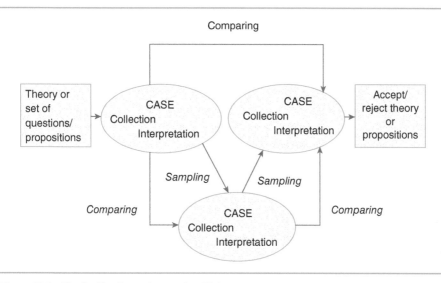

Figure 11.4 Replication through use of multiple cases

Source: Adapted from Flick, 2006

Chapter 6) is important, or if it is feared that each study may produce quite divergent results, then it is safest to maximize the number of studies. The key here will not be to aim for measures of statistical significance but for at least some semblance of reliability and credibility.

TOP TIP 11.2

If you are undertaking a doctoral qualification, you may have the time and resources to conduct a multiple case study. If, however, you are studying at Masters or even undergraduate level, you are best advised to stay clear of multiple case studies. This is mostly because the number of cases needed to reach data saturation is impossible to predict in advance, and you may overrun your timescales for completing your research.

DATA COLLECTION SOURCES

One of the features of case study research is its flexibility. Hence, adjustments might be made during the data collection process by deciding to make use of additional data collection sources, an approach that Eisenhardt (1989: 539) refers to as 'controlled opportunism'. Yin (2009, 2012) suggests that there are broadly six main sources of case study data, each of which have their own strengths and weaknesses, which are summarized in Table 11.3. It should be noted that these sources are not mutually exclusive, with a good case study tending to use multiple sources of evidence. Note that each of these data collection sources is discussed in detail in later chapters.

Table 11.3   Six sources of evidence and their strengths and weaknesses

Source of evidence	Strengths	Weaknesses
Documentation (see Chapter 20)	Stable – can be reviewed repeatedly Unobtrusive – not created as a result of the case study Exact – contains precise details of names, positions, events Broad coverage – long span of time, events and settings	Access – problems of confidentiality in many organizations Reporting bias – reflects (unknown) bias of document author
Archival records (see Chapter 19)	(Same as above for documentation) Precise and quantitative	(Same as above for documentation)
Interviews (see Chapter 15)	Targeted – focus directly on case study topic Insightful – provide original and illuminating data	Danger of bias due to poorly constructed questions Response bias inaccuracies due to poor recall Reflexivity – interviewee gives what interviewer wants to hear
Direct observation (see Chapter 16)	Reality – covers events in real time Contextual – covers context of events	Time-consuming and costly Narrow focus – unless broad coverage Reflexivity – event may proceed differently because it is being observed
Participant observation (see Chapter 17)	(Same as for direct observation) Insightful into interpersonal behaviour and motives	(Same as for direct observation) Bias because investigator unwittingly manipulates events
Physical artefacts (see Chapter 19)	Insightful into cultural features Insightful into technical operations	Selectivity – may be based upon idiosyncratic choices

Source: Adapted from Yin, 2009

■■ ACTIVITY 11.3 ■■

A new Managing Director takes over at Zenco, a manufacturer of engine parts for the automobile industry. His first decision, in a major cost-cutting exercise, is to scrap the headquarters' Reception desk and make the staff who work in it redundant. In its place, visitors have to complete their own security passes and use the internal company telephone directory to inform their client that they have arrived. After six months, you are asked by the MD to carry out a small case study on how the new system is working.

1.   What kind of research questions would you seek to address?
2.   Which of the following data gathering methods would you use: survey, observation, interview, archival records? Would you favour just one of these methods or use a combination?

Suggested answers are provided at the end of the chapter.

QUALITY IN CASE STUDIES: VALIDITY AND RELIABILITY

ENHANCING THE QUALITY

As we have seen in other research methods, and already in this chapter, the issues of validity and reliability are never far from the surface. They are probably of particular importance for the case study method because of the reliance on data that is generated from either limited or particular samples or situations.

Construct validity

Construct validity refers to the quality of the conceptualization or operationalization of the relevant concepts (Gibbert, Ruigrok and Wicki, 2008), that is, the extent to which the study investigates what it claims to investigate (Denzin and Lincoln, 1994). However, as Yin (2009) points out construct validity is particularly problematic for case studies, because of the difficulty of defining the constructs being investigated. For example, let us say that a researcher is asked to investigate the extent to which team work within groups of social workers and between groups has improved over a 12-month period. The problem here is how the concept of team work is defined, leaving the danger that the researcher will base this on his or her subjective impressions. This can only be avoided if the researcher:

- Operationally defines the concept 'team work' at the outset (particularly in the context of the project, in this case, social work).
- Selects appropriate measurement instruments and/or data sources for the defined concept (for example interviews with members of the social work team or focus groups).
- Uses multiple sources of data in a way that encourages divergent lines of inquiry (for example, interview data and documentation).
- Establishes a chain of evidence during the data collection process (linking findings and recommendations to the data, providing evidence that the two are connected).
- Evaluates the draft case study report through feedback from key informants (who in this case are likely to include managers of social work units or departments).

Internal validity

This issue arises with causal (as opposed to descriptive) case studies where the researcher is attempting to show that event x led to outcome y. As we saw in Chapter 6, in research designs that attempt to demonstrate causality, the dangerous impact of extraneous variables always threatens. Taking our previous example of team work within the group of social workers, we may be trying to 'prove' that

INTERNAL VALIDITY

improvements have occurred as a result of an intensive training programme in team building initiated by senior management. The challenge will be to find significant associations between the training programme and better team work and that the recent introduction of 'flat' management structures (in this case, an extraneous variable) was not the main source of improvement.

Another threat to internal validity comes from the problem of making inferences from the data, when it is simply not possible to actually observe the event. Hence, the researcher will 'infer' that something has occurred based upon case study interview data or documentary evidence. But is it logical and safe to make this inference? Gibbert et al. (2008) suggest three measures for enhancing internal validity. First, case study researchers should formulate a clear *research framework* that demonstrates that variable x leads to outcome y. Secondly, through *pattern matching*, researchers should compare empirically observed patterns with either predicted ones, or with patterns identified in previous studies (Denzin and Lincoln, 1994; Eisenhardt, 1989). Thirdly, *theory triangulation* allows the researcher to verify the findings from multiple perspectives (Yin, 2009).

External validity

This addresses one of the most problematic issues faced by the case study approach – whether its findings can be generalized beyond the study itself. Of course, not all would agree that generalizability should be a goal of research. Lincoln and Guba (2000) assert that generalizations inevitably alter over time, so that they become of only historical interest. There are no absolutes and all 'truth' is relative. But Schofield (2000) argues that generalizing is also becoming important in qualitative research. This is partly because the approach is increasingly being used in high profile studies often linked to evaluation. Funding agencies for large-scale projects also want to see that findings have a wider applicability than to just the project itself.

EXTERNAL
VALIDITY

Taking our example of team work in the social workers group, to what extent are we able to say that if the training programme did, in fact, help towards better team work, the programme would have a similar impact in other project groups within the organization, or, indeed, in quite different organizations? Gomm et al. (2000) point out that a significant amount of case study research does, indeed, try to make claims for studies that go beyond the original case. They also claim that case study research should be directed towards drawing general conclusions. But how, in practice, should this be done?

The problem faced is that the data collected in the case study may not be representative of the population as a whole (or merely representative of those features that are the focus of the research). Nevertheless, Gomm et al. (2000) advise that researchers can improve the empirical generalizability of a case study by:

- Providing evidence about the 'fit' of key characteristics between the sample and the population (for example, showing that our group of social workers are typical of social workers in general – we could mention age, gender composition, qualifications, experience, management structure, etc.); if information about the population is not available, a warning should be issued about the risks of generalizing from the particular case study.
- Using a systematic selection of cases for study, that is, making efforts to ensure, if possible, that cases are typical of the population. Too often cases are chosen on a convenience basis only.

Yin (2009) also defends case studies by pointing out that safer grounds for making generalizations can be established if a study is replicated three or four times in different circumstances. Dooley (2002) advises that external validity can be strengthened by relating the findings from one or multiple cases back to the literature, showing that the results are theoretically feasible or are supported by similar empirical studies.

Before accepting this, however, it is worth noting Lieberson's (2000) note of caution. Referring to what he calls 'small-*N*s' (a small number of cases), he warns that it is a bad basis from which to generalize. This is because causal propositions are either *deterministic* or *probabilistic*. In the case of determinism, it is argued that 'If x, then y', that is, the presence of a given factor will lead to a specified outcome. Probabilistic perspectives are more modest, claiming that 'the presence of x increases the likelihood of y occurring or its frequency'. The problem with small-N studies is that probabilistic measurement is ruled out because of the small size of the sample – which leaves us with deterministic measurement.

Lieberson (2000) uses the example of drink-driving and accidents. Cases can be shown where drunken drivers are involved in accidents, generating a deterministic relationship between the dependent variable (accidents) and the independent variable (alcohol consumption). But there are also cases where sober drivers have accidents and drunk drivers do not. Small-N studies cannot deal with interaction effects between variables (for example, the interaction between alcohol consumption and driving speed, or running through a red light), because they arbitrarily assume that such interactions do not operate. According to Lieberson, exceptionally rigorous practices are required to avoid these methodological pitfalls. If a small number of cases is selected, then it makes a great deal of difference whether the outcomes are the same in each case, or not. A defensible solution for generalization occurs where:

- One variable is constant across all cases – so, the same independent variable, *x*, leads to the same dependent variable, *y*, over a range of cases.
- The dependent variable is different across the cases, and all but one independent variable is constant – so pointing to that independent variable as the cause of the changes.

→ **TOP TIP 11.3** ←

If your case is one organization, and it was chosen by convenience, say, because you or a relative works there, this should alert you to thinking carefully about how typical or representative your case is of the general population. Single case studies are best used as exploratory rather than confirmatory studies. Be very cautious about generalizing and note the limitations of your study.

Reliability

Conditions for reliability are met if the findings and conclusions of one researcher can be replicated by another researcher doing the same case study. Bryman (2007a) supports this approach, arguing that case study generalization is made more feasible by team research where a group of researchers investigate a number of cases. As we have seen, this can only be achieved if researchers conscientiously document procedures through what Yin (2009) calls case study protocols and case study databases. As discussed earlier, a protocol is a plan of data collection instruments and also the procedures for using these instruments (which subsequent researchers can follow). The production of a protocol forces the investigator to think not only about how the final case study report might be completed, but also its intended audience. Yin (2009) recommends that a protocol should contain the following sections:

RELIABILITY

- An overview of the case study project, including objectives and theoretical issues.
- Field procedures, including: access to the case study 'sites' and people; general sources of information; back up procedures including eliciting help, if needed, from colleagues; timescales; and contingency plans – for example, if interviewees decide not to cooperate.
- Case study questions, table templates for collecting data and the potential sources of information for answering each question.
- A structure and guide to the final report.

ANALYSING THE EVIDENCE

The case study approach can be one of the most productive in terms of collecting data, but here the problems can often begin. In contrast to other methods, such as experimental design, there is less experience and fewer developed strategies for analysing case study data. Nevertheless, there are some general approaches that can be used with effect. We will look, first of all, at some general strategies, and then at some specific analytical methods.

General strategies

There are, essentially, two ways in which the case study evidence can be analysed. The first is to analyse the data on the basis of the original theoretical propositions and the research objectives that flowed from them. The other is to develop a descriptive framework once the case study has been completed. Yin (2009, 2012) recommends that the former is preferable.

Theoretical propositions

One of the purposes of theory is to assist the researcher in making choices between what is worth investigating and what wisely should be ignored (recall Chapter 1). Hence, the objectives and questions of the study are very likely to have been guided by its theoretical underpinning. For example, a case study exploring the introduction of 'moral education' into the curriculum would first delve into the meaning and history of moral education in a variety of contexts as well as examining the origins of moral education in some of the principles and theories of virtue ethics. At the analysis stage itself, data can be compared and contrasted with what the theoretical models have predicted, and suppositions made about the extent to which the original propositions can be supported or rejected. In the curriculum example, any problems arising from the curriculum innovation might be linked back to where the new programme strayed from some of its underpinning ethical principles.

Descriptive framework

This approach, as its name implies, is more descriptive than analytical, and can be used perhaps when a case study is chosen for a subject or issue for which an underlying theoretical proposition is not obvious. The descriptive framework can operate perhaps to identify the types of cases for which further, more quantitative analysis, should be applied. Of course, once the case research is completed, it might become more obvious as to what theoretical models are relevant and need to be addressed.

Analytical methods

Since one of the objectives of data analysis is to find relationships and contrasts between variables, some techniques are presented here that facilitate this process.

Pattern matching

The logic behind pattern matching is that the patterns to emerge from the data, match (or perhaps fail to match) those that were expected. Figure 11.5 illustrates two possible scenarios. With *non-equivalent dependent variables as a pattern*, a research study may have a number of dependent variables or outcomes that emerge from it. If, before the research is carried out, a number of predictions about the expected dependent variables are made, and are subsequently found, then this supports the internal validity of the study. Hence, in Figure 11.5 dependent variables A, B and C are predicted, resulting from changes in one or more independent variables.

PATTERN MATCHING

Another type of pattern matching approach is the use of *rival explanations as patterns*. Here, several cases may be known to have a certain outcome, but there may be uncertainty as to the cause, that is, which independent variable is the determining one. Each of the different theoretical positions must be mutually exclusive, so finding the presence of one position excludes the presence of any other.

Take the example of a charitable organization that wants to understand the factors that increase its donation receipts (dependent variable). Case study research is initiated that explores several cases of positive fluctuations in its income stream. It finds two cases when extensive media coverage of a national overseas disaster leads to a 40 per cent short-term rise in donations. A rival theoretical position, that media advertising produces a higher income stream, is found to be inconclusive – on some occasions income rises modestly, on other occasions hardly at all. Hence,

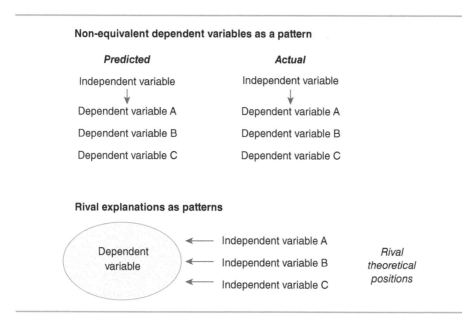

Figure 11.5   Pattern matching of case study data

the theoretical position, that donations are a product of media coverage of disasters, is accepted. Case Study 11.2 provides an illustration of how pattern matching can be used.

— CASE STUDY 11.2 —

A case study of team working

A year ago, the CopyMatch printing company faced mounting financial losses and decided that it needed to restructure its organization. Its sales representatives earned most of their income through incentive bonuses and, therefore, tried to maximize both their number of clients and sales per client. But often this meant that they took very specialist and small-scale orders that were time consuming to set up, and therefore unproductive and costly to execute. This, of course, was of little concern to the sales 'reps' since they were maximizing their own income.

As part of the restructuring, the workforce was divided into five teams, each of which contained different combinations of sales representatives, production managers, production supervisors and print workers. Through these cooperative teams it was intended that sales representatives would be influenced and informed by those more knowledgeable of the production cycle. The company wanted to monitor the impact of the reorganization and set up a research project, based upon this single case study. The dependent variables (outcomes) of the reorganization were predicted as:

More orders will be fulfilled to specified times.
Estimates of customer satisfaction will rise and there will be fewer customer complaints.
Larger-scale print runs will be undertaken.
Levels of employee satisfaction will rise.

The research study measured the impact of each type of team (non-equivalent independent variables) to find whether the new structure was more effective than the old one, and which combination of workers had the greatest effect on outcomes.

— ACTIVITY 11.4 —

For Case Study 11.2:

1. Suggest an appropriate case study design. For example, what would you choose as the source of measurement?
2. What are the independent variables? Would you treat the project as one case, or each of the teams as sub-cases?

Suggested answers are provided at the end of the chapter.

We saw in Case Study 11.2 that all the predicted independent variables were present, lending considerable weight to the validity of the assertion that the use of production teams increases efficiency, productivity and customer and employee satisfaction. If, however, even just one of these outcomes was not found, the initial proposition could not be supported. Conversely, if another company also used this type of team organization and came up with equivalent results, then this replication of the findings would lend further weight to the proposition.

Explanation building

This strategy is a special kind of pattern matching, but is less structured. Let us say that we want to find an explanation for a problem – to reveal its underlying causes. If these are not to be either subjective or anecdotal, it helps if these causes are located within some sort of theoretical proposition. We would first of all make an initial statement or proposition based upon this theoretical position. Next, we would compare the findings of an initial case study against this proposition, and amend the proposition if necessary. Another case study is taken and the proposition amended, etc. The process is repeated as many times as is considered necessary. At all times it is essential that rival explanations are also considered and solid grounds sought for accepting or rejecting them.

EXPLANATION
BUILDING

Time-series analysis

In time-series analysis, data on dependent or independent variables are traced over time so that predicted patterns can be compared with the actual patterns that emerge and inferences drawn. What is important here, is that valid indicators are selected that match the objectives of the study. Case Study 11.3 provides an illustration.

CASE STUDY 11.3

Time-series analysis

A large-scale retail park is built on a green-field site on the periphery of a medium-sized city. The impact of such a development is measured over time, so a time-series analysis is appropriate here. As usual, we start with a theoretical position or proposition, in this case, that the retail park will impact on the nearby town and locality in a number of ways. First, it will increase the pace of mid-town urban degeneration, in the first place by the closure of various shops and stores, followed, in time, by changing patterns of urban residence – higher income families moving out towards the suburbs. Secondly, increased urban degeneration will increase crime patterns in this locality. Thirdly, traffic flows will change with new congestion 'blackspots' emerging in feeder roads to the retail park. Data are collected on an annual basis over five years through observation, local government records and crime statistics.

ACTIVITY 11.5

In Case Study 11.3 identify the independent and dependent variables. To what extent can you be sure that changes in the dependent variable result from the impact of the independent variable and not from other factors?

Suggested answers are provided at the end of the chapter.

Case Study 11.3 is an example of an *interrupted time-series* because the data on, say, patterns of retail spending in the inner city are known before the retail park is built and can be compared with those after its completion. Using a *complex time-series*, we could postulate that a negative trend in a set of data points will be followed by a rise. Using our retail example, we could predict that after a period of several years, the cheap rents and land prices in the inner city (plus state grants and programmes) will attract new entrepreneurs, small businesses and service industries, resulting in urban regeneration.

Another form of time-series analysis is the use of *chronologies*, tracing events over time. The aim here is to compare the chronology of predicted events with what actually occurs. A theoretical proposition may predict that one set of events should be followed by another and that the reverse sequence is impossible; similarly, it may predict that one event should be followed by another after a prescribed period of time. Thus, chronologies not only allow for a description of events, but also for the analysis of causes.

Programme logic models

This combines both pattern matching and time-series approaches. Here, it is postulated that an initial event (independent variable) will produce an intermediate result which, in turn, will produce a final outcome (dependent variable). So, for example, improvements in health and safety procedures in a factory might, indeed, produce better safety standards and lower accident rates. The final result of this might be less disruption to production (through sickness and absence) and higher levels of worker satisfaction, both leading to higher productivity levels. Pattern matching would predict a number of dependent variables (worker satisfaction and higher productivity) as outcomes whilst the time-series approach would measure these outputs over time.

COMPOSING CASE STUDY REPORTS

REPORTING
CASE STUDY
RESEARCH

We will deal with the skills in writing business research reports in general in Chapter 24, but here we will focus on some of the skills and issues that are specific to the case study approach. Given that, as we have seen, the planning and execution of case studies is one of the least systemized of all the research approaches, this, in principle, leaves the case study report also less precisely structured. Nevertheless, following some of the ideas below will help.

Know your audience

Typical recipients of case study reports may be business managers, teachers, health professionals, government planners and policy makers, community leaders and special interest groups. As with any report, it is essential that you know whom you are writing for and what it is that they are interested in and what they want to know.

Sometimes case studies can be particularly effective when read by non-specialist or non-technical readers because their descriptive basis and findings can be both illuminating and memorable. For example, consider the relative impact of two reports on the effect of government aid programmes on developing nations. One report is based on a thorough statistical analysis and plentiful quantitative data presented in tabular form. The other report is a case study of an African village showing both the dramatic fall in the mortality rate following the installation of a clean water supply but also the continuing grinding levels of under-employment and poverty.

— ACTIVITY 11.6 —

Which of the reports just described do you think will have the greatest impact on: (a) public opinion; (b) government opinion?

Clearly, government opinion is more likely to be influenced by facts, statistics and rational analysis, while the public tend to favour more of the 'human element' that would emerge through the case study of the African village. Imagine the potential impact if the African village report was taken up and illustrated through a television programme.

➤ TOP TIP 11.4 ◄

One type of audience we have not mentioned so far are the readers and examiners of dissertations and theses. If you are conducting a case study as part of an academic programme then this type of audience will be interested, among other issues, in the theoretical propositions on which the study is based, and the extent to which your analysis supports claims that are consistent with the evidence. Also, ensure that you have addressed and provided details of the case study approach to research in the dissertation or thesis methodology chapter under the theme of Research Design.

You must ensure that you are actually writing for an audience and not for yourself. This is a particular danger if you are conducting a case study within your own particular work environment, or in a situation within which you have a strong emotional connection. Take, for example, a voluntary worker with an AIDS charity conducting a case study into how a particular group of HIV-infected men and women support each other. The danger is that the final report deals with a catalogue of issues that have worried the voluntary worker for some time. But if the report is aimed at changing public perceptions and attitudes towards HIV-infected people, then it must objectively address these wider social values and interests if it is to have any chance of changing peoples' opinions.

Types of case study report

Case study reports are usually written, but, in principle, they can also be presented orally, or through photographs, film or video. If a case study is not subject

TYPE OF CASE STUDY	REPORT STRUCTURE		
Single case study	Case study description and analysis		
Multiple case study	Cross-case analysis and results	Appendix: Narrative Case Study 1 Narrative Case Study *n*	
Multiple case study: without narrative	Case study 1	Question 1 Question 2	Answer Answer
	Case study 2	Question 1 Question 2	Answer Answer
Multiple case study: Integrated	Cross-case issue 1 – data and analysis from all cases Cross-case issue 2 – data and analysis from all cases		

Figure 11.6 Four written forms of case study

COMPOSING
THE REPORT

to confidentiality, then it can also be placed on the Web for wider public dissemination. Indeed, if the intended audience is a public one, it would be difficult to find a better delivery medium than the Web. In general, whether presented as a traditional document, or via the Web, written communication is likely to be the most familiar medium to both writer and reader. Dooley (2002) suggests that two types of report are popular with case study researchers. The first is *reflective reporting* where the researcher uses literary devices to bring the case alive for the reader. The researcher's voice is apparent. The second is *analytical reporting* which uses a more detached writing style (the researcher's voice is either silent or subdued). The analytic report tends to adopt a conventional structure: introduction, review of the literature, methodology, results and discussion (similar to Linear-Analytic in Figure 11.7). This figure gives examples of four structures that can be used for the generation of written reports, broadly following typical case study design formats. For the classic single case study, the report simply consists of the description and analysis of the data. In the multiple case study, the main body of the report could begin with narrative descriptions of each of the case studies, but these can be bulky and could be confined to the appendices. In this case, the main body of the report would consist of the analysis and supporting data of the cross-cases. A more focused approach would be to present the findings in the form of a question and answer format for each of the case studies. Here, the reader is then in a position to go to those questions of particular interest for each of the cases. This can be both efficient in terms of the reader's time and allow the reader to draw comparisons across each of the studies. The fourth example takes this a stage further using an integrated approach that looks at each issue in turn (using each case study to supply the underlying data and analysis).

Yin (2009) warns that the selection of one of these approaches for the final report needs to be made during the design of the case study and not as an afterthought, and should be contained in the case study protocol.

LINEAR-ANALYTIC	THEORY BUILDING
Statement of problem	
Literature review	
Methodology	Theory/model
Findings/analysis	
Conclusions	

COMPARITIVE	SUSPENSE
Case study 1: description A	Answer
Case study 1: description B	Background
	Alternative explanations

CHRONOLOGICAL	UNSEQUENCED (example)
Event A	Product development
Event B	Health and safety improvement
Event C	Business planning
	Human resource development

Figure 11.7   Alternative written report structures

➤ TOP TIP 11.5 ◄

If undertaking a case study as part of an academic programme, you may need to think of also producing a report for the organization or community you have studied. This might have been negotiated as part of your entry to gain their collaboration. This would not, in all probability, be your final dissertation or thesis, which would be too long, but a short summary or Flash Report. A typical size for this would be in the region of 2,000–3,000 words.

Written report structures

A number of alternative report structures are possible, depending on the audience and what the researcher is trying to achieve (see Figure 11.7). If, for example, the final case study report is being written for a largely academic audience, then the *linear-analytic* structure would probably be acceptable, since its format would be readily recognized by academics. These structures could be used with any of the single or multiple case studies just discussed.

The *comparative* structure takes the same case study and repeats it two or more times, comparing and contrasting the results. This could be done through beginning each time with different underpinning theoretical models, allowing the case to be viewed from an alternative perspective. These repetitions are typical of pattern matching approaches.

The *chronological* structure simply takes a series of events over time and sets them out in sequence. It should not be supposed, however, that this approach is purely descriptive – it can also be used both from explanatory and exploratory studies. For example, setting out a logical sequence of events may not only describe them, but provide insights into linkages and causes.

With the *theory building* structure the purpose is to build a series of chapters or sections that develop a theoretical perspective behind the case study. The theory may serve an explanatory purpose, seeking connections between cause and effect, or an exploratory one, suggesting new research questions and propositions.

The *suspense* structure is probably one of the most valuable in a business environment because it begins with the 'answer' or key findings of the case study. This is what managers, planners and the sponsors of research want to know. Subsequent chapters provide the background to the study and may even look at alternative perspectives on the findings.

Finally, in the *unsequenced* structure, the actual sequence of sections or chapters has no particular significance for the report. Findings can be presented in any order, provided that they are compatible. So, in Figure 11.7, the unsequenced example illustrates a case study of a company where each section can be presented independently in its own right, with no requirement for sequencing the sections in a particular order.

The final case study in this chapter brings together many of the principles of case study design that we have discussed. These include the role of theoretical propositions, the design of clear research methodologies and data gathering tools and the use of multiple sources of evidence.

CASE STUDY 11.4

Japanese transplant companies in the UK

A major theoretical theme of management–worker relations in Japanese (transplant) firms based in the UK, is that of strong management control (hegemony) based upon sophisticated recruitment policies, surveillance and performance monitoring. This is facilitated by a compliant local environment with national and local state bureaucracies, development corporations and trades unions eager to offer cooperative working arrangements in exchange for inward foreign (Japanese) investment.

A case study was carried out (Elger and Smith, 1998) working on the hypotheses (based upon previous research) that:

Despite the use of 'green-field' sites and inexperienced labour, recruitment and retention of labour still poses problems for Japanese transplant companies.

In response to these circumstances, management policies are not neatly pre-determined but involve debate, conflict and often piecemeal innovation.

Management policies among Japanese transplants are influenced not only by local and national environments, but by patterns of ownership and company traditions.

These sources of differentiation help to explain the variations in the ways in which managers respond to common problems within a shared labour market.

Table 11.4   Personnel and production practices in the case study plants

Practice	Company name			
	Copy Co.	PCB Co.	Assembly Co.	Car-part Co.
Team briefing	+	+	P	+
Performance appraisal	+	P	X	+
Formal consultation	X	+	X	+
Use of temporary workers	+	+	X	+
Performance-related pay	+	+	X	+
Systematic hiring policy	X	X	X	P
Operator responsible for quality	+	+	+	+

Key: + = practice exists; P = partial application; X = practice does not exist.

A research methodology for the case study was established with the selection of four Japanese green-field transplant companies, all based in Telford, a 'new town' in the West Midlands of the UK. Ten per cent of managers in these companies were interviewed, plus a number of other 'key informants' in the locality. Documentary evidence and observational data were gathered on both corporate policies and the local labour market. The impact of 'location' as an independent variable was controlled for by holding it constant – that is, by using a set of case study companies from the same location. So, by focusing on four companies operating in the same labour market, it became feasible to identify key features of this environment that impact on their labour relations. It also became possible to explore the impact of individual company policies and strategies on the management of labour relations.

Data on the production and personnel policies in each of the four case study workplaces were gathered using a template (see Table 11.4).

The authors acknowledge that the data need to be treated with some caution:

> Of necessity, this table captures only a snapshot of what are evolving patterns of employment practices, and the uniform terminology glosses over important differences in the implementation and meaning of the various features in the different workplaces. (Elger and Smith, 1998: 193)

But the evidence (from the Table and from the interviews) shows that in all four transplant companies, managers are implementing procedures for quality management. But the form taken by quality and just-in-time measures varies significantly between the factories. Thus, the case study highlights the danger of treating specific transplant workplaces as merely exemplars of generalized Japanese ways of working. There seemed to be no uniform or systematic set of personnel policies designed to shape and induct new recruits. Rather, employee policies seemed to emerge in a much more ad hoc way, in response to emerging problems and pressures, often based around the problems of recruitment and retention of young labour. The case study data reveal that transplant operations are embedded within the influences of the local as well as the national economy and are influenced by the distinctive nature of local labour markets, patterns of trades unionism and employer organization and the politics of local state and development agencies.

Source: Adapted from Elger and Smith, 1998

The case study reveals a number of typical issues in case study design. The following Activity asks you to identify what they are.

— ACTIVITY 11.7 —

In Case Study 11.4, identify the following:

1. The theoretical underpinning of the case study.
2. The number and type of data collection sources.
3. Protocols used for data collection.
4. The analytical method: pattern matching, explanation building or time-series.
5. The extent to which the original hypotheses are supported or refuted.

Suggested answers are provided at the end of the chapter.

Summary

- Case studies are used for a variety of subjects, including organizational performance, evaluating relationships between individuals, teams or departments and project implementation.
- Case studies are often deductive in character, beginning from a theoretical premise or stance.
- They should be used when there is no opportunity to control or manipulate variables, but when there is an interest in explanations and analysis of situations or events.
- While procedures are not as well defined as those for experimental research, case study research should involve the development of an initial hypothesis or set of questions, and the design of research tools, protocols and field procedures.
- Case studies can involve single or multiple units of analysis (individuals, departments, objects, systems, etc.) in combination with single or multiple case designs.
- In case studies, researchers should aim to collect multiple sources of evidence that should evolve into a chain of evidence, linking research questions, data, analysis and case study reports.
- Data for case studies are typically collected from multiple sources including documentation, archives, interviews and direct or participant observation.
- Internal validity in case studies is strengthened by pattern matching, explanation building and time-series analysis. Reliability is strengthened by multiple replication of the same or similar cases.

REVIEW QUESTIONS

1. Suppose you are planning to undertake a study into the strategies that small companies should adopt to achieve success. You know you are going to undertake a national survey. What arguments could you use for also including ten case studies of successful small companies?
2. In selecting case studies, what would be the advantages in choosing cases that were divergent in terms of their features?
3. How many case studies is enough?

FURTHER READING

Yin, R.K. (2012) *Applications of Case Study Research*, 3rd edn. Thousand Oaks, CA: Sage. An ideal complementary text to books on case study theory in that it provides detailed examples of descriptive case studies, explanatory case studies and cross-case synthesis.

Yin, R.K. (2009) *Case Study Research: Design and Methods*, 3rd edn. Thousand Oaks, CA: Sage. Yin is widely recognized as one of the leading authorities on case study design. There is no better starting point.

Stake, R.E. (2005) *Multiple Case Study Analysis*. New York: The Guilford Press. Examines single cases but then goes on to using multiple cases, and the application of cross-case analysis. Three international multiple case study examples are also provided.

Gomm, R., Hammersley, M. and Foster, P. (eds) (2000) *Case Study Method: Key Issues, Key Texts*. London: Sage. Not for the novice researcher, this book explores some of the complex issues associated with case study research, including external validity and the generation of theory.

JOURNAL RESOURCES

Lee, W., Collier, P.M. and Cullen, J. (2007) 'Reflections on the use of case studies in the accounting, management and organizational disciplines', *Qualitative Research in Organizations and Management: An International Journal*, 2(3): 169–178. Discusses the merits of unique cases and singular forms of evidence within a single case; the comparability of case studies with tools in other areas; and methods of theorizing from case studies.

Patton, E. and Appelbaum, S.H. (2003) 'The case for case studies in management research', *Management Research News*, 26(5): 60–71. Suggests that case studies are an important approach in organizational research both for generating hypotheses for quantitative studies, and for generating and testing theory.

Rowley, J. (2002) 'Using case studies in research', *Management Research News*, 25(1): 16–27. Explains when case studies are the ideal method, how to design case studies and issues around validity and reliability.

Suggested answers for Activity 11.2

1. The implicit working hypothesis is that taxi-dance halls are dens of vice and corruption.
2. The multiple sources of evidence used include observation (of people arriving, their means of transport, the look and demeanour of both clients and taxi-dancers, etc.), and interviews with clients, taxi-dancers and the owners of the halls.
3. This is a matter of interpretation! Clearly, however, the hypothesis that the halls are merely vice dens is too simplistic. Both the taxi-dance girls and their clients reveal a wide mixture of hopes, aspirations and incentives.

━━ Suggested answers for Activity 11.3 ━

1. Research questions might include: (a) What is the attitude of customers towards the new system? (b) What is the attitude of staff to the system? Does the system work – are customers able to understand and use it?
2. Data collection methods could include covert observation of the customers as they arrive to see how easily they manage to use the new system. Later, a selected sample of customers could be interviewed as they left the building to ascertain their views on the system. The views of staff could be tapped through a small-scale survey using a structured questionnaire (perhaps distributed in the next issue of the company newsletter).

━━ Suggested answers for Activity 11.4 ━

1. The source of measurement would include the number of orders filled to specific timescales, levels of customer satisfaction, the scale of print runs and the levels of employee satisfaction.
2. Independent variables include the new team structures, but you would need to look out for other extraneous variables that might confound the results (for example, do some teams contain more experienced workers?). Since the project is looking at the impact of different combinations of workers (compared to the old one) then sub-cases would be used, comprising each of the new team structures. One sub-group could comprise the old structure which could then act as a control to see if the more collaborative team approach was, indeed, more effective.

━━ Suggested answers for Activity 11.5 ━

The new retail park is acting as an independent variable on its environment, within which dependent variables include urban degeneration, traffic congestion and crime. One of the challenges here is to measure the impact of the retail park itself, since there are likely to be many other independent variables at work. Taking just traffic as an example, car ownership tends to rise over time, so will add to traffic congestion.

━━ Suggested answers for Activity 11.7 ━

1. The theoretical underpinning of the study revolves around the literature on management–worker relationships in Japanese transplant companies.
2. Data collection sources include secondary sources (previous studies), interviews with ten per cent of company managers, some key informants in the locality, documentary evidence on company policies, plus observational data.
3. The protocols used for data collection are illustrated in the template in Table 11.4.
4. The analytical method comprises a form of explanation building.
5. The original hypothesis could be accepted on the basis of the results.

12

DESIGNING EVALUATIONS

CHAPTER INTRODUCTION

Chapter outline

The focus of evaluation 297

Schools of evaluation 304

Data collection sources 309

Data collection tools 311

Quality issues in evaluation 316

Planning the evaluation report 318

Enhancing the impact of evaluation 319

The ethics of evaluation 322

Keywords

Kirkpatrick

Impact analysis

Force-field analysis

TQM

Formative evaluation

Summative evaluation

Repertory grid

Critical incidents

Chapter objectives

After reading this chapter you will be able to:

- Describe the purposes of evaluations.
- Distinguish between the different schools of evaluation.
- Identify suitable data collection sources.
- Design valid and reliable evaluation tools.
- Produce readable and informative evaluation reports.
- Adhere to ethical principles in conducting evaluations.

EVALUATION

Often surveys (Chapter 10) can be used to evaluate public perceptions of a product or service. Equally, a case study approach (Chapter 11) can be adopted, which consists of the evaluation of, say, a new factory system or process. Evaluation involves the systematic collection of data about the characteristics of a programme, product, policy or service. As part of this process, evaluation will often explore what needs to be changed, the procedures that are most likely to bring about this change, and whether there is evidence that change has occurred (Warr et al., 1970). Indeed, as Clarke (1999) points out, while the purpose of basic research is to discover new knowledge, evaluation research studies show how existing knowledge is used to inform and guide practical action. A significant amount of evaluation research revolves around training or professional development programmes, and some of the chapter will focus on this area. However, as Kaufman and Keller (1994) make clear, evaluation has tended to focus too much on the effects of training and not enough on other performance improvement interventions such as strategic planning, organizational development, diversity, team working and mentoring.

EVALUATION
RESEARCH

Interest in the process of evaluation can be traced back to the 1970s and was strongly influenced by the work of Donald Kirkpatrick, who focused on the evaluation of programmes. The emphasis was often on the accuracy, or otherwise, of evaluation measuring techniques, and was strongly positivist in orientation (Lincoln, 1985). In recent years, with the expansion of action learning, work-related learning and self-development programmes, learning is now seen as arising *within* and *through* the work situation rather than just through formal programmes. Hence, for evaluation, the focus has shifted to a certain extent away from measurement and towards issues of *what* is evaluated, *why* and *for whom*. This includes issues around subjectivity and the ethics of evaluation.

It has been suggested by Campbell (1997) that the process of evaluation suffers from a lack of accurate and complete information, bad information or untimely information, that is, a lack of information when it is really needed. In this chapter, then, we will look at different sources for collecting data for evaluation, and the design of valid and reliable tools for use in the field. We will also look at ways of enhancing the quality and accuracy of evaluation studies and therefore the chances of them being accepted by their sponsors – so that the effort of planning and implementing an evaluation study produces positive outcomes.

THE FOCUS OF EVALUATION

In his original, seminal work, Kirkpatrick (1959) made recommendations for evaluation that have laid the basis for thinking about the subject ever since. He argues that, in essence, the evaluation of training programmes should concentrate on four levels:

- *Level 1, Reaction:* evaluating the reactions of trainees to the programme (usually by the use of a questionnaire). This determines their level of satisfaction with the programme.
- *Level 2, Learning:* measuring the knowledge, skills and attitudes that result from the programme and which were specified as training objectives. The extent of learning can be tested through assessment.
- *Level 3, Behaviour:* measuring aspects of improved job performance that are related to the training objectives.
- *Level 4, Results:* relating the results of the training to organizational objectives and other criteria of effectiveness such as better quality, productivity, safety or profits.

According to Kirkpatrick (2005), the evaluation of training programmes is important for a number of reasons: (a) to justify the existence and budget of the training department by showing how it contributes to the organization's objectives and goals; (b) to decide whether or not a programme should be continued; (c) to gain information on how to improve programmes in the future. Unfortunately, as Bramley and Kitson (1994) suggest, in the UK and USA over 80 per cent of training is only evaluated at Level 1, with participants commenting on how much they enjoyed or thought they benefited from the programme. This information is gathered through the issue of evaluation forms or, in modern jargon, 'happiness sheets'. However, even if evaluation is at this level, negative responses might prompt training designers to improve a programme (Pershing and Pershing, 2001).

EVALUATION
FOR TRAINING
PROGRAMMES

Yet it is probably Level 3 that is most important. At Level 1 participants can enjoy a programme but their performance may remain the same. At Level 2 they may be able to show an increase in knowledge but maintain the same behaviours. Rowe (1995) distinguishes between three levels of work-related outputs at Level 2:

- Knowledge (understanding of a subject or skill).
- Skill (the practice of the skill itself).
- Competence (showing one's ability in applying a skill).

As Rowe points out, competence often means 'the minimal standard required', whereas in many work situations what is needed is excellence in performance. Also, many highly competent teams will include incompetent individuals. Perhaps, then, it is the competence of teams that we should be evaluating.

It is at Level 3 that improved job performance and behaviour can be measured. Kirkpatrick (2005) suggests that to do this, if possible a control group should be used against which the performance of the trained group can be compared. There should be a time gap before measuring post-course performance to give time for behaviours to change. Evaluation should be both before and after the programme and as many stakeholders as possible should be contacted: course participants, their line managers, their subordinates and other relevant parties. Costs as well as benefits should also be considered.

TOP TIP 12.1

Before the training intervention, discuss with participants or programme sponsors what the intended success factors of the training intervention will be. For example, if success is seen as 'improved performance', what, precisely, must be improved and to what level? How will performance be measured both before the training intervention and afterwards? How will external factors such as changing market conditions be taken into account?

PROGRAMME
EVALUATION
EXAMPLE

At Level 4, evaluating results presents a challenge particularly if a control group is not used. However, even with a control group, as we saw in Chapter 6, it is possible to use faulty designs such as the use of non-equivalent control groups. Sound designs include the use of a group that receives the training with a control group, with both groups taking both a pre-test and a post-test. Yet, the question of what is to be tested has to be decided. Furthermore, the use of a control group that is pre-tested and post-tested but receives none of the benefits of training raises ethical questions. One solution would be to conduct the pre- and post-tests, but for the control group to then get the benefit of the training programme.

Bramley and Kitson (1994) caution that the problems of evaluating at Levels 3 and 4 are not well understood. Measuring changes in job performance, for example, is problematic, partly because of the amount of work involved in designing measurement criteria. They proceed, however, to offer some solutions. As Figure 12.1 shows, cost–benefit analysis is one way of measuring the benefits emerging from a programme, described as a list of performance indicators.

Behaviours expected of, and benefits to, trainees

Improved and new skills, leading to:

- Improved job prospects
- Higher earnings
- Access to more interesting jobs
- Improved job satisfaction

Behaviours expected of, and benefits to, supervisors and line managers

Improved and new skills, leading to:

- Increased output
- Higher value of output
- Greater flexibility and innovativeness
- Likelihood of staying longer
- Less likelihood of sickness/stress
- Less likelihood of absence
- Less need to supervise
- Increased safety

Benefits to customers

- Better quality work
- Less need to return work
- More 'on time' deliveries

Figure 12.1   Cost–benefit analysis of a proposed training event

Source: Adapted from Bramley and Kitson, 1994

Taking Figure 12.1, think of ways of measuring some of the performance indicators listed. What sort of data should be collected? Are some indicators easier to measure than others?

Suggested answers are provided at the end of the chapter.

Kaufman and Keller (1994) also offer some further developments to the Kirkpatrick model, arguing that the original four-level model fails to take into account the broader impact of interventions on society. Hence, they add a Level 5 which requires organizations to measure this. They also modify some of the other Kirkpatrick levels. So, at Level 1, instead of just participant reaction to an intervention, they include an evaluation of the value and worth of the resources put into the programme, and the efficiency of the methods and tools used. Level 3 becomes application instead of behaviour, that is, whether participants are able to apply what they have learned on the job. Hence, an organization that introduces a new programme aimed at increasing diversity awareness, would evaluate the training programme in terms of whether people considered it used an appropriate amount of resources (Level 1), whether it was being implemented according to its design and objectives (Level 2), whether it succeeds in reducing or eliminating sexist or racist behaviour (Level 3) and what payoffs this achieves for the organization (Level 4) and society (Level 5).

An alternative approach to the evaluation of training and development programmes is offered by Brinkerhoff (2006) who suggests two basic steps: a) identify the few trainees who have been the most successful following the training; b) interview both the successful and least successful trainees to try and understand and analyse their stories. While Kirkpatrick's approach typically comes after the training intervention, for Brinkerhoff (2006) the first stage is to plan the evaluation which can comprise either a formative, summative evaluation or both. Step 2 involves identifying the critical success factors that the programme is meant to

Table 12.1   Five levels of evaluation

Level	Kirkpatrick	Kaufman & Keller	Kaufman & Keller focus
5		Societal contribution	Societal and client responsiveness, consequences and payoffs
4	Results	Organizational payoff	Organizational contributions and payoffs
3	Behaviour	Individual or small group payoff	Individual and small group (products) utilization within the organization
2	Learning	Individual or small group payoff	Individual and small group mastery and competence
1	Reaction	Process acceptability and efficiency	Methods, means and processes acceptability and efficiency
		Resource availability and quality	Availability and quality of human, financial and physical resources inputs

achieve. So, for example, how will the training intervention change the performance of the employee? How will it affect the goals of the organization? At Step 3, a survey is administered to identify those employees who have achieved the greatest success and those who have achieved least. This involves implementing a scoring system to identify these two groups. Step 4 involves interviewing successful and least successful employees by asking some simple, basic questions such as:

- What, if anything, has changed as a result of the training intervention?
- How has the intervention changed your job-specific behaviour?
- Did the intervention result in any worthwhile outcomes?

The results from this stage allow for Step 5 at which conclusions are reached as to the impact of the programme in terms of its overall achievements, whether some elements of the programme were more successful than others, and the value of outcomes generated. It also allows for answers to the fundamental question: did the benefits outweigh the costs?

Another way of evaluating the effectiveness of a programme is through impact analysis. Here, all stakeholders get together before the start of the programme and discuss its objectives and the behaviours that are likely to change as a result. Through a snowballing process, each participant is asked to write down the three results they see as most important. These are pinned to a noticeboard, then reorganized into clusters or themes. Each cluster is then given a title, and stakeholders asked to award 10 points across the clusters so that a ranking of clusters is achieved. Having done this, enabling and inhibiting factors are discussed to create a force-field analysis. Finally, stakeholders discuss how the purposes of the programme can be evaluated. The following case study provides yet another approach to programme evaluation, and one that is widely used in business and organizational contexts.

FORCED FIELD
ANALYSIS

CASE STUDY 12.1

Programme evaluation through force-field analysis

A hospital senior management team has planned a programme of workshops spread over 12 months, the purpose of which will be to instigate major organizational change. Before this can happen, the programme itself must be evaluated. If this proves successful, then the change programme will be cascaded down through the entire organization.

To prepare for the evaluation, the participants carry out a snowballing process which crystallizes sets of enabling and inhibiting factors that may influence the programme's likely impact on the rest of the organization. The participant evaluators (and programme planners) convene an *impact workshop* during which they come up with four factors that are likely to restrain the spread and success of the programme and four factors that are driving for its full implementation. As Figure 12.2 shows, leadership is seen as both a restraining *and* a driving force, that is, there are groups of managers in favour of change and those who oppose it.

Use of the force-field analysis process and diagram allows the participants to debate and analyse the various strengths of the restraining and driving forces. As a result, the budget for the change management programme is re-examined (evaluated) to see if it is sufficiently large. The impact workshop is reconvened after three months and the on-going programme evaluated against the driving and restraining forces that have been anticipated to see what remedial action needs taking.

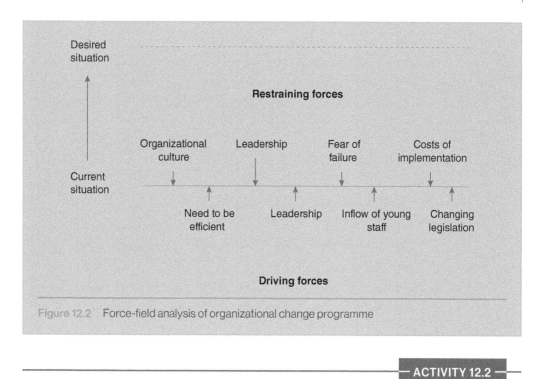

Figure 12.2 Force-field analysis of organizational change programme

—— ACTIVITY 12.2 ——

Take a programme or change process with which you are familiar and conduct a force-field analysis on it. This works better if you are able to conduct the evaluation with colleagues who are also familiar with the programme/process. How useful is force-field analysis as an evaluation method?

An increasingly popular focus of evaluation is through the Total Quality Management (TQM) process, the European model of which is set out in Figure 12.3. As Bramley and Kitson explain, each of these nine elements can be analysed in terms of an organization's progress towards TQM. Hence, leadership is defined as 'How the executive team and all other managers inspire and drive total quality TOTAL QUALITY MANAGEMENT as the organization's fundamental process for continuous improvement' (Bramley and Kitson, 1994: 14). Since the focus of evaluation is results, this is at Level 4 of Kirkpatrick's (1959) model.

Focusing on outputs, however, may cause us to miss other important features that deserve evaluation. Easterby-Smith (1994), for example, argues that it is virtually impossible to understand a programme without evaluating the *context* in which it takes place. This might include why the programme was sponsored or devised in the first place (and any differences between overt and hidden agendas), and the different aims and objectives of the various stakeholders. Another focus of evaluation could include *administration*. This includes the processes that occur before the training (for example, nomination for the training, selection of participants) and what happens once the training is complete (such as follow-up activities). The selection of candidates is often an illuminating place to start. They may find themselves on a programme because they have been identified as a 'high flier', but alternatively it may be because they have been underperforming on the job, and need help.

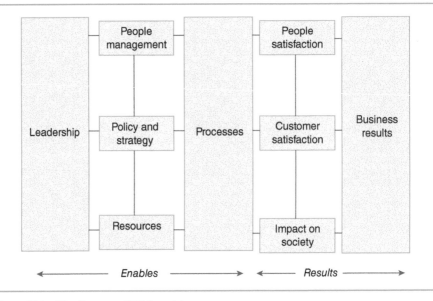

Figure 12.3 The European TQM model

Source: Bramley and Kitson, 1994

Evaluation schemes that concentrate narrowly on inputs and outputs of programmes are in danger of missing vital, often illuminating information on *processes*. Process evaluation may involve merely observing what is occurring and keeping a narrative record of events. But it may go further than this, trying to understand the programme or event from the perspective of participants. Another element of process evaluation might be to focus on interactions between facilitators and participants or between participants themselves. Process evaluation may not only describe events, but seek to *interpret* what is happening. Table 12.2 provides an overview of all the many different types of evaluation, some of which we have mentioned above.

Two of the evaluation types in Table 12.2, formative and summative, have a long pedigree. Scriven (1967) uses these terms to describe educational curricula, and the terms have been widely used in an educational context ever since. Formative evaluation is undertaken to provide feedback to people who are trying to improve something. It is often relatively informal, with the evaluator working alongside practitioners to identify the strengths and weaknesses of a programme or intervention. In contrast, summative evaluation aims to determine the overall effectiveness of a programme or project, and to provide a judgement on whether it should continue to run. Summative evaluation is usually more formal in character, with the evaluator operating in a more independent role. In formative evaluation, feedback to practitioners may be written or provided through discussions, but in summative evaluation feedback is usually in the form of a formal, written report to the commissioning body.

EVALUATING A
PROGRAMME
OF RESEARCH

➤ TOP TIP 12.2 ◄

In planning the evaluation of a programme or teaching/training intervention, consider using not only summative but also formative evaluation. This allows you to explore how the programme evolves over time, generating a dynamic and richer picture of change.

Table 12.2   Types of evaluation and their defining question or approach

Focus or type of evaluation	Key questions or approach
Accreditation (validation) focus	Does the programme meet minimum standards for accreditation (validation)?
Comparative focus	How do two or more programmes rank or compare on specific indicators, outcomes or criteria?
Compliance focus	Are rules and regulations followed?
Context focus	What is the social, economic, political and cultural environment within which the programme operates?
Cost–benefit analysis	What is the relationship between programme costs and programme benefits (outcomes) expressed in monetary terms?
Criterion-focused evaluation	By what criteria (quality, costs, client satisfaction) should the programme be evaluated?
Decision focus	What information is needed to inform specific future decisions?
Descriptive focus	What happens in the programme? What can be observed?
Effectiveness focus	To what extent is the programme effective in attaining its goals? How can the programme be more effective?
Efficiency focus	Can inputs be reduced and the same level of output maintained? Can outputs be increased with no increase in inputs?
Formative evaluation	How can the programme be improved (during its planning and delivery phases)?
Goal-based focus	To what extent have the programme goals been attained?
Impact focus	What are the direct and indirect impacts on participants, the organization, the community?
Input focus	What resources (money, staff, facilities, technology, etc.) are available and/or necessary?
Knowledge focus	What can be learned from this programme's experiences and results to inform future efforts?
Longitudinal focus	What happens to the programme and to participants over time?
Needs assessment	What do clients need and how can these needs be met?
Norm referenced approach	How does this programme population compare to some specific norm or reference groups on selected variables?
Outcomes evaluation	To what extent are desired clients/participant outcomes being attained? What are the effects of the programme on clients or participants?
Process focus	What do participants experience on the programme? How can these processes be improved?
Quality assurance	Are minimum standards (of teaching/training/healthcare, etc.) being provided? How can quality be monitored and demonstrated?
Summative evaluation	What is the overall merit or worth of the programme? Should it be modified? Should it be continued?

Source: Adapted from Patton, 1982

Take a look at the various types of evaluation in Table 12.2. Which of these would you consider selecting for your own evaluation projects? Can several approaches be combined at the same time?

Clearly, these different approaches to evaluation stem from differences of opinion as to what evaluation is for. Such differences can be classified into schools of evaluation, to which we now turn.

SCHOOLS OF EVALUATION

Easterby-Smith (1994) categorizes the various approaches to evaluation into four schools of thought: experimental, systems, illuminative and goal-free. To these we can add: decision making, goal-based, professional review and interventionist (see Figure 12.4). It is worth noting the views of Ballantine et al. (2000) that the philosophy underlying an evaluation has a great influence on how it is conducted, the tools used and also its goals. So, evaluations that focus on technical issues (such as computer information systems) are likely to be summative and formal in approach, regarding people as automata, or mere cogs in a process (see experimental and systems evaluation). In contrast, the more moral approach to evaluation is likely to be more formative and human-centred (see illuminative and goal-free evaluation). Clearly, implicit in some of these approaches are some of the ontological and epistemological assumptions discussed in Chapter 2.

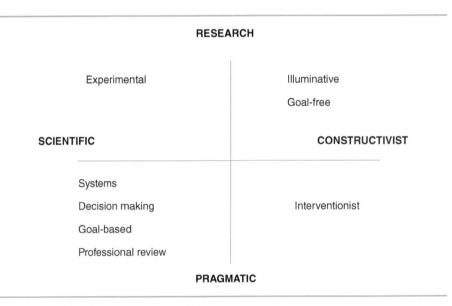

RESEARCH

Experimental	Illuminative
	Goal-free
SCIENTIFIC	**CONSTRUCTIVIST**
Systems	
Decision making	Interventionist
Goal-based	
Professional review	

PRAGMATIC

Figure 12.4 Model of schools of thought in evaluation

Source: Adapted from Easterby-Smith, 1994

The role of the evaluator is likely to be quite different according to which type of evaluation process is being followed. For example, in more formal, 'scientific' approaches, the evaluator may often be an independent and detached 'outsider' providing feedback to a commissioning body. In constructivist or more naturalistic approaches, the evaluator may work quite closely with practitioners in a more collaborative, participatory style, acting not only as an evaluator but as a facilitator of change. The evaluator is expected to enter the evaluation setting free of pre-determined views, and hence is unlikely to start with a particular research design or set of research questions. These emerge as part of the process of inquiry. Evaluators approach the research context with an open mind.

Experimental evaluation

Experimental evaluation seeks to demonstrate that any observed change in behaviour or outcomes can be attributed to the intervention (for example, the training or development provided). There is an emphasis on research design and quantitative measurement, and sometimes the use of control groups and treatment groups – just as we would expect to see in any, typical, experimental approach. Clarke (1999) posits the example of a training programme for the unemployed. An evaluator may attempt to measure the causal effect of the programme by comparing the future employment records of those who participated in the programme with unemployed adults living either in the area where no training is provided, or residing in the same area but receiving no training.

EXPERIMENTAL
DESIGN

Easterby-Smith (1994), however, cautions that there are a number of reasons why experimental evaluation may have limited applications. For example, if statistical techniques are going to be applied, sample sizes must be sufficiently large (see Chapter 9). If control groups are used, they must be properly matched to the experimental group; even when associations between variables can be identified, there is still the problem of showing causality, that is, that changes in one variable led to changes in the other. Clarke (1999) also argues that experimental evaluation faces all the kinds of problems that typify experimental research in general. For example, there may be differential attrition rates between the experimental and control groups, meaning that the two groups are no longer equivalent. Furthermore, the research may actually serve to create inequalities between the two groups, since one group receives the treatment and the other does not. This can work in unexpected ways. For example, if the control group learns that it *is* a control, members may be tempted to perform better than the experimental group; conversely, they may feel deprived and resentful and their performance may deteriorate.

Systems evaluation

In the *systems* approach, there is emphasis on specifying the objectives of the evaluation, with identifying outcomes, and on providing feedback on these outcomes to those providing the training. An example of the systems approach process is provided by Campbell (1997), who describes a schema for conducting an evaluation (see Table 12.3).

Table 12.3   An evaluation schema based on the systems approach

Part 1 Plan the evaluation

1.1   Determine evaluation requirements

1.2   Specify evaluation purposes and objectives

1.3   Identify sources of information

1.4   Prepare an evaluation schedule with stakeholder involvement

Part 2 Collect and interpret information/data

2.1   Prepare and pilot test instrument(s)

2.2   Administer instrument(s)

2.3   Collect and tally data

Part 3 Prepare recommendations and an action plan

3.1   Formulate recommendations

3.2   Draw up a plan for corrective action

3.3   Write a report

Source: Campbell, 1997, adapted from L'Angelle, 1996

A typical example of systems evaluation would be where evaluators are brought in to investigate the effectiveness of a new financial accounting system. Objectives might be discussed with stakeholders and defined as:

- How robust is the system – does it 'crash'?
- Does its functionality match the original specifications?
- How 'user-friendly' is the system, and what are its implications for staff development and training?

A structured evaluation schedule is then drawn up containing questions matched against design specifications. An interview schedule is also designed so that issues can be explored with those who work on the system. Once the data have been collected, they are analysed and a formal report prepared containing recommendations for change.

One of the criticisms of the systems approach is that it represents rather a mechanistic view of the world that fails to recognize that objectives, for example, can never be neutral. Critics of the approach would point out that objectives tend to be selected by one particular social group (for example, often senior managers) and reflect the vested interests of such groups. A systems approach to evaluation may also fail to pick up the subtleties and complexities of both the products and processes of training or systems because it does not recognize that such complexities exist.

Goal-based evaluation

Like systems evaluation, goal-based evaluation is focused on the achievement of pragmatic outcomes. Here, however, the emphasis is not so much on designing systems to measure outcomes, but on identifying any discrepancies between planned and actual goals. This evaluation approach has been extensively used by educationalists from the behavioural school, who believe that the outcomes of programmes should be expressed in behavioural terms (for example, 'the learner should be able to *demonstrate* the ability to plan a project'). This does, however, raise questions about the extent to which from what is observed in terms of human behaviours can be inferred what people are actually thinking. It also assumes that the stated goals of a programme against which outcomes are to be evaluated can be accepted at face value. Yet people may hold tacit goals that they choose not to articulate or are not consciously aware of. Furthermore, there are issues of democracy and power relationships: who selects the goals that are to be evaluated? Whose interests do they represent?

Decision making evaluation

The decision making approach suggests that evaluation should be structured by the decisions that need to be made – often by top decision makers or managers. This resolves one of the evaluator's dilemmas of not always knowing at whom the evaluation should be directed (House, 1980). A drawback is that it can often ignore other potentially interested parties and stakeholders, although this can be overcome to some extent by gathering evaluative data from groups outside the original sponsors of the evaluation. As an evaluation approach it makes extensive use of survey methodology, often using tools such as questionnaires and interviews.

Professional review: validation and accreditation

Many professional associations for people such as lawyers, accountants, doctors, social workers, consultants and human resource managers set professional standards and then assess and accredit individual members of the profession against these standards. Indeed, possession of the prerequisite accreditation is often the passport required for entry into the profession. If professional training and assessment are delivered by organizations (such as institutions of higher education) external to the professional association itself, then the association is likely to set in motion evaluation (validation) processes to assure the quality of the training and professional development programmes.

In many countries, validation is seen as an essential quality assurance process to ensure appropriate standards for courses delivered by colleges and universities. In the UK, for example, the Quality Assurance Agency for Higher Education sets out a code of practice for the approval, monitoring and review of programmes (QAA, 2000). Hence, higher education institutions are charged with the task of ensuring that programmes are compatible with the goals and mission of the institution and with its academic planning and resources. In the course of the approval (validation) process, institutions are asked to give consideration to:

- The design principles underpinning the programme.
- The definition and appropriateness of standards in accordance with the level and title of the award.
- The resources needed and available to support the programme.
- Anticipated demand for the programme.
- Monitoring and review arrangements.

- The length of time for which approval is granted (which will normally be between one and five years).
- The contents of the programme specifications.

Ongoing monitoring will normally be undertaken by the department delivering the programme and will include the use of student feedback (often through evaluation forms), student progress information, reports from accrediting or other external bodies and examiners' reports (an important form of external evaluation of assessment standards).

Illuminative evaluation

Illuminative evaluation takes a much more flexible and open-ended approach. Rather than focus on measurement, it seeks the views of participants, recognizing that there are 'multiple perspectives' on any matter under scrutiny. So, in evaluating the success of a city's crime prevention scheme, the process might elicit the views of the police authority that launched the scheme, social workers, community groups and teachers as to its effectiveness. Illuminative evaluation will seek to promote communal awareness about a programme, rather than aiming to achieve pre-specified outcomes, results and recommendations. In terms of methodology, it is often associated with the case study approach we discussed in Chapter 11 and will tend to use qualitative methods such as in-depth interviews and direct observations of programme activities.

A danger of using illuminative evaluation, apart from the time and costs involved, is that clients and sponsors may want more than just 'illumination', but rather results that can lead to action. These do not always emerge from approaches of this kind. Furthermore, as with the case study approach in general, the results may be heavily influenced by the subjective views of the evaluator. As House (1980) warns, illuminative evaluation faces the difficulty of proving its authenticity and confidence in its outcomes.

Goal-free evaluation

Goal-free evaluation suggests that evaluations should totally ignore the formal objectives of a programme, since these may fail to reflect what is actually happening. Indeed, according to Scriven (1973), knowing the goals of a programme will bias the evaluator. The evaluation, then, should aim to look for unanticipated outcomes and, above all, processes. So this may mean observing pre-course planning meetings, mixing with participants socially and discussing the training event with them afterwards. In terms of research paradigms, goal-free evaluation may typify a constructivist approach, exploring how participants make sense of their experiences. Ballantine et al. (2000) support this approach, arguing that evaluation should look less at financial measures, and more at subjective views where personal judgements are made explicit. The results of this approach to evaluation may reveal illuminating insights but may not always produce results that can easily be implemented. There are also the dangers of the objectivity of evaluations being compromised by evaluators becoming too involved in events.

Interventionist evaluation and action research

This encompasses a number of different approaches, but here we will focus on two of the most widely used. In contrast to experimental evaluation that uses predefined objectives and measuring instruments, *responsive* evaluation concentrates on a programme's activities rather than its planned intentions, and explores the different stakeholder perspectives involved. Responsive evaluation, as the name implies, is more likely to be adaptive as the needs and circumstances around a programme change. Rather than act in a detached capacity, responsive evaluation favours the evaluator in a more involved, interventionist mode, often working in close collaboration with programme staff and participants.

Another approach to interventionist evaluation is *utilization focused* evaluation. Here, the stress is on the importance of identifying the motives of key decision makers before deciding on what types of information need to be collected. So evaluators must discuss with stakeholders both before, during and after the programme what it is that they need to know and the ends to which the emerging data may be put. This has much in common with action research (see Chapter 13), in which practitioners set out to solve problems through planning, implementing and evaluating change processes and strategies.

Both approaches have in common a commitment to achieve a direct impact on a programme and those involved in it. One problem with interventionist evaluation is that it might become too adaptive to changing situations, with evaluators becoming too involved with clients to maintain detachment and objectivity.

➤ TOP TIP 12.3 ◄

In selecting which of the above evaluation approaches to adopt, reflect first of all on your research philosophy. In terms of epistemology, do you believe that there is an objective 'truth' that can be measured? In which case, you could consider using experimental evaluation. On the other hand, if you adopt a more interpretivist paradigm, then illuminative evaluation might be more appropriate.

DATA COLLECTION SOURCES

There are many channels available for collecting data, and the type of medium used will often depend on the objectives of the evaluation. Easterby-Smith (1994) suggests that there are three kinds of medium available, all of which are discussed in detail in other parts of this book. The media comprise: the use of *informants*, where data are collected through, for example, questionnaires (Chapter 14); direct *observations* by the evaluator of what is taking place (Chapters 16 and 17); and accumulated *records* of what has taken place in the past (Chapter 19). In this section, then, we will only look at some ideas that are specific to the evaluation process.

Informants

Easterby-Smith (1994) classifies informants into four categories: direct participants, observers, controls and stakeholders.

- *Direct participants* are the programme delegates and the tutors or facilitators. Depending on the extent of their involvement, it might also include programme sponsors or the colleagues of programme participants.
- *Observers* may include course participants, if they are able to become sufficiently emotionally detached to be able to comment on the outcomes and processes objectively. The views of managers and sponsors can be useful in commenting on the effectiveness of a programme in terms of its impact on the subsequent work performance of learners.
- *Controls* are identical to the people in the experimental group, except that they do not receive the intervention. Using this approach, it is possible, in principle, to measure the effectiveness of a training or development programme. As we saw in Chapter 6, however, it is often difficult to find two groups that can be matched in this way and also difficult to control for the effects of extraneous variables.
- *Stakeholders* are those who do not have direct contact with a programme but have a legitimate interest in it none the less. Top managers, for example, may be very interested in the success of a sponsored MBA programme because it is hoped that some 'high fliers' will emerge that are vital for medium-term succession-planning at executive level.

Observations

Evaluating a training session or project by observing it may appear not only a perfectly sensible but also a fairly unproblematic approach. As we will see in Chapters 16 and 17, however, there are different ways of observing, including overt and covert observation and evaluating a programme or project by joining it as a participant or from the outside as a non-participant. Covert observation whether as a participant or looking in from the outside may reveal information that would not emerge if participants knew they were under scrutiny. Of course, the fact that they are being observed secretly raises ethical issues that require addressing.

Whichever approach is adopted, it is simply not possible to observe everything that occurs. Those that advocate using a video recorder to solve this problem forget that even this medium is selective in what it can 'see'. Of course, observing, taking notes and using video and audio media all help to build data sets that can provide a more comprehensive (reliable) picture for subsequent analysis. For practical purposes, it may be necessary to be selective in collecting data, which may involve a number of approaches including:

- *Time sampling* involves making 'snapshot' observations over a period of time. For example, as part of a job evaluation study a shopfloor packer could be observed every 20 minutes against the categories: walking, packing, discussing, requesting, taking instructions, absent.
- *Incident sampling* involves looking for critical incidents that might have an important impact on what is being evaluated. For example, a training programme may involve arguments and hostility between participants that could be documented.
- *People sampling* involves observing a sample of people in the belief that the sample selected is representative of the population from which it is drawn. So, in evaluating the impact of a new bonus scheme, a number of people who had recently received bonuses would be observed to evaluate whether this had had any impact on their behaviour or performance.

- *Analytical categories sampling* involves looking for, and recording, instances of specific behaviours or verbal interchanges. A classic example of this is the work of Bales (1950), who observed interactions among groups to determine broad categories of group behaviour comprising asking questions, attempted answers to these questions, followed by either positive or negative reactions.

Methods of recording the data collected using these techniques are examined in detail in Chapters 16 and 17.

Accumulated records

While the use of informants and observations requires the collection of data in the field, it is possible to evaluate programmes on the basis of data that were collected in the past. Examples of typical sources include:

- Programme or project plans and specifications.
- Communications between those responsible for the commissioning, planning or delivery processes.
- Comments written on flipcharts.
- Emails between participants.

Records, for example, might also show that it is taking participants longer than in the past to achieve a particular programme objective – based on this fact, personnel records might be checked to see if recruitment standards were being observed (Campbell, 1997). Sometimes, it is the lack of recorded information that might be significant – for example, the fact that few participants completed the pre-course activities that were vital to the programme's success. Accumulated records are an example of unobtrusive measures that are discussed in more detail in Chapter 19. Having identified appropriate sources, the next step is actually to collect the data.

DATA COLLECTION TOOLS

There are a wide variety of tools available for collecting evaluation data, some of the commonest techniques including questionnaires and interview schedules. Since these are discussed in considerable depth in Chapters 14 and 15 respectively, they will be discussed only briefly here. As in any type of questionnaire, the content must be designed to be both valid and reliable. In Figure 12.5, for example, 18 questions are asked about a training programme – probably a sufficient number to produce a reliable estimate of people's opinions. Note that Campbell (1997) calls this not a questionnaire but an opinionnaire, since it is eliciting participants' opinions about a training programme.

It is worth noting, however, the concern of Campbell (1997) who warns against too much reliance being placed on the use of numerical ratings and statistical calculations in evaluation questionnaires. He cautions that the data on the feelings and opinions collected remain subjective.

Directions: Please read the following 13 statements and indicate your level of disagreement or agreement by making a check mark in the column that corresponds to your opinion. Add a written comment to support your opinion on the line provided below each statement.

STATEMENTS	STRONGLY DISAGREE	DISAGREE	AGREE	STRONGLY AGREE
1 Learning objectives were adequately discussed at the beginning of sessions	❑	❑	❑	❑
Comment				
2 Including learning objectives on instructional materials enhanced learning	❑	❑	❑	❑
Comment				
3 The instruction included all that was necessary to perform	❑	❑	❑	❑
Comment				
4 Sufficient opportunities were provided to practise the skills taught	❑	❑	❑	❑
Comment				
5 The instructor encouraged trainee involvement	❑	❑	❑	❑
Comment				
6 The instructor was available for help when needed	❑	❑	❑	❑
Comment				
7 The instructional methods used (lecture-discussion, demonstration, etc.) helped me learn	❑	❑	❑	❑
Comment				
8 The audio-visual media used (PowerPoint slides, DVDs, etc.) and training aids used helped me understand	❑	❑	❑	❑
Comment				
9 The instructional materials used (books, modules, job performance aids, instruction sheets, etc.) helped me learn	❑	❑	❑	❑
Comment				
10 The criterion-referenced performance tests helped me become proficient	❑	❑	❑	❑
Comment				

| 11 | The training environment enhanced my motivation and helped me learn | ❑ | ❑ | ❑ | ❑ |

Comment

| 12 | All the necessary tools and equip-ment were available | ❑ | ❑ | ❑ | ❑ |

Comment

| 13 | The facilities in which training took place supported my learning | ❑ | ❑ | ❑ | ❑ |

Comment

Directions: Please write your answer to items 14 to 18 on the lines provided

14   What subject/topics should be added?

15   What subject/topics should be deleted?

16   What part of the training was most helpful?

17   What part of the training was least helpful?

18   What changes do you recommend for the future?

Your feedback will remain confidential and your assistance is greatly appreciated.
THANK YOU.

Figure 12.5   Sample opinionnaire

Source: Adapted from Campbell, 1997

Assessment tests

It is important to differentiate between assessment and evaluation. Put simply, we evaluate products, policies, programmes, etc., but we assess people. So what is the connection between evaluation and assessment? The answer is that we can evaluate the success of a programme by assessing what people have learned from it in terms of knowledge, skills or comprehension – and above all, performance. Hence, controlling for other variables, if post-course assessments reveal that new skills and knowledge have been acquired, we can attribute this (through evaluation) to the training programme itself. Thus, the outcomes of assessment can comprise an important element of the evaluation process.

Repertory grid

The repertory grid technique is based upon the original work of Kelly (1955), who argued that people's behaviour is influenced by the way in which they classify what is going on around them. People construe and interpret events, noting features of a series of events that characterize some and are particularly uncharacteristic of others. In doing this, they erect constructs involving similarity and contrast. So, if someone is construed as having leadership qualities, this would imply they shared similar characteristics to other people seen to have this quality *and* contrast with characteristics shown by people with no leadership ability. But this does not imply that the person identified as a leader would be seen in this light by everyone. Constructs are personal, with different individuals giving different interpretations of events or characteristics. They are also hierarchical, with some constructs seen as more important than others. In particular, *core* constructs allow an individual to maintain their sense of identity and continuing existence, while *peripheral* constructs can be altered without any change in core structures. Some (permeable) constructs may change on the basis of new evidence, but other constructs (impermeable) prove more resistant to change. Hence, a technique is used, the repertory grid, to elicit these constructs for analysis and interpretation. Since the result of using this technique is the production of quantitative data, repertory grids have proved popular for evaluating the outputs from training programmes in terms of people's views, behaviours or perceptions.

REPERTORY
GRID ANALYSIS

Using an example (Figure 12.6), let us say we want to evaluate an organization's appraisal system through the perspectives of an employee. Designing a questionnaire or interview schedule might bias the evaluation towards the issues and concerns of the evaluator. Using personal construct theory, however, this should not

							Significant ELEMENTS of the appraisal			
							Pre-appraisal planning	Appraisal: reviewing progress	Appraisal: agreeing objectives	Post-appraisal: documenting/signing
							1	2	3	4
CONSTRUCTS	Motivating	1	2	3	4	Demotivating	3	3	4	3
	Helpful	1	2	3	4	Unhelpful	1	3	3	3
	Quick	1	2	3	4	Time-consuming	4	1	3	1
	Encouraged analysis	1	2	3	4	Encouraged feeling	2	4	4	3
	Creative	1	2	3	4	Destructive	1	3	4	3

Figure 12.6   Repertory grid showing an individual's constructs of an appraisal

occur. The employee is asked to identify a set of events connected to her recent appraisal that were of particular significance to her (Elements in Figure 12.6). She is asked to identify what it was about these elements (constructs) that had been of particular significance to her. Hence, for example, she decided that she had found some elements motivating whilst others were demotivating. She then uses the grid to allocate a score between 1 and 4 against each of her constructs for each of the elements.

Just glancing at Figure 12.6 reveals some quite startling results. We can see that the appraisee found nearly all aspects of the appraisal process either fairly or completely demotivating. The reasons for this are not hard to identify. While she found the preparation of the documentation for the appraisal very helpful (perhaps in focusing her thoughts and identifying her achievements) if time-consuming, the actual appraisal itself obviously did not go well. She found the reviewing of progress and the setting of new work objectives not at all helpful – indeed, destructive. Feelings rather than analysis emerged – and probably very negative feelings at that.

This is a relatively simple example of a repertory grid, with some detailed and complex examples benefiting from the use of especially designed computer software programs. Nevertheless, it serves to illustrate the power of allowing someone to identify their own constructs and interpretation of events. From an evaluation perspective, it allows us to identify which aspects of the appraisal programme may need review and overhaul – in this case, not the documentation, but the interaction dynamics between appraiser and appraisee. Perhaps we should continue the evaluation by looking at the appraiser's personnel records – is he sufficiently trained?

Critical incidents

A critical incident is something that produces an emotional response (whether positive or negative) in a person (Gray et al., 2000). As an evaluation tool, this is a qualitative approach that asks participants to comment on such events, often through the use of a log or diary (see next section). There may be a pact between evaluators and participants before the start of the evaluation process whereby such diaries are acknowledged to be confidential, with participants revealing and commenting on only those critical incidents they are willing to divulge.

CRITICAL
INCIDENTS

The analysis of critical incidents may also be useful in the workplace itself. Here the effectiveness of a training or development programme is evaluated (say, by managers or supervisors) when they see how staff respond to critical incidents following a training programme.

Learning logs

We have already seen how logs or diaries can be used to keep a note of critical incidents. But they can also be used by participants to keep a note of any events, incidents, thoughts, learning outcomes or unanticipated results of a programme. This can often provide a rich source of illuminative data for evaluation – providing that participants are willing to divulge the contents of such logs. Questionnaires, and to a less extent, observations, are very common in evaluation studies. The use of repertory grids, critical incident analysis, and learning logs, etc., however, are far less common. This is a pity because they all have the potential for generating rich and illuminating data.

QUALITY ISSUES IN EVALUATION

One of the challenges of evaluations is that there are no precise rules on how to plan and implement them. Judgement is called for. As Patton (2002) warns, an inevitable trade-off will be faced between gathering as much data as possible (and then face the costs of doing so) or reducing costs, time and hence data, but then reducing confidence in the evaluation findings. Looking at a problem in depth may produce detailed results but leave other problems unanswered; conversely, examining a range of problems might provide insufficient depth to be able to arrive at any sensible conclusions. So, especially at the planning stage, an evaluator needs to decide on what aspects of a programme should be evaluated, and whether all the outcomes require scrutiny or only selected elements. The evaluator's role, then, may be to get stakeholders or sponsors to narrow the focus of the evaluation to a more feasible list of questions.

The quality of any evaluation process is also deeply influenced by the familiar issues of validity, reliability and objectivity. Let us look at each of these in turn, within the context of the evaluation process.

Validity

As we saw in Chapter 6, for a research instrument to be valid, it must measure what it was intended to measure. Sometimes face validity may be sufficient, that is, the extent to which an instrument *looks* as though it will measure what it is intended to measure. This rather unscientific approach is held in low regard by measurement experts. Patton (2002), however, advises more optimistically that it may have some value. It may, for example, help managers and those responsible for implementing evaluation findings to have confidence in the evaluation instrument – and hence in the evaluation results. House (1980) suggests that goal-based evaluations often offer high levels of face validity because their objectives are made explicit to all concerned.

VALIDITY

One of the most sought after measurements is that of predictive validity, that is, the extent to which the results of an evaluation can be used to predict events, usually the impact of a programme on participant performance. As we saw earlier, one of the weaknesses of many evaluation studies is that they tend to focus on whether participants liked, or thought they benefited from, the programme rather than measuring whether new skills or attitudes resulted.

As Patton (2002) points out, validity may be threatened when observation methods are being used and participants know that they are being observed. This is because they may behave quite differently in situations where they are not observed. This suggests that covert observation may be more valid and reliable (although ethical considerations then arise). Yet, it needs to be borne in mind that even covert observation only picks up observable behaviours and not what is in people's minds. The data, therefore, are selective. Validity may be improved by long-term observations where observers and participants get to know one another (Longitudinal focus, see Table 12.2).

House (1980) contends that systems evaluation often tends to produce valid and reliable evidence because data are produced in a way that lends them to replication by other evaluators. Contrast this with other evaluation approaches where data can involve large elements of personal interpretation. Reay (1994) provides a useful example (Case Study 12.2) of what can, at least potentially, go wrong when the evaluation process fails to address validity issues.

CASE STUDY 12.2

Invalid evaluation – getting it wrong on a Friday afternoon

A company training department trained workers in the goods depot to stock-take every Friday afternoon. All aspects of stock-taking were demonstrated and explained and at the end of the course there was an evaluation which gathered data on the costs of the training programme (including down time and the costs incurred in lost production when trainees were not working), the likely savings through increased productivity and an assessment of what people had actually learned. The evaluation 'proved' that the course was successful.

Then, one Friday afternoon, the depot became extremely busy and the stock-taking was not done. Next week chaos resulted as the computer systems failed to cope with out-of-date information. The result was that orders were not met and customers complained.

Why had this happened? The reason was that nobody had explained to the stock-taking employees that stock-taking was *important* on a Friday afternoon. They had simply assumed that it was something they did when they weren't busy. The evaluation had been invalid. It hadn't asked the question: 'Do these people know *why* they are performing this task?' The evaluation had failed to spot a vital missing training objective.

Source: Adapted from Reay, 1994

ACTIVITY 12.4

Using the summary of evaluation types in Table 12.1, suggest which evaluation approaches were applied in Case Study 12.2. Are there any additional ones that you think *should* have been applied?

Suggested answers are provided at the end of the chapter.

Reliability

Recalling Oppenheim (1992), for a research instrument to be reliable it must be consistent. So to prove the reliability of an evaluation tool, we could attempt to confirm its findings by looking at other data sources. For example, say a study found that a once popular course was now receiving quite negative evaluations. It might be prudent to look at documentation on the kinds of participants coming on the programme – they might be more experienced or senior than previous participants and not find the course of particular value or sufficiently demanding. Reliability can also be measured by giving the data to another trainer or evaluator to see if they reach similar conclusions (inter-judge reliability).

Essentially, as Patton (2002) advises, a trade-off exists between the size and significance of a programme and the amount of evaluation error that can be tolerated. In the case of a summative evaluation of, say, a major national education programme, involving large amounts of expenditure, we would want to see a robust evaluation involving reliable instruments (or at least as reliable as possible) using a large sample. In contrast, a small-scale training programme involving few people might only require a relatively informal, formative evaluation to highlight areas for improvement, reliability not being a major point of concern.

Objectivity

Concern for objectivity may be particularly strong from evaluators who believe in forms of 'scientific' or experimental evaluation and an emphasis on measurement, manipulation of variables, quantifiable outputs and distance (physical and critical) from what is being observed. But, as Patton dryly comments: 'Distance does not guarantee objectivity; it merely guarantees distance' (2002: 575). This issue, according to Patton, is not one of objectivity as such, but is about the credibility of the evaluator and the extent to which fairness and balance are addressed. This may mean abandoning any positivist notion that there is one objective 'truth' out there, and instead focusing on people's multiple perspectives and interpretations of events.

Certainly, there are dangers when those designing and delivering a programme are also those who conduct the evaluations. There may be a sense of ownership that might be difficult to overcome. Either evaluators must be aware of the danger of subjectivity and try to address it, or they could bring in external consultants to conduct the evaluation. Of course, even when all the issues of validity, reliability and objectivity have been addressed, we may end up with the 'so what?' conclusion. If evaluation results tell us that 82 per cent of respondents scored a programme as either 'excellent' or 'good' what does this really tell us? Probably not very much. As Patton (2002) suggests, the outcomes of evaluation have to be compared with something else for them to have any meaning, such as:

- The outcomes of similar programmes.
- The outcomes of the same programme delivered on a previous occasion.
- The outcomes of model programmes in the same field.
- The stated goals of the programme.
- External standards developed by professional bodies.

Hence, evaluation should be seen less as a 'snapshot', than a measurement of indicators over time.

PLANNING THE EVALUATION REPORT

Evaluation reports may have a multiplicity of potential audiences with quite different needs. Funding agencies, steering groups and managers may be interested in technical issues arising from evaluation, not least because some of these may require action. This does not mean that they need all of the report – they may prefer an executive summary – but they will expect that the technical detail is available should they need it. Programme clients may not require so much technical detail but will want to know the evaluation's findings and its impact on themselves personally. Morris et al. (1987) present a summary (Figure 12.7) of the kinds of communication methods that can be used to report evaluation findings to different groups.

Clearly, some of the formats suggested in Figure 12.7 require the production of quite formal and large-scale documents. If effective action is to result from these reports, it is important that they are properly structured, a typical example being a table of contents, an executive summary, the main body of the report and appendices. Campbell (1997) suggests the following outline, described in Figure 12.8.

Remember, you will have to write clearly and concisely for your intended audience (see Chapter 19). Make as much use of figures and tables as is feasible, as these provide accessible summaries of the data and serve to break up the text. Planning the evaluation report may include allowing time for the review (evaluation!) of the report by a colleague or a helpful member of the intended audience, so that errors, inconsistencies and misunderstandings can be eliminated.

ENHANCING THE IMPACT OF EVALUATION

Having completed an evaluation, how can you ensure that its findings lead to change or improvements? As Patton (2002) points out, the key is getting the right information to the people who need it and also encouraging those people to actually make use of the information in forging policy and decision making. This may not always be easy. Evaluations may be 'ritualistic', conducted so that an agency can delay having to make a decision on a difficult subject (Weiss, 1984). One, obvious, approach is to ensure that the evaluation report is of high quality and worth reading and acting on. For example, make sure that conclusions and recommendations actually fit the data and are compatible with the objectives of the evaluation study. Campbell (1997) also strongly recommends the production of action plans, providing precise details of remedial measures required and their timing.

A key factor here is making sure that these findings do not come as a shock to the programme or evaluation sponsors. People do not like surprises, particularly when money and resources have been invested in a policy, system or programme.

A number of steps can be taken to improve the probability of an evaluation being accepted:

- Involve sponsors in formulating the objectives and the design of the evaluation to gain their interest and commitment.
- Get commitment from senior stakeholders in advance of the evaluation that action will be taken on the basis of results.
- Consider establishing a steering group to monitor and help the evaluation project and get senior stakeholders onto the group if possible to increase its credibility.
- Keep sponsors informed of outputs (particularly unexpected ones) as they occur.

Consider producing several reports, one for each type of audience. Senior managers, as we have seen, may not have either the time or the inclination to read complete reports and may prefer an executive summary. But take care to ensure that

Possible communication form Audience/users	Technical report	Executive summary	Technical/professional paper	Popular article	News release/press conference	Public meeting	Media appearance	Staff workshop	Brochure/poster	Memo	Personal discussions
Funding agencies	•	•									•
Programme administrators	•	•	•	•	•			•		•	•
Board members, trustees		•		•							
Advisory committees	•	•	•								
Political bodies		•		•							
Community groups				•		•					
Current clients				•		•	•				
Potential clients											
Programme providers		•		•				•	•	•	•
Media					•	•					

Figure 12.7   Communication methods for a variety of audiences

Source: Adapted from Morris et al., 1987

Cover page

Typically includes a fully explanatory report title, specifies when the evaluation was conducted, when the report was prepared and who it was submitted to. It may also identify those who prepared it, reviewed and approved the report.

Table of contents

Lists all headings in the report, especially the evaluation objectives and attachments/appendices by page number.

Acknowledgements

Identifies colleagues' professional contributions and provides an expression of thanks.

When appropriate, the source(s) of financial support is recognized.

Part 1 – Summary

Sometimes called an Executive Summary – for those who are too busy to read the full report.

1.1   Introduction – background information, etc.

1.2   Purpose of the evaluation

1.3   Objectives of the evaluation

1.4   Summary of the evaluation project

    1.4.1   A brief presentation of evaluation procedures, including a summary statement on the collection as well as the analysis of information and data

    1.4.2   The conclusion(s) drawn from the information and data

    1.4.3   The recommendations made

Part 2 – Report body

2.1   Evaluation of objective 1

    2.1.1   Description of evaluation activities – how the evaluation was conducted, development and validation of the instrument(s), collection of information and numerical data, etc.

    2.1.2   Responses, including tables and figures

    2.1.3   Analysis and interpretation of the information and data

    2.1.4   Conclusion(s) formed and recommendation(s) made for the objective

2.2   Evaluation of objective 2

    2.2.1   Etc.

    2.2.2   Etc.

    2.2.3   Etc.

2.3   Plan for corrective action

Part 3 – Appendices

3.1   Instrument(s) used in the evaluation, i.e., reaction form, questionnaires, etc.

3.2   Presentation of raw data (if too bulky for main report)

Figure 12.8   Format for an evaluation report

Source: Adapted from Campbell, 1997

different versions contain similar content and recommendations – the difference should be one of presentation. Ensure that not only managers receive the report but all other relevant stakeholders.

THE ETHICS OF EVALUATION

ETHICS IN
EVALUATION

Ballantine et al. (2000) provide a framework of considerations to be taken into account in any attempt to mount an ethical approach to evaluation. Referring to the work of Habermas (1972), they warn that society is becoming less aware of ethical choices because these are being rationalized as either technical or economic decisions. Science is being absorbed into this discourse and presented as politically neutral and theoretically objective. According to Habermas (1972), however, knowledge always serves the vested interests of one group or another. Ballantine et al. (2000) therefore suggest five constraints (based on the work of Kettner, 1993) that can set the conditions for a 'truly moral dialogue'. These comprise:

- *The generality constraint:* participation in a discourse or discussion must be as wide as possible, and present the views of all affected interest groups.
- *The autonomous evaluation constraint:* participants must be allowed to introduce and challenge any assertions and any interests stated.
- *The role taking constraint:* participants must give equal weight to the interests of others alongside their own interests.
- *The power constraint:* a participant should not appeal to any hierarchical authority to legitimate their argument.
- *The transparency authority:* participants must openly declare their goals and intentions.

To illustrate these, Ballantine et al. (2000) present a real life example from the City of London that is summarized in Case Study 12.3.

CASE STUDY 12.3

Short supply of ethics at the Stock Exchange

In the late 1980s and early 1990s, the London Stock Exchange invested £80 million in Taurus, a major new information systems project. The project failed and the system was never completed. Ballantine et al. (2000) suggest that this was due to a failure to engage in rational moral discourse (discussion) during its evaluation, design and development.

The *generality constraint* was met during the project to the extent that there were a large variety of stakeholders (the Stock Exchange itself, its stockbroking member firms both large and small, company registrars and other financial institutions). One of the problems, however, was that these stakeholders held conflicting requirements. The *autonomous evaluation constraint* played a significant part in the demise of the project because the planning process was quite well developed before participants really began to challenge its rationale and make their own case. The design team were motivated by largely technical considerations and failed to question whether the project was actually worthwhile.

There is little evidence that the *role taking constraint* was adhered to because the more powerful stakeholders (institutional investors) paid little attention to the interests of smaller parties (for example, private investors and small stockbroking firms). Indeed, the inability of different stakeholders to take the views and interests of others seriously was one of the main reasons that led to the Taurus project's collapse. The result was that rather than the creation of one seamless system, about 17 alternative systems were welded together. The *power constraint* was not met because, although the chief executive of the Stock Exchange had wanted to stop the project, it had already gained too much momentum and support from the international banks. Finally, in terms of the *transparency authority*, it is clear that not all participants' objectives were made explicit from the start.

Ballantine et al. caution that if the managers and designers involved in the project had paid more attention to a moral discourse, then the political and ethical issues at stake might have been given more consideration. The result would have been either a project that was more in line with what stakeholders wanted, or the project would have been suspended long before it was, and losses minimized.

Source: Adapted from Ballantine et al., 2000

Taking the information provided in Case Study 12.3, and using Ballantine et al.'s five constraints, describe a 'truly moral' and ethical process of collaboration and dialogue that could, in principle, have led to a more positive outcome.

Using some of the principles outlined in the discussion of constraints, above, Ballantine et al. (2000) have constructed a framework for the ethical evaluation of a programme. While they focus this on information systems, it also offers a useful guide for evaluations of any kind (see Figure 12.9). They argue that there are six general factors that influence the choice of evaluation approach: philosophy, power, culture, management style and the kind of evaluator and resources available (see left column in Figure 12.9). As we saw earlier, different schools of evaluation (and therefore philosophical approaches) have a direct bearing on what is evaluated, the purpose of evaluation and the tools used.

So, in Figure 12.9, the left hand side of each of the ranges represents a more expert and controlling approach to evaluation, while the right hand side emphasizes participation and learning. The framework can be used to consider the amount of thought given to ethics by each of the evaluation approaches. According to Ballantine et al. (2000), the more ethical approaches are to be found at the right end of each of the ranges, because more consideration is given to the views of those on the receiving end of the evaluation process. But the authors acknowledge that there may be organizational circumstances when priorities other than ethical factors may be uppermost.

The ethical framework can be used to provide guidance on how ethics can be incorporated into the decision making process. It can also be used as a check on internal consistency, to see whether ethical approaches are consistent across all six influences.

Ethical attributes Evaluation influences	Purpose of evaluation	Process of evaluation	People affected by the evaluation
Philosophy	Summative Formative	Positivist Interpretivist	Automata Human
Culture	Control Learning	Ritualistic Purposeful	Organizational Individual
Management style	Covert Overt	Implicit Explicit	Directive Consensual
Power	Manipulative Emancipate	Autocratic Democratic	Dictatorial Participative
Evaluator	Judgemental Assist	Investigative Collaborative	Control Facilitate
Resources	Minimalist Comprehensive	Limited Sufficient	Constrain Enable

Figure 12.9   A framework for ethical evaluation

Source: Ballantine et al., 2000

Summary

- Evaluation involves the systematic collection of data about the characteristics of a programme, product, policy or service.
- The focus of evaluation can be on trainees' reactions to a programme, how much new knowledge they have gained, how much this is transferred into better job performance and other organizational criteria.
- Like most approaches to research, evaluation involves different schools or perspectives, ranging from experimental and quasi-experimental with an emphasis on the measurement of outcomes and quantifiable data, to illuminative perspectives with a focus on processes and the multiple perspectives of participants.
- Data can be collected from various informants and through observations, involving a wider range of stakeholders than just participants.
- Data collection tools include questionnaires, assessment tests (since an important outcome of evaluation is a measurement of what participants have actually learned), learning logs and documentation of critical incidents.
- The principles of validity, reliability and objectivity apply as much to evaluation as they do to many other aspects of research.
- The impact of evaluation is enhanced if stakeholders are kept informed of outcomes as they arise – particularly if they are going to be unwelcome or unexpected. Care should be taken to avoid redundancy of information, providing different stakeholders with different versions of evaluation reports on the basis of what they need to know.
- Evaluation that fails to take into account ethical issues will often be doomed to failure. Ethical approaches include a focus on the individual needs of people rather than the goals of organizations, on making the purpose of the evaluation transparent to those being evaluated, and encouraging participation in the evaluation process.

REVIEW QUESTIONS

1. Why is it that so much evaluation is undertaken at the level of reaction (Level 1 of Kirkpatrick's model)?
2. Explain the pros and cons of making more use of control groups in evaluation studies. If 'objectivity' is the goal, what other approaches can be implemented, other than the use of control groups?
3. How would you present the negative results of an evaluation study to the client who commissioned it? Think of this in terms of timing, impact on respondents and other stakeholders, impact on the client, and ethical codes of research practice.

FURTHER READING

Russ-Eft, D. and Preskill, H. (2009) *Evaluation in Organizations: A Systematic Approach to Enhancing Learning, Performance and Change*. Cambridge, MA: Persius Publishing. Discusses the evolution of evaluation as a method and offers a wide range of approaches to data collection including surveys, focus groups and observation. Suggests strategies for implementing effective evaluation programmes in organizations.

Rossi, P.H., Lipsey, L.W. and Freeman, H.E. (2003) *Evaluation: A Systematic Approach,* 7th edn. Thousand Oaks, CA: Sage. Provides a wide range of evaluation approaches including collaborative and empowerment evaluation. Packed with examples.

Patton, M.Q. (2002) *Qualitative Research and Evaluation Methods*, 3rd edn. Newbury Park, CA: Sage. Still one of the best books on qualitative methods, with a substantial section on models of evaluation.

Clarke, A. (1999) *Evaluation Research: An Introduction to Principles, Methods and Practice*. London: Sage. Deals with a range of evaluation paradigms, and data collection methods and provides some case studies of evaluation in the education, healthcare and criminal justice systems.

JOURNAL RESOURCES

Sormunen, M., Saaranen, T., Tossavainen, K. and Turunen, H. (2012) 'Process evaluation of an elementary school health learning intervention in Finland', *Health Education,* 112(3): 272–291. Describes an action research project involving process evaluation of a school programme. Demonstrates the importance of pre-planning the evaluation.

Eduardo Tasca, J., Ensslin, L., Rolim Ensslin, S. and Alves, M.B.M. (2010) 'An approach for selecting a theoretical framework for the evaluation of training programs', *Journal of European Industrial Training*, 34(7): 631–655. A study into the ways in which training programmes have been evaluated, including the main journal sources where evaluation results have been published.

Marsden, D. and Littler, D. (2000) 'Repertory grid technique – An interpretive research framework', *European Journal of Marketing*, 34(7): 816–834. Demonstrates application of the repertory grid to a study of consumer behaviour.

Suggested answers for Activity 12.1 (Selected examples)

Table 12.4   Type of evaluation and data collected

Focus or type of evaluation	Type of data collected	Ease or difficulty of measurement
Accreditation (validation)	Market research data (is the programme needed?); course structure and content; module descriptions and objectives; links to other courses; resources supplied (including staff and their qualifications), etc.	Usually a significant quantity of data has to be collected. Evaluators (validation panels) will look for accuracy and coherence of data.
Compliance	Case studies of breaches of regulations; performance indicators for compliance – e.g. speed of performance, customer satisfaction rates, etc.	Data may be hidden by those organizations seeking to escape compliance. Costs of data collection may inhibit the setting up of robust systems, but in some cases systems may be required by legislation.
Formative evaluation	Participant evaluation forms; tutor observation and self-reflection.	How honest are the participants? How self-reflective are tutors? Are a sufficient number of indicators used?
Quality assurance	Minutes of meetings; evaluation of accuracy and completeness of staff and student handbooks; student evaluations; resources etc.	The data may not be particularly complex, but the quality assurance exercise may demand large quantities!

Suggested answers for Activity 12.4

The main evaluation approach seems to have been confined to a cost–benefit analysis. Perhaps a more prudent approach would have been to evaluate the outcomes, goals or the effectiveness of the programme. A descriptive focus might also have illuminated what was actually happening to participants when taking the course.

13

ACTION RESEARCH AND CHANGE

CHAPTER INTRODUCTION

Chapter outline

What is action research? 329

The action research process 332

The role of researchers and participants 338

Methods of data gathering 339

Validating action research 342

Ethics and action research projects 343

Some of the limitations of action research 345

Keywords

Participatory action research

Action science

Cooperative inquiry

Critical colleagues

Ethics

— Chapter objectives —

After reading this chapter you will be able to:

- Distinguish between action research and other research methodologies.
- Distinguish between the variety of approaches within action research.
- Plan a project, keeping in mind some of the potential limitations of action research.
- Describe the processes involved in conducting an action research project, and methods for gathering data.

Action research methodology symbolizes much of what modern research is about – analysing the world but also trying to change it. Whereas some research paradigms may be content to add to the store of knowledge, action research asks the question: 'What can I do about it?' In addressing real world problems, the action researcher becomes directly involved in the research process as a change agent, devoted not only to studying organizations, communities and processes but also to improving them. Contrast this with other research paradigms where the researcher is seen as a detached scientist, intent on avoiding any action that might bias or tarnish the results. Action research, in contrast, is committed and intentional but also informed and systematic. Lincoln (2001) sees strong connections, for example, between action research and constructivism, both of which claim the impossibility of value-free knowledge. But action researchers do not simply throw themselves into the research process. As we will see, there are planning, implementation and ethical issues that need addressing.

The term 'action research' was first coined by Lewin in 1946, by which he meant a process through which theory building and research on practical problems should be combined. Given the context of post-war reconstruction in which the theory was developed, it is not surprising that Lewin viewed action research as a way of improving social behaviour and encouraging social change. But his approach to such change was similar to the contemporary, traditional, scientific paradigm in that it recognized the value of experimentation and the importance of creating knowledge. But, while traditional science begins with substantial knowledge about hypothetical relationships, action research begins with very few facts. Lewin also argued that it was important to conduct social experiments in natural, social settings, not in the artificial world of controlled laboratory environments. Action research is also gestaltist in origin, that is, it sees issues as only being understood not through the study of a single variable, but within a holistic, complex social system.

Unfortunately, Lewin never wrote a systematic statement of his views before his death in 1947. Hence, as Dickens and Watkins (1999) note, there is still no definitive approach to action research and no unified theory. However, according to Bowling (1997, cited in Badger, 2000), Lewin's concept of action research as a means of social engineering has now been replaced by one that emphasizes raising awareness, empowerment and collaboration. There are still, however, a number of disparate definitions and characterizations of action research. McKay and Marshall (2001) even claim that the practice of action research is somewhat enigmatic, with few guidelines for action researchers to follow. This chapter, however, hopes, within the constraints just identified, to offer some guidelines to practice.

WHAT IS ACTION RESEARCH?

The term action research is a generic one and has been used to describe a bewildering range of activities and methods. In brief, however, action research is an approach that focuses on action and research simultaneously and in a participative manner (Coghlan and Brannick, 2010). Within this approach there are varied methodologies, each with their own priorities and modes of inquiry (although there are as many overlaps and similarities between the approaches as there are distinctions). Some, for example, focus on how communities can enact change, particularly challenging issues such as injustice and social exclusion. Others are based in a more organizational context and may include how professional practitioners can improve their own professional practice (McNiff and Whitehead, 2011).

ACTION
RESEARCH

All approaches, however, have at least three common features:

- Research subjects are themselves researchers or involved in a democratic partnership with a researcher.
- Research is seen as an agent of change.
- Data are generated from the direct experiences of research participants.

A mode of action research that takes this latter point particularly seriously is *participatory action research* (PAR). McTaggart (1997) warns that participation is much more than mere involvement. Authentic participation means immersing people in the focus of the enquiry and the research method, and involving them in data collection and analysis. One of the primary aims of PAR is to transform situations or structures in an egalitarian manner. Hence, it has been used to deal with issues such as inner-city and rural poverty, education, mental health, disability and domestic violence. In the 1990s, however, PAR has also been taken up as a legitimate research approach by powerful agencies such as government departments, universities and multinational companies. In 1999, for example, the World Bank commissioned a 'Consultation with the Poor' involving over 20,000 people in 23 countries. Gaventa and Cornwall argue that the key element in PAR is a process of reflection, social learning and the development of 'critical consciousness' (2001: 76). This is particularly so among oppressed groups of people, where non-experts play a central role (Park, 2001).

PARTICIPATORY
ACTION
RESEARCH
JOURNAL

PARTICIPATORY
ACTION
RESEARCH

In contrast, another type of action research is what Coghlan (2001) terms '*insider action research*', in which managers or other professionals are engaged in action research projects in their own organizations or contexts. McNiff and Whitehead (2011) contrast the kinds of questions practitioner-researchers might ask with those posed by external social scientists (see Table 13.1)

Often, action research projects are undertaken as part of an academic programme of study such as an executive MBA. The kinds of issues addressed often include systems improvement, organizational learning and the management of change. One of the advantages of adopting insider action research is that managers and professional practitioners have an intimate knowledge of the organization being studied – they know its culture, its jargon and its personal networks. They can also participate freely in discussions or merely observe what is going on without people necessarily being aware that they are being researched. On the other hand, it may be difficult at times to maintain a sense of detachment and it may sometimes prove difficult for an insider to cross departmental, hierarchical or network boundaries.

Table 13.1   Differences between outsider and insider questions

Outsider (social science) questions	Insider (action research) questions
What is the relationship between nurses' practice-based knowledge and the quality of patient care?	How do I study my nursing practice for the benefit of patients?
Does management style influence worker productivity?	How do I improve my management style to encourage productivity?
Will a different seating style increase audience participation?	How do I encourage audience participation through the use of different seating arrangements?

Source: Adapted from McNiff and Whitehead, 2011

➤ **TOP TIP 13.1** ◄

GRAY ON
GETTING A
SPONSOR

If you are considering undertaking an insider action research project, the first step is to ensure that you gain a sponsor for your project before you start. The sponsor may offer financial backing for the project, but at a minimum, should be someone who will give it 'political' backing, that is, they are willing to speak up for the project when asked. This sponsor should, preferably, be a senior manager and someone respected and well 'networked' within the organization.

An alternative approach is *external action research*, where the researcher may be independent of the professional context, but work within it and alongside professional practitioners (for example, business leaders, managers, trainers or health professionals) to achieve change. Hence, action research is a process of collaboration for bringing about change. The exact nature of this collaboration, however, may be problematic.

━ ACTIVITY 13.1 ━━━

Examine each of the following statements, only two of which are typical of action research statements. Which are they?

1. What is happening here?
2. How can I improve the quality of my professional practice?
3. How can this research method be improved?
4. What implications does my research have for all practitioners in my profession?

Suggested answers are provided at the end of the chapter.

Another approach to action research is *action science*, which attempts to integrate practical problem solving with theory building and change. Friedman (2001) acknowledges that it is difficult to locate a single, comprehensive definition of action science, but suggests that it involves a form of social practice which integrates both the production and use of knowledge in order to promote learning with and among individuals and systems. The objective of action science is to help practitioners to 'discover the tacit choices they have made about their perceptions of reality, about their goals and about their strategies for achieving them' (Friedman, 2001: 160). To achieve this, communities of practice are created in which both practitioners and researchers make explicit their interpretations, which can then be made subject to rigorous testing for their validity.

Gummesson (2000) divides action science into *societal action science* and *management action science*. The former is concerned with the kinds of macro social, political and economic issues that arise, say, when a company is threatened with closure. This could involve, for example, a participatory study by groups of workers who are directly threatened by the closure. Such an approach stems from a belief that research should not lie in the hands of 'professional experts', who will have their own agendas and subjective biases.

Management action science is focused on a company as a business. Here, the action researcher has the difficult task of tackling issues and producing results that are of value to both science and to business. Thus, from a theoretical perspective, the action researcher will seek to contribute to knowledge, understanding and theoretical perspectives. But this must also be knowledge that can be applied and 'validated in action' (Gummesson, 2000: 119). This means that the life of the action scientist is often prone to role conflict and ambiguity. Another aspect of management action science is that it is interactive, that is, it requires close collaboration between the researcher and the company client. Again, this may pose problems for the researcher who may be pressurized to change original research designs in the interests of producing short-term actionable results.

Some important differences between participant action research and action science are highlighted by Whyte (1991). Action science focuses more heavily on interpersonal relationships, but also requires the intervention team to keep control of both the intervention and the research process (often as detached observers). In contrast, participatory action research, for example, involves greater sharing of control between practitioners and researchers.

Finally, *cooperative inquiry* is related to action research in that both focus on research with people rather than research on people. Where cooperative inquiry differs is in the way collaboration between researchers and participants takes place. Heron and Reason describe how co-subjects become 'immersed in and engaged with their action and experience' (2001: 180). They develop a degree of co-openness to what is happening through deep experiential engagement, often generated through music, drawing, drama and dance.

This relationship between theory (usually produced by academics) and practice (the domain, normally of practitioners), has been seen in dichotomous terms of theory versus practice (Swanson, 2001). For Short (2006), the gap has many different names: the research-practice gap; the implementation gap; the research-practice divide; the theory-practice void; and the 'disconnect' between researchers and research consumers. Research driven research for researchers is termed Mode 1 research. However, one of the potential benefits of action research is that it provides opportunities for bringing researchers and practitioners together where research objectives and research designs are jointly negotiated and implemented – Mode 2 research (Gray, Iles and Watson, 2011).

We can see, then, that action research involves quite a varied range of approaches to research both in terms of the relationship between researcher and participants

Table 13.2   Sectors where action research projects have been used

Sector	Type of project
Education	School curriculum Evaluation Classroom processes Parent participation
Health	Infant health programmes Drug abuse programmes Health promotion projects Community health projects
Social work	Youth programmes Parenting programmes
Organizational development	Planning Change processes Training programmes Human resource development
Urban and economic development	Urban planning projects Community planning projects Housing needs surveys Youth housing needs

Source: Adapted from Stringer, 2013

and the focus of the research itself. Table 13.2 provides a summary of the kinds of action research projects that have been undertaken in different sectors.

THE ACTION RESEARCH PROCESS

PARTICIPATORY
ACTION
RESEARCH AS
PRACTICE

McNiff et al. (1996) caution that it is wise at the outset to be very realistic about what action research can achieve. You may also have to recognize that it is easier to change your own perspectives and professional practice than that of others. The success of an action research project will depend, in large measure, on your success with working with other people, so you need to identify the range of people who will be involved. These will certainly include participants, who may include colleagues or fellow employees. It is essential to pay very close attention to gaining access and to maintaining relationships. This is helped by keeping participants informed about the progress of the research and by thanking them for their assistance. But other possible collaborative sources might include:

- Critical colleagues, those who work with you and who may be willing to discuss your research, critically but supportively. It is advisable to negotiate the ground rules for engagement at the start of the project.
- Adviser/mentor/tutor, whose role is to challenge your thinking so that the direction of the project can be refocused or ideas reshaped.

- Action research colleagues, who may be fellow students on a taught programme or colleagues in a professional development programme. These people are key for providing support and sharing information and resources.
- The validating group of colleagues, managers or fellow professionals who may be used to comment critically on the outcomes of the project (see Validating action research p. 342).

Failure to engage the cooperation of people who can give you advice and support may actually endanger your project (see Case Study 13.2).

➤ TOP TIP 13.2 ◄

It may help to bring all or some of these people together in a more formal structure such as a project Steering Group. The Steering Group could have Terms of Reference for what it has been set up to achieve, a chairperson (possibly the project sponsor – see Top Tip 13.1), representatives of the participants involved in the project, and, of course, the action researcher(s). This would be typical of a Mode 2 research project with close collaboration between academics and practitioners.

EXAMPLE:
TERMS OF
REFERENCE

As Stringer (2013) shows, the aim of action research is not to present finalized 'answers' to problems, but to reveal the different truths and realities (constructions) held legitimately by different groups and individuals. People with identical information will interpret it in different ways, depending on their previous experiences, world view and culture. The task of action researchers, therefore, is to bring people with divergent views and perceptions together so that they can collectively formulate a joint construction.

The action research process itself, as originally conceived by Lewin, is a cyclical one, working through a series of steps including planning, action and observing and evaluating the effects of that action. Note that these stages overlap, meaning

Image 13.1   Gaining collaboration through a steering group

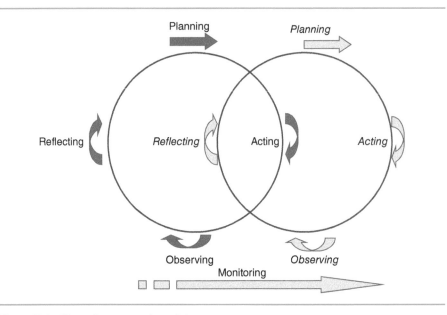

Figure 13.1   The action research model

that some activities are running in parallel with each other. For example, a team could plan a project, and begin to execute some change, but then modify these plans on the basis of lessons learnt through action. Each of these steps is continually monitored to make adjustments as needed (see Figure 13.1). McTaggart (1997) suggests an alternative approach. Rather than see this as an entire project, a good way to begin is to collect some initial data in an area of general interest (a reconnaissance), then to reflect before making a plan for action. Hence, execution (albeit on a small scale) precedes planning.

While this section has looked at action research as a neatly planned and orderly process, Dickens and Watkins warn that this is not always the case and that 'it can go forward, backward, and all directions at once' (1999: 135). We will explore each of the core action research stages in more detail next.

Planning: getting the focus right

Choosing a focus for the action research project may, at first sight, seem a relatively simple task, yet it is one that often causes researchers the most difficulty. This is because there are often so many issues that could be addressed, the problem is prioritizing between them. One of the keys to identifying a suitable research topic is having a sense of commitment to improvement (McNiff et al., 1996). If undertaking research within your own professional practice, you could, for example, ask yourself questions such as:

ACTION
RESEARCH
FOCUS

- How can I reduce my stress levels at work?
- How can we improve the quality of the consultancy and advice we give in the organization?
- How can we achieve better working relationships within the company's project teams?

But there is an important difference between focusing on an issue that you consider vital or interesting and one that can actually be practically addressed. You must, then, also consider the matter of feasibility – do I have the time, access to participants and resources to actually tackle this issue and to bring about change? If the answer to the above question is 'Yes' then you will probably want to start with at least a tentative working hypothesis: 'If I do this, then it is likely that X might happen'. Unlike experimental research, this is not an attempt to identify causal relationships between variables. It is trying to identify the kinds of actions that can lead to positive change.

This means meeting with stakeholders to obtain a consensus on the actions that are planned. As Stringer (2013) makes clear, it is essential that the voices of all are heard, so that appropriate goals can be set. For planning purposes, the focus becomes one of establishing:

- Why activities are required.
- What actions need to be taken.
- How tasks are to be accomplished.
- Who is to be responsible for each activity.
- Where the tasks are going to be performed.
- When the activities are going to commence and when they are to be completed.

Mumford (2001) advises that a formal 'action' document should be drawn up with precise specifications of processes, objectives and outputs, and that this should be signed by both management and the researcher and given to all interested parties. Avison et al. (2001) refer to such a document as 'action warrants' that define the authority under which action can be taken, specifying the balance of authority between researchers and internal organizational participants. Sometimes projects may not begin with an action warrant because they are relatively informal or the precise nature and scope of the problem have not been defined, or it is initially not seen as serious. Once the problem and research objectives become clearer, then an organization may decide it needs the sort of formal control structures that an action warrant can specify.

In aiming to get the focus of the research project right, it is vital to make our own personal values explicit, so that we can explore the relationship between these values and our own behaviour. Although we all have value systems, we may be forced by organizational constraints to act in ways that contradict them. For example, a headteacher might espouse democratic forms of work organization, but act in quite authoritarian ways towards teachers. Action research:

> is a way of working that helps us to identify the things we believe in and then work systematically and collaboratively one step at a time, to making them come true. (McNiff et al., 1996)

— ACTIVITY 13.2 —

In planning your own action research project: (a) make a list of the likely participants (other than yourself); (b) identify those who might be prepared to give you critical advice and support; (c) select a suitable action research subject; and (d) formulate a provisional hypothesis for the project.

If you are coming into an action research project from the outside, you will need to make contact with key stakeholders and interest groups as quickly as possible.

These groups might include not only those people most directly concerned with the issue, but also managers and sponsors. It may also be necessary to contact, and get to know, unofficial opinion leaders or gatekeepers.

Acting: gathering evidence

Having identified the focus of your research, the next step is deciding what sort of actions to initiate and then what data to gather. It is usually best to focus on the kinds of performance indicators that show whether you, or others who are the focus of your research, are being effective in initiating change or not. Hence, if you were looking at improving communications between yourself and a group of clients, then you could try to locate critical incidents of when communication was progressing well, and when it was subject to problems. Data collection should be as comprehensive as possible, because important insights may only emerge once the data are being analysed. This means that you may have to use a wide range of data gathering tools, such as interviews (individual and focus groups), participant or non-participant observation, informal meetings and document analysis. For every piece of data, ensure that you record the date, time, place and the people who were present. Transcripts of conversations and records of meetings should be authenticated by getting them signed by a relevant participant.

The main problem is knowing how much data to gather without the process becoming unwieldy and unmanageable. As usual, the key is aiming to achieve a representative selection from the possible range of data. So, if you are trying to investigate the working relationships of a team of 12 school inspectors, one approach would be to choose four of them, if you were sure that they were typical of the group as a whole. Stringer (2013) also advises you should ensure that the diversity of groups in a social setting are represented. For example, in conducting an action research project among the parents of school children, it would be important to ensure that different social classes and ethnic groups were represented.

Stringer also suggests four alternative frameworks for assisting the data gathering process, namely:

- Interpretative questions. Participants might be encouraged to work through these in order to extend their understanding of the problem. These questions might include: what are the key elements of the problem? How is the problem affecting us? Who is being affected?
- Organizational review. Participants should focus on analysing various features of their organization, including: the general mission or purpose of the organization; its goals and objectives; the structure of the organization, including roles and responsibilities and the efficiency or otherwise with which they are conducted; the factors that inhibit the enactment of these responsibilities.
- Problem analysis. This is similar to concept mapping, only here participants are asked to identify the problem itself, the antecedents that led up to it and the major consequences that have ensued.
- Concept mapping. This is used by stakeholders to understand how different key elements in the problem relate to each other. The facilitator begins by drawing a word that sums up the central problem. Participants then add new labels to the chart that represent other elements associated with the problem. They then decide how the issues are linked. An example of a concept map is illustrated in Figure 13.2.

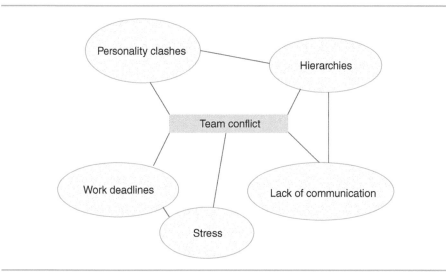

Figure 13.2   The data gathering process: concept mapping of team conflict within a workplace

Observing: analysing the impact

Since action research is about taking action and often involves experimentation, action researchers have to take note of the impact of their actions. This might include providing authentic descriptions of what has been achieved. These may be either factual (for example, transcripts of conversations), subjective (such as, diaries and personal reflections) or fictionalized accounts that preserve the anonymity of participants but are used to highlight issues explicitly.

On the other hand, the impact analysis might take the form of meetings of stakeholders to examine what has been achieved. This is not a case of looking at the techniques and procedures that guide action research, but exploring the sense of unity that inspires people to work together towards a common good (Stringer, 2013). There should be opportunities for participants to discuss their contributions and to describe what they will do and the way in which they will go about it. The key to action is participation, a shared intent, positive working relationships and inclusivity. Of course, disagreements and antagonisms might arise. The role of the action researcher is to maintain a neutral stance and to act as a mediator to heal conflict.

→ TOP TIP 13.3 ←

In meeting with stakeholders, try to ensure that participants are well briefed before stakeholder meetings and ensure that there are no sudden 'shocks' in terms of news about the project. People do not often react positively to the unexpected. Between meetings, consider keeping stakeholders briefed through either newsletters (in the case of very large projects) or emails.

GRAY ON
KEEPING
STAKEHOLDERS
INFORMED

Reflecting: evaluating the impact of the project

As we have seen, the aim of action research is the attainment of change. So how will you evaluate that change has actually taken place? The best approach, before you even start the project, is to identify what criteria constitute evidence of change. Then, select a piece of evidence from the data that you think demonstrates this change and have the evidence judged (validated) by others. For example, in an action research school project aimed at reducing pupil absentee levels, the indicator of change would be improvements, over time, in attendance rates.

EXAMPLE:
PROJECT
OUTCOME

The individual action researcher is not in a position to say whether their actions have had an impact – it is for participants in the project to judge for themselves. But action research is not just about fostering change in organizations, it is about generating learning among the action research participants. This too needs to be a focus of reflection – what was learned, what is its value, can it be applied elsewhere?

Having cycled through the planning, acting, observing and reflecting stages (often a number of times), what should the action researcher have to show for it? Coghlan (2001) suggests that the outputs of action research should include evidence of:

- How researchers engaged in the steps of action research, how they recorded their data and how they were a true reflection of what was studied.
- How they challenged and tested their own assumptions and interpretations of what was happening on a continual basis.
- How they accessed different views of what was happening, showing both confirming and contradictory interpretations.
- How these interpretations and analyses were grounded in academic theory and how this theory both confirmed and challenged the analysis.

In contrast, Stringer (2013) argues that good action research projects have no well-defined ending. Instead, new realities emerge that extend the process of inquiry. In the pupil attendance example, mentioned above, the project might discover high levels of pupil boredom, so motivating and generating pupil engagement might become the focus of a new action research project. What people also should do is celebrate their achievements. Mumford (2001), however, talks explicitly about 'getting out' of the action research setting through the action researcher successfully handing over the knowledge needed by the group he or she has been working with, so that they can continue to solve their own problems. Hence, successful action research projects are not just about bringing about change in organizations, communities or networks, but about changing and empowering people.

PARENT
EMPOWERMENT
PROGRAMME

THE ROLE OF RESEARCHERS AND PARTICIPANTS

In contrast to many other research methodologies, in action research the role of the researcher is seen as more of a facilitator than an 'expert'. Stringer (2013) contrasts action research with surveys, which he says are often limited in scope and frequently biased by the agendas and perspectives of the people who commissioned or constructed them (Stringer, 2013), that is, Mode 1 research. In action research, the researcher is a catalyst for achieving change by stimulating people to review their practices and to accept the need for change. But the researcher is not there to offer blueprints but to enable people to develop their own analysis of the issues facing them and the potential solutions. This might mean getting people to consider a range of possible solutions and their consequences. Once a plan has been decided,

Table 13.3   Elements that contribute to community relationships in action research

Working principle	Principle as implemented in action research community
Relationships	Promote feelings of equality for all involved Maintain harmony Resolve conflicts openly Encourage cooperative relationships
Communication	Listen attentively to people Be truthful and sincere Act in socially and culturally appropriate ways Regularly advise others as to what is happening
Participation	Enable significant levels of involvement Enable people to perform significant tasks Provide support for people as they learn to act for themselves Deal personally with people rather than with their representatives or agents
Inclusion	Maximize the involvement of all relevant individuals Ensure cooperation of other groups, agencies and organizations Ensure that all relevant groups benefit from activities

Source: Adapted from Stringer, 2013

the role of the action researcher is to help in its implementation through analysing any weaknesses in the plan and by helping to locate resources (including human resources and the development of the necessary skills for the plan's success).

Given the facilitative role of the action researcher, the relationships and working processes between researcher and participants are of central importance. According to Stringer (2013), action research seeks to develop and maintain non-exploitative social and personal relationships and to enhance the social and emotional lives of those who participate. It is organized in democratic, therapeutic and equitable ways that should engender a community spirit. Table 13.3 summarizes some of the key elements that contribute to this.

————————————▷ **ON THE WEB 13.1** ◁————————————

Take a look at the wealth of action research sources at:

http://www.goshen.edu/soan/soan96p.htm

Evaluate some of these sources and note any that may be of value in the future.

METHODS OF DATA GATHERING

After planning the action research project, the next question is how to gather the data. As in most research methods, a variety of techniques are available, many of them already discussed in some detail in this book. The key, however, it to ensure that data gathering is systematic and provides a permanent record of what has taken place. As usual, it is important to use a variety of methods if possible to allow for triangulation.

ACTION
RESEARCH
APPROACH

Diaries

Whatever data gathering tool is used, it is probably advisable for the researcher to keep a diary throughout the action research project as it can, as a minimum, provide a factual description of events, dates and people. But diaries are useful for a whole number of other purposes, including providing:

- An *aide-mémoire* of short notes for later reflection.
- A detailed portrait of events to provide a 'thick description' for later reports.
- A reflective account through which the researcher makes tentative interpretations of events, or through which the researcher records personal feelings and anxieties in order to try to understand them.
- An analytical tool that could contain a framing of the original research focus and a provisional analysis of the data as they are gathered.

If the action research project is a collaborative one, then it is also possible to write collaborative diaries. These can be written independently, and so provide a way of triangulating and checking for different recall or interpretations of events. Alternatively, they could be written interactively. The Internet offers some flexible facilities here. For example, one researcher could send an email offering opinions or reflections on a topic to a co-researcher who would reply; the original researcher would reply to this, and so on. Hence, an interactive document is produced around a specific theme. Once the theme is exhausted, one of the researchers could send an email on another subject. Alternatively, using a computer-based discussion forum, a group of action researchers or project participants could debate and comment on subjects through a continuous flow of threaded discussions or they could engage in a group Skype debate.

Observations, interviews and questionnaires

Entire chapters of this book have been devoted to these data gathering methods and it is not the intention merely to repeat what has already been said. However, one way in which action research uses these methods differently, is that they are used in collaboration with others. Take the example of a group of consultants who frequently have to make presentations to company chief executives. They could set up an action research project in which they observe and video each other's practice presentations and give feedback. Action research is often linked to personal development.

It is usually unwise to use a questionnaire in action research unless there are really good reasons for doing so. This is because they do not help to generate the forms of collaborative problem solving that action research requires. But the use of questionnaires is valid for discovering information that could not be ascertained in any other way, or for evaluating the effect of an action research intervention – again, if data cannot be gathered using other methods.

Photography, audio and video recordings

These media can be used either to stimulate discussion or recall events during the research process, or as a means of capturing evidence in data gathering. In the case of the research process, participants may sometimes need visual evidence to remind them of a situation or just to stimulate ideas. Photographs or video can be used to present evidence of changes that perhaps the action research project has achieved. In the case of video, this is particularly true if we are talking about changes in human behaviour.

Audio is valuable because it can be used as a kind of talking diary that captures an entire conversation (McNiff et al., 1996). Of course, this will often mean that an audio file will have to be transcribed before it can be analysed. You may find it useful either to play the file to your critical friends, or to show them the transcript of the conversation.

PHOTOGRAPHY
IN ACTION
RESEARCH

Memory work

Memory work is used to uncover and analyse earlier understandings of social behaviour in personal and professional situations through the framework of current understanding. First used by feminist researchers, participants write stories about events or situations they have experienced in their lives. These narratives, which are written in the third person to create a sense of detachment, are then discussed and analysed by the group. Each member of the group then rewrites their original text in the light of the comments they have received. In the final phase, the original and rewritten texts of all group members are compared by the group. According to Schratz (1996), what is important is that the memory work process allows the group to explore issues and to learn.

MEMORY
WORK

An illustration of how action research data collection methods can be used in practice is given in Case Study 13.1.

— CASE STUDY 13.1 —

Improving children's health through action research

The aim of the action research project was to improve the provision of child health surveillance in a community context (doctor's surgeries rather than hospitals) and to develop a written framework for child health surveillance. The study was conducted over a 12-month period in 28 surgeries within one health district. Participants comprised between two and 11 primary care staff from each surgery, including at least one doctor and health visitor.

As is typical of action research projects, data were collected using a variety of methods, namely: direct observation of baby clinics by the research team, questionnaires to parents, semistructured interviews with team members and analysis of child healthcare surveillance reviews recorded in personal child health records. The 28 practices were randomly assigned to two groups comprising 14 practices in each, with one of the groups used for the action research study, the other being the control.

In the action research group, action researchers facilitated team meetings in each practice at four-monthly intervals. At these meetings, the data collected from the observations, questionnaires and interviews were discussed. This allowed the teams to analyse how child healthcare surveillance could be improved and what kind of changes should be made.

The results did not reveal a statistically significant difference between the two groups of practices in terms of parent satisfaction or return rate of child health surveillance reviews. But the teams involved in the action research project did decide to make changes in aspects of their professional practice. Communication and the use of child health records improved, and health visitors reported a greater feeling of empowerment. A framework for child health surveillance was developed that was acceptable to the practice teams.

Source: Adapted from Hampshire, 2000

Given the research aim in Case Study 13.1, to what extent do you think that action research was the appropriate research methodology?

Suggested answers are provided at the end of the chapter.

VALIDATING ACTION RESEARCH

Given that action research can involve the quite personal observations and analysis of the researcher, using small samples or individual case studies, the issue of validation is certainly no less important for this than for other research methodologies. According to McNiff et al. (1996), the purpose of validation in action research is to:

- Test out key arguments with a critical audience to identify where there is a lack of clarity or focus.
- Sharpen claims to new knowledge and ensure that the data match these claims.
- Develop new ideas.

The starting place for establishing claims for the validity of action research is with the researcher. McNiff (1988) suggests that the researcher needs to demonstrate publicly that he or she has followed a system of disciplined inquiry. This includes checking that any judgements made about the data are reasonably fair and accurate.

Validation can be quite an informal process, but may also involve the use of formal groups, especially selected to scrutinize the outcomes of an action research project. These could include critical colleagues, advisers or mentors, or fellow action research colleagues working on the project. If formal groups are used, it is important to ensure that participants both understand and can empathize with the context of the research. Ideally, the group should also contain members from outside the context who can provide a more detached and independent perspective. For example, an action research project at a Job Centre, where the aim is to help unemployed people find work, might include staff at the Centre who advise clients and some unemployed clients themselves. But the project steering committee could also include a representative from the local Chamber of Commerce, representing local employers.

Waterman (1998) argues that the process of validation in action research is strengthened by the 'to-ing and fro-ing' between the elements in the action research spiral (planning, acting, observing and reflection). Typically, action researchers are not satisfied with one turn of the action research spiral but will repeat the process several times, allowing for the refinement of ideas and practices.

Of course, not all of those involved in action research would agree that validity is a necessary or feasible objective. Lincoln and Guba (1994), you may recall, argue that instead of validity, the aim, certainly of qualitative research, should be to establish the credibility of the research through forging confidence in the accuracy of its interpretations. As Grønhaug and Olson (1999) note, if the validity of research is founded on a notion of scientific knowledge, based upon rigorous testing of falsification, then action research may prove lacking. However, claims for the generalizability of findings may be made on the basis of systematic comparison of such findings with the results from other settings, and by conducting more research to examine the robustness of the generalizations. In a sense, this is not too dissimilar to Flick's (2006) notion of case study replication (see Figure 11.4 p. 277).

ETHICS AND ACTION RESEARCH PROJECTS

The issue of ethics has been raised in nearly every chapter of this book, and this chapter is no exception. Action research is deeply embedded in an existing social organization, and failure to respect the general procedures of that organization will jeopardize the process of improvement. Badger (2000) suggests that, at least superficially, action research seems to pose few ethical dilemmas because it is based on a philosophy of collaboration for the mutual benefit of researchers and participants. Lathlean (1994, cited in Badger, 2000) contrasts action research with the 'smash and grab' approach of both positivist and interpretative traditions, who complete their study and leave their subjects to 'clear up the mess'. Taking note of ethical principles for action research, however, still involves the usual array of requirements for negotiated access, confidentiality and allowing participants the right to withdraw.

ETHICS IN
ACTION
RESEARCH

Negotiating access

Access needs to be negotiated at various levels: within organizations or communities, with individuals and with parents, guardians or supervisors.

Organizations and communities

You will probably first need to negotiate access to organizations or communities or to management in your own organization. After establishing contact, you will need to define your aims and objectives and get their agreement, in writing, to your research project. Be honest about what you are about to do, and if your objectives change, notify the sponsors immediately. Also note the warning of Coghlan and Brannick (2010) that doing action research in your own organization is a political act which might even be construed by some as subversive.

Participants

Make it clear that they are not 'subjects' but participants and co-researchers. You are studying yourself in relation to them or their relationship to others. Either way, they are central to your research. However, while most commentators on action research tend to emphasize the democratic and inclusive nature of the action research process, Avison et al. (2001) argue that either practitioners or researchers have the upper hand in most aspects of control and authority. Their relationship, then, is not balanced in a democratic sense, so opening up the potential for the abuse of power, influence and authority.

Parents, guardians or supervisors

Particularly if you are dealing with parents or guardians you need to inform them in writing of your intentions and to elicit their agreement, also in writing. You need to ensure that your research does not infringe any equal opportunities or human rights legislation.

⇢ **ON THE WEB 13.2** ⇠

Take a look at the UN Convention of the Rights of the Child at:

http://www.unicef.org/crc/crc.htm

Look particularly at issues of non-discrimination (Article 2), best interests of the child (Article 3), freedom of expression (Article 13), disabled children (Article 23) and education (Articles 28 and 29).

Maintaining an ethical stance
Promise of confidentiality

You need to make it clear that you will not reveal any information that is confidential or sensitive in nature, unless prior permission is obtained. If organizations and individuals are content to allow you to use the names of participants then you can do this, but otherwise use numbers or initials for identification. You also need to protect the confidentiality of your data, by getting other participants to check both the data and your interpretation of them for accuracy and balance. In some work situations, however, merely describing someone's role in an organization might immediately identify an individual. You need to negotiate or warn these individuals before publishing any report.

The right to withdraw

Research participants must know that they can withdraw from the research at any time, and this right to withdraw must be respected. Lathlean (1994, cited in Badger, 2000), however, notes that action research might involve the use of observation of group activity from which individuals could not withdraw, especially when the activity is related to collective working practices.

Communication

Keep participants informed about the objectives of the project and how it is progressing. One idea is to produce project reports, but limit the distribution of these only to the relevant interested parties. Communication should be used as a means of eliciting and encouraging suggestions and participation.

Maintaining good faith

Never take anything for granted and try to anticipate areas where possible misunderstandings could arise. Check with people to see if their interpretations are the same as yours. Indeed, Mumford (2001) suggests that participants should be actively involved in writing up any final report or recommendations. Participants should also be consulted as to how descriptions of the action research project are to be published (Coghlan and Brannick, 2010).

By following these criteria it should be possible to ensure that the outcomes are objective and truthful in the sense that the understanding of meaning is directed towards the achievement of a possible consensus among actors (Winter, 1996). However, as Tickle (2001) points out, action researchers often face a practical dilemma between keeping all participants informed of what is happening and maintaining confidentiality.

Taking note of the ethical issues outlined above, return to your plan for your action research project and include a set of ethical principles that you will need to address. In doing this, consider any documentation in the organization that deals with these issues and make yourself aware of any processes (such as gaining permission for conducting the research from senior managers or committees). Make a note of any ethical problems you potentially face in your research diary, and maintain a reflective record of how you deal with them.

SOME OF THE LIMITATIONS OF ACTION RESEARCH

While we have identified the effectiveness of the action research approach in particular settings, like any research paradigm, it has its potential drawbacks and limitations. Hampshire (2000) reports on action research projects in the field of primary healthcare, where significant amounts of time and effort have to be expended on maintaining collaborative networks. Since action research studies, typically, take longer to complete than other approaches, staff turnover and people leaving the project can be disruptive. Also, while new knowledge generated through studies may lead to practical results, these may not be widely reported in the academic literature – hence, they do not reach the public domain, and their application to other situations may be limited. As we have seen, another problem is that of generalizability. Many action research projects are fairly unique or idiosyncratic in nature. Badger also warns that due to its very contextual focus, action research may only be capable of allowing 'tentative generalization' (2000: 202). On the whole, action researchers seem fairly divided as to whether generalization of the results of an action research project is either feasible or, indeed, worthwhile.

LIMITATIONS
AND ETHICS

An honest evaluation of an actual action research project is presented by Waterson (2000) in the next case study.

The real world – when an action research project goes wrong

In the mid-1990s in the UK, the role of social services departments was changed from being an assessor and provider of social care, to an assessor only, with care being purchased from public and private sector sources, depending on which was most appropriate. This new policy generated new forms of work responsibility and management priorities. Waterson (2000) reports on three phases of an action research project within one social service region that explored issues of organizational progress in making these changes, problems that required solving, and strategic questions that had emerged.

Despite the commitment of the researcher and the care with which the research was planned and undertaken, major problems ensued. During the latter phases of the project, the preliminary findings were forcefully challenged by the main management client. Interestingly, he objected to the qualitative nature of the research reports and appeared to want a more positivistic, deductive perspective, including the use of statistics. New statements had to be inserted into the report at the insistence of senior managers. The final circulation of the report was restricted to a small number of senior managers, not to all the many staff involved in providing information, as had been agreed at the outset. Partly as a result of these difficulties, the impact of the project was minimal.

Why did this disappointing outcome occur? Waterson is instructive in pointing to some of the causes. She argues that one problem was the multiple agendas of those involved in the project. The task of the researcher is to create knowledge that is reliable and trustworthy. The ground-level social workers, however, were primarily preoccupied with the immediate needs of their clients. Senior managers faced the challenges of implementing a radical government policy. These multiple agendas eventually led to conflicts that the action research reports emerging from the project simply could not hide. As Waterson succinctly comments, there is an underlying assumption in action research that researchers are powerful change agents when, in fact, it is senior managers who have the power to block change. She therefore recommends that action researchers:

Use an independent mentor to provide support and advice.
Bring in co-workers (researchers).
Engage more proactively in contact with senior managers.
Establish a steering group with the involvement of an external researcher.
Make explicit at the outset the sort of action research model that is being used.
Discuss strategies for making sure that the validity of all participants' contributions is recognized and that ways of handling conflict are planned.
Emphasize that research findings on their own cannot achieve change.

ACTIVITY 13.5

Evaluate the recommendations at the end of Case Study 13.2. Do you agree with them? Are they all practical? Are there any other recommendations that you would make to strengthen the potential success of an action research project?

Summary

- Action research is used to address real world problems, with the researcher becoming actively involved in the research process as a change agent.
- Often, action researchers are professional practitioners who use action research methodology as a means of researching into and changing their own professional practice.
- Action research involves a cyclical process of planning, acting, observing and reflecting.
- Methods of data collection include: diaries and logs; documents; observations; questionnaires; interviews; memory work (writing stories about events); and the analysis of photographs, audio and video recordings.
- The data gathered through action research can be validated through eliciting the views of critical colleagues, advisers or mentors or fellow action researchers.
- Action research must avoid the 'smash and grab' mentality. The usual ethical principles must be adhered to, including negotiating access, promises of confidentiality, guaranteeing the right of participants to withdraw and checking to see if participants agree with the interpretations emerging from the research.
- One of the drawbacks of action research is that it often takes considerable resources, including time, to complete. Also many action research projects tend to be fairly unique and difficult to generalize. However, claims for generalizability may be strengthened by the replication of findings across a number of contexts.

1. Undertaking a project that involves 'action' (say, the use of interviews) and research (the adoption of a theoretical stance, data gathering and analysis) does not necessarily make it an action research project. Discuss.
2. How valid is the claim that action research is superior to all other research methodologies when it comes to the improvement of professional practice?
3. What are the dangers of undertaking an action research project in an organization which the researcher is a member of?
4. Examine the assertion that generalizing from an action research project is neither feasible nor valid.

— FURTHER READING —

Stringer, E.T. (2013) *Action Research*, 4th edn. Thousand Oaks, CA: Sage. A comprehensive and practical guide for those intending to conduct an action research project.

Coghlan, D. and Brannick, T. (2010) *Doing Action Research in Your Own Organization*, 3rd edn. London: Sage. Provides practical advice on selecting and framing a project, as well as the advantages and potential pitfalls of researching in your own organization.

Reason, P. and Bradbury, H. (eds) (2001) *Handbook of Action Research: Participative Inquiry and Practice*. London: Sage. Aptly called a Handbook since this very comprehensive volume contains chapters on the many approaches to action research as well as a wide range of case studies.

Whyte, W.F. (ed.) (1991) *Participatory Action Research*. Newbury Park, CA: Sage. Describes some of the principles of participatory action research, which are then illustrated through a series of case studies.

— JOURNAL RESOURCES —

Davison, R.M., Martinsons, M.G. and Ou, C.X.J. (2012) 'The roles of theory in canonical action research', *MIS Quarterly*, 36(3): 763–796. Describes how Canonical action research (CAR) addresses real-world problems and aims to improve organizational performance by combining scholarly observations with practical interventions.

French, S. (2009) 'Action research for practising managers', *Journal of Management Development*, 28(3): 187–204. Discusses the various definitions of AR and also offers a model for how an AR business research project can be conducted.

Altrichter, H., Kemmis, S., McTaggart, R. and Zuber-Skerritt, O. (2002) 'The concept of action research', *Learning Organization,* 9(3): 125–131. Discusses the lack of accepted definition of action research and argues for continuing flexibility.

— SUMMARY OF WEB LINKS —

http://www.goshen.edu/soan/soan96p.htm

http://www.unicef.org/crc/crc.htm

Suggested answers for Activity 13.1

Action research asks 'What is happening here?' and is a process that seeks to improve the professional practice of the action researcher and those colleagues who take part in the project. Since the focus is often highly localized and contextual, it does not usually make strong claims for generalizability and, hence, would rarely claim to be able to change practices across a profession.

Suggested answers for Activity 13.3

Since the focus of the project is on improvement and change within a professional context, action research would appear to be an ideal methodology. This methodology encourages the active engagement of a range of participants who, through the action research process, come to value their contribution and to 'own' the changes that are made.

PART C

Data Collection Methods

Contents

14. Questionnaires   351
    Why use questionnaires?   353
    Designing questionnaires   354
    Designing Internet and
    Web-based questionnaires   370
    Piloting questionnaires   372
    Maintaining quality: validity
    and reliability   374
    Questionnaire administration   376

15. Interviewing   381
    Why use interviews?   382
    Selecting interview approaches   384
    Designing credible interviews   388
    Interviewing skills   390
    Group interviews   401
    Using telephone interviews   404
    Ethical issues   405

16. Non-participant Observation   411
    Approaches to observation   413
    Gathering and recording
    observational data   416
    The process of observation   426
    Validity and reliability issues   430
    Presenting observational data   431
    Ethical issues in observational
    studies   432

17. Ethnography and Participant
    Observation   437
    The origins of ethnography   439
    Guidelines for fieldwork   441
    Gathering data: participative
    observation and field notes   448
    Gathering data: interviewing   451
    Gathering data: digital media   452
    Ethical principles in ethnography   453
    The ethnographic self   455
    Feminist ethnography   457
    Critical ethnography   459

    Sculpting the truth in ethnographic
    accounts   461
    Recording the miracle   463

18. Focus Groups   467
    The uses and benefits of focus
    groups   469
    The limitations of focus groups   471
    Organizing focus groups – an
    overview   472
    Focus groups and research design   485
    Special issues in focus group
    research   488
    Epistemological considerations
    and focus groups   490
    Ethical considerations and focus
    groups   494

19. Unobtrusive Measures   497
    Identifying physical measures   498
    Documents   502
    New unobtrusive measures:
    digital archives   502
    Ethical issues in using digital
    technology   506

20. Secondary Analysis   513
    Advantages and disadvantages
    of using secondary data   515
    Sources of secondary data   516
    Qualitative data sources   524
    Secondary data analysis   525
    Criteria for selecting a data set   527
    A systems approach to using
    secondary data   528
    Secondary data methodologies   530
    Secondary data in mixed
    methodologies   531
    Ethical considerations in secondary
    analysis   532

14

QUESTIONNAIRES

CHAPTER INTRODUCTION

Chapter outline

Why use questionnaires?	353	Piloting questionnaires	372
Designing questionnaires	354	Maintaining quality: validity	
Designing Internet and		and reliability	374
Web-based questionnaires	370	Questionnaire administration	376

Keywords

Q-sort	Sequencing questions
Classification questions	Response categories
Filter questions	Instructions
Open questions	Web-based questionnaires
Closed questions	Piloting

Chapter objectives

After reading this chapter you will be able to:

- Plan and design valid and reliable questionnaires.
- Describe the processes involved in collecting primary data, including piloting.
- Demonstrate the skills for writing appropriate individual questions and designing questionnaires.
- Write appropriate documentation to accompany questionnaires.

QUESTIONNAIRES

As an important data gathering tool, questionnaires are used as part of many of the research methodologies described in Part B of this book. Indeed, it is difficult to imagine a large-scale survey (Chapter 10), for example, without the use of a carefully constructed questionnaire. Similarly, case studies (Chapter 11) can use a combination of data gathering tools, with the use of questionnaires, sometimes in the form of an interview schedule (see Chapter 15).

Questionnaires are research tools through which people are asked to respond to the same set of questions in a pre-determined order. Since questionnaires are one of the most widely used primary data gathering techniques, considerable space will be devoted here to their design and construction. Many people in the business and educational worlds have had experience in data gathering using questionnaires, but fewer are knowledgeable about how difficult it is to construct questionnaires that are valid, reliable and objective. It is thus relatively easy to produce reports and recommendations based upon the most spurious of data. Hopefully, after reading this chapter you will understand many of the pitfalls of questionnaire design so that you can avoid them.

Questionnaires should be used when they fit the objectives of the research. Hence, in a case study that involves seeking the in-depth opinions and perspectives of a small number of respondents, a highly structured questionnaire might be completely inappropriate. Here you might want to construct an interview schedule containing open-ended questions, adopting a descriptive approach. But where the audience is relatively large, and where standardized questions are needed, the questionnaire is ideal, and will allow, if this is required, an analytical approach exploring relationships between variables. For example, a health district survey on the availability and types of mental health services would be able to determine not only the general awareness of such services, but statistical variations in awareness according to geographical location, income level and social class. Of course, in many cases questionnaires will be only one tool used in the general research effort. The research design may plan for a wide-scale survey using questionnaires, to be followed up by in-depth structured interviews or observations with a target sample identified to be of interest by the survey. For example, following the survey mentioned above, the health district might conduct a series of focus groups with the users of mental health services to gain insights into customer perceptions.

In this chapter we will explore some of the essential principles in questionnaire design, including how to write appropriate questions, whether to use open or **closed questions**, how to sequence questions and questionnaire layout. We also look at some of the more specific principles behind designing Web or Internet questionnaires, and how questionnaires of any kind should be administered.

QUESTIONNAIRES

WHY USE QUESTIONNAIRES?

Questionnaires are perhaps one of the most popular data gathering tools, probably because they are thought by many researchers to be easy to design. This belief, as we shall see, is not necessarily supported by the evidence. As Gillham (2007) points out, the popularity of questionnaires is also probably based on some of their inherent advantages. For example:

- They are low cost in terms of both time and money. In contrast to, say, interviews, questionnaires can be sent to hundreds or even thousands of respondents at relatively little cost.
- The inflow of data is quick and from many people.
- Respondents can complete the questionnaire at a time and place that suits them. Contrast this with interviews, when it can be difficult to find convenient times to meet the respondent.
- Data analysis of closed questions is relatively simple, and questions can be coded quickly.
- Respondents' anonymity can be assured. But Gillham (2007) rightly notes that in small-scale surveys, this can be largely nominal in character – it may not be difficult for the researcher to recognize the responses of individuals. But real anonymity can also be double-edged. If you do not know who has not responded, to whom do you send reminders?
- There is a lack of interviewer bias. There is evidence that different interviewers get different answers – because of the way in which they place different emphasis on individual words in questions and because of the different probes (additional questions) that they follow up with.

Of course, not surprisingly, using questionnaires also has its drawbacks. Unless we can make completing the questionnaire intrinsically rewarding, the response rate can be depressingly low. This is even more of a danger if questionnaires are too long. Gillham (2007) advises that questionnaires should be limited in length to four to six pages, otherwise the return rate may be adversely affected. Few people greet receiving a questionnaire with unbounded enthusiasm, particularly long ones. Most people find verbal communication easier than using the written word, yet questionnaires demand a certain level of literacy. But there is no opportunity to ask questions. For example, a respondent might tick 'Strongly agree' to the statement: 'Shared values are important to my organization'. If we were able to follow up this response in an interview, we might ask what these values are, and how they actually manifest themselves in practice. In questionnaires, respondents might also give flippant, inaccurate or misleading answers, but the researcher is not in a position to detect this. In contrast, the face-to-face interview might reveal underlying problems through observing body language or the verbal tones of the respondent.

GOOD & BAD
SURVEYS

— ACTIVITY 14.1 —

Take a questionnaire that you have designed, preferably quite recently. Was it less than six sides in length? Was it well designed and easy for respondents to complete? Were the answers, in your view, honestly given? Overall, how successful was the questionnaire in eliciting the required data and how could you explain its success or failure?

DESIGNING QUESTIONNAIRES

GUIDE TO
QUESTIONNAIRES

Questionnaires reflect the designer's view of the world, no matter how objective a researcher tries to be. This is true not only for the design of individual questions, but often about the very choice of research subject. Furthermore, what we choose *not* to ask about, may just as easily reflect our world view as what we include in the questionnaire. It is important, then, that, as a researcher, you are aware of this and try, as far as possible, to be objective. Indeed, it is the values, perceptions and interests of the respondent that you should be attempting to capture, and the questionnaire should reflect this as much as possible. In this section, we will look at the design of individual questions, including open and closed questions, the sequencing of questions and questionnaire layout.

Writing individual questions

POOR
QUESTIONS

Piloting a questionnaire usually helps to eliminate or at least reduce questions that are likely to mislead. So, getting five or six people, who are similar in key characteristics to the target audience, to read the questions can often identify errors, weaknesses or ambiguities. This is because people may read and interpret questions in quite distinct ways. It is naive to believe that standardized questions will always receive standardized, rational responses. Nevertheless, it helps if questions are phrased in ways that are clear, concise and unambiguous (to everyone in the sample), and free from jargon and abbreviations. While the overall content, style and structure of the questionnaire must satisfy the respondent, each individual question must stand on its own merits. Arksey and Knight (1999) provide a useful list of what to avoid when constructing individual questions.

Prejudicial language: Try to avoid language that is prejudicial or contains sexist, disablist or racist stereotyping. A question that annoys, irritates or insults a respondent may affect the way they respond to questions that follow – if they decide to complete them at all! For example, the question: 'What is your marital status?' may annoy those who live with partners or who are not living in a heterosexual relationship (assuming that the society allows only heterosexual marriages).

Imprecision: Avoid vague phrases such as 'average', 'regularly' and 'a great deal' since they are likely to be interpreted in different ways by different respondents. For example, one person might feel that going to the gym once a week is 'often', while another who goes three times a week construes this as 'regularly'.

Leading questions: These suggest a possible answer and hence promote bias. Questions such as 'Why do you think the government has been successful in the past three years?' are leading because they are making an assumption with which the respondent may not necessarily agree.

Double questions: These should be avoided because they are impossible to answer. For example, if the question: 'Do you like chocolate and strawberry ice-cream?' receives a reply of 'Yes' you would be unclear as to whether this relates to both of the ice-cream flavours or just one of them.

Assumptive questions: Avoid questions that make assumptions about people's beliefs or behaviours. For example, 'How often do you drink alcohol?' makes an assumption about the respondent's drinking habits which may be entirely false (and even hurtful – see prejudicial language, above).

Hypothetical questions: Try to avoid hypothetical questions such as: 'Suppose you were asked to ...' since these have been shown to be poor predictors of people's actual subsequent behaviour. A useful check on whether the content and structure of a question is right is to ask whether a respondent would understand why the question was being asked within the overall context of the study. Arksey and Knight (1999) also argue that such questions can generate insightful data when people have some direct knowledge or experience of the subject being discussed.

Knowledge: Make sure that the group that has been targeted to answer the questions has the knowledge actually to do so. Sometimes it may be necessary to provide people with some background information if the subject is quite technical – for example, questions on IT systems, or mobile phone technology.

Memory recall: People may have difficulty recalling what has occurred even quite recently. If, say, you are constructing some questions around recent newsworthy events, then it would be appropriate to present respondents with a list of such events before asking them questions about them.

In determining how to ask individual questions consider the following:

- Even if the question can be understood (in the literal sense), can the researcher's intentions be inferred? So, if the researcher asks: '*What do you like*?' is it possible to understand what kind of beliefs or attitudes the study is focusing on?
- Can the question be misunderstood? Does it contain difficult or unclear phraseology?
- Is the question misleading because of unstated assumptions or unseen implications?
- Is the wording biased? Is it emotionally loaded or slanted towards a particular kind of answer?
- Is the question wording likely to be objectionable to the respondent in any way?
- Can the question be asked in a more direct or a more indirect form?
- Are double questions avoided?
- Are leading questions avoided?
- Is attention paid to detail – e.g. overlapping categories such as 'age 30–35, 35–40'
- Do questions avoid taxing respondents' memories?
- Can the questions be shortened?
- Are categories such as 'Don't Know' and 'Not Applicable' provided?
- Will the words used have the same meaning for all respondents, regardless of nationality, language, culture, etc.?
- Is the frame of reference clear – e.g. if asking how often, is the range of possible responses made obvious?
- Do questions artificially create opinions on subjects where respondents really do not have any?
- Is personal wording preferable (e.g. 'How do *you* feel?), or impersonal (e.g. 'How do you think people feel?'). The first is a measure of attitudes, the second a measure of respondents' perceptions of other people's attitudes.
- Finally, just to emphasize the importance of question wording, consider the study by Schuman and Presser (1981). When asked what they consider 'the most important thing for children, to prepare them for life', 61 per cent chose the alternative '*to think for themselves*', when this was offered to them from a list. However, when no list was provided, only 4.6 per cent volunteered this answer. Lists then, may remind respondents of material they might not otherwise have considered and give a clear indication of what the researcher is interested in. But lists may also omit items that, otherwise, the respondent would have reported (Kenett, 2006).

→ TOP TIP 14.1 ←

How do you construct a comprehensive list that includes all the necessary concepts? A thorough review of the relevant literature and previous studies is a good starting point. But to ensure your list of concepts is complete, you could also run a focus group (see Chapter 18) in which you could elicit comments (validation) of your concepts. Using a focus group comprising subject matter experts will also help in the identification of concepts that are missing.

Developing questions to measure a construct

As indicated above, the development of individual questions is a skilful process. However, as we shall see later, to increase reliability we normally have to use more than one question to measure a construct accurately. This might be relatively straightforward when eliciting customers' views on the quality of a physical entity such as a can of baked beans. Here we can ask questions about the aesthetic design of the can, the taste and texture of the beans and their 'value for money'. But what about more service-related subjects such as service efficiency, staff friendliness, hospital cleanliness, etc.? How do we go about measuring a construct when even the very definition of the construct itself may be vague or even unknown to us? Ekinci and Riley (1999) suggest that using the Q-sort methodology can be of considerable assistance here. The Q-sort approach falls into three stages:

Q-METHOD-
OLOGY

- Stage 1: Create construct definitions. It is important that these should have a high degree of face validity so they need to be derived from previous studies or from expert opinion.
- Stage 2: Create sets of statements that are designed to represent the definition.
- Stage 3: Test the statements against the definitions by getting participants to combine the statements with the definitions on a 'free sort' basis, with the option 'don't know' or 'no opinion'.

CASE STUDY 14.1

Applying the Q-sort methodology

A hotel chain wishes to conduct a customer survey on the quality of staff behaviour and attitudes to customers and the reliability of services. Using some well known articles in the field of hospitality management, definitions of appropriate staff behaviour and attitudes were developed, followed by a definition for reliability of hotel services. Each definition was written onto a card – but without any title. For example, a card contained a definition of reliability but the card did not have 'Reliability' as a title. This card read: *It is the hotel's regularity and consistency in performing services which inspires confidence and trust to customers. In operational terms this means keeping promises, trustworthiness in transaction and efficiency of recovery process if anything goes wrong.* Another

INTRODUCTION TO
Q-METHODOLOGY

card was created for the response 'don't know'. Five positive and five negative statements were then developed for each of the two categories, making 20 statements in all.

Thirty participants took part in Stage 3 of the process. All the cards were shuffled to create a random order and each participant was then asked to place the statement cards against one of the two definition cards or the 'don't know' option. The results of each participant's choice were noted. From these data it was possible to calculate what proportion of respondents agreed that a statement described the definition.

In interpreting the results, a definition is only deemed to be legitimate if at least two state-ments are accepted as describing it. Secondly, for a statement to be legitimate, at least 70 per cent of the sample must allocate it to the same definition. Ideally, a minimum of four to six statements should be obtained for each definition (construct) in order to obtain internal con-sistency for the scale. Table 14.1 illustrates the results for each statement. We can see that for the construct 'Staff behaviour and attitude' there are six statements that yield a recognition rate of about 70 per cent. For the reliability construct three statements are deemed satisfac-tory. Hence, the Q-sort process has helped in the development of nine statements that are deemed adequate for measuring two constructs used to measure customer satisfaction within the hotel industry.

Table 14.1 The frequency of staff behaviour/attitude and reliability statements (acceptable statements appear with an asterisk)

Staff behaviour and attitude statements	Frequency (%)
*Staff don't know what they were doing	82
*Staff displayed effortless expertise	82
*Staff seemed to anticipate what I needed	76
*Staff recognized you	73
*Staff didn't care whether you were pleased or not	73
*Staff were willing to explain things when I asked	70
Staff seemed to want to get rid of me when I asked questions	68
If they didn't like you it was hard to get service	68
Staff were committed to pleasing customers	65
You were always treated like a stranger	46
You were always treated the same	41
If you wanted something you had to ask twice	31
Reliability statements	
*The hotel did not deliver any of its promises	80
*The hotel always delivered what it promised	78
*You had to constantly dispute items on the bill	71
The billing was always clear and accurate	66
They apologized for the mistakes and rectified the problems	59
They neither apologized nor made any attempt to rectify the problem or offered compensation	56
I always expected a screw-up with room reservations	49
When they told me how long it was going to be, I left it to fate and forgot about waiting	46
I didn't expect any problem with room reservation	44
When they told me how long it was going to be, I believed them	17

Source: Adapted from Ekinci and Riley, 1999

Using classification questions

One type of question often required by a survey is the classification question, dealing with, for example, the name, sex, age, status, etc. of the respondent. These are important for providing the basis for analysing associations between variables (for example, a respondent's gender and attitude towards sexual harassment issues in the workplace). These questions should be introduced by a gentle 'It will help us in further analysis if you would tell us a little about yourself'. Take care not to run the risk of alienating the respondent by prying for information that is not, subsequently, needed. For example, is it necessary to know the respondent's exact age, or would a response within a range of ages suffice? People may also be reluctant to reveal details of their salary, particularly to a stranger within their own organization. It may be easier to obtain their response to a question on job grade that may provide an indirect indication of salary.

→ **TOP TIP 14.2** ←

Response rates will be maximized if the curiosity and interest of respondents is 'grabbed' on the first page of the questionnaire. Hence, it is usually best to place the important, but less than exciting, classification questions at the end of the questionnaire. People may be pleased to complete them because they have already invested time in responding to the questionnaire's main themes.

ACTIVITY 14.2

Anyone can write a questionnaire? Evaluate the questions in the short questionnaire shown in Figure 14.1.

Suggested answers are provided at the end of the chapter.

Drafting the question content

Clearly, in writing questions issues such as validity need to be borne in mind. Hence, the content of the questionnaire needs to cover the research issues that have been specified. But Foddy (1993) points out that this is by no means a simple matter. A series of precise steps must be followed:

- The researcher has to be clear about the information required and encode this accurately into a question.
- The respondent must interpret the question in a way that the researcher intended.
- The respondent must construct an answer that contains information that the researcher has requested.
- The researcher must interpret the answer as the respondent had intended it to be interpreted.

Unfortunately, as Foddy (1993) comments, there is ample opportunity for the process to break down at any stage, with resulting threats to validity. Even if the respondent understands the question, there also needs to be some confidence that

1. State your age

   Under 20   20–25   25–30   Over 30

2. What are your views on appraisal?

3. Do you consider appraisal to be vital for organizational development or a way of wasting time?

   Yes   No

4. Do you consider that appraisal should be:
   - Integrated with training plans
     so people are better trained?
   - Linked to the reward system
     so everyone earns more money?

   1

   2 Please tick one

5. Without effective 'best practice' appraisal the organization cannot prosper

   Yes

   No

6. Give details on the number of appraisals conducted within the organization over the recent time period

7. How many of your appraisals have you failed?

8. How often do you think that people should be appraised: (a) once a year (as now);
   (b) twice a year; (c) once every two years; (d) never (the scheme should be abandoned);
   (e) other (please specify)

Name:

Department:

Salary:

Complete and return

Figure 14.1   Example questionnaire

LAYOUT AND
WORDING

he or she will know the answer, and that they will be willing to provide it. For example, in understanding school truancy, classroom teaching assistants would be able to answer questions on factors that trigger truancy behaviour, but might not be able to answer questions on truancy rates for the whole school. In deliberating about question content ask yourself the following questions:

- Is the question necessary? Just how will it be useful?
- Are several questions needed on the subject matter of this question?
- Do respondents have the information necessary to answer the question?
- Does the question need to be more concrete, specific and closely related to the respondent's personal experience?
- Is the question content sufficiently general and free from spurious concreteness and specificity?
- Is the question content biased and loaded in one direction, without accompanying questions to balance the emphasis?
- Will the respondents give the information that is asked for?

Cannell (1985) deals with the issue of how to ask difficult or embarrassing questions. Referring to the work of Barton, he illustrates a number of ways in which the cooperation of respondents can be maintained. The possible approaches are illustrated in Table 14.2, in which, by means of illustration, a set of hypothetical questions are asked about whether a respondent sabotaged the organization's intranet.

Drafting the answer

Decide on how you want people to respond and stick with it. So, if you require respondents to *tick* their responses, get them to do this throughout the questionnaire, rather than to also incorporate *underlining* and *circling*. In general, people seem to be used to box-ticking. The golden rule is that it should be absolutely clear how the respondent is to complete the questionnaire.

Table 14.2   Approaches to asking the embarrassing question: 'Did you sabotage the intranet?'

Approach	Question
Casual approach	Do you happen to have sabotaged the intranet?
Give a numbered card	Would you please read off the number on this card which corresponds to what became of the intranet [*Hand card to respondent*]:
	(a) It went down of its own accord (as usual)
	(b) I hacked into it and programmed a bug to make it self-destruct
	(c) Other (what?)
The Everybody approach	As you know, many people are tempted to sabotage the intranet these days. Do you happen to have done it recently?
The Other People approach	(a) Do you know any people who have sabotaged the intranet?
	(b) How about yourself?
Sealed Ballot technique	We respect your right to anonymity. Please complete this form, indicating whether or not you sabotaged the intranet, seal it in the envelope and place it in the box marked 'Secret Ballot'

Source: Adapted from Cannell, 1985

Types of question

With the above warnings in mind, we can now move on to look at the types of questions that can be posed in a questionnaire. Oppenheim (1992) suggests that a funnel approach can often be used, whereby the questionnaire starts off with a broad set of questions and then progressively narrows down the questions to target specific areas. This is sometimes achieved by **filter questions** that are designed to exclude some respondents. So, for example, in a survey of employee commuting experiences, a question might be posed: Have you ever had difficulty in getting to work? If the answer is 'Yes', then more market research questions follow; if the answer is 'No' then the respondent is routed to a later part of the questionnaire on different transport issues. The main body of the questionnaire, however, will comprise either open or closed questions. It should be noted that different formats can be used for questions. Using a variety of such formats adds interest and can even help increase questionnaire response rates. Let us look at some now.

Open questions

Open questions have no definitive response and contain answers that are recorded in full. Hence, the questionnaire must be designed in such a way that respondents are able to provide such a response without the restriction of lack of space. Open questions often begin with words such as 'How', 'Why', 'What', etc.

OPEN QUESTIONS

The advantage of open questions is the potential for richness of responses, some of which may not have been anticipated by the researchers. But the downside of open questions is that while they are easy to answer they are also harder to analyse. At first sight much of the information gathered may seem varied and difficult to categorize. Generally, the solution to this is the use of **coding** and the adoption of a **coding frame**.

Open questions may lead to interesting or unexpected responses, so, as we saw in Chapter 10 follow-up questions called probes or probing questions can be used (if the questionnaire is administered by an interviewer). These probes should be general in nature, and should not try to lead the respondent – for example, 'Could you say a little more about that accident report?'; 'How do you feel about those new operational procedures?' Probing questions can also be used to add some clarity where the interviewer has not understood a response. Clearly, it is easier to ask probing questions when conducting a structured interview than when using a postal questionnaire.

PROBING QUESTIONS

The simplest form of open question is the specified response, as illustrated in Question 1.

QUESTION 1: SPECIFIED RESPONSE QUESTION

What aspects of the government's healthy living campaign do you find the most useful? Please write in. _____

What aspects of the government's healthy living campaign do you find the least useful? Please write in. _____

(You could follow up each response with a 'Why?' question.)

—————————————————————> **TOP TIP 14.3** <—————————————————————

GRAY ON
USING OPEN
QUESTIONS

In making use of open questions, give careful consideration to how you intend to analyse the qualitative data that results from them. How much qualitative data do you expect to generate? Do you have the time and resources to handle it? What approach to qualitative data analysis do you intend to adopt?

Closed questions

A closed question is one to which the respondent is offered a set of pre-designed replies such as 'Yes/No', 'True or False', multiple-choice responses, or is given the opportunity to choose from a selection of numbers representing strength of feeling or attitude. In contrast to open questions, closed questions may restrict the richness of alternative responses, but are easier to analyse. They also make it easier to compare the views of one group with another. Closed questions can be useful in providing respondents with some structure to their answers. There are a number of approaches to asking closed questions.

CLOSED
QUESTIONS

List questions: These provide the respondent with a list of responses, any of which they can select. This approach avoids making the answering of a questionnaire a test of memory. If list questions are being presented as part of a structured interview, then prompt cards can be used which list responses and which are shown to respondents. So, rather than read out Question 2 and rely on respondents to remember each item accurately, a card is given to them that reproduces the question and the possible responses.

—————————————— **QUESTION 2: LIST QUESTION** ——————————————

What do you think is the most important influence on the success of the organization in the next two years? Please tick as many responses as you think accurate.

Changes in government policy affecting the legal regulation of the market ☐

The entry of new competitors to the market ☐

The impact of the company's current reorganization strategy ☐

Foreign exchange rates ☐

While the list will, clearly, influence the direction of people's responses, this does not make the approach invalid. If the questionnaire is concerned with issues that require recall of information, the list might act as a useful memory-jogger. But it must be recognized that influencing respondents in this way may affect their response to any later open questions.

Category questions: These are designed so that only *one* response is possible. For structured interviews there can be any number of categories, provided a prompt card is used. But for self-administered questionnaires and telephone questionnaires Fink (2003) suggests a maximum of no more than five alternative responses (see Question 3).

QUESTION 3: CATEGORY QUESTION

How often in an average week do you use our e-banking facilities? Please tick one response.

Never	☐
Once	☐
2–3 times	☐
4–5 times	☐
6 times or more	☐

Ranking questions: This requires the respondent to **rank** responses in order. With this kind of question it is important to make the instructions for completing the question clear and explicit. Be aware that more than seven or eight items in the list may make it too complex for many respondents to complete. For face-to-face interviews use will have to be made of prompt cards and for telephone interviews, items should be limited to no more than three or four. Note that an 'other' category is also provided to catch any features not mentioned in the list (see Question 4).

QUESTION 4: RANKING QUESTION

Please indicate in the boxes provided which features you believe are the most important when visiting our superstore (1 indicating the most important, 2 the next most important, etc.) Please leave blank those features that have no importance at all.

Ease of car parking	☐
Low prices	☐
Friendly staff	☐
Store loyalty card	☐
Variety of goods	☐
Other (please specify)	☐

Scale questions: Scale or rating questions are used to measure a variable, and comprise four types of scale: **nominal**, **ordinal**, **interval** and **ratio**. A common type is the Likert scale on which respondents are asked to indicate how strongly they agree or disagree with a series of statements (see Question 5). This is an example of an ordinal scale. Further details of all these scales are presented in Chapter 22. Most Likert scales use either a four- or five-point scale (see Figure 14.2).

QUESTION 5: SCALE QUESTION (ORDINAL)

As a loyal electricity customer we would like to know your views on the service we provide. Please put one ✓ for each of the following statements

	Strongly Agree	Agree	Disagree	Strongly Disagree
I have been pleased with the emergency 24-hour call out service	☐	☐	☐	☐
Electricity prices have been competitive with gas prices	☐	☐	☐	☐

Figure 14.2   An ordinal scale

Other forms of scaling can also be used. The number of response categories, for example, can be changed. Common formats are 'True/False', 'Yes/No'. Another approach would be to get respondents to mark a point on a continuum. Question 6 seeks responses on the quality of helpline support. Czaja and Blair (2005) warn, however, that this approach can lead to complexities at the data analysis stage. For example, do we calculate the average rating; combine parts of the scale into high, medium and low categories; or use a threshold that indicates a trend in one direction or another?

———————————————— **QUESTION 6: CONTINUUM SCALE** ————————————————

Please circle one number that reflects your opinion of our helpline support

Quick	1	2	3	4	5	6	7	8	9	10	Slow
Friendly	1	2	3	4	5	6	7	8	9	10	Discourteous
Informative	1	2	3	4	5	6	7	8	9	10	Confusing

Figure 14.3   A continuum scale

Oppenheim (1992) provides a useful table comparing the advantages and disadvantages of open and closed questions, reproduced in Table 14.3. Note that often a questionnaire will use a mixture of both open and closed questions. Indeed, it is often useful to follow up a closed question with an invitation to add comments.

Sequencing questions

There should be a logical flow to the sequence of questions, just as you would expect in a formal written text. Such a flow will aid the respondent in understanding individual questions and the overall purpose of the questionnaire. One way of designing the flow of questions is to use a flowchart, as shown in Figure 14.4.

Oppenheim (1992) points out that after reading the accompanying documentation that tells them all about the survey, respondents may be quite eager to answer some of the questions. Therefore, the last sort of question they want to see is what is presented in many surveys – a list of personal questions about age, gender, rank, status (work and marital, etc.). These types of questions should be kept to nearer the end of the questionnaire, and should be preceded by a short statement explaining that this data is needed for making statistical comparisons, so the respondent's

Table 14.3   The advantages and disadvantages of open and closed questions

Advantages	Disadvantages
Open questions	
Freedom and spontaneity of the answers	Time-consuming
Opportunity to probe	In interviews: costly of interviewer time
Useful for testing hypotheses about ideas or awareness	Demand more effort from respondents
Closed questions	
Require little time	Loss of spontaneous response
No extended writing	Bias in answer categories
Low cost	Sometimes too crude
Easy to process	May irritate respondents
Make group comparison easy	
Useful for testing specific hypotheses	

Source: Adapted from Oppenheim, A.N. (1992) *Questionnaire Design, Interviewing and Attitude Measurement,* 2nd edn. Continuum, an imprint of Bloomsbury Publishing Plc.

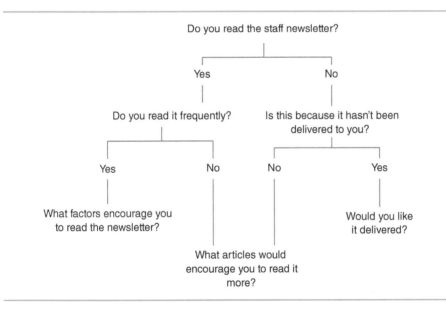

Figure 14.4   Flowchart for planning of question sequences

help would be appreciated. De Vaus (2002) argues that questions that should come first include those that are easily answered, factual questions and those that are obviously key to the purposes of the survey. Indeed, as Dillman (2007) points out, if the covering documentation has highlighted the key themes of the questionnaire, it is sensible to start with questions that deal directly with the theme. He also suggests that special attention be given to the first question since this will help determine whether the questionnaire is answered or put in the wastepaper bin.

Other useful advice includes going from easy to more difficult questions and from more concrete to abstract. Any sensitive questions should be left until the end. Where possible, a variety of answering formats should be used to provide interest, some additional advice on the sequencing of questions being:

- Is the answer to the question likely to be influenced by the content of preceding questions?
- Is the question led up to in a natural way? Is it in correct psychological order?
- Does the question come too early or too late from the point of view of arousing interest and receiving sufficient attention, avoiding resistance, etc.?

ACTIVITY 14.3

Take a questionnaire that has been designed either by yourself or a colleague (it could be the one you used for Activity 14.1). Evaluate individual questions. Are they clear, concise and unambiguous? Are they in grammatical English? Would the intended audience be able to answer them in terms of their knowledge of the subject? Are instructions on answering the questions clear? Is the sequencing of questions appropriate?

Providing response categories

Asking a question like 'What employment sector did you work in before your present job?' is asking for trouble. It might both confuse the respondent ('What do they mean – sector?') or the respondent might be uncertain as to whether their classification is acceptable. So, for the question cited, it would be appropriate to provide a list of categories such as: Finance, Retailing, Education, Commerce, Agriculture, Other (please specify), etc. Providing these categories also yields a standardized set of responses that will make the data easier to analyse. Note that we have been careful to provide an 'Other' category, just in case. Some common response category statements are provided by Czaja and Blair (2005) and are summarized in Table 14.4.

Table 14.4   Common response category quantifiers

Category	Quantifiers
Opinions	Very satisfied/Somewhat satisfied/Somewhat dissatisfied/Very dissatisfied Very important/Somewhat important/Not too important/Not at all important Oppose/Support
Knowledge	Very familiar/Somewhat familiar/Not too familiar/Not at all familiar True/False
Frequency of events or behaviour	Always/Frequently/Seldom/Never Often/Sometimes/Rarely/Never Per day/Per week/Per month/Per year/Never
Ratings	Excellent/Good/Fair/Poor Got better/Got worse/Stayed the same Very fair/Fair/Unfair/Very unfair High/Medium/Low

Source: Adapted from Czaja and Blair, 2005

Questionnaire layout

One way of improving the rate of response to a questionnaire is by making it as attractive as possible. Hence, factors such as the general layout, choice of paper, line spacing and answering directions should be considered. So, the way of answering multiple-choice questions should be consistent throughout – for example, ticking boxes or circling numbers. Boxes or lines should be provided for open question responses. It is best to avoid making the questionnaire too cramped as this can be off-putting to respondents.

Dillman (2007) warns against unconventional designs, such as printing on both sides of paper with a staple to bind the pages together, or using landscape (horizontal) orientation. He argues strongly for a booklet format which, he says, is understood automatically by respondents. With this format, people start on page 1 and turn over to page 2 which is to the left of page 3. If the budget is tight, then it is legitimate to print on one side only and to staple sheets together. Carroll (1994) suggests that other typographical issues require careful consideration such as:

- Putting boxes around groups of questions.
- Shading multiple-choice questions.
- Selecting clean, clear typefaces.
- Using lines to take the respondent's eye from question to response.
- Numbering all questions and sections.

Dillman (2007) cautions that questions should not be written on the cover page which should contain an interesting title or graphic to attract the attention of the reader. Below the illustration the purpose of the questionnaire should be outlined, and a message provided that explains the value of the study and states that the opinions of the respondent are important. If the questionnaire is part of a study linked to an organization or part of an academic programme, then the name and contact details of the organization should go at the base of the front page. Figure 14.5 provides an example from an online questionnaire that was part of an actual study.

Writing a set of instructions

Most questionnaires will also contain, probably at the start, a set of instructions for completing them. This is important, and it should not be assumed that respondents will all know that they should, say, only tick one choice for each question. Unless instructions are made absolutely specific, it is almost certain that questionnaires will be returned completed incorrectly resulting in a loss of data. Cohen and Manion (2011) even suggest that with postal questionnaires it is advisable to repeat the instructions. Carroll (1994) supports this idea, arguing that providing additional instructions for groups of questions will help the response rate.

One of the problems with instructions is that they are either not read or are misread. Dillman (2007) suggests that respondents can be helped by careful use of typography and design. De Vaus (2002) suggests that, to improve the flow of a questionnaire, the following instructions should be considered:

Triggers for Business Success ◄─── Title

We are currently undertaking a research study to find out about the triggers for Small and Medium sized Businesses' success and are interested in your opinions. This study is being undertaken by the University of Surrey on behalf of Kingston Smith, one of the UK's largest accountancy firms. The findings will be used to better advise businesses on how to grow and make them more successful.

◄─── Use of the findings

We would be really grateful if you could answer the 60 questions in this questionnaire. This should take about 20 minutes to complete.

◄─── How long it will take

Please click on the answer which most closely matches your view for each question. If you wish to add further comments, you will be able to do so in space provided at the end of the questionnaire. If you decide to take part, you are still *free* to withdraw at any time without giving a reason. If you choose to withdraw your answers will not be saved. All information you provide will be treated in the *strictest confidence* and will be *anonymous*. Your identity and that of your business cannot be linked to your answers.

◄─── The Research ethics

The answers from your questionnaire and those from others will be used as data for a research study report and to write academic articles.

◄─── Outputs

If you have any questions or would like further information, please do not hesitate to email our research officer [name and email address here].

We hope that you will take part and will find completing the questionnaire interesting and thought provoking. When you have completed the questionnaire, you will be asked whether you wish to submit your responses. Please feel free to email [name and email address of research officer] to request a summary of the research findings.

◄─── Incentive for taking part

To help and take part, please click on the link to the questionnaire [add link to questionnaire] by [date here].

◄─── Return date

Thank you for your help

Professor David E Gray, Professor MNK Saunders and Harshita Goregaokar

The Business School
University of Surrey

Figure 14.5   Example of a questionnaire cover page

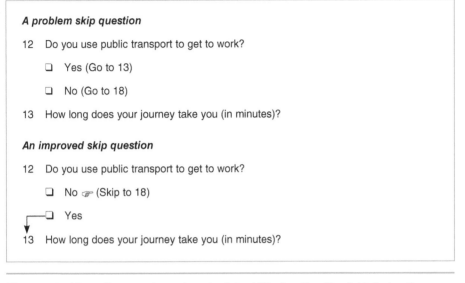

A problem skip question

12   Do you use public transport to get to work?

   ❑   Yes (Go to 13)

   ❑   No (Go to 18)

13   How long does your journey take you (in minutes)?

An improved skip question

12   Do you use public transport to get to work?

   ❑   No ☞ (Skip to 18)

   ❑   Yes

13   How long does your journey take you (in minutes)?

Figure 14.6   Uses of typography and emphasis to aid the functionality of skip instructions

Source: Adapted from Dillman, 2007

- General instructions, dealing with the purpose of the questionnaire, assurances of confidentiality, how and when to return the questionnaire.
- Section introductions when the questionnaire is divided into subsections.
- Question instructions (e.g. tick only one response).
- 'Go to' instructions.

Dillman (2007) refers to these 'go to' instructions as 'skip instructions' and argues that they are important because they avoid respondents reading or completing questions that do not apply to them. But in self-administered questionnaires the problem is getting people to read the skip instructions correctly. Figure 14.6 illustrates a poorly constructed skip question and an improved version. Note that in the improved version, the 'No' response is presented first and respondents re-routed if necessary. Instructions are in bold and a pointed finger used for emphasis.

Similarly, the use of spacing can help to improve the understanding of a question, as illustrated in Figure 14.7. See how a quite densely packed question is laid out so that different elements are separated.

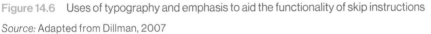

➤ TOP TIP 14.4 ◄

Researchers who are new to questionnaire design tend to give little thought to helping respondents in completing the questionnaire. Re-read your questionnaire. Is it clear how a respondent should complete it? If, say, you want just one response from a list of five choices, have you stated this? Ask for feedback on the quality of instructions at the piloting stage.

A problem question

1. When you joined the company, what was your major ambition (a) promotion;
   (b) job satisfaction; (c) a rise in salary; (d) learning a new skill; (e) None of these?
   Mark.

2. How long have you now worked for the company? _____ Years

An improved question

❶ When you joined the company, what was your major ambition? Mark one answer.

   ❑   Promotion

   ❑   Job satisfaction

   ❑   A rise in salary

   ❑   Learning a new skill

   ❑   None of these

❷ How long have you now worked for the company?

   _____ Years

Figure 14.7   The uses of spacing to help identify groups of elements

DESIGNING INTERNET AND WEB-BASED QUESTIONNAIRES

WEB BASED
SURVEYS

As we saw in Chapter 10, the advent of the Internet and World Wide Web has transformed the way in which many surveys are conducted. Given that many organizations, particularly larger ones, have good connections to the Internet, the use of online surveys is especially advantageous in terms of convenience and access to large samples and populations.

Email questionnaires

Email questionnaires (often used as part of surveys) are relatively easy to compose but offer fewer opportunities to provide visual stimulation or interactivity. It is difficult, for example, to use the kind of skip patterns discussed in the previous section. On the whole, the principles of email questionnaire design are very similar to many of those concerned with paper-based design. Dillman (2007) suggests the following strategies:

- Use multiple contacts (e.g. preliminary email, questionnaire email, 'thank-you' email, etc.)
- Personalize all email contacts, do not send them via a listserv. One reason for this is that a response would be sent to all others on the list – so much for confidentiality!
- Keep the covering (introductory) text brief, avoiding the need for the respondent to scroll down the page.

- Suggest alternative ways to respond, such as printing out the questionnaire and completing it by hand. Some respondents may feel insecure about email responses, which can always be checked by an employer.
- Limit column width to 70 characters to decrease the likelihood of text wrapping around to the next line.
- Start with an easy but interesting question.
- Provide instructions on completing questions, such as putting an X inside the brackets.
- In the case of non-response, include a replacement questionnaire with the reminder message.

Web-based questionnaires

Web-based questionnaires offer many facilities for questionnaire design that are not available in traditional, paper-based formats, such as the use of drop-down menus, pop-up instruction boxes and sophisticated skip patterns. They can track response processes such as the order in which respondents proceed through the questionnaire, and whether they viewed a question but chose not to answer it. One of the more popular Web-based survey tools, SurveyMonkey, for example, offers the following functionality:

- A range of question types (including multiple choice, rating scales, drop-down menus).
- Question forcing (requiring the respondent to answer a question before they can proceed). But note that these may sometimes frustrate or even anger respondents (Albaum, Wiley, Roster and Smith, 2011).
- Choices of colour, size and style of font.
- Tracking facilities to see who responds and follow-up messages to those who do not.
- Data downloaded into either spreadsheet or database format ready for analysis.

➤ ON THE WEB 14.1 ◄

Go to the SurveyMonkey website at:

http://www.surveymonkey.com/

To understand more about how the software works, take a look at one of the video tutorials.

However, the very flexibility of the Web makes the opportunities for making design errors all the greater, which may, in turn, affect response rates. It is extremely easy to get 'lost' in a website, at which point many users exit the site quickly. Respondents must also be able to provide information in a way that reflects their genuine views, including 'don't know' responses (Market Research Society, 2010). Hence, following some simple design instructions is all the more important. Dillman (2007) makes a number of recommendations:

- Introduce the Web questionnaire with a welcome screen that is motivational, that emphasizes the ease of responding, and shows how to proceed.
- Provide a login to limit access to the site to the selected sample.
- Choose a first question that is easy and stimulating to answer.
- Present questions in a similar format to that used in a conventional questionnaire.

- Use colour appropriately and not just for the sake of it.
- Unless you are sure that all respondents have the same screen configuration, test the Web pages on different screen resolutions and Web browsers to ensure that the appearance is always the same.
- Use drop-down boxes sparingly and identify each with a 'click here' instruction.

All questionnaires, whether paper-based, email or Web-based need careful piloting before dissemination to a wider audience. In the case of Web-based questionnaires, it is best if a paper-based version is piloted first to produce a final version ready for putting online. But once online this Internet version should also be piloted to see if respondents find it easy to use. Note that while your questionnaire may appear neat and tidy on your own screen, words may appear out of place on some users' screens if they are using a Web browser different to your own. Piloting using a variety of Web browsers is therefore a sensible step.

ON THE WEB 14.2

Take a look at the following website, which contains a wide variety of Web-based questionnaires:

http://www.accesscable.net/~infopoll/Library.htm

Now find examples of:

- Accompanying documentation, including information letters.
- Different question formats (open/closed; listing questions; category questions; ranking questions; scale questions).
- The use of skip questions.
- Face sheet information.
- The use of response category quantifiers.

Also take a look at Sample Web Questionnaires at:

http://www.surveysystem.com/websurveys.htm

PILOTING QUESTIONNAIRES

QUESTIONNAIRE
PILOTING

Research instruments such as interview schedules can be modified if certain questions appear to be ineffective, but questionnaires, particularly if used for large surveys, are a 'one-shot' attempt at data gathering. It is therefore essential that they are accurate, unambiguous and simple to complete. As we saw in Chapter 10, piloting is vital. Judicious piloting will reduce the incidence of non-response to the questionnaire. Gillham (2007) suggests that it is wise to pilot at least 50 per cent more questions than you need so that confusing or unreliable questions can be thrown out at this stage. What else should be piloted? Well, basically, anything and everything! But you could consider the:

- Instructions given to respondents.
- Style and wording of any accompanying letter.

- Content of face-sheet data, that is, respondents' names, addresses, etc.
- Formality or informality of the questionnaire in terms of tone, presentation, etc.
- Length of the questionnaire – if too long, is the response rate likely to be reduced?
- Sequence of questions.
- Quality of individual questions in terms of whether they are understood and answered in a way that was intended.
- Scales and question format used, for example, Likert scales, Yes/No responses, etc.

Oppenheim (1992) even suggests that the tables for the data analysis phase of the final report should be piloted (that is, dummy tables written) before the questionnaire is issued. This might highlight new issues or problems that could require consideration and inclusion in the questionnaire itself.

De Vaus (2002) suggests that evaluation is important in a number of design areas, including checking for:

- The ability of a question to discriminate. If everyone responds with the same answer to a question this is often not very useful, since one purpose of using a questionnaire is to examine the diversity of views on a subject.
- The validity and reliability of questions.
- Redundancy, so if it is found that two questions measure the same thing, one of them can be dropped.
- The response set. With some respondents, a pattern of answering Likert-type questions quickly sets in. So, if they tick 'Strongly agree' for, say, the first three questions, this response becomes habitual and they tick all remaining questions with this response. To avoid this happening, it is wise to alternate responses, for example, by using a negative statement on which the respondent will have to disagree.

Who can help you with piloting? Gillham (2007) advises trying out your initial list of questions with one or two people who are not part of the target group. Explain that you are trying to get the questions right, and that they should indicate where a question is unclear. Even sit with them as they look through the questions, noting their comments and your own observations on a spare questionnaire. Once you have amended the questionnaire, re-trial it with another two or three people who are similar to, but not part of, the target group. The procedure is the same, but this time also ask for improvements, deletions and additions. You are now ready to start designing the layout of the questionnaire.

Of course, if the survey is delivered via the Web, in addition to the issues raised above a whole new set of problems have to be faced. As we saw earlier, the design of Web-based surveys offers both flexibility but also opportunities to get things spectacularly wrong. As in any software development, it is sensible to design and pilot a prototype of the final site, so that user problems can be identified. Issues to look at here include the use of colour, on-screen instructions, navigational routes (especially for skip questions) and how respondents handle inputting their responses to questions (do they know what to do?). Observation at the piloting stage with respondents actually using the website questionnaire may also reveal some entirely unanticipated problems. Case Study 14.2 provides an example of how piloting can help to improve a questionnaire.

—— CASE STUDY 14.2 ——

Questionnaire piloting to get it right

A research project is set up to study public attitudes towards the decriminalization of certain categories of drugs. The study starts with the question:
Would you say that most people think that certain 'soft' drugs should be decriminalized?

1. Yes
2. No
3. Don't know/not sure

Piloting the questions reveals that:

Most respondents cannot report in general what 'most people' think, they only know what they, personally, think.
Some people did not understand the concept 'decriminalize'.
Some could not differentiate between 'soft' and 'hard' drugs.
Respondents resisted selecting between just 'Yes' and 'No' and wanted an opportunity to express their feelings between alternatives.

The question then was modified to read:
Do you think that people arrested for the possession of drugs such as cannabis are sentenced fairly: (a) almost always; (b) most of the time; (c) some of the time; (d) never?

Piloting shows that this is an improvement because it asks people what they themselves think, and it is more specific about the type of drugs being discussed. It also provides a range of categories. Its disadvantage is that it has become too specific and shifted away from the central theme of the original question, decriminalization.
The third and final version becomes:

Please indicate your view on each of the following statements:

Fining someone for possession of cannabis is: Very fair, Fair, Unfair, Very unfair.

Imprisoning someone for possession of cannabis is: Very fair, Fair, Unfair, Very unfair.

Fining someone for dealing in cannabis is: Very fair, Fair, Unfair, Very unfair.

Imprisoning someone for dealing in cannabis is: Very fair, Fair, Unfair, Very unfair.

—— ACTIVITY 14.4 ——

Take one or a small number of questions from a questionnaire you are designing and pilot it/them with a sample audience. Amend the question(s) on the basis of the responses and advice given. Pilot the amended question(s). Amend them again. How similar is the third version of the question(s) to what you started with?

MAINTAINING QUALITY: VALIDITY AND RELIABILITY

RELIABILITY &
VALID
QUESTION-
NAIRES

Since questionnaires are one of the most popular instruments for data gathering, you will not be surprised that we pause yet again to discuss the issues of validity and reliability.

Validity

We saw earlier in this chapter that the validity of a questionnaire can be affected by the wording of the questions it contains. But even if individual questions are valid, a poor sequencing of questions or confusing structure or design of the questionnaire can all threaten its validity.

The questionnaire must cover the research issues both in terms of content and detail. Recall Figure 6.6 in Chapter 6 which shows the dangers of a questionnaire not covering the research area (Zone of Neglect) and some questions being asked that are irrelevant to the study (Zone of Invalidity). It should be noted that asking spurious, irrelevant questions increases the length of a questionnaire, which in turn, may reduce the number of responses. If the response rate becomes too low, this may limit the generalizability of the findings, and hence external validity.

As we saw in Chapter 10, two threats to the validity of postal questionnaires are the extent to which respondents complete the questionnaires accurately, and the problem of non-response. Accuracy can be checked by interviewing a sample of respondents, and probing for how carefully they have answered the questionnaire. For non-response, again follow-up interviews can be used for those who did not reply, and their responses compared with those who did answer the questionnaire to see if the two sets of responses are similar. If they are, it suggests that the responding and non-responding populations are the same, and there is no threat from this source to the validity of data collected.

➤ TOP TIP 14.5 ◄

The validity of questionnaires is greatly assisted if you start from the basis of a set of clear and concise research questions. You can then formulate, say, three or four questions in the questionnaire that seek to gather data for each research question. In this way, you are achieving a tight match between your questionnaire and what you are attempting to research. If you find a question within the questionnaire that does not address one of your research question themes, ask yourself: should this question be here? Do I need it? If the answer is, 'No', eliminate the question. But if the answer is, 'Yes', you will need to return to your research questions and modify or add to them so that your new question is addressed.

Reliability

In terms of questionnaire design, a high reliability means that if you measured something today, you should get the same results at some other time, assuming that what is being measured has not changed (Black, 1993). As we discussed in Chapter 6, reliability is a measure of consistency and can include measures of

- Stability (over time).
- Equivalence (administering two versions of a test instrument to the same people on the same day).
- Inter-judge reliability.

The extent of this consistency is measured by a reliability coefficient using a scale from 0.00 (very unreliable) to 1.00 (perfectly reliable). In practice, a score of 0.9 is generally deemed to be acceptable. There are several ways in which this coefficient can be calculated. One of the most common is Cronback's alpha, which presents the average of all possible split-half correlations, and so measures the consistency of all items, both globally and individually.

QUESTIONNAIRE ADMINISTRATION

CONTEXTS OF
QUESTIONNAIRE
USE

Even the best-designed questionnaire will not create an impact if care is not taken with its administration, one of the fundamental objectives of which is to maximize the return rate. We examine next some of the techniques associated with different kinds of survey methods that were discussed in Chapter 10.

Self-administered questionnaires

Postal questionnaires

It is usual for a questionnaire to be accompanied by a letter. Getting the content, style and tone of this letter right is just as important as achieving the quality of these elements in the questionnaire. Indeed, since respondents will probably read the letter first, it could be argued that it is even more important. It is essential that you get the respondent's name, initials and preferred title absolutely right. Documentation sent to women should usually be titled Ms unless you know that they prefer another form.

The letter should cover issues such as the aims of the research, its importance (particularly its importance to the respondent's company or organization, if applicable), how long it will take to complete, and an assurance of confidentiality. The name of the sponsor or researcher should appear on the letterhead, and details of where to return the questionnaire should appear both on the letter as well as the questionnaire itself. Above all, the letter should be as brief and concise as possible, and should contain a note of thanks for the questionnaire's completion. If there are instructions that you particularly need to emphasize, state them as part of a postscript as people often notice these below the main text.

Saunders et al. (2012) list six further techniques that researchers will find useful:

- Ensure that questionnaires and letters are printed and envelopes properly addressed.
- Make a pre-survey contact with recipients either by email, post or phone to warn them that the questionnaire is on its way.
- Post the questionnaire and covering letter to arrive at a convenient time.
- One week after the initial posting, send out the first follow-up reminder letters to all recipients.
- Send the second follow-up reminder to those who have not responded after three weeks.
- Post out a third follow-up if the response rate is low.

Of course, before reminders can be sent, it is necessary to know who has not responded. A useful technique is to number the questionnaires, but this will not work if anonymity has been promised to respondents. In this situation, a 'scattergun' approach may be necessary, reminding all respondents but apologizing in advance to those who have already responded.

Table 14.5   Likely timing of responses for postal survey

Distribution	Timing (P-day)*	Responses
First posting	P-day + 10 days	50 per cent of final return
First reminder	P-day + 17 days	80 per cent of final return
Second reminder	P-day + 27 days	A few more

* P-day = Postal-day, i.e. the initial posting.

When sending reminders, emphasize the importance of the study and do not imply that the initial response has been poor – imply the contrary, if anything (providing this is truthful). When prompting, it is important not to be apologetic. Enclose another copy of the questionnaire and another stamped addressed envelope in case people had not received or had 'mislaid the original'. In terms of responses and timings, Table 14.5 suggests a typical pattern. It can be seen that after just over two weeks you will have received about 80 per cent of what will prove to be your final total. You will know by this point whether your final return rate is going to be successful, or not.

Postal questionnaires should be sent by first-class post and include a stamped addressed envelope. If the questionnaire is going to an individual in their home, Gillham (2007) suggests Thursday as the best day for posting as people have more time at weekends. Letters to organizations should be sent on Mondays or Tuesdays so that they can be completed at work.

Delivery and collection questionnaires

Since questionnaires are to be collected, clearly one of the prime factors is to ensure that respondents know exactly when this will occur. Saunders et al. (2012) advise that, when conducting research in an organization, response rates can be dramatically improved by calling all respondents to a meeting in the organization's time, explaining the purpose of the questionnaire, and getting it completed before people leave the meeting. A box near the exit to the room for collecting questionnaires may help to assure confidentiality.

Online questionnaires

As we saw earlier, online questionnaires can be administered either by email or via the Web. For emails, it is relatively easy to obtain people's email addresses, but to contact a sample of respondents 'cold' would risk the accusation of 'spamming', that is, sending unsolicited messages. Another danger is that anonymity will be lost as respondents can be identified by their email addresses.

Nevertheless, emails can be used effectively for surveys either by including the questions in the main body of the email or sending the questionnaire as an attached document. Including questions in the body of an email message makes the questionnaire simple to return, but there is little opportunity for using the kind of layout and design that encourages the completion of a questionnaire.

If you are, say, conducting a survey within an organization that uses one software application standard, then you may be able to attach the document in a word processed application version that can be read by all. If the survey is cross-organization there will be risks that not everyone will be able to read the attachment, so including questions in an email is the safest approach. After this, procedures for sending reminders are the same as for postal questionnaires.

Interviewer-administered questionnaires

Structured interview

Since structured interviews involve face-to-face contact, one of the essential administrative factors is arranging meetings with respondents, and improving the chances of respondents turning up for the interview. This chance will be increased if respondents are contacted in advance of the meeting and advised of dates, times and location, etc. If the structured interview involves some open as well as closed questions, it might be advisable to tape record the interview since transcribing verbal dialogue is difficult unless you are skilled at shorthand. The use of tape recorders involves ethical issues including confidentiality, so you must ask permission before using one. Once interviews are completed, times for any return visits should be arranged. Further details of interview techniques are given in Chapter 15.

Telephone questionnaire

For telephone questionnaires it is important that respondents know when they are to be interviewed, so they must be contacted by post and given clear details of dates and times (including the likely length of the interview). When calls are unsuccessful, the reasons should be noted, such as the fact that the respondent has moved or did not pick up the telephone. In the latter case, call three more times at different times of the day.

Summary

- Designing individual questions involves a rigorous process of analysis to avoid ambiguity, leading questions, double questions and simply misleading questions.
- Questions must be clearly linked to the purpose of the research (as specified in the accompanying letter or documentation).
- Questionnaires should start with questions that are easy to answer, interesting and transparently linked to the purpose of the research.
- Questionnaire layout and the use of typography can make a questionnaire easier to complete and more appealing to respondents, enhancing the response rate.
- Clear, well set out instructions on completing the questionnaire can also boost the response rate.
- Web and email questionnaires offer a new and potentially powerful tool, but also require additional design skills.
- All questionnaires, whether paper-based, email or Web-based, require thorough piloting which will include evaluation of accompanying documentation, instructions, individual questions, types of question, question sequencing, the use of scales and skip instructions – basically, everything!

REVIEW QUESTIONS

1. In many research studies, a questionnaire is just a tool looking for a job. Discuss.
2. Should classification questions (for example, asking a respondent's age, gender, etc.) be placed at the beginning or at the end of a questionnaire? Justify your choice.
3. Suggest four reasons as to why piloting a questionnaire is important.
4. Why may forcing respondents to answer all questions reduce response rates?

FURTHER READING

Brace, I. (2008) *Questionnaire Design: How to plan, structure and write survey material for effective market research*. London: Kogan Page. Covers planning the questionnaire, formulating questions and questionnaire design (including online questionnaires). As the title suggests, written from a market research perspective.

Colton, D. and Covert, R.W. (2007) *Designing and Constructing Instruments for Social Research and Evaluation*. San Francisco, CA: Jossey-Bass. An easy-to-read and accessible book for students who are new to questionnaire design as well as the more experienced. Contains guidelines for reviewing and revising questionnaires to enhance their validity and reliability.

Gillham, B. (2007) *Developing a Questionnaire*, 2nd edn. London: Continuum. A small and simply written book that provides an excellent introduction to the subject. Includes chapters on questionnaire design, distribution, data presentation and the analysis of open and closed questions.

De Vaus, D.A. (2002) *Surveys in Social Research*, 5th edn. London: George Allen & Unwin. See specifically Chapter 7 on constructing questionnaires and Chapter 8 on administering questionnaires.

JOURNAL RESOURCES

Corchon, S., Watson, R., Arantzamendi, M. and Saracíbar, M. (2010) 'Design and validation of an instrument to measure nursing research culture: The Nursing Research Questionnaire (NRQ)', *Journal of Clinical Nursing*, 19(1–2): 217–226. Describes the development of a self-administered questionnaire, including the identification of concepts, piloting of a first draft, and survey launch and further refinement.

Ashman, I. (2007) 'An investigation of the British organizational commitment scale: A qualitative approach to evaluating construct validity', *Management Research News*, 30(1): 5–24. By challenging the validity of the British Organizational Commitment Scale, draws lessons for improving validity in instrument design.

Elaydi, R. (2006) 'Construct development and measurement of indecisiveness', *Management Decision*, 44(10): 1363–1376. Discusses how an instrument to measure 'indecisiveness' was constructed and validated, demonstrating some of the general principles of scale construction.

SUMMARY OF WEB LINKS

http://www.accesscable.net/~infopoll/library.htm

http://www.surveysystem.com/websurveys.htm

1. An *ambiguous* question since the categories overlap. Also *impertinent* in two ways – the fact that age is asked for (why is this necessary?) and the curt way in which this is demanded.
2. *Vague* and therefore probably unreliable.
3. *Double question* and therefore also ambiguous.
4. *Loaded question.*
5. *Double negative.* It also contains the phrase 'best practice' – what does this mean?
6. Demands either *memory recall* (if the person is in a position to know the answer) or an expectation that they have the *knowledge*, which may not be the case.
7. *Impertinent.*
8. *No instructions.* It is unclear how to complete an answer – ticking or circling? The fact that only one answer can be given is assumed, but should be made explicit.

Finally, the questionnaire contains no introductory paragraph or explanation of its purpose. It asks for respondents to give their name, which does not appear necessary, and asks for their salary, which is both unnecessary and impertinent. It offers no assurances of confidentiality, does not explain what is going to be done with the information and is unclear as to where it can be returned (and when).

15

INTERVIEWING

CHAPTER INTRODUCTION

Chapter outline

Why use interviews?	382	Group interviews	401
Selecting interview approaches	384	Using telephone interviews	404
Designing credible interviews	388	Ethical issues	405
Interviewing skills	390		

Keywords

Structured interviews   Rapport
Semi-structured interviews   Active listening
Non-directive interviews   Probes

Chapter objectives

After reading this chapter you will be able to:

- Describe and choose between structured, semi-structured, non-directive, focused and informal interviews on the basis of the objectives of the research.
- Select between using interviews and self-completed questionnaires.
- Produce valid and reliable interview schedules.
- Conduct an interview skilfully, tactfully, safely and ethically.

An interview is a verbal exchange in which one person, the interviewer, attempts to acquire information from and gain an understanding of another person, the interviewee. The latter may be invited to talk about their own attitudes, beliefs, behaviours or experiences, as a citizen, consumer or employee (Rowley, 2012). Very often, the interviewer will have on hand a set of written questions which are posed in a structured and methodical fashion (a structured interview). Alternatively, these questions might only be used as an *aide-mémoire*, to remind the researcher of the key areas that need probing. In either case, interviews often make use of questionnaires, so this chapter has much in common with Chapter 14. However, whereas the previous chapter focused on the design of questionnaires, this chapter looks at one way, the interview, in which they can be used. Hence we are shifting, to some extent, from product (the questionnaire) to process.

Interviewing may pose challenges because of the human interaction between the interviewer and respondent. The interviewer has to pose questions (in either a structured, semi-structured or unstructured format), listen to (and data capture) the responses (either by audio or video recording or taking notes) and pose new questions. If the interview format is relatively unstructured, then these questions have to be constructed 'on the fly'. The interviewer may also not only be listening to the verbal responses, but be noting other elements of the interview process such as the body language of the interviewee. However, despite the challenges involved, the well-conducted interview is a powerful tool for eliciting rich data on people's views, attitudes and the meanings that underpin their lives and behaviours.

In this chapter, we will examine some of the different interview approaches, and look at some of the essential interviewing skills you will need to acquire. We will also look, briefly, at telephone interviews, and conclude with some thoughts on ethical issues in interviewing.

WHY USE INTERVIEWS?

There are a number of situations in which the interview is the most logical research technique. If the objective of the research, for example, is largely exploratory, involving, say, the examination of feelings or attitudes, then interviews may be the best approach. The use of semi-structured interviews also allows the researcher to 'probe' for more detailed responses where the respondent is asked to clarify what they have said. This phenomenological approach, then, is concerned with the *meanings* that people ascribe to phenomena. Interviewing is a basic form of human activity, in which language is used between two human beings in the pursuit of cooperative inquiry. Indeed, narratives have been a major way down the ages in which people have sought to capture their experience. As Reason (1981) comments:

> The best stories are those that stir people's minds, hearts and souls and by so doing, give them new insights into themselves, their problems and their human condition. (1981: 50)

At the route of interviewing, then, is the intent to understand the lived experiences of other people, and the meaning they make of that experience (Seidman, 2013).

Interviews are also useful where it is likely that people may enjoy talking about their work, families, communities, feelings or relationships, rather than filling in questionnaires. An interview allows them an opportunity to reflect on events without having to commit themselves in writing, often because they feel the information may be confidential. They may never have met the researcher and may feel concerned about some of the uses to which the information may be put. Also, with questionnaires the concise meaning of a question may not always be clear, whereas with an interview meanings can be immediately clarified. For example, in undertaking a business survey, the author once posed the question: 'How long has your firm been in business?', which elicited the response: 'What, do you mean just trading or actually being in profit?' Potentially, at least, interviews can produce a greater response rate because questions like this can be made explicit.

As Cohen and Manion (2000) point out, the interview can serve a number of distinct purposes. First, it can be used as the means of gathering information about a person's knowledge, values, preferences and attitudes. Secondly, it can be used to test out a hypothesis or to identify variables and their relationships. Thirdly, it can be used in conjunction with other research techniques, such as surveys, to follow up issues. For example, a survey by a sports shoe company might find a relationship between age and the tendency to purchase certain kinds of trainer. The company might then follow this up with structured interviews among a sample of people from the original survey to explore in more depth the values and motivation behind these buying patterns.

Interviews are also preferable to questionnaires where questions are either open-ended or complex, or where the logical order of questions is difficult to predetermine. But whether an interview is successful in eliciting the range and depth of answers required will depend in large part on the skills of the interviewer.

Essentially, the interview is the favoured approach where:

- The research objectives are based upon understanding experiences, opinions, attitudes, values and processes.
- There is a need to attain highly personalized data.
- Opportunities for probing are required.
- A good return rate is important.
- Respondents are not fluent in the native language of the country, or where they have difficulties with written language.

In contrast, standardized questionnaires are more powerful where:

- Large numbers of respondents must be reached.
- Better reliability of data is desired.

Table 15.1 Comparison of interviews and self-administered questionnaires

Characteristics	Interviews	Self-administered questionnaires
Provide information about	As for questionnaires, but potential for exploring in more depth.	Attitudes, motivation, opinions, events.
Best at	Exploring stories and perspectives of informants.	Testing the validity of a hypothesis.
Richness of responses	Dialogue between interviewer and respondent allows for nuances to be captured and for questions to be clarified and adapted or improvised. Long interviews common.	Questions cannot be modified once printed, and nuances of respondent's voice cannot be heard. Long questionnaires rarely acceptable.
Ethics	Interviewers know whom they have interviewed, although transcripts can be anonymized.	Anonymous questionnaire responses can be assured.
Sample size	With the exception of telephone interviews, less suitable for wide coverage.	If generalizing to a population, samples often have to be large.
Time cost Planning and design	Devising interview guide, piloting, etc., may be less of an issue.	Devising questionnaire (checking validity and reliability), piloting, etc. may be very time-consuming.
Operation	Arranging interviews, travelling, establishing rapport – all time-consuming.	Distributing questionnaire.
Data transcription	Typically 7–10 hours for 1 hour interview.	Usually swift, especially where optical readers are used.
Data analysis	Time needed usually underestimated.	Usually swift (unless there are many open-ended questions).
Money costs	High if includes interviewers, travel costs, memory sticks or cards, batteries, transcription of digital recordings.	Mainly costs of printing, distributing and receiving questionnaires. Looks cheap per questionnaire, but looks more expensive if return rate low.

Source: Adapted from Arksey and Knight, 1999

A summary of some of the pros and cons of interviews and self-administered questionnaires is presented in Table 15.1.

SELECTING INTERVIEW APPROACHES

There are several different types of interview, so the choice of interview technique will depend in large part on the aims and objectives of your research. Indeed, one of the purposes of the interview may be to determine these research objectives themselves. There may also be occasions when more than one interview type is used for a research project.

Interviews may be divided into six categories:

STRUCTURED
AND
UNSTRUCTURED
INTERVIEWS

- Structured interviews.
- Semi-structured interviews.
- Non-directive interviews.
- Focused interviews.
- Informal conversational interviews.
- Problem-centred interviews.

Before looking at these approaches in detail, it is worth noting that Roulston (2010) links the type of interview used and the processes involved to the researcher's philosophical position. Hence, she distinguishes between research interviews that are:

- Neo-positivist. The 'skilled' interviewer asks good questions, takes on a neutral role to avoid bias and generates data to produce valid findings.
- Romantic. The interviewer establishes rapport and an empathetic connection with the interviewee and gets him or her to generate self-disclosure and in-depth interpretations of their world.
- Constructionist. The interviewer and interviewee co-construct the data through unstructured and semi-structured interviews, working together to make sense of the research topic.

Consider these epistemological positions when looking at the six interview approaches, discussed below.

Structured interviews

Structured interviews are often used to collect data for quantitative analysis, and use pre-prepared questionnaires and standardized questions, that is, the same questions are posed to all respondents. Responses are recorded by the interviewer on a standardized schedule, and, while there is some interaction between interviewer and respondent, this is kept to a minimum. Ideally, questions are read out in the same tone of voice so as not to influence answers. Hence, structured interviews are similar to the use of questionnaires, except that the interviewer poses the questions; this is one way in which the researcher hopes that direct contact will increase response rates compared with postal or online questionnaires. Structured interviews are often used as a precursor for more open-ended discussions such as non-directive interviews.

THE
STRUCTURED
INTERVIEW

Semi-structured interviews

Semi-structured interviews are non-standardized, and are often used in qualitative analysis. The interviewer has a list of issues and questions to be covered, but may not deal with all of them in each interview. The order of questions may also change depending on what direction the interview takes. Indeed, additional questions may be asked, including some which were not anticipated at the start of the interview,

SEMI
STRUCTURED
INTERVIEWS

as new issues arise. Responses will be documented by note taking or possibly by recording the interview.

The semi-structured interview allows for probing of views and opinions where it is desirable for respondents to expand on their answers. This is vital when a phenomenological approach is being taken where the objective is to explore subjective meanings that respondents ascribe to concepts or events. Such probing may also allow for the diversion of the interview into new pathways which, while not originally considered as part of the interview, help towards meeting the research objectives.

Non-directive interviews

Non-directive interviews are used to explore an issue or topic in depth and questions are not, generally, pre-planned. Clearly, though, the researcher must have a notion of the objectives of the research and, therefore, what issues are going to be addressed in the interview. The format of the interview will be such that the respondents are allowed to talk freely around the subject. The input of the interviewer is mainly confined to checking on any doubtful points and rephrasing answers to check for accuracy of understanding. Like semi-structured interviews, non-directive interviews tend to collect data for qualitative analysis.

Focused interviews

FOCUSED
INTERVIEWS

The focused interview is based upon the respondent's subjective responses to a known situation in which they have been involved. The interviewer has prior knowledge of this situation and is, thus, able to re-focus respondents if they drift away from the theme. An analogy would be the celebrity television interview in which the interviewer has already analysed the interviewee's autobiography and wishes to probe certain issues in more depth.

Informal conversational interviews

CONVERSATIONAL
INTERVIEWS

The informal conversational interview relies on the spontaneous generation of questions as the interview progresses. This is the most open-ended form of interview technique. One of the advantages of this approach is the flexibility it offers in terms of what path the interview takes. Indeed, the interviewee may not even know an interview is taking place. This, though, will rule out the taking of notes during the interview. In cases where the fact that an interview is taking place *is* known, it is appropriate to take notes or to use a digital recorder.

One of the drawbacks of the conversational interview is the danger of the 'interviewer effect', that is, the interviewer may begin to influence the course and direction of the interview. Another disadvantage is that it may take some time before the interviewer has posed similar questions to the set of people being interviewed. Finally, the data collected through conversational interviews may be difficult to analyse because different questions have been asked of different people. As a result, the researcher will have to sift through the data to find emerging patterns.

A summary of the characteristics of the different types of interview is provided in Table 15.2.

Table 15.2 Characteristics of structured, semi-structured and unstructured interviews

Structured	Semi-structured	Unstructured (non-directive, focused and informal conversation)
Quick to data capture	Slow and time-consuming to data capture and analyse.	As for semi-structured.
Use of random sampling	The longer the interview, the more advisable it is to use random sampling.	Opportunity and snowball sampling often used. In organizations, targeting of 'key informants'.
Interview schedule followed exactly	Interviewer refers to a guide containing mixture of open and closed questions. Interviewer improvises using own judgement.	Interviewer uses *aide-mémoire* of topics for discussion and improvises.
Interviewer-led	Sometimes interviewer-led, sometimes informant-led.	Non-directive interviewing.
Easy to analyse	Quantitative parts easy to analyse.	Usually hard to analyse.
Tends to positivist view of knowledge	Mixture of positivist and non-positivist.	Non-positivist view of knowledge.
Respondents' anonymity easily guaranteed	Harder to ensure anonymity.	Researcher tends to know the informant.

Source: Adapted from Arksey and Knight, 1999

> **TOP TIP 15.1** ◀

Non-directive, focused and informal conversational interviews are great for collecting a large amount of qualitative data. However, before you decide on one of these approaches, make sure that you have decided on what approach you intend to adopt for data analysis – see Chapter 23.

GRAY ON PICKING AN INTERVIEW STYLE

Problem-centred interviews

The problem-centred interview combines an open approach with minimal interview structuring in the first phase of the interview, followed by a second semi-structured phase which allows the interviewer to set a focus. In the first phase, then, open questions are posed to elicit stories and narrations that are structured by the interviewee themselves. Scheibelhofer (2008) provides an example of this in her study of Austrian migrants who had settled in New York. In this research the first, narrative phase was considered pivotal as she was interested in the constructions of migration from the interviewees' perspectives. So, she initiated the interviews with phrases such as:

INTRODUCTION TO PROBLEM CENTRED INTERVIEWING

> Could you please tell me everything that is involved in you coming to New York and how your life went since then? I will listen and make some notes and will not interrupt you until you have finished. Please take as much time as you feel necessary and tell me all the details that you remember that, in your opinion, are connected to your living in New York. (Scheibelhofer, 2008: 407)

After the interviewees have finished their stories, the researcher then asks open questions (based on the notes they took during the first phase), related to the topics the interviewee has brought up but had not elaborated on. This second set of questions often gets the interviewee to further narrate. Following these questions the interviewer then asks a set of questions that had been prepared before the interview usually related to the interviewee's level of education, job biography, ties with relatives and friends and future aspirations.

Problem-centred interviews are particularly appropriate when the focus is on personal biography and getting respondents to narrate their personal perspectives on a theme.

DESIGNING CREDIBLE INTERVIEWS

One of the prime driving forces behind the design of interviews is the search for credibility by ensuring that the findings can be trusted, which includes issues of validity and reliability. But since interviews often come from a more qualitative perspective, it would be a mistake to apply these concepts rigidly. Instead, we might want to also make use of other indicators of credibility. We also need to ask some familiar questions about the extent to which the findings from the interview study can be generalized to a wider population.

Validity

As we saw in Chapter 6, validity means that an instrument must measure what it was intended to measure. In the case of structured and semi-structured interviews, the issue of validity can be directly addressed by attempting to ensure that the question content directly concentrates on the research objectives. For informal conversational, focused and non-directive interviews, the issue of validity is more problematic because, by their very nature, the direction questions take will depend, in large part, on the responses of the interviewee. In a sense, instead of these approaches commencing with a rigid set of objectives, the subject matter emerges inductively from the interview itself. But the research will need to ensure that if any research questions require addressing, this is achieved by the end of the interview.

According to Arksey and Knight (1999), validity is strengthened by:

CONDUCTING
RESEARCH
INTERVIEWS

- Using interview techniques that build rapport and trust, thus giving informants the scope to express themselves.
- Prompting informants to illustrate and expand on their initial responses.
- Ensuring that the interview process is sufficiently long for subjects to be explored in depth.
- Constructing interviewing schedules that contain questions drawn from the literature and from pilot work with respondents.

Another important issue of interview design is that of external validity, that is, as we have seen, the extent to which findings from a study can be generalized. As we saw in Table 15.1, interviews are best used when the study is relatively small scale, since interviewing very large samples can be both expensive and time-consuming. Hence, external validity may be restricted. On a practical note, Rowley (2012) suggests that a good rule-of-thumb is to aim for around 12 interviews of approximately

30 minutes in length, or the equivalent, say, six to eight interviews of around an hour. For a more extended study, a second phase of interviews can be conducted. Arksey and Knight (1999) offer two practical principles that can be adopted in making a more plausible case for generalizing from interview findings:

- Try to select a sample that allows for a subject to be viewed from all relevant perspectives.
- Keep increasing the sample size, or sub-samples that represent different perspectives, until no new viewpoints are emerging from the data. A sample size of eight is often sufficient, although a survey should then be used to verify the data.

In a practical sense, this means that interview data need to be studied and analysed as they are collected, until it is clear that perspectives are being repeated and data saturation reached.

Reliability and bias

For a research instrument to be reliable it must *consistently* measure what it set out to measure. There is, at least, some potential for such consistency when an interview is standardized, with the same questions being asked of each respondent. However, even with standardized questions the issue of interviewer bias comes into play – does the interviewer ask the questions in the same way and with the same tone of voice with all respondents? In other words, what must be avoided is the 'interviewer effect'.

Interviewer bias can creep into the interview situation in many subtle, and not so subtle, ways. An interviewer, for example, might (unconsciously) give less time to shopfloor workers when conducting an interview than to supervisory and management grade employees. Similarly, prompt cards might be issued to shopfloor workers but not to 'more intelligent-looking' office workers. The only way to avoid this kind of systematic error is to standardize not only the interview schedule, but the behaviour of the interviewer. This is especially important if interviews are being conducted by more than one person. This does not mean that all interviews will be identical, since sometimes an interviewer will have to depart from a script to provide guidance or clarification. The skill of the interviewer is to provide such explanation without influencing the answer of the respondent.

Oppenheim (1992) suggests a number of ways in which bias occurs, namely:

- Departures from the interviewing instructions.
- Poor maintenance of rapport with the respondent.
- Altering factual questions.
- Rephrasing of attitude questions.
- Careless prompting.
- Biased probes.
- Asking questions out of sequence.
- Biased recording of verbatim answers.

One way of avoiding, or at least minimizing, interviewer bias is to require all interviewers to follow the same protocol. Hence, a set of guidelines might be drawn up which ask the interviewer to read the questions *exactly* as they are written, to repeat a question if asked, to accept a respondent's refusal to answer a question without any sign of irritation, and to probe in a non-directive manner. The following Case Study gives a practical example of how bias can occur if guidelines such as these are not followed.

— CASE STUDY 15.1 —

Interviewer bias – it can drive you to drink!

THE GREAT
DEPRESSION

In 1929, during the Great Depression, a New York researcher hired several interviewers to ask destitute people about their situation. Several years later the researcher reviewed some of the interviews. He noticed that the responses of one interviewer attributed most of the causes of destitution to economic factors such as unemployment, while the responses of another interviewer focused on problems with alcohol abuse. The researcher located the two interviewers and talked to them. He found that the first one was a socialist and the second, a prohibitionist. There was, thus, a strong suggestion that the causes of bias were located in the behaviour of the interviewers.

Source: Adapted from Beed and Stimson, 1985

— ACTIVITY 15.1 —

STEPHEN FRY
INTERVIEW

Record a 'serious' television interview. From the content of the interview look for evidence of interviewer bias in the content of the questions, the way in which they are expressed, or the non-verbal behaviour of the interviewer. Political interviews, of course, are not necessarily intended to exemplify the degree of objectivity of a research interview, but they may illustrate the issue of bias more clearly.

More quality indicators

We have looked so far at validity and reliability as factors that enhance the credibility of an interview study. We need, however, to find some alternative, or at least additional, sources of quality. One important indicator is *consistency*, showing how the research has been conducted and the plausibility of the researcher's actions and analysis. The study should also provide evidence of *accuracy*, showing that the data is a fair representation of what informants have actually said. This might mean checking with interviewees that they have not been misinterpreted. Finally, the study must attempt to demonstrate *neutrality*, showing that the researcher is aware of the possible confounding effects of their own actions and perceptions and that these, as far as possible, have been accounted for.

INTERVIEWING SKILLS

Interviewing is a skill that must be learned through experience and practice. Of course, the respondent must first of all agree to be interviewed, and this might depend on a number of factors. Getting an interview might depend upon:

- *Your status:* Are you 'internal' to the organization, or, say, someone completing a research project as part of an academic programme? If you are an internal researcher, how senior are you in the organization – and particularly, how senior compared to the interviewee?
- *The project:* Is the project of interest to the potential respondent? Is there a potential pay-off (such as a copy of the research or a summary of the main findings)?
- *Yourself:* Do you seem trustworthy, personable and professional?

Hence, the quality of any initial contact with potential interviewees is of vital importance. Be clear about how much time is needed for the interview. Assure the interviewee of confidentiality, and invite them to indicate their availability over, say, the next two weeks. If they are unwilling or unable to be interviewed face-to-face, consider using telephone interviews or Skype. Once agreement is obtained, there is some preparatory work to be done, after which there are a number of techniques that help in the interviewing process.

Getting started

Preparing for the interview

Interviews cannot be rushed. Wengraf (2001) advises that you should arrive at least 30 minutes before the scheduled interview to make the necessary preparations and put aside at least an hour after the interview to make field notes. So, a 45-minute interview, for example, could take up to 2–3 hours to complete. Only by allowing yourself a clear stretch of time will you be assured that the interview will be conducted in a stress-free and unhurried fashion.

Wengraf (2001) sets out a schedule that should be followed, even before the day of the interview. About three weeks before, it is sometimes useful to get respondents to complete a pre-interview questionnaire dealing with demographic issues (for example, age, occupation and other details) so that the interview can focus on more substantive matters. Or you may have requested material from the respondent, and you will need time to read and reflect on it. About 7–10 days before the interview, you need to contact the respondent to make sure that they are still available, provide final confirmation about the exact location of the interview, and respond to any last-minute queries or concerns. The day before the interview you need to check that you have all the material you need at your disposal, and especially that you have an up-to-date version of your interview schedule. A summary of these actions is presented in Figure 15.1.

→ TOP TIP 15.2 ←

Make sure that any equipment, such as a digital recorder, is working and that you have spare batteries, plenty of blank memory cards, cables to the electricity supply and extension leads, note paper, pens and perhaps two bottles of mineral water in case you or the interviewee gets thirsty.

Preliminaries at the start of the interview

The first task of the interviewer is to explain the purpose of the interview, who the information is for, how the information is going to be handled (including issues of confidentiality), why the information is being collected and how it will be used. This should not require a long speech, but should be done quickly and simply. Above all, the importance of the information should be stressed. If the research has been commissioned by a particular division or department of the organization this should be made clear. Ask permission to record the interview.

Also ensure that the seating arrangements are acceptable to both parties. Sitting closely and face-to-face can feel confrontational and threatening. It is usually best to face each other but at a slight angle (see Image 15.1). Having some furniture such

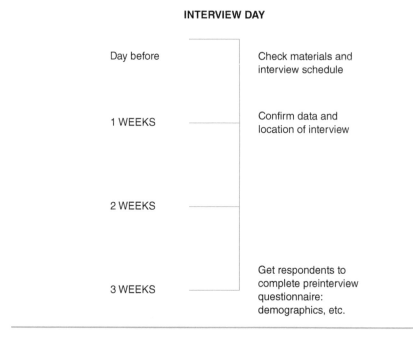

Figure 15.1   Pre-interview timeline

as a table between the interviewer and respondent also provides something on which to place note paper and creates safe 'distance' between the parties. The seating should also be arranged so that the interviewee cannot read forthcoming questions or any notes that are being made.

Building rapport with the respondent

Rapport means an understanding, one established on a basis of respect and trust between the interviewer and respondent. To establish a rapport it is particularly important to make the respondent relaxed and to get the interview off to a good start. This means you should:

- Describe how the interview will be conducted, how long it should last and the general subjects that are to be covered.
- Ask for permission to record the interview (and listen attentively for responses and note body language).
- Make guarantees of confidentiality.
- Ask if the respondent has any questions.

Rapport is described by Oppenheim (1992) as an elusive quality, and one that often only experienced and skilled interviewers possess. If an interviewer has little rapport, the respondent may be unwilling to answer questions or may cut the interview short. If the interviewer has too much rapport he or she may soon find themselves cast in the role of social worker or counsellor. The secret is to remain objective, professional and detached yet relaxed and friendly (who said that interviewing was easy?!)

Image 15.1   Ideal set up versus confrontational set up

→ **TOP TIP 15.3** ←

Before commencing an interview, it is very important to get your interviewee as relaxed as possible. When relaxed, they are more likely to provide you with rich, honest and illuminating data. Smile and be relaxed yourself. Make sure that the respondent knows about the purpose of the interview so that they are put at ease. Start off with easy questions or questions that the respondent is more likely to enjoy answering.

Conducting the interview

Impression management

Oppenheim (1992) warns that an interviewer creates an impression on the respondent, even before he or she opens their mouth. Features such as general appearance, mode of dress, accent (see next section), hairstyle, ethnicity and social background may all play a part. Different respondents will be affected in different ways. If an interviewer wears an expensive business suit and interviews top management, this might be acceptable, but would the interviewer receive the same reaction in the machine shop? As Oppenheim warns, however, there are no hard and fast rules here. Production line workers might be quite intrigued about being interviewed by someone in a suit and tie.

The key is that the interviewer should be aware of the process of impression management, and should try to avoid giving expression to her or his own distinctive style. The aim is for bland, social neutrality.

Use of language

One problem that needs to be borne in mind is that words can have different meanings to different people. In the UK, especially, there are difficulties stemming from the way different social classes use vocabulary. The word 'dinner', for example, has a meaning that is different in middle- and working-class language, or regions of the UK, where for some it is the meal eaten around the middle of the day, while for others it is consumed towards the end. In a business setting, the word 'management' may have different connotations. Managers themselves, for example, may see it as a way of steering the company (in the interests of *all* employees) towards profit and efficiency. Some employees, however, may view the word more negatively in terms of interference and control from 'above'. The key is making use of language that is accessible to your audience. Kvale (1996) suggests hanging about the environment in which the interviews are to be conducted to get an introduction to local language and routines.

Maintaining control of the interview

Since time is usually of the essence, it is important that the interviewer keeps control of the interview, minimizing long-winded responses and digressions. Patton (2002) argues that control is maintained by:

- Knowing what the interview is seeking to find out.
- Asking the right questions.
- Giving appropriate verbal and non-verbal feedback.

This means listening carefully to responses and channelling the interview back onto the right tracks if necessary. As Patton (2002) warns, it is not enough to have an excellent list of questions if the respondent is permitted to stray from the point.

ACTIVITY 15.2

Consider the following exchange:

Interviewer: Could you tell me something about your feelings when voluntary redundancies were called for?

Respondent: The request for redundancies came in a letter to all of us just before Christmas last year. They were asking for 200 people to go, out of a workforce of just 850. Quite a few people I know were very interested in the package on offer from day one.

Is the response an acceptable reply to the question?

Suggested answers are provided at the end of the chapter.

Verbal and non-verbal communication should be used to provide appropriate feedback. If, for example, the respondent is on-track, head nodding, the active taking of notes and the occasional verbal acknowledgement, should all help. Similarly, the use of a silent probe, remaining quiet when further elaboration of a point is desired, is quite valid. If the respondent is straying off the point, then the usual cues such as head nodding should cease, and a new question interjected as soon as the respondent hesitates. As Patton (2002) warns, it may sometimes become necessary to actively intervene with a statement such as: 'Can we stop there. I just want to check that I fully understanding something you just said'. Then ask a question aimed at a more targeted response.

GRAY ON
WHEN TO
INTERRUPT AN
INTERVIEW

→ TOP TIP 15.4 ←

Do not be embarrassed about interrupting the interviewee if this means getting the interview back on track. But one of the skills of interviewing is knowing what is relevant and irrelevant as the interview progresses (so think back to your research objectives or general theme!).

Improvising when necessary

In semi-structured or unstructured interviews, improvisation may be the key to success. According to Wengraf (2001) the interviewer may have to improvise between 50 and 80 per cent of the time with new questions on the basis of the planned questions asked. To improvise effectively, Arksey and Knight (1999) offer the following tips:

- Vary the question order to fit the flow of the interview.
- Vary the phrasing of the questions to help the conversation seem natural.
- Let the interview seem to go off track.
- Build trust and rapport by putting something of the interviewer's self into the interview, possibly by raising similar or different experiences.

Improvising, of course, is a skill that needs to be built through experience. One of the essential elements of improvising is the use of probes, that is, follow up questions that arise 'in the moment' in response to the answers being given by respondents. This requires active listening skills (see below) and an ability to recognize an avenue that is worth exploring. A probing question might be worth posing if, say, a respondent hints that they can tell a more detailed story or give illuminating comments about the theme being researched.

—ACTIVITY 15.3—

Having used a semi-structured or unstructured approach, go through the transcripts and note where you improvised. What was the result? How else could the question or comment have been phrased to improve the response? Was the eventual outcome a success? Should you continue with this approach, or adopt a more structured one?

Asking questions

As with the case of questionnaires, interview questions should be phrased so that their meaning is unambiguous, and they should be delivered in as neutral a tone of voice as possible. As we saw in Chapter 13, there are also certain ways of formulating questions that must be avoided. These include questions that:

- Contain jargon.
- Use prejudicial language.
- Are ambiguous.
- Lead the respondent.
- Include double questions.
- Contain hypothetical statements.
- Probe personal or sensitive issues.
- Require memory recall or knowledge the respondent does not possess.

Cluster groups of questions that deal with similar issues, and then sequence these blocks of questions in a logical order. How many questions should be asked? Rowley (2012) recommends that a semi-structured interview schedule with around six to 12 well-chosen questions is a good starting point. Each question might have two to four sub-questions or prompts which can be used flexibly by the interviewer to ensure that the interviewee explores the main theme in sufficient depth.

> **TOP TIP 15.5** <

The type and quality of questions you ask are at the core of a successful interview. So, having drafted a set of questions, try them out on friends or peers to see if they 'work'. Do they avoid the kinds of problems identified above? Are they clear and unambiguous?

Active listening skills

Active listening involves attentive listening, that is, not just listening to the words that are being said, but also to the tone and emphasis. Attentive listening also means that the respondent should be doing most of the talking! If attentive listening is achieved, it should be possible to pick up new or significant themes that can be probed with new questions. Sometimes silences or incomplete statements can reveal more than what is actually said. Attentive listening involves identifying these incomplete replies and following them up.

It should be remembered that an interview is not a normal conversation and therefore the usual norms of human interaction do not necessarily apply. Where in normal conversation it might be acceptable to occasionally glance at one's watch or look away, in interviews a far greater degree of attentiveness is required. This means listening to and interpreting the meaning of what is being said, but also noting the tone and delivery of the dialogue to pick up any traces of irritation, confusion or boredom.

Observing and reflecting

Like listening, careful observing helps to detect information on how the interview is progressing. Observation of the respondent's body language, for example, is important to detect important clues on the respondent's concentration level, motivation to continue with the interview and whether she or he is at ease. If negative signs are detected, it may mean changing the sequencing of questions, bringing easier or less controversial ones up the order.

Of course, self-observation (reflection) is just as important. Self-understanding helps us to make our questioning and probing more sensitive. If, for example, the interviewer knows that he tends to dominate most natural conversations, he might make a conscious effort to hold back and leave spaces for the respondent to fill.

Testing and summarizing understanding

A useful approach is occasionally to repeat back to the interviewee what you believe they have just told you. This is particularly important if there are statements or issues that are not fully understood. A summary needs to be accurate, focused and succinct – not a long-winded ramble. If the respondent comments on the summary, listen carefully for their response since it may, in obvious or subtle ways, differ to your summary. If this happens, summarize again (and keep summarizing) until agreement and clarity are reached.

Closing the interview

It is at this point that you should check that you have asked all the questions that you intended. It is worthwhile asking the interviewee if they have any questions or final comments that they would like to make.

It is important that both you and the respondent leave the interview with a positive sense of achievement. Even if you feel less than elated by the data you have gathered, thank the interviewee for their help and their valuable observations. Then describe what happens next, particularly in terms of whether the respondents will be needed for checking the accuracy of transcripts, and the reporting process and follow-up work. It is worth noting that interviewees often make some of their most interesting and valuable points once they think that the interview is over. Interviewers should not then suddenly scramble for note paper, but should remember and note these remarks once the respondent has left the interview setting.

Recording and transcribing data

There should be no short cuts when it comes to recording data. The analysis stage is made redundant if the data have not been collected carefully. Patton (2002) suggests that, no matter what the kind of interviewing style used, and no matter how carefully interview questions are worded, all is wasted unless the words of the interviewee are captured accurately.

TRANSCRIPTION
SYMBOLS

Taking notes may be useful for a number of reasons, since it:

- Can help in the formulation of new questions.
- Provides a means for locating important quotations during later analysis.
- Is a non-verbal behaviour that helps pace the interview, providing the interviewee with a cue that they have said something significant.

Note taking, however, is much harder than it sounds, especially since making handwritten notes is a slow and often inaccurate process. Many people now type, but even here some are quicker than others. You will also be observing the respondent and thinking of the next question. It is probably best to jot down key words and occasional verbatim comments. It is usually better to make notes in conjunction with an audio or video recording. Particularly in the case of the former, it should be possible to note the digital recorder counter number where a key statement has been made.

→ TOP TIP 15.6 ←

The use of a digital recorder is vital for conducting interviews. Not only does it record the essential data, it permits the interviewer to concentrate on the process of listening, interpreting and re-focusing the interview. Using a digital recorder, though, is not always without its problems. In the workplace, respondents may, initially, feel uneasy about being recorded. They will need reassurance as to confidentiality. In terms of the ethics of research, they should also be given the right to turn off the recorder at any time.

Give some careful consideration to the recording equipment you will need. Ensure you have enough digital storage capacity for the length of interview. Always make use of an external microphone rather than relying on the digital recorder's internal microphone, as this will give you superior sound reproduction.

Test out the quality of reproduction of your digital recorder by making practice recordings at different distances from the microphone. What is the furthest distance that gives you a quality of recording from which you can comfortably transcribe? If you are doing group interviews, will you need two microphones?

Patton (2002) suggests that the ideal objective is to achieve a full transcription of the interview. This process, however, is both expensive and time-consuming, with perhaps each hour of live interview requiring between 7 and 10 hours of transcribing. Nevertheless, there is really no substitute for being able to see all the transcribed data at a glance during the analysis stage of the research. If it is simply impractical to achieve full transcription, one option is to use notes taken at the interview to locate key quotations or passages that can be accessed on the recording for transcription.

Writing up the report

There are many ways of converting transcripts and other interview data sources (such as the researcher's own notes) into a credible and accessible report. However, certain approaches add weight to the research outputs while others detract from them. Rowley (2012), for example, recommends that reports should contain a table that outlines the basic profile of interviewees, in terms of their job role, qualifications, experience, gender and any other criteria that might be considered relevant. This profile serves to demonstrate to the reader that the interviewees have the necessary authority or knowledge to comment on the subject.

Another issue is when or how to use quotations. Too often, inexperienced researchers pepper the page with quotations, trying to get the quotations themselves to carry the main burden of the argument. This approach never works because no attempt has been made by the researcher to link the quotations to an argument or theme; indeed, the over use of quotations usually means that the researcher has made little or no effort to actually identify the themes that have emerged from the data. The left hand column in Figure 15.2, then, illustrates the 'death by quotation' approach, while the right hand column illustrates an example of a more appropriate approach. Quotations, then, must be used to support and illustrate themes not to explain the themes themselves.

Do not use quotations that are merely descriptive and where the researcher just summarizing or synthesizing transcript data does the job. Use quotations where the way in which the respondent has commented is vibrant, exciting, controversial, or surprising. So, in commenting on the introduction of a new pain control drug in an accident and emergency ward, the following phrase might be summarized by the researcher as part of the theme, rather than as a quotation: 'The new drug came through its trials satisfactorily, and was known to be a cost-effective substitute for the range of pain relief drugs we have been using'. However, this might be considered for

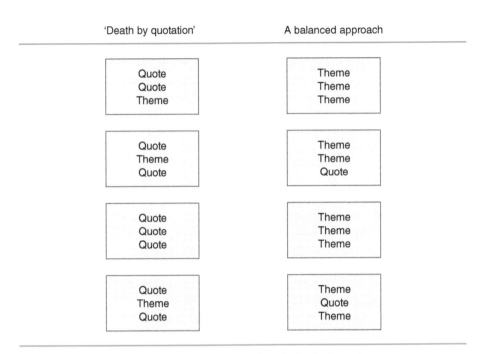

'Death by quotation'	A balanced approach

Quote
Quote
Theme

Theme
Theme
Theme

Quote
Theme
Quote

Theme
Theme
Quote

Quote
Quote
Quote

Theme
Theme
Theme

Quote
Theme
Quote

Theme
Quote
Theme

Figure 15.2   The 'pacing' of quotations from interviews in the final report

use as a quotation: 'As a health professional I consider the relief of pain as one of one of my prime functions. It's why I became a nurse – to help people. I knew from what I'd read in the medical press that this new drug could be special. I didn't realise how special'.

Finally, some advice on how to make use of contentious comments or where there is a divergence of opinion. Novice researchers are often inclined to see counter-views as reducing the clarity of the findings and may attempt to hide them. This is a mistake. As Rowley (2012) makes clear, disagreements should be reported because they enhance the findings demonstrating a richness of results.

Dealing with problem respondents

Interviewing presents a wide variety of potential difficulties. Within the workplace, people may be very reluctant to answer questions connected with their job responsibilities because they may feel vulnerable. Why am I being asked about my job? Why have *I* been picked out? What are they going to do with the information? Similarly, they may be nervous about expressing their views about issues and subjects connected with the company, and may be tempted to provide answers they think are wanted (socially desirable responses) rather than what they actually believe. Also, unless the research is seen to be officially sponsored by the organization in some way, it might be viewed as irrelevant snooping. If the research *is* sponsored, the level of this sponsorship within the organization hierarchy may prove a factor in eliciting cooperation.

Knowledge questions can also prove to be an embarrassment if people do not know the answer, particularly if they are supposed to be subject matter experts. For example, if interviewing a lawyer and they have forgotten a vital detail in the law. The interviewer must never show surprise at a wrong answer or hint what the correct answer should be. Keep a look out for body language that signals discomfort, anger or irritation, and be prepared to switch questions or even to curtail the interview. Table 15.3 provides a simple summary checklist of dos and don'ts of conducting interviews.

Conducting multicultural interviews

It is worth considering the implications of conducting interviews with people who are of a different ethnic, social or cultural group to that of the interviewer. We have seen the importance of building rapport between the two parties, and the significance of impression management and the use of language. It is extremely easy for any of these elements to go wrong unless the interviewer is aware of, and prepared for, the kinds of problems that can arise. Vazquez-Montilla et al. (2000) talk about the need for *culturally responsive* interviewing that is more sensitive to and aware of multi-ethnic cultural perspectives, and they introduce the notion of 'Triple A' (AAA) practices: authenticity, affinity and accuracy.

Working with Hispanic families in Florida, USA, the researchers found that their own Hispanic backgrounds were vital in establishing authenticity since the researchers were able to 'validate their ethnic match and cultural backgrounds' (Vazquez-Montilla et al., 2000: 4). To accomplish this task they were able to make reference to specific cities, events, characteristics of their native country, foods, etc. Since respondents were made aware of the interviewer's shared cultural perspectives, they became more confident that their message would not be misunderstood. Affinity was established through the interviewer spending time building up a knowledge of the community, often through community agencies and groups. During the interviews, the interviewer attempted to match the respondent's conversational and interaction style, terminology and gestures (although stopping short of mirroring exaggerated mannerisms which would probably appear mocking and offensive). To enhance accuracy, interviewers made themselves aware of basic language terms used by participants by keeping a list of words and idiomatic expressions commonly used by the group. A second researcher always validated the analysis so that cultural stereotyping was avoided.

Keats (2000) suggests that some cultures would find the following actions unacceptable:

- Sending a woman to interview a man.
- Sending a man to interview a woman.
- Sending a person of one religion to interview a person of a different religion when factions from each are in conflict.
- Making direct rather than circuitous replies.
- Looking directly into a person's face when speaking.

Table 15.3   Checklist of dos and don'ts of interviewing

DO	DON'T
Establish clearly what the interviewee thinks.	Do not give an indication to the interviewee of *your* meanings and understandings or appear to judge their responses.
Provide a balance between open and closed questions.	Do not ask leading questions or questions to which it is easy for interviewees to simply agree with all you say.
Listen carefully to all responses and follow up points that are not clear.	Do not rush on to the next question before *thinking* about the last response.
If necessary, either to gain interviewer thinking time or for the clarity of the audio recording, repeat the response.	Do not respond with a modified version of the response, but repeat exactly what was said.
Give the interviewee plenty of time to respond.	Do not rush, but do not allow embarrassing silences.
Where interviewees express doubts or hesitate, probe them to share their thinking.	Avoid creating the impression that you would prefer some kinds of answers rather than others.
Be sensitive to possible misunderstandings about questions, and if appropriate repeat the question.	Do not make any assumptions about the ways in which the interviewee might be thinking.
Be aware that the respondent may make self-contradictory statements.	Do not forget earlier responses in the interview.
Try to establish an informal atmosphere.	Do not interrogate the interviewee.
Be prepared to abandon the interview if it is not working.	Do not continue if the respondent appears agitated, angry or withdrawn.

Source: Adapted from Arksey and Knight, 1999

With the spread of globalization, many people now live in multicultural societies so it is more than likely that you will need to address some of these multicultural issues in your own research. For example, in an educational setting, you might interview the parents of recent immigrant children. Working in a health setting, you might interview consultants, nurses or ancillary workers who are first or second generation immigrants.

DOS & DON'TS OF INTERVIEWING

GROUP INTERVIEWS

So far we have assumed a one-to-one situation between an interviewer and single respondent, but, of course, other combinations are possible. Group interviews can comprise a number of different formats, including multiple interviewers, joint interviews and focus groups. An advantage of using group interviews is that costs can be drastically reduced, while the chance of non-response is reduced to about zero. But a drawback is that the social nature of responding may have an influence. Furthermore, as Dillman (2007) reports, group interviews using a questionnaire may invoke test-taking behaviour. He observed respondents checking through questions after completing them and even changing their answers.

Multiple interviewers

It can be very useful to have more than one interviewer present since different roles can be performed. For example, one interviewer can act as chairperson, controlling the pace and direction of the interview, while the other takes notes. At the end of the interview, each researcher can compare thoughts and observations to ensure that nothing has been missed.

Joint interviews

Joint interviews involve one researcher talking with two people simultaneously about one phenomenon. This can facilitate collecting differing or corroborating perspectives of the one event. Having both parties present can also allow for them to fill in details that the other has omitted. Against this must be set the danger of interviewees diverting each other's attention, or one respondent dominating the interview.

Focus groups

FOCUS GROUP
EXAMPLES

Focus groups originated in market research in the 1950s when people were brought together so that their attitudes to new products could be tested. Today, focus groups are still used for this purpose, but their popularity has spread to wider aspects of research. They can be a low-cost way of collecting data, but require a considerable amount of cooperation and enthusiasm from participants. Focus groups are now such a useful method of conducting interviews and collecting data that Chapter 19 is devoted them.

So far we have assumed that interviews can be successfully conducted either in an unstructured manner or through the use of various types of question-naires or interview schedules. However, there may be some special groups for which these techniques will either be inappropriate or entirely ineffective. Case Study 15.2 provides an illustration of some more creative and imaginative approaches.

→ **TOP TIP 15.7** ←

When running a focus group, be prepared for unexpected comments and even the expression of views you find unhelpful or even distasteful. Do not get drawn into expressing your own opinion. You are there to facilitate the session and elicit the views of others. Remain as calm and as neutral as possible. Welcome the expression of all opinions and keep the digital recorder running!

Secret boxes, soap operas and spiders

Punch (2002) reports on a research study she carried out that explored young people's perceptions of their problems, coping strategies and help-seeking behaviour. The sample was drawn from young people both living at home and in residential care. The interviews were conducted using single-sex friendship groups of five people. Clearly, because of the private nature of their problems and often their difficulty or unwillingness to articulate their worries, some innovative approaches were required. These included:

INTERVIEWING
YOUNG PEOPLE

A 'secret box': The young people were asked to write down any current or recent problem and to post their anonymous response into a box. This was then sealed with sticky tape with the assurance that responses would only be read by the researcher after the completion of the last interview with each sample. It was also shaken up to ensure that the last response would not be on the top. Respondents were also permitted either to write a response or to post a blank piece of paper. This process both assured anonymity but also that questions would not be asked about the responses. Typical concerns to emerge concerned puberty, grief at the death of a close relative and illegal activities (drinking, drug taking and stealing). However, one of the limitations of this technique is that, because of anonymity, it is impossible to probe any of the responses.

Stimulus material – video clips from soap operas: Three short clips from recent soap operas were recorded onto one video tape, each one depicting a typical problem that young people have to cope with. During a group interview, each of the clips was discussed in relation to young people's coping strategies. They were firstly asked how the people in the clip had coped. Secondly, they were asked how they would cope in similar circumstances. Punch describes these video clips as visual vignettes. The clips were highly effective in sparking off memories of personal experiences and provided a stimulus for discussions. One of the drawbacks was the time it took to locate appropriate clips and the time taken up by the clips in the interview sessions.

Stimulus material – problem letter pages: These were used in a similar way as video clips to discuss issues such as eating disorders, sexual activity and depression.

Stimulus material – task-based activities: A grouping and ranking exercise was used where the young people grouped 20 different problems written on plain index cards and placed them into three piles: big, middle and small worries. Then each pile was ranked from the most to the least worry. This was then used to provoke a group discussion about the nature of different problems. Spider diagrams were also used. Using a large sheet of paper, 'coping with problems' was circled in the middle and each person was asked to add a 'leg' indicating how they dealt with problems. Thus, the diagrams were used to build information and allow for issues to be probed in greater depth.

Source: Adapted from Punch, 2002

Consider the following questions in relation to Case Study 15.2:

1. Why were the interviews conducted with single-sex friendship groups?
2. In developing a simple protocol that you could use for each of the above activities, how would you explain each activity, and how would you provide the necessary reassurances?

Suggested answers are provided at the end of the chapter.

USING TELEPHONE INTERVIEWS

We looked briefly at telephone interviews in Chapter 9 in the context of conducting telephone surveys. One of the main advantages of conducting interviews by telephone is the low cost. They also tend to be conducted more quickly, another important benefit. However, research by Irvine (2011) suggests that compared to face-to-face interviews, in telephone interviews respondents tend to talk for shorter bursts of time, providing slightly less depth and elaboration. A potential disadvantage of telephone interviews is the fear that the refusal rate may be higher. Indeed, Vigderhous (1981) lists a number of non-response outcomes (see Table 15.4).

Research by Vigderhous (1981) found that for telephone interviews, response rates are better during the early evening between 6pm and 6:59, irrespective of the day of the week. The month is also significant. Schedules in spring (March, April and May) and autumn (September, October and November) are generally more successful than summer or winter months. While a study using 250,000 diallings found no significant difference between time, day or month, a somewhat cautionary finding was that only 8 per cent of dialling attempts resulted in a completed interview (Kerin and Peterson, 1983).

Image 15.2   Telephone interviews – a traditional medium

TELEPHONE
INTERVIEWS

But whatever the time or month, interviewers will need to adopt a professional telephone manner, especially to strike up a rapport. For a long interview, it is usually best to make a preliminary call to set up a time for the interview.

In terms of questions, all but the most complex kinds can be asked over the telephone. Indeed, one of the strengths of telephone interviews over questionnaires is

Table 15.4   Temporary non-response and non-response to telephone interviews

Response	Comment
Busy	The number dialled by the researcher was busy
Callback	The interviewer was asked to call back at a more convenient time
No answer	The dialled number keeps ringing but with no answer
No responsible party	The phone is answered but by someone who is underage, disabled (deaf) or drunk/incapable of reasoning
Other language	The phone is answered but the interviewer is unable to communicate due to language difficulties
Partially completed	The interview is partially completed but respondent does not have time to complete
Quit	The respondent refuses to continue after hearing one or several questions

Source: Adapted from Vigderhous, 1981

Table 15.5   Example of explanations given by telephone interviewers

Respondent's comments	Typical interviewer's replies
What's the purpose of the survey?	The questions are about your attitude to [*give name of topic*]. It will give us a better idea of [*what to do/how to improve things/what the firm, department, etc. should concentrate on in the future*]. I'm doing this as part of my work for [*name your institution*]. All your replies will be treated in confidence.
How will the survey be used?	A summary of the findings will go to [*add name of sponsor*]. A short version of the survey will be available to our respondents at [*give Web address*].
How did you get my number?	Your number was chosen by a computer which randomly generates a list of numbers. Your name was provided by a professional association/club [*name association/club*].
Why don't you want to talk to [*someone of the opposite sex, someone older or younger*] rather than me?	I need to make sure I have a good mix of men and women, younger and older people. You have been chosen because this helps us to achieve this mix.
Hmm. I'm still not sure	If you want to check [*our/my*] credentials, why not call [*give name and number of sponsor*] and I'll call back later.

Source: Adapted from Arksey and Knight, 1999

that the interviewer can help respondents with any misunderstandings or difficulties they have. Response rates can also be raised if the interviewer has a slick, persuasive manner and can give encouragement. Table 15.5 provides a summary of the kinds of responses commonly given.

Using Skype for interviews

Of course, in addition to telephone interviews you now have the option of using Skype which offers the benefit of video and audio calls which are free of charge if the respondent is also on Skype. For video calls you will, of course, need a web cam which may come already installed in your computer or purchased as an add-on facility. The quality of video feedback will depend, in part, on the quality of web cam equipment being used and the data transfer rate at both ends. For example, interviewing someone in a developing country may suffer from glitches in picture and sound quality and the occasional crashing of the system. That apart, using the visual element of Skype offers the possibility of generating much better inter-personal communication, the development of greater trust and, as a result, more rounded and detailed responses than would have been the case in just using a telephone.

RECORDING
SKYPE
INTERVIEWS

ETHICAL ISSUES

No matter the type of interview used, the central ethical issue surrounding data collection through interviews is that participants should not be harmed or damaged in

Table 15.6   Action that can be taken for conducting an ethical interview

Ethical issue	Actions
Promises and guarantees	State what the interviewee will gain. Ensure that if a copy of the report is promised, it is delivered.
Risk assessment	Consider in what ways might the interview put people at risk in terms of: • Stress • Hostility from line-managers, peers, etc.
Confidentiality	Reflect on the extent to which promises of confidentiality can *actually* be met.
Organizational permissions	Consider whether you have the 'right' to interview respondents. Are permissions necessary?
Data access and ownership	Evaluate who has the right to access data and for what purpose. Who 'owns' the final report in terms of intellectual property rights?
Mental health	Consider how the mental health of the interviewer and interviewee may be affected by conducting the interview.
Advice	Appoint an adviser on ethical matters during the course of the study.

Source: Adapted from Patton, 1990

any way by the research. If a respondent becomes anxious or upset during the course of an interview, the session should be immediately abandoned. We have already seen that confidentiality should be offered to respondents when completing questionnaires, so, clearly, the same respect should be afforded to those participating in interviews. Furthermore, interviewees have the right not to answer individual questions or to terminate the interview before its completion. It is also important that interviews are not used as a devious means of selling something to the respondent.

One of the problems is that, as Patton (2002) comments, effective interviewing opens up the interviewees' thoughts, knowledge and experience to both the interviewer, but also the interviewees themselves. Hence, after a good interview, the interviewees know more about themselves and their situation than they did before. This, in itself, may be quite therapeutic (or not as the case may be), but the purpose of research is to collect data, not to change people or opinions. A key ethical consideration is that of **informed consent**. In some countries, for example the USA, written consent is required even when the research is small-scale or only involves structured, closed-question interviews. An example of an informed consent form is given in Figure 15.3.

Having taken steps to ensure informed consent, what are the practical considerations that help to ensure that an interview is ethically conducted? Table 15.6 sets out some issues and suggested ethical solutions.

Ethical issues might arise in any number of unexpected ways. For example, in dealing with particularly difficult or sensitive topics, the respondent might ask for practical guidance or advice. It should be noted that the interviewer is not a counsellor, and should avoid being drawn into this type of discussion. The proper course of action would be to offer contact details for those kinds of organization that could provide help. These would include advice bureaux, voluntary organizations, support networks and telephone helplines.

CONSENT FORM

Beechwood Academy

Evaluation of anti-bullying policy

This consent form is designed to check that you understand the purposes of the study, that you are aware of your rights as a participant and to confirm that you are willing to take part

---

Please tick as appropriate

	YES	NO
1. I have read the leaflet describing the study.		
2. I have received sufficient information about the study for me to decide whether to take part.		
3. I understand that I am free to refuse to take part if I wish.		
4. I understand that I may withdraw from the study at any time without having to provide a reason.		
5. I know that I can ask for further information about the study from the research team.		
6. I understand that all information arising from the study will be treated as confidential.		
7. I know that it will not be possible to identify any individual respondent in the study report, including myself.		
8. I agree to take part in the study.		

Signature: Date:

Name in block letters, please:

I confirm that quotations from the interview can be used in the final research report and other publications. I understand that these will be used anonymously and that no individual respondent will be identified in such report.

Signature: Date:

Name in block letters, please:

Figure 15.3 Example of an informed consent form

Source: Adapted from Arksey and Knight, 1999

Summary

- Interviews can be divided into six categories ranging from the informal conversational to the completely structured.
- The choice of approach will depend on the objectives of the research, with structured interviews eliciting more quantitative data and unstructured, qualitative.
- The danger of bias in interviews stems not only from the type of questions asked but the way in which they are articulated by the interviewer.
- Interviewing is a skill and includes the ability to build rapport with respondents while maintaining detachment, and observing and listening in order to keep control of the interview.
- Ethical issues are of paramount importance since confidentiality may be more difficult to maintain than in other forms of data gathering, such as postal questionnaires.

REVIEW QUESTIONS

1. When conducting an interview, suggest at least three ways in which rapport can be established at an early stage.
2. Is it best to prepare probing questions in advance or to be spontaneous?
3. To transcribe or not to transcribe. What is your view and why?
4. If a respondent becomes visibly upset during an interview, what should your first response be?
5. For long distance interviews, which would be your preference, telephone or Skype, and why?

INTERVIEWING

FURTHER READING

Seidman, I. (2013) *Interviewing as Qualitative Research: A Guide for Researchers in Education and the Social Sciences*, 4th edn. New York: Teachers College Press. Covers interviewing from a phenomenological perspective, the ethics of qualitative interviewing and the relationship between data gathering and analysis.

King, N. and Horrocks, C. (2010) *Interviews in Qualitative Research*. London: Sage. As well as offering guidance on designing and conducting interviews, this book also looks at the epistemology and ethics of interviewing.

INTRODUCTION FROM KING & HORROCKS

Roulston, K. (2010) *Reflective Interviewing: A Guide to Theory and Practice*. London: Sage. As the title implies, a book that provides a useful blend of theory and practice. Includes chapters on writing interview questions and designing studies that use interviews.

Kavale, S. and Brinkmann, S. (2008) *Interviews: Learning the Craft of Qualitative Research Interviewing*, 2nd edn. Thousand Oaks, CA: Sage. Deals with the 'hows' and 'whys' of research interviewing with the new edition containing a discussion of new developments in qualitative interviewing including conversational and narrative analysis.

Keats, D.M. (2000) *Interviewing: A Practical Guide for Students and Professionals*. Buckingham: Open University Press. A simple but practical guide to interviewing skills that includes the structure of interviews, interpreting responses, and chapters on interviewing children, adolescents, the aged and people with disabilities.

Arksey, H. and Knight, P. (1999) *Interviewing for Social Scientists*. London: Sage. Easy to read, but detailed and comprehensive. This book shows how to design an interview study and provides essential advice on how to conduct a successful interview.

── JOURNAL RESOURCES ──

Rowley, J. (2012) 'Conducting research interviews'. *Management Research Review*, 35(3–4): 260–271. Covers three areas: designing and planning interviews, conducting interviews, and making sense of interview data. Within these sections, 11 questions often asked by novice researchers are posed and answered.

Granot, E., Brashear, T.G. and Motta, P.C. (2012) 'A structural guide to in-depth interviewing in business and industrial marketing research', *Journal of Business & Industrial Marketing*, 27(7): 547–553. Presents a structural guide for data collection in a participant-oriented, business-to-business context.

Jepsen, D.M. and Rodwell, J.J. (2008) 'Convergent interviewing: a qualitative diagnostic technique for researchers'. *Management Research News*, 31(9): 650–658. Introduces the convergent interviewing technique and describes the method of selecting the interview subjects.

── Suggested answers for Activity 15.2 ──

While the response does offer factual information, the question is probing for the respondent's feelings, and so the response received is inappropriate.

── Suggested answers for Activity 15.5 ──

1. Clearly, because of the often personal nature of some of the discussions, single-sex groups are more appropriate for the interviews.
2. Any research protocol should be simple and easy to use. It could, perhaps, take the form of a single side of A4 paper to be given to the respondent, containing the purpose of the research and a short list of instructions. Assurances of confidentiality could be given at the top of the pro forma and at the end (as reinforcement). The researcher could repeat these assurances orally.

16

NON-PARTICIPANT OBSERVATION

CHAPTER INTRODUCTION

Chapter outline

Approaches to observation	413
Gathering and recording observational data	416
The process of observation	426
Validity and reliability issues	430
Presenting observational data	431
Ethical issues in observational studies	432

Keywords

Overt observation

Covert observation

Field notes

Non-participant observation

Structured observation

Observation schedule

Chapter objectives

After reading this chapter you will be able to:

- Describe some of the advantages and disadvantages of the structured observational approach.
- Select a structured observational approach appropriate to a given research objective.
- Analyse and interpret observational data.
- Produce observational data that are valid and reliable.
- Use structured observational methods in an ethical manner.

OBSERVATION & RESEARCH

NON-PARTICIPANT RESEARCH

NATURALISTIC OBSERVATION

Observation (especially if informed by ethnographic principles – see Chapter 17) can involve a deep and often long-term engagement in the field of study. Indeed, some researchers can become so close to their subjects that the fact that they were researchers was sometimes forgotten (at least for a time, until they attempted to disengage from the field and end the study). While a wide variety of data-gathering tools can be used in participant observation, field notes are common and typical because they allow for the documenting of speech, observations and also personal reflections. In non-participant observation, however, the researcher aims to maintain a position of detachment and independence from subjects, keeping a physical and emotional distance from the group, business, or community they are researching. Achieving this detachment, however, is easy to espouse but much harder to do in practice.

McBurney and White (2009) distinguish between participant and naturalistic (non-participant) observation. Naturalistic observation is conducted in such a way that the subjects' behaviour is disturbed as little as possible by the observation process. Another term for naturalistic research is non-reactive research. This term suggests that the researcher strives not to bias or influence behaviour or responses by their own presence. An essential ingredient of non-participatory observation is

Image 16.1   Doing observational research

careful record keeping (McBurney, 1998), particularly the use of checklists or observational schedules to note behaviour. Sometimes behaviour might be recorded using audio or visual media. But in non-participation observation, both structured and unstructured approaches to data gathering are common.

Observation is not simply a question of looking at something and then noting down 'the facts'. Observation is a complex combination of sensation (sight, sound, touch, smell and even taste) and perception, through which we develop schemas, the mental structures we use to organize and simplify our knowledge of the world around us. They affect what we notice, how we interpret things and how we make decisions and act. We use them to classify things, such as when we 'pigeon-hole' people. They also help us forecast, predicting what will happen. We maintain our view of the world (and ourselves) by selective attention to information that confirms our schemas and by selective inattention to information that disconfirms our schemas. Hence, a ringing sound in the office might be a telephone or the fire alarm! On hearing such a sound, we would have to use some experience from the past as a guide to interpreting it, and to give it meaning as a guide to action.

The interpretation of 'meaning' is one of the benefits but also potentially one of the drawbacks of the observation method. On the positive side, observation provides an opportunity to get beyond people's opinions and self-interpretations of their attitudes and behaviours, towards an evaluation of their actions in practice. For example, we might ask people their views about working with the opposite sex and find that, through a questionnaire and a set of interviews, most state that they find this constructive and rewarding. A researcher, however, spends a month in the organization listening to conversations and observing behaviour and finds barely concealed hostility and 'backbiting' among a significant proportion of male shop-floor workers against their female counterparts. You may have noted that eavesdropping in this way raises many ethical questions. The ethics of observation will be discussed later in this chapter.

As we shall see, one of the drawbacks of observation is that the interpretation of what is observed may be influenced by the mental constructs of the researcher (including their values, motivations, prejudices and emotions). We often 'see' what we want to see and disregard other phenomena that could prove important. Secondly, if stationed among those who are being observed, the researcher may begin actually to influence events. Furthermore, while the data gathered from observation are often rich in evidence, extracting themes and concepts from the data can be quite challenging.

The observational method is often associated with ethnographic methodology in that it studies people in their natural settings or 'fields'. Ethnography, however, can also entail the use of other methods such as in-depth interviewing, and the analysis of personal documents. Ethnography and participant observation are discussed in detail in Chapter 17. In this chapter we will focus on non-participation observation.

SOCIOLOGICAL NON-PARTICIPANT OBSERVATION

APPROACHES TO OBSERVATION

Observation involves the systematic viewing of people's actions and the recording, analysis and interpretation of their behaviour. Saunders et al. (2012) differentiate between participant and structured observation. Participant observation is largely

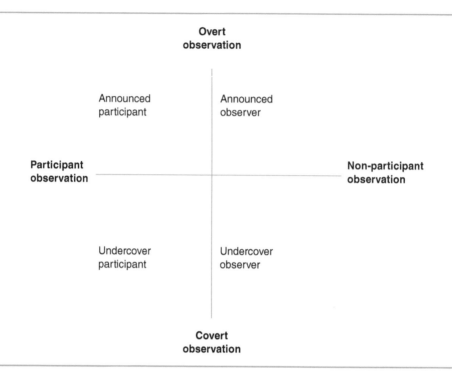

Figure 16.1   Observation research roles

NON-
PARTICIPANT
OBSERVATION
IN CASE
STUDIES

qualitative and emphasizes the meanings that people give to their actions, while structured observation is largely quantitative and focuses on the frequency of their actions. Mintzberg (1970) refers to structured observation as a methodology which combines the flexibility of open-ended observation with the discipline of seeking certain types of structured data. Within each of these categories the researcher can either collect the data covertly by hiding their identity, or collect the data overtly (see Figure 16.1).

Overt and covert observation

OBSERVATION:
OVERT &
COVERT

Overt observation is where those being observed are aware that the observation is taking place. For example, a medical researcher could be brought into a hospital department to investigate why there have been outbreaks of bacterial infection. The researcher's presence would be made clear to everyone and their cooperation requested. By contrast, covert observation is where they are unaware of this. One of the arguments in favour of covert observation is that people may change their behaviour when they know they are being observed, thus threatening the validity of the results. The problem with covert observation, of course, is that it can be construed as unethical. Consider your own feelings – how would you feel if you discovered that someone, perhaps in your own organization, and, say, with the approval of management, had been observing you performing some element of your work. Douglas (1976), however, considers it legitimate to conduct covert observations since people try to obscure the truth through misinformation, evasions, lies and 'fronts'.

In practice, the extent to which participants in a research project are informed that they are being observed ranges from full disclosure to no disclosure at all, with many projects somewhere in the middle. As Berg (2006) comments, some subjects are so sensitive that it might be impossible to carry out research by any other means. It is worth noting that most communication within organizations today takes place via email and that all these messages are stored and can be analysed. The laws on how this is done, and what consequences result, vary between countries, but, in a sense, covert observation is now part of our everyday lives. If covert observation is undertaken, it is essential that confidentiality is still respected. Hence, the names and locations of those being observed should not be revealed to any sponsor of the research. Case Study 16.1 provides an illustration of how covert observation can produce unexpected findings. Note that the case study is also an example of non-participant observation.

CASE STUDY 16.1

How smart is covert observation?

A company running a Holiday Village has just introduced a smart card for its customers so that the customer can:

- Check in on arrival using the smart card without having to get out of the car.
- Pre-book facilities such as bicycle hire and the hire of tennis courts.
- Open their lodge door.
- Use the card instead of making credit card or cash transactions.

A covert non-participant researcher with knowledge and expertise in smart card technology enters the Village as a 'guest' to observe the 'customer experience' in using the cards. As a covert observer she is able to note some of the problems guests experience with the system including:

- A court booking system that does not use real time updating, thus allowing double booking of the system.
- Aspects of the system failing to be fully functional when the volume of customers exceeds capacity.

The full interpretation of systems failures depends on the researcher's knowledge of computer systems and, at times, her ability to phrase questions that are deemed as acceptable coming from a fellow customer.

Source: Slack and Rowley, 2001

ACTIVITY 16.1

Examine Case Study 16.1. Is covert observation justified here? Could the study have been conducted using overt observation with the same success?

Suggested answers are provided at the end of the chapter.

GATHERING AND RECORDING
OBSERVATIONAL DATA

OBSERVATIONS
IN PSYCHOLOGY

Before examining how researchers can gather observational data, we should first ask: what actually constitutes data? Burgess (1984), using the example of a study in a school, provides a list of potential data sources (see Table 16.1). Any of these data features could be followed up by more focused questions dealing with each area in more detail. While there are a variety of ways in which observational data are collected, two of the most widely used are the writing of field notes and the use of more structured data collection methods.

Making field notes

Taking field notes is an important process whether the approach comprises the use of non-participant observation (as in this chapter) or participant observation and ethnography (Chapter 17). In both cases similar processes may be followed. However, in the case of ethnography, the volume of data may be more extensive as engagement in the field is generally longer. While ethnographers will almost certainly keep comprehensive field notes, they will tend to eschew the kinds of quantitative data gathering of structured observation. Non-participant observation studies may use field notes, structured observation methods or both. However, the style of notes created by non-participant and participant (particularly ethnographic) methods may contain subtle differences. As we shall see in Chapter 17, ethnographic field notes are likely to include the actions and reflections of the researcher.

FIELD NOTES &
MEMOS

According to Bailey, field notes are 'the backbone of collecting and analyzing field data' (2007: 80). They are absolutely essential to the success of fieldwork, and comprise everything the fieldworker believes to be of importance. The danger of taking field notes is to fail to note a situation in the belief that it will always be recalled at a later date. The field researcher should guard against this kind of

Table 16.1   Features of social situations as a basis for observational data sources

Data features	Features of a school
Space	Layout of classrooms and offices
Actors	The people involved in the situation and their names
Activities	The various activities of people in the setting
Objects	The physical elements present such as furniture and its position in the room
Acts	The actions of individuals
Events	Activities such as school assemblies
Time	The time sequence of the school, such as lessons, breaks and lunch hours
Goals	The activities people are attempting to accomplish
Feelings	Emotions in particular contexts

Source: Adapted from Burgess, 1984

optimism. In general, field notes should be written up immediately following the observation. Bailey (2007) suggests that field notes develop out of an analytic process. First, the researcher must attempt to mentally capture and remember as much detail as possible: who was in the field setting, what did they look like, what did they say, how did you feel about them, etc. These constitute mental notes, which can be recalled later to aid the production of jotted notes. Jotted notes comprise observations taken in the field that act as a kind of *aide-mémoire* for the later production of more comprehensive field notes, of which there are several components (as illustrated in Figure 16.2):

- *Primary observation – chronological log:* Raw data (i.e., no explanations or analysis) of observations on people, their surroundings, behaviours and conversations. Each set of field notes is dated and the time of occurrence noted. It is important to distinguish between actual verbatim quotations and approximate recall of conversations. You could, for example, put all real quotations in quotation marks and leave the general paraphrasing of conversations without such quotations.
- *Reflection and recall:* Some of these will be stimulated from jotted notes and some recalled during the process of writing up field notes. Sometimes objects or events do not seem important at the time but are then recalled when they occur again.
- *Pre-analysis data – ideas and inferences:* Themes and insights may start to emerge. Do not try to censor yourself at this stage, but write down anything that occurs to you – even when in the field. Indeed, Burgess (1984) advises the use of wide margins for field notes so that there is space to add preliminary categories. Make sure that a distinction is maintained between observational and analytical notes, even though they may be written at virtually the same time.
- *Experiential data – impressions and personal feelings:* These can often be a useful source of analytic insights at a later stage. So write down everything you can think of, including your feelings about events, people, conversations and your interpretations of your emotional reactions. These kinds of notes might be kept in the form of a diary.
- *Forward planning:* This might involve planning to revisit the field to collect missing data or to plan the next stage of the research project.

Once the field notes are completed, they can be written up along with any visual media that have been collected, such as photographs or audio tapes, and held as a permanent record. Burgess (1984) also recommends the drawing of diagrams to show, for example, the arrangements of furniture and people's sitting positions (especially for the recording of groups). Even at this stage, people, events or instances might be recalled that did not appear in the field notes, but which can now be recorded. This permanent written record (Figure 16.2) provides the basis for the primary analysis of the data.

What do field notes actually look like? Obviously, there are no rigid rules that define the answer. But it should be noted that too much data is better than too little. It is also usually far from clear when in the field as to which data are going to be relevant and which of little value. Hence, try to be as comprehensive as possible. Like all note-taking, the way in which field notes are written up will depend on the researcher. Some wait until they have left the observational setting and write up their notes immediately. Others make cryptic notes during the observation and translate these later into field notes, usually as a computer file. In terms of content, field notes should contain:

FIELD NOTES

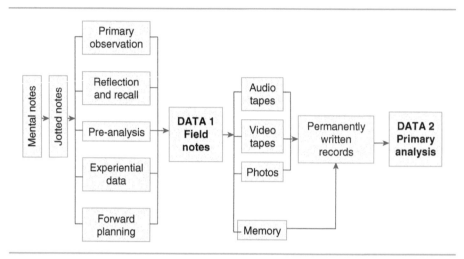

Figure 16.2   The data gathering process

Source: Adapted from Ellen, 1987

- Key quotations, reproduced verbatim.
- Details of the physical appearance of inhabitants: gender, height, physical build, age, ethnicity, clothes, style of hair, appearance of jewellery, etc.
- Observation of verbal behaviours such as the verbatim text of conversations, the characteristics of the speech and the speaker (use of slang or technical language); who does most of the talking and whose suggestions are followed and whose ignored; who interrupts and who does not; the tone of the conversation (polite, bored, hostile, formal, indifferent, etc.).
- Observation of non-verbal behaviours such as body language – facial expressions, body posture (arms folded in front is usually a defensive posture), how they move (confident or diffident?), length and frequency of eye contact.
- The time of events and activities.
- The alteration of names and places to assist in the promotion of confidentiality (but a list of pseudonyms should be kept so the same name can be allocated to each term used).
- The researcher's views and feelings at the time of the observation.

In making field notes, Berg (2006) also suggests that the researcher:

- Records key words and phrases while in the field.
- Makes notes about the sequence of events.
- Limits the time spent in the field, since every hour will take 4 hours to write up (at least).
- Writes up full notes immediately on exiting the field. It is not worth undertaking any further observation until this is done.

The reproduction of field notes can be accomplished quite simply using a word processing program. Alternatively, you might consider using a specifically designed software program that provides facilities for data storage and later content analysis. These days, many people will simply type notes directly into an electronic tablet such as an iPad because they are small enough to be discrete.

Having described in some detail the process of observing and writing up field notes, it is worth heeding de Laine's (2000) words of caution. She argues that in producing field notes, the researcher brings personal meaning to the account created. In other words, field notes are not 'raw data' in the simple sense, but details that are sieved from all the possible data through the researcher's mental constructs, understandings and interpretations. An (abridged) example of the author's field notes from a research project are presented in Figure 16.3. Note the attempt to capture key quotations, details of physical appearance of participants at the meeting, observations of behaviours and the researcher's own reflective thoughts.

Image 16.2   Observation in action

—— ACTIVITY 16.2 ——

Examine the notes in Figure 16.3. Are they sufficiently detailed to give you an accurate picture of the event? How useful are the Reflective Comments of the researcher? What do they reveal about the researcher's own stance towards the subject being discussed? Might these views bias what the researcher observes and records?

——➤ TOP TIP 16.1 ◄——

In making field notes, try to suspend your natural judgements as to what is appropriate to note and what is inappropriate. This is because what is relevant only becomes transparent during the transcription and analysis process. So note down as much as possible.

GRAY ON
MAKING
FIELD NOTES

—— ACTIVITY 16.3 ——

Go to a busy environment (such as a train station or high street) and spend ten minutes observing people in action, and listening to their conversations. During the observation make as comprehensive a set of field notes as you can, and write these up as soon as is practicable. Examine your completed field notes. Do they accurately reflect what you observed? What was the ratio between time observing and time taken to write up? Note, you may need to get ethical permission for this activity if you are undertaking research as part of an academic programme.

Consultancy project: Youth Offending Panel meeting

Background[1]

These observational notes were taken as part of a consultancy project undertaken for a Youth Offending team who wanted to gauge public opinion on the work they were doing to integrate youth offenders back into their local communities. This integration was done through 'reparations' work, getting youth offenders to work in the community.

Venue: The Centre, Old Building

Time in: 19.20

Time out: 20.36

Observations	Reflective comments
Modern building, low sloping roof. Three 'official' looking people standing outside (19.04) chatting to each other. Inside the Centre, chairs arranged in a semi-circle. Two display notice boards have been set up, one illustrating the work of the Youth Offending Board, the other, photographs and accounts of 'Community Reparations' by young people (such as clearing ditches, rebuilding fences, etc.) Two police officers (one male and one female) ensure that all chairs are covered by leaflets. By 17.21 seven members of the public are seated, two look at the Community Reparations noticeboard and another chats to the female police officer.	I feel 'attentive' rather than nervous. Not sure how this evening is going to unfold or how it is going to contribute to the research (the survey and two focus groups). All seems well organised but numbers low. Is this going to be seen as a success or failure?
A man is fixing up the projector for the presentation. Tea/coffee are being served at a counter. 19.25 Some of the audience are glancing at leaflets, including the questionnaire developed for the consultancy project. Three people seem to discuss in a friendly way the demographic details requested in the questionnaire. Overheard: 'It's all about grammar: *Eats, Shoots and Leaves*'. Lady could be English teacher! Her partner is filling in the questionnaire. 19.29 16 people seated and 5 standing near the noticeboards or coffee hatch.	[Get the impression they do not want to fill the questionnaire in]. Ah! The name of a book on grammar. Hopefully not an error in the questionnaire. The hall has filled up quickly. Numbers now seem better.
19.35 Start. 29 people in the audience. Introductions made by male police officer. Then talk by CS, of the Community Youth offending team Audience: some couples, some single people both male and female. Overwhelmingly white, middle-aged to elderly. Casually dressed. Serious concentration. No smiling. One young lady making notes. CS describes felling of foliage from footpaths with 'good work' being done by Community Reparations after local woman had been stabbed by man with knife while walking. Audience is still and polite. 'I don't think we are about humiliating young people. But we take a robust stance and get them to put something back'. 19.58 Presentation finishes.	He doesn't use microphone. Engaged with audience. Good speaking voice; hand gestures. Eye contact. Who is she – a reporter? He seems to be delivering a message of 'reconciliation' rather than punishment, but as subtly as he can. Appears not to want to alienate the audience.

Question and Answer session.	
'Why haven't we heard of you before? Where have you been? Why don't we hear more about you in the media?' [Handed a microphone]' I'm not going to say anything else' [laughter].	
'Is this county liberal in having a low custodial rate?' CS responds.	Challenge.
'Do you have figures?'	
'Who supervises the offenders?'	
CS: 'We tend to recruit people with the right skills. For example, bona fide carpenters. One offender did carpentry and went on to do a course at the local college.	Tells a story – gives a case study.
'They seem to come and go as they please. It doesn't seem to be a deterrent against crime'. Who's monitoring them?	More challenge.
'How many are actually caught for graffiti?' [Hear, hear!]	Is there a right-wing tendency here who, so far, has been too shy to speak out?
[Applause from 2 members of audience]. A cry from somewhere: 'The police are never around!'	Are they gaining confidence? Where is this going?
Police officer intervenes: 'I think we should leave this to the second part of the meeting, the Panel'.	Heading off the opposition!
'It is good that people are working with young people to show them a different way'. [Lady sitting with smartly dressed man].	Liberals hit back!???
A couple in the back row seem critical of the meeting. The woman was one of those who applauded the graffiti comment. Lots of frowns.	More of the 'silent majority'?
'Offending kids are spending a day with the Fire Service. How do non-academic kids at school get these same opportunities?'	Not sure what point was being made here.
Police officer responded by giving examples of how non-academic kids were encouraged into vocational courses. Other police officer talked about tackling low levels of anti-social behaviour.	Police seemed anxious to get back to stressing positive outcomes of scheme.
Voting for subject for next Panel meeting.	
• How courts deal with anti-social behaviour (0 votes)	So, the 'law and order' section set the agenda for the next meeting!
• Sentencing options and how they are decided (18 votes)	
• The role and responsibilities of volunteer magistrates (0 votes)	
20.36 CS thanks people for coming and closes meeting. Some leave, others mill around in small groups having conversations.	

[1]Location and people anonymous for reasons of confidentiality.

Figure 16.3   Field notes and reflective comments of researcher

Structured observation

STRUCTURE &
OBSERVATION

Structured observation aims to observe and record behaviour in a holistic and systematic way, usually making use of an observation guide or coding schedule. Given that the coding schedule often has to be constructed, some researchers may enter the field and conduct unstructured observation first, in order to develop the right categories for the observation guide. To minimize bias, the observer seeks to be as unobtrusive as possible, so that subjects are either unaware of his or her presence, or at least feel at ease in carrying out their activities. Whether the observation is being conducted by the researcher, or by other individuals or research teams, training is often undertaken as the process of observing and noting specific behaviours is often complex and demanding.

The advantages and drawbacks of structured observation

In contrast to the use of field notes, structured observation is more quantitative in nature. A typical example in the workplace would be a time-and-motion study where someone is observed performing a task and their actions noted on a pre-designed pro forma. Structured observation has a number of distinct advantages:

- It should result in more reliable data because the results can be replicated either by the same researcher at a different time, or by other researchers.
- It allows data to be collected at the time they occur and does not have to rely on the recall of participants or their interpretation of events.
- It collects data that participants themselves may not realize are important.

Against this must be set the disadvantages that:

- The researcher must be at the place where the events are occurring and at the appropriate time.
- Only overt actions can be observed, from which often subtle inferences have to be made.
- The coding schedule might impose an irrelevant framework on what is being observed.
- As Mintzberg (1970) comments, it is often difficult to categorize observations. In his study of managerial work, for example, he raises a number of examples. In coding a meeting called to resolve a conflict between two manufacturing executives, does he code this under 'manufacturing' or under 'personnel'? There is also the problem of 'double-talk'. Hence, a manager might give one type of information ('I'm holding the meeting even though you cannot be there') may actually be conveying quite a different message ('I don't want you at the meeting').

Constructing coding schedules

CODING
SCHEDULES

Coding schedules are structured schemes using pre-determined categories for recording observable events. They range from quite simple approaches, such as a system based upon time, to quite complex event systems. Robson (2002) suggests that before a coding schedule is selected, the first phase of a structured observation approach will be an exploratory one, often using other techniques such as interviews or questionnaires.

Coding schedules can be developed by the researcher (an onerous task) or use made of existing schedules. A common time scheme, the Flanders interaction analysis (IA) system, has been widely used in educational research for many years to illustrate the interaction between teachers and pupils. In Table 16.2 the Flanders system has been adapted for a situation where interaction is taking place between work-based employees. This could be on the basis of peer group interaction, for example, a project team working on the development of a new software system, or a manager–subordinate interaction. Table 16.2 provides an example of the latter.

In using the Flanders system an interval coding system is used where a code is selected for every three seconds of interaction. Figure 16.4 illustrates a typical coding sheet, showing that, so far, three minutes of interaction have been logged, with a code number noted for every three seconds. In the first minute, it can be seen that most of the conversation is led by the manager either making comments (5) or giving directions (6). In the third minute, the manager asks a question (4), the subordinate responds (8), and the manager criticizes this response (7).

The Flanders interaction analysis system is an example of an interval coding scheme since data are collected at pre-determined time periods. Other categories of coding scheme include event coding when a tally is made only when an event occurs. Figure 16.5 illustrates alternative ways in which this can be done. In (a) we have a

Table 16.2   Flanders interaction analysis system

Categories

1. **Manager accepts subordinate's feelings.** Accepts and clarifies an attitude or the feeling tone of a subordinate in a non-threatening manner. Feelings may be positive or negative. Predicting and recalling feelings are included.

2. **Manager praises subordinate.** Praises or encourages subordinate's action or behaviour. Jokes that release tension, but not at the expense of another individual; nodding head, or saying 'mm hm?' or 'Go on' are included.

3. **Manager uses subordinate's ideas.** Clarifying, building or developing ideas suggested by subordinate. Manager's extensions of subordinate's ideas are included but as the manager brings more of his/her ideas into play, switch to category 5.

4. **Manager questions.** Asking a question about content or procedure, based on manager's ideas, with the intention that the subordinate will answer.

5. **Manager discusses.** Manager gives facts or opinions about content or procedures; expresses own ideas, gives own explanations, or cites an authority other than the subordinate.

6. **Manager gives directions.** Directions, commands or orders with which the subordinate is expected to comply.

7. **Manager criticizes subordinate.** Statements intended to change subordinate's behaviour from non-acceptable to acceptable patterns: bawling someone out; stating why the manager is doing what she/he is doing; extreme self-reference.

8. **Subordinate response.** Talk by subordinate in response to manager. Manager initiates the contact or solicits subordinate's statement or structures the situation. Freedom for subordinate to express own ideas is limited.

9. **Subordinate-initiated response.** Talk by subordinate that they initiate. Expressing own ideas; initiating topic; freedom to develop opinions.

10. **Silence and confusion.** Pauses, short periods of silence and periods of confusion which cannot be understood by the observer.

Source: Adapted from Flanders, 1970: 34

1	5	5	5	5	5	9	9	9	9	5	5	5	5	6	6	6	5	5	9	9
2	7	7	7	4	4	4	7	7	7	7	7	7	7	7	5	5	5	5	5	5
3	4	4	4	8	8	8	8	7	7	7	7	5	5	5	5	9	9	9	7	7
4																				
5																				

Figure 16.4   Analysis of dialogue between manager and subordinate using the Flanders interaction analysis system

(a) Simple checklist

Event	1	2	3
	///	////	/

(b) Sequence record

Event	2	2	1	3	1	1	1	2	3

(c) Sequence record on timescale

Elapsed time (min)	0	5	10	15	20	25	30
Event	1	2	322	1	12	2	1

Figure 16.5   Alternative ways of event coding

simple array of events labelled 1 to 3. When each event occurs, it is tallied. Hence, we can see that event 2 occurred more frequently than event 3. Knowing the number of times an event occurred is often enough. In (b) the sequence record gives us not only how often an event occurred, but the sequence of events. This can often be more useful at the analysis stage than knowing the simple frequency. The sequence record on timescale (c) adds a further layer of detail, showing not only how often events occurred and their frequency, but also the time intervals between these events.

— CASE STUDY 16.2 —

Using structured observation

In a classic study, Mintzberg (1970) describes a structured observation approach to identify the work role of the typical manager. In doing this, he used three data gathering methods: a *chronology record*, a *mail record* and a *contact record*. In the chronology records, times and basic activities were noted and cross-referenced with the other two records. An abbreviated version of each of the three records is provided below.

Table 16.3   Chronology of activities

Time	Medium	Reference	Duration (in hours)
8.20	Call	A	0.02
8.22	Desk work	1-7	0.3
8.40	Unscheduled meeting	B	0.2
8.55	Call	C	0.1
9.00	Scheduled meeting	E	0.5

The chronology record provided a basic overview of the entire working day and showed at a glance the distribution of telephone calls, scheduled and unscheduled meetings, tours (informal wanderings around the workplace) and desk work. The mail record logs the nature of the mail received (today this would probably be mostly emails as well as some paper-based communications) and what was done with it.

Table 16.4   Mail record

No.	Form	From	Purpose	Attention	Action taken
1.	Letter	Trade organization	Request to speak	Read	Reply: decline
2.	Clipping	Salesman	Solicitation	Skim	
3.	Letter	External board	Notice of meeting	Read	
4.	Periodical		Business news	Skim	Forward advertisement to production supervisor

Finally, the contact record provides details of meetings, telephone calls and tours. IC stands for 'instant communication', that is, current information was transmitted quickly. If the terms used appear somewhat strange, this was because they were chosen at the time of the observation. Later, the number of categories was reduced and some categories renamed.

Table 16.5   Contact record

No.	Medium	Purpose	Participants	Initiation	Duration	Place
1	Call	Informed event	Manufacturing manager	Opposite	0.02	Office
2	Unscheduled meeting	Informed IC	Assistant	Opposite	0.2	Office
3	Call	Informed IC	Chairman	Self	0.1	Office
4	Scheduled meeting	Ceremony	Retiring employee	Personnel officer	0.5	Office

After five weeks, the data on each manager were consolidated into one table for comparison. Hence, it was possible to deduce the proportion of managerial time devoted to meetings, desk work, tours and phone calls, as well as looking at variations between individuals.

Source: Mintzberg, 1970

Wodarski, Feldman and Pedi (1975) conducted an experiment to see if different structured observational systems came up with different results. The study involved six non-participant observers scoring anti-social behaviour among school children by observing the children's behaviour on videotape. The behaviour to be rated comprised: pro-social (behaviour directed towards the completion of the group task or towards participation in group activities); non-social (behaviour not directed towards completion of the group task but which did not interfere with the activities of other children); and anti-social (behaviour which prevented other group members from participating in group activities). System 1 observational system required observers to rate the first behaviour observed at the beginning of a ten-second interval; System 2 required observers to look at a child for a ten second interval and if he/she exhibited anti-social behaviour to score this (other behaviours were not recorded); for System 3 observers watched the child for 10 seconds and recorded all three behaviours, but only once per interval; System 4 involved observers recording all anti-social behaviour by a child each time it occurred. Wodarski et al. (1975) found that in terms of results, there was no significant difference between using any of the four observational systems.

THE PROCESS OF OBSERVATION

Training observers

As the Wodarski et al. (1975) study illustrates, the process of conducting structured observation can be quite complex and demanding. Hence, it should come as no surprise that when a number of observers are used for a study, training is often essential. This is important not just because people will be expected to carry out the observational task competently. It is also important to achieve as high a degree of validity and reliability as possible (see validity and reliability issues below). Particularly where a large number of coding categories are used, observers will need to memorize the code numbers so well that, in the field, they can note down the code while simultaneously observing the behaviours occurring in front of them (Jungermann, Hahn and Ferger, 1981). Martinko and Gardner (1990), for example, describe their study which used 41 observers. All were required to attend a two-day training session in which the trainee's ratings were compared to a standardized set of ratings developed by the researchers. Only those trainees whose overall agreement with the standardized coding reached at least 85 per cent, were allowed to proceed as observers. McKenzie (2006) also advises that observers need to visit the target areas they are going to observe and practise coding.

In constructing an observational schedule, it makes sense if you can make use of experts or experienced people who have an insight or experience in the theme or context being researched. For example, in conducting a structured observation of clinical practice in a hospital ward (the provider–patient interaction), it might help to elicit the advice of clinical practitioners such as doctors, nurses or ancillary workers who may provide insights into the kind of themes that are worthy of observation.

Deciding on what to observe

It is impossible to observe everything that takes place in a situation, so it helps if the researcher is able to partition activities to focus on key areas. For example, in researching customer behaviour at an international airport, the researcher might select particular locations or sub-groups of customers for study. Observation might be conducted by personally mingling with the subjects, but, equally, might occur through filming or videoing activities or viewing the results of closed circuit television monitoring. If the observation is 'live', Berg (2006) suggests some strategies for collecting data:

- Take in the physical setting by visiting the environment that people will be observed in. This allows an opportunity to get acquainted with the activities of the target group, and draw up first impressions and points of reference.
- Develop relationships with inhabitants. We have seen that guides may help here, but whether they are available or not, it is important to strike up a rapport with the inhabitants. If the observation is announced, it is sensible to provide a brief description of the purpose of the research, but it is best to avoid technical details. It is also wise to provide assurances of confidentiality at an early stage, and perhaps to possess a letter of introduction supporting the project. A key objective will be to quickly establish relations beyond those with the guides.
- Track, observe, eavesdrop and ask questions. Tracking comprises following guides around their daily tasks, and watching their activities and interactions with others. Eavesdropping can offer opportunities for picking up vital new data, but one problem may be understanding the language used, especially if the information is couched in the jargon or technical language of the organization, location or neighbourhood.
- Locate sub-groups and 'stars'. Sub-groups may exist on the basis of personal relationships, job roles, or mutual interests, and may contain central figures or stars. Locating stars and establishing good relationships with them may be important in opening doors and soliciting the cooperation of the group. However, as Patton (2002) points out, organizations may be rife with political conflicts between various groups and sub-groups. This may sometimes lead to a group trying to align itself with the researcher as part of its conflict with other groups.

But it is not just a question of how to conduct an observation but what to observe. Table 16.6 offers some suggestions.

You will probably have noted when looking at Table 16.6 that a considerable amount of observation also includes interpretation. If, for example, you notice a particularly high specification desktop computer, you might assume that the person sitting behind it was of a high status. But there again, you might be entirely wrong. The owner might be off sick and the person sitting at the desk, a temporary worker. The next Case Study illustrates this point.

CASE STUDY 16.3

The impact of gaudy colours

A researcher conducted some non-participant observational research in a home for elderly people. One of her strong initial impressions was the paint-work – lots of strong colours such as red, black and orange. She found the colours gaudy and reported in her field notes that they made her feel 'jumpy'. However, as she spent some time in the home she learned that the ageing process means that we become less able to distinguish softer colours. Hence, the bright colours were needed by the elderly residents for them to be able to see and enjoy them. When interviewed, the residents stated that they liked the colours. The researcher was able to reflect that it is important not to base interpretations only on her own reactions to phenomena.

Source: Adapted from Bailey, 2007

Table 16.6 Examples of what to observe when entering field settings

Subject	Comments
Lighting	Lighting conveys social meaning, and may influence the way in which individuals interact with the setting and with each other. For example, loving couples prefer subdued lighting, sports people usually bright, specialist lights.
Colour	Colours help create a mood. Are they garish, bold, soft, well coordinated? What purpose might they serve?
Smell	What does the smell convey: food, pets, children, cars, chemicals, cleaning fluids? Does it have the scent of a family home, business, hospital? Sense for smells early on entry to the setting because people adjust to smells after time.
Sound	What sort of sounds are there: machinery, cars, crying babies, bird song, music? Do people react to the sounds or are they ignored? Are the sounds used to convey information? Does the volume of sound rise, fall or stay constant? Like smell, be aware of sound early on entry as the ability to detect sounds falls with exposure.
Objects	Pay attention to objects such as: furniture, computers, machinery, tools, books, pictures and other decorations. Are the objects in good or poor condition? What sort of 'statement' do the objects make? What do they convey in terms of status?
Weather and temperature	Note any relationship between temperature and moods and behaviours. Are there more people on the neighbourhood streets when it is hot?

Source: Adapted from Bailey, 2007

ACTIVITY 16.4

Carry out a small-scale exercise with a fellow researcher. Select a place to conduct non-participant observation. It could be a restaurant, library, park, etc. Spend about 20 minutes during which time you both take field notes using the criteria in Tables 16.1 and 16.6. Leave the field setting and complete your field notes. Working independently, begin to interpret your notes. When you are both ready, compare your interpretations. How similar are they? What do you disagree about? What has caused this difference in interpretation? Are either of you willing to re-interpret your data on the basis of the discussion? What evidence would you base this re-interpretation on?

Observing non-interactive data sources: unobtrusive measures

UNOBTRUSIVE RESEARCH

So far, we have discussed non-participant observation in the context of social settings such as workplaces and communities with observation mainly focused on interactions between people. However, as we shall see in more detail in Chapter 19, researchers can also observe what are called unobtrusive measures, non-reactive sources which do not involve human interaction. Unobtrusive measures include outcroppings, documents and folktales.

Outcroppings

Outcropping is a geological term referring to a portion of bedrock that has become exposed on the surface, that is, something that protrudes or sticks out (Fetterman, 2010). Outcroppings in urban contexts include high rise buildings, graffiti on the station walls, litter and the hypodermic syringe lying on the pavement. The researcher can make judgements about the relative wealth of an area by observing these outcroppings. But making assumptions based on this kind of evidence can be dangerous. So, for example, a school trophy cabinet full of silver cups might suggest a successful institution in which learning and academic excellence are valued. On the other hand, the large number of trophies might act as 'cover' for a school where sport is emphasized over academic standards. Like all unobtrusive measures, outcroppings need to be analysed alongside other data sources.

Site documents

More will be said about using secondary materials and documents in Chapter 20. However, here we will focus on some of the approaches to using documents when the researcher is dealing with specific communities, organizations or events. Documents come in a bewildering variety of styles and formats, ranging from the 'formal' to the 'informal'. At the informal end, there may be 'lay' accounts of life in the organization including fictional literature, diaries, autobiographies and letters (Hammersley and Atkinson, 2007) to which we might add blogs, tweets and personal pages on social media sites.

Of course, not all sites will readily offer up documents or materials for the researcher to use. Groups with literacy problems, or transient people, may leave few written materials. For example, there are few published diaries written by people who have been 'down and out' since many never become reintegrated into society. Even in localities where the researcher might reasonably expect to get access to documents, such access may be barred by gatekeepers, or maybe the documentary evidence is fragmentary or missing. Records themselves are not neutral. Stoler (2010) warns that researchers should view archives, for example, not as sites of knowledge retrieval, but of knowledge production, as monuments of what states choose to store. Archives, therefore, are cultural agents of 'fact' production and of state authority. What constitutes an archive, what form it takes, and its system of classification, reflects critical features of state power.

Proxemics and kinesics

Harrigan (2008) defines proxemics as the study of our perception and the structuring of interpersonal and environmental space, while kinesics refers to positions of the body, head and limbs. Proxemics focuses on the socially defined distance between people, while kinesics focuses on body language. So, employees whose offices are located physically distant from their line manager, may experience only a tenuous relationship with him or her. Similarly, seating arrangements at meetings have a social meaning with those exercising power (such as 'the boss' or chairperson) typically sitting at the head of the table. The fieldworker needs to record these observations, but put them in a larger context for interpretation (Fetterman, 2010). Sensitivity to body language may also allow the ethnographic researcher to generate hypotheses and add a layer of understanding to fieldwork. For example, observing that a manager keeps his arms folded across his chest when talking to female colleagues but not with males, might suggest a nervousness around women. Harrigan (2008: 138) describes the use of a coding scheme for noting the *'rich mosaic of actions, gestures and postures'* when observing human interactions or activities.

VALIDITY AND RELIABILITY ISSUES

Validity

With internal validity, given the often high degree of personal interpretation in observation, it may be difficult to prove conclusively that the data gathered are sufficiently objective to represent a true reflection of events. This, however, may be assisted if the researcher is able to display a sound understanding of the organization or context being researched because she or he actually works in it. In other words, they are a practitioner–researcher (see Chapter 12).

In the case of external validity, the very individuality of some observations may make it difficult to generalize the findings to other situations. Many observational research projects take the form of case studies and, as such, suffer from all the problems of generalization normally associated with the case study approach, one being small sample size. While Brewer (2000) concedes that it is essential not to exaggerate the generalizability of findings obtained from one or two fields, this does not mean that generalization should be ruled out. Cases, for example, can be carefully selected on the basis of their potential for being representative of the population (so the researcher must be aware of, and have access to, multiple field sites). Secondly, cases can be studied in one field that are similar to cases in another, or a series of longitudinal studies can be taken to build up a historical, comparative perspective.

Claims for generalizability are also strengthened if the researcher is able to stay in the field long enough to observe or experience the full range of routines and behaviours that typify the case. If this is not practically possible, then **time sampling** becomes necessary, in which all activities are recorded during a specified period. This should allow the observer to identify frequent routine activities, and irregular events that are special or abnormal.

Hammersley (1992) argues that, while validity and reliability are important issues, they are not sufficient. In considering the value of a study, plausibility and credibility must also be taken into account. In writing reports, researchers have the duty to present sufficient evidence that may convince an audience – given the existing state of knowledge. The more central a claim is to the core arguments of the research, the greater the breadth and depth of evidence that must be provided.

Reliability

As we have seen, one of the problems with observation is that different researchers may see different objects, phenomena and human behaviours when observing the same event. Similarly, each researcher may give different interpretations of an event when seeing it on different occasions. One way of reducing this unreliability is to record the observed events in some way so that the data can be reviewed and, if necessary, re-interpreted. The recording of data through a structured notation system is important here because it reduces the danger of human error in the recall of events. Experienced researchers tend to keep very comprehensive notes, as some details that appeared hardly relevant at the time of the observation may later prove to be crucial. Again, reliability will be increased by this more structured process.

Another way of improving the reliability of a study is through the process of triangulation, that is, the use of multiple methods of data collection. Triangulation is a word drawn from the world of surveying, where measurement is taken from three or more different points in order to identify a particular area with accuracy. According to Begley (1996) triangulation comes from a positivist frame of reference, which assumes, as we have seen, that a single reality or 'truth' can be found. But this does not mean that only quantitative data are relevant. Both quantitative and qualitative data can be combined to form a coherent picture.

In principle, then, triangulation reduces sources of error by gathering data from multiple sources, or using a variety of methods or theoretical approaches. But while it may reduce the chance of error, it does not eliminate it. Indeed, using a number of inappropriate data gathering methods, or using more than one badly trained observer, does not improve research reliability! So, just as in the selection of one research approach or method, using multiple methods still requires making them congruent with the research questions being asked. As Begley (1996) puts it:

> Unfortunately, many neophyte researchers 'use triangulation' without either explaining or rationalizing their decisions, seeming to expect that the mere fact that they are utilizing this approach will magically solve all problems of bias, error and invalidity. (Begley, 1996: 127)

PRESENTING OBSERVATIONAL DATA

In contrast to other research approaches, observational research does not leave the writing up of results to a later stage – it is an ongoing process right from the start. This permits the researcher to interact with the data, to expose gaps in knowledge and identify where further investigation is required. Important issues in the presentation of data include: what to write; how to write it; and what kinds of claim can be made for the status of the account.

What to write

There can be no prescriptive rules on this, but accounts could include:

- The context of the study (physical setting, history, etc.).
- The number of participants.
- The activities taking place.
- The division of labour and hierarchies.
- Significant events.
- Member's perspectives and meanings.
- Social rules and basic patterns of order.

Quotations should be used to provide the reader with an opportunity to verify some of the claims made in the report, but should not be too numerous as to be intrusive. Reports can also include photographs, charts, leaflets and other visual media.

Writing for the audience

We will look at some of the essential skills of report writing in Chapter 24, so these will not be examined in any detail here. For reporting on observational research, all the basic rules of report writing stand: use language that the audience understands; engage the reader's interest through the use of rich, vivid descriptions; and make connections from data analysis to the theory clear.

Determine the status of the writing

Researchers, and particularly ethnographic researchers (see Chapter 17), are divided as to the level of credibility they should assign to their report. Those who adhere to more positivistic traditions tend to argue for the authenticity of their research as a reflection of 'how it really is' in the field. Postmodernists, of course, challenge this view, arguing that any version of events is just one among multiple perspectives and interpretations. In extreme postmodern accounts, ethnographers even hold back from interpretation, allowing the text to 'speak for itself'. Certainly, researchers who use structured observation methods are probably more likely to see their quantitative data as offering an 'objective' measure of reality.

ETHICAL ISSUES IN OBSERVATIONAL STUDIES

ETHICS IN
OBSERVATIONAL
RESEARCH

While we have raised ethical concerns in looking at the use of other research methods and instruments, ethical issues are certainly no less important here. One of the justifications for covert observation is that, by omitting informed consent, it 'protects' subjects from any of the potentially negative effects of knowing that they are being observed. This might include apprehension or nervousness. Another argument is that all researchers assume a 'variety of masks' depending on where they find themselves, so covert observation is no different. The notion of 'net gain' is cited, whereby the benefits of the research outweigh the risks of the covert method. Diener and Crandall (1978), however, point out that the costs and benefits of research are often both impossible to predict and difficult to measure. Herrera (1999) also has little sympathy with the net gain argument, suggesting that some subjects may discover their involvement and might be disturbed by the revelation – not least that they learn of their own naiveté (recall Cassell's (1982) point about unasked for self-knowledge in Chapter 4). It is probably best if covert methods are only used where there is no alternative, such as where gatekeepers impose impossible barriers or where access is closed.

ETHICAL
COVERT
RESEARCH

As we saw in Chapter 4, most professional associations that concern themselves with research draw up ethical codes of conduct. If a researcher is commissioned, sponsored or provided with access to a site through one of these associations, then she or he will be required actually to sign up to the code. The British Sociological Association's statement of ethics, for example, provides guidelines on:

- *Professional integrity:* Members should seek to safeguard the interests of those involved or affected by their work. They should recognize the boundaries of their own competence and not accept work they are not qualified to carry out.
- *Relations with and responsibility to research participants:* The physical, social and psychological well-being of participants should not be adversely affected. Participation should be on the basis of informed consent, and participants should understand how far they will be afforded anonymity and confidentiality. Special care must be taken when dealing with groups that are vulnerable by virtue of age, social status or powerlessness. If research is covert, anonymity of participants must be protected and, if possible, informed consent obtained post hoc.

- *Relations with and responsibility towards sponsors and funders:* The obligations of sponsors and researchers should be clarified in advance of the research. Researchers should not accept conditions that are contrary to their professional ethics or competence. During the research, sponsors or funders should be informed of any departure from the terms of reference.

→ **ON THE WEB 16.1** ←

For a more detailed description of ethical guidelines see the British Sociological Association's website at:

http://www.britsoc.org.uk/about/ethic.htm

Also take a look at the ethical guidelines on covert observation for the National Health and Medical Research Council of Australia at:

http://www.nhmrc.gov.au/publications/humans/part17.htm

Our final case study illustrates an actual use of covert observation (both participative and non-participative within the same study) and the uses of multiple sources of evidence.

CASE STUDY 16.4

The role of observation in market research

In certain situations, observation is the only way of obtaining information on customer behaviour, especially where the influences on that behaviour are subconscious. A study was undertaken to develop guidelines for the siting of middle-market restaurant outlets in order to maximize the number of potential consumers passing by at lunch-times. The location was three interconnecting streets in a suburb of South London. The study was in two stages. First, an observation of consumer movements around the high street. Secondly, a series of visits to the restaurants as covert observers during the lunch period.

In Phase 1, a range of factors was assessed to see if they had any influence on consumer traffic flows in general and on restaurant usage. These included: the curve of the road, the sunny side of the street, pedestrian crossings, public transport sites, the gradient of the street and the types of shops in the vicinity of the restaurant. Counts of consumer traffic were conducted for 15-minute periods, focusing on strategic areas such as those near pedestrian crossings, the top and the bottom of the hill, near banks with cash withdrawal facilities, etc.

During Phase 2 the restaurants in the study were visited four times at lunch-time and detailed notes taken of customers using classifications such as: types of customer (individuals, couples, families, similar age groups); dining purpose (business, family treat, celebration, romantic one-to-one); style of dress (formal or casual); and mode of transport (walk, taxi, car, bus, etc.). By analysing the types of customer in the restaurant, it was then possible to assess if there was a positive relationship between the type of customer on the streets and the type of customer in the restaurants. In other words, the study was assessing whether the restaurant was situated in the right place.

It was found that, to maximize the flow of potential customers going past the restaurant at lunch-times, the outlet ought to be situated: on a central site rather than at the far end of the high street, on the sunny side of the street, on the inner rather than the outer curve of the street, and near transport links appropriate to the outlet's key market segments (customers).

Source: Adapted from Boote and Mathews, 1999

ACTIVITY 16.5

Examine the observational design in Case Study 16.4. Could the data gathering have been done in any other way? How effective would this alternative method have been in terms of the validity of the data? What dangers are there of observer bias in the study and how could they be controlled for?

Suggested answers are provided at the end of the chapter.

Summary

- Observation is more than just 'seeing'; it also involves complex combinations of all the senses and the interpretation of observed events.
- Observation can be overt or covert and involve the active participation of the observer or non-participation.
- One of the challenges of the observational approach is the gathering of data, particularly if the observer is a covert participant.
- Field notes should be as comprehensive as possible and should be taken either as events are observed or as soon as possible afterwards.
- Observational methods will often be triangulated with other research approaches, such as interviews and questionnaires.
- For structured observation, coding schedules will be used based on the principle of either noting events over a period of time or noting when an event occurs.
- Ethical issues arise, particularly where covert observation is being used. Researchers may do well to make use of a code of ethics drawn up by the relevant professional body, if such a code exists.

REVIEW QUESTIONS

1. To what extent does observation provide a better approach to the study of behaviours than interviews and surveys?
2. Compare the advantages and disadvantages of conducting covert and overt observation.
3. Why should field notes be written up immediately after the field observations?
4. List three advantages of using structured observation. What are the drawbacks, and how can these be accommodated?
5. What is the role of unstructured observation as a precursor to structured observation?

OBSERVATION

FURTHER READING

Podmore, V.N and Luff, P. (2012) *Observation: Origins and Approaches in Early Childhood*. Maidenhead: OUP. While aimed specifically at teachers, this book does, nevertheless, cover a wide spectrum of observation themes including both qualitative and quantitative approaches to observation, media and data collection and ethics.

Bailey, C.A. (2007) *A Guide to Field Research*, 2nd edn. Thousand Oaks, CA: Pine Forge Press. Not only is it clearly written, this book contains a host of valid and informative examples of practical experiences in the field.

Wragg, T. (1999) *An Introduction to Classroom Observation*, 2nd edn. London: Routledge. A useful book, especially for teachers seeking to research their classroom practice.

JOURNAL RESOURCES

Walshe, C., Ewing, G. and Griffiths, J. (2012) 'Using observation as a data collection method to help understand patient and professional roles and actions in palliative care settings', *Palliative Medicine*, 26(8): 1048–1054. Places qualitative observational data collection methods in their methodological context and provides an overview of practical issues to consider when using observation as a method of data collection.

Geraghty, J. (2012) 'Smoking behaviour and interaction: The observation process in research', *British Journal of Nursing*, 21(5): 286–291. Acting as a 'partial participant' rather than a full one, the researcher shows how she conducted an observational study, including details of the room layout to explain the observational process.

Cotton, D.R.E., Stokes, A. and Cotton, A. (2010) 'Using observational methods to research the student experience', *Journal of Geography in Higher Education*, 34(3): 463–473. Describes the uses of observations in an educational setting and provides three cases studies.

SUMMARY OF WEB LINKS

http://www.britsoc.org.uk/about/ethic.htm

http://www.nhmrc.gov.au/publications/humans/part17.htm

Suggested answers for Activity 16.1

If the observation was overt, then customers might act in ways that might hide or obscure their inability to cope with some aspects of the system.

Suggested answer for Activity 16.5

Certainly, data could have been collected in other ways – for example, through a market research survey of customer attitudes to the sighting of the new restaurant. But would the return rate be adequate? Would the responses be honest? With observations, however, one of the dangers is observer bias. One way of controlling for this is through the use of multiple observers, who would each observe independently and then compare both their raw data and analysis.

17

ETHNOGRAPHY AND PARTICIPANT OBSERVATION

CHAPTER INTRODUCTION

Chapter outline

The origins of ethnography	439
Guidelines for fieldwork	441
Gathering data: participative observation and field notes	448
Gathering data: interviewing	451
Gathering data: digital media	452
Ethical principles in ethnography	453
The ethnographic self	455
Feminist ethnography	457
Critical ethnography	459
Sculpting the truth in ethnographic accounts	461
Recording the miracle	463

Keywords

Ethnography

Participant observation

Fieldwork

Reflexivity

Natural settings

Postmodernism

Feminist ethnography

Critical ethnography

Positionalities

Chapter objectives

After reading this chapter you will be able to:

- Describe the origins of ethnography as a data gathering method.
- Distinguish between ethnography and structured observational methods.
- Outline the circumstances when ethnography is the most appropriate approach.
- Plan and conduct ethnographic fieldwork, selecting the field, gaining access, building rapport and getting out.
- Conduct ethnographic research ethically.
- Handle identity and know when and how to weave 'the self' into ethnographic accounts.
- Write an ethnographic account that is authentic and credible.

WHAT IS
ETHNOGRAPHY?

Ethnography is a qualitative research method that seeks to understand cultural phenomena that reflect the knowledge and meanings that guide the life of cultural groups within their own environment. While the origins of ethnography lie in the socio-cultural anthropology of the nineteenth century, it is now widely used in sociology, communications studies, educational and medical research, and history – subjects where the intention is to study people, ethnic groups and cultures. However, ethnography remains a contested and, in the view of Jordan and Yeomans (1995), an often loosely used term. Hammersley and Atkinson (2007: 1) see ethnography as:

> ... a particular method or sets of methods. In its most characteristic form it involves the ethnographer participating, overtly or covertly, in people's lives for an extended period of time, watching what happens, listening to what is said, asking questions....

For Willis and Trondman (2000: 5) it is

> ... a family of methods involving sustained social contact with agents, and richly writing up the encounter, respecting, recording, representing at least partly in its own terms, the irreducibility of human experience.

Ethnographers, then, as participant observers, look at and record people's way of life and take an **emic** (folk or inside) and **etic** (analytic or outside) approach to describing communities and cultures. The research is carried out in natural settings and is sympathetic to those settings. Traditionally those involved in ethnographic research spend long periods of time in the place of study, and are able to produce thick written cultural descriptions that communicate the information found in the field, or, in the words of Fetterman (2010: 1) 'a credible, rigorous and authentic story'. While in the past, ethnographers may have travelled to distant places to study 'exotic' tribes or groups, contemporary ethnography can concern itself with more mundane locations such as shopping malls, libraries, parks, workplaces, households, communities, cities and even information systems and cyberspace.

Image 17.1   The old and the new – both are legitimate sites for ethnography

Ethnographic accounts seek to be both descriptive and interpretive. Description is important because a high level of detail is essential. Interpretation is equally important because the ethnographer must determine the significance of what he or she observes. Ethnographic research typically employs three kinds of data collection methods: observation, interviews and documents, often employing all three methods in a single study. These in turn produce three kinds of data: quotations, descriptions and excerpts of documents. The aim of ethnographic research is to produce narrative descriptions that help to tell 'the story' (Hammersley, 1990). Ethnographic methods can help in the development of constructs, themes or variables, but ethnography is also used to test theory. Indeed no study, ethnographic or otherwise, can be conducted without recourse to theory whether scholarly or personal (Fetterman, 2010).

One of the key decisions at an early stage is the extent to which the researcher is going to be a participant in the study, which can vary from complete immersion alongside those being observed, or complete detachment (or at least an attempt at detachment) with the role of spectator. Participation helps the researcher to develop an insider's perspective on what is happening. However, the researcher must also observe what is happening (whilst reflecting on their own involvement and biases). The key to ethnographic research, then, is skilfully combining the role of participant and observer.

ETHNOGRAPHY
OR
OBSERVATIONAL
RESEARCH

THE ORIGINS OF ETHNOGRAPHY

The origins of ethnography are often attributed to the pioneering fieldwork of Polish anthropologist Bronislaw Malinowski. Published in 1914, in his seminal work, *The Argonauts of the Western Pacific*, Malinowski devotes a whole section of the book to explaining the process of gathering data through meticulously documented observations and interviews. He explained that, to have a thorough understanding of a different culture, anthropologists must have daily contact with their informants and become immersed in the culture which they are studying. The goal, then, was to understand the 'native's point of view'. To achieve this, not only must the anthropologist collect data, there needs to be an emphasis on inter-pretation. The link between data collection and the writing of ethnographic monographs is meticulous field notes. According to Roldan (2002), Malinowski increased the validity of his ethnography by including in the text fieldwork data, information about the research process and theoretical assumptions.

Although its origins lie in the field of anthropology, ethnography was soon taken up by sociologists, a move pioneered by the Chicago School at the University of Chicago in the 1920s, 1930s and 1940s. The primary assumption for the Chicago School was that qualitative methodologies, especially those used in naturalistic observation (such as ethnography), were best suited for the study of urban, social phenomena. It was through the Chicago School that ethnography and symbolic interactionism became closely associated. The phrase symbolic interactionism was first coined in 1937 by Blumer (1969), although the approach to social analysis is largely credited to the work of George Hubert Mead during his time at the University of Chicago. Blumer (1969) argued that, in essence, humans act towards things (including fellow humans) according to subjectively attributed meanings which are interpreted reflexively and subjectively. The combination of ethnography and symbolic interactionism led to the writing of several classic texts such as W.F. Whyte's *Street Corner Society* (1943) and E. Goffman's *Asylums* (1961). Ironically, the teaching of fieldwork methods at the University of Chicago was limited, with ways of organizing ethnographic research being largely acquired 'on the hoof' (Shaffir, 1999).

In recent years, ethnography has witnessed great diversification with differ-ent approaches being adopted, guided by different epistemological concerns and ethnographic practice, including long-term in-depth studies, through to con-densed fieldwork, consultancy work or participation in political struggles (Atkinson and Hammersley, 1994). There has also been a growing application of ethnography beyond anthropology and sociology into applied fields such as edu-cation, health and social policy. Sometimes associated with these more applied forms of ethnography have been moves towards collaborative research, stem-ming not just from a desire for engagement with practice, but also from an epis-temological concern that ethnography has privileged the researcher – as the implied Narrator – over the Other, the object of the ethnographer's gaze. Hence, the accounts produced by researchers are viewed as constructions that reflect the presuppositions and the socio-historical conditions in which they were pro-duced. Under the influence of various forms of antirealism such as constructiv-ism (Guba, 1990) or poststructuralism (Denzin, 1990; Lather, 1991), claims for ethnographic accounts have become more sceptical. In the late 1980s and early 1990s, for example, a postmodern turn in anthropology challenged anthropolo-gists to question their own assumptions and write more reflexively. An example here is auto-ethnography (Reed-Danahay,_1997) which has been encouraged by postmodern theory to draw out the narrative of participant observation and relationships in the field through personal stories (of the researcher) as a reliable mode of expressing findings from the field (Coffey, 1999) and as a credible, adjunct data source (Possick, 2009).

Anderson (1999: 456), however, is sceptical of what he terms the nihilist excesses of the postmodern turn, its hyper-reflexivity, and its 'clever, self-absorbed and evasive writing', serving to undermine empirical ethnographic work. He does, though, claim that some of its more positive insights will eventually be absorbed into what he calls analytic ethnography, an empirical approach linked to eth-nomethodological traditions. He is also optimistic about the future of ethnography, pointing to the growth of ethnographic research in the 1990s, within a broader range of academic disciplines. Hence, it is possible, for the first time, to talk about educational ethnography, medical ethnography, policy-oriented ethnography and even performance ethnography. Denzin and Lincoln (1994) also talk about the flowering of ethnographic 'moments' through which US social science has passed or is passing. Anderson (1999), however, sees this less as a succession of movements, but more of a diversification of ethnography. Indeed, ethnography remains a highly complex and contentious discursive field (Atkinson and Hammersley, 1994) at the 'intersections of communication, culture and identity' (Berry, 2011: 169).

GUIDELINES FOR FIELDWORK

It is fieldwork that is the most defining characteristic of ethnographic research (Fetterman, 2010). While classic ethnography could involve from six months to two years or more in the field, modern ethnography can involve studies where the researcher visits a site for, say, a two-week period every few months or so during a study lasting two or three years. Fieldwork involves an outsider angling for insider knowledge. Hence, fieldworkers ride the lines between and across multiple boundaries, with the result that the journey can be emotionally uncomfortable or in the words of Irwin (2006: 160) 'exceedingly edgy'. Doing fieldwork involves a number of stages including deciding what field or context in which to conduct the research, getting access and gaining acceptance within the field, conducting the fieldwork itself and leaving the field (getting out) in as ethical and acceptable a way as possible.

PREPARING FOR FIELDWORK

→ TOP TIP 17.1 ←

If ethnographic studies can involve immersion in the field for long periods, even several years, you need to think carefully before you embark on this type of research. It might be appropriate, say, for someone undertaking research as part of their employment, or as part of a doctorate. Indeed, as we shall see in some of the case studies that follow, some have been implemented as part of a PhD. However, for those studying, say, at Masters level the long periods required would normally rule out this kind of research undertaking.

Selecting the field

The nature of the setting chosen for the study may be decided before the research problem has been fully resolved. In some studies, however, the collection of ethnographic data may itself help in the definition of the research problem. Data collection and analysis may also lead to the identification of new themes that require different and additional sites for study. Settings contain cases for study but the two are not necessarily synonymous. Hence, cases may be studied in a particular setting, but researchers may have to study aspects of a case across multiple settings (Hammersley and Atkinson, 2007). For example, youth gangs could be studied in street settings, but a study might also need to explore their links with other outside groupings such as social workers and the police. How and why cases are chosen (sampled) will be determined by the kinds of criteria discussed in Chapter 9. So, given the qualitative and intensive nature of most ethnographic research, and the use of only a few sites, sampling design will be mostly based upon typical sites (Schneider, 2006a).

As Hammersley and Atkinson (2007) point out, sampling decisions must also be taken within cases, particularly in relation to time, people and context. For time sampling, it is obvious that the researcher cannot be in the field for 24 hours a day; so some choices have to be made in terms of when to enter the field. In a factory setting, for example, this could be sampling during day shifts, evening shifts and night shifts. Time phases are also an issue. Schneider (2006a) recommends that, for applied ethnographic studies (for example, studies that evaluate projects or programmes) observations should continue through at least one cycle related to the research problem. So, a study of the effects of government funding on agency programmes might observe the impact through a complete budget year. Sampling within a case (for example a study within an organization) will also involve selecting among people, which could involve ensuring different categories, based on gender, race, educational qualifications or social class, were all represented in the study. Within a setting, people may act differently according to the context. So, for example, within the setting of a university, students may act differently depending on whether they are attending a lecture, studying in the library or socializing with friends. Sampling design, then, will have to take this into account.

Gaining access

Central to gaining access to a site is the attitude of gatekeepers who can help or hinder the research depending upon their views as to the validity of the research and its impact on the welfare of people they work with. Reeves (2010) distinguishes between formal and informal gatekeepers. In her study of sex offenders within a probation hostel, the main formal gatekeeper was the hostel manager and his immediate line manager within the Probation Service. As Reeves (2010) notes, she was fortunate in that she was able to make initial contact through a friend (her informal contact) who had worked with this manager. Duke (2002) supports this view, asserting that gaining access to sites is much easier when personal contacts can smooth the path and where the researcher is known to have some knowledge or experience of the area. Zaman (2008) for example, relates how he decided to undertake his research at the teaching hospital where he trained as a physician, using his identity as an ex-student to gain access. However, even once access has been negotiated, further informal gatekeepers also need to be approached before site members will fully participate in a study (Reeves, 2010).

It will certainly be easier to gain entry if the researcher has empathy with those being studied. This does not mean necessarily agreeing or disagreeing with them, but it does mean avoiding the adoption of judgemental attitudes. Patton

(2002) suggests that a reciprocity model of gaining entry is valuable, where both researcher and participants come to see mutual advantages emerging from the observational process. This, of course, may be a pious hope. As Hall (2000) points out, especially when working with disadvantaged groups (for example street gangs), an outsider's curiosity might be construed as objectionable and patronizing – the first few weeks of fieldwork can sometimes be a miserable experience for the researcher.

The issue of gender may be significant to gaining access. Gurney (2002) comments that being a female researcher in a male-dominated environment may aid not only formal but also informal access as women are regarded as 'warmer' and less threatening than men. Hence, gatekeepers may not demand the same level of assurances from women researchers prior to granting formal access. Conversely, women may find entry problematic because of a perceived lack of professionalism or credibility (Gurney, 2002). However, as Mulhall (2003) asserts, an effort can be made to rectify this position by dressing for the occasion, and deferring (within limits) to the authority and cultural expectations of gatekeepers.

→ TOP TIP 17.2 ←

Negotiating access may take longer than you anticipate. As part of your research planning, make sure that you give yourself sufficient 'lead time' in setting up your observation.

Gaining informed consent

Informing people in the research setting of what you are doing, and eliciting their consent, is seen as good practice by most researchers. Diener and Crandall (1978) suggest that fully informed consent should include:

- Describing the overall purpose of the research.
- Telling the participants about their role in the study.
- Stating why they have been chosen.
- Explaining the procedures, including the amount of time required.
- Clearly stating the risks and discomforts.
- Stating that the participants may withdraw at any time.

As we saw in Chapter 15 (recall Figure 15.1), getting participants to sign a consent form is also prudent. This, of course, implies that covert observation cannot be undertaken. Bailey (2007) argues that achieving a cooperative relationship with a group more than compensates for what is lost through reactivity (between researcher and those being researched). However, the impact of the researcher's presence and interactions needs to be reflected in field notes and analysis. Note that even after permission has been granted it can be withdrawn at any time and that this must be respected. Of course, there are often circumstances when informed consent is simply impractical. Burgess (1984) notes that in research in public settings (sports events, parents' evenings, church services, etc.) access cannot be negotiated with every participant.

OBTAINING
INFORMED
CONSENT

Becoming invisible

The researcher may become 'invisible' due to the length of time they are involved in the project, by immersing themselves into the norms and behaviours of the group being studied, or simply by hiding the fact that they are researchers. Young researchers, for example, would have greater success in integrating themselves as workers/researchers in a fast food retail outlet than, say, researching the activities of a rambling club where membership tends to be much older. As Berg (2006) points out, however, there are reasons why invisibility is a danger. If, for example, you go 'undercover' to research, say, criminal activities within an organization, you need to ensure that you do not become implicated yourself! On the whole, though, invisibility means that participants cease to be consciously aware of the researcher's presence, and therefore act more naturally.

Building rapport

Rapport is concerned with 'getting there' and 'being there' and is often associated with themes such as empathy, immersion, participation, friendship, honesty, collaboration, trust and loyalty (Springwood and King, 2001). In the field, researchers seek to develop close interpersonal relationships with key informants based upon mutual respect and shared understandings. Berger (2001), for example, describes how she shared her personal stories with those engaged in her fieldwork studies, generating relationship formation and exchange between them. However, while this may appear simple at a surface level, in practice the achievement of rapport may be challenged where researchers find themselves having to hide their identities, or where their views and values clash with those they are researching. Westmarland (2001) for example, reports on her ethnographic study of the police where she witnessed a number of examples of police violence against an attempted suicide victim, a drug addict and others. As Reeves (2010) notes, while the researcher may be anxious to establish and maintain rapport in order to generate good quality data, respondents do not have these concerns. Hence, in her study of convicted criminals living in a probation hostel, even though respondents were comfortable with her presence, they continued to tell her half-truths, lies and stories in order to give her an image they wanted to portray. Achieving rapport then, does not necessarily lead to honest responses.

Handling identity – reflexive positioning

REFLEXIVITY

In undertaking participant observation one of the challenges is to maintain a balance between 'insider' and 'outsider' status. To gain a deep understanding of people's lives it is essential that the researcher gets not only physically but also emotionally close to them – but how then does the researcher maintain a professional 'distance'? Achieving this is often affected by issues such as the gender, race, social class and the education of the researcher compared to that of the people being researched. Burgess (1984) also adds that age can sometimes be an issue – is it practical for researchers of more advanced years to observe youth gangs, for example? As one set of researchers put it:

> The more one is like the participants in terms of culture, gender, race, socio-economic class and so on, the more it is assumed that access will be granted, meanings shared, and validity of findings assured. (Merriam et al., 2001: 406)

To remain an 'outsider' would be to fail to gain the kind of rapport that is needed to make this method a success. The participant observer, in a sense, needs to be both inside and outside the setting. Indeed, Merriam et al. (2001) argue that the boundaries between the two positions are not simple or clearly delineated. Being inside or outside is relative to a whole host of cultural and social characteristics and is a position that can shift over time. According to Hall (2000), the best the ethnographer can achieve is to negotiate a position in which one is in some way 'at home' and considered as 'one of us' without becoming completely immersed.

Positioning is a concept used in the analysis of narratives that allows researchers to explore how people make sense of themselves and construct their own identities (Possick, 2009). Using processes such as self-reflection, self-criticism and agency, participants can choose a position among the variety of positions available and/or generate new positions by performing narratives with the audience. One position is that of the autobiographical, an approach that seeks to acknowledge the effects of the researcher's personal and intellectual biography on all stages of research through the process of reflexivity (Hugill, 2012; Mickelson, 2011). According to Possick (2009) while many researchers engage in reflection, much remains unpublished or separate from the main data analysis. In cases of research on sensitive topics, where there are strong emotional reactions and ethical dangers, this self-censorship is particularly glaring. Possick (2009) urges that auto-biographical elements be included in the foreground of research not the background. This, then, is one aspect of positioning. The personal account includes thoughts and feelings about the informants, the physical elements in the field, relevant autobiographical events and a variety of 'unstructured musings about the research experience' (Possick, 2009: 862).

Getting out

While ethnographers have written quite extensively on entering a field of study and on developing rapport with participants, less is known about leaving the field (Lofland and Lofland, 1995). When to leave may have been planned early on in the project or it might result from the 'Things to do' portion of field notes getting ever smaller, or when fewer insights are emerging. Leaving the field of observation involves both the physical and emotional disengagement of the researcher. This is particularly the case if the observation has been conducted over a lengthy period of time and the researcher has developed empathy and commitment to the inhabitants. Prior to disengagement, the researcher should warn the community of members that this exit is imminent. The withdrawal is probably best handled in a series of stages. Rock (2001) agrees that quitting the field is never easy. Ethnographic research involves 'emotional enmeshment' (Possick, 2009: 868). For one thing, the researcher will have invested a considerable portion of themselves cultivating relationships and even friendships but these are now to be shed.

> The ethnographer who courted others, who had seemingly limitless time to listen, is now revealed as a person who can no longer be bothered and is in a hurry to be off. (Rock, 2001: 36)

To make matters worse, the ethnographer is off to expose what has been learned to the whole world. No wonder people can feel *used*. In leaving the field, you might like to consider paying attention to the following elements:

- Make the fact that you will leave the field explicit at the start (that is, your project has a finite length)
- Indicate the date of your leaving several weeks before the event so there are no surprises
- Remind respondents of your leaving date several days before it arrives
- Hold a leaving 'event' to celebrate the project (but also remind others of your imminent departure)
- Organize emotional support for yourself (see next)

→ **TOP TIP 17.3** ←

GRAY ON INSIDER PARTICIPATORY RESEARCH

If undertaking insider participant research (especially if it is covert), consider using either your supervisor or another confidante as an adviser or 'critical friend'. Use this person to discuss any problems you may be having, particularly in maintaining your sense of detachment and objectivity. You may also want to discuss any issues or incidents that raise ethical considerations.

CASE STUDY 17.1

Ethnography, reciprocity and getting too close?

Ortiz (2004) describes an ethnographic study in which he researched the isolated world of the wives of professional athletes using sequential interviewing, participant observation, personal documents and print media accounts. He travelled thousands of miles across the USA during the process. As a result

> I necessarily minimized involvement in other areas of my personal life. As a result, their world was my world for more than three years. (p. 470)

His impression management style was one of 'muted masculinity', offered in direct contrast to the hegemonic masculinity so common in the sports world. Hence, he became regarded as a man of a 'different kind' by many of the women whose lives were socially isolated. The establishment of reciprocity in his collaborative relationship with the women included babysitting, hanging curtains, running errands, shopping with them and even house-hunting. Over time, this closeness generated data that included secrets, gossip and occupationally relevant information (about their husbands).

Through sequential interviewing, critical topics were constantly emerging, but each new tantalizing piece of information became critical data that he felt he had to follow up with more interviews. Thus he got himself into an endless cycle of compulsive data collection. Even when he terminated a relationship he agreed to keep in touch with the respondent. He discovered, however, that staying in touch served to open up a Pandora's box of new information.

The therapeutic nature of the interview sessions also seemed to act as an added incentive for the wives to stay in touch with the researcher. Hence, although he knew he needed to make an effort to distance himself 'constant reminders of the wives and their marriages continued to pull me back into their isolated world' (Ortiz, 2004: 479). He finally arrived at a point where he began to feel emotionally exhausted and trapped and terminated contact. Although this process left him with feelings of guilt, he concludes that 'going native' is not always a mistake, especially if collaborative relationships are mutually beneficial.

— ACTIVITY 17.1 —

How does Ortiz (2004) justify his 'compulsive data collection'? Can/should the researcher be both an ethnographer and an informal therapist? What steps should be taken to maintain ethical boundaries?

The field as a construction

In the previous section we explored fieldwork from a practical perspective, the researcher simply entering the field with an 'open mind', similar to Glaser and Strauss's (1968) notion of fieldwork as a 'clean slate' where the researcher is free of prior experience. However, as Funder (2005) warns, this notion ignores the degree to which we are socialized and institutionalized into adopting ways of structuring and labelling the world we explore. For example, talking about the field of environment and development, we talk of *sustainable* resource management practices and *unsustainable*, so establishing categories of people who live sustainably or unsustainably.

> This framing of the world through our pre-conceived ontologies often takes place through dichotomies: When addressing the environment and development problems, we frequently approach the world as divided into the poor and the wealthy, the rural and the urban, the community and the state, the traditional and modern, the natural and the degraded. Although we may attempt to overcome some such dualisms, they are powerful notions that to a large extent provide our only means of negotiating the world. (Funder, 2005: 2)

This Western pattern of knowledge production now permeates Asian societies as well where, in some ways, Western science came to structure and to some extent even create Asian societies, through the process of giving names to (classifying) ethnic groups, and by drawing maps (creating national boundaries). In terms of knowledge, 'modern' methods of resource management (i.e. Western) were privileged above 'traditional' methods. Funder (2005) describes his ethnographic study of a coastal zone management project in Thailand where he first sought to identify community members to interview, dividing them into 'participants' and 'non-participants' and subsequently developing new categories of 'fishermen' and 'non-fishermen', 'Buddhist' and 'Muslim' households. He reflects that this categorization rested on his own embedded notion of communities as essentially heterogeneous, stratified entities, steeped in struggles over control of natural resources. However, this underlying conflict perspective was one into which he had been socialized through many years of interaction with teachers and peers at his 'left-leaning' university. Similarly, Brunt (2001) raises problematically the notion of community. Communities consist of people who consider themselves to be part of the same history or destiny, but this notion is based on symbols and attitudes, not necessarily concrete urban neighbourhoods or villages. Hence, ethnographers should not necessarily go off in search of a physical community. People have multiple identities and may regard themselves as members of multiple communities irrespective of where they work or live.

GATHERING DATA: PARTICIPANT OBSERVATION AND FIELD NOTES

Participant observation involves not only gaining access to the field and building rapport, it also means producing written accounts and descriptions of what was observed. A vital stage in this process is the production of field notes, that is, writings that are produced in close proximity to the field. Proximity may mean geographical closeness, but more important is temporal proximity, the fact that field notes are written more or less *contemporaneously* with the events, experiences and interactions they describe (Emerson, Fretz and Shaw, 2001). As representations of what they purport to represent, field notes are necessarily *selective*. The ethnographer writes about what he or she thinks is important, omitting what appears to be less significant. Hence, field notes are never a complete record of what happened (Atkinson, 1992). As Emerson et al. (2001) comment, there are considerable differences between what different ethnographers write about and the role of field notes in their research. For some ethnographers, field notes both record what they observe and also record their own actions, questions and reflections. Others, however, keep a distinct separation between field notes as recordings (data) and their own reactions and interpretations.

FIELD NOTES

Emerson et al. (2001) distinguish between several types of field notes that vary in their purpose and detail. *Mental notes*, for example, are a conscious attempt to recall features such as the physical character of a place, who said what to whom, who moved to where (Lofland and Lofland, 1995). These may lead to *jotted notes*, the commitment to writing key words and phrases overheard while the ethnographer is in or at least very close to the field. These jotted notes may be used later as memory joggers when it comes to constructing a more detailed account. The timing and openness of making jotted notes will depend on the relationship between the researcher and his or her subjects. Fieldworkers may need to be sensitive when it comes to jotting down notes on issues that subjects might regard as confidential or embarrassing.

An important and contested issue is the place of the ethnographer's personal feelings within field notes. In the past, ethnographers have tended to confine descriptions of their personal feelings, reactions and anxieties to personal journals and diaries (see below). From the 1960s, however, most sociological ethnographers have supported the inclusion of personal accounts within core field notes (Emerson et al., 2001). Recording one's emotions during a research project enables the ethnographer to read through field notes and to identify any biases and prejudices that may have crept in, as well as noticing changing views and perspectives over time (Lofland and Lofland, 1995). At its most extreme form, in auto-ethnography, the researcher seeks to integrate their private and social experiences through personal introspection, their own 'lived emotional experience' of events and interactions (Ellis, 1991: 25). It is a form of ethnography where the researcher radically alters their positioning by becoming a research subject (Reed-Danahay, 1997).

Before their use in the report writing process, field notes need to be revised and edited, partly to ensure that extraneous elements are excluded and also that anonymity of those within the account is preserved. But they are also edited to ensure that they are more comprehensible to a wider audience (particularly when field notes are later incorporated into finished texts). Hence, context and background may be added to events (Emerson et al., 2001). Other ethnographers, however, prefer to retain the sanctity of the original field notes and will therefore avoid or minimize these editorial changes. Ethnographers, then, integrate field notes into finished accounts in different ways. What Emerson et al. (2001) call an excerpt strategy, field notes are separated from commentary and interpretation by indenting or using italics; field notes, then, are offered as fragments of 'evidence' composed close to the events themselves. An alternative approach is to weave together the field notes and the interpretation, what Emerson et al. (2001) call an integrative strategy. In this style, field notes and ideas merge into a flowing prose written with 'a single authorial voice' (Emerson et al., 2001: 364). This voice, however, is not uniform. It contains within it the multiple voices of local people and the divergent views arising from their different roles and positions.

Diaries are similar to field notes, but are, naturally, structured by date and can be in a written format or oral (audio recorded). In written format they may include words but also photographs or diagrams. As Hall (2008) points out, there is no standard format for diaries. They can be used by the researcher to record events as well as their own personal reflections, or given to respondents to log events in their lives. For example, a diary could be given to a newly qualified teacher so they can keep a record of their feelings, critical incidents and introspective reflections on their own experience as they develop their professional practice (Bailey, 1983). Given that such diaries will be read by others (for example fellow practitioners or researchers) it is important ethically that this lack of privacy is made explicit at the start (Hall, 2008). The following case study provides an example of an ethnographic diary kept by a researcher investigating opportunities for the Irish dairy industry in Indonesia and Vietnam by undertaking visits to people's homes. Note both the diary entries and also the analytic 'insights' as well as the impact that photographs add to the piece.

— ACTIVITY 17.2 —

Examine Case Study 17.2. Imagine the diary without the presence of the photograph, then ask yourself what the photograph adds to the account. Does the use of photographs add further ethical issues to ethnographic reporting?

CASE STUDY 17.2

Example of an ethnographic diary

Wednesday March 21 – Jakarta

Home Visit 1 - Sifa Age 12

After a hair raising 45 minute journey by Ojek through the streets and side streets of Jakarta we arrive at our first home visit in the West of the city. Sifa is a 12-year-old school girl who lives with her family (Mum, Dad and two siblings). It soon becomes apparent that neither Mum and Dad are home but this is just a typical day.

Sifa comes home from school everyday around 12.30 and is the head of the household while her parents are at work. Her own day started at 5.30am with morning prayers and she was in school from 6.30am. The first thing that you notice about Sifa's home is how little furniture there is – in fact there is virtually none. In the main living room we sit on the floor with Sifa and discuss her day and what she typically eats.

Stay Slim

Surprisingly, for a girl who is so slight, Sifa reveals one of her main dietary concerns is not to put on weight! She wants to stay slim and this does influence her attitude to dairy foods. Sifa tries not to drink too much milk because "milk makes you fat".

Despite Sifa's weight concerns she does tell us one of her favourite snacks in school is Nestle's Bear Brand. A milk drink that Sifa regularly drinks to give her energy.

INSIGHT

Female teenagers in Indonesia are very weight conscious and believe milk is fattening. Female teenagers believe one of the main benefits of dairy products is that they 'fill you up' and give you energy during what are very long days.

The report in its entirety can be viewed at:
http://www.bordbia.ie/eventsnews/ConferencePresentations/2012/DairyIndustrySeminar/
Ethnographic%20Visits%20Diary%20Report%20-%20Rory%20McDonnell,%20Bord%20Bia.pdf

Figure 17.1

Source: King, H. (2012*) Indonesia and Vietnam: An Ethnographic Study Exploring the Consumer Landscape and Opportunities for the Irish Dairy Industry. Bord Bia: Dublin.*

GATHERING DATA: INTERVIEWING

Ethnographic interviewing can be distinguished from other forms of interviewing in that it encourages interviewees to shape the questions being asked and possibly even the focus of the study, resulting in data being a co-production between interviewer and interviewee (Heyl, 2001). Rubin and Rubin (2005: 4) refer to this as a conversation in which the interviewer gently guides a 'conversational partner'. The key is a concern with the meanings of actions and events to the interview subjects themselves. Kvale (1996) offers two alternative metaphors of the research interviewer: one as a *miner* and the other as a *traveller*. The miner gathers up objective data that are 'out there' ready to be discovered and culled. For the traveller, the interview is a journey from which stories will emerge, stemming from conversations the researcher will have along the way. The route may be planned ahead of time, but it will inevitably take unexpected twists and turns. What the traveller elicits in new knowledge depends on his/her ability to connect with people and to build relationships.

The origins of ethnographic interviewing go back to the Chicago School of sociology in the 1920s and the 1930s and particularly to the work of Robert Park and his call for graduate students to get out into the city and 'get the seat of your pants dirty in real research' (Bulmer, 1984: 97). What researchers need to know is what goes on behind the faces of other human beings, the personal secrets that the researcher has to discover to understand the world in which people live. The Chicago School's pioneering of informal interviews and observational techniques stood in sharp contrast to the large scale standard surveys being used by sociologists at the time (Heyl, 2001). Life history fits within this tradition because of its focus on the meanings the interviewees give to their life experiences and circumstances. The data that emerge can be analysed only by paying attention to *what* is said, *how* it is said and by showing ways in which the how and why are interrelated (Holstein and Gubrium, 1995).

Following what became known as the linguistic, postmodern turn in the 1980s and 1990s, many feminists and multicultural researchers found ethnographic

Image 17.3   Data gathering in the field

interviewing particularly attractive because they allowed for the gathering of data in relationships based upon empathy and egalitarianism (Stacey, 1988), providing opportunities to hear people's

> ideas, memories and interpretations in their own words, to hear differences among people and the meanings they construct, and to forge connection over time to the interviewees. (Heyl, 2001: 374)

Fine (1994) takes this a stage further, suggesting that researchers and informants should take time to check out what is, and is not, happening between them including whose story is being told and with what interpretation. As we will note in Case Study 17.5 however, Stacey's personal experiences have led her to call into question this equality, given the researcher's freedom to exit the world they are researching.

So, what does all this mean in practice? In conducting ethnographic interviewing Heyl (2001) recommends that the interviewer should:

ETHICS,
INTERVIEWS,
FIELD NOTES

- Listen well and respectfully, developing an ethical engagement with participants
- Acquire a self-awareness of his/her own role in the construction of meaning within the interview process
- Be aware of the ways in which both the ongoing relationship and broader social contexts affect participants, the interview process and potential outcomes
- Recognize that what emerges from the interview process is only partial knowledge

GATHERING DATA: DIGITAL MEDIA

So far we have looked at quite traditional approaches of gathering data in ethnography – observation and interviews – but, of course, we now have at our disposal advanced, technological media that are ideal for data collection and interacting with social worlds. These include media for capturing images such as digital cameras and video recorders, and include the use of smart phones since these also contain digital recording facilities. Proponents of visual-based methods argue that complex experiences cannot be captured by textual interpretations alone (Pink, 2006) and help to provide a comprehensive and enriching exploration of the social worlds of both researcher and participants (Lenette and Boddy, 2013). Ruby (2007) describes an ethnographic study of Oak Park, an upper-middle class suburb of Chicago renowned for its success in creating and maintaining diversity. Rather than produce a book, Ruby created an interactive and nonlinear work with video clips, still photographs and text, and in one case, a 30-minute video on DVD. The work was reflexive in that the subject of his research was his hometown.

DIGITAL
ETHNOGRAPHY

━━━━━━━━━━━━━━ ➤ **ON THE WEB 17.1** ◄ ━━━━━━━━━━━━━━

To see the Chicago ethnographic study go to the following link and type Oak Park in the search box.

http://www.der.org/

At the Documentary Educational Resources you will also see many other examples of ethnographic film making and recording.

However, it is not just ethnographers who make use of digital media. For example, giving participants digital cameras to take photographs of their daily working lives, Warren (2012) describes how people are able to document, through this visual medium, 'how people work here' – what is referred to as 'photo voice'. The researcher then discusses the photographs with the participant. Ethnographic research does only use digital media to record the field, digital media are themselves becoming a field of study. In other words, ethnographers have become increasingly interested in digital media such as blogs, internet forums and social media sites and the ways in which people use and interact through and within them (McKie and Ryan, 2012).

ETHICAL PRINCIPLES IN ETHNOGRAPHY

Ethnographic research faces particular challenges when it comes to conducting research ethically. As Chapter 4 sought to demonstrate, the benefits of research should outweigh the potential harm. Yet, as Murphy and Dingwall (2001) point out, one of the difficulties in ethnography is that risks are likely to be indirect and also open to interpretation. Research participants may experience anxiety, stress, damage to self-esteem and feelings of guilt or a loss of friendship when ethnographers withdraw from a study (as Case Study 17.3, below, shows). One of the most significant differences between ethnography and, say, risk in pure science, is temporal positioning. In experimental science, the risk of harm is largely concentrated in the experiment itself. In ethnography, however, the greatest risk arises at the time of publication (Murphy and Dingwall, 2001). Research participants may feel wounded or offended by published ethnographic material, often in ways that were unanticipated by the ethnographer (Ellis, 1995). Ethnography has particular problems when it comes to guaranteeing anonymity. As Murphy and Dingwall (2001) state, ethnographic studies often involve a single setting or a very small number of settings; field notes and interview transcripts invariably record sufficient detail to make participants identifiable.

While IRBs are almost without exception strict when it comes to the need for the signing of consent forms, in ethnographic studies this is not always feasible, since researchers have no control over who enters the field of observation. This is further complicated by the emergent nature of ethnographic research design where the objectives and subjects of the research may not be fully formed at the start. Fassin (2006) is critical of the role of IRBs and particularly their regulation of ethnographic research, claiming that their rules are more applicable to biomedical experiments than to social science. According to Fassin (2006), their restrictions reduce the quality of research and hence the potential of research for social utility. For example, in researching people dying of AIDS in a South African hospital, discussing the purpose of his research with someone lying on a stretcher did not seem feasible, let alone humane. Although Ellis (2007) agrees that the rules of IRBs are helpful, she is critical, arguing that their rules are grounded on the premise that research is being done on strangers. This is often not the case in ethnography. The following case study reveals a poignant story of how the publication of a researcher's book led to anger and rupture between her and the community she was reporting.

INFORMED
CONSENT: IRB

━ **CASE STUDY 17.3** ━

Challenges in ethnographic research

Carolyn Ellis relates her experiences in conducting an ethnographic study in a place she calls Fishneck, a small US community about 10 miles from the nearest town and a world she describes as one of oyster shells, fish plants, trailers, crab pots, extended families, reported violence and speech that combines a rural dialect and old English provincialisms. On many visits from 1972 up until 1986 she spent much of her time with one extended family – two parents and 13 children and their immediate families and in-laws. She was honest with them that she was a researcher, but over time this was largely forgotten by the community. As Ellis (1995: 71) comments: 'Who thought about research when there were funerals to go to, floods to escape, killings to be straightened out, sick babies to tend, welfare checks that didn't arrive on time, and doctors (always doctors) to visit?' She saw herself as a 'realist' ethnographer, seeking to describe the community 'as it was'. In doing so, she kept out of the story, especially events that might reflect badly on herself such as practices that allowed her to get a 'scoop' while pretending to maintain distance. When her book, *Fisher Folk* (1986) was published, she didn't acknowledge to the Fishneckers that there was a book coming out and gave little thought to the Fishneckers responding to it. In this she was entirely wrong.

Ellis was not the only person researching Fishneck. Another was a sociologist from a nearby college who she calls Professor Jack. Three years after its publication, she is told that Professor Jack has got hold of a copy of her book, hated it, and had read portions of it to Fishneckers who themselves were angry about its contents (and with Ellis). She decided to make a return visit, and was shocked by her reception. There are accusations that she made a million dollars from the book (in fact she made nothing), and despite using pseudonyms, people were able to identify each other. As one person comments: 'That was a lot of nonsense you wrote. I know you was writin' 'bout me'. Flicking through the book, Ellis reflected, shamefully, that she had written about underage sexual impropriety and portrayed their ignorance of contraception and their lack of literacy. Some people now refused to talk to her, regarding their friendship as over.

Ellis reflected on her return to the field and was able to make three recommendations for ethnographers:

Researchers should put more of themselves into the research, showing themselves in dialogue and tell more stories about their experiences in the community. This would counter the tendency of social researchers to privilege what they say about others over what others say about themselves.

Researchers should pay more attention to emotional responses of themselves and those they research while they are in field settings and while they write.

Researchers should take care when using grounded theory to force data into patterns that may not be there. Although the patterns that emerged had explanatory value, they presented life as lived more simply than day-to-day experiences warranted.

Ellis concludes by seeing the emerging narrative as not one of difference between researcher and her subjects, but one of connectedness between Fishneckers and herself. Indeed, having friends helped ward off feelings of being 'the lone fieldworker in a distant land' (Ellis, 2007: 9). She believes that this might help her to call on the ethics of care, empathy, personal relationships and community and to embrace personal accountability to assess her knowledge claims. The problem was not one of being a friend. It was not living up to the obligations of friendship (Ellis, 2007).

Source: Adapted from Ellis: 1995, 2007

Following reflections on her experience, to what extent would it be accurate to call Ellis a 'realist' ethnographer? What are the implications of this discussion for the ethics of ethnographic practice?

→ **TOP TIP 17.4** ←

If conducting research which has to be approved by an IRB, be aware that ethnographic research may prove a challenge in terms of getting ethical approval. Be cautious about making assurances of gaining consent and achieving reciprocity as these might prove difficult to keep.

Issues of power also come into play. Some postmodernists, for example, have rejected the researcher's right to interpret experience other than their own – hence, the growth of auto-ethnography. Auto-ethnography, however, does not escape ethical problems since it presents the actions of others from the author's perspective. Ellis (2007) also points out that when writing about oneself, we also write about others and so run the risk of these people becoming recognizable to readers. Murphy and Dingwall (2001) ask: what is the basis of the auto-ethnographer's authority to represent others, and should the permission of these others be sought? A number of practical steps are suggested that may increase the likelihood that ethnographic research will adhere to ethical codes, namely:

AUTO-
ETHNOGRAPHY

- Remove identifying information about respondents at the earliest opportunity
- Use pseudonyms for respondents (recognizing that for small scale communities or settings, these may not be effective)
- Reduce or eliminate non-relevant details about the setting and individuals (to reduce the danger of anonymity being breached)
- Consider undertaking ethnographical research in collaboration with research subjects
- Separate out the data from the researcher's interpretations so that the nature of this interpretation is open to scrutiny by others
- Consider putting more of the researcher's own presence into the research, including own emotional responses (i.e., the ethnographic self)

THE ETHNOGRAPHIC SELF

Conventional ethnography has emphasized the *other* lives that are being observed, analysed or produced (Coffey, 1999), the ethnographer serving as a biographer of others. However, the ethnographer is simultaneously involved in biographical work of their own because they are part of, and interacting with, the field setting. Hence, it is important to recognize the reflexive nature of social research, that is, we are part of the social world that we study (Allen, 1997). As Hammersley and Atkinson (2007) point out, this is not a methodological commitment – it is an existential fact. So, rather than attempting to eliminate the effects of the researcher, we should set about understanding them. Fieldwork, then, cannot be accomplished without attention to the roles of the researcher including their social roles and relationships and how the identity of the researcher is constructed and recast during the course of the fieldwork (Coffey, 1999). The self is not so much complete and rounded as partial and multiple which has implications for how the self interconnects with others in the field. In the end, the choice is probably not between immersion or not, but a recognition that the self is the product of sets of complex negotiations, influenced by social norms and expectations of others in the field.

Shaffir (1999) criticizes the formulaic accounts of field research prior to the 1970s with ethnographers subsequently starting to deviate from the stance that the researcher can adopt a value-free position. The façade, no matter how neatly construed, prevents the researcher from examining his or her own cultural assumptions and also from analysing the personal experiences that inevitably shape research processes and outcomes. Hence, researchers began to pay attention to their own social and emotional experiences including

> the anxieties and frustrations, the exhilaration and pride in achievement, as well as the disappointments and failures. Such disclosures would provide a richer and more detailed insight into the world of research. (Shaffir, 1999: 680)

Yet the degree to which the researcher places him or herself within the ethnographic 'story' is open to debate. Furthermore, while some support the value of immersion within the field, Hammersley and Atkinson (2007) sound a note of caution, arguing for the importance of intellectual distance in order for the researcher to conduct analytical work. But openness and honesty and worthy goals are not necessarily easy to achieve as Case Study 17.4 shows.

CASE STUDY 17.4

The challenges of 'getting in'

Shaffir (1999) relates how ethnographic research requires some measure of role playing and acting involving the presentation of particular images of one's self. This kind of self-presentation cannot be calculated completely in advance but often evolves during the research process. Shaffir describes his ethnographic study among a group of Hasidim Jews. He was honest in telling them that he was a sociologist and did not pretend that he wanted to become a Hasid. However, he gradually discovered that deception was nonetheless inherent in the ethnographic encounter. For example, he began to wear the black felt yarmulke (skullcap) and donned tefillin (small leather boxes containing scrolls of parchment inscribed with verses from the Torah) when attending morning prayer services. But this was not complete dissimulation because he genuinely found himself being drawn to this community, impressed by their warmth and friendliness. So he was not a completely calculating observer. He was that and more – his self-presentation being influenced by both academic and personal considerations. Yet he was always an outsider, and recognized by the community as one. It is important to recognize that there is a boundary which it is not possible (despite sometimes personal wishes) to cross. Whereas previously he thought of this barrier as reflecting his lack of research skills, he has now come to accept it.

Source: Adapted from Shaffir, 1999

Shaffir reflects on his self-identity within his chosen setting. How much of these reflections do you think should go into his ethnographic account?

FEMINIST ETHNOGRAPHY

Feminist ethnography is one of the feminist research methodologies (recall Chapter 2) and is, in fact, considered by some to be particularly appropriate to feminist research (Klein, 1983; Stanley and Wise, 1993). Feminist research is research carried out *for* women (Webb, 1993), to confront women's oppression, which can only be addressed if power differentials between researchers and the researched are broken down. What makes ethnography feminist is its explicit concern with reflexivity and the social positioning of the researcher in relation to research subjects. Reflexivity and self-examination are both important values in feminist research (Huisman, 2008; McNamara, 2009), as is the idea of reciprocity – researchers and participants are equal and both should benefit from the research. However, there are a wide range of perspectives within feminist methodology as well as tensions and divisions. As Williams (1993) warns, feminist ethnography is diverse in respect of both topic and method, indicating ontological and epistemological differences.

Another feature of feminist research, and particularly feminist ethnographic studies, is the stance of intimacy. Becoming intimate with a subject allows for the creation of an emotional connection. While the Chicago School of sociologists warned of the dangers of 'over-rapport' and recommended striking a balance between empathetic participation and complete engagement, existential ethnographers of the 1960s and early 1970s such as Goffman, argued for complete emersion to penetrate fronts (Irwin, 2006). In a seminal work, Oakley (1981) argued that remaining detached while research subjects bared their souls merely served to perpetuate inequalities between researchers and subjects. Feminist researchers began to argue for more emotional connection. However, as other feminist researchers have noted, intimacy and friendliness can be false and easily manipulated by the researcher to obtain rich data (Ellen, 1987). In an intimate study in which she dated and then married her key informant (involved in the world of professional tattooing), Irwin (2006) notes that she experienced

FEMINIST RESEARCHERS – RAPPORT ETHICS

> marginality, conflicting loyalty pulls, professional and personal angst, moments of intense pleasure and joy, as well as devastating bouts of self-doubt and failure. (Irwin, 2006: 160)

Her conclusion, however, is unequivocal – 'Becoming intimately close to setting members can do more harm than good' (Irwin, 2006: 160).

Stacey (1988), in what has become a very influential article in this field, also raises concerns. Feminist scholars have favoured ethnographic methods as ideally suited to feminist research because of their contextual, experiential approach to knowledge. It is also a method that draws on what many regard to be female strengths, namely: empathy and human concern, a commitment for social justice, and a reciprocal relationship between knower and known. According to Stacey

(1988), however, this is ironic, since, she claims, ethnographic methods subject research subjects to greater risks of exploitation, betrayal and abandonment by the researcher than, say, positivist research methods. Fieldwork constitutes an intervention into a system of relationships that the researcher is far freer than the researched to leave. Case Study 17.5 takes up this theme in more detail.

CASE STUDY 17.5

'Getting close' – a cautionary tale

Huisman notes the contribution of Stacey (1988) in challenging the assumptions about feminist ethnography and pointing out that qualitative research methods do not necessarily mitigate the dangers of exploitation in research. In a study conducted with Bosnian Muslim refugees, Huisman (2008) outlines three tensions she experienced and addresses how these tensions were related to her shifting and sometimes contradictory position as a woman, a researcher, a friend, a graduate student, and as a person who was straddled between two social classes.

   The ethnographic case study was conducted involving participant observation and in-depth interviews with 30 refugees from seven Bosnian Muslim families (14 women, 10 men and 6 children) who had lived between 2 and 6 years in the United States. Thirteen interviews were also conducted with social services providers, community leaders and community members who worked directly with the Bosnian families. Huisman, who was completing her doctorate, spent a year in the field (1999–2000) before conducting any interviews. The second phase (2000–2002) involved intensive observations (in the homes of participants), in-depth interviews, community involvement and informal conversations.

   Trusting relationships were established with key people within the Bosnian Muslim community, through whom other participants were recruited through a snowball sampling process (recall Chapter 9). Huisman felt it was important to spend a lot of time with participants to increase her own understanding of Bosnian culture and to avoid power imbalances stemming from her own culture. She conducted observations of participants in their homes and at social events, observing everyday interactions, conflicts, decision making processes and gender displays. But from day one, conducting this research was a struggle. On the one hand she wanted to complete her doctorate. On the other hand she felt a need to move slowly in order to develop trust and empathy with participants. Her rising feeling of contradictory positionalities was exacerbated by a growing closeness to the women in the study who began to view Huisman as a friend. But to the researcher the relationships felt asymmetrical (in terms of power relations) and inauthentic, knowing that she would eventually leave this community behind, an act that might be seen as a betrayal (the 'getting out' problem discussed above). The situation came to a head when, at the end of a two hour meeting, a participant who she had visited almost every Thursday for a year said: 'Does this mean that you are not going to visit me anymore?', resulting in the researcher's feelings of guilt, empathy and frustration.

   Huisman (2008) comments reflexively that she became too involved in the daily lives of the Bosnian women. In a later research study, she shows how this reflexivity has revealed to her a new strategy that can avoid, or at least minimize, some of the problems arising in the Bosnian study. She undertook the new project with a team of researchers, so there was less intensity between herself and the study participants. The team was also multidisciplinary, bringing broader perspectives, theories and methodologies into the project. As a result, even after three years she has not run into the kinds of ethical problems she faced in the Bosnian study.

Source: Adapted from Huisman, 2008

In Case Study 17.5, explore how the feminist positions of reflexivity and reciprocity are analysed by the researcher. What important lessons emerge for conducting ethnographic research?

CRITICAL ETHNOGRAPHY

Ethnography has a unique capability for getting close up to sites of exploitation and oppression and hence offers the ethnographic researcher a unique opportunity for constructing emancipatory practices (Lather, 1986), probably one reason why it has been embraced by feminism (Jordan and Yeomans, 1995). However, this has not always been its role. Said (1989) argues that modern anthropology retains a theoretical perspective and conceptual framework that has been shaped by colonialism and imperialist domination. Social anthropology and colonialism were contemporaneous because colonial power made the subjects of anthropological study accessible. But the relationship was deeper than this. According to Asad (1973) anthropology was defined by its willingness to adapt to colonial ideology. The British state, for example, embraced anthropology because it allowed for the collection of information and data on its subject territories. In the words of Kabbani (1986: 62) it was 'the colonial cataloguing of goods; the anchoring of imperial possessions into discourse'.

Bourgois and Schonberg (2009: 17) criticize the use of ethnography in fieldwork, objecting to the ways in which ethnography tends to focus on intricate details, while sometimes overlooking the 'implications of structures of power and of historical context' because these are not immediately recognizable in the everyday. Ethnography, then, has to ask how power is exercised in concrete human relations (Denzin, 1999). Conventional ethnography tends to grasp only the phenomenon of everyday life without apprehending the causal processes and generative mechanisms that drive them. Symbolic interactionism and ethnomethodology, for example, have helped to create a methodological individualism and an atomistic viewpoint (Jordan and Yeomans, 1995) and so apprehend only surface appearances instead of locating ethnographic research within a broader political economy and power relations.

For Denzin (1999) ethnography should articulate identifiable cultural and political issues including injustices based upon race, class, gender and sexual orientation. 'It should criticize how things are and imagine how they could be different' (Denzin, 1999: 513). Smith (1987) seeks to do this through what she calls institutional ethnography, where inquiry begins with the work organization within which

CRITICAL ETHNOGRAPHY

people are embedded. Jordan and Yeomans (1995) argue, however, that critical ethnography has been more successful in addressing academic audiences than those it purports to engage with for social change. To achieve a more emancipatory ethnography, Jordan and Yeomans (1997) recommend drawing on the process of action research (as discussed in Chapter 13). What action research offers is the redefinition of the relationship between the researcher and the researched. In action research, the role of the professional researcher is severely circumscribed, hence avoiding the privileging of the ethnographer. Action research is also a comfortable partner to ethnography because it is a form of research conducted by practitioners to improve rationality and social justice (Kemmis, 1993). The following case study explores some of the political and ethical problems faced by a critical management research study, conducted through ethnography.

CASE STUDY 17.6

The challenges of abiding by ethical codes

One of the issues facing many ethnographic researchers is that of access, especially to organizations where gatekeepers may be suspicious and concerned that organizational practices will become exposed to public scrutiny. Furthermore, they may not see any benefits from becoming involved in long-term, in-depth research given the demands this makes on organizational time. Access is particularly difficult for researchers who follow a critical perspective. Alcadipani and Hodgson (2009) relate a study during which one of the authors, a proponent of critical management studies (CMS), faced a range of severe ethical dilemmas.

The main research aim was to conduct a critical ethnographic study exploring organizational change on individuals working in an industry in decline, the newspaper industry. Negotiations for access started with three distinct but interconnected organizations: RedPaper, FailCo and OneCo. RedPaper is a regional newspaper that was moving production from one printing site (FailCo) to another (OneCo) at a cost of £45m. After sending a proposal to the managing director (MD) of RedPaper, it was four months before the researcher received a reply giving the go ahead but at a meeting the MD stated: 'You can only do interviews. You will need to send all questions you will ask people in advance. I will select the questions you can ask and the people you can speak to'. The researcher replied he could not accept this due to methodological and ethical constraints. Finally, it was agreed that the researcher would shift the focus of the research to the printing sites.

A new proposal was submitted covering FailCo and OneCo. However, the print director (PD) of RedPaper commented that access to FailCo would be difficult due to poor relations between the companies. He added: 'they might think you are spying for us'. He also commented: 'You will be my eyes and ears in this project – you will be our man on the ground'. The researcher was extremely unhappy with these remarks but decided to keep quiet. The RedPaper MD made it clear to those at OneCo that they would collaborate with the researcher. As the researcher comments, as a CMS-orientated researcher, it felt uncomfortable taking advantage of hierarchical structures of control, the self-same structures that critical management studies sought to critique.

The fieldwork itself was no less problematic. A customary response to requests for consent was: 'F*ck off mate, you always ask this sh*t. Of course I agree pal'. People answered questions but there were doubts as to whether this was a free choice. In the field the researcher routinely witnessed instances of sabotage, bullying and racism towards Asian workers and managers. An HR manager asked for information about this, but the researcher chose not to divulge any information on the grounds that it would breach the ethical guidelines underpinning the research. But as the researcher comments: 'This was a paradoxical situation because to protect some people from harm I keep silent about people's attitudes and actions that were clearly harming others'. Ironically, despite feelings of guilt, adherence to the ethical guidelines allowed the researcher to keep the research going – despite his *critical* research commitments. The researcher concludes that during fieldwork, researchers face situations that are beyond what ethical guidelines would predict. As a result he faced a constant tension between adherence to ethics, his desire to keep the research going, his commitment to critical management studies, and his conscience.

Source: Adapted from Alcadipani and Hodgson, 2009

In Case Study 17.6, as a *critical* management studies researcher, what steps, if any, could the researcher have adopted, that were different to the ones actually taken? What would have been the consequences?

SCULPTING THE TRUTH IN ETHNOGRAPHIC ACCOUNTS

Ethnographic studies can provide nuanced, comprehensive reports on a particular problem or set of problems, but the results of ethnographic research are often regarded as lacking in validity, reliability and generalizability (LeCompte and Goetz, 1982). Taking reliability, ethnography deals with natural settings where the idiosyncrasy of themes may be difficult to replicate elsewhere. However, because human behaviour is never static this is a problem faced by all research methods. LeCompte and Goetz (1982) advise that, while settings cannot be replicated, ethnographers should work instead to generate, refine and validate the constructs they are seeking to study. If this is done well, then other researchers can work to replicate these constructs in other settings. But the ethnographer's findings are influenced by the investigator's social role within the research site; other researchers can only attain comparable findings if they develop a corresponding social position or have partners who can do so (LeCompte and Goetz, 1982). Internal reliability is aided by the use of multiple researchers in the field and by peer examination of ethnographic accounts. The latter requires that the researcher provides sufficient primary data in the account so that others can gauge the correspondence between data and interpretation (Wolcott, 1994).

In principle, one of the strengths of ethnography is the high internal validity derived from long periods in the field, continual data analysis and the refining of categories to match these categories to reality. Secondly, interview instruments are closely informed by the language and 'natural' categories used by participants, while observation is conducted in natural settings that reflect the reality of the subjects' everyday experiences. However, given the intimate nature of most ethnographic research and the rapport built between researcher and subjects, researcher bias can seriously skew the results (Schneider, 2006b). This is one reason why reflexivity is used to make the researcher's views (biased or otherwise) as transparent as possible. The credibility of informant reports in interviewing must also be scrutinized. Since respondents may lie, exaggerate or omit data, the researcher may wish to elicit independent corroboration from multiple informants (LeCompte and Goetz, 1982).

Short and Hughes (2009) argue that the social sciences have made considerable progress in improving the reliability of data through developing more sophisticated protocols and instruments, triangulating data sources, and sampling targeted populations. However, validity remains a problem because studies of 'moving targets of social life' such as families, peer groups, neighbourhoods and institutions can never fully capture their reality (Short and Hughes, 2009: 398). The best that we can do is take snapshots. Short and Hughes argue that ethnographic methods are often necessary to determine how conclusions based on quantitative data translate to the everyday life of groups and individuals. Taking the example of a quantitative study on the violence of street gangs, Short and Hughes (2009) posit that what this achieves is uncontextualized self-reports of individual behaviour. In contrast, their ethnographic study (eliciting 17,000 pages of narrative data) looked at respondents in situations and relational processes and interactions in which violent behaviour both occurred or was avoided. As well as violence, the study also observed gang members finding 'ways out' of behaving violently, fieldwork thus showing how and perhaps why differences occur in ways that quantitative data do not.

An example of how an ethnographer strove to increase the validity of his research is provided by one of the originators of ethnography, Malinowski himself. Roldan (2002) describes how Malinowski used three analytical procedures to improve the validity of his research: triangulation or comparison of distinct data sources (using several informants) and different methods (interviews and observations); a constant validity check by looking for both consistencies and inconsistencies in the data and the seeking of alternative descriptions and explanations; and analytic induction or the acknowledgement of negative evidence. In the text he also introduced cases as descriptions of typical or a-typical beliefs. Above all, he was meticulous in reading his text, checking, coding, indexing, sorting, rearranging and merging information from his field notes in order to produce his analysis. He was also careful to check informants' reports against more objective evidence such as observations wherever possible.

External validity (generalizability) is always going to be a challenge for ethnographic research (even assuming the researcher sees this as worthy of effort), because ethnography examines a particular setting within its historical and present-day context. However, as Schneider (2006a) points out, by using the same general methods and examining the same kind of organizations, studies can achieve a certain level of replicability. Comparing and contrasting such studies might reveal nuanced differences but also patterns that repeat across contexts.

Image 17.4   A street gang – one of the 'moving targets of social life'

While this may seem similar to replication across case studies, it is different because ethnographic research involves long-term engagement in the field. LeCompte and Goetz (1982) agree, arguing that the key of achieving external validity is the identification and description of those characteristics of a phenomenon that are salient for comparison with other, similar types.

RECORDING THE MIRACLE

The ethnographic report (the ethnography) attempts to be as holistic and encompassing as possible, the success or failure of the report depending on the degree to which it rings true for participants in the field (Fetterman, 2010). A written report is the most common type of ethnography output, but a wide variety of other media are also possible, including charts, diagrams, photographs and various audio and visual digital media including websites. Whatever media are used, producing the account can be a daunting experience, trying to translate a vivid world of noises, sights, smells and a world of embodied people where the visual is imported into an oral, written medium (Rock, 2001). The danger is that the analysis can become too much like storytelling in which the imagination is allowed to dominate and where fragments, simplifications and gaps can be glossed over in an attempt to give coherence to the data (Rock, 2001).

➤ **ON THE WEB 17.2** ◄

For an example of how an ethnographic report combines text with both historic and contemporary photographs to describe the culture of US Everglades 'Gladesmen' see:

http://www.evergladesplan.org/pm/progr_master_rec_plan_gladesmen.aspx#report

In the report, note the use of both maps and photographs.

A fundamental question is whether the self remains invisible in the writing of the ethnographic account, becomes part of the account, or is the entire subject of the account (auto-ethnography). Certainly, feminist ethnography places importance on the emotional dimension of research and the crafting of self-conscious, self-revelatory and confessional accounts. As Coffey (1999) points out, these confessional or biographical stories can be presented as parallel but separate texts, or can be woven into the account itself. Although some see this as somehow polluting the narrative, Atkinson (1990) argues that this mingling of text creates greater authenticity and presents multiple voices.

Adopting a first-person position limits the perspective to what the ethnographer witnessed, experienced or knows. However, the first-person stance locates the ethnographer firmly within the group or community he or she is studying (Emerson et al., 2001). In contrast, a third-person account where the ethnographer is invisible from the account achieves a tone of detachment, distance and objectivity. However, the danger here is that the ethnographer can easily slip into an omniscient viewpoint, privileging the ethnographer's account above all others. Different approaches and examples based in a hospital setting on a study of providing patients with 'bad news' about their medical condition is presented in Table 17.1.

NARRATIVE
ETHNOGRAPHIC
RESEARCH

Table 17.1   Positioning the presence of the researcher

Positioning	Illustrative text
Invisible	The doctor was observed to enter the room, looking serious. He asked the child's mother to take a seat and waited until she had made herself comfortable.
Present but separate	The nurse said, 'I'm sorry but there is no easy way of telling you this'. Then she paused. I felt myself part of a highly charged situation and felt uncomfortable.
The text itself (auto-biographical)	For me, giving bad news to patients was always the toughest but still a very necessary part of the job. I suppose it's something you just get used to.

Summary

- Ethnography is a qualitative research method that seeks to understand cultural phenomena that reflect the knowledge and meanings that guide the life of cultural groups within their own environment.
- The origins of ethnography lie in anthropology and later sociology but today can be found in a wide range of disciplines including communication studies, history and cultural studies.
- Doing fieldwork involves deciding on what field or context in which to conduct the research, getting access and gaining acceptance within the field, conducting the fieldwork itself and leaving the field (getting out) in as ethical and acceptable a way as possible.
- Data gathering involves participant observation, interviews and also the use of documents and other unobtrusive measures.
- Conducting ethically principled research is a particular challenge for ethnographers, given their often long-term engagement in the field and the development of close relationships and friendships with those that they observe.
- Ethnography demands that not only do researchers immerse themselves in the field, but they also act reflexively when collecting data; the ethnographer's interactions with others in the field become part of the data.
- The ethnographic report (the ethnography) attempts to be as holistic and encompassing as possible. The success or failure or the report depends on the degree to which it rings true for participants in the field.
- In the ethnographic account, the researcher's positionality can be invisible, present but separate in the text, fully integrated into the account, or the account itself.

REVIEW QUESTIONS

1. Why is reflexivity a key component of ethnographic research? How does the researcher become reflexive?
2. What are the advantages and disadvantages of a feminist anthropology in the construction of ethnographic knowledge?
3. Establishing rapport within the field setting can be a double-edged weapon. Why do you think that this is a particular challenge in ethnography?
4. Why is it so challenging to undertake ethical ethnographic research? What steps would *you* take to make your ethnographic research ethical?
5. Should ethnographic studies pay attention to issues of validity and reliability? If not, what should they pay attention to?
6. Positionality is important in ethnographic research. To what extent should the presence of the researcher be part of the ethnographic account?

FURTHER READING

Pink, S. (2013) *Doing Visual Ethnography*, 3rd edn. London: Sage. Explores the potential of photography, video and hypermedia in ethnography and social research. Provides a reflexive approach to practical, theoretical and methodological issues.

Madden, R. (2010) *Being Ethnographic*. London: Sage. A clear and useful book that draws heavily on the author's own experience of undertaking ethnographic research.

Fetterman, D.M. (2010) *Ethnography: Step-by-Step*, 3rd edn. Thousand Oaks, CA: Sage. Apart from guiding the reader in the essentials of collecting, maintaining and interpreting data, this book also takes on the theme of technology and ethnography.

Hammersley, M. and Atkinson, P. (2007) *Ethnography: Principles in Practice*, 3rd edn. London: Routledge. This classic account of ethnography presents examples from ethnographic research, with the aim of linking theory and practice. Offers guidance on gaining access to the field, interviewing, recording and analysing data and the role of ethics.

Atkinson, P.A., Delamont, S., Coffey, A.J., Lofland, J. and Lofland, L.H. (eds) (2007) *A Handbook of Ethnography*. London: Sage. A book that presents previously published articles on a wide range of issues including symbolic interactionism and ethnography, grounded theory and ethnography, ethnographic interviewing and ethics in ethnography.

Taylor, S. (2002) *Ethnographic Research – A Reader*. London: Sage. Presents ten articles that introduce students to a broad range of ethnographic research studies in the social sciences.

Coffey, A. (1999) *The Ethnographic Self: Fieldwork and the Representation of Identity*. London: Sage. In this much referenced text, the author explores the relationship between the self and ethnographic fieldwork, particularly focusing on the personal, emotional and identity issues that emerge in undertaking prolonged fieldwork.

JOURNAL RESOURCES

Evans, G. (2012) 'Practising participant observation: An anthropologist's account', *Journal of Organizational Ethnography*, 1(1): 96–106. Provides an anthropological viewpoint on the debate about the uses and abuses of the method of ethnography in the field of commercially motivated research.

Gallant, M. (2008) 'Using an ethnographic case study approach to identify socio-cultural discourse: A feminist post-structural view', *Education, Business and Society: Contemporary Middle Eastern Issues*, 1(4): 244–254. Uses a case study, ethnographic approach to identify dominant socio-cultural discourse using a feminist post-structural lens.

Vinten, G. (1994) 'Participant observation: A model for organizational investigation?', *Journal of Managerial Psychology*, 9(2): 30–38. Addresses and refutes some of the critiques of participant observation.

18

FOCUS GROUPS

CHAPTER INTRODUCTION

Chapter outline

The uses and benefits of focus groups	469
The limitations of focus groups	471
Organizing focus groups – an overview	472
Focus groups and research design	485
Special issues in focus group research	488
Epistemological considerations and focus groups	490
Ethical considerations and focus groups	494

Keywords

Focus groups

Sampling

Research design

Moderation

Ethics

--- Chapter objectives ---

After reading this chapter you will be able to:

- Describe the origins and purpose of focus groups.
- Identify situations in which the use of focus groups is appropriate.
- Plan a focus group including selecting participants.
- Develop appropriate questions for a focus group.
- Facilitate the running of a focus group, taking into account epistemological and ethical principles.
- Plan approaches to data analysis.

UNDERSTANDING
NATURALISTIC
OBSERVATION

A focus group is essentially an organized discussion among a selected group of individuals with the aim of eliciting information about their views. The purpose is to gain a range of perspectives about subjects and situations. While similar to group interviewing they are not the same. In group interviews, a number of people are interviewed at the same time. In focus groups, however, the purpose is to generate interactions and discussions within the group. Indeed, through the provision of a 'safe' environment, focus groups aim to promote self-disclosure among participants, through generating group dynamics within discussions (Freeman, 2006). In the realm of qualitative research, focus groups lie somewhere between naturalistic observation and individual interviews (Seal, Bogart and Ehrhardt, 1998).

MARKET
RESEARCH
EXAMPLE

Focus groups were first developed in the 1940s by Robert Merton at the Bureau of Applied Social Research in the USA, an organization dedicated to mass communication research. After that, academics rather lost interest, but focus groups were taken up with enthusiasm by the practitioner, market research community in the 1950s. In the 1980s they were rediscovered by the academic community (Krueger and Casey, 2009) since when they have been an essential part of qualitative social research, exploring people's opinions, beliefs and perceptions about products, services, ideas and concepts (Freeman, 2006). They are used in many different fields, including:

- Marketing research where corporations are interested in the views of consumers about their products or services, as well as their perceptions about price, retail environments and their reactions to advertising
- Academics including sociologists, psychologists, and health, education, management and organizational behaviour researchers
- Political scientists and governments who want to gauge public opinion to proposed new policies
- Marginalized groups or people with inadequate literacy or language in the dominant culture that limits the use of more traditional research methods such as interviews

Today, focus groups are no less popular with marketing specialists. For example, some multinational corporations have specialist facilities dedicated to testing products with consumers. Products are arranged in dedicated rooms and the eye movements of focus group participants are measured (they wear special spectacles) as they enter the room to see which products attract their attention. Focus group meetings follow at which their choices, and the reasons for them, are discussed. The

Image 18.1
A focus group in action

name of the organization is not revealed, so that participants' responses are not influenced. These specialist facilities are usually located in towns or cities in which the demographics are ideal – a mix of income groups and ethnicities so that heterogeneous samples can be picked. As we will see in this chapter, the choice of samples is often an important theme in focus groups.

THE USES AND BENEFITS OF FOCUS GROUPS

One of the most beneficial features of focus groups is their 'robust versatility for shedding light on almost any topic or issue' (Stewart et al., 2007: 42). Compared to large scale surveys, for example, they can be assembled relatively quickly and cheaply and provide data which researchers can begin analysing almost immediately the focus group session is finished. They also provide opportunities for the clarification of responses, for posing additional probing questions and for the observation of non-verbal responses such as gestures, smiles and frowns (Stewart et al., 2007). Unlike research methods such as interviews, focus groups allow for the synergistic building up of data as respondents add to the views expressed by others. Indeed, a research study by Seal et al. (1998) suggested that interviews may be better used to identify the range and depth of individual values and beliefs, but group settings may be better at generating discussion around shared and unshared attitudes and experiences.

FOCUS GROUPS: FOCUS INTERVIEWS

Focus groups can be used at the exploratory stage of a study (Krueger, 1988), for example, when the themes or boundaries of a subject are unknown or unclear, and when the key constructs for investigation need to be identified. For example, a local education authority wants to develop a greater understanding of why pupil absentee levels in its area have risen steeply over the last five years. Before it conducts a survey through a questionnaire, it needs to ascertain the main themes and issues the survey instrument is going to address. A focus group made up of parents, and another of pupils, might begin to identify a range of valid themes. Focus groups, then, are a useful starting point for exploring respondents' views about objects and events, allowing for the subsequent design of closed-end survey items. This combination of focus groups followed by a survey, is of course, an example of mixed methods research discussed in Chapter 8. Focus groups can also be used at the confirmatory stage of research. For example, when marketing research has yielded inconclusive results about a product, focus groups can tease out more subtle sources of a product's appeal or lack of it. While Basch (1987) suggests that focus groups are not useful for traditional hypothesis testing, Stewart et al. (2007) argue that it is common for focus groups to be used for the purpose of developing hypotheses that may be later tested quantitatively.

Focus groups allow researchers to explore the feelings, attitudes, beliefs, prejudices, reactions and experiences of a subject, in a way that would not be so accessible through other approaches such as observation, interview or survey. Sometimes these views might be held individually and be independent of a social setting, but often they will emerge from social interactions with other individuals and groups. For Morgan and Krueger (1993), focus groups can be particularly effective when there are issues of power within the group, when the culture of a group is of interest, and when researchers want to explore the degree of consensus around a subject. Indeed, Kitzinger (1995) points out that focus groups are particularly useful when researching cross-cultural issues and ethnic minorities because the technique is sensitive to detecting cultural variables. However, as Winslow, Honein and Elzubeir (2002) warn, what is assumed to work in, say, Western societies may not transfer across other cultures.

Focus groups can achieve what Lindlof and Taylor (2002) call a chain or cascade effect, where listening to other people's memories and experiences, triggers ideas in other participants. This is particularly the case where participants realize that they share a common experience, and feel that their views are validated and supported by others. So, for example, children who have been the victims of abuse might be more willing to talk about their experiences in front of others who have shared a similar traumatic experience. Above all, focus groups help to clarify similarities and differences between the opinions and values held by participants (Freeman, 2006). According to Kitzinger (1994, 1995), focus groups can:

- Facilitate the collection of data on group norms
- Encourage a greater variety of communication between participants
- Provide insight into the operation of group/social processes in the articulation of knowledge
- Encourage open conversations about sensitive subjects that might be left less developed through a one-to-one interview
- Use conflict between participants to clarify *why* they believe what they do
- Explore turning points in arguments when people change their minds and document how facts and stories operate in practice
- Encourage participation from people who do not want to be interviewed on their own
- Facilitate discussions on sensitive or taboo subjects such as bereavement or sexual violence
- Help to empower and motivate participants as part of an action research project

However, some commentators also note some of the limitations of focus groups, or advocate their use with caution.

THE LIMITATIONS OF FOCUS GROUPS

One of the limitations of focus groups is that moderators have less control or influence over processes and outcomes, than if, say, the data were being collected through an interview (Morgan, 1997). The conversations, discussions and even arguments can take on a flow and life of their own. However, if the moderator were to step in to redirect the flow of dialogue, this would defeat the point of the exercise. But this means that some focus group members may come to dominate the discussions, whilst others may say little or nothing unless prompted. As Kitzinger (1994) points out, one of the downsides of group dynamics is that the group may censor deviations from group norms or standards. For example, in her description of focus groups studying the effect of media messages about AIDS (see Case Study 18.3), if someone knew too much about how HIV is transmitted, they were met with suspicion and cries of 'How come you know so much about this?'

Locating and persuading respondents to take part may also be a challenge. An interview, particularly if it is structured, may take only a few minutes to complete. A focus group session, however, might take up at least an hour, or often longer. It may be necessary, therefore, to offer some kind of incentive such as gift vouchers, a prize draw or similar inducement. As Kitzinger (1995) also points out, focus groups are not appropriate when it is essential to maintain confidentiality, since, by design, views are expressed in a group environment.

As discussed in 'Epistemological considerations and focus groups', below, one of the drawbacks of focus groups is that they are often composed of convenience samples, hence limiting the generalizability of the results. Indeed, as Stewart et al. (2007) caution, people who are willing to travel to a focus group location and give up one or two hours of their time, may be quite different to the population under discussion, at least on dimensions such as compliance and deference. Furthermore, the responses of members of the group are not independent of each other, which further limits the generalizability of the results.

There may be further difficulties at the analysis stage. The discursive nature of the data often means that summarization and interpretation of the results can be challenging. The results may also have been contaminated by the moderator providing cues as to what kinds of answers are desirable, certainly a danger if the moderator is inexperienced. Table 18.1 provides a summary of the strengths and weaknesses of using focus groups.

Table 18.1   Summary of strengths and weaknesses of the focus group approach

Strengths	Weaknesses
Affords the opportunity to identify collective perspectives	Potential for breach of confidentiality
Discussion in the group allows for validation of ideas and concepts	Conflicts may arise in the group that are difficult to manage
Allows access to culturally and linguistically diverse groups	Success is dependent on the skills and experience of the moderator
Allows access to a wide range of participants	Complexity of monitoring verbal and nonverbal responses of participants
Can become a catalyst for change both during and after the focus group	

Source: Adapted from Halcomb et al., 2007

PLANNING &
DESIGNING
FOCUS GROUPS

ORGANIZING FOCUS GROUPS – AN OVERVIEW

Figure 18.1 outlines the steps required in planning and organizing a focus group, each of which is discussed in more detail below.

Identify problem/formulate research question

Focus groups are not just an open discussion. They do, as their name implies, have a focus, hence they must have an agenda and seek answers to a specified problem. Defining a problem allows for the generation of a clear statement about the kinds of information needed and what kinds of research methods are most appropriate. For example, a problem that requires the measurement of the effectiveness of a new anti- flu medicine is best answered by an experimental design, not a focus group. However, a problem that involves whether motorists understand and empathize with a new anti-drinking and driving television campaign could be addressed through focus group research. Specifying the research problem in turn helps in the development of research questions and subsequently the writing of questions to be posed in the focus group itself.

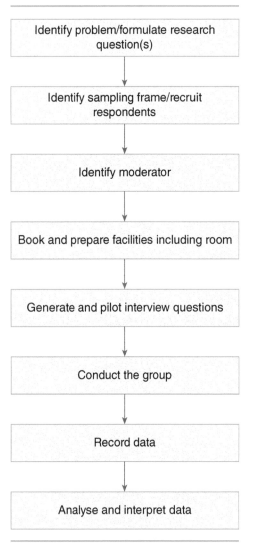

Figure 18.1 Steps in the design and running of a focus group

Source: Adapted from Stewart et al., 2007

Identify sampling frame/ recruit participants

As we saw in Chapter 9, a sampling frame is the operational definition of the population. While it is important to have a sound sampling frame in large scale research such as surveys, this is less important for focus groups because it is less easy to generalize beyond the focus group to the population. Hence, the sampling frame needs to be only a good approximation to the population of interest (Stewart et al., 2007). So, if the research was concerned with gauging the views of owners of small and medium sized enterprises (SMEs), using membership lists of local Chambers of Commerce would suffice. However, in doing this, you need to consider and acknowledge that membership organizations like Chambers of Commerce may represent a disproportionate number of certain types or sizes of organization, so the sample may not be truly representative.

The diversity, or otherwise, of a group may be difficult to plan. A highly diverse group, say in terms of social class, status or seniority (for example, fans from the same football club), might reveal a wide range of viewpoints, but only if participants are sufficiently relaxed and confident to speak in each other's presence. Conversely, a highly heterogeneous group (for example, all members of the same professional association) might bond well and elicit contributions from all members – but responses might be bland and somewhat repetitive. Morgan (1988) suggests that focus group members prefer to meet with those who they consider have similar characteristics and levels of knowledge to themselves. Groups should also be homogenous in terms of culture and language (Strickland, 1999) while Halcomb, Gholizadeh, DiGiacomo, Phillips and Davidson (2007) argue that consideration should also be given to gender and age. In some non-Western cultures, it is considered impolite for younger people to proffer opinions that are different to those of older members of the group. The diversity or homogeneity of focus groups may partly be determined by the epistemological stance of the researcher – see 'Epistemological considerations and focus groups', below.

WORKING
IN OTHER
CULTURES

From a practical perspective, Kahan (2001) suggests that homogeneity helps focus groups generate interactions, so *multiple* homogenous groups can be used, each group selected to represent different kinds of stakeholder or status level. Similarly, Krueger and Casey (2009) argue for the use of three or four focus groups with each type of participant so that patterns and themes can be identified and data saturation achieved (see Chapter 23). When recruiting for focus groups where the views of a wider community are needed, Kahan (2001) suggests that some people are, by the nature of their job, well-informed about community opinions. These people include: village council members, teachers, ministers, high school students, elected officeholders, and family doctors.

Recruiting participants to a focus group takes more organizing than most other forms of data gathering method, partly because a group of people must be identified and invited. MacIntosh (1981) recommends that the ideal size for this group should be between six and eight participants, with the session lasting between one and two hours, while Krueger (1994) recommends between six and 12 members. The first step in recruiting to a focus group is screening for eligibility, often on factors such as demographics: age, gender, occupation, community role, etc. When the research requires different kinds of focus group, this screening is essential. Having identified participants, they can be contacted by letter, email or personally. This communication will set out the overall purpose of the research and make clear that a focus group discussion is involved. The importance of the individual's participation should be noted, as should any reward structure such as payment if any is provided. The date, start and end times of the focus group should be given, with the time of arrival normally 20–30 minutes prior to the start. On a practical note, Stewart et al. (2007) suggest recruiting slightly more people than needed in case some participants drop out. Indeed, some researchers have reported that up to 20 per cent of participants fail to attend (Beaudin and Pelletier, 1996). Having invited participants, it is also prudent to follow this up with a telephone call or email the day before the focus group meeting to reduce the likelihood of 'no shows'.

FOCUS GROUP
INVITATION

─────────────────────── ➤ **TOP TIP 18.1** ◄───────────────────────

Avoid using large groups of participants. Generally, a group size of about six is ideal. Larger numbers make the group dynamics harder to manage and may divert you from the purpose of the exercise, eliciting data for analysis.

Identify moderator and others

Moderators must be appointed who fit the needs of the group taking part in the focus group (Krueger and Casey, 2009). So, for example, a moderator skilled in and empathetic to working with children with special needs might not be suited to running a focus group for web designers. But whatever the subject under discussion, the moderator should be an experienced facilitator, not necessarily a subject matter expert (Langer, 2001). When working with a group from a particular ethnic group or culture, Halcomb et al. (2007) suggest that the moderator is ethnically similar to this group, a perceived similarity that might assist in reducing communication barriers. But whatever their 'fit' with participants, all moderators should understand, and be able to work with, unfolding group dynamics, and be able to 'orchestrate' the workings of the group. This might mean encouraging quieter members to speak, calming down more vociferous members who like to dominate discussions, and ensuring that the group keeps on task (see Table 18.2 below).

─────────────────────── ➤ **ON THE WEB 18.1** ◄───────────────────────

Take a look at bad focus group moderation in action at:

http://www.youtube.com/watch?v=0sSZTWp21Fk

The question of structure is also important. Moderators will need to concentrate on structure and direction when seeking to control dominant group members, but will probably flex into a more unstructured style once the group has developed its own dynamics. Neveril (2004) and Hunter, Bailey and Taylor (1994) offer between them a range of approaches that a moderator should use:

COMMON
MODERATOR
MISTAKES

- Make a good first impression. Establish the tone by making eye contact, smiling etc.
- Be clear about intensions and expectations. Introduce self. Welcome the participants. State clearly what the focus group is about and establish ground rules (see Table 18.2). Explain what will come out of it (e.g. a report or article). Do *not* ask if there are any questions at this point as this may lead to a long discussion that delays the start
- Create a comfortable atmosphere for participants. Ensure temperature is at the right level, seats comfortable, lighting acceptable
- Be awake – listen, look, sense what is happening in the room
- Be your natural self – avoid being over formal
- Use clear language
- Request personal stories
- Use self-disclose to encourage self-disclosure of participants
- Be comfortable with silences
- Bring to the fore patterns (consistencies and inconsistencies)
- Be culturally sensitive
- Have fun

Table 18.2   Ground rules established by the moderator

Ground rule	Comment
Ask for permission to use video or digital recording equipment	Get acceptance and 'buy in'. If anyone objects they are free to leave.
Ask people to speak up	Mumbling will not help quality of video or audio recordings or group interactions
Address each other, not the moderator	Emphasize that this is a discussion and not an interview
Listen while others are speaking	Establish respect for others' contributions
Take it in turns to speak	Again, a sign of respect but also necessary to help quality of video or audio recordings
Make the timings clear, especially when the session will finish – and keep to it	Sessions that overrun the designated time can seriously upset participants

Image 18.2   Facilitator using a flipchart to elicit discussion

---

→ **TOP TIP 18.2** ←

Keeping discussions 'on topic' can sometimes be quite a challenge, even for experienced moderators. The use of a flipchart can help here. The list of topics introduced at the beginning of the session can be noted on the flipchart, so everyone can see the agenda. New themes that emerge during the discussion can also be added as the group progresses. However, do use flipcharts sparingly and spend a minimum of time standing in front of them so as not to appear to dominate the group.

STAYING
ON TOPIC

In addition to a moderator, Kahan (2001) also suggests the use of a rapporteur whose job it is to take notes (subject to the approval of the participants) especially in circumstances where the sensitivity of the discussion makes video or audio recording unethical or unfeasible. The rapporteur should use a laptop or tablet to take notes – including notes on non-verbal communication and participant interactions (Halcomb et al., 2007). When the topic is highly technical, for example the siting of a nuclear power station, then a subject matter expert might be used to provide detailed information to group participants. Generally, those who commission the research should be discouraged from attending as they have too much of a vested interest in the results and merely add to the number of observers. Once the session has ended, the moderator and rapporteur should get together and discuss the quality of the field notes (see 'Record data', below). Napolitano, McCauley, Beltran and Philips (2002) also suggest the use of an assistant moderator whose role it is to take notes not on the verbal discourse but to observe and record group dynamics. Stewart et al. (2007) call this role an observer who must sit away from the main group so they are seen to be independent of the group. They should be introduced by name only as more detail might reveal too much about the purpose of the research and bias responses.

Book and prepare facilities including room

Location is important, with a 'neutral' venue being preferable to avoid participants having a particular response to a building or setting (Powell and Single, 1996). For example, a research project seeking to investigate community responses to how the judicial system deals with youth crime, might meet in a community hall, but not near the locations where the majority of street robberies take place. This would also fit with the advice of Winslow et al. (2002) that the setting should be similar to one in which the target group would normally congregate. The nearer the location is to participants' home or workplace, the more likely they are to attend. Travel time is typically more critical than distance. Psychology also plays a part. If a location is perceived to be in, say, an area of deprivation where personal safety might be an

Image 18.3   Different focus group set ups

issue (particularly for young people and women), then this might affect both numbers who will attend the focus group and its composition.

Having booked meeting facilities it is essential to ensure that seating arrangements aid rather than hamper group discussions. Seats arranged in a horseshoe shape, so participants face each other, encourages discussion. However, particularly if they do not know each other, some groups prefer a barrier such as a table between them. Cultural issues may play a part. Halcomb et al. (2007) point out that the Asian style of focus group would customarily provide a desk for people to sit at because this would be seen as a welcome physical defence without which participants would feel uncomfortable.

Generate and pilot interview questions

We examined some of the principles of question design in Chapter 14. Here, then, we discuss some of the more specialist issues in relation to question design for focus groups, the first of which is: How many questions should be asked in a focus group? Krueger and Casey (2009) advise about 12 questions for a two hour focus group session. Stewart et al. (2007), however, suggest that the more complex the topic, the more emotionally charged the topic or the greater the heterogeneity of the group, the fewer the questions that can be covered. Given that one of the key purposes of focus groups is to encourage discussion, questions will be open in nature. So, questions might take a format such as:

FOCUSING ON QUESTIONS

- When you saw the news about X, what was your immediate response?
- What did you think when you first saw Y?
- What do you feel now when you recall Z?

Note that these questions are quite general and do not draw attention to any specific dimension or aspect. More specific questions do, indeed, add a dimension. Hence:

- When you saw the news about the earthquake, what were your immediate thoughts about the effectiveness of the emergency services?
- What did you think about its aesthetic appeal when you first saw the new Porsche?
- What do you feel now when you recall the negative attitude of your teachers?

There needs to be a balance between general and more specific questions. Here a number of commentators recommend a 'funnel' approach as a frame for questioning (Morgan, 1997). Through this method, an introductory question is used to stimulate group discussion, allowing the moderator to gain an insight into the basic opinions of the group. After this, questions gradually narrow with transition questions before core, key questions are posed. A final 'catch all' question provides closure to the session. Stewart et al. (2007) offer a similar approach, arguing that questions should move from the general to the specific and from the most important to the less important. Figure 18.2 (a) provides a simple illustration. However, in practice, questions may begin with the general and move to the specific, but after that the direction of the group discussion may lead the questioning in unexpected directions (see Figure 18.2 (b), in this example, never getting back to the general).

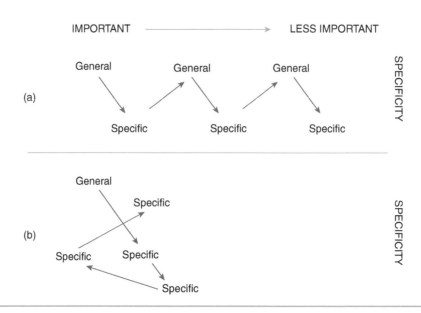

Figure 18.2   Questioning framework from the general to the specific

Source: Adapted from Stewart et al., 2007

Whatever direction it takes, the focus group plan should at least plan for the funnel flow suggested. Table 18.3 provides an illustration of the kinds of questions posed by an autism outreach organization with a focus group of parents with autistic children discussing how the organization can best help parents. Notice that some of the questions follow Napolitano et al. (2002) who advise that concrete statements should be followed by shorter questions.

Krueger and Casey (2009) offer two additional possible ending questions. The first is: 'All things considered', an attempt to determine the final position of each individual in the group on areas of critical concern. The second is the summary question. The moderator gives a short oral summary of the discussion and participants are asked to comment on its completeness and accuracy. For example, 'Today we have explored the issue of wind farm power generation and the greening of technology. Most of the group are in favour of wind farms but are sceptical about their long term effectiveness. Would this be a fair summary of what has been said?'

Speaking in public, and especially on subjects where viewpoints are polarised, may make some people particularly reticent to speak. The moderator may notice people not completing sentences or looking as though they want to speak without actually doing so. Here probing questions can be vital. These can take a variety of forms. A simple one is the use of positive gestures and noises ('Uh-huh') just to keep a respondent talking so there is depth to their response. Another kind of probe is when the moderator repeats what the contributor has said: 'What I understand from that is....', a technique which often elicits a further piece of dialogue. The moderator can also probe by asking for examples or personal stories from people's experience.

Table 18.3   Questions posed in focus group using funnelling approach

Introductory Question	Please tell us your first name and what it was that motivated you to come to this meeting.
General Question	Autistic children generally have support from a variety of professional teams including doctors, teachers, psychiatrists etc. What kind of support does your child have?
Specific Question	What were the greatest needs and most important issues that you encountered when your child was first diagnosed with autism?
Specific Question	Some people find it very difficult to cope with their autistic child, particularly if they are in mainstream education and thus spend a lot of time in the family environment (in the evenings and at weekends). What kind of further assistance would you benefit from doctors, teachers, psychiatrists, therapists or others? What prevents you from accessing further help?
Specific Question	As you know, we are going to implement a new outreach programme to support parents. Think back to your experiences of support services. What advice would you like to give us?
Final Question	Is there anything else that anyone feels we should have talked about but didn't?

Source: Adapted from Halcomb et al., 2007

As in the development of all data gathering instruments, the piloting of focus group questions is vital. This could be through a mock focus group, ideally with a group of people who are typical of the intended participants. Krueger and Casey (2009), however, warn that such a group might be difficult and time consuming to arrange. Better would be to get together a few people who fit the proposed focus group demographics. Test whether it is easy to ask the questions without having to read them and ascertain whether participants actually understand the questions. The moderator who is going to be used in the focus groups should be the person who poses the questions – testing how they pose the questions and also, vitally, how they facilitate the discussion that follows.

Conduct the group

Observe participants as they enter the room and notice non-verbal communication taking place, whether people are talking to each other and the subject of conversations. Use this information, if relevant, as a guide to who should sit next to each other. Avoid letting friends sit next to one another since cliques can soon form. Once the focus group has assembled, the role of the moderator becomes central, this being to:

CONDUCTING
THE GROUP

- Introduce him or herself, including their credentials, that is, their justification for moderating the meeting
- Provide some personal information (to 'connect' with the group)
- Explain the purpose of the focus group
- Provide reassurances about confidentiality (within constraints)

- Ask permission for the use of a digital recorder (if required)
- Mention logistical issues such as the approximate length of the session, when breaks are going to be taken, and the location of facilities such as toilets and safety features such as fire exits
- Make clear the ground rules of the session (recall Table 18.2)

▶ TOP TIP 18.3 ◀

It is best if demographic information on participants (for example, their age, gender, job descriptions) is collected before the focus group starts rather than during the discussions (Clark, 2009); this is also the time to get ethical approval forms signed by participants.

GOOD
MODERATION

The moderator poses the pre-planned questions and essentially orchestrates the workings of the group. In doing this, moderators must show an even hand, not favouring one group member over another. Table 18.4 offers a range of possible behaviours that the moderator may have to respond to. Members may have their own interests which may, or may not, coincide with the interests of the researcher. The moderator needs to be aware that he or she may have to impose a structure or agenda on the group which may divert them from what the groups consider to be significant.

⌐ CASE STUDY 18.1 ¬

Getting a focus group to focus

Kahan (2001) reports on a study where the process within the focus groups at first went badly wrong. The research concerned public attitudes towards the strengthening of river dykes in the Netherlands, particularly the views of environmental groups who protested on the grounds that these would harm the environment. The political debate became so heated that the minister concerned commissioned a study to determine whether the previously established security level (dyke height) was too conservative.

    The questioning approach was to avoid beginning directly with the main policy issue and instead to start with a general topic and later move to specifics. So, researchers began by asking participants about how the river landscape fits with their image of the country, how important it was and in what ways they enjoyed the landscape. Unfortunately, in the first focus group, composed of political activists, researchers admit that the agenda was quickly taken over by these activists who launched into a set of prepared speeches. After an hour the researchers called for 'time out', explained the purpose of the research and, in effect, asked the group to begin again. Having vented their anger, the group readily agreed and the next 90 minutes went according to plan.

Source: Adapted from Kahan, 2001

⌐ ACTIVITY 18.1 ¬

Considering the above case study, were the researchers right to allow the session to continue for an hour before calling 'time out'? What else could they have done?

Image 18.4
Focus group

Table 18.4   Possible difficult behaviours in a focus group

Behaviour	Why it occurs	Moderator's response
The Heckler	Argumentative, attention-seeking	Don't get drawn in or counter-heckle. Keep the group calm. Move on with the agenda.
The Challenger	Trying to get own view adopted. Seeking to get the moderator's advice	Determine reason/background to the question. Throw question open to the group
The Chatterbox	An extrovert. Highly informed, or otherwise. Attention-seeking	Slow them down with some questions. Bring in other members of the group with their questions or comments
The Rambler	Strays off the subject; uses long stories which lack a point	Ask for the point of story; when pauses, restate the question or move the agenda on
The Mute	Shy, bored or indifferent	If shy give them time to 'settle in' to the group; if bored, find what they are interested in; if indifferent, ask a provocative question
The Sceptic	Sceptical about the value of the topic or the views expressed about it	Acknowledge viewpoint; probe for reasons underneath it. Re-explain purpose of research and value of outputs
The Moaner	Gripes about a 'pet hate'. Sometimes these hates can be legitimate	If 'on subject' explain how the research may find answers. If 'off subject' offer discussion outside focus group session
The Expert	Some people are genuine subject matter experts; others attention-seekers or deluded	For experts, draw on their expertise (without allowing them to dominate); for attention seekers, reduce or stop eye contact and eliminate positive reinforcement of comments
The Enemy	Is hostile (to the subject, fellow group members or the moderator) or aggressive	If not spotted before commencement of the group, call a break, and invite to leave

→ **TOP TIP 18.4** ←

GRAY ON
FOCUS
GROUPS:
USING A
MODERATOR

Especially if you are new to conducting empirical research, seriously consider engaging the services of an experienced moderator. Firstly, this will enable you to concentrate on your role as a researcher: listening, observing and recording data. Secondly, if group dynamics take an unexpected turn (for example, if participants become upset or angry), the moderator will be able to take appropriate action, either to calm tensions, or in extreme circumstances to close the focus group early. If you are undertaking an academic dissertation, then consider teaming up with a fellow student who is also using a focus group and provide each other with support – they moderate your focus group and you moderate theirs.

Record data

Capturing group discussions (and interactions between participants) can be achieved in a number of ways, each of which has its advantages and disadvantages. Here, we deal with three approaches, namely memory, field notes and audio-recordings.

Memory

Memory is one of the least reliable forms of data recording since it is so fallible. However, especially if equipment fails to work (for example, digital recorders), it may be the only form of recording available. If there are at least two researchers working in the group, they should get together immediately after the focus group has finished to agree and write up some notes.

Field notes

You will recall that we discussed the use of field notes in Chapters 7 and 15 in relation to observational research. For focus groups, however, there are some additional issues that need to be borne in mind particularly since we are concerned with collecting data from groups rather than individuals. Hence, given that there are multiple voices and interactions taking place, the research team must decide in advance what it is they want to capture. This could include:

- Selected themes with a number of key quotes
- Observation of group interactions including emotional responses
- Turning points where views change

Krueger and Casey (2009) offer three approaches to taking field notes.

MEANING OF
DESCRIPTION

- *Record notes and quotes.* Here the researcher draws a vertical line down the page and creates two columns: notes and quotes. Key ideas are captured under notes, with as close to verbatim quotes as possible on the right hand page. As the moderator moves on to the next question, the researcher draws a horizontal line and begins a new section.
- *Rich description.* Here the attempt is to capture the conversation word for word as closely as possible. Spaces are used to separate contributions of each speaker.
- *Speaker identification.* With long transcripts it can become difficult to identify individual speakers. Here field notes are used to identify who is speaking, with the first few lines of what they say. These can later be matched to the transcript and the names of speakers added.

Whatever note-taking method is employed, Krueger and Casey (2009) recommend that notes should always include the following information:

- The name of the study
- The date/time/location of the focus group
- The type and number of participants
- The names and roles of researchers
- A diagram of seating arrangements including a first name or code for each participant

---

→ **TOP TIP 18.5** ←

To help transcribers, start the focus group by introducing yourself and then get all participants to do likewise. Transcribers can then put a name to each voice.

Audio recordings

We discussed using digital recorders in Chapter 15. These, however, were for use in recording the views of individual respondents. Recording the discussion of group participants offers special challenges, not least of which is that sometimes people will be talking at the same time. It is vital, therefore, that the quality of the recording is at its best. Whatever type of digital device you intend to use, go to the focus group location and try it out before the focus group event. If the device is placed, say, in the middle of a table, will the voices of all contributors be heard? It helps here if you use an external microphone. It is also best to use the highest quality recorder and digital format such as Stereo High Quality (SHQ). Paying more for equipment and sound card will ultimately save on transcription costs.

Approaches to data analysis

In one sense, the analysis of data emanating from focus group discussions is no different to any other kind of data. However, a number of qualifications have to be made. Focus group analysis tends to start immediately after the first focus group has been completed – data collection and analysis are concurrent (Krueger and Casey, 2009). This also helps in the generation of questions since it will become obvious sooner rather than later as to which questions are generating illuminating responses and which are not. This section rounds off this overview of organizing focus groups by looking at some technical aspects of data analysis. The next section deals with some philosophical issues.

The first of these technical issues is identifying the unit of analysis. For focus groups, it is the group that is the unit of analysis and not the individuals that comprise it – hence, the aim of data analysis will be to capture the views expressed by the *group* as a whole. This means not only an analysis of the raw data but also of the interactions and group dynamics (Kitzinger, 1995). Given the open nature of questions posed to focus groups, and the fact that group dynamics and interactions may become part of the data set, analysing focus group data can be quite a challenge. One way of handling group analysis, particularly when multiple focus groups are used, is by using a grid (Miles and Huberman, 1994) where groups are plotted on the vertical axis and question numbers on the horizontal axis, as in Table 18.5. To achieve this, each question needs to be asked in each focus group (although as we noted earlier, sometimes a question schedule will be modified progressively from one focus group to another, as some questions are seen to work better than others).

— CASE STUDY 18.2 —

Getting a blend of professionals together

The aim of the research project described by Zimmerman et al. (2010) was to seek to understand the kinds of factual and other information that different professionals prefer and emphasize when faced with an emergency situation, and the communication skills required. The focus groups concerned two potential terrorism scenarios: a terrorist attack involving the hypothetical release of sarin (a synthetic chemical and nerve agent), and another attack involving the release of smallpox, both in confined physical spaces, namely, a train, train station and a bus depot. Two separate focus groups were held for each type of attack. Each focus group concentrated on three issues:

> How participants respond to such events
> How events are defined geographically
> How variations arise in information used by participants from different professional groups

By understanding how people react to a terrorist attack, researchers expected to gather insights into how professionals refine scenario design and their responses to the crisis.

Focus group participants consisted mainly of professionals from emergency planning and response teams and were selected through snowball sampling (recall Chapter 9). Hence, initial contact was made with individuals in government agencies, utilities and the health professions with experience in emergency response. They in turn suggested other professionals. Given the complexity of the topic, the researchers felt that a size of 6–8 people was appropriate, that is, a small group. Participants were not known to each other. The duration of the groups was typically between 1.5 and 2.5 hours, with the setting in a conference room in the offices of a university. The room had plain white walls and participants were seated around a rectangular table. The ethical requirements of the university institution were adhered to. The sessions were manually transcribed rather than recorded.

The moderator directed the discussion according to a pre-planned agenda. Firstly the research director introduced the objectives and rationale of the study, including the nature of risk communication and some of the challenges. The characteristics of the effects of sarin and smallpox were outlined. Then the moderator presented a series of tables which describe the desired behaviour of the general public associated with an attack, and details of actual behaviour. The framework provided the basis for group discussion. Questions posed included: What information is needed to influence behaviour? How should the message be worded? Who should deliver the message?

In terms of results, participants recommended merging some of the time periods presented in the framework to avoid repeating the same information for different time periods. Secondly, the nature of the space (confined or otherwise) was critical in shaping the message given to the public. Thirdly, the professionals spoke different languages and emphasized different information needed in responding to the crisis.

Source: Zimmerman, Restrepo, Culpen, Remington, Kling, Portelli and Foltin (2010)

— ACTIVITY 18.2 —

Explain why the use of focus groups might be particularly relevant to discussions of risk communication. Can you think of other scenarios where groups of professionals might come together through focus groups to discuss issues relevant to researchers?

FOCUS GROUPS AND RESEARCH DESIGN

As we saw in Chapter 6, research design comprises an overarching plan for the collection, measurement and analysis of data. A research design, then, could comprise the use of only one focus group. However, as we saw in Chapter 17, one of the purposes of qualitative research is to achieve a degree of data 'saturation', a point where the last focus group does not provide or promise new knowledge (Flick, 2006). Data saturation lends credibility to the research, hence it is usual to use at least three or four focus groups as part of a research design (which may, of course, also include other data gathering methods as part of a mixed methods design). Krueger and Casey (2009) distinguish between a number of alternative designs, depending on the purpose of the research.

Programme or product development design

Krueger and Casey (2009) pinpoint three phases in a programme or product design when focus groups can be useful. The first is when researchers seek to understand more about the product or programme. If this was, say, a training programme, then this would often be called the needs assessment stage (see Figure 18.3). One or more focus groups helps the researcher to understand the needs of consumers or employees which helps in the development of a series of prototypes (samples or models, built to test a product or programme), which are themselves pilot tested (evaluated) by focus groups. The prototype most favoured by the focus groups is then developed into the 'final' stage model which again is evaluated by focus groups.

If, say, the authority responsible for promoting waste recycling among domestic households wanted to implement a popular and successful scheme, it might first start by organizing a series of focus groups aimed at understanding customer

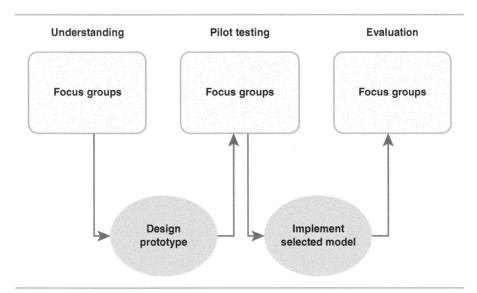

Figure 18.3   Research design for product or programme development

Table 18.5   Grid to facilitate comparison of data across focus groups

Group	Q1	Q2	Q3	Q4
1	Data Q1 Group 1	Data Q2 Group 1	Data Q3 Group 1	Data Q4 Group 1
2	Data Q1 Group 2	Data Q2 Group 2	Data Q3 Group 2	Data Q4 Group 2
3	Data Q1 Group 3	Data Q2 Group 3	Data Q3 Group 3	Data Q4 Group 3
4	Data Q1 Group 4	Data Q2 Group 4	Data Q3 Group 4	Data Q4 Group 4

Local resident	0	0	0	0	Saturation?

0 = one focus group

Figure 18.4   Single-category design

Source: Adapted from Krueger and Casey, 2009

interests, motivation (to recycle or not) and concerns. Developing an understanding of customer interests helps in the design of various approaches which include the provision of different prototype designs for 'wheelie' bins for unwanted newspapers and food, each of which are tested in a selected district for three months. The most practical designs are subsequently 'rolled out' (implemented) throughout the town, but the authority still evaluates the results through more focus groups to ensure popular 'buy in' to the scheme and to see if it can be improved – see next section.

Programme or product evaluation design

The above example shows how focus groups can be used iteratively in the development process. In this section we look at how they can be used to evaluate final products or programmes. Krueger and Casey (2009) offer a range of designs including a Single-category design, Multiple-category design, Double-layer design and Broad spectrum design. We will take the example of waste recycling in the above section and apply it to each of these designs.

Single-category design

The wheelie bins are used across the town, but the local authority knows from evaluation reports that some districts seem to be using the bins more than others, and there are also variations even on individual roads. The authority, then, wants to evaluate how residents are using the bins, and how less committed residents can be brought into the scheme. Using a Single-category design (residents as the category), information rich residents are recruited to, say, four focus groups. After the groups have been held and the data analysed, if data saturation is reached, the focus groups stop; if new information is being obtained from the fourth group, another group is held, and so on until there is saturation (see Figure 18.4)

Multiple-category design

The local authority might have a suspicion that certain variables are at play and that these influence residents in their decision on whether to recycle or not. One variable might be age, hence, focus groups are organized for three age groups: 18–39; 40–64; 65+. In addition, it is believed also important to gain the views of recycling bin collectors since they have the opportunity to witness residents' behaviour and may have some interesting views. However, since this is a small group, only one focus group will be necessary (see Figure 18.5).

Double-layer design

If the local authority believes that not only age but social class has an influence on recycling behaviour, then it will adopt a double-layer design, using the same age categories, but this time across, say, three layers (districts), each district chosen because of its known socio-demographic features. Figure 18.6 illustrates the resulting design.

Local resident 18–39 age group	0	0	0
Local resident 40–64 age group	0	0	0
Local resident 65+ age group	0	0	0
Recycling bin collectors	0		

0 = one focus group

Figure 18.5   Multiple-category design

Source: Adapted from Krueger and Casey, 2009

District 1 Local resident 18–39 age group Local resident 40–64 age group Local resident 65+ age group	0 0 0	0 0 0	0 0 0
District 2 Local resident 18–39 age group Local resident 40–64 age group Local resident 65+ age group	0 0 0	0 0 0	0 0 0
District 3 Local resident 18–39 age group Local resident 40–64 age group Local resident 65+ age group	0 0 0	0 0 0	0 0 0

0 = one focus group

Figure 18.6   Double-layer design

Source: Adapted from Krueger and Casey, 2009

Broad spectrum design

The domestic waste recycling example is typical of the type of issue that can involve a wide spectrum of public opinion and interests. In these cases, the public authority may seek to canvas the views of those groups who have a keen interest in the subject, before then ensuring that less key, but by no means unimportant groups are also taken into account. The key groups may sometimes be over sampled as they will provide a benchmark against which the other groups can be measured (Krueger and Casey, 2009). In our recycling example, it might be the 'refusenik' groups that provide the baseline, since it is achieving changes in their behaviour that the scheme must achieve. Other groups that must also be sampled could include the managers of the recycling plants, scheme administrators, ecologists and scientists with expertise in recycling theory. Figure 18.7 provides an illustration.

SPECIAL ISSUES IN FOCUS GROUP RESEARCH

While one of the benefits of using focus groups is their versatility, working with some types of audience or certain kinds of themes throws up particular challenges. In this section we will look at using focus groups with children and with international, culturally diverse audiences, before exploring how focus groups can be used to explore difficult and embarrassing issues.

Focus groups with children and young people

FOCUS GROUPS WITH CHILDREN

In the UK, before working with children, moderators and others involved with a focus group will have to be checked through the Criminal Records Bureau (CRB) in order to receive their CRB certificate, evidence that the applicant has not been barred from working with vulnerable groups. Before talking to young people moderators may have to seek permission from parents or teachers. Beyond these important legal issues, moderators will only be effective if they are comfortable with working with children. With very young children it may be appropriate to use pictures and objects to stimulate discussion, or to use role play or games. In terms of homogeneity, it is better to arrange for groups of a similar age, as different age

Resident 'refuseniks'	0	0	0	0	0
Recycling plant managers	0	0			
Recycling scheme administrators	0				
Ecologists	0				
Scientists	0				

0 = one focus group

Figure 18.7   Broad spectrum design

Source: Adapted from Krueger and Casey, 2009

Image 18.5   Children/young people in a focus group

ranges do not mix well together. Krueger and Casey (2009) recommend an age range of no more than two years within the group. Clearly, questions should address issues that are age appropriate as well as socially appropriate. Clark (2009) warns that asking children to disclose uncomfortable or discriminating information among peers is ill-advised.

Even before the questions are posed, it is essential to relax the group, perhaps by engaging in conversational topics such as sport, music, or favourite television programmes. The moderator should also model the kinds of behaviours that demonstrate the sharing of ideas. Thus it often helps with a youth audience if the moderator is also from this age group, provided they have been given sufficient and detailed instructions on how to conduct the group. Working with young people, moderators may find themselves having to overcome scepticism about the process, since young people may be suspicious about the motives of the research and the credence taken of their views. Hence, trust has to be built.

SUCCESS WITH CHILDREN AND YOUNG PEOPLE

Focus groups and international audiences

When moderating a focus group overseas, it is better to conduct the group in the local language even if English is a commonly used second language in the country. This ensures that all participants both understand the questions and can respond fluently. Focus group organizers also need to be sensitive to aspects of power and status. In some cultures, where respect for authority and age is paramount, younger people and those who perceive themselves as lower in status may hesitate to contribute.

Discussing sensitive issues

It is important here for the moderator to set the right tone from the start. Since participants may be embarrassed, the moderator can lighten the atmosphere by divulging a knowledge or interest in the subject. For example: 'The first time I visited a sexually transmitted disease clinic ....' As Stewart et al. (2007) advise, a useful

BULLYING FOCUS GROUP

way of deflecting sensitivity is to get participants to comment on the views or experiences of friends or colleagues rather than themselves. This, however, may not always be practical since participants might be required here to have more intimate knowledge of others than they actually possess.

EPISTEMOLOGICAL CONSIDERATIONS AND FOCUS GROUPS

EPISTEMOLOGICAL
CONSIDERATIONS

According to Sayre (2001), three epistemological perspectives are relevant to the qualitative analysis of focus group data.

- Firstly, social constructivism claims that reality and the meanings people accord to it are socially constructed. Focus group researchers that hold this approach tend to emphasize how group members collaborate and reach a consensus on how shared meanings about events, products or themes are constructed.
- In contrast, qualitative researchers from a constructionist persuasion, reject the notion that there is a single reality. Instead, knowledge is seen as provisional and context dependent. Hence, strategies are adopted that favour reflexivity and the articulation of the researcher's perspectives as a legitimate element of the analysis. Constructs such as robustness, credibility, dependability and transferability are seen as key (Lincoln and Guba, 1994).
- Then there is interpretivism which notes the views expressed by participants but refuses to take them at face value, preferring to compare words with other data such as non-verbal communication (facial expressions, tone of voice, etc.). Those who adhere to an interpretivist stance are more likely to use rapporteurs to make observations and produce notes of these. This approach seeks consumer stories as powerful tools for understanding how consumers construct meaning and make decisions. Hence, textual data are read, analysed for interpretation and re-read and reanalysed.

To the three epistemological positions outlined above, Freeman (2006) discusses a fourth – a 'realist' approach. Qualitative researchers who favour 'realism', seek to represent reality (Hammersley, 1992) and analyse data to discover pre-existent categories and consistency of meaning. There may be a concern for producing convincing evidence of validity and reliability, so that the findings can be considered 'true'.

Exploring the impact of epistemological positions on focus groups, Freeman (2006) takes the work of Krueger (1994) to highlight a realist position and Kitzinger (1995) who takes a constructionist stance to illustrate four areas of interest, namely, group membership and sampling, homogeneity and heterogeneity in group composition, interaction within groups and generalizability of results (for a summary see Table 18.6).

Realist and constructionist approaches to focus groups

Let us look at each of these elements in turn.

Group membership and sampling

From his realist perspective, Krueger (1994) is critical of the use of convenience samples and pre-existing groups, warning of the dangers of using groups where

Table 18.6   Methodological tensions between constructionist and realist perspectives

	Kitzinger (contextual constructionism)	Krueger (realism)
Group membership	Pre-existing groups useful for providing 'naturalistic' exchanges	Pre-existing groups should be avoided, given their potential for bias; random sampling of participants recommended
Homogeneity	Weak: helpful when participants have diversity of status. Homogenous groups generate too much conformity	Strong: groups should be homogenous with regard to key variables for sub-group comparisons
Interaction	Strong: interaction is a central analytical resource	Weak: interaction is useful for generating discussion on the topic of interest
Generalizability of results	Weak: theoretical insights potentially transferable, but this must be decided by the reader	Strong: with a number of homogenous groups, results may hold for the population the groups are drawn from, given the random sampling of participants

Source: Adapted from Freeman, 2006

people know or work with each other. One reason is that these groups will have their own pre-existing dynamics, and can be influenced by formal and informal hierarchies. But a more important problem posed by convenience sampling is the threat to external validity (see 'Generalizability of results', below). From her constructionist perspective, however, Kitzinger (1995) champions the use of pre-existing groups (for example, people who work together), arguing that there is no single reality waiting to be revealed. Using pre-existing groups allows for observation of fragments of interactions between participants that approximate to naturally occurring interactions yielding data that might have been gathered through participant observation.

CONVENIENCE
SAMPLING

Homogeneity and heterogeneity in group composition

Krueger (1994) warns against heterogeneity in group composition as this acts as a threat to external validity. He advises that participants should be segmented into relevant sub-groups using a series of focus groups for each sub-group. So, if the study is concerned with the views of healthcare professionals and managers towards the issue of clinical governance in the health service, then there should be separate sub-groups for doctors, nurses and managers, etc. This helps in the analysis of differences between sub-groups, and increases the external validity of comparisons made between sub-groups, since knowledge of such differences has currency beyond the study to a broader population. However, there is a concern that homogeneity may inhibit discussion, especially when there are power or status differences between group participants. In the above example, for instance, would nurses speak so freely when there are doctors or consultants in the group? In contrast, for Kitzinger (1995) issues of external validity are of less concern since she is interested in situated discourses rather than shared perceptions of population samples

(Freeman, 2006). While she acknowledges that status differences may inhibit some participants, this does not mean that people's 'real' thoughts will not emerge.

Interaction

For Krueger (1994) interaction is a functional device for ensuring that data are gathered. But for Kitzinger (1995) interaction is a central analytical resource and intrinsically valuable in itself. It is one of the defining features of focus groups as a research method. When group dynamics work well, co-participants (sic) act as co-researchers, taking the discussion in unexpected directions (Kitzinger, 1994). Interactions in group work also allow for the generation of theory rather than the mere testing of it.

Generalizability of results

According to Krueger (1994) with an adequate number of homogenous focus groups with randomly selected participants, results may be generalizable to populations from which the groups were drawn. As would be expected, Kitzinger (1995) is more cautious about making claims for external validity, arguing for transferability based upon the theoretical saturation of data segments. At this point, it is up to the reader to make a judgement as to the credibility of these claims (Freeman, 2006). Hence, results are more likely to yield conceptual insights and illumination rather than generalizability (Kitzinger, 1995). Stewart et al. (2007) also consider focus group results to be idiosyncratic and therefore difficult to generalize. However, this does not mean they lack value – indeed, they possess the kind of ecological validity not found in other kinds of research such as traditional surveys. Having compared and contrasted realist and constructionist stances, Case Study 18.3 provides an illustration of a constructionist approach based on a study by Kitzinger herself.

ECOLOGICAL
VALIDITY

CASE STUDY 18.3

AIDS Media Research Project

Kitzinger (1994) describes how focus groups were used as part of a three-pronged study of the production, content and effect of media messages about AIDS. Focus groups were used to examine how media messages are processed by audiences and constructed, including not just what they thought, but *how* they thought and *why*. The research also explored how diverse identities and social networks impact on these perceptions. A total of 52 discussions were conducted comprising 351 participants, with each group consisting on average of 6 participants, with discussions lasting about 2 hours. The sampling approach used pre-existing groups, clusters who knew each other as neighbours, work colleagues or through socializing. Flatmates, colleagues, family and friends are just the kinds of people who might 'naturally' discuss topics like AIDS (Kitzinger, 1994). Their familiarity with each other meant that they were more likely to comment on incidents that were familiar to all of them, and also to challenge the contradictions between what was being professed as a belief and how people actually behaved.

To promote discussion, the moderator employed several group exercises. For example, at the start of the session, participants were asked to play a 'news game', whereby they were divided into two teams, each team using a pre-selected set of photographs taken from actual TV news bulletins to write their own news bulletin. Later, they were provided with a pack of cards containing statements about who might be at risk from AIDS, and were asked, as a group, to sort the cards into piles indicating the degree of 'risk' for each 'type of person'. Kitzinger has used card games with groups as diverse as peace campaigners (asking them about gender and violence), old people in residential care (assigning degrees of importance to statements about the quality of their care) and with midwives (asking them to describe how they perceived their professional role). It is not the final layout of the cards that is important – it is the process of getting there.

Through these focus groups, participants argued, boasted, made faces at each other, told stories and on one occasion, sang songs. There was also teasing, joking and the acting out of viewpoints – for example, acting out the 'look' of an AIDS carrier (contorting their faces, squinting and shaking). As Kitzinger (1994) comments, focus groups can reach the parts other methods cannot reach, revealing dimensions of understanding that remain untapped by other methods such as interviews or questionnaires. However, she does not claim that focus groups are more 'authentic' than other data sources; merely that all talk through which people generate meaning is contextual.

Source: Adapted from Kitzinger, 1994

— ACTIVITY 18.3 —

Think about a subject about which you have strong views and managing a focus group containing people with opposite views. What strategies would you adopt to maintain a detached role as group moderator?

Phenomenology and focus groups

We saw in Chapter 2 and in the realist/constructionist example above, that a researcher's epistemological stance can have a profound influence on their choice and application of research method. Bradbury-Jones, Sambrook and Irvine (2009) discuss this in relation to phenomenology and the use of focus groups. The primary objective of phenomenology is to investigate and describe phenomena as consciously experienced, people's 'natural attitude', prior to critical or theoretical reflection (Husserl, 1983: 51). The underlying belief is that it is best to research phenomena through the eyes of the person(s) having the experience. Another important feature of descriptive phenomenology is that of phenomenological reduction, achieved through the performance of 'bracketing', that is, withholding the impulse to make judgements or assumptions about the world, and looking at phenomena in their essence. However, according to Heidegger, the attempt by Husserl to guarantee a truth undistorted by human interpretation is misdirected (Polkinghorne, 1983). To be human is to be interpretive, with the interpreter always bringing their own experiences and frames of reference to their understanding of the phenomena. Hence, understanding is based upon interpretation of phenomena not on a description of them (Bradbury-Jones et al., 2009).

PHENOMENOLOGY

Where does this leave the role of focus groups? In a critique of nursing research, Webb and Kevern (2001) argue that focus groups and phenomenology are incompatible. Since the goal of phenomenological research is to get individuals to describe their experiences in as uncontaminated a way as possible, the use of research methods that involve groups is inappropriate since individuals will be influenced by the views of others. However, Bradbury-Jones et al. (2009: 666) distinguish between Husserl's descriptive and Heidegger's interpretive (hermeneutic) phenomenology, arguing that, since Husserlian phenomenology aims to adopt a detached position, using any kind of group approach to data collection may be 'skating on thin ice'. However, since Heideggarian phenomenology is not concerned with the uncontamination of participant accounts, the use of focus groups should not be discounted. Indeed, interpretive phenomenology, as its name implied, is concerned with interpretation. For Bradbury-Jones et al. (2009) the researcher does not arrive at an objective description of the phenomenon being studied. Instead, during data gathering, the researcher shapes the interview, but in turn is shaped by it. Hence, in focus groups, the researcher is engaged in a process of 'reciprocal interpretation with participants' (Bradbury-Jones et al., 2009: 667). Focus groups may also be relevant to phenomenological research in that the approach may help researchers to bracket their assumptions when they are challenged by group members. The researcher, then, is able to arrive at a clearer, and richer understanding of the phenomenon under study (Bradbury-Jones et al., 2009).

ETHICAL CONSIDERATIONS AND FOCUS GROUPS

SPECIAL ETHICAL
CONSIDERATIONS

Ethics were discussed in detail in Chapter 4. However, there are some specific issues that concern the ethical conduct of focus groups that will be outlined here. The first is that ethical principles, while of course a challenge within all approaches to research, pose particular problems for focus groups. An obvious one is that confidentiality is difficult to keep since statements made by participants will be heard in a public forum. Confidentiality therefore can be promised only within certain constraints. The potential for breaches of confidentiality, then, needs to be highlighted on ethical consent forms (Smith, 1995). Krueger and Casey (2009) recommend that these forms are presented when participants first arrive and before the focus group begins, when a member of the research team can explain the protocol orally and answer questions in a confidential manner. This can be especially helpful when participants have literacy problems. Confidentiality can also be assisted if participants refer to themselves and others only by first name.

Using groups or teams of participants from the same organization or sector may have far-reaching consequences once the focus group is over. Barbour (1999) suggests that this is factored in during sample selection to identify and avoid combinations of groups where conflict is likely to occur. During the focus group, some participants might voice opinions that are upsetting to others. One of the roles of the rapporteur, apart from taking notes, is to monitor the comfort level of participants (Halcomb et al., 2007) to ensure they are not becoming too stressed. Sometimes upset may result from statements containing misinformation. The role of the moderator is to provide accurate information – possibly through debriefing or the distribution of information leaflets at the end of the session (Kitzinger and Barbour, 1999). In the final analysis, adhere to one of the basic ethical principles in research – do no harm!

Summary

- Focus groups are ideal ways of exploring people's beliefs and perceptions about products, services and concepts and are used in a wide variety of contexts including marketing, social policy and health and education management
- Focus groups are not group interviews. Rather they aim to achieve a cascade effect where the utterances of one participant triggers ideas in others
- Focus groups have many strengths, but may pose challenges where confidentiality is key and where success is dependent on the skills of the moderator
- Typically focus groups will comprise between six and eight participants and will last between one and two hours
- The choice of homogenous or heterogeneous samples, and the claims made for the results, will be influenced by the epistemological stance of the researcher
- Researchers will often use three or four focus groups or more until data 'saturation' is achieved
- Questions must be carefully designed and piloted with the number of questions dependent on the complexity of the topic and the experience of the moderator. Funnelling is often used with general questions being posed before specific ones
- Ground rules for the conduct of the focus group must be explained and adhered to, particularly timings and respect for others in the group

REVIEW QUESTIONS

1. To what extent do the benefits of focus groups outweigh the disadvantages?
2. Why is the role of the moderator so vital to the success of focus groups?
3. Why is the beginning of the focus group so critical to its success? What makes for an effective start?
4. Explain how the funnel approach is used to design the flow of questions.
5. What is a probe? Give some examples of probing phrases or approaches.
6. Explain how the epistemological stance of a researcher can affect areas such as sample selection in focus groups and claims for external validity.

FOCUS GROUP

FURTHER READING

Liamputtong, P. (2011) *Focus Group Methodology: Principles and Practice*. London: Sage. Covers, in commendable detail, essential topics such as focus group methodology, and the practicalities of running a successful focus group. In addition, there is a useful chapter on using focus groups on sensitive topics and with vulnerable groups. Each chapter concludes with a series of tutorial questions for discussion and an extensive list of sources for further reading.

LIAMPUTTONG
CHAPTER 7

Krueger, R.A. and Casey, A. (2009) *Focus Groups: A Practical Guide for Applied Research*, 4th edn. Thousand Oaks, CA: Sage. Provides a useful guide for planning a focus group, the kinds of questions to ask and how to moderate a group. Although written from a sociological perspective, the advice can be applied to any kind of research topic.

Morgan, D.L. (1997) *Focus Groups as Qualitative Research.* 2nd edn. Thousand Oaks, CA: Sage. At less than 100 pages, this book is short and accessible. It provides an overview of social science approaches to using focus groups, and contains a useful section that compares the use of focus groups with individual interviews.

JOURNAL RESOURCES

Carlsen, B. and Glenton, C. (2012) 'Scanning for satisfaction or digging for dismay? Comparing findings from a postal survey with those from a focus group-study', *BMC Medical Research Methodology*, 12(1): 134–141. Discusses a study where a discrepancy in findings between focus groups and a questionnaire reflects characteristics of the two different research methods.

Rodriguez, K.L., Schwartz, J.L., Lahman, M.K.E. and Geist, M.R. (2011) 'Culturally responsive focus groups: Reframing the research experience to focus on participants', *International Journal of Qualitative Methods*, 10(4): 400–417. Illuminates the advantages of using culturally responsive focus groups (CRFGs) in data collection.

Stokes, D. and Bergin, R. (2006) 'Methodology or "methodolatry"? An evaluation of focus groups and depth interviews', *Qualitative Market Research: An International Journal*, 9(1): 26–37. A study that suggests that group processes may have an influence on the consensus view expressed in focus groups, which may not be representative of respondents' individual views.

19

UNOBTRUSIVE MEASURES

CHAPTER INTRODUCTION

Chapter outline

Identifying physical measures 498

Documents 502

New unobtrusive measures:
digital archives 502

Ethical issues in using digital
technology 506

Keywords

Unobtrusive measures

Accretion

Organizational documents

Digital archives

Ethics

— Chapter objectives —

After reading this chapter you will be able to:

- Distinguish between unobtrusive measures and other research approaches.
- Describe the advantages of unobtrusive measures over more interactive methods.
- Select between different unobtrusive measures for conducting research.
- Demonstrate how to access data archives on the Internet.

UNOBTRUSIVE
RESEARCH

So far, we have concentrated on interactive research methods such as surveys, case studies, interviews and observations. Unobtrusive measures, however, involve the use of non-reactive sources, independent of the presence of the researcher, and include documentary evidence, physical evidence and archival analysis. The term archive derives from the ancient Greek aekheion, which means a house that is the residence of the superior magistrates, the archons, those that command. This house was where official documents were stored and where the archons acted as both guardians and interpreters of the documents. Here, the principle was created that archives require that documents are stored in one place (Featherstone, 2000).

UNOBTRUSIVE
MEASURES

These archives exist in a wide variety of formats and can consist of files, maps, drawings, films, sound recordings and photographs. While libraries tend to provide access to published materials, archives hold unique unpublished records. But, as Sleeman (2002) points out, with the growth of electronic environments such as the Internet, what is 'unique' and 'published' or 'unpublished' is increasingly blurred. Web pages, for example, can contain links to many other sites or pages, challenging the notion of a document as an integral and independent record.

As we have seen, interactive measures carry with them various inherent problems, such as the dangers of interviewer bias, the possibility of research tools of questionable validity and reliability, or reactivity between the interviewer and interviewee. Unobtrusive measures, because they are dealing with 'dead' data, in principle, are unlikely to face the risk of reactive measurement effects.

But, as we shall see, unobtrusive measures pose other risks if used on their own. Some materials, for example, tend to survive better than others, so their representativeness is open to question. To ensure reliability, it is often prudent to use unobtrusive measures in conjunction with other approaches.

In this chapter we will look at various kinds of unobtrusive measures and how they can be of value to the researcher. We will then examine a number of typical sources of unobtrusive measures.

IDENTIFYING PHYSICAL MEASURES

TRACE
MEASURES

From the prehistoric cave paintings of early man to the Great Wall of China, medieval cathedrals or the discarded fast food containers of modern times, human beings have left behind physical evidence of their existence. According to Webb et al. (2000), these physical or **trace** measures can be divided into four broad categories: natural and controlled **accretion measures**, and natural and controlled erosion measures.

Image 19.1   Physical traces left by early man

Natural accretion measures

Accretion takes place where there is a build up of deposits of materials or evidence. Within the context of ancient worlds, for example, this could include the accumulation of shards of pottery. In a more modern context, it could include the build up of piles of litter, or, say, the amount of dust gathering on some files or equipment, showing how little they are being used. An often-quoted example is that of graffiti appearing on the surfaces of (usually) urban features such as walls or buildings. Lee (2000) provides examples of research where graffiti have been used to analyse relationships and attitudes between different ethnic gangs, and how the graffiti delineated certain 'zones of tension' between groups.

But accretion measures could also include more innocent examples, such as the number of plastic cups accumulating in waste bins around an office. We are not interested, however, in these materials for themselves, but for what they might reveal about aspects of human behaviour. In the case of the plastic cups, we could use them to come to a tentative estimate of the number of breaks taken by office workers, as the following case study shows.

─ **CASE STUDY 19.1** ─

Natural accretion measures – cold coffee!

After trade union pressure, an office manager agrees to install a vending machine for hot and cold drinks. After only a month, through casual observation, he becomes concerned that the vending machine is encouraging a 'take a break' mentality, and that too many staff are losing focus on their work. He decides to carry out a short study to see if his hypothesis is correct.

He first of all notes where people consume their drinks, and finds that there are two areas: at the vending machine itself, which has now become a sort of social area, and at people's personal desks. Using unobtrusive measures, once staff have left work at the end of the day, he goes around the office, collecting used plastic cups from the waste bins. He finds over 50 cups in the bin next to the vending machine, but a total of over 200 in individual staff bins.

The next day, he covertly observes six members of staff consuming their drinks to make an average estimate of the time they spend on each break. In doing this, however, he finds that it is only those people who congregate around the vending machine who actually stop to talk. Those who take their drinks back to their desks continue immediately with work, taking a drink when they can. Indeed, he now recalls that when he delved into individual waste bins the previous evening, many contained grey-brown slops in the bottom. This is another unobtrusive measure – the fact that many staff had been so busy, their tea or coffee had gone cold and had to be poured into the bin! Since these people are clearly working rather than taking a break, the manager concludes that the vending machine is probably increasing productivity, not reducing it.

ACTIVITY 19.1

Take another look at Case Study 19.1.

What evidence is there that the manager used a triangulation of methods?

How accurate would the study have been if the manager had only used unobtrusive measures? Would the data have been reliable if he had conducted the research using, say, an interview schedule?

Suggested answers are provided at the end of the chapter.

Image 19.2   Material left at Vietnam veterans war memorial

Another example of natural accretion measures comes from Patton (2002), who refers to Palmer's study of letters and remembrances laid at the Vietnam Veterans Memorial. She took samples of material left at the memorial and then located and interviewed the people who had left it. The combination of both the materials and the interviews allowed a powerful analysis to be written of the effects of the Vietnam War on the veterans who had survived it.

Controlled accretion measures

This is where the researcher tampers with the materials that are connected to the accretion comparison. Webb et al. (2000) give the example of researchers who tested advertising exposure using the 'glue-seal method'. Here, a small glue spot was inconspicuously placed between the pages of a magazine close to the binding. After the magazine had been read, the researchers could detect, by noting whether the seals had been broken, which pages had been opened fully and looked at and which had not. This method was developed because of the tendency in question-naire surveys for respondents to falsely claim they had read or viewed an advertise-ment. But as Webb et al. note, this controlled accretion measure is rather limited in its effectiveness. It does not, for example, allow researchers to determine precisely which advertisement was seen, only which pair of pages. It also yields no data on how long an advertisement was looked at, or indeed, if it was actually viewed at all.

A more modern example of controlled accretion is the use of the Web. Many organizations make use of a Web counter to keep a tally of how many 'hits' they are receiving on their website. Sophisticated software is also now available to provide data on how long a person stayed on the site, which pages they viewed, and whether the hit came from inside or outside the organization. Where a company has a web-site that contains information that people may genuinely want (reports, articles, economic or business data, etc.), then it can grant access to the site only through visitors having to complete an online pro forma about themselves. The company can now develop a detailed profile of its potential customers that it then targets with its marketing materials.

Natural erosion measures

Here, there is a degree of selective wear or deterioration on the material being stud-ied. For example, examining the wear and tear on office carpet tiles may reveal the density of human 'traffic' in a particular section of a library. Similar deterioration in a department store might reveal the location of the most popular goods. Observation (see Chapters 16 and 17) might also be used to confirm these findings.

If, for example, you wanted to discover the most popular resources used by learn-ers in an organization's Open Learning Centre, a sensible approach would be to check the records of how often a book, video or CD Rom had been borrowed. But this is only an indirect measure, since it tells us nothing about the extent to which the resource has actually been used. Here, unobtrusive natural erosion measures could be used, checking the wear and tear on the learning materials. So, we could compare how many times page corners had been turned down on different study guides and handbooks. Playing some of the Centre's training videos might soon reveal which ones seem rather worn out. One problem, of course, is that with the move towards digital technology, such signs of wear and tear will be virtually impossible to detect.

Controlled erosion measures

In this case, it is possible to use or manipulate the extent to which something wears out against some other experimental variable. Say, for example, a company hired people to distribute its leaflets door-to-door around neighbourhoods. How does it know that the leaflets are being delivered? Using controlled erosion measures it could estimate the rate at which the distributors' shoes wore out, by taking a measurement of sole depth before they started the job and, say, after 3 months. Of course, there are many potential intervening variables here, not least of which is the extent to which staff used their shoes during their leisure time. The answer here would be to issue 'company' shoes so that this could be controlled for.

DOCUMENTS

REPOSITIONING
DOCUMENTS

Documents are some of the most frequently used unobtrusive measures and include a wide variety of personal, organizational and institutional documents, and state financial, political and legal records. We can distinguish between two types of documents: running records and episodic records. Running records include organizational documents, actuarial records and political and judicial records. In contrast to running records that tend to be in the public domain, episodic records such as personal diaries are discontinuous and tend to be private. Hence, they are often more difficult to access. Webb et al. (2000) suggest three main classes: sales records, industrial and institutional records, and personal documents. To these we can add: visual and mass media records, and institutional investigations. Many types of documents are examples of what are termed 'secondary sources' which are discussed in more detail in Chapter 20 *Secondary Analysis.*

NEW UNOBTRUSIVE MEASURES: DIGITAL ARCHIVES

So far, we have looked at quite traditional forms of unobtrusive measures, many of which include the collection of documents (of various descriptions), usually located in one place. But because of problems of access, many document archives are under-utilized by researchers. After all, if the archive that you need is hundreds or even thousands of kilometres away, you are going to have to do some serious personal planning to see it. The growth of the Internet and the World Wide Web, however, is changing this. It is also worth considering another new and digital source of information, closed circuit television, as yet another modern source of unobtrusive information.

The Internet

The Internet and World Wide Web are already making an impact on how archives are accessed.

In the long term it may well be that the greatest contribution which the Internet makes to research is to provide easier access to archives. (Sleeman, in Dochartaigh, 2002: 220)

Archives were once one of the most inaccessible research resources, and just discovering which resources were held in which archive could be a major research activity in itself. Today, however, the Internet allows archivists to put information about their collections into the public arena. The next stage, which is happening with many archives already, is then to put the collection itself onto the Web. With the provision of a search facility, it becomes possible to search for archival information from your work desk. On the Web 19.1 provides some useful examples.

INTERNET
RESEARCH

One factor that distinguishes archives from published sources, is that collections are presented so that the context and original order of the materials is maintained. This is an attempt to preserve the authenticity of the archive and its value to researchers. One of the dangers of the Web is that it can allow the user multiple access to documents at different levels. Archivists are conscious of this danger, hence, they often show the researcher how a holding was created. The use of Web links also allows for documents to be linked to one another in a variety of ways, each of which demonstrates different relationships and contexts.

➤ ON THE WEB 19.1 ◄

Take a look at the following websites, each of which provides you with access to archives of government and business information.

Euromonitor (http://www.euromonitor.com/default.asp): This site is a global information provider of strategic analysis and market statistics for dozens of global industries.

National Archives and Records Administration of the United States (NARA) (http://www.nara. gov): This site provides a research room that gives details of its records, plus a search tool, NARA Archival Retrieval Locator (NAIL), for locating archival sources across the USA.

Public Records Office, England (PRO) (http://www.pro.gov.uk): A site that contains over nine million files that are searchable through a multi-level catalogue. The database includes legal and government archives.

The National Archives of Australia (http://www.naa.gov.au): This site holds federal government records on defence, immigration, security and intelligence, naturalization and other issues.

EAN (European Archival Network) (http://www.european-archival.net): A site, organized alphabetically and geographically, for searching for European archives.

As well as websites dealing with general government and business information, there are a growing number of sites that offer access to statistics. Sleeman (2002) distinguishes between two kinds of site:

- *Statistics websites*: These are the websites of agencies (often government agencies) that collect statistics and make them available online. Not only can data tables be viewed, the sites often provide tools with which the data can be manipulated and analysed.
- *Data archives*: These provide indexes to data sets gathered from a wide variety of research projects and organizations, often allowing users to download full data sets for analysis on their own computers.

On the Web 19.2 provides you with an opportunity to explore examples of each type of website.

━━━━━━━━━━━━━━━━━━━━▶ **ON THE WEB 19.2** ◀━━━━━━━━━━━━━━━━━━━━

Statistics websites

US Census Bureau (http://www.census.gov): Provides data on the US population, income, housing, and economic and government statistics.

Statistical Resources on the Web (http://www.lib.umich.edu/libhome/ documents.center/ stats.html): A vast guide with links to economics, politics and sociology sources.

Data archives

National Digital Archive of Datasets (NDAD) (http://www.ndad. ulcc.ac.uk): Provides access to computer data sets of UK government departments and agencies.

ICPSR (The Inter-university Consortium for Political and Social Research) (http://www. icpsr.umich.edu): Provides access to the world's largest archive of computerized social science data.

Monitoring technology

Many workplaces are now becoming penetrated by a growing infrastructure of technology capable of monitoring work performance. Leaving aside, for a moment, any ethical issues, the data generated from such technology are not only of value to the organizations that had it installed, but also to researchers – if they are able to gain access to it. Davies (2001) discusses both the range and power of the emerging technologies, including miniature cameras that monitor employee behaviour, 'smart' ID badges that track an employee's movements in a building, and telephone management systems analysing the patterns of telephone use and the destination of calls.

Advances in location tracking now mean that geostationary satellite-based systems can send information on the precise location of an employee or vehicle back to a tracking centre. In the growing IT industry, employee use of their computer can also be monitored and measured, including the number of keystrokes they have been making, which websites they have accessed and the amount of time the computer was idle during the day. Many businesses routinely analyse their employees' email. Software can be used for analysing an organization's entire email traffic phrase by phrase, including a search for specific key words. In telephone call centres, software monitors the length and content of calls and the timing and duration of employee toilet and lunch breaks. Software can also monitor how often a call worker uses a customer's name and how often they try to overcome a potential customer's initial objection to a sale.

Closed circuit television (CCTV) equipment is also now becoming commonplace where people travel, shop, socialize and even work. According to Davies:

> Once viewed as a blunt tool of surveillance, CCTV in the space of fifteen years is now seen as an integral design component of the urban and the work environment. (Davies, 2001: 13)

Image 19.3   CCTV equipment in use – an example of monitoring technology

Certainly CCTV is now becoming an integral component in modern retailing. Kirkup and Carrigan (2000) relate how CCTV is being used for:

- *Security*: To deter shoplifters and pickpockets and also to detect fraudulent activities among staff.
- *Safety*: To see who is still in a building after a fire or security alert.
- *Training*: Allowing a retailer to capture the behaviour of both staff and customers that can then be used in staff development programmes.

But it is the research dimension where CCTV can provide a valuable mechanism for understanding consumer behaviour. For example, it can help retailers (or the researchers they commission) to:

- Analyse customer flows.
- Evaluate the impact of store refits.
- Identify ways of increasing store penetration.
- Measure dwell-time in different departments or on specific displays.
- Understand the nature of interactions between staff and customers.

In short, CCTV allows the retailer to explore the relationships between the profile of shoppers, their level of involvement in browsing and trialling, and the nature of their response to different stimuli (Kirkup and Carrigan, 2000). Digital technology can now be used both to gather and to analyse data. Software called 'The Observer', for example, allows for the computerized coding of observations, and the production of video 'highlights'.

→ ON THE WEB 19.3 ←

Take a look at the specifications for The Observer software and what you can do with it at:

http://www.noldus.com/products/index.html

ETHICAL ISSUES IN USING DIGITAL TECHNOLOGY
Ethics and the Internet

ETHICS IN
ONLINE
RESEARCH

Once email communication has occurred between people, it remains available for other people to access in the future. In the case of newsgroups this can be for days or weeks, but for mailing lists it can be for as much as two years. These posts and archives, then, can be used by researchers as documents for analysis, and form a potentially rich source of data. Sixsmith and Murray (2001), however, raise some intriguing ethical issues linked specifically to research using the Internet.

Accessing voices

The ethical obligations of researchers go beyond the need merely to protect participants. It is also necessary to involve those in the research process whose voices are rarely heard in research, and for whom the new digital media provide a unique opportunity for communication. This could include socially disadvantaged groups, people with disabilities or children. For Flietas (referenced in Sixsmith and Murray, 2001), email and Internet chatrooms may be perfect communication tools to address this problem. However, some of the potential ethical difficulties researchers face in accessing and using Internet postings were discussed in Chapter 4.

Gaining consent

As we saw in Chapter 4, an important feature of ethical considerations is that participants give their fully informed consent. An exception to this principle is observational research in which behaviour in the public domain may be observed without consent, so that natural behaviour can be observed in its context. But in 'observing' email and Internet communications, are researchers similarly free from seeking consent? As Sixsmith and Murray (2001) comment, this is a highly contentious issue. Some researchers believe that all posts on the Internet are in the public domain and are, therefore, available for research purposes without the need for consent. But as Sixsmith and Murray warn (and as we noted in Chapter 4), such a practice could lead to distrust and anger amongst discussion forum participants and would be highly damaging. Yet, if researchers do consult the discussion group, they run the risk of alerting participants to the fact that they are being observed and this may alter the dynamics of the group interaction. The observation would no longer be unobtrusive in the strictest sense. But Sixsmith and Murray conclude that the best course of ethical action is for researchers to consult the introductory notes or charters of electronic forums.

Even when following these kinds of guidelines, if undertaking research through a discussion list it is prudent to contact the list moderator to gain permission for the research. Even if permission is granted, researchers need to be aware that their activities may not be greeted with approval by all members on the list. In joining a discussion group, researchers should announce their presence as researchers. But later on, other new members will be unaware of this intrusion unless researchers post reminders of their presence. Of course, they will also have access to the posts of those who left messages but subsequently left the group. These people will be unaware that their comments are being used by researchers.

Respecting privacy

The ethics of research stipulate that the privacy and anonymity of participants must be respected during the research process (American Psychological Association, 1992). However, in practical terms, distinguishing between what is private and public behaviour can be difficult, since some private behaviour (for example, private conversations, intimate behaviour, etc.) can be observed in public places. Hence, the concept of privacy needs to be understood within its specific social setting.

In the case of discussion list posts, the researcher has to establish whether these are made in a public or private context. The problem here is that participants may tend to regard their posts as public (to the group) but private as far as outsiders are concerned. Since many posts are made from home-based computers, participants may tend to assume that their privacy will be respected. It may be useful, then, to distinguish between discussion groups, where privacy is probably assumed, and mailing lists where posts may be transmitted to hundreds or thousands of subscribers. Since the latter are available to everyone on the Internet, it is fairly safe to assume that they can be regarded as being in the public domain.

ETHICS OF
INTERNET
RESEARCH

Ensuring anonymity

In using archived posts for research analysis, the anonymity of participants should be preserved. Any information that could identify the originators of the post should be removed, including names or pseudonyms used, as well as the names and locations of lists and newsgroups. The problem here, however, is that the removal of this kind of information also limits the possibilities of thick description, that is, relating the research data with features such as the age, nationality and occupation of participants. Despite this problem, it is respect for ethical principles that should take priority.

Avoiding misinterpretation

In analysing data, it is important that the researcher does not misrepresent the participant's meaning or views. This can be a particular danger when using data from discussion forums or archives because the data available may be incomplete (often old posts are deleted by the moderator or writers themselves). Another problem is that the discussion group data may not represent the entire communication process, since some participants will exchange emails privately.

To reduce the danger of misinterpretation, tracts of related messages need to be considered as a group, especially since messages are often related to each other in a thread. This allows for the discursive context of a message to be considered through a more grounded interpretation.

Identifying ownership

This is a complex issue. Do posts or archives belong to the poster (author), the discussion group or the observer (who may be a researcher)? Issues of intellectual property rights and the Internet are contentious and, as yet, still largely unresolved.

JISCmail (2008), for example, a UK discussion list for the academic community, states that ownership of an email sent to a forum within the JISCmail community remains with the poster of that email. The sender also retains the moral right to be named as the author of the work. But JISCmail also warn that the poster of a message gives JISCmail permission to reproduce, distribute and archive their message as appropriate. JISCmail users may also read, save, download and print all messages sent within the JISCmail system. Hence, sending a message to a public, online discussion list is rather like sending a letter to the editor of a newsletter – it would be regarded as intended for publication, unless there was a stipulation by the sender that this was not the case. But in sending a message to a discussion group, the sender still retains 'moral rights' to work and would expect that:

- The message is not changed or reworded if forwarded on to others without the author's permission.
- The message is not quoted out of context in a way that would mislead people or damage the author's reputation.
- The name of the original sender would always be acknowledged.

Attributing authorship

It is the convention always to attribute authorship when making a direct quotation from someone's work. But what if the source is a discussion group? We have seen that JISCmail (2008) regards emails as similar to published works so that any quotation should include a credit to its source. However, as we have seen, this contradicts people's right to anonymity. The solution here is to request the author's permission before making long quotations.

Ethics and monitoring technology

Many of the above issues, particularly those relating to privacy, are also raised by the growth of monitoring technology, such as CCTV cameras and other surveillance media. Carrigan and Kirkup (2001) argue that the researcher's main responsibility is to those that are observed, but there are also responsibilities to other groups, namely:

- The client who has commissioned the research.
- The general public who may not want to be filmed in certain shops (for example, chemists, opticians or lingerie stores).
- Innocent bystanders, since modern surveillance cameras have a 360° field of vision and are capable of filming well beyond their intended zone.
- The police or legal system if criminal activities are observed.
- Employees who may be concerned that recordings of their good or bad behaviour will affect their pay or promotional prospects.

The challenge is in reconciling the interests of these disparate groups. The objective of the research might be monitoring flows of customer traffic within the store to observe interest in particular displays. But later, the store management (clients) might request the recordings to examine employee behaviour. This abuses the privacy rights of the employee and reneges on the purpose of the research. If employees become aware of this kind of potential for abuse, they may become uncooperative, which then threatens the reliability and validity of subsequent research. However, the wishes of clients are difficult to ignore since they are the financial sponsors of the research. One way out of these difficulties is through the design of ethical frameworks.

Ethical frameworks

Laczniak (cited in Carrigan and Kirkup, 2001) suggests an ethical framework through which, if any of the following questions can be answered negatively, then the action is probably unethical:

- Does action A violate the law?
- Does action A violate any general moral obligations: justice, beneficence, self-improvement, etc.?
- Is the intent of action A evil?
- Are any major evils likely to result from action A?
- Is a satisfactory alternative, action B, which produces equal or more good with less evil than action A, being knowingly rejected?
- Does action A infringe the inalienable rights of the participant?
- Does action A leave another person or group less well off, and is this person or group already relatively under-privileged?

The purpose of this framework is to sensitize researchers to the factors that are important in dealing with ethical issues. For example, if employees are monitored while customer behaviour is being recorded, is the framework being violated? The answer is 'Yes'. While no evil is being intended, we cannot be assured that no evils will arise from the action because there is no way of knowing whether employers will use the video evidence against employees. Hence, it becomes important to look for other defence mechanisms.

Professional codes of conduct

We have seen in previous chapters that many professional associations that rely on research have put in place their own professional codes of conduct. In the case of market research, for example, this is provided by the Market Research Society's (MRS) Code of Conduct which in turn is based upon the International Code of Marketing and Social Research Practice. In terms of establishing rules on the uses of video and other recording equipment, the MRS stipulates that:

- The researcher *must* [original emphasis] inform employees about any recording or monitoring methods (e.g. tape recording, video recording and presence of a mirror or a camera) both at recruitment and at the beginning of an interview, giving the employee the option not to proceed. This also applies to instances where remote monitoring is used.
- Any audio or video recordings *must not* [original emphasis] be released by a researcher or research agency unless explicit permission has previously been obtained from all the employees involved. Where such permission is to be obtained the researcher must ensure that employees are given as much relevant information as possible about the future use of the data, in particular:

    To whom they are to be given.

    To whom they are likely to be shown.

    For what purposes they are likely to be used.

- Any recorded data collected for research purposes *must* [original emphasis] not be used for any non-research purpose (Market Research Society, 2010).

However, as Carrigan and Kirkup (2001) note, as yet, many professional codes contain few specific references to the use of CCTV in retail settings. They also exclude the need to inform individuals where observation techniques or recording equipment are being used in a public place. Unfortunately, one of the difficulties is in the definition of a 'public place', with some organizations arguing that this includes the workplace, thereby gaining exclusion from codes of conduct. Conversely, employees and their trade unions or professional associations may disagree with this broad definition. The codes of conduct of some television companies suggest that when filming in an institution there is no obligation to seek agreement when people are shown incidentally, randomly or anonymously. However, Carrigan and Kirkup (2001) argue that employees are not anonymous in this sense and so deserve equal rights of privacy. Where employees are the specific subject of the surveillance where standards of service are being evaluated, further safeguards are needed. For example, the video material should not subsequently be used for purposes other than the original objective (hence, it should not be used for disciplinary purposes). Staff should also be informed that filming is going to take place. The professional code of the European Society for Opinion and Market Research (ESO-MAR) stipulates that participants must be asked to give their permission for the use of video recordings for non-research purposes and should be given the opportunity to have the media deleted. If researchers pass a video on to a client it must be labelled with appropriate restrictions.

➤ ON THE WEB 19.4 ◄

Take a look at the Market Research Society's Code of Conduct at:

http://www.mrs.org.uk/

Click on Code/Guidelines, and look in particular for guidelines dealing with employees.

See also the website of the European Society for Opinion and Market Research at:

http://www.esomar.nl/guidelines/Tapeandvideo.htm

Ethical contracts

Since many professional codes are still trying to catch up with the ever-changing developments in technology, Carrigan and Kirkup (2001) suggest that an important safety net can be provided by ethical contracts. These make transparent the roles and responsibilities of all stakeholders, including the researcher, before any research is undertaken through:

- Clarifying the aims and nature of the research.
- Identifying, with stakeholders, any potential conflicts that may arise.
- Drafting resolutions to these problems.
- Seeking the explicit agreement of all those affected.

If, at any point, a stakeholder wishes to act outside of the contract, the agreement of all other stakeholders must be sought.

There are, however, differences between employees and customers as subjects of surveillance research in that employees can be identified by the researcher or by their client. As such, the researcher has a particular responsibility to ensure anonymity for these individuals, or at least informed consent. Staff should be given assurance about the objectives of the research and should be allowed open access at all times to the CCTV control room. These objectives should not include using surveillance for non-research purposes such as disciplinary action, and permission for filming (although not necessarily its timing) should be sought.

Seeking the permission of customers is much more problematic. First, it would be simply impractical to ask all customers individually for their agreement. Secondly, there might be circumstances when the researcher might not want customers to know that they were being filmed since this might affect their subsequent behaviour. Most market research codes of practice allow researchers to withhold this information to reduce the risk of bias. But permission would have to be obtained if the researcher wished to pass on video footage to any third party. If a recording is passed on to a client, it should be labelled with appropriate restrictions that the recipient should be made aware of. It is also important that the video data are not held for longer than the purposes for which they were collected. Kirkup and Carrigan (2000) suggest a maximum time period of 31 days for CCTV footage, after which it should be destroyed.

Summary

- Unobtrusive measures involve the use of non-reactive sources such as files, photographs, videos, sound recordings and drawings, and now the Internet.
- Unobtrusive measures include the analysis of physical accretion and erosion measures, and the use of documents that include a wide range of organizational, business and personal records.
- One of the advantages of using unobtrusive records is that they deal with 'dead' data, and they do not pose the risk faced by many other research methods of reactive measurement effects such as interviewer bias, or socially conditioned responses by participants.
- An important source of unobtrusive measures are documents that include running records (such as actuarial, political and judicial records) and episodic records (such as sales records and personal records).
- Unobtrusive measures carry with them their own inherent problems in that documents, for example, may be stored selectively, survive selectively and be inaccurate and incomplete.
- The growth of the Internet and monitoring technology such as CCTV means that the scope for research using unobtrusive measures is increasing at a rapid rate. However, the new technology also brings with it new ethical challenges which require recognizing the interests of disparate groups. The use of ethical contracts may be one way of reconciling these different interests.

REVIEW QUESTIONS

1. A researcher seeks to identify the radio stations that people listen to in his home town. Using an unobtrusive measures approach, he goes to five of his local garages where cars are being repaired, and finds what radio stations car radios are tuned to. He could have used a survey approach. Why do you think he chose unobtrusive measures in this case?
2. Thinking of media in your own home or office, are there any documents, videos, photographs or other media that are now in a format that cannot be 'read'? What does this tell you about the vulnerability of digital and other records?
3. Why is it prudent to use other data gathering methods when using unobtrusive measures?

─ FURTHER READING ─

Webb, E.J., Campbell, D.T., Schwartz, R.D. and Sechrest, L. (2000) *Unobtrusive Measures.* Thousand Oaks, CA: Sage. Something of a classic, it was in this book that the term unobtrusive measures was originally coined and described with elegance, clarity and intriguing examples. First published in 1966, Sage have helpfully republished a revised version of the book in their Sage Classics series.

Lee, R.M. (2000) *Unobtrusive Measures in Social Research.* Buckingham: Open University Press. Given that the pioneering work of Webb et al. was written in 1966, this is a welcome and very much updated discussion of the subject. It also contains a useful chapter on unobtrusive measures and the Internet.

─ JOURNAL RESOURCES ─

Marrelli, A.F. (2007) 'Unobtrusive measures', *Performance Improvement*, 46(9): 43–47. Application of unobtrusive measures in performance technology is outlined, including their advantages and disadvantages.

Kiofas, J.M. and Cutshall, C.R. (1985) 'The social archeology of a juvenile facility: Unobtrusive methods in the study of institutional cultures', *Qualitative Sociology*, 8(4): 368–388. A study that uses content analysis of graffiti collected from the walls of an abandoned Massachusetts juvenile correctional facility.

─ SUMMARY OF WEB LINKS ─

http://www.naa.gov.au

http://www.census.gov

http://www.esomar.nl/guidelines/Tapeandvideo.htm

http://www.euromonitor.com/default.asp

http://www.european-archival.net

http://www.icpsr.umich.edu

http://www.lib.umich.edu/libhome/documents.center/stats.html

http://www.nara.gov

http://www.ndad.ulcc.ac.uk

http://www.noldus.com/products/index.html

http://www.mrs.org.uk/

http://www.pro.gov.uk

http://www.statistics.gov.uk

─ Suggested answers for Activity 19.1 ─

Triangulation of methods is evidenced by the fact that the researcher uses observation (of where people consume their drinks), as well as using the unobtrusive indicators. This, certainly, helps towards the reliability of the study.

Using an interview method would probably not have worked here because the honesty of replies could not be assured – and would the manager have believed them?

20

SECONDARY ANALYSIS

CHAPTER INTRODUCTION

Chapter outline

Advantages and disadvantages of
using secondary data 515

Sources of secondary data 516

Qualitative data sources 524

Secondary data analysis 525

Criteria for selecting a data set 527

A systems approach to using
secondary data 528

Secondary data methodologies 530

Secondary data in mixed
methodologies 531

Ethical considerations in
secondary analysis 532

Keywords

Secondary data analysis

Secondary data sources

Primary data

Secondary data

Ethics

— Chapter Objectives —

After reading this chapter you will be able to:

- Define what is meant by secondary data.
- Evaluate the advantages and disadvantages of using secondary data.
- Describe the sources of secondary data such as national and local government records, the records of agencies and business organizations, etc.
- Describe the kinds of secondary sources available such as census returns, financial records, annual reports, policy documents, newspaper articles, diaries, biographies, etc.
- Implement a systems approach to making use of secondary sources.
- Undertake secondary data analysis ethically.

SECONDARY
ANALYSIS

There are numerous definitions of secondary data often involving quite subtle differences, suggesting that there is an overall lack of consensus as to what the term actually means (Smith, 2006). According to Heaton (1998), secondary analysis involves the use of existing data, collected for the purpose of a prior study, in order to pursue a research interest which is distinct from the original work. This may comprise a new research question or an alternative perspective on the original question. However, for Schutt (2007), even re-analysis of one's own data for a new purpose constitutes secondary analysis. Whatever the definition, secondary analysis involves the use of data that have already been gathered or compiled and may involve the use of new statistical approaches or theoretical frameworks (Smith, 2006). Secondary sources may be analysed in conjunction with primary data sources (such as surveys, interviews, observations etc.) or instead of primary data. In terms of the kinds of sources, secondary data may be gleaned from census returns, government records at national and local level, business organizations (including financial records, annual reports, minutes of board meetings, policy documents), scientific papers, human resource records, newspaper articles, websites or social media. Secondary sources can provide a rich insight into the history of an institution, its mission, its presentation of self and how others perceive it (Schneider, 2006a). Whether sources are considered primary or secondary depends on the relationship of the researcher to them. So, if the data were collected by the researcher, they may be considered primary data. If collected by one researcher but used by another, the latter considers them secondary data. However, as we shall see, if a researcher returns to their own data set at a later date, but with new research questions or theoretical framework, some researchers would regard this as secondary data analysis. Hence, the distinction between primary and secondary data analysis is not always clear cut. Finally, it should not be overlooked that a literature review is itself an example of secondary data analysis.

QUALITATIVE
SECONDARY
ANALYSIS

→ **TOP TIP 20.1** ←

If you are undertaking an academic qualification such as a Master's degree, check as to whether you are permitted to conduct (a) a dissertation using only secondary data sources or (b) a dissertation as a review of the literature. Some institutions insist on the use of primary data only. This, however, takes a somewhat limited perspective since, as we shall see, secondary sources can offer a rich seam of data.

ADVANTAGES AND DISADVANTAGES OF USING SECONDARY DATA

The Internet has brought professional researchers and students instant access to sources and volumes of data sets that previous generations could only just imagine. However, this is a two-edged sword, since researchers now have to distinguish between what is valid and useful data and what is garbage. Hence, in deciding whether to make use of secondary sources, researchers need to weigh up the pros and the cons involved. While secondary data analysis is increasingly considered a legitimate and valuable way of conducting research, the potential disadvantages and problems mean that this must be done with care.

WHAT IS SECONDARY ANALYSIS

Advantages

- Cost. The data have already been collected by another individual or research team. Even if the data set has to be purchased, its cost is likely to be less than would have been incurred if the data had been collected from scratch.
- Time is another factor. The researcher can get on with data analysis rather than go through the processes of research design, instrument design, data gathering, data entry and data cleaning. By being timely, studies using secondary data can be of more interest to policymakers who need up-to-date information (Hofferth, 2005).
- Breadth and scale of data sets available. These include national surveys and data that have been collected on a longitudinal basis. Secondary data are also available in greater quantity allowing for the use of more powerful statistical tests (Rabinovich and Cheon, 2011).
- Replication. If the data are publicly available, they will give scholars the opportunity to carry out replication studies to fine tune or validate initial findings (Welch, 2000).

IMPORTANCE OF SECONDARY ANALYSIS

- Explaining change and evolution. Since data often cover long periods of time, they can be useful in generating developmental explanations about a phenomenon and the changes to it that have occurred.
- Detachment. Secondary analysis may allow for the viewing of a data set with more objectivity that might be difficult to achieve for the original researcher (Szabo and Strang, 1997).
- Professionalism. Data often come from sources developed by teams of professional researchers who have many years of experience in research design and data collection (Boslaugh, 2007).
- Social benefits. Secondary analysis is unobtrusive (see Chapter 19) in that additional data are not collected from individuals, hence protecting their privacy (provided that anonymity is preserved). It also means that sensitive, vulnerable or hard-to-reach populations do not have to be contacted again.
- Convenience for student researchers. It has been suggested that the use of secondary data is a particularly convenient approach for student researchers (Szabo and Strang, 1997), given that they often have to complete dissertations to very demanding timescales.

Disadvantages

- Data might be incomplete, obsolete, inaccurate or biased. In the case of the latter, for example, sources may tend to offer published studies where statistical significance has been found; a way of addressing this is to also use unpublished studies.
- Mismatched objectives/questions. Secondary data have been collected with reference to specific research questions which may not be those of the team seeking to use them for secondary analysis. Or they may have been collected with reference to one geographical area whilst the team is interested in another. The data set may also have been

developed with reference to a set of variables that do not closely match those required by the new research. For example, the data set may have collected categorical data but the research requires continuous data. There is also no opportunity for the researchers to ask supplementary questions (Szabo and Strang, 1997). This can partially be overcome at the validation stage by getting someone who closely matches the demographic profile of the original research sample to comment on the new analysis.

- Data quality. A potentially serious drawback is that the researcher does not know how or how well the data were collected; for example, response rates may have been low, or the data gathering instruments may have contained errors or inconsistencies that call into question the validity and reliability of the data. Thorne (1994) argues that when the researcher is not part of the original research team, secondary data sets are best utilized only by experienced researchers. However, Szabo and Strang (1997) advise that these problems can partly be overcome by the researchers establishing effective communication with the original researchers to glean information on the research context.

- Data mining. The availability of secondary data may mean that the researcher snoops around the data looking for themes of interest, rather than commencing with a set of research questions or hypotheses. Hofferth (2005) advises that if this is the case, while the data can be used in an exploratory fashion to develop a hypothesis, to test a hypothesis, alternative data should be sought. Alternatively, the data could be split into two separate sub-samples, the first one used for exploration and the second for hypothesis if the intention is testing.

- The cost of learning a new data set. It takes time to become familiar with a data set through getting to know the questions, the documentation and the structure of data files. This is why, for large-scale data sets, organizations often provide training courses to familiarize potential users with the data.

SOURCES OF SECONDARY DATA

SOURCES OF
SECONDARY
DATA

Given the wide range of subject disciplines, it would be simply impractical to provide a comprehensive description of secondary data sources for all of them (some discipline-specific sources are suggested under Further Reading). Instead, what follows is a range of examples illustrating the breadth and the utility of using secondary data:

- Archives and gateways
- Personal documents
- Organizational documents
- Professional and technical reports
- Political and judicial records
- Visual and mass media
- Academic sources
- Official statistics

Note, however, that these categories are not distinct and that there will often be some overlap between them.

Archives and gateways

Archival research is described by Welch (2000: 197) as 'an archaeological process in that it involves the discovery and interpretation of fragmentary evidence'. Archival data can be created by individuals for their own purposes (for example, diaries, letters, photographs, weblogs and discussion list postings – see Personal documents) or by organizations (see Organizational documents). Fischer and Parmentier (2010) suggest that archival data have mainly been used to help the development and understanding of the research context (to supplement interviews and observational data), rather than as a main source of data themselves. However, archival data are fast becoming a viable source largely because an ever increasing amount is now available over the Internet.

In using archival data, Welch (2000) offers a five-stage process:

- Discovery. Establishing the location of an appropriate collection is not always a simple task. In the case of an organization, for example, staff turnover means that corporate memory is often lost – current employees are unaware of the existence of archival evidence. Or the company's records may not be in its own keeping – they may be in national archives for example (see: http://www.nationalarchives.gov.uk/records/).
- Access. Even if a collection is located, there may be restricted access to it or the collection may be private. Companies, for example, have no obligation to make their records publicly available. It may be a case of trying to negotiate access.
- Assessment. Once accessed, it then becomes necessary to evaluate the quality of the sources.
- Sifting. This means sorting the documents into a meaningful or systematic order either in terms of chronological order or by theme or category.
- Cross-checking. This is used for verification purposes. Hence, data triangulation is adopted by cross-checking sources from more than one collection. Methodological triangulation means cross-checking sources by using an alternative strategy – for example, interviews.

Personal documents

Personal records include letters, diaries, autobiographies, biographies and oral histories. Brewer (2000) suggests a way of classifying personal records across two dimensions. The first is whether the records are primary (compiled by the author) or secondary (containing data obtained from someone else's primary document). A second dimension is contemporary (compiled as a document at the time) or retrospective (produced as a document after the event). Using these dimensions, we get four categories, as illustrated in Figure 20.1.

As Brewer warns, making generalizations from such documents can be problematic, especially if they are personal documents about one individual. There may be more possibility of generalizations if the documents can be shown to be representative or typical of a group. The contents of personal documents should also be evaluated for distortion, misrepresentation, exaggeration and omission.

Organizational documents

Organizational documents include a large array of sources that can include: board minutes, the minutes of annual general meetings, corporate annual reports, correspondence files including emails, staff records, financial statements, press releases, advertisements, magazine articles, ratings websites, etc. A company, for example, might collect data on employee headcount, employee turnover, promotions and absenteeism. In terms of finance, many organizations are interested in knowing the

CONTEMPORARY PRIMARY Compiled by the writer at the time		CONTEMPORARY SECONDARY Transcribed from primary sources at the time	
Personal	**Official**	**Personal**	**Official**
Letter Audio recording of a talk Suicide note	Court record Census Minutes of a meeting	'Ghosted' autobiography Edited transcript of a talk, letters etc.	Research using the census
RETROSPECTIVE PRIMARY Compiled by the writer after the event		RETROSPECTIVE SECONDARY Transcribed from primary sources after the event	
Personal	**Official**	**Personal**	**Official**
Diary Autobiography Life history Oral history	Novels Historical archives Film archives	Research using diaries Biography using the subject's autobiography	Medical records Parish records Judicial records Newspaper reports

Figure 20.1   Sources of personal records

Source: Adapted from Brewer, 2000

size of their borrowing and the costs of financing it, turnover compared to profits and share price movements. Hakim (2000) also points to health service records, school records, membership records of trade unions and voluntary associations, records of births, deaths and marriages, police, court and prison records. Such records tend to be updated over time. Hakim also suggests that these types of records are expanding with the spread of computerized management information systems. One of the distinct advantages of using them is their non-reactivity. While the information may sometimes be inaccurate or incomplete, at least it is not usually manipulated by the producer of the data in the knowledge that the material is going to be studied. Hakim (2000) suggests that administrative records can provide the basis for longitudinal studies, quasi-experimental designs, international comparisons and studies of organizations and their development of policy.

On the negative side, there are at least two sources of potential bias: selective deposit and selective survival. Hence, which records, documents or materials are archived by an organization will depend both on the policy of that organization but also on the extent to which that policy is implemented by its employees. In most modern organizations there exists a store of 'official' records, such as legal and financial documents, company reports, rules and regulations, staff handbooks and human resource records. But in addition, there will exist a wealth of less official 'grey' materials such as emails, memoranda, minutes of meetings, team plans, marketing ideas, etc. that are an integral part of the knowledge base and thinking of the organization. Many of these will be stored on the computer hard drives of designated employees (company secretary, HR manager, Director of Marketing, etc.) or shared networks, or are created and stored by individuals. What is stored or shared (often via email attachments) and what is discarded will often be a matter of individual choice, rather than organizational policy. Hakim (2000) warns that researchers who use organizational records will often find that vital data are missing, or that they have to contact employees to have the data interpreted or explained to them, to avoid erroneous assumptions.

Developments in computer technology have made the chances of records surviving both better and worse. We are all familiar with how the ravages of time have destroyed many ancient records. Those artefacts that we can see in museums have survived because of their composition (stone or clay rather than paper or wood, for example), or just by luck. Computers allow us to store vast amounts of data efficiently – or do they? There are many ways in which computers hinder the survival of data and records. First, there is plentiful evidence of computer failure – systems crash and backups fail. Secondly, there is the problem of incompatible computer systems; if, say, an organization moves to a single computer platform, what happens to the data on the discontinued system? Thirdly, there is technical obsolescence. In theory, computer systems are upwardly compatible, so that upgraded computers can read the data on older systems. But in the case of the original 5-inch floppy disk, these data can only be read if they were copied to a hard drive. Similarly, how many of today's videos will be available for viewing in 10 years' time when all transmission equipment is digital and most VCRs have broken down?

Apart from the impact of computers on data survival, organizations themselves are subject to mergers, takeovers and closures, all of which impact on whether data survive or are discarded. For example, if a company is taken over by another, which of its records would the new owner want to retain? Since the aggressor company already has its own legal, financial, operational and HR set up, it would probably not want to retain all of the captured company's records. It is not only large companies where data and documents are destroyed. Many small organizations fail to survive beyond their first few years of existence. In addition to the casual destruction of records as organizations move or merge, there is also the risk of the deliberate destruction of material where this highlights the errors that organizations have made.

→ **TOP TIP 20.2** ←

In exploring organizational archives, reliability can be improved by comparing the data with that from other sources, such as newspaper or other media reports, customers or suppliers. This does not eliminate the risk that records are biased through selectivity, but it does at least reduce it.

USING
ORGANISATIONAL
ARCHIVES

Professional and technical reports

Professional reports are used to gather information that is useful to an audience in the workplace (or profession). If this report also comments in some way on technology, then it is more likely to be called a technical report. Professional and technical reports might be commissioned by professional associations, governments or large corporations and might be completed by consultants, academic research institutions or government departments. Baake (2007) comments how technical reports can include sub-genres such as feasibility studies, which investigate a subject to analyse whether it is acceptable or not; similar to this, recommendations reports balance a number of different options before making a recommendation. Technical reports may be large scale and national. For example, should a country electrify its train system? Or they may be focused on orientation. For example, what type of student record system should a university install? Technical and professional reports allow the researcher an insight into the aspirations, values and worries of an organization or government.

Political and judicial records

The study of voting statistics and opinion polls is now almost an element of popular culture, and certainly one that is common in the mass media. Political pundits and researchers are interested not only with voting intentions, or the total votes cast for a particular party or candidate, but also with a breakdown of votes cast by region, locality, age group and social class. Voting behaviour is studied because it is seen by some as a 'window' into the hearts and minds of people as electors, citizens, workers and consumers. This assumes, of course, that people do not vote tactically, that is, they vote for the party of their genuine political choice, and not for another party to keep the party they dislike most out of office. Other political records include the speeches and voting behaviour of members of the government legislature (see On the Web 20.1). These are of interest not only to political commentators but also to professional lobbyists hired as consultants by businesses, interest groups and campaigning organizations. Another source for gauging the views of politicians is interviews or comments in the media through television programmes and the press. Particularly if a source is an article written by a journalist, one has to be especially conscious of the threats to validity through biased reporting and hidden agendas.

Image 20.1　Political records include data on voting behaviour

One potentially useful source of data that justifies more consideration is the use of evidence from legal and judicial investigations. Many governments, for example, set up special commissions to investigate large-scale disasters (such as rail crashes) or public inquiries into the siting of a new airport. It is not so much the subject focus of these inquiries that is of interest, but what the debate and dialogue reveals about the roles of organizations, institutions and pressure groups that attempt to influence the state. Of course, one of the dangers is not knowing the extent to which witnesses have been screened or specially selected, and what evidence has been submitted and what withheld.

➤ ON THE WEB 20.1 ◂

See text and videos of UK parliamentary debates at:

http://www.parliament.uk/business/publications/hansard/

Visual and mass media records

Industrial societies are now awash with visual images in the mass communication media, many of which can provide a novel source of data, worthy of investigation and analysis. These include advertisements, newspaper photographs, textbooks, comics and magazines, postcards and product packaging. If we take advertisements first, consider whether groups such as ethnic minorities or women are depicted in ways that are obviously different. Lee (2000) refers to the work of several researchers that suggests that real differences do exist. In some countries, visual images of black people, for example, are under-represented in advertisements, and where they appear, this is often in stereotypical roles as sportspeople or musicians. When black and white people appear in the same advertisement, they are rarely interacting with one another (Lee, 2000).

Academic sources

These include academic journals, doctoral theses and dissertations (recall Chapter 5). Whether they offer secondary data depends on the approach taken. Some articles, for example, may be purely conceptual, presenting, evaluating and reformulating concepts and theories; as such they may contain little or no data, but they may provide a comprehensive literature review of what has already been written. However, empirically based articles will contain data, but their use in secondary analysis will depend on the extent to which the original data is presented. Due to challenges of space, empirical articles may offer summaries of the data rather than the data files themselves. It will be a matter of judgement as to whether these summaries or meta-analyses are a valid and reliable representation of the underlying data.

ACADEMIC
SOURCES

Reference books are often a useful source of secondary material and are diverse in terms of both titles and content. Scott (1990) distinguishes between three types (although he acknowledges that there are overlaps between them). Firstly, directories, that typically list inhabitants of an area or members of an organization or association. Secondly, almanacs, an annual calendar of dates and information related to those dates. While they originally provided religious and astronomical data, modern almanacs have been extended to include the weather and political events. The famous *Whitaker's Almanack*, published since 1868, includes a wealth of information on many subjects including average life expectancy in every country, extensive data on every country in the world, and directory listings on educational institutions, clubs, and media. Thirdly, Scott (1990) describes yearbooks, which, as the name implies, are an annual publication that aims to bring a subject area up-to-date, presenting the same basic information each year. So, for example, the *Global Compact International Yearbook* (2011) describes the strategic policy initiative of the United Nations for businesses that are committed to aligning their strategies with ten principles in the areas of human rights, labour, environment and anti-corruption.

→ **ON THE WEB 20.2** ←

See the *Global Compact International Yearbook* at:
http://www.unglobalcompact.org/news/

Official statistics

Official statistics are collected by governments through their various agencies and departments and can provide a rich source of specialized data for the researcher. Another important benefit is that they are often collected over long periods of time and hence offer the opportunity for longitudinal studies. There may, however, be a number of drawbacks to using official statistics including:

- The scale of government surveys requires large numbers of interviewers who may not receive sufficient training; this may lead to a lack of standardization and interviewer bias
- Resource limitation may inhibit the timely and accurate reporting of results

Table 20.1 provides examples of the kinds of large scale statistical data sets available.

Table 20.1 Sites for large scale survey data

Organization	Scope and subjects	Links to other data archives/data sets
Office for National Statistics (ONS) at www.statistics.gov.uk	Subjects comprise: Agriculture and the Environment; Business and Energy; Children and Education; Crime and Justice; Economy; Government; Health and Social Care; Labour market; People and Places: Population; Travel and Transport	Annual Business Survey (ABS). The ABS is the ONS's financial information survey which covers approximately two thirds of the UK economy. The survey samples UK businesses, and other related establishments, according to their employment size and industry sector.
Data.gov.uk at www.data.gov.uk	Brings together in one searchable website over 8,000 data sets from central government departments and public and local authorities.	Department for Communities and Local Government Department of Health Home Office

Organization	Scope and subjects	Links to other data archives/data sets
The UK Data Archive at http://www.data-archive.ac.uk/	The UK Data Archive is curator of the largest collection of digital data in the social sciences and humanities in the UK.	The Economic and Social Data Service (ESDS) is a national data service providing access and support for an extensive range of key economic and social data, both quantitative and qualitative, spanning many disciplines and themes. Includes Eurobarometer Survey Series – a programme of cross-national and longitudinal comparative social research conducted on behalf of the European Commission, designed to monitor social and political attitudes. British Household Panel Survey (BHPS). The main objective of the BHPS is to further understanding of social and economic change at the individual and household level in Britain, and to identify and forecast such changes and their causes and consequences in relation to a range of socio-economic variables.
The National Centre for Social Research at www.natcen.ac.uk	NatCen is an independent not-for-profit organization, dedicated to making an impact on society and advancing the role of social research in the UK. Since its foundation in 1969 it has grown to become Britain's largest independent social research organization with a team of 350 permanent staff and a field force of 1200 freelance interviewers.	The British Social Attitudes survey, which has been conducted annually since 1983, asks a sample of over 3,000 people (selected through random probability sampling) about what it is like to live in Britain and how they think Britain is run. The survey tracks people's changing social, political and moral attitudes and informs the development of public policy. Topics include work, transport, health, education, government spending and voting habits, as well as religion, racism and illegal drugs.
NHS: the Information Centre for Health and Social Care at http://www.ic.nhs.uk/statistics-and-data-collections	The statistics and data collection site contains survey data on a wide variety of subjects including: health and lifestyles, hospital care, mental health, social care, and the NHS workforce.	Links to Office for National Statistics and the Department of Health.
The Organization for Economic Cooperation and Development (OECD) at http://www.oecd.org/	The OECD provides statistical data on a huge range of world topics, themes including agriculture, the economy, education, energy, science and technology, and trade.	Not applicable.

CASE STUDY 20.1

Imaginative use of secondary data sources

This case study presents two research studies that made imaginative use of secondary sources. In the first, Barker (2006) describes her study of why American states use prison confinement differently in response to crime, using three case studies: California (which imprisons 455 inmates per 100,000 population), Washington (262 inmates per 100,000 population) and New York (343 inmates per 100,000 population). While different, these are examples of typical case sampling – Louisiana's rate, for example, is 803 inmates per 100,000. Barker (2006) contends that these state variations can, in part, be explained by levels of citizen participation, with wider participation tending to keep prison levels lower. The study was conducted purely on the basis of secondary sources which included: transcripts from town hall meetings; letters to public and political leaders; public hearing testimony; state constitutions; penal codes; legislative bill files; governors' papers; state agency reports and memos; legislative committee reports; oral histories; newspaper clippings; statistical information; state histories; and social and political histories.

In the second study, Zubrzycki (2011) investigates, looking at Poland as an example, how nationalist mythology is created and sustained. She argues that national mythology is structured by historical events but also embodied in visual and material cultures, which in turn frame national subjects' understanding of the present. However, the extent to which national mythologies can shape national identity or mobilize people towards nationalistic action depends on the specific historical contexts in which they are employed. In conducting this analysis, Zubrzycki conducted both ethnographic and archival research. The ethnographic research, conducted in the course of 40 months over 20 years, included participant and non-participant observation of religious events, popular festivals, historical commemorations, national holidays, political demonstrations, touristic excursions and museum visits. For secondary data, she used primary texts (poetry, textbooks, newspaper editorials); iconographic materials (icons, paintings, prayer cards, postcards, photographs, graffiti and advertisements); audio-visual materials (photographs, films and amateur videos, radio broadcasts, music and soundtracks); and artefacts (flags, jewellery, crosses, monuments and devotional objects).

ACTIVITY 20.1

As Case Study 20.1 shows, secondary analysis can be conducted alongside other methodologies such as ethnography. What are the benefits of doing this? What are the drawbacks?

QUALITATIVE DATA SOURCES

USING
SECONDARY
DATA

The potential gains (and also some of the drawbacks) of using secondary analysis of qualitative data have gained increasing attention in recent years (Hammersley, 2010) particularly in the USA and to a lesser extent in Europe and Australia (Heaton, 2008). A major landmark in the development of the archiving of qualitative data came in 1994 with the setting up of Qualidata, the world's first organization for promoting archiving and reusing qualitative data, established at the University of Essex (see On the Web 20.3). Since then, in the UK, the Economic and Social Research Council (ESRC) now requires researchers to deposit qualitative data sets from primary research which it has funded (Heaton, 2008).

► ON THE WEB 20.3 ◄

Take a look at the website for the Economic and Social Data Service (ESDS) at:

http://www.esds.ac.uk/qualidata/

Under 'Which Service?' you can select from government, international, longitudinal or Qualidata. The ESDS government site offers data on health, consumption, ethnic differences and employment. ESDS international provides access to international macro data sets and help for users in acquiring international micro data sets. ESDS longitudinal includes data sets on the British Household Panel Survey, the English Longitudinal Study of Ageing, and the Longitudinal Study of Young People. The ESDS Qualidata site provides access to qualitative data from across the UK. In all of the sets, useful information is provided as to the authors of the study and their affiliations (institution), as well as background details on the dates of the fieldwork, the type of observational unit (for example, individuals), the population sampled and methodology. User guides to using the data are often provided, as are notes on how the data were cleaned and checked for gaps or errors.

► ON THE WEB 20.4 ◄

For a comprehensive list of guides for the Economic and Social Services data sets go to:

http://discover.ukdataservice.ac.uk/?sf=User%20guides

SECONDARY DATA ANALYSIS

The secondary analysis of qualitative data derived from previous studies includes the analysis of materials such as semi-structured interviews, responses to open-ended questions in questionnaires, field notes and research diaries (Heaton, 2008). Heaton (2004) argues that secondary data analysis involves a focus on *non-naturalistic* qualitative data and can be distinguished from documentary analysis, which involves working with *naturalistic* or 'found' materials such as autobiographies, personal diaries and photographs. However, some types of qualitative sources such as life stories and diaries can be classified as either secondary or documentary sources, depending on the extent to which the material was shaped by the involvement of the researcher (Heaton, 2008). Heaton (2004) offers a typology of approaches to qualitative secondary data analysis, which are dependent on the extent to which the aims of the primary and secondary data analysis converge or diverge:

SECONDARY
DATA ANALYSIS

- *Re-analysis*. Data from a previous study are re-examined to confirm and validate the original findings.
- *Supplementary analysis*. A more in-depth look is taken of emergent issues or elements of the data that were not explored in the original study.
- *Supra analysis*. The aims and focus of the secondary study transcend those of the original study.
- *Amplified analysis*. Two or more existing qualitative data sets are compared and contrasted.
- *Assorted analysis*. Re-use of existing qualitative data is carried out alongside the collection and analysis of primary data for the same study.

As with quantitative data analysis, there are disadvantages or at least dangers in using qualitative data. For example, there may be a potential lack of fit between the data available and the objectives of the secondary analysis and a lack of knowledge about the contexts through which the data were collected (Thorne, 1998). As a result, the data sets are either difficult to interpret or the analysis may be strewn with errors. Hammersley (2010) counters this by arguing that even in conducting primary research such as interviews, there is always a sense in which interview data are co-constructed between researcher and respondent. We should not assume, then, that the researcher knows and understands everything about the interview context and that interpretation is error-free. To address the problem of context Gladstone et al. (2007) suggest that researchers should try to get access to original audio/video tapes or transcripts as well as background information on interviewers including their age, gender, race and social class. It also helps to know how participants were recruited as well as information about gatekeepers and issues of access.

Anything that helps the researcher feel close to 'having been there' and to imagine the emotions and cognitions of participants and researchers during data collection is particularly valuable (Hinds et al., 1997). In qualitative research, secondary analysis creates the potential to intensify the effects of researcher bias (the bias of the original researcher, compounded by the bias of the secondary researcher). Thorne (1998) also cautions that most qualitative data sets are sufficiently small to harbour all sorts of statistically improbable conditions, creating the potential for exaggerating the influence of convincing peculiarities within the data. A further line of criticism is epistemological. Mauthner et al. (1998) argue that because the original context in which the data were produced cannot be recreated, the normal criteria against which qualitative data can be evaluated cannot apply. Indeed, qualitative data are the products of the reflexive relationship between researcher and researched which means that secondary analysis can only be legitimately applied to methodological exploration. Fielding (2000), however, counters this argument saying that the problems associated with the analysis of secondary data are not epistemological but practical, above all having to deal with incomplete data.

(RE) USING
QUALITATIVE
DATA

— CASE STUDY 20.2 —

Reusing qualitative data sets

Bishop (2007) offers a reflexive account of reusing qualitative data accessed through the ESDS Qualidata website on the topic of convenience foods and choice and particularly the phenomenon of individuated eating of processed foods. The study used two qualitative data sets: Blaxter's *Mothers and Daughters* (2004) and Thompson's *The Edwardians* (2005) to explore attitudes and practices about early forms of processed foods and about food choices at meals. Blaxter's work revealed a preference for 'proper' meals as opposed to eating processed foods which were regarded as snacks. Thompson's *Family Life and Work Experience before 1918*, carried out between 1970 and 1973, was the first national oral history interview study to be carried out in Britain, with people who were born before 1911. Bishop (2007) discusses how Thompson's data has detailed descriptions of social practices at meals, who ate together, manners, the allocation of food and the availability of tinned food.

After preliminary data exposure and reading of transcripts and the sociology of food literature, Bishop formulated a number of research questions, including:

What range of attitudes towards convenience foods is expressed?
Under what conditions is the use of convenience foods accepted?
How do these attitudes vary across time, age of respondents and social class?

Data analysis revealed a number of categories such as: types of food, cooking techniques, definitions of 'good' food, plus reference to tinned food, convenience and processed foods. Bishop comments that one of the advantages of the Edwardian data is its size and representativeness. Hence, it is possible to pose questions such as: do expressions of individual choice at meals vary with occupation, region or gender? However, she is also aware of the limitations of her data. For example, the *Mothers and Daughters* sample is narrow, including only women in social classes IV and V (partly or unskilled occupations) in one Scottish city. She is therefore cautious about generalizing from this base. However, given that in the UK convenience foods are associated in the public mind with laziness, low morals and lower social class, it seemed particularly germane to focus on attitudes to convenience foods expressed by members of lower socio-economic groups.

Bishop (2007) concludes by reflecting not on the differences between primary and secondary data analysis but on the similarities. For example, in undertaking her project with secondary data, defining questions, locating data and sampling proved to be very similar to if she had collected the data herself. What was most familiar was the process of working back and forth: from questions to data and back; from one data source to another; and from data to explanation and back. She describes this as a *bricolage* made systematic by reflexivity. Yet there were also differences. While all qualitative data are constructed within a context, reusing the data creates new dimensions across time.

Source: Adapted from Bishop, 2007.

— ACTIVITY 20.2—

What does Bishop mean by *bricolage?* How does reflexivity help towards creating this *bricolage?*

CRITERIA FOR SELECTING A DATA SET

Once a data set has been located, the next step is to judge whether it is 'fit for purpose' which means evaluating the quality of the secondary material in relation to the aims of the proposed study. Hofferth (2005) offers a number of suggestions:

EVALUATING
DATA SETS

- Does the design of the study fit the research questions? We saw in the section on 'Advantages and disadvantages of using secondary data' (above) that there can often be a mismatch between the research questions of the current study and those of the original research. Furthermore, were the data collected from a sample of the population fitting to the current study?
- Are the sample sizes for the sub-group of interest large enough? Even if the size of the original sample is large, the number of cases of a particular category may be much smaller.
- Are the methods and research tools used in the study appropriate? The data may need statistical adjustments, for example using tools that take multiple levels of analysis into account.

- Can missing data be explained and adjusted? The researcher needs to know why the responses to a question do not have as many cases as are in the full sample. Is this due to survey instruments that make use of skip patterns that sort respondents into different groups and routes them to specific questions; or is it because the respondent did not know the answer or refused to answer the question?
- Does the data set have the measures needed? The data set may have information on the topic, but are the properties of the scales and indices used acceptable in the field? What information is provided on the validity and reliability of the scales used? For example, analysis relying on self-reports may not be acceptable to some research sponsors or publications.

Figure 20.2 offers an assessment tool for judging the value of a document for secondary data analysis.

A SYSTEMS APPROACH TO USING SECONDARY DATA

One of the challenges facing researchers is not so much in finding secondary data, but rather in deciding how to put limits on what is collected. It is thus essential to put in place coherent strategies for collecting data, especially when the role of the data is central to a research project (Fischer and Parmentier, 2010). Furthermore, as we have seen, one of the problems faced by researchers is that mismatches often arise between the secondary data that are accessed, and the kinds of data required by the research questions posed within a project. One way of minimizing this problem is making use of a systematic process. Fischer and Parmentier (2010) suggest that the researcher starts by creating an inventory of the kinds of archival material they could access and then examine selections of the data in order to familiarize themselves with the phenomenon of interest. Boslaugh (2007) and Smith (2006) suggest some additional stages, saying that the researcher should:

1. Define the focus of the research.
2. Specify the population that is to be studied.
3. Specify the variables that are to be included in the analysis, for example, age, educational attainment and unemployment rates, etc.
4. Decide on what kind of records are appropriate to the study. For example, national longitudinal surveys, personal diaries, photographs, etc.
5. Create a data list of the sources that are most appropriate to the research focus. At this point, since these sources are unlikely to provide a perfect fit, it will become necessary to either revise the data requirements, or the research focus to fit the sources.
6. Evaluate the data set to identify problems such as missing data, or out of range values. In doing this, it will be necessary to ask the following questions:
   i. What was the original purpose for which the data were collected?
   ii. What kind of data are they, and how were they collected? Who collected the data (for example, were they professional researchers?)?
   iii. What kind of questions were used and how rigorous were piloting procedures?
   iv. What were the sampling strategies and the response rates? What groups, if any, were excluded from the data and does this matter?
   v. When were the data collected – are they timely?
   vi. What kind of cleaning or recoding procedures have been applied to the data?
7. If problems cannot be eradicated, look for another data set.

Criteria for determining the general quality of primary study data set			
Ready access to study documents/ team?	Yes		No
- Tapes of interviews - Hard copies - Field notes - Memos and interpretive notes			
	Satisfactory	Unable to determine	Unsatisfactory
Credentials of team members conducting primary study			
Completeness of data set	Yes		No
- Available documents are complete - Transcriptions are accurate - Typographic errors are minimal - Software is appropriate			
Ability to assess quality of interviewing	Satisfactory	Unable to decide	Unsatisfactory
- Interviewing quality - Interview responses in depth - Focus/meaning of responses can be determined			
Able to assess sampling plan	Yes		No
- Type of sampling plan clear (e.g. convenience, purposive, etc.)			
	Present in sufficient depth	Unable to determine	Not present in sufficient depth
Criteria for determining fit of secondary research question			
	Likely	Not sure	Unlikely
Study sample could be expected to experience concept/situation			
	Similar	Somewhat similar	Not similar
Proposed research question is similar to that of primary study			
	Yes		No
Data set of sufficient quality, completeness and fit with secondary research questions			

Figure 20.2   Criteria for evaluating the use of secondary qualitative data

Source: Adapted from Hinds et al., 1997

It is important to know whether any theoretical model lay behind the research project since this will influence the kinds of data collected. A further issue is knowing how the data were collected. If they were collected, say, through telephone interviewing, how were respondents selected; and how was adjustment made for the bias introduced because not all households own a telephone? What was the response rate and how were non-respondents followed up? As we saw in On the Web 20.3, organizations providing secondary data offer guidance on many of these issues as a matter of course.

SECONDARY DATA METHODOLOGIES

There are a number of alternative approaches to the analysis of secondary data that will depend partly on the nature of the secondary sources themselves, and also on the aims of the research project. Presented next are two common approaches.

Meta-analysis

META-
ANALYSIS

While researchers can summarize prior studies on a particular theme through literature reviews, the aim of meta-analysis is to subject those studies to the rigour of statistical tests. For example, meta-analysis may be used to critically evaluate the results and claims made by previous studies. So meta-analysis might examine whether the results of previous research are meaningful (depending on the size of the sample and the magnitude of values obtained) and whether the findings support the conclusions reached. It is essential that meta-analysis begins with well formulated research questions and the operationalization of constructs (Rabinovich and Cheon, 2011), allowing the researcher to hone in on relevant data sets to address the research questions.

— CASE STUDY 20.3 —

Using secondary data to conduct a meta-analysis

Glass (1976) reports on a meta-analysis project used to integrate the outcome evaluation literature in psychotherapy and counselling. Through an extensive literature search, nearly 400 controlled evaluation studies on the effects of psychotherapy were found, each described in quantitative or quasi-quantitative terms. More crucially, each study reported on the 'effect size', that is, the mean difference between the outcome variable between treated and untreated subjects, divided by the within group standard deviation. Hence, a study could be described as having a .5, a .75 or a –.25 standard deviation effect of therapy. Other features reported by the studies included the duration of therapy (hours), the experience of therapists (years), the diagnosis of patients (neurotic, psychotic), and the type of therapy (Freudian, behaviour modification, client-centred, etc.), the organization of the therapy (individual or group), and the type of outcome measured (anxiety, self-concept, physiological stress, etc.).

In terms of findings, the average size of the overall effect size measures was about two-thirds standard deviation above the control group mean of the outcome variable. While the impact of the four different types of therapy were not greatly different, overall therapy could be expected under average conditions to move subjects from the 50th percentile to the 75th percentile of the untreated population. What emerges from this meta-analysis (and which would not emerge from the mass of individual studies) is that for all the superiority claimed by one therapy over another, 'the available evidence shows essentially no difference in the average impact of each class of therapy' (Glass, 1976: 7). Glass concludes that often the proofs within research reside in a vast literature, making meta-analysis an important methodological approach.

Source: Adapted from Glass, 1976

—ACTIVITY 20.3—

In Case Study 20.3, the meta-analysis focuses on nearly 400 quantitative studies. What would be the challenges (apart from the volume of data) of conducting a meta-analysis of a similar number of qualitative studies?

Event studies

Event studies, as the name implies, evaluate the impacts caused by the occurrence of events on dependent constructs. For example, a study could evaluate the impact of the privatization of a public service, or the impact of global warming on the sustainability of land use in developing countries. One of the first tasks in event studies is to define the event itself and the period over which the event has occurred. So, in the case of privatization, is the focus going to be on one year after the event, two years, or more? Sources for event studies might include the use of financial reports, company data and press releases, but Rabinovich and Cheon (2011) warn that these may contain important gaps, making it necessary to gather data from individuals who have been directly involved in the event. This is an example of combining secondary analysis with primary data (see 'Secondary data in mixed methodologies'). Researchers will then have to consider the criteria for the measurement of the dependent constructs. For example, how do we define what is meant by 'sustainability'? This allows researchers to identify how these constructs change as a result of the events.

EVENT DRIVEN
RESEARCH

SECONDARY DATA IN MIXED METHODOLOGIES

It has been assumed so far that studies make use of secondary data sets alone. However, secondary data analysis can be conducted before, in addition to, or after other research approaches. Secondary analysis, for example, can identify themes and help to generate hypotheses that are then tested through a survey; conversely, empirical testing done through a survey can be followed up by post hoc secondary data analysis that offers additional insights into the original research questions (Rabinovich and Cheon, 2011; Heaton, 1998). Secondary analysis, then, is used as part of a validation process. This is particularly useful when the empirical research throws up spurious or unexpected findings. In using secondary data as part of a mixed methodology, the kinds of opportunities offered by mixed methods research designs, but also some of the challenges, are the same as those discussed in detail in Chapter 8, *Research Design: Mixed Methods.*

— CASE STUDY 20.4 —

Using secondary data in a mixed methods study

A study by McKenna and Hasson (2002) illustrates how mixed methods can include the use of secondary data. Hospitals in Ireland faced a shortage of experienced midwives, so the study sought to investigate the feasibility of introducing a healthcare assistant grade into the midwife workforce. The study began with secondary analysis in terms of a comprehensive search of the literature (using online bibliographies), to uncover any previous investigations in this area. The search revealed very few investigations. The study itself used several approaches: the Delphi technique, a postal questionnaire, and the analysis of secondary data. This combination of strategies helped the researchers to validate the findings.

The Delphi technique involves a series of 'rounds' through which a discussion group of research participants attempts to reach a consensus on an issue, each round building on the results of the previous one. The first round participants were asked to list eight non-midwifery tasks they carried out as part of their normal duties. In round two, participants were asked to identify which of these tasks could be allocated to a midwifery assistant. Then, using the literature and the responses from Round One of the Delphi, a questionnaire was constructed to survey respondents' views on issues such as staff turnover, skill mix and the role of midwife assistants. Results showed that most respondents felt that staff turnover was triggered by low morale and by staff shortages.

The secondary data analysis was then conducted using workload and staffing levels data for the period 1985–97. The results revealed an increase in midwifery workloads, partly due to rising birth rates. At the same time there was a rise in sickness rates, particularly amongst the more qualified midwives, and a rise in the number of resignations. Hence, the secondary data was highly effective in supporting the views of midwives expressed in the Delphi sessions and through the questionnaire that workloads had increased and staff numbers fallen.

— ACTIVITY 20.4 —

Returning to Figure 8.1 in Chapter 8, which of the mixed methods designs most closely aligns with the study described in Case Study 20.4?

ETHICAL CONSIDERATIONS IN SECONDARY ANALYSIS

At first sight it may appear that ethical considerations are irrelevant or minimal in secondary analysis because there are no face-to-face interviews or observations of human behaviour taking place. However, as Gladstone et al. (2007) point out, the issues of informed consent and confidentiality are not eliminated – they are just highlighted in different ways. Thorne (1998) asks whether posing new questions of previously collected data violates the consent obtained when the original study was conducted, perhaps one reason why Hinds et al. (1997) suggest that researchers should seek permission from the primary study participants for the secondary analysis of their data. Thorne (1998) also advises that secondary analysts should familiarize themselves with the actual and potential privacy needs of individuals and

ETHICAL &
REPRESEN-
TATIONAL
ISSUES

populations in the databases they employ. For example, informants in studies dealing with living with cancer might assume that their responses will help to inform health professionals about the subjective experience of cancer illness; but imagine their distress if they learn about a secondary analysis that is probing their accounts for words indicating the presence of a 'cancer-prone personality' (Thorne, 1998). As Gladstone et al. (2007) advise, researchers need to be able to defend their judgement as to the scope of the original consent and the conditions under which secondary analysis is appropriate. Institutional Review Boards now often make provision for participants to give their consent to the future use of data for other purposes.

Summary

- Secondary analysis involves the use of existing data, collected for the purpose of a prior study, in order to pursue a research interest which is distinct from the original work.
- Secondary sources include census returns, government records at national or local level (such as finance, welfare, employment), and the records of agencies and business organizations.
- The advantages of using secondary data include costs and time saved in not having to undertake primary research, the breadth and depth of (quantitative) data sets available, and the fact that vulnerable or hard to reach populations do not have to be re-interviewed.
- The disadvantages include the fact that the data might be incomplete, inaccurate or obsolete and there may be a mismatch between the data and the new research questions.
- Large scale sources of quantitative data sets include: the Annual Business Survey, the British Household Panel Survey, the British Social Attitudes Survey.
- Qualitative data sets are now available at the Qualidata website.
- The criteria for selecting a secondary data set include questions such as: Does the design of the study fit the research questions? Are the sample sizes for the sub-group of interest large enough? Are the methods and research tools used in the study appropriate? Can missing data be explained and adjusted?
- Ethical considerations for using secondary data include researchers being able to defend their judgement as to the scope of the original consent and the conditions under which secondary analysis is appropriate.

REVIEW QUESTIONS

1. How useful is it to distinguish between primary and secondary data?
2. What are the advantages and drawbacks of using secondary sources?
3. What advantage does data gathering using secondary sources have over conducting interviews?
4. How can the use of secondary data sources be mixed with other research methodologies? What are the benefits of the mixed approach?
5. In using secondary data sources, researchers are one step away from the primary researcher's field. What steps can researchers take to breach this gap?

FURTHER READING

Vartanian, T.P. (2011) *Secondary Data Analysis (Pocket Guides to Social Work Research Methods)*. Oxford: Oxford University Press. Primarily aimed at social workers, this text outlines the pros and cons of using secondary data, and provides an introduction to 29 of the most used data sets in social work.

Trzesniewski, K.H., Donnellan, M.B. and Lucas, R.E. (2010) *Secondary Data Analysis: An Introduction for Psychologists*. American Psychological Association. As the title implies, this book is mainly for psychologists and covers different fields of study including adult and adolescent development, cross cultural psychology and political beliefs and actions. The book encourages a critical perspective on making use of secondary data.

Hakim, C. (2000) *Research Design,* 2nd edn. London: Unwin Hyman. Although mainly focused on the general principles of research design, Chapter 2 provides some help on meta-analysis and secondary analysis.

JOURNAL RESOURCES

Jones, D.E., Feinberg, M.E., Cleveland, M.J. and Cooper, B.R. (2012) 'A multidomain approach to understanding risk for underage drinking: Converging evidence from five data sets', *American Journal of Public Health*, 102(11): 2080–2087. Examines the independent and combined influence of major risk and protective factors on youths' alcohol use, using five large data sets. The results combined using meta-analytic techniques.

Rabinovich, E. and Cheon, S-H. (2011) 'Expanding horizons and deepening understanding via the use of secondary data sources', *Journal of Business Logistics*, 32(4): 303–316. Outlines the use of secondary data analysis in addressing challenges in logistics and supply chain research. A review of the logistics and supply chain literature identifies six important methodologies that can be useful for secondary data generation and analysis.

Popkess, A.M. and McDaniel, D. (2011) 'Are nursing students engaged in learning? A secondary analysis of data from the National Survey of Student Engagement', *Nursing Education Perspectives*, 32(2): 89–94. Using a descriptive, correlation design, the study incorporated a secondary analysis of National Survey of Student Engagement data collected during 2003.

SUMMARY OF WEB LINKS

http://www.nationalarchives.gov.uk/records/

http://www.parliament.uk/business/publications/hansard/

http://www.unglobalcompact.org/news/

www.statistics.gov.uk

www.data.gov.uk

http://www.data-archive.ac.uk/

www.natcen.ac.uk

http://www.ic.nhs.uk/statistics-and-data-collections

http://www.oecd.org/

http://www.esds.ac.uk/qualidata/

PART D

Analysis and Report Writing

— Contents —

21.	Getting Started Using SPSS	537
	Getting around the SPSS interface	538
	Naming and defining variables	543
	Entering and modifying data	547
	Navigating the Windows interfaces	548
	Handling missing data	549
	Recoding or transforming data	550
	Exporting into MS Word	551
	Getting help	551
22.	Analysing and Presenting Quantitative Data	553
	Categorizing data	554
	Data entry, layout and quality	558
	Presenting data using descriptive statistics	562
	Analysing data using descriptive statistics	566
	The process of hypothesis testing: inferential statistics	569
	Statistical analysis: comparing variables	572
	Statistical analysis: associations between variables	582

23.	Analysing and Presenting Qualitative Data	601
	Elements of qualitative data analysis	603
	Analysing qualitative data	607
	Other approaches to qualitative analysis	621
	Quality in qualitative analysis	622
	Software for qualitative data analysis	625
24.	Writing up the Research	631
	The report writing process	633
	The report structure	637
	Ethical and legal considerations	649
	Developing a writing style and tone	652
	Undertaking a review process	655
25.	Preparing for Presentations and Vivas	659
	Preparing the presentation	660
	Structuring the presentation: beginning, middle and end	662
	Structuring the presentation – the density of ideas	663
	Creating interest in presentations	665
	Delivering the presentation	666
	Team presentations	668
	Preparing for and surviving vivas	670

21

GETTING STARTED USING SPSS

CHAPTER INTRODUCTION

Chapter Outline

Getting around the SPSS interface 538

Naming and defining variables 543

Entering and modifying data 547

Navigating the Windows interfaces 548

Handling missing data 549

Recoding or transforming data 550

Exporting into MS Word 551

Getting help 551

Keywords

SPSS

Quantitative data

Defining variables

Data entry

Data analysis

Recoding data

— Chapter objectives —

After reading this chapter you will be able to:

- Use the main functions of the SPSS interface
- Name and define variables
- Input data into SPSS
- Handle missing values
- Recode and transform data
- Use the Analyze function
- Use SPSS in a confident manner

SPSS (originally called Statistical Package for the Social Sciences), was first launched in 1968 and today is one of the most widely used and respected computer programs for the analysis of quantitative data that is able to deliver the analysis and presentation of:

- Descriptive statistics: frequencies and cross-tabulation
- Bivariate statistics: means, t-tests, ANOVA, correlation and non-parametric tests
- Prediction of numerical outcomes: linear regression
- Prediction for identify groups: factor analysis, cluster analysis

However, for inexperienced researchers, the thought of having to make use of a statistical program like SPSS often induces feelings of fear, stress and dread. This, though, should not be the case as this chapter sets out to prove. Here we will introduce you to some of the main features of SPSS such as how to input data, how to use menus and tools to conduct data analysis, how to create tables and charts, and how to export output into external documents such as Word. It will not get into details about what kind of statistical tests to use as this is the subject of Chapter 22, *Analysing and Presenting Quantitative Data*.

GETTING AROUND THE SPSS INTERFACE

Before we take a look at entering data into SPSS we are going to take a tour around some of the most useful features of the SPSS interface.

ACTIVITY 21.1

Launch SPSS either from your computer desktop (if the SPSS icon appears there) or by going to **Start** and locating SPSS from the menu. Once launched, you will see the screen as illustrated in Figure 21.1 (or a similar interface, depending on what version of SPSS you are running).

SPSS USER
INTERFACE

Figure 21.1 illustrates one of the main ways of viewing data in SPSS, namely, **Data View** which displays your actual data and any new variables you choose to create. Another view of data is called **Variable View** where the variables are listed down the side of the screen with their characteristics (name, type, etc.) along the top (see Figure 21.5). Notice in Figure 21.1 that the interface contains both rows and columns for data. In Data View, the columns represent the different variables in your study, while the rows represent each case. So, for example, if your questionnaire contains the variables gender, age and hatred of spiders, then there will be a column for each of these variables. Row 1 would be for all the responses from your first case (for example your first questionnaire), and Row 2 for the responses from the next case (questionnaire), and so on.

Like any Windows-based program, SPSS offers a range of dropdown menus (see Menu bar in Figure 21.1) and shortcut items (see Toolbar). On the Menu bar you will notice dropdown menus such as **File, Edit, View** and **Analyze.** We will focus here on these four menus since they deal with some of SPSS's basic but essential features.

— ACTIVITY 21.2 —

On the menu bar click on **File**. You should see a dropdown menu as in Figure 21.2. This shows that you can start a new file, open an existing file that you created or imported earlier, **Save** a file you have created, **Print** the window or **Exit** the program.

— ACTIVITY 21.3 —

On the menu bar click on **Edit**. You should see a dropdown menu as in Figure 21.3. The Edit menu allows you to insert a new variable (vertical columns), or to insert a new case (horizontal rows). So, say last week you set up an SPSS file containing responses to a survey you are conducting. Today a new set of questionnaires have just been returned. Each questionnaire represents a new case that you will want to add to your data set, so you will want to use the **Insert Cases** function.

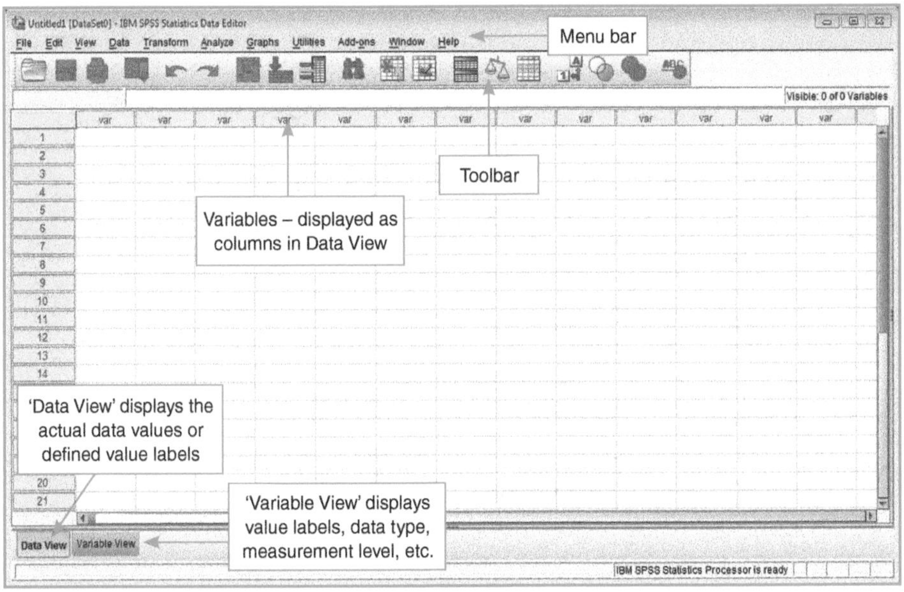

Figure 21.1   The SPSS interface – Data Editor window in Data View

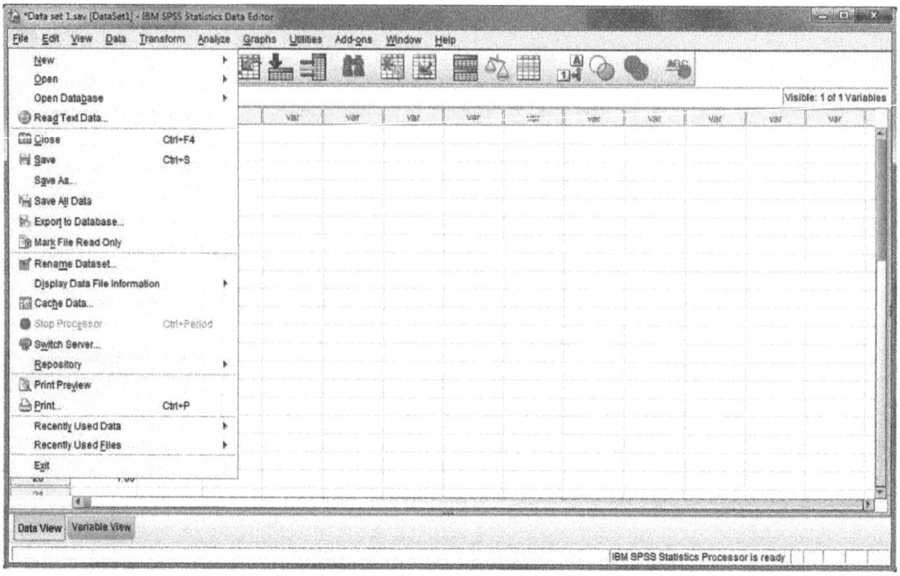

Figure 21.2   The File menu in Data View

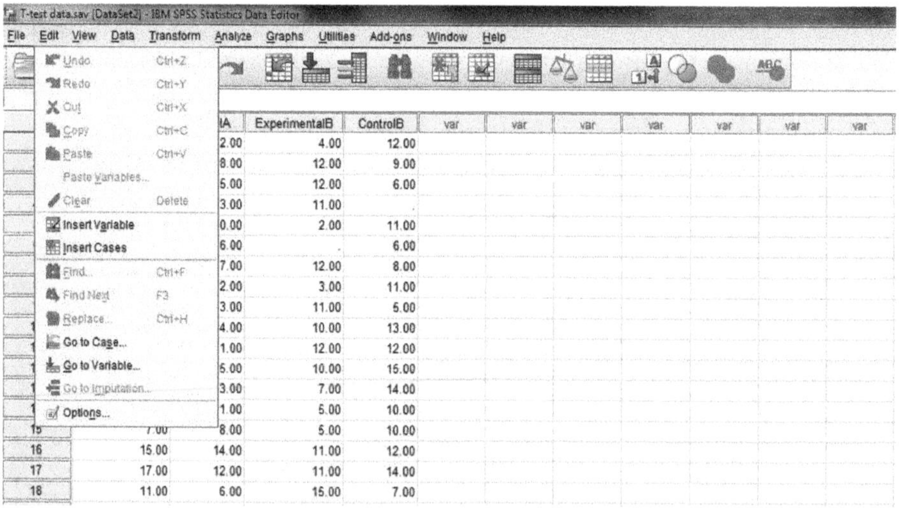

Figure 21.3   The Edit menu in Data View

→ **ON THE WEB 21.1** ←

For a useful introduction to the SPSS interface and for ways of inputting or importing data
into SPSS, go to:

http://www.youtube.com/watch?v=msl7xf0tlnE

— ACTIVITY 21.4 —

On the menu bar click on **View**. You should see a dropdown menu as in Figure 21.4. The **View** menu allows you to customize the Toolbar, change the look of the fonts, and remove or put back grid lines to the page. The **Variables** option allows you to switch to **Variable View** and back again to **Data View**. You can also do this by toggling between the Data View and Variable View buttons at the bottom left of the screen.

— ACTIVITY 21.5 —

On the menu bar click on **Analyze**. You should see a dropdown menu as in Figure 21.5. The Analyze menu is the place where all statistical analysis is conducted. Some of the most commonly used functions here include Descriptive Statistics (which includes Frequencies and Cross tabulations – a crosstab being a summary table), Regression analysis and Non-parametric statistics (including t-tests). We will explain and get you to use many of these statistical tools in Chapter 22.

DATA ANALYSIS

— ACTIVITY 21.6 —

On the menu bar click on **Graphs**. You should see a dropdown menu as in Figure 21.6. As its name implies, the **Graphs** menu allows you to create a variety of graphs and charts from your data, including histograms, bar charts and pie charts. Again, you will have an opportunity to use many of these graphing functions in Chapter 22.

Figure 21.4   The View menu in Data View

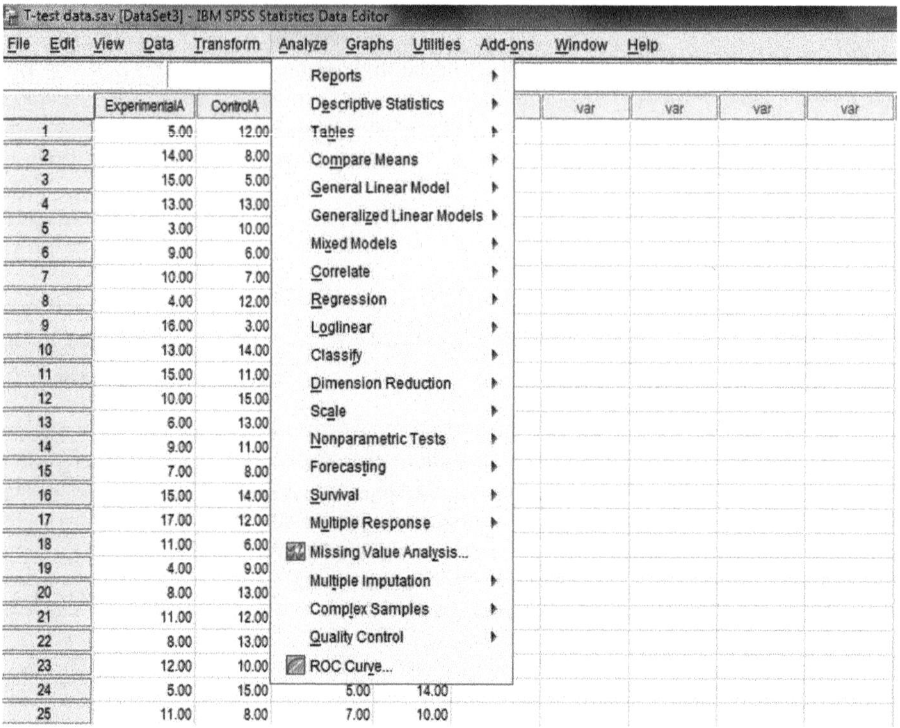

T-test data.sav [DataSet3] - IBM SPSS Statistics Data Editor

File Edit View Data Transform Analyze Graphs Utilities Add-ons Window Help

	ExperimentalA	ControlA	Reports ▶		var	var	var	var
			Descriptive Statistics ▶					
1	5.00	12.00	Tables ▶					
2	14.00	8.00	Compare Means ▶					
3	15.00	5.00	General Linear Model ▶					
4	13.00	13.00	Generalized Linear Models ▶					
5	3.00	10.00	Mixed Models ▶					
6	9.00	6.00	Correlate ▶					
7	10.00	7.00	Regression ▶					
8	4.00	12.00	Loglinear ▶					
9	16.00	3.00	Classify ▶					
10	13.00	14.00	Dimension Reduction ▶					
11	15.00	11.00	Scale ▶					
12	10.00	15.00	Nonparametric Tests ▶					
13	6.00	13.00	Forecasting ▶					
14	9.00	11.00	Survival ▶					
15	7.00	8.00	Multiple Response ▶					
16	15.00	14.00	Missing Value Analysis...					
17	17.00	12.00	Multiple Imputation ▶					
18	11.00	6.00	Complex Samples ▶					
19	4.00	9.00	Quality Control ▶					
20	8.00	13.00	ROC Curve...					
21	11.00	12.00						
22	8.00	13.00						
23	12.00	10.00						
24	5.00	15.00	5.00	14.00				
25	11.00	8.00	7.00	10.00				

Figure 21.5   The Analyze menu in Data View

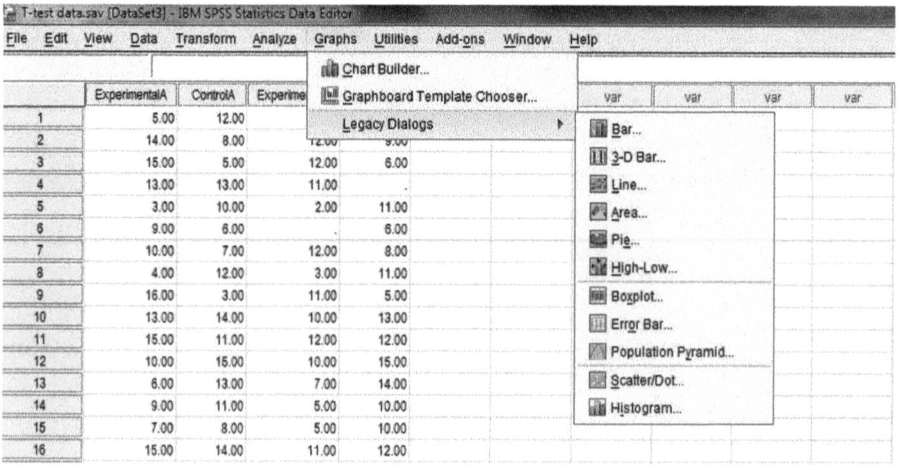

T-test data.sav [DataSet3] - IBM SPSS Statistics Data Editor

File Edit View Data Transform Analyze Graphs Utilities Add-ons Window Help

	ExperimentalA	ControlA	Experime	Chart Builder...		var	var	var	var
				Graphboard Template Chooser...					
1	5.00	12.00		Legacy Dialogs ▶	Bar...				
2	14.00	8.00	12.00	9.00	3-D Bar...				
3	15.00	5.00	12.00	6.00	Line...				
4	13.00	13.00	11.00		Area...				
5	3.00	10.00	2.00	11.00	Pie...				
6	9.00	6.00		6.00	High-Low...				
7	10.00	7.00	12.00	8.00	Boxplot...				
8	4.00	12.00	3.00	11.00	Error Bar...				
9	16.00	3.00	11.00	5.00	Population Pyramid...				
10	13.00	14.00	10.00	13.00	Scatter/Dot...				
11	15.00	11.00	12.00	12.00	Histogram...				
12	10.00	15.00	10.00	15.00					
13	6.00	13.00	7.00	14.00					
14	9.00	11.00	5.00	10.00					
15	7.00	8.00	5.00	10.00					
16	15.00	14.00	11.00	12.00					

Figure 21.6   The Graphs menu in Data View

NAMING AND DEFINING VARIABLES

Having gained a 'feel' for the SPSS interface, you are now ready to enter data. However, before you do this you need to set up names for your variables and tell SPSS how you want the variables coded. This process of defining variables is done in the **Data Editor** window which, as we saw earlier, consists of two areas: **Data View** and **Variable View** (see Figure 21.1 above). Each column in the **Data View** is given the default label of **var**. You will be changing this when you name your own study's variables.

→ TOP TIP 21.1 ←

Pallant (2010) rightly suggests that researchers should create a codebook, the purpose of which is to provide an outline of the instructions needed to convert the data gathered as part of the study into a format for input into SPSS. Essentially the two main stages comprise:

CODE BOOK

- Defining and labelling each of the variables
- Assigning a number for each possible response

For examples of defined variables and assigned numbers see Table 21.1, below. To define your variables, click on the Variable View tab. Note that in Variable View the variables are listed down the left-hand column (gender, age etc.), with the characteristics of each variable (Type, Width, Decimal places, etc.) along the top of the screen – see Figure 21.7. Taking each of the variables in Figure 21.7, we will now see how each can be modified and how some key variables need to be defined in more detail.

Name

There are specific rules for naming variables. Hence, each variable:

- Must be unique (so you could have Attitude 1 and Attitude 2, but not two data sets called Attitude)
- Must begin with a letter and not a number
- Cannot include symbols or punctuation (?, ", &, %)
- Cannot include words that are used in commands (all, eq, ne, le, to, lt, by, or, gt, and, with, ge)
- Cannot contain blank spaces
- Must not end with a full stop
- Cannot exceed 64 characters

	Name	Type	Width	Decimals	Label	Values	Missing	Columns	Align	Measure	Role
1	id	Numeric	8	0	Identification nu...	None	None	8	Right	Nominal	Input
2	gender	Numeric	8	0	Gender	{1, Male}...	None	8	Right	Nominal	Input
3	age	Numeric	8	0	Age	None	None	8	Right	Nominal	Input
4	mar	Date	11	0	Date married	None	None	8	Right	Scale	Input
5											

Marriage.sav [DataSet3] - IBM SPSS Statistics Data Editor
File Edit View Data Transform Analyze Graphs Utilities Add-ons Window Help

Figure 21.7 The Variable View window

Table 21.1 Examples of full and abbreviated variable names

Full name	SPSS abbreviated variable	Coding instructions
Identification number	id	Subject identification number (each case, for example, questionnaire, will be given its own identification number
Gender	Gen	1 = male; 2 = female
Age	age	In years
Marital status	marital	1 = single; 2 = married; 3 = divorced; 4 = civil partnership; 5 = separated; 6 = remarried; 7 = widowed
Married (date)	mar	Date
Residence	res	1 = detached house; 2 = semi-detached house; 3 = flat; 4 = bungalow
Highest level of education	ed	1 = primary; 2 = secondary; 3 = undergraduate; 4 = post graduate
Type of business	bus	1 = corporate; 2 = SME; 3 = voluntary
Employment	emp	1 = full time; 2 = part-time; 3 = unemployed
Training	train	1 = classroom; 2 = coaching; 3 = mentoring; 4 = distance learning

━━ **ACTIVITY 21.7** ━━━

Under **Name**, type in an abbreviated variable name, using the variables for your study devised in your codebook. So, for example, your study might require the variables 'gender', 'age' or 'highest level of education'. Table 21.1 offers some examples of typical variables often used in research studies. The Table gives a full variable name, an abbreviated version of the name that you type into SPSS, plus some coding instructions, and is typical of the kind of information described in a codebook.

Type

DEFINING
VARIABLE
TYPES

SPSS insists on what are termed *strongly typed* variables, that is, variables that are defined according to the type of data they will contain. Because of this, it is important to ensure that all the data in any field are consistent. Variable types include:

- **Numeric**. A variable whose values are numbers. The name Numeric appears automatically in the Type column, largely because this default option is what is required in most cases. **Binary** variables are a special subset of numeric variables and include yes/no, male/female, and 0/1. It is clearly not possible to perform a calculation on yes/no or male/female; but this does become possible if they are recoded into numeric values such as assigning a value of 1 to female and 0 to male. It is then quite simple to calculate what proportion of the sample are male and female.
- **String**. Value of a variable that is not numeric. String is also used for numbers that cannot be used as part of a calculation – for example, telephone numbers or postcodes. String numbers, then, need to be treated differently to numbers. You could use these as numbers and calculate them but the results would be meaningless!
- **Date**. A numeric variable the values of which are displayed in one of several calendar-date or clock–time formats.

To change from **Numeric** to one of the other options simply click in the cell and a box will appear from which you can select other options – see the **Variable Type** box Figure 21.8.

Width

The default value for **Width** is 8 which is sufficient for most situations. It only becomes necessary to expand this value if your variable has very large values or if you have selected a **String** variable that contains more than 8 letters. Figure 21.8 below shows where you can change to **String** in the **Variable Type** and where you can modify the **Width**.

Decimals

The default value for **Decimals** is 2, that is, numbers are presented to 2 decimal places. If you want to change this, you will need to go into Options. Click on **Edit/ Options/Data**. In the **Data** tab you will see **Display Format for New Numeric Variables**. You can then, for example, change the **Decimal Places** option to 0. This means that all data will be displayed as whole numbers, simplifying the appearance of data files. You can also change the **Decimals** value for individual variables just by clicking on its **Decimals** tab in **Variable View** and clicking the up or down arrows.

→ **ON THE WEB 21.2** ←

For more on naming variables go to:

http://www.indigorose.com/webhelp/ams/Tips/Naming_Variables.htm

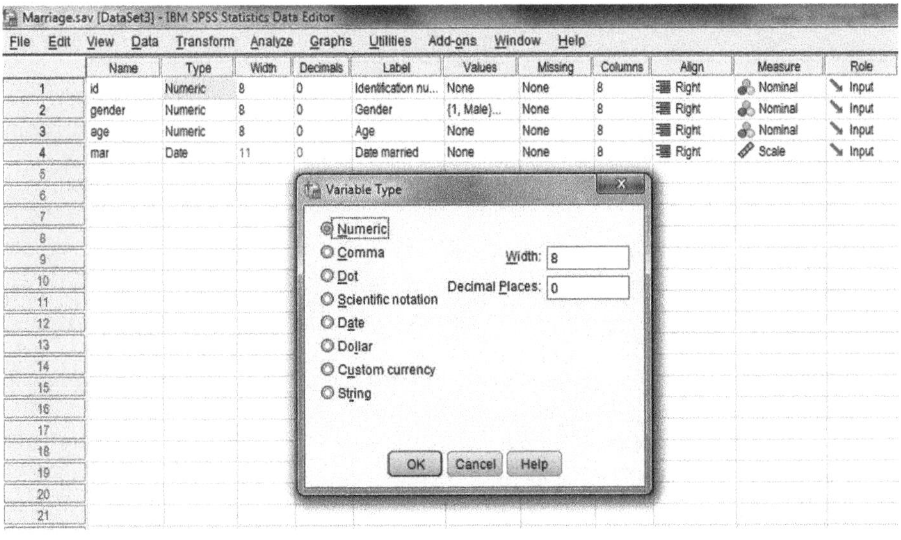

Figure 21.8   Changing the variable Type

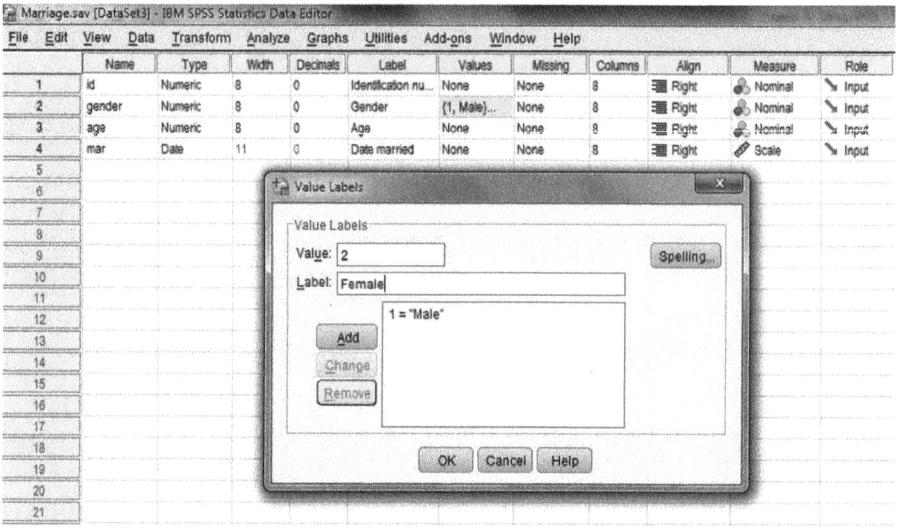

Figure 21.9   The Value Labels box after '1' has been added to Value and 'Male' to Label

——— **ACTIVITY 21.8** ———————————————————————————————————————

For each of the variable names you have created under **Name**, you need to give each Name a variable Type. The default Type is **Numeric**. If you wish to change this, just click on the cell containing the word **Numeric** and a dialogue box will appear (see Figure 21.8). Click on the appropriate radio button. If you need to, adjust the Width and Decimal Places and then click on **OK**.

Label

The **Label** column provides an opportunity to input a longer and more comprehensive label compared to the one used in the **Name** column (see the left-hand column in Table 21.1).

Values

The **Values** column allows you to define your values. Take, for example, 'Gender' as in Table 21.1. The following procedure allows you to create values for this variable.

1. In the Gender row, click on the three small dots in the right-hand side of the box in the Values column.
2. Click in the box marked **Value**. Type in 1.
3. Now click on the box marked Label. Type in **Male**.
4. Click on **Add**.
5. Now click on **Value** again and add 2.
6. Now click on the box marked **Label**. Type in **Female**. (see Figure 21.9)
7. To finish click on **OK**.

Missing

Any missing data will be recognized by SPSS, so it is not necessary to do anything about the **Missing** column. However, if you intend to specify missing values (for example, 'not applicable'), then this must be specified in the **Missing** column. Hence, 99 = not applicable (N/A). But to ensure that SPSS does not include the value in statistical analysis, the N/A value must be accounted for. Click on the three dots in a cell in the Missing column and choose **Discrete missing values** in the dialogue box. Type the value 99. Then click on **OK**.

MISSING DATA

➤ TOP TIP 21.2 ◄

Conducting statistical research can involve creating a number of data sets, on each of which various statistical analyses may be carried out. It is sensible to keep a list of data files, and also records of the analyses that were performed. Perhaps you could keep a section of your codebook for this purpose.

ENTERING AND MODIFYING DATA

Entering data

Having created your labels and given them values, you are now ready to enter your data. To help you do this, we are going to get you to enter some data, based upon the variables set up in the previous section. The data set will be very small as the idea is to give you experience in inputting data – not to give you typing or mouse fatigue!

1. Click on **Data View**. A window should appear that contains all of your defined variables listed at the top of each column.
2. Click on the first cell – the first row of the first column.
3. Type in your data.
4. Move the cursor into the next cell (first row, second column) by clicking the Tab key or using the mouse. Enter the data.
5. Complete the data input across the row.
6. Click on the first cell of the second row of the first column.
7. To correct any mistakes, simply click in the relevant cell and type in the correct value.

Modifying data

There may be times when you need to modify your data file. Here you will need to make sure that you are displaying **Data View**.

Delete a case

Move the cursor to the case (row) you wish to delete, positioning the cursor to the left of the screen in the row containing the case number. Click to highlight the row, then click on **Edit** and then on **Clear**.

Delete a variable

Move the cursor to the variable (column) you wish to delete, positioning the cursor above the column. Click to highlight the column, then click on **Edit** and then on **Clear**.

NAVIGATING THE WINDOWS INTERFACES

Apart from the Menus and Toolbar, SPSS allows you five different ways of viewing your data: **Data Editor**, the **Viewer**, the **Pivot Table** editor, **Chart Editor** and the **Syntax Editor**. Note that when using SPSS you will have a number of windows open at the same time. One of these is going to be the **Data Editor** because this contains the file that is being analysed. Once you begin to analyse data, the **Viewer** window will open because this is where the results of analysis are displayed. It can, at first, seem rather confusing having so many windows open at the same time. However, navigation is made easy. To have a particular window on top, simply click the name of the window where it appears at the bottom of the screen. You can perform the same operation by clicking on the **Window** drop down menu which will list all the windows that are open. Just click on the one that you want. Now let us look at each of the windows interfaces in turn.

The Data Editor window

The **Data Editor** window displays the contents of a data file with variables in the columns and each case in the rows. In the **Data Editor** you can open a data file, save a file, create a new file, enter data, make changes to existing data and run statistical analyses. As we saw earlier, the Data Editor is made up of two screens: the **Data View** and the **Variable View**.

The Viewer window

When you conduct statistical analysis, the **Viewer** window will launch automatically and should look like the output in Figure 21.10. Note that the **Viewer** is not

Figure 21.10   Output in the Viewer window

the same as the **Data Viewer** which, as we have seen, is a spreadsheet into which you enter your data. **Viewer** presents the output from statistical analysis. Hence, the left-hand pane contains a list of all the analyses that you have conducted, allowing you to easily navigate your way back and forth between outputs. In the right-hand pane are the results from the analysis. You can see more examples of outputs in the Worked Examples in Chapter 22.

The Pivot Table Editor window

The tables that appear in the **Viewer** window (which SPSS calls pivot tables) can be reformatted and also turned into graphs. To modify one of these pivot tables, double-click on it to be taken to the **Pivot Table Editor**. Here you can change the fonts used in the table, and alter column widths, to improve the table's overall appearance. To create graphics from the results, double-click on a table, then right click on the mouse to see the graphing options.

The Chart Editor window

As we saw above, you can create graphics in the **Viewer** window using the **Pivot Table Editor**. However, if you wish to make modifications to graphics you need to do this in the **Chart Editor** window. Simply double-click on your chart and this will launch the **Chart Editor** in which you can change the type of graphic used as well as the fonts, colours and the patterns within the graphs.

The Syntax Editor window

The SPSS windows format makes life relatively easy because of its graphical interface. However, behind the windows façade, the system is running computer code in the form of a special command language or syntax. In most circumstances, you have no need to gain access to this. However, for more advanced users, it is possible to access and modify the basic commands by using the **Syntax Editor**.

HANDLING MISSING DATA

It is unfortunate but true that data sets often contain missing data, often because respondents forget or refuse to answer some questions. In long, online questionnaires, for example, fatigue might set in and many respondents might omit to complete the last sections. It is important, then, to check data files for any missing data. This is done by running **Descriptives** to find out what proportion of values is missing for each variable. If this results in finding a variable with a lot of missing data, you need to consider whether this is just a random outcome, or whether there is a systematic flaw in the data gathering instrument. For example, many people may be reluctant to indicate what salary they earn.

The next step comes in deciding how to deal with the missing values. Clicking on **Options** presents a number of choices some of which are more appropriate than others.

- **Exclude cases listwise** option includes cases only if they have full data on all of the variables listed in the **Variables** box for that case. So, if a respondent, say, provides data on all the variables except their age, this one missing piece of data will preclude the case from the analysis. Hence, choosing **Exclude cases listwise** can limit your sample size. A lot of missing data on one variable might indicate that there are fundamental problems with it and it was not worth using (for example a survey question was poorly worded).

- **Exclude cases pairwise** option excludes cases only if they are missing the data required for a specific analysis. Pallant (2010) suggests using this option unless there are compelling reasons for doing otherwise.
- **Replace with mean** option calculates the mean value for the variable and gives every missing variable this value. Pallant (2010) warns that this option should never be used as it can severely distort the results of your analysis, particularly if there are many missing values.

RECODING OR TRANSFORMING DATA

RECODING
DATA

No matter how carefully you have planned your data design there will come a time when you will want to work with some variables in different formats or to collapse the number of categories of a categorical variable. So, for example, say you collected data on a population's salary level, but now find that your data tells you the results are widely dispersed. Ideally, you would like to divide the data into three categories of high, middle, and low income groups. This kind of data manipulation is called recoding or transforming. Before recoding a variable it makes sense to back up your data by saving it under another name. In recoding a categorical variable:

1. From the menu, click on **Transform**, and then on **Recode**. Then click on **Into Different Variables** to open up the **Recode** window. Note the importance of recoding into 'different variables' as failure to do this will result in a loss of the original variable which you may need for later analysis.
2. Select the variable that is to be recoded (Income), moving it into the **Input Variable-> Output Variable** box. In the **Name** box, type a new name for the new variable (for example, **LowIncome**). Click on **Change**.
3. Click on the button **Old and New Values** to create the new codes.
4. Click the second **Range** (lowest through) radio button to activate its field.
5. Click in the **Lowest through** range and type 15000.
6. Click on the **Value** field under **New Value** and type: 1. Now all incomes of less than 15000 will be assigned a value of 1.
7. Click on **Add**. Notice that in the definition of the old and new values now appears in the **Old->New** window.
8. Repeat this process for the middle and high income groups.
9. Click **Continue**. The **Old and New Values** window now closes and the original **Recode into Different Variables** window is displayed.
10. In the field for **Output Variable Name** type: **incrange**
11. In the field for the **Output Variable Label** type: **Income Range**
12. Click **Change**. The new name is now listed in the **Numeric Variable->Output Variable** box as **salary->incrange**
13. Click **OK**. The **Recode** window closes and **Data View** is now displayed, with a new column on the right for **incrange**

Recoding can also be used for combining two categorical variables together. Say, for example, that you have collected data for three categories of organization: small and medium enterprises (SMEs), large corporations, and voluntary sector organizations. You now find that most of the responses have come from SMEs and voluntary sector organizations with very few from corporates. Using the approach described above, you can merge the SME and corporate data into a new variable (which you could label 'Private sector') with the voluntary sector as the second variable.

➤ TOP TIP 21.3 ◄

Before recoding data, it is essential to back-up your data set by saving it under another name. This ensures that any transformations done to the data do not modify your data set in ways you did not anticipate (or want!). Secondly, when recoding, do not recode variables into the same name. Doing this deletes your existing data (hence, the initial warning to save your data set under another name for back-up) and it destroys the history of the data. Always create a new variable to contain the new codes.

EXPORTING INTO MS WORD

It is easy to export a chart or the output from statistical analysis into MS Word. In copying a graph, the simplest way is to use a copy and paste procedure. Note that if the graph requires editing, this should be done in SPSS as once it is imported into MS Word the most you can do is resize the graph. To copy and paste the graph:

1. Select the graph to be copied (click on the graph itself)
2. In the main SPSS menu click on **Edit > Copy Special >Image (JPG, PNG).** Click on **OK.**
3. Open your MS Word document and place the cursor at the point where you want to insert the graph.
4. In the MS Word menu click on **Home > Paste > Paste Special** and select **Picture (JPEG).**

Similarly, if you have statistical output tables (as in Figure 21.10) you can import selected tables into Word simply by the following process:

1. Select the data set table to be copied (click on the table itself).
2. In the main SPSS menu click on **Edit > Copy Special.** Click on **OK.**
3. Open your MS Word document and place the cursor at the point where you want to insert the table.
4. In MS Word, click on **Home > Paste (Keep Source Formatting)**

GETTING HELP

SPSS provides you with a number of useful Help facilities. Clicking on the Help menu allows you to search on topics, or you can click through the Tutorial pages. A series of case studies are provided to explain themes in more depth. However, in addition to SPSS itself, there are many tutorials on the Web. If you want to supplement what you have studied in this chapter with more information on getting started using SPSS, then go to Google and type: SPSS beginners youtube. This will take you to a range of short video clips on some of the basics of using SPSS.

Summary

- It is suggested that, at an early stage, you create a codebook in which you should define the labels for your variables, and assign a number for each possible response.
- Two of the most useful and important tabs are **Data View** (in which you can view and modify your data) and **Variable View** (in which you can add and modify your variables).
- From the **Edit** menu you can insert new variables and insert new cases (for example, when new questionnaires are completed by respondents).
- The **Analyze** menu offers you a wide range of statistical tools many of which are described in Chapter 22.
- After conducting a statistical analysis you will see the results displayed in the **Viewer** window. Double clicking on a pivot table allows you to change the appearance of tables. Right clicking allows you to create graphs.
- Recoding or transforming data can involve splitting a data set into more categories, or collapsing two or more categories into one.
- It is relatively easy to export SPSS output into MS Word, largely by using the copy and paste function.
- Help on using SPSS is available in the program, but also consider some of the useful video tutorials available in YouTube.

REVIEW QUESTIONS

1. What purpose does a codebook serve? What might be the consequences of not bothering with a codebook?
2. Describe why it is useful to keep a log of the statistical analyses conducted.

FURTHER READING

Pallant, J. (2010) *SPSS Survival Manual: A Step by Step Guide to Data Analysis Using SPSS*, 4th edn. Maidenhead: Open University Press/McGraw-Hill. From basic through to advanced techniques, this excellent book is written in a clear, accessible style.

Field, A. (2013) *Discovering Statistics Using SPSS*, 4th edn. London: Sage. A book that not only teaches how to use SPSS but delivers instruction about how to use statistical analysis at the same time. Highly detailed and probably more for the advanced user.

22

ANALYSING AND PRESENTING QUANTITATIVE DATA

CHAPTER INTRODUCTION

Chapter outline

Categorizing data 554

Data entry, layout and quality 558

Presenting data using descriptive statistics 562

Analysing data using descriptive statistics 566

The process of hypothesis testing: inferential statistics 569

Statistical analysis: comparing variables 572

Statistical analysis: associations between variables 582

Keywords

Categorizing data

Data entry

Descriptive statistics

Distributions

Hypotheses

Inferential statistics

Significance

Correlation analysis

Regression

Chapter objectives

After reading this chapter you will be able to:

- Prepare quantitative data for analysis.
- Select appropriate formats for the presentation of quantitative data.
- Choose the most appropriate techniques for describing data (descriptive statistics).
- Choose and apply the most appropriate statistical techniques for exploring relationships and trends in data (correlation and inferential statistics).

As we have seen in previous chapters, the distinction between quantitative and qualitative research methods is often blurred. Take, for example, survey methods. These can be purely descriptive in design, but on the other hand, the gathering of respondent profile data provides an opportunity for finding associations between classifications of respondents and their attitudes or behaviour, providing the potential for quantitative analysis.

One of the essential features of quantitative analysis is that, if you have planned your research tool, collected your data and now you are thinking of how to analyse it – you are too late! The process of selecting statistical tests should take place at the planning stage of research, not at implementation. This is because it is so easy to end up with data for which there is no meaningful statistical test. Robson (2002) also provides an astute warning that, particularly with the aid of the modern computer, it becomes much easier to generate elegantly presented rubbish, reminding us of GIGO – Garbage In, Garbage Out (Robson, 2002).

The aim of this chapter is to introduce you to some of the basic statistical techniques. It does not pretend to provide you with an in-depth analysis of more complex statistics, since there are specialized textbooks for this purpose. It is assumed that you will have access to a computer and an appropriate software application for statistical analysis, particularly SPSS. Note that in this chapter, rather than offer you Activities, Worked Examples using statistical formulae will be provided. In some cases, these will be supported with data from the book's website (see: www.sagepub.co.uk/gray3e) so that you can apply some statistical tests to 'real' data.

→ **TOP TIP 22.1** ←

BASIC
STATISTICS
LESSON

If you are relatively new to statistics, try to get access to someone more experienced than yourself to act as a guide or mentor. Also, of course, if you have an academic supervisor, ensure that you maintain regular contact and ask for advice. As suggested in Chapter 21, there are also many useful online tutorials on statistics on YouTube. If you are new to statistics, you might find it helpful if you add the word 'basic' to 'statistics' in the YouTube search engine.

CATEGORIZING DATA

The process of categorizing data is important because, as was noted in Chapter 6, the statistical tests that are used for data analysis will depend on the type of data being collected. Hence, the first step is to classify your data into one of two categories, categorical or quantifiable (see Figure 22.1). **Categorical data** cannot be quantified numerically but are either placed into sets or categories (nominal data) or ranked in some way (ordinal data). Quantifiable data can be measured numerically, which means that they are more precise. Within the quantifiable classification there are two additional categories of interval and ratio data. All of these categories are described in more detail below. Saunders et al. (2012) warn that if you are not sure about the level of detail you need in your research study, it is safest to collect data at the highest level of precision possible.

CATEGORICAL DATA ANALYSIS

In simple terms, these data are used for different analysis purposes. Table 22.1 suggests some typical uses and the kinds of statistical tests that are appropriate.

As Diamantopoulos and Schlegelmilch (1997) point out, the four kinds of measurement scale are nested within one another: as we move from a lower level of measurement to a higher one, the properties of the lower type are retained. Thus, all the statistical tests appropriate to the lower type of data can be used with the higher types as well as additional, more powerful tests. But this does not work in reverse: as we move from, say, interval data to ordinal, the tests appropriate for the former cannot

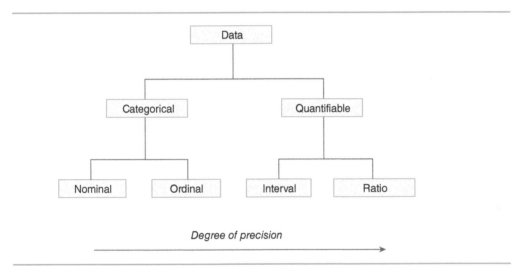

Figure 22.1   Types of categorical and quantifiable data

Table 22.1   Measurement scales and their uses

	Nominal	Ordinal	Interval	RATIO
Example of usage	Type of firm	Customer preference	Temperature	Sales
	Type of product	Organizational hierarchy	Blood pressure	Costs
	Location of organization	Attitudes		Number of customers
Statistical tests	Non-parametric tests			Parametric tests

Which category describes where the employee works?	(Tick one)
Retail department	❏
Warehouse	❏
Accounts	❏
Personnel	❏

Figure 22.2   Types of questions that yield nominal data

Table 22.2   Number of employees per department (nominal scale)

Department/location	Frequency
Retail	67
Warehouse	62
Accounts	15
Personnel	16

be applied to the latter. For categorical data only, non-parametric statistical tests can be used, but for quantifiable data (see Figure 22.1), more powerful parametric tests need to be applied. Hence, in planning data collection it is better to design data gathering instruments that yield interval and ratio data, if this is appropriate to the research objectives. Let us look at each of the four data categories in turn.

Nominal data

NOMINAL
SCALE

Nominal data constitute a name value or category with no order or ranking implied (for example, sales departments, occupational descriptors of employees, etc.). A typical question that yields nominal data is presented in Figure 22.2, with a set of data that results from this presented in Table 22.2. Thus, we can see that with nominal data, we build up a simple frequency count of how often the nominal category occurs.

Ordinal data

ORDINAL
MEASURE

Ordinal data comprises an ordering or ranking of values, although the intervals between the ranks are not intended to be equal (for example, an attitude questionnaire). A type of question that yields ordinal data is presented in Figure 22.3. Here there is a ranking of views (Sometimes, Never, etc.) where the order of such views is important but there is no suggestion that the differences between each scale are identical. Ordinal scales are also used for questions that rate the quality of something (for example, very good, good, fair, poor, etc.) and agreements (for example, Strongly Agree, Agree, Disagree, etc.). The typical results of gathering ordinal data are taken from Figure 22.3 and presented in Table 22.3.

How often have you felt like insulting a customer?	(Tick one)
Every day	❏
Once a week	❏
Sometimes	❏
Never	❏

Figure 22.3   Types of questions that yield ordinal data

Table 22.3   Frequency table showing number of responses on attitude questionnaire (ordinal)

Staff tendency to insult customers	Number of responses
Every day	10
Once a week	15
Sometimes	11
Never	4

Interval data

With quantifiable measures such as interval data, numerical values are assigned along an interval scale with equal intervals, but there is no zero point where the trait being measured does not exist. For example, a score of zero on a traditional IQ test would have no meaning. This is because the traditional IQ score is the raw (actual) score converted into a mental age divided by chronological age. Another characteristic of interval data, is that the difference between a score of 14 and 15 would be the same as the difference between a score of 91 and 92. Hence, in contrast to ordinal data, the differences between categories are identical. The kinds of results from interval data are illustrated in Table 22.4, delivered as part of a company's aptitude assessment of staff.

INTERVAL MEASURE

Ratio data

Ratio data are a subset of interval data, and the scale is again interval, but there is an absolute zero that represents some meaning, for example, scores on an achievement test. If an employee, for example, undertakes a work-related test and scores zero, this would indicate a complete lack of knowledge or ability in this subject! An example of ratio data is presented in Table 22.5.

RATIO SCALE

This sort of classification scheme is important because it influences the ways in which data are analysed and what kind of statistical tests can be applied. Having incorporated variables into a classification scheme, the next stage is to look at how data should be captured and laid out, prior to analysis and presentation.

Table 22.4   Frequency table showing number of employees scoring within various ranges on IQ test

Scores	Frequency
76–80	1
81–85	0
86–90	4
91–95	10
96–100	21
101–105	25
106–110	48
111–115	18
116–120	11
121–125	4
126–130	1
131–135	2
136–140	1

Table 22.5   Frequency distribution of employee scores on an in-house work-related test

Scores range	Frequency
0–4	4
5–9	13
10–14	15
15–19	12
20–24	8

DATA ENTRY, LAYOUT AND QUALITY

Data entry involves a number of stages, beginning with 'cleaning' the data, planning and implementing the actual input of the data, and dealing with the thorny problem of missing data. Ways of avoiding the degradation of data will also be discussed.

Cleaning the data

SPSS ERROR
CHECKING

Data analysis will only be reliable if it is built upon the foundations of 'clean' data, that is, data that have been entered into the computer accurately. When entering data containing a large number of variables and many individual records, it is easy to enter a wrong figure or to miss an entry. One solution is for two people to enter data separately and to compare the results, but this is expensive. Another approach is to use frequency analysis on a column of data that will throw up any spurious figures that have been entered. For example, if you are using numbers 1 to 5 to represent individual codes for each of five variables, the frequency analysis might show that you had also entered the number 8 – clearly a mistake. Where there are

Table 22.6   Data matrix from survey showing data coding for each variable

Case	Id	Department	Length of service	Seniority
Case 1	1	5	3	2
Case 2	2	2	1	3
Case 3	3	3	12	2

branching or skip questions (recall Chapter 14) it may also be necessary to check that respondents are going through the questions carefully. For example, they may be completing sections that do not apply to them or missing other sections.

Data coding and layout

Coding usually involves allocating an identification number (Id) to data. Take care, however, not to make the mistake of subsequently analysing the codes as raw data! The codes are merely shorthand ways of describing the data. Once the coding is completed, it is possible to collate the data into groups of less detailed categories. So, in Case Study 22.1 the categories could be re-coded to form the groups Legal and Financial and then Health and Safety.

The most obvious approach to data layout is the use of tables in the form of a data matrix. Within each data matrix, columns will represent a single variable while each row presents a case or profile. Hence, Table 22.6 illustrates an example of data from a survey of employee attitudes. The second column, labelled 'Id', is the survey form identifier, allowing the researcher to check back to the original survey form when checking for errors. The next column contains numbers, each of which signifies a particular department. Length of service is quantifiable data representing actual years spent in the organization, while seniority is again coded data signifying different scales of seniority. Thus, the numerical values have different meanings for different variables. Note that Table 22.6 is typical of the kind of data matrix that can be set up in a software program such as SPSS, ready for the application of statistical formulae.

Case Study 22.1 illustrates the kind of survey layout and structure that yields data suitable for a data matrix (presented at the end of the case study). Hence, we have a range of variables and structured responses, each of which can be coded.

━ CASE STUDY 22.1 ━

From survey instrument to data matrix

A voluntary association that provides free advice to the public, seeks to discover which of its services are most utilized. A survey form is designed dealing with four potential areas, namely the law, finance, health and safety in the home.

Question: Please look at the following services and indicate whether you have used any of them in the last 12 months.

	Yes	No	Not sure
Legal advice	❑	❑	❑
Financial advice	❑	❑	❑
Health advice	❑	❑	❑
Advice on safety in the home	❑	❑	❑

The data are collected from 100 respondents and input into the following data matrix using the numerical codes: 1 = Yes; 2 = No; For no data or non-response the cell should be left blank.

Id	Legal	Finance	Health	Safety
Respondent 1	1	2	2	2
Respondent 2	2	1	1	1
Respondent 3	1	0	0	0

Note that in Case Study 22.1 Respondent 3 has ticked the box for 'Legal advice' but has failed to complete any of the others – hence, a '0' for no data has to be put in the matrix.

Dealing with missing data

Oppenheim (1992) notes that the best approach to dealing with missing data is not to have any! Hence, steps should be taken to ensure that data are collected from the entire intended sample and that non-response is kept to a minimum. But in practice, we know that there will be cases where either a respondent has not replied or has not answered all the questions. The issue here is one of potential bias – has the respondent omitted those questions they feel uneasy about or hostile to answering? For example, in answering a staff survey on working practices, are those with the worst records on absenteeism more likely to omit the questions on this (hence, potentially biasing the analysis)?

It might be useful to distinguish between four different types of missing values: 'Not applicable' (NA), 'Refused' (RF), 'Did not know' (DK) and 'Forgot to answer' (FA). Making this distinction may help you to adopt strategies for coping with this data loss. Table 22.7 illustrates examples of these responses.

You may note that the categories for non-response chosen may depend largely on the researcher's inferences or guesswork. How do we know that someone forgot to answer or simply did not know how to respond? Of course, if many people fail to answer the same question, this might suggest there is something about the question they do not like – in which case, this could be construed as 'Refusal'. You may decide to ignore these separate categories and just use one 'No answer' label. Alternatively, you might put in a value if this is possible by taking the average of other people's responses. There are dangers, however, in this approach, particularly for single item questions. Note that some statisticians have spent almost a

Table 22.7 Distinguishing between different types of non-response

Response	Recorded for value
Question answered by wrong or inappropriate person, e.g. line manager of intended respondent	Not applicable
Rude message instead of response	Refused
All questions answered except one	Forgot to answer
All questions answered accurately but one left blank	Did not know

Please indicate your age by ticking the appropriate box:	
18–24	[ ]
25–34	[ ]
35–44	[ ]
45–54	[ ]
55–64	[ ]
65+	[ ]

Figure 22.4 Section of questionnaire compromising an age profile

lifetime pondering issues of this kind! It would be safer if missing data were entered for a sub-question that comprised just one of a number of sub-questions (for which data were available). Note, also, that this becomes unfeasible if there are many non-responses to the same question, since it would leave the calculation based on a small sample.

Avoiding the degradation of data

It is fairly clear when non-response has occurred, but it is also possible to compromise the quality of data by the process of degradation. Say we were interested in measuring the age profile of the workforce and drew up a questionnaire, as illustrated in Figure 22.4. One problem here is that the age categories are unequal (for example, 18–24 compared with 25–34). But a further difficulty is the loss of information that comes with collecting the data in this way. We have ended up with an ordinal measure of what should be ratio data and cannot even calculate the average age of the workforce. Far better would have been simply to ask for each person's exact age (for example, by requesting their date of birth) and the date the questionnaire was completed. After this, we could calculate the average age (mean), the modal (most frequently occurring) age and identify both the oldest and youngest worker, etc.

Table 22.8   Appropriate use of charts and graphs for frequency data

	Bar chart	Pie chart	Histogram	Frequency polygon
Nominal	+	+		
Ordinal	+			
Interval			+	+
Ratio			+	+

Source: Adapted from Black, 1999: 306

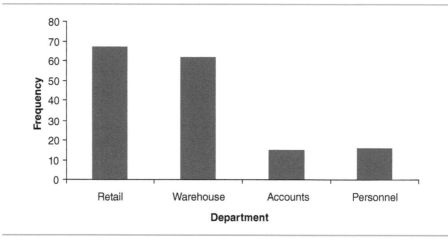

Figure 22.5   Bar chart for the nominal data in Table 22.2

PRESENTING DATA USING DESCRIPTIVE STATISTICS

One of the aims of descriptive statistics is to describe the basic features of a study, often through the use of graphical analysis. Descriptive statistics are distinguished from inferential statistics in that they attempt to show what the data is, while inferential statistics try to draw conclusions beyond the data – for example, inferring what a population may think on the basis of sample data.

Descriptive statistics, and in particular the use of charts or graphs, certainly provide the potential for the communication of data in readily accessible formats, but the kinds of graphics used will depend on the types of data being presented. This is why the start of this chapter focused on classifying data into nominal, ordinal, interval and ratio categories, since not all types of graph are appropriate for all kinds of data. Black (1999) provides a neat summary of what is appropriate (see Table 22.8).

Nominal and ordinal data – single groups

As we saw earlier, nominal data are a record of categories or names, with no intended order or ranking, while ordinal data do assume some intended ordering of categories. Taking the nominal data in Table 22.2, we can present a bar chart (Figure 22.5) for the frequency count of staff in different departments.

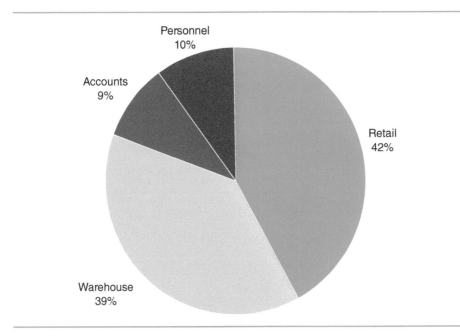

Figure 22.6   Pie chart of the nominal data in Figure 22.2

Figure 22.6 shows that this same set of data can also be presented in the form of a pie chart. Note that pie charts are suitable for illustrating nominal data but are not appropriate for ordinal data – obviously, because it presents proportions of a total, not the ordering of categories.

Interval and ratio data – single groups

Interval and ratio data describe scores on tests, age, weight, annual income, etc., for a group of individuals. These numbers are then, usually, translated into a frequency table, such as in Table 22.3. The first stage is to decide on the number of intervals in the data. Black (1999) recommends between 10 and 20 as acceptable, since going outside this range would tend to distort the shape of the histogram or frequency polygon. Take a look at the data on an age profile of the entire workforce in an e-commerce development organization, presented in Table 22.9. The age range is from 22 to 43, a difference of 21. If we selected an interval range of 3, this would only give us a set of seven age ranges and conflict with Black's (1999) recommendation that only a minimum of 10 ranges is acceptable. If, however, we took two as the interval range, we would end up with 11 sets of intervals, as in Table 22.10, which is acceptable. We then take this data for graphical presentation in the form of a histogram, as in Figure 22.7.

Nominal data – comparing groups

So far, we have looked at presenting single sets of data. But often research will require us to gather data on a number of related characteristics and it is useful to

Table 22.9   Age profile of e-commerce development company

Age	Frequency	Age	Frequency
22	1	33	10
23	2	34	4
24	3	35	3
25	6	36	2
26	5	37	4
27	11	38	2
28	15	39	2
29	7	40	0
30	9	41	0
31	3	42	1
32	4	43	0

Table 22.10   Frequency table for age range (interval) data

Age range	Frequency	Age range	Frequency
22–23	3	34–35	7
24–25	9	36–37	6
26–27	16	38–39	4
28–29	22	40–41	0
30–31	12	42–43	1
32–33	14		

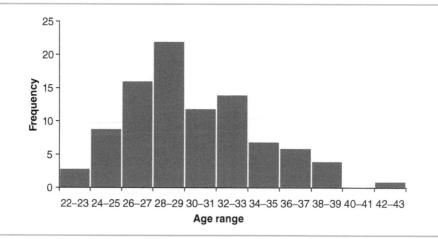

Figure 22.7   Histogram illustrating interval data in Table 22.10

be able to compare these graphically. For example, returning to Table 22.2 and the number of employees per department, these may be aggregate frequencies, based on the spread of both male and female workers per department, as in Figure 22.8.

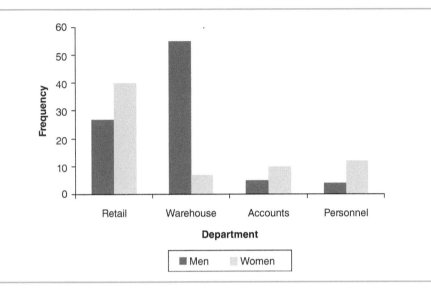

Figure 22.8   Bar chart for nominal data with comparison between groups

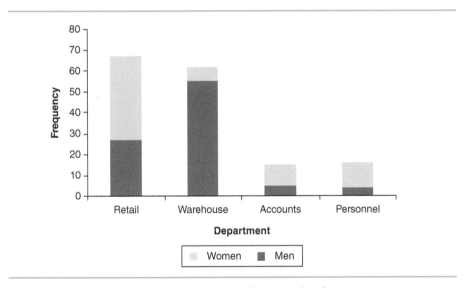

Figure 22.9   Stacked bar chart for nominal data with comparison between groups

Another way of presenting these kind of data is where it is useful to show not only the distribution between groups, but the total size of each group, as in Figure 22.9.

Interval and ratio data – comparing groups

It is sometimes necessary to compare two groups for traits that are measured as continuous data. While this exercise is, as we have seen, relatively easy for nominal data that is discrete, for interval and ratio data the two sets of data may overlap and one hide the other. The solution is to use a frequency polygon. As we can see in

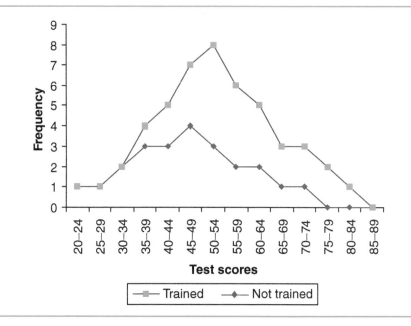

Figure 22.10 Frequency polygons for two sets of continuous data showing test scores

Figure 22.10, we have two sets of continuous data of test scores, one set for a group of employees who have received training and another for those who have not. The frequency polygon enables us to see both sets of results simultaneously and to compare the trends.

Two variables for a single group

You may also want to compare two variables for a single group. Returning once more to our example of departments, we might look at the age profiles of the workers in each of them. Figure 22.11 shows the result.

ANALYSING DATA USING DESCRIPTIVE STATISTICS

A descriptive focus involves the creation of a summary picture of a sample or population in terms of key variables being researched. This may involve the presentation of data in graphical form (as in the previous section) or the use of descriptive statistics, as discussed here.

Frequency distribution and central tendency

Frequency distribution is one of the most common methods of data analysis, particularly for analysing survey data. Frequency simply means the number of instances in a class, and in surveys it is often associated with the use of Likert scales.

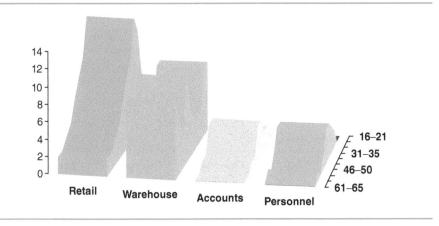

Figure 22.11   Solid polygon showing data for two variables: department and age

Table 22.11   Percentage of respondents answering for each attitude category over a two-year period

	Strongly Agree	Agree	Disagree	Strongly Disagree	Total
2012	14	40	32	14	100
2013	21	33	26	20	100

So, for example, a survey might measure customer satisfaction for a particular product over a two-year period. Table 22.11 presents a typical set of results, showing what percentage of customers answered for each attitude category to the statement: 'We think that the Squeezy floor cleaner is good value for money'.

Comparing the data between the two years, it appears that there has been a 7 per cent rise in the number of customers who 'Strongly Agree' that the floor cleaner is good value for money. Unfortunately, just to report this result would be misleading because, as we can see, there has also been a 6 per cent rise in those who 'Strongly Disagree' with the statement. So what are we to make of the results? Given that the 'Agree' category has fallen by 7 per cent and the 'Disagree' category by 6 per cent, have attitudes moved for or against the product? To make sense of the data, two approaches need to be adopted.

- The use of all the data, not just selected figures that meet the researcher's agendas.
- A way of quantifying the results using a single, representative figure.

This scoring method involves the calculation of a mean score for each set of data. Hence the categories could be given a score, as illustrated in Table 22.12.

All respondents' scores can then be added up, yielding the set of scores presented in Table 22.13, and the mean, showing that, overall, attitudes have moved very slightly in favour of the product.

Since the data can be described by the mean, a single figure, it becomes possible to make comparisons between different parts of the data or, if, say, two surveys are

Table 22.12   Method of scoring each response category in order to calculate the mean score

	Strongly Agree	Agree	Disagree	Strongly Disagree
	4	3	2	1

Table 22.13   Calculation of mean scores for attitude categories to discover attitude trends over a two-year period

	Strongly Agree (4)	Agree (3)	Disagree (2)	Strongly Disagree (1)	Total	Mean
2012	56	120	64	14	254	2.86
2013	84	99	52	20	255	2.97

carried out at different periods, across time. Of course, there are also dangers in this approach. There is an assumption (possibly a mistaken one) that the differences between these ordinal categories are identical. Furthermore, the mean is only one **measure of central tendency**, others include the **median** and the **mode**. The median is the central value when all the scores are arranged in order. The mode is simply the most frequently occurring value. If the median and mode scores are less than the mean, the distribution of scores will be skewed to the left (positive skew); if they are greater than the mean, the scores are said to be skewed to the right (negative skew). So, while two mean scores could be identical, this need not imply that two sets of scores were the same, since each might have a different distribution of scores.

Having made these qualifications, this scoring method can still be used, but is probably best utilized over a multiple set of scores rather than just a single set. It is also safest used for descriptive rather than for inferential statistics.

Measuring dispersion

In addition to measuring central tendency, it may also be important to measure the spread of responses around the mean to show whether the mean is representative of the responses or not.

There are a number of ways of calculating **measures of dispersion**:

- The **range**: the difference between the highest and the lowest scores.
- The *inter-quartile range*: the difference between the score that has a quarter of the scores below it (often known as the first quartile or the 25th **percentile**) and the score that has three-quarters of the scores below it (the 75th percentile).
- The *variance*: a measure of the average of the squared deviations of individual scores from the mean.
- The *standard deviation*: a measure of the extent to which responses vary from the mean, and is derived by calculating the variation from the mean, squaring them, adding them and calculating the square root. Like the mean, because you are able to calculate a single figure, it allows comparisons to be made between different parts of a survey and across time periods.

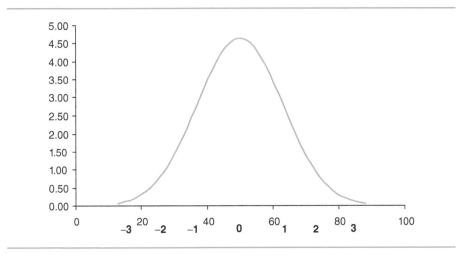

Figure 22.12   The theoretical 'normal' distribution with mean = 0

Normal and skewed distributions

The **normal distribution** curve is bell-shaped, that is symmetrical around the mean, which means that there are an equal number of subjects above and below the mean (x–). The shape of the curve also indicates the proportion of subjects at each of the standard deviations (S, 1S, etc.) above and below the mean. Thus in Figure 22.12, 34.13 per cent of the subjects are one **standard deviation** above the mean and another 34.13 per cent below it.

In the real world, however it is often the case that distributions are not normal, but **skewed**, and this will have implications for the relationship between the mean, the mode and the median. A distribution is said to be skewed if one of its tails is longer than the other. Where the distribution is positively skewed, it has a long tail in a positive direction (to the right) and the majority of the subjects are below, to the left of the mean in terms of the trait or attitude being measured. With a negative skew, the tail is in a negative direction (to the left) and the majority of subjects are above the mean (to the right).

THE PROCESS OF HYPOTHESIS TESTING: INFERENTIAL STATISTICS

We saw in Chapter 3 that the research process may involve the formulation of a hypothesis or hypotheses that describe the relationship between two variables. In this section we will re-examine hypothesis testing in a number of stages, which comprise:

- Hypothesis formulation.
- Specification of significance level (to see how safe it is to accept or reject the hypothesis).
- Identification of the probability distribution and definition of the region of rejection.
- Selection of appropriate statistical tests.
- Calculation of the test statistic and acceptance or rejection of the hypothesis.

Hypothesis formulation

As we saw in Chapter 3, a hypothesis is a statement concerning a population (or populations) that may or may not be true, and constitutes an inference or inferences about a population, drawn from sample information. Let us say, for example, that we work for a marketing company conducting some research on the ownership of laptop computers in Western Europe. We conjecture that per capita ownership in the UK is likely to be greater than that in France. If we had unlimited time and resources, we could survey both populations. For practical considerations, of course, we have to sample. If we took random samples for both the UK and French populations and found that ownership was 18 per cent in the UK and 12 per cent in France, our conjecture would be confirmed by the evidence. Or would it?

First, we run the danger of sampling error, with the smaller the sample size the greater the potential for this error. Secondly, we can never 'prove' something to be true, because there always remains a finite possibility that one day someone will emerge with a refutation. Hence, for research purposes, we usually phrase a hypothesis in its null (negative) form. So, rather than state:

The ownership of laptop computers will be greater in the UK than in France.

We say:

The ownership of laptop computers will not be greater in the UK than in France.

Then, if we find that the data for ownership is greater for the UK than in France, we can reject the **null hypothesis**.

Hypotheses come in essentially three forms. Those that:

- Examine the characteristics of a single population (and may involve calculating the mean, median and standard deviation and the shape of the distribution).
- Explore contrasts and comparisons between groups.
- Examine associations and relationships between groups.

For one research study, it may be necessary to formulate a number of null hypotheses incorporating statements about distributions, scores, frequencies, associations and correlations.

Specification of significance level

Having formulated the null hypothesis, we must next decide on the circumstances in which it will be accepted or rejected. Since we do not know with absolute certainty whether the hypothesis is true or false, ideally we would want to reject the null hypothesis when it is false, and to accept it when it is true. However, since there is no such thing as an absolute certainty (especially in the real world!), there is always a chance of rejecting the null hypothesis when in fact it is true (called a **Type I error**) and accepting it when it is in fact false (a **Type II error**). Table 22.14 presents a summary of possible outcomes.

What is the potential impact of these errors? Say, for example, we measure whether a new training programme improves staff attitudes to customers, and we express this in null terms (the training will have no effect). If we made a Type I error then we are rejecting the null hypothesis, and therefore claim that the training does have an effect when, in fact, this is not true. You will, no doubt, recognize that we do not want to make claims for the impact of independent variables that are actually false. Think of the

Table 22.14   Potential errors in hypothesis testing

Situation in the population

Decision made on null hypothesis	Hypothesis is true	Hypothesis is false
Hypothesis is rejected	Type I error	Correct decision
Hypothesis is not rejected	Correct decision	Type II error

implications if we made a Type I error when testing a new drug! We also want to avoid Type II errors, since here we would be accepting the null hypothesis and therefore failing to notice the impact that an independent variable was having.

Type I and Type II errors are the converse of each other. As Fielding and Gilbert (2006) observe, anything we do to reduce a Type I error will increase the likelihood of a Type II error, and vice versa. Whichever error is the most likely depends on how we set the significance level (see following section).

Identification of the probability distribution

What are the chances of making a Type I error? This is measured by what is called the **significance level**, which measures the probability of making a mistake. The significance level is always set before a test is carried out, and is traditionally set at either 0.05, 0.01 or 0.001. Thus, if we set our significance level at 5 per cent |(p = 0.05), we are willing to take the risk of rejecting the null hypothesis when in fact it is correct 5 times out of 100.

DISTRIBUTIONS & PROBABILITY

All statistical tests are based on an **area of acceptance** and an **area of rejection**. For what is termed a **one-tailed test**, the rejection area is either the upper or lower tail of the distribution. A one-tailed test is used when the hypothesis is directional, that is, it predicts an outcome at either the higher or lower end of the distribution. But there may be cases when it is not possible to make such a prediction. In these circumstances, a **two-tailed test** is used, for which there are two areas of rejection – both the upper and lower tails. For example, for the z distribution where p = 0.05 and a two-tailed test, statistical tables show that the area of acceptance for the null hypothesis is the central 95 per cent of the distribution and the areas of rejection are the 2.5 per cent of each tail (see Figure 22.13). Hence, if the test statistic is less than -1.96 or greater than 1.96 the null hypothesis will be rejected.

Selection of appropriate statistical tests

The selection of statistical tests appropriate for each hypothesis is perhaps the most challenging feature of using statistics but also the most necessary. It is all too easy to formulate a valid hypothesis only to choose an inappropriate test, with the result – statistical nonsense! The type of statistical test used will depend on quite a broad range of factors.

First, the type of hypothesis – for example, hypotheses concerned with the characteristics of groups, compared with relationships between variables. Even within these broad groups of hypotheses different tests may be needed. So a test for comparing differences between group means will be different to one comparing differences between medians. Even for the same sample, different tests may be used depending on

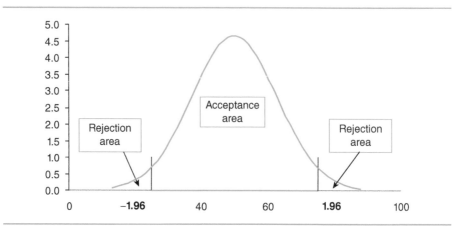

Figure 22.13 Areas of acceptance and rejection in a standard normal distribution with $\alpha = 0.05$

the size of the sample. Secondly, assumptions about the distribution of populations will affect the type of statistical test used. For example, different tests will be used for populations for which the data are evenly distributed compared with those that are not. A third consideration is the level of measurement of the variables in the hypothesis. As we saw earlier, different tests are appropriate for nominal, ordinal, interval and ratio data, and only **non-parametric tests** are suitable for nominal and ordinal data, but **parametric tests** can be used with interval and ratio data. Parametric tests also work best with larger sample sizes (that is, at least 30 observations per variable or group) and are more powerful than non-parametric tests. This simply means that they are more likely to reject the null hypothesis when it should be rejected, avoiding Type I errors. Motulsky (1995) advises that parametric tests should usually be selected if you are sure that the population is normally distributed. Table 22.15 provides a summary of the kinds of statistical test available in the variety of circumstances just described.

In the sections that follow, we will take some examples from Table 22.15 and apply them for the purpose of illustration.

STATISTICAL ANALYSIS: COMPARING VARIABLES

In this section and the one that follows, we will be performing a number of statistical tests. It will be assumed that readers will have access to SPSS.

Nominal data – one sample

In the following section we will look at comparing relationships between variables, but here we will confine ourselves to exploring the distribution of a variable. First, if we assume a pre-specified distribution (such as a normal distribution), we can compare the observed (actual data) frequencies against **expected** (theoretical) **frequencies,** to measure what is termed the **goodness-of-fit**.

Let us say that a company is interested in comparing disciplinary records across its four production sites by measuring the number of written warnings issued in the

Table 22.15 Guide to selection of statistical tests

Survey objectives	Type of Data		Potential statistical test
	Independent variable	Dependent variable	
For objectives with one dependent and one independent variable			
Compare departments in frequency of issue of written warnings	Nominal: groups (departments)	Nominal (number of written warnings)	Chi-square, **Fisher's exact test**
Compare an experimental and control group in their attitudes after 'anti-smoking' campaign	Nominal (dichotomous): groups (experimental and control)	Quantifiable (attitude scores)	One-sample *t*-test, dependent *t*-test and independent *t*-test; Wilcoxon signed-ranks test; Wilcoxon rank-sum test
Compare attitudes across five company departments to new working practices	Nominal: more than two values	Quantifiable (attitude scores)	**One-way analysis of variance** (using the *F*-test)
Determine if high scores on measurement of confidence predict high scores on test of ability	Quantifiable (attitude scores)	Quantifiable (knowledge scores)	Regression (when neither variable is dependent or independent, use correlation)
For objectives with two or more independent variables			
Compare manual and white collar staff in experiment and control groups with respect to attitudes	Nominal (manual and white collar)	Quantifiable (attitude scores)	**Analysis of variance (ANOVA)**
Determine if length of service and salary level relate to attitudes	Quantifiable (length of service and salary level)	Quantifiable (attitude scores)	Multiple regression
Compare men and women in experimental and control groups in their attitudes when their salary level is controlled	Nominal (gender and group) with confounding factors (salary level)	Quantifiable (attitude scores)	Analysis of covariance (ANCOVA)
For objectives with two or more independent and dependent variables			
Compare men and women in experimental and control groups in their attitude and knowledge scores	Nominal (gender and group)	Quantifiable (scores on two measures: attitudes and knowledge)	Multivariate analysis of variance (MANOVA)

Source: Adapted from Fink, 2003

Table 22.16 Contingency table of data for analysis

| | Cases | |
Site	Observed O_i	Expected E_i
A	12	29
B	68	29
C	14	29
D	22	29
Total	116	116

Table 22.17 Analysis of data in Table 22.16

Site	Observed O_i	Expected E_i	$\dfrac{(O_i - E_i)^2}{E_i}$
A	12	29	9.97
B	68	29	52.45
C	14	29	7.76
D	22	29	1.69
Total	116	116	71.86

past two years. We might assume that, since the sites are of broadly equal size in terms of people employed, the warnings might be evenly spread across these sites, that is, 25 per cent for each. Since the total number of recorded written warnings is 116 (see Table 22.16), this represents 29 expected warnings per site. Data are gathered (**observed frequencies**) to see if they match the expected frequencies. The null hypothesis is that there will be no difference between the observed and expected frequencies. Following our earlier advice, we set the level of significance in advance. In this case let us say that we set it at $p = 0.05$. If any significant difference is found, then the null hypothesis will be rejected. Table 22.16 presents the data in what is called a **contingency table**.

The appropriate test here is the **chi-square distribution**. For each case we deduct the expected frequency from the observed frequency and square the result and divide by the expected frequency; the chi-square statistic is the sum of the totals (see Table 22.17).

Is the chi-square statistic of 71.86 significant? To find out, we look the figure up in an appropriate statistical table for the chi-square statistic. The value to use will be in the column for $p = 0.05$ and for 3 **degrees of freedom** (the number of categories minus one). This figure turns out to be 7.81, which is far exceeded by our chi-square figure. Hence, we can say that the difference is significant and we can reject the null hypothesis that there is no difference between the issue of written warnings between the sites.

Note, however, that the expected frequencies do not have to be equal. Say, we know through some prior research that site B is three times as likely to issue warnings as the other sites. Table 22.18 presents the new data.

Table 22.18   Example of a one-sample chi-square test with uneven expected frequency

Site	Observed O_i	Expected E_i	$\dfrac{(O_i - E_i)^2}{E_i}$
A	12	19.33	2.78
B	68	58.00	1.72
C	14	19.33	1.47
D	22	19.33	0.37
Total	116	116.00	6.34

Here we find that the new chi-square statistic is only 6.34, which is not significant. Diamantopoulos and Schlegelmilch (1997) warn that when the number of categories in the variable is greater than two, the **chi-square test** should not be used where:

- More than 20 per cent of the expected frequencies are smaller than 5.
- Any expected frequency is less than one.

If the numbers within **cells** are small, and it is possible to combine adjacent categories, then it is advisable to do so. For example, if some of our expected frequencies in Table 22.14 were rather small but sites A and B were in England and site C and D in Germany, we might sensibly combine A with B and C with D in order to make an international comparison study.

Nominal groups and quantifiable data (normally distributed)

Let us say that you want to compare the performance of two groups, or to compare the performance of one group over a period of time using quantifiable variables such as scores. In these circumstances we can use a **paired *t*-test**. If we were to have two different samples of people for which we wish to compare scores, then we would use an independent ***t*-test**. *T*-tests assume that the data are normally distributed, and that the two groups have the same variance (the **standard deviation** squared). If the data are not normally distributed then usually a non-parametric test, the **Wilcoxon signed-ranks test**, can be used – although, as we shall see, *t*-tests can be used even when the distribution is not perfectly normal. The *t*-test compares the means of the two groups to see if any differences between them are statistically significant. If the **p-value** associated with *t* is low (< 0.05), then there is evidence to accept the alternate hypothesis (and reject the null hypothesis), that is, the means of the two groups are statistically different.

Say that we want to examine the effectiveness of a stress counselling programme. Taking a simple before and after design (recall Chapter 6 for some of the limitations of this design), we get respondents to complete a stress assessment questionnaire before the counselling and then after it. We can see from the data set provided (see the book's website and the link to Data sets: *t*-test data) that in a number of cases the levels of stress have actually increased! But in most cases stress levels have fallen, in some cases quite sharply. Worked Example 22.1 shows how we can use SPSS to see if this is statistically significant.

WORKED EXAMPLE 22.1

DATASET

Type the gain scores for both the experimental and control groups into an SPSS data file. Before we begin any data analysis, we need to determine the normality of the data distribution, since this will influence whether we should use parametric or non-parametric statistical tests. Remember that parametric tests are the more powerful, but can only be used if the data are relatively normally distributed.

Turn to the book's website (www.sagepub.co.uk/gray3e) and click on [Data sets] and then [T-test data] and save the data. Open the data set in SPSS.

1. Click on [Analyze], then on [Descriptive statistics] followed by [Explore].
2. Click on Experimental A and Experimental B and move them into the [Dependent List] box by clicking on the arrow.
3. In the [Display] section make sure that [Both] is ticked.
4. Click on [Statistics] and then on [Descriptives] and [Outliers]. Click on [Continue].
5. Click on the [Plots] button. Then under [Descriptive] click on [Histogram]. Select [Normality plots with tests] and [Continue].
6. Click on the [Options] button and in the [Missing values section] select [Exclude cases pairwise]. To complete the process click on [Continue] followed by [OK].
7. You should then see the data as presented in the outputs below.

CASE PROCESSING SUMMARY

| | Cases | | | | | |
| | Valid | | Missing | | Total | |
	N	Percent	N	Percent	N	Percent
Experimental A	93	100.0%	0	0.0%	93	100.0%
Experimental B	91	97.8%	2	2.2%	93	100.0%

DESCRIPTIVES

			Statistic	Std. Error
Experimental A	Mean		10.4301	.36674
	95% Confidence Interval for Mean	Lower Bound	9.7017	
		Upper Bound	11.1585	
	5% Trimmed Mean		10.4779	
	Median		11.0000	
	Variance		12.509	
	Std. Deviation		3.53676	
	Minimum		2.00	
	Maximum		18.00	
	Range		16.00	
	Interquartile Range		5.00	
	Skewness		–.208	.250
	Kurtosis		–.487	.495

				8.4176	.34805
	Mean			8.4176	.34805
	95% Confidence	Lower Bound		7.7261	
	Interval for Mean	Upper Bound		9.1090	
	5% Trimmed Mean			8.3907	
	Median			8.0000	
	Variance			11.024	
Experimental B	Std. Deviation			3.32019	
	Minimum			2.00	
	Maximum			16.00	
	Range			14.00	
	Interquartile Range			5.00	
	Skewness			.026	.253
	Kurtosis			–.875	.500

EXTREME VALUES

			Case Number	Value
Experimental A	Highest	1	81	18.00
		2	17	17.00
		3	88	17.00
		4	9	16.00
		5	77	16.00[a]
	Lowest	1	80	2.00
		2	82	3.00
		3	5	3.00
		4	19	4.00
		5	8	4.00
Experimental B	Highest	1	78	16.00
		2	18	15.00
		3	81	15.00
		4	62	14.00
		5	57	13.00[b]
	Lowest	1	19	2.00
		2	5	2.00
		3	82	3.00
		4	80	3.00
		5	38	3.00[c]

a. Only a partial list of cases with the value 16.00 are shown in the table of upper extremes.
b. Only a partial list of cases with the value 13.00 are shown in the table of upper extremes.
c. Only a partial list of cases with the value 3.00 are shown in the table of lower extremes.

TESTS FOR NORMALITY

ANDERSON-
DARLING
TEST & SHAPIRO-
WILK TEST

	Kolmogorov-Smirnov[a]			Shapiro-Wilk		
	Statistic	df	Sig.	Statistic	df	Sig.
Experimental A	.091	93	.056	.984	93	.320
Experimental B	.133	91	.000	.961	91	.008

a. Lilliefors Significance Correction

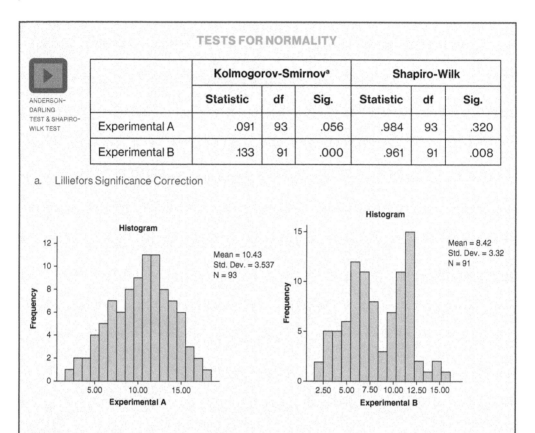

Histogram — Experimental A
Mean = 10.43
Std. Dev. = 3.537
N = 93

Histogram — Experimental B
Mean = 8.42
Std. Dev. = 3.32
N = 91

KOLMOGOROV-
SMIRNOV

In the Descriptives output, note the statistic for 5% Trimmed Mean. SPSS removes the top and bottom 5 per cent of cases and recalculates this new mean, to see if extreme scores (outliers) have much impact. In our example above, the mean and trimmed means are very similar so we should not be concerned about outliers distorting the results. The output also provides values for *skewness* and *kurtosis*. Skewness provides an indication of the symmetry of the distribution and (as discussed above) can be reported as positive (if scores are clustered to the left) and negative (if clustered to the right). Kurtosis refers to the peakness or otherwise of the distribution. Values of less than 0 indicate a relatively flat distribution, that is, too many cases at the extremes (as in Experimental A example).

The table labelled Test for Normality contains the Shapiro-Wilk statistic, which is generally used for samples ranging from 3 to 2000. Above 2000 the Kolmogorov-Smirnov statistic is generally used to test for the normality of the distribution. A result where the Sig. value is more than 0.05 indicates normality, while a result that is less than 0.05 violates the assumption of normality. Given that the sample size in this study is below 100 we will use the Shapiro-Wilk statistic. In the above table we can see that the statistic for Experimental A is above 0.05 indicating normality, whereas the statistic for Experimental B is below 0.05 violating the assumption of normality. Does this mean that we must use a non-parametric test? Not necessarily. For sample sizes over 30, Pallant (2010) suggests that violation of the normality assumption should not lead the researcher to panic, with use of parametric tests being permissible. The next step is to take a look at the results for Skewness and Kurtosis in the Descriptives table. As long as these are between –1.0 and +1.0, we can assume that the distribution is sufficiently normal for the use of parametric tests.

Hence, we apply the procedure for a paired sample *t*-test as follows:

1. Click on [Analyze] then on [Compare Means] and then on [Paired Samples *T*-test].
2. Click on the variables Experimental A and Experimental B and on the arrow to move them into the [Paired Variables] box.
3. Click on [OK]. You should see the output as presented below.

PAIRED SAMPLES STATISTICS

		Mean	N	Std. Deviation	Std. Error Mean
Pair 1	Experimental A	10.3736	91	3.50444	.36736
	Experimental B	8.4176	91	3.32019	.34805

PAIRED SAMPLES TEST

		Paired Differences							
		Mean	Std. Deviation	Std. Error Mean	95% Confidence Interval of the Difference		t	df	Sig. (2-tailed)
					Lower	Upper			
Pair 1	Experimental A – Experimental B	1.95604	2.11299	.22150	1.51599	2.39609	8.831	90	.000

The procedure for interpreting these results is as follows.

1. Look at the Paired Samples Tests, at the right-hand column labelled Sig. (2-tailed) which gives the probability value. If this is less than 0.05 then we can assume that the difference between the two scores is significant. In our case the Sig. = 0.00 so the differences in the stress scores is, indeed, significant.
2. Establish which set of scores is the higher (Experimental A or Experimental B). The box Paired Samples Statistics gives the mean for each set of scores. The mean for Experimental A was 10.3736 while that for Experimental B was 8.4176. We can therefore conclude that the counselling programme did, indeed, help to reduce stress.

NORMALITY TEST

Now a note of caution. Although we obtained differences in the two sets of scores (and the Sig. result suggests that this did not occur by chance alone), we must be careful when it comes to attributing causation. We also need to take into account other factors that could explain the fall in stress levels – refer to Design 3: One group, pre-test/post-test in Chapter 6. The researcher should try to anticipate the kinds of contaminating factors that could confound the results. One approach would be to improve the research design – for example, by introducing a control group that does not receive the intervention (in this case the stress counselling).

Nominal groups and quantifiable data (not normally distributed)

In the section above we looked at differences in normally (or near normally) distributed data. But what if the data do not satisfy the assumptions required for statistical tests based on normal distribution? Let us say that we are exploring the attitudes of men and women towards the purchase of skin care products. Do women prefer these types of product more than men? Figure 22.14 provides an example of part of a survey dealing in attitudes towards personal grooming. The resulting data from this imaginary survey are provided on the book's website (see Data sets: Mann-Whitney U data).

The data are captured into an SPSS file, with each questionnaire being allocated its own Id number. Male respondents are allocated the code 1 and females 2. The response of each person is allotted a score by adding their responses. Note that in Figure 22.14, question 3 has been posed in a negative form to encourage respondents to think more carefully about their answers. This needs to be allocated a score of 1. Hence, the total score for this respondent would be coded as 6. Total scores for each respondent range from 4 to 20.

Personal grooming survey				
1	Sex	○√ ○	Male Female	Please tick which applies

SECTION A: SKIN CARE PRODUCTS

Please indicate through the following statements your attitude towards skin care products. Using the scale provided, write the number that indicates how you feel about each statement.

Strongly disagree		1 2 3 4 5	Strongly agree
1	2	Skin care products help my self confidence.	
2	1	Skin care products are an essential purchase for me.	
3	5	Skin care products are a waste of money.	
4	2	Skin care products improve my looks.	

Figure 22.14   Example of a portion of a survey on skin care products

---

WORKED EXAMPLE 22.2

DATASET

MANN-
WHITNEY
U TEST

Turn to the book's website (www.sagepub.co.uk/gray3e) and click on [Data sets] and then on [Mann-Whitney] and save the data. Open the data set in SPSS.

First of all, we test for whether the data are normally distributed (see Worked Example 22.1 for how to test for this). Note that as we have both a dependent variable (attitude) and independent variable (sex), you can generate data for both male and female groups by moving the categorical variable (sex) into the [Factor List] box in the [Explore] dialogue box.

Looking at the Kolmogorov-Smirnov statistic in the Tests for Normality table below, we note that the figure for Sig. is 0.00, indicating that the assumption of normality has been violated. Rather than an independent t-test, we now need to make use of its nonparametric alternative, the Mann-Whitney U.

TESTS FOR NORMALITY

	Sex	Kolmogorov-Smirnov(a)			Shapiro-Wilk		
		Statistic	df	Sig.	Statistic	df	Sig.
Attitude	1	.298	32	.000	.815	32	.000
	2	.167	68	.000	.909	68	.000

a. Lilliefors Significance Correction

The procedure for the Mann-Whitney U test is as follows:

1. Click on [Analyze], then on [Nonparametric Tests], followed by [2 Independent Samples].
2. Click on the dependent variable [Attitudes] and the arrow to move it into the [Test Variable List] box.
3. Click on the categorical (independent) variable [sex] and the arrow to move this into the [Group Variable] box.
4. Click on the [Define Groups] button. In the [Group 1] box input the number '1', and in the [Group 2] box, input '2' to match sex Id numbers in the data set. Click on [Continue].
5. Click on [Mann-Whitney U] box under the label [Text Type].
6. Click on [Options] and then [Descriptive]. Then click on [Continue] and finally, [OK].

You should see the output as presented below.

TEST STATISTICS (A)

	Attitude
Mann-Whitney U	492.500
Wilcoxon W	1020.500
Z	–4.419

(a) Grouping Variable: Sex

RANKS

	Sex	N	Mean Rank	Sum of Ranks
Attitude	1	32	31.89	1020.50
	2	68	59.26	4029.50
	Total	100		

To analyse the data, look at the Test Statistics box for the value of Z and the significance level. The Z value has a significance level of 0.000. Given that this figure is lower than the probability value of 0.05, we can say that this result is significant. Since the result is significant we now need to make reference to the [Ranks] box and particularly the differences between the mean ranks, commenting on which is higher (in our example, it is females).

Note that the **Mann-Whitney U test** is also useful in other situations. Say, for example, we employ two different training programmes that teach the same topic and want to see which is the most effective. If it cannot be assumed that the data come from a normal distribution, we would use the Mann-Whitney U test to compare the test scores of the two sets of learners.

STATISTICAL ANALYSIS: ASSOCIATIONS BETWEEN VARIABLES

This section examines situations where the study contains two independent variables of the same type (nominal, ordinal, interval/ratio). Table 22.19 illustrates the different kinds of measurement of association between two variables, depending on the type of variable involved.

Associations between two nominal variables

Sometimes we may want to investigate relationships between two nominal variables – for example:

- Educational attainment and choice of career.
- Type of recruit (graduate/non-graduate) and level of responsibility in an organization.

You will recall in the discussions about chi-square, above, that we used the statistic to see whether the distribution of a variable occurred by chance or not. Chi-square is appropriate when you have two or more variables each of which contains at least two or more categories.

Let us say that a research team is studying a coaching programme and that a set of interviews with coachees (the recipients of coaching) have indicated that, when it came to a choice of coach, many (both males and females) expressed positive preferences for female coaches. Given that these comments were made by several respondents, the researchers turned to the quantitative data to see whether this was true. Table 22.20 illustrates the observed values, that is, the data set that shows the gender of coach selected by both female and male coachees. We can see that in both cases, both male and female coachees did, indeed, choose more female than male coaches. But is this difference significant? To find out, we need to use the chi-square statistic. Worked Example 22.3 shows how SPSS can be used for this data analysis.

Table 22.19 Summary of statistical tests available for measuring association between two variables

Association	Measure
Between two nominal variables	Cramer's V
Between two ordinal variables	Spearman rank-order correlation (where the relationship is non-linear)
Between interval and/or ratio scale variables	Pearson's product moment correlation (where the relationship is linear)

Table 22.20   Observed values for coach–coachee matching by gender

| | | GenderCoach | | |
		Male	Female	Total
GenderCoachee	Male	64	67	131
	Female	31	39	70
Total		95	106	201

Turn to the book's website (www.sagepub.co.uk/gray3e) and click on [Data sets] and then on [Chi-square] and save the data. Open the data set in SPSS.

DATASET

1. Click on [Analyze] and then on [Descriptive Statistics] followed by [Crosstabs].
2. Click on one of the variables, for example [GenderCoachee], and then click on the arrow to move this variable to the [Rows] box. Then click on [GenderCoach] and then the arrow to move this to the [Columns] box.
3. Click on the [Statistics] button, followed by [Chi-square] and [Phi and Cramer's V]. Then click on [Continue].
4. Having clicked on the [Cells] button, click on [Observed] in the [Counts] box. In the [Percentages] box, click on [Row], [Column] and [Total].
5. Click on [Continue], followed by [OK]. You should see the output as illustrated below.

GENDERCOACHEE * GENDERCOACH CROSSTABULATION

| | | | GenderCoach | | Total |
			Male	Female	Male
Gender Coachee	Male	Count	64	67	131
		% within GenderCoachee	48.9%	51.1%	100.0%
		% within GenderCoach	67.4%	63.2%	65.2%
		% of Total	31.8%	33.3%	65.2%
	Female	Count	31	39	70
		% within GenderCoachee	44.3%	55.7%	100.0%
		% within GenderCoach	32.6%	36.8%	34.8%
		% of Total	15.4%	19.4%	34.8%
Total		Count	95	106	201
		% within GenderCoachee	47.3%	52.7%	100.0%
		% within GenderCoach	100.0%	100.0%	100.0%
		% of Total	47.3%	52.7%	100.0%

In analysing the above output, the first step is to ensure that one of the assumptions of the chi-square test has not been violated, that is, that the expected cell frequency should never be less than five. We can see from the footnote (b) under the Chi-Square Tests table that 0 per cent of cells have an expected count of less than 5 – so we have not violated the assumption. In the study we are discussing, the minimum expected count is, in fact, 33.08.

CHI-SQUARE TESTS

	Value	df	Asymp. Sig. (2-sided)	Exact Sig. (2-sided)	Exact Sig. (1-sided)
Pearson Chi-Square	.382(b)	1	.536		
Continuity Correction(a)	.221	1	.638		
Likelihood Ratio	.383	1	.536		
Fisher's Exact Test				.556	.320
Linear-by-Linear Association	.380	1	.537		
N of Valid Cases	201				

a. Computed only for a 2 x 2 table
b. 0 cells (.0%) have expected count less than 5. The minimum expected count is 33.08

SYMMETRIC MEASURES

		Value	Approx. Sig.
Nominal by	Phi	.044	.536
Nominal	Cramer's V	.044	.536
N of Valid Cases		201	

a. Not assuming the null hypothesis.
b. Using the asymptotic standard error assuming the null hypothesis

When interpreting chi-square it is usual to make use of the Pearson Chi-square value (as in the Chi-Square Tests table). However, when, as in this case, we have a 2 by 2 table, it is necessary to use the Continuity Correction, which compensates for the overestimation of chi-square when using a 2 by 2 table. To be significant, this value needs to be .05 or smaller. In our case, this value is .221 so we need to conclude that this is not significant. Hence, although both male and female coachees have selected a larger number of female than male coaches, there is no statistically significant association between coachee's and coach's gender.

Correlation analysis: principles of measurement

Correlation analysis is concerned with associations between variables. Correlations are sometimes confused with regression. As Fink (2003) makes clear, however, correlation is concerned with describing relationships (for example, between X and Y), while regression predicts a value (say, X based on a value of Y). When an association is measured numerically, we get a correlation coefficient that gives the strength and the direction of the relationship between two variables. In addition to the strength of a relationship, we might also be interested in the direction of an association such

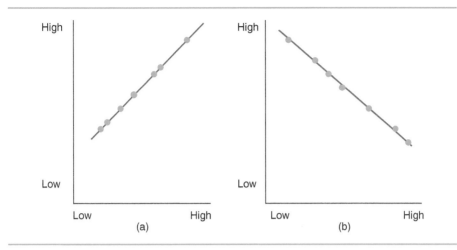

Figure 22.15   Perfect positive correlation (left) and perfect negative relationship (right)

as being positive or negative. Such relationships can be the basis of some very important questions in organizational and social analysis. For example,

- Is there a positive relationship between the introduction of performance management techniques and a specific group of workers' morale? (Relationship: performance management/morale)
- Is there a relationship between size of company (measured by size of workforce) and efficiency (measured by output per worker)? (Relationship: company size/efficiency)
- Is there a positive relationship between health and safety procedures and output? (Relationship: health and safety procedures/output)

The most commonly used coefficients assume a linear relationship between the variables, with Figure 22.15 illustrating an idealized form of 'perfect' linear correlation. Measured numerically, this would give a perfectly positive correlation coefficient of +1.0 for (a) and a perfectly negative correlation of -1.0 for (b). Figure 22.16, however, shows a much more likely type of correlation where the variables are highly positively correlated. The points shown all fall close to a cigar-shaped envelope. The thinner this envelope, the stronger the correlation, while the broader the envelope, the weaker the correlation. Where the points are scattered so much as to appear entirely random, then the correlation is likely to be zero, or close to it.

When, as is usually the case, we obtain figures that are somewhere between 0.00 and 1.0, what do we make of different results? Cohen (1988) suggests a range of descriptions, as illustrated in Table 22.21.

The correlation coefficient is calculated in a number of ways, depending on the type of data being used. This section focuses on bivariate relationships, that is, associations between just two variables. Calculating a correlation for a set of data should only be done when:

- The subjects are independent and not chosen from the same group.
- The values for X and Y are measured independently.
- X and Y values are sampled from populations that are normally distributed.
- Neither of the values for X or Y is controlled (in which case, linear regression, not correlation, should be calculated).

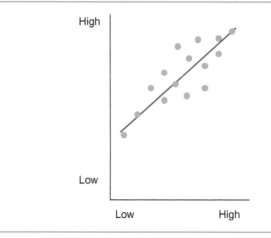

High

Low

Low   High

Figure 22.16   Example of a highly positive correlation with cigar-shaped envelope

Table 22.21   Strength of association based upon the value of a coefficient

Correlation figure	Description
0.10–0.29	Small
0.30–0.49	Medium
0.50–1.00	Large

Table 22.22   Three simplified sample sets of data illustrating Spearman's rho (r_s)

$r_s = +1.00$		$r_s = 0.04$		$r_s = -1.00$	
x	y	x	y	x	y
1	1	1	3	1	7
2	2	2	4	2	6
3	3	3	7	3	5
4	4	4	5	4	4
5	5	5	1	5	3
6	6	6	2	6	2
7	7	7	6	7	1

Source: Adapted from Black, 1999

Associations between two ordinal variables

Sometimes it is not possible to give values to variables, only ranks (1st, 2nd, 3rd, etc.). Table 22.22 illustrates three possible simple correlations, showing extremes of correlation (+1.00 and -1.00) and one slight correlation in the central column.

Let us now take the example of a case where two interviewers are judging the rankings of 10 applications for a new company post. Each interviewer allocates a rank from 1 to 10 for each person. Do they agree? To what extent are their judgements correlated? For data that are ranked, or in circumstances where relationships are non-linear, **Spearman's rank-order** correlation, often known as Spearman's rho, can be used. Let us now look at how SPSS can be used to calculate this kind of association between ordinal variables.

SPEARMAN
CORRELATION

— WORKED EXAMPLE 22.4 —

Turn to the book's website (www.sagepub.co.uk/gray3e) and click on [Data sets] and thenon [Spearmans rho] and save the data. Open the data set in SPSS. To calculate Spearman's rho:

DATASET

1. Click on [Analyze], followed by [Correlate] and then [Bivariate].
2. Select the two variables, Mr Jones and Mrs Smith, and click on the arrow to move them to the [Variables] box.
3. In the [Correlation Coefficients] area, tick the [Spearman's rho] box and untick Pearson.
4. Click on the [Options] button and for [Missing Values] click on [Exclude cases pairwise].
5. Click on [Continue] and then [OK].

You should then see the output as in the Correlations table below.

CORRELATIONS

			MrJones	MrsSmith
Spearman's rho	MrJones	Correlation Coefficient	1.000	.779(**)
		Sig. (2-tailed)	–	.000
		N	30	30
	MrsSmith	Correlation Coefficient	.779(**)	1.000
		Sig. (2-tailed)	.000	–
		N	30	30

** Correlation is significant at the 0.01 level (2-tailed)

Pallant (2010) advises that the first data to check is the N number. Is it correct for the number of cases? You need to know if there is missing data so that you can, if possible, locate it. Next, consider the direction of the relationship – is there a negative sign in front of the correlation coefficient value? See Table 22.22 for an example of a negative correlation. Then you need to determine the strength of the relationship. Using Table 22.21, we can see the value of .779 is a very strong relationship. Finally, you need to consider the significance level – did this value appear by chance alone? Pallant (2010) notes that care must be taken in not confusing significance with the strength of the relationship. With small samples (such as N=30) moderate correlations may not reach a traditional significance level of p<.05. Conversely, with larger samples (N=100+), small correlations may reach statistical significance.

Associations between numerical variables

PEARSON
CORRELATION

It is often the case that organizational researchers want to explore potential associations between variables such as income or age and various human activities such as spending patterns. Another use would be comparing sales figures against the number of sales representatives a company employs – do sales rise as more representatives are used? When exploring relationships between numerical data (interval and/or ratio) such as sales figures, age or income, then we can use the **Pearson product-moment** correlation. Note, however, that this statistical test is only appropriate if the relationships between variables are linear. In some circumstances there may be strong associations between variables but the relationship may be C or E-shaped. The Pearson product-moment correlation would not be able to detect this. For non-linear associations it is best to use the Spearman's rho calculation (as above).

WORKED EXAMPLE 22.5

DATASET

Let us take the example of a cosmetics company that wants to know if there is any association between the sales of one of its face creams and the weather conditions. Are people put off from using face cream if the weather is wet? To discover if there is a relationship, the company looks at sales figures and annual rainfall patterns over the past 30 years.

Turn to the book's website (www.sagepub.co.uk/gray3e) and click on [Data sets] and then on [Pearson product-moment] and save the data. Open the data set in SPSS. Before conducting a correlation, it is prudent to firstly generate a scatterplot in order to provide a visual check on the relationship between the two variables. The scatterplot also enables a check to be performed on the assumptions of linearity (the assumption that there is a straight line between variables and homoscedasticity (all variables have the same finite variance)). In other words, the output demonstrates some kind of relationship between the variables rather than being completely random. To create a scatterplot in SPSS:

1. From the menu, click on [Graphs] and then [Legacy Dialogs] and then [Scatter/Dot].
2. Click on [Simple Scatter] and then [Define].
3. Click on what you consider the dependent variable (in this case Sales) and click on the Arrow to move the variable to the Y-axis box.
4. Next click on [Rainfall] to move this variable into the X-axis box.
5. Finally, click on [OK]. You should see the output as illustrated by Figure 22.17.

Analysing the results of the scatterplot, it seems that there is a moderately negative correlation between the two variables rainfall and face cream sales. In considering the results take care to look for outliers, that is, data points that are away from the main cluster of points. Extreme outliers sometimes mean that the data have been entered incorrectly and this may influence the analysis. Scatterplots, however, do not yield definitive answers – it is necessary to make use of the appropriate statistical test. Given that the relationship is linear rather than curvilinear, it is appropriate to make use of the Pearson product-moment for these two variables. Before undertaking this, Pallant (2010) recommends that you should select [Edit] from the menu, then [Options] and make sure that there is a tick in the box labelled [No scientific notation for small numbers in tables]. The rest is straightforward:

1. Click on [Analyze] followed by [Correlate] and then [Bivariate].
2. Click on the arrow to move the variables into the box marked [Variables].
3. In [Correlations Coefficients] the [Pearson] box should be the default option so leave it as it is. If you needed a test for non-linear data, then you should choose the [Spearman rho] available here.

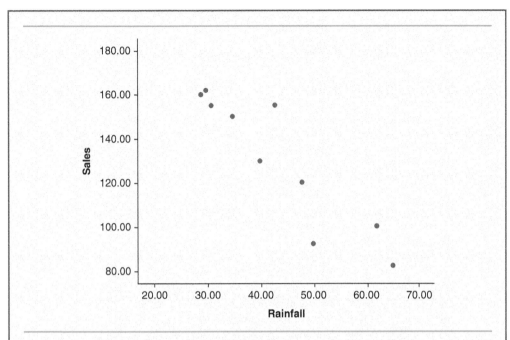

Figure 22.17 Scatterplot illustrating relationship between rainfall and face creams

4. Click on the [Options] button and then for [Missing Values] choose the [Exclude cases pairwise] box. If you wish, under [Options] you can also display means and standard deviations in the output.
5. Click on [Continue] and [OK]. The output should match the data outputs below.

DESCRIPTIVE STATISTICS

	Mean	Std. Deviation	N
Rainfall	48.17	11.228	30
Sales	132.47	28.311	30

CORRELATIONS

		Rainfall	Sales
Rainfall	Pearson Correlation	1	−.813(**)
	Sig. (2-tailed)		.000
	N	30	30
Sales	Pearson Correlation	−.813(**)	1
	Sig. (2-tailed)	.000	
	N	30	30

**Correlation is significant at the 0.01 level (2-tailed).

In analysing these results follow these steps:

1. Check that the number of cases (N) are correct and that there is no missing data. In our case N = 30.
2. Check whether the correlation figure is positive or negative. In the table above, for example, you will see a figure of –.813 which, obviously, is a negative correlation showing an inverse relationship between the two variables (when rainfall is high, face cream sales are low, and vice versa).
3. Next determine the strength of the relationship. As indicated earlier, this can range from –1.00 to 1.00, with a correlation of 0 indicating no correlation at all (refer to Table 22.21 above). We can see that –.813 is a very strong relationship.
4. Calculate how much variance the two variables share by determining the coefficient of determination. The variance expresses how much of the variation in one variable is due to the other variable. This is calculated by squaring the r value and multiplying by 100. In our example we take .813 x .813 = 66 per cent.
5. Report on the statistical significance. In the figure above, this is given as significant at the 0.01 level. Note, however, that the level of significance does not indicate how strongly the two variables are correlated. It indicates how much confidence we should have in the results that have been obtained. With small samples (e.g. N = 30), we might obtain strong correlations but still not reach statistical significance. Conversely in large samples (N = 100) relatively small associations can yield significance.

Relationship between continuous dependent variable and numerous independent variables

Regression analysis

REGRESSION
ANALYSIS

Regression analysis is a suitable statistical technique when one continuous interval or ratio variable is identified as a *dependent* and one or more continuous interval, ratio or categorical variable is defined as an *independent* variable (Tabachnick and Fidell, 2001). The primary purpose of regression analysis is to test the effect of one or more independent variable on one dependent variable. In other words, regression analysis is used to measure the relationship between the dependent and independent variable and assess significance of this relationship. The second objective of regression analysis is to obtain a formula to predict the value of the dependent variable for a new case based on knowledge of one or more independent variable. Regression analysis is different from correlation analysis because correlation assesses only the relationship between the two variables which tend to move together in the same (positive) or opposite (negative) direction. Correlation analysis has no assumption that one variable (independent) is affecting the other variable (or dependent variable). For example correlation analysis can be used to measure the relationship between advertising expenditures (independent variable) and price (dependent variable). The research aim for the correlation analysis is to find out if advertising expenditures and sales are positively related. For the linear regression, the research aim is to establish whether advertising expenditure has a statistically significant influence on sales as a dependent variable. If so, how much would be the effect of advertising expenditures on sales?

Regression analysis is a family of techniques including simple regression, multiple regression and other forms of regression. When the analysis includes only one independent (e.g. advertising expenditures) and one dependent variable (sales), the term refers to simple regression. When the analysis includes multiple dependent variables (advertising expenditures and price) and one dependent variable the terms refer to multiple regression. When data are skewed, one or more independent variables are measured by ordinal scales or when the dependent variable is a categorical one (e.g. yes, no) one of the non-linear regression techniques such as logistic regression may be suitable for testing the effect of an independent variable on a dependent variable (Pallant, 2010). Some of the research questions that linear regression analysis can address are:

- how well a set of independent variables is able to predict a particular dependent variable
- which variable in a set of independent variables is the best predictor of a dependent variable; and
- whether a particular independent variable (advertising expenditures) is still able to predict a dependent variable (sales) when the effects of another variable are controlled for (e.g. price).

Regression analysis produces a regression coefficient called R^2 (r-square) which is similar to the correlation coefficient. As for the correlation analysis, the square of the correlation coefficient shows the proportion of variance in the two variables. As for the regression analysis, the r-square value shows the percentage of variances in the dependent variable explained by the independent variable(s). The r-square value range from 0 to 1 is similar to the positive correlation coefficient but it does not take a negative value even though some independent variables (e.g. price) may have a negative influence on the dependent variable. A value of 0 indicates that the independent variable has no influence on the dependent variable. A scatterplot showing the regression line, r-square value, the relationship between dependent and independent variable are illustrated in Figure 22.18.

Taking into account the previous example, if the r-square value is 0.60, this means that the regression model including advertising expenditures and price explains 60 per cent of the variance in sales. This finding also suggests that unexplained variance in the regression model is 40 per cent. Most statistical programmes also compute if the r-square is statistically significant at the 0.05 probability level.

Regression analysis produces the r-square value as well as a regression equation (or a regression model). The regression equation is the formula for computing an estimation value for the dependent variable based on the value of the independent variable. For simple linear regression analysis, there are only two values in the equation for a straight line as shown below:

$$Y = a + b^*(X)$$

$$Y = 2000 + 0.30^*(400)$$

In the regression equation, Y is the intercept or the dependent variable that the equation is attempting to predict, a is a constant and b is the slope of the line or the regression coefficient. To predict the value of the dependent variable (Y) such as

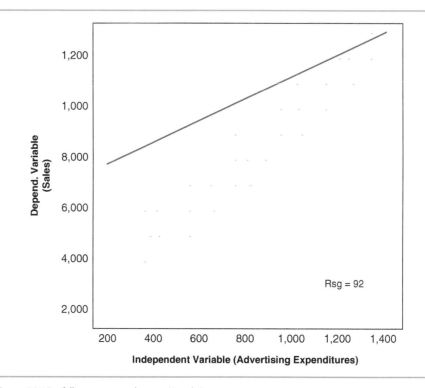

Figure 22.18   A linear regression scatterplot

sales when only the value of the independent variable is known (e.g. advertising expenditure = 400), the analysis would multiply the value of the regression coefficient (0.30) and add the constant (2000).

Assumptions of regression

Regression analysis makes a number of assumptions about the data. Both the independent and dependent variables should be taken from ratio or interval scales. The dependent variable can also be a unique form of nominal data called dummy variable (e.g. agree, disagree). The relationship between the dependent and independent variables must be *linear* rather than curved. Regression analysis is very sensitive to outliers (very extreme scores comparing to the mean scores) and the nature of underlying relationships between the variables. *Multicollinearity* occurs when the independent variables are highly correlated within themselves and the dependent variable (Pallant, 2010). In addition, the variance of the residuals about predicted dependent value scores should be the same for all predicted values (*homoscedasticity*).

The sample size is an important issue for regression analysis for two reasons. Firstly, producing reliable and valid results and secondly, generalizing the findings of regression analysis to the research population. As commented by Pallant (2010) different authors tend to give different guidelines concerning the number of cases required for the regression analysis. One of the most practical criteria for the sample size is N > 50 + 8iv (where iv indicates the number of independent variables). If you have four variables you will need at least 82 respondents.

To illustrate the use of multiple regression, a customer satisfaction survey in the restaurant industry will be used as the dependent variable. Service quality and food quality are the two independent variables. The literature in this area suggests that if customers feel that they receive good quality service and food in a restaurant they are likely to be satisfied with the overall visit experience. In this example, we are interested in exploring how well the service quality and value for money are able to predict scores on a measure of overall satisfaction. Accordingly in this example two questions will be addressed

Q1.   How well do service quality and food quality predict overall visit satisfaction?

Q2.   Which is the best predictor of overall visit satisfaction: service quality or food quality?

The variables and measures used in this example are as follows. Overall visit satisfaction was measured by a 7-point scale where (1) indicates extremely dissatisfied and (7) indicates extremely satisfied. The measures of service quality and food quality used two 7-point scales ranging from (1) being extremely poor to (7) being extremely good. DATASET
The example covers only the use of Standard Multiple Regression for the purpose of simplicity and criticism that has been addressed at the use of Stepwise and Hierarchical Multiple Regression techniques (Pallant, 2010). These techniques can be explored by looking at other text.

Go to the book's website at: www.sagepub.co.uk/gray3e and click on the button [Data sets]. Select the [Regression] data set. Once the data are opened in SPSS follow the next set of steps.

1. Click on [Regression], then click on [Analyze] and then on [Linear].
2. Click on your continuous dependent variable (overall visit satisfaction) and then move it into the [Dependent] box.
3. Click on the two independent variables: food quality and service quality and move them into the [Independent] box as shown in Figure 22.19 below.

Figure 22.19   Moving the independent variables food quality and service quality into the Independent variable box

1. Make sure [Enter] is selected in the [Method] section.
2. Click on [Statistics] button. Tick the box marked [Estimates, Confidence intervals, Model fit, Descriptives, Part and Partial Correlations] and [Collinearity Diagnostics].
   Then tick the [Casewise diagnostics] and [Outliers outside 3 standard deviations] in the [Residuals] section. Click on [Continue].
3. Click on the [Options] button. Then under the [Missing Values] section click on [Exclude cases pairwise]. Click on [Continue].
4. Click on the [Plots] button.
   Then click on [*ZRESID] and move this to the [Y] box.
   Click on [*ZPRED] and move this to the [X] box.
   Tick the [Normal probability plot] option under the section of [Standardized Residual Plots]
5. Click on [Continue]
6. Click on the [Save] button. Then under the [Distances] section tick the [Cook's] and [Mahalanobis] box to identify multivariate outliers. Click on [Continue].
7. To complete the process click on [OK].

You should then see the output generated from this procedure as presented below.

CORRELATIONS

		Overall Visit Satisfaction	Food Quality	Service Quality
Pearson Correlation	Food Quality	.573	1.000	.606
	Service Quality	.504	.606	1.000
	Overall Visit Satisfaction	.	.000	.000
Sig. (1-tailed)	Food Quality	.000	.	.000
	Service Quality	.000	.000	.
	Overall Visit Satisfaction	402	402	402
N	Food Quality	402	402	402
	Service Quality	402	402	402
	Overall Visit Satisfaction	1.000	.573	.504

MODEL SUMMARY[b]

Model	R	R Square	Adjusted R Square	Std. Error of the Estimate
1	.606[a]	.368	.364	.972

(a) Predictors: (Constant), Service Quality, Food Quality
(b) Dependent Variable: Overall Visit Satisfaction

ANOVA[a]

Model		Sum of Squares	df	Mean Square	F	Sig.
1	Regression	219.195	2	109.598	115.967	.000[b]
	Residual	377.086	399	.945		
	Total	596.281	401			

a. Dependent Variable: Overall Visit Satisfaction
b. Predictors: (Constant), Service Quality, Food Quality

COEFFICIENTS[a]

Model	Unstandardized Coefficients		Standardized Coefficients	T	Sig.	95.0% Confidence Interval for B		Correlations			Collinearity Statistics	
	B	Std. Error	Beta			Lower Bound / Upper Bound	Zero-order	Partial	Part	Tolerance	VIF	
(Constant)	1.348	.307		4.388	.000	.744	1.953					
Food Quality	.466	.055	.423	8.460	.000	.357	.574	.573	.390	.337	.633	1.581
Service Quality	.327	.066	.248	4.945	.000	.197	.457	.504	.240	.197	.633	1.581

(a) Dependent Variable: Overall Visit Satisfaction

COLLINEARITY DIAGNOSTICS[a]

Model	Dimension	Eigenvalue	Condition Index	Variance Proportions		
				(Constant)	Food Quality	Service Quality
1	1	2.967	1.000	.00	.00	.00
	2	.022	11.642	.52	.67	.00
	3	.011	16.504	.47	.33	1.00

(a) Dependent Variable: Overall Visit Satisfaction

CASEWISE DIAGNOSTICS[a]

Case Number	Std. Residual	Overall Visit Satisfaction	Predicted Value	Residual
39	–3.052	3	5.97	–2.967

(a) Dependent Variable: Overall Visit Satisfaction

RESIDUALS STATISTICS[a]

	Minimum	Maximum	Mean	Std. Deviation	N
Predicted Value	4.05	6.90	5.62	.739	402
Std. Predicted Value	–2.124	1.723	.000	1.000	402
Standard Error of Predicted Value	.058	.114	.082	.019	402

Adjusted Predicted Value	4.03	6.93	5.62	.739	402
Residual	-2.967	2.153	.000	.970	402
Std. Residual	-3.052	2.215	.000	.998	402
Stud. Residual	-3.071	2.221	.000	1.001	402
Deleted Residual	-3.004	2.165	.000	.977	402
Stud. Deleted Residual	-3.104	2.232	.000	1.004	402
Mahal. Distance	.421	4.513	1.995	1.350	402
Cook's Distance	.000	.039	.003	.005	402
Centred Leverage Value	.001	.011	.005	.003	402

(a) Dependent Variable: Overall Visit Satisfaction

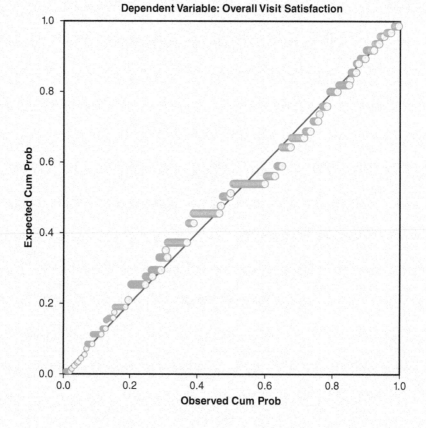

Normal P-P Plot of Regression Standardized Residual

Dependent Variable: Overall Visit Satisfaction

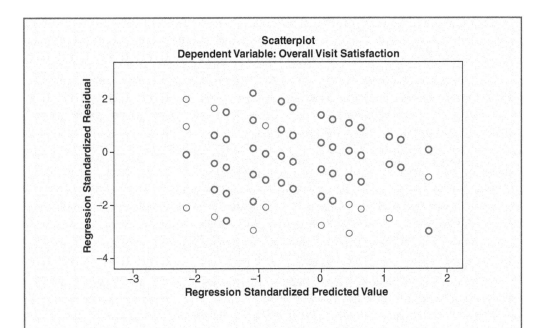

The procedure for interpreting these results is as follows.

1. Before we begin to interpret the regression results, check if the data meets the linear regression test assumptions. In doing so:

   - Look at the table labelled as *Correlations* to find out **Multicollinearity**. As the correlation between the two independent variables (0.61) as well as the correlations between the two independent variables and the dependent variable (0.50 and 0.57) are not too high, we can conclude that multicollinearity is not a problem in the model. The SPSS programme also produces collinearity diagnosis on the variables as part of the multiple regression procedure as shown in the table labelled *Coefficients*. Two values are given in relation to multicollinearity: Tolerance and VIF (Variance Inflation Values). These values are related to each other and therefore reporting one of them (e.g. VIF) would be sufficient. If VIF values are large (higher than 10), it would indicate possibility of multicollinearity which is not the case here as the VIF values in our regression model (1.58) are well below the cut-off value of 10.

   - Check the **normality, linearity** and **outliers** assumptions by inspecting the residuals *scatterplot and the normal probability plot*. No major deviations from normality will be present if the plot lies as a reasonably straight diagonal line from bottom left to top right in the Normal Probability Plot which is the case here. Linearity can be checked using the *Scatterplot of the standardized residuals*. You would expect that the pattern of residuals will be distributed roughly as rectangular rather than curvilinear or higher on one side than the other. Linearity seems to be supported in this model by looking at the scatterplot of the standardized residuals. Finally, the presence of outliers can also be detected by inspecting the scatterplot and the table titled *Casewise Diagnostics*. This illustrates information about cases that have absolute standardized values above 3.0. Since in a normally distributed sample we would expect only 1 per cent of cases to fall outside this range, and there is only one case here, outliers therefore do not cause concerns in this model.

2. To evaluate the success of the regression model, look at the **R-square** in the *Model Summary* box. This shows how much of the variance in overall visit satisfaction is explained by food quality and service quality. In this case the value is 0.368 which means that service quality and food quality explain 36.8 per cent of the variance in overall visit satisfaction. This is a good result. To assess the statistical significance of the results it is necessary to check *the ANOVA statistics* (F=115.967) table and the p value (Sig = 0.000). As can be seen from this example the model is statistically significant at the 0.001 probability level.

3. The final step in interpreting the results of the regression model is to determine which of the independent variables contribute to the prediction of the dependent variable. This information can be found in the output box labelled *Coefficients*. Although this table provides a wide range of information, in order to compare the contribution of independent variables in predicting the dependent variable, check the statistics under *Beta* in the *Standardised Coefficients* column. In this case, the largest beta value is 0.42 which is the food quality. This is followed by service quality (0.25). As can be seen from the t scores and probability values, food quality (t = 8.460, Sig = 0.00) and service quality (t = 4.945, Sig = 0.00) are also statistically significant at 0.005 probability level in predicting overall visit satisfaction. These statistics indicate each variable makes a significant unique contribution to the prediction of the dependent variable. The Beta value for service quality is slightly lower (0.25), indicating that it made less of a contribution. You should note that absolute Beta values are used when ranking the contribution ability of independent variables in predicting the dependent variable in regression analysis. The sign of the Beta value (positive or negative) also indicates the direction of the relationship (positive or negative) between independent and dependent variables which is similar to correlation analysis. For more information about how to interpret the findings of regression analysis you can look into major statistics books in the references provided at the end of the chapter.

Summary

- The selection of statistical tests should be made at the design stage of the research and not as an afterthought.
- Data can be classified into categorical data (which includes nominal and ordinal) and quantifiable data (which includes interval and ratio). The types of data yielded by a study will determine the kinds of analysis and statistical tests applied to them.
- Data may be presented descriptively through the use of pie charts, bar charts and histograms or through the use of descriptive statistics. The latter focus on themes such as the distribution of the data and its dispersion.
- Inferential statistics are used to draw conclusions from the data and involve the specification of a hypothesis and the selection of appropriate statistical tests.
- Some of the inherent danger in hypothesis testing is in making Type I errors (rejecting a hypothesis when it is, in fact, true) and Type II errors (accepting a hypothesis when it is false).
- For categorical data, non-parametric statistical tests can be used, but for quantifiable data, more powerful parametric tests need to be applied. Parametric tests usually require that the data are normally distributed.

REVIEW QUESTIONS

1. What practical steps can be taken to avoid the degradation of data during the questionnaire design stage?
2. Why is the use of parametric tests usually preferred to the use of non-parametric?
3. In testing the safety of a drug, is it better to avoid a Type I or a Type II error? Why?
4. What role does the Kolmogorov-Smirnov statistic play in choice of statistical tests? What other statistics can be used to supplement K-S?

FURTHER READING

Wetcher-Hendricks, D. (2011) *Analyzing Quantitative Data: An Introduction for Social Researchers*. Hoboken, NJ: Wiley. Guides readers through the essentials of data analysis including organizing raw data to using descriptive statistics and tests of significance.

Pallant, J. (2010) *SPSS Survival Manual*, 4th edn. Maidenhead: OUP/McGraw-Hill. Now a standard text, largely because it is so clear and user-friendly.

Fielding, J. and Gilbert, N. (2006) *Understanding Social Statistics*, 2nd edn. London: Sage. Comprehensive and clearly articulated. Illustrates how to perform statistical calculations using SPSS.

Hosker, I. (2002) *Social Statistics: Data Analysis in Social Science Explained*. Taunton: Studymates. A very short and simple text for those truly terrified by statistics.

Black, T. (2001) *Evaluating Social Science Research*, 2nd edn. London: Sage. Provides a clearly written introduction to evaluating research projects. The last chapter (in the second edition) contains a very useful introduction to using Excel as a data analysis tool.

JOURNAL RESOURCES

Russo, F. (2011) 'Correlational data, causal hypotheses, and validity', *Journal for General Philosophy of Science,* 42(1): 85–107. Discusses how to make sense of correlational data coming from observations and/ or from experiments, and how to establish when correlations are causal and when they are not.

Campo, M. and Lichtman, S.W. (2008) 'Interpretation of research in physical therapy: Limitations of null hypothesis significance testing', *Journal of Physical Therapy Education*, 22 (1): 43–48. Points out some of the limitations of null hypothesis significance testing and offers some alternatives.

Wynd, C.A., Schmidt, B. and Schaefer, M.A. (2003) 'Two quantitative approaches for estimating content validity', *Western Journal of Nursing Research*, 25(5): 508–518. Suggests a quantitative method for improving the content validity of an instrument.

QUANTITATIVE
APPROACHES

SUMMARY OF WEB LINKS

www.sagepub.co.uk/gray3e

23

ANALYSING AND PRESENTING QUALITATIVE DATA

CHAPTER INTRODUCTION

Chapter outline

- Elements of qualitative data analysis — 603
- Analysing qualitative data — 607
- Other approaches to qualitative analysis — 621
- Quality in qualitative analysis — 622
- Software for qualitative data analysis — 625

Keywords

Induction

Coding

Reflexivity

Content analysis

Thematic analysis

Grounded theory

Narrative analysis

Conversational analysis

Discourse analysis

─ **Chapter objectives** ─

After reading this chapter you will be able to:

- Describe some of the principles of qualitative data analysis.
- Select appropriate qualitative analytical methods, including grounded theory approaches.
- Apply qualitative methods to produce valid, reliable and trustworthy data.
- Make use of the 'voice' of the researcher.

MILES &
HUBERMAN
CHAPTER 1

We saw in Chapter 2 that while some research methodologies tend to utilize either quantitative *or* qualitative methods, very often both are used. This is because qualitative data can provide rich descriptions and explanations that demonstrate the chronological flow of events as well as often leading to serendipitous (chance) findings. According to Miles and Huberman (1994) qualitative studies have a quality of 'undeniability' because words have a more concrete and vivid flavour that is more convincing to the reader than pages of numbers. However, qualitative analysis has been criticized for being lacking in methodological rigour, prone to researcher subjectivity and based on small cases or limited evidence. We will explore how qualitative analysis addresses such problems later in this chapter.

Qualitative analysis is (or should be) a rigorous and logical process through which data are given meaning. Through analysis, we can progress through an initial description of the data then, through a process of disaggregating the data into smaller parts, see how these connect into new concepts, providing the basis for a fresh description. As we saw in Chapter 2, there are different approaches to qualitative research, including grounded theory, ethnography and phenomenology, researchers often using a combination of approaches in a research project. One of the challenges of qualitative research is that there are no widely accepted rules about how qualitative data should be analysed, other than that the approach is generally inductive and involves the coding of data.

Another major issue is the extent to which data should be analysed. As Strauss and Corbin (1998) point out, some researchers believe that the data should not be analysed at all, but should merely be presented. This allows the data to 'speak for themselves', untainted by the potential subjective interpretations of the researcher. Other qualitative researchers are concerned, however, with accurate selection, synthesis and description of the data, but in as detached and objective a way as possible. Other researchers are more concerned with theory building, interpreting the data to build concepts and categories that can be brought together into theoretical frameworks. In contrast, some researchers see qualitative research as primarily being about storytelling and description (Wolcott, 1994).

In this chapter we will look at approaches to how data can be analysed, looking particularly at content analysis and grounded theory methods and also including some increasingly influential approaches such as the use of narratives, conversational analysis and discourse analysis. The important issues of reliability and validity will also be addressed, particularly from the stance of those who favour interpretivist and naturalistic approaches.

➤ **TOP TIP 23.1** ◄

Many people who are new to qualitative research collect their data and then wonder how to analyse it. This is too late in the day! Plan for the qualitative data analysis method you intend to use at the design phase of the research process. This is essential, because some approaches to data analysis will influence the ways in which data are collected and the phases in which they are analysed.

ELEMENTS OF QUALITATIVE DATA ANALYSIS

There is what may seem at first sight, a quite bewildering number of approaches to the analysis of qualitative data (some of which will be discussed in this chapter) and no clear rules on which approach to adopt in different circumstances. Thankfully, however, there are a few general principles to qualitative data analysis that should be understood and applied, whatever the approach to data analysis being adopted. These include analytic induction, the principles and practices of coding, the place of **secondary data analysis** and the reflexivity of the researcher. We will look at each of these in turn.

Analytic induction

As we saw in Chapters 2 and 3, induction involves the collection and analysis of data from a range of individual cases in order to identify patterns from them for the development of conceptual categories. As Figure 23.1 illustrates, the process of analytic induction involves a number of defined stages. Essentially, starting from at least an approximate definition of a research question, cases are examined to see if they are

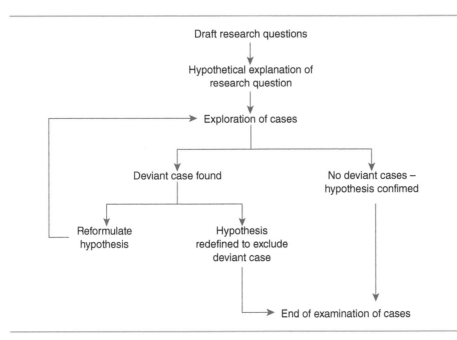

Figure 23.1   The process of analytic induction

Source: Adapted from Bryman and Bell, 2007

UNDER-
STANDING
THEORETICAL
SAMPLING

consistent with a hypothetical explanation of the research question. If no deviant cases are found, then the hypothesis can be confirmed. If, however, cases emerge that are inconsistent with the hypothesis, then either the hypothesis has to be rewritten (and new cases examined), or the hypothesis itself is redefined to exclude the deviant case.

As Bryman and Bell (2007) contend, analytical induction is an extremely rigorous method of data analysis because if a single case is inconsistent with the hypothesis, then either further data have to be collected, or the hypothesis has to be reformulated. The selection of cases also needs to be sufficiently diverse for the theory that emerges to be adequately tested. So while **theoretical sampling** makes use of cases that add weight to the development of a concept, analytical induction deliberately chooses negative or deviant cases to disconfirm a hypothesis (Flick, 2009).

Steps in the coding process

TRANSCRIBING
YOUR OWN
DATA

Unlike quantitative data analysis where the statistical tools are well understood, in qualitative analysis there are no hard and fast rules for how data should be coded. There are, however, a number of useful principles that should be applied, irrespective of whether you are using grounded theory, content analysis or any other method.

- *Transcribe the data*: Field notes from observations or reflective diaries should be written up into a format that can be easily read. Hastily written field notes, for example, should be typed into a document. Assuming that interviews have been tape recorded, these should be transcribed. Whether you do this yourself, or pay for the service, may partly be determined by your budget. While typing up the transcript yourself may be time-consuming and laborious, it does develop a familiarization with the data at an early stage.
- *Collect/code/collect*: Avoid waiting until all data are collected before starting the coding process, start as soon as possible. Coding allows you to become familiar at an early stage with the issues emerging from the data. Identifying these themes also helps with theoretical sampling (selecting new cases on the basis of theories and concepts emerging from the analysis).
- *Familiarization*: Read through all field notes, documents and transcripts but suspend the temptation to interpret. Get a general flavour of what is happening. Perhaps at this point make some general notes as an *aide-mémoire* in your research diary on what seemed interesting, unusual or perhaps significant.
- *Focused reading*: Next comes a more focused reading of the data, this time underlining key words or phrases and making notes in the margins. The underlined words/phrases are the beginning of the coding process. You might also allot a word or phrase (code) that summarizes or seems pertinent to a particular passage. Notes might include reminders to yourself or reflective thoughts on puzzles or passages that throw up the unexpected.
- *Review/amend codes*: On the second reading, begin to modify your codes. If two or more codes seem to apply to the same phenomenon, then remove one of them. If a code relates to a concept in the literature, then make use of the literature category or description. Are some of the codes hierarchical? In other words, is one concept a sub-category of another? Generate as many codes as seem logical. These can always be amended or rationalized at a later stage.
- *Generating theory*: Look for connections between categories and concepts that are emerging from the data. Do they amount to a set of theoretical principles? Do they relate to any theoretical models in the literature? Develop hypotheses about some of these connections and return to the literature to see if they can be confirmed by the evidence. Some of the principles outlined here will be demonstrated when we look at the use of grounded theory in qualitative data analysis.

However, even when these principles are applied consistently and with care, a common accusation levelled at qualitative data analysis is that the coding tends to fragment the data, losing the connection between the text and its context. For example, in presenting a quote from a respondent, the reader loses the context within which it appeared. The narrative flow of what people say is lost. This is one of the reasons why narrative analysis as a form of qualitative data analysis has gained in popularity in recent years.

➤ TOP TIP 23.2 ◄

In analysing qualitative data, make sure that you don't end up merely using isolated quotations from a number of respondents as if they contained some significant meaning. You have to move beyond description to include an analysis and interpretation of the data. Any verbatim quotations should be used as a way of supporting this analysis.

MOVING BEYOND QUOTATION

Analysing secondary data

While most of this chapter is concerned with the analysis of primary data gathered in field settings (for example, through observations or interviews) it is important to also recognize that researchers can have access to data in the form of documents and other resources where the data has been collected (and in some cases analysed) by others (recall Chapter 20). For quantitative researchers, secondary analysis can involve the use of both documents and official statistics. For qualitative researchers, secondary data analysis primarily involves the analysis of another researcher's qualitative data or documents. While the re-analysis of quantitative data sets has been common in policy analysis and in the interpretation of key business decisions, its use in qualitative analysis has been much more modest (Fielding, 2004). The purpose, however, remains similar – to perform additional, in-depth analysis of a sub-set of the original data; or to apply a new perspective or conceptual focus to the data.

UK DATA ARCHIVE

Bryman and Bell (2007) suggest a checklist that researchers should use when making use of documents (for both quantitative and qualitative secondary analysis). The criteria include:

- Who produced the document?
- Why was it produced?
- Is the material genuine and produced by someone who could write authoritatively and objectively on the subject?
- Can the events or accounts presented in the document be corroborated by other evidence?

To these we can add a concern about ethics. Are safeguards in place to honour any commitments made by the original researchers to the research subject? Whatever promises were made about confidentiality need to be followed during the secondary data analysis.

As we saw in Chapter 20, secondary data analysis offers the researcher a number of advantages, particularly in terms of saving cost and time. Furthermore, where a subject is particularly sensitive, researchers can make use of previously gathered secondary data, rather than having to re-interview participants. Secondary analysis is not, however, without its detractors. Mauthner et al. (1998) contend that since qualitative data are the result of a reflexive relationship between the researcher and the researched (see the following section), the conditions under which the data were collected are inescapable. This means that secondary data analysis can only be valid if limited to methodological exploration. Attempts to go beyond this by attempting, say, to establish new analytical themes from the data are inappropriate. Fielding (2004), however, sees this as less of an epistemological than a practical problem since qualitative researchers have always had to monitor the effects of contextual features whether performing primary or secondary analysis. Vital evidence for judging the validity of an analytical point may well be sometimes missing from archived data – but the same can be said of primary data too.

Reflexivity – the voice of the researcher

REFLEXIVITY

Reflexivity is a concept used to describe the relationship between the researcher and the object of research (Brannick and Coghlan, 2007), and has been discussed by social scientists for over 30 years, influenced in the main by feminist researchers and those from hermeneutic and critical theory traditions (recall Chapter 17). It has mainly been applied to the collection of qualitative data, usually through interviewing (Ryan and Golden, 2006). Reflexivity involves the realization that the researcher is not a neutral observer, and is implicated in the construction of knowledge. Far from being a disinterested bystander, the researcher is seen as someone whose observations are by their very nature, selective, and whose interpretations of results are partial. Coffey (1999), for example, argues that researchers need to be aware of how fieldwork data gathering and ethnographic writing construct, reproduce and implicate selves, relationships and personal identities. The problem is that many researchers fail to recognize this. In the words of Mauthner and Doucet, in many research accounts, the researcher is 'rendered invisible as are the interpersonal, social and institutional contexts' (2003: 415). This process, they contend, has been made even worse by the growth in the use of computer-assisted qualitative data analysis programs which have given an air of scientific objectivity to what remains a fundamentally subjective and interpretive process.

REFLEXIVITY IN NURSING

There are, essentially, at least two forms of reflexivity.

- Epistemological reflexivity where the researchers reflect on their assumptions about the world and about the nature of knowledge. So they will ask themselves questions such as: how has the research question limited or distorted what was found? How could the study have been conducted differently?
- Personal reflexivity, where the researcher reflects upon how their personal values, attitudes, beliefs and aims have served to shape the research. This might also involve a personal reflection on how the research process impacted and changed the stance taken by the researcher. It involves honesty and openness and locates the researcher firmly within the dynamic of the research process, or in the words of Dupuis (1999), in a continuous, intentional and systematic self-introspection.

Mauthner and Doucet (2003) note that while reflexivity has been increasingly seen as important, the research methods literature has been relatively silent on steps for achieving it. However, some practical approaches could include:

- Designing research that involves multiple investigators. This can encourage dialogue and the critical interchanges of ideas – pushing researchers to make transparent their epistemological positions and personally held beliefs.

- Writing a reflexive journal. Lincoln and Guba (1994) recommend that this should include writing: (1) a daily schedule describing the logistics of the study; (2) a log of methodological decisions and changes; and (3) a personal diary recording reflections with particular reference to one's values and interests.
- Reporting research perspectives, values and beliefs in any research report. Dupuis (1999) recommends that this is done pre and post data collection so that changes in personal feelings can be made explicit.

Weber (2003), however, notes some of the potential dangers of reflexivity.

- Narcism. We become so wrapped up in self-introspection, that it becomes the actual focus of the study.
- Self-righteousness. We start to denigrate the work of other researchers who, for whatever reason, do not engage in reflexivity.
- Nihilism. We see that our research is limited in more and more ways. We become so conscious of the constraints on our research, the indeterminacy of theory, the limitations of research methods and the assumptions and biases that underlie our work that we become paralysed.
- Arrogance. We dismiss any work that can be generalized, arguing that every research context (including, or even particularly, our own) is unique.

While apposite, these warnings are perhaps aimed at those researchers at the more extreme wings of the reflexivity movement. For the rest of us, we should embrace reflexivity to the extent that it is in line with our attitudes towards epistemology and our principles of research design and practice.

ANALYSING QUALITATIVE DATA

Analysis involves the process of breaking data down into smaller units to reveal their characteristic elements and structure (Dey, 1993: 30). Descriptions can lay the basis for analysis, but we need to go beyond description: we want to interpret, to understand and to explain. Through analysis, however, we can also gain new insights into our data. Data can be broken down into their constituent parts, and connections made between these concepts, providing the basis for new descriptions (see Figure 23.2).

As we have seen, there are a wide range of approaches to qualitative analysis, some being more deductive in approach (such as content analysis) and others heavily inductive. Inevitably, the various approaches also differ in the mechanics of data analysis, including the attitude taken to the fragmentation of data.

Content analysis

One of the most common approaches to analysing qualitative data is through content analysis. Essentially, this involves the making of inferences about data (usually text) by systematically and objectively identifying special characteristics (classes or categories) within them. The attempt to achieve a measure of objectivity in this process is addressed by the creation of specific rules called *criteria of selection* which have to be established before the data can be analysed. In contrast to this, with grounded theory (see the following section) no a priori criteria are assumed, with these emerging through the process of data collection and analysis itself. Hence, at

FLICK ON
CONTENT
ANALYSIS

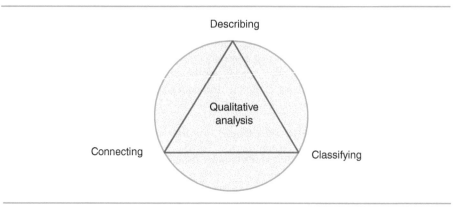

Figure 23.2   Qualitative analysis as a circular process

Source: Dey, 1993

the risk of over-simplification, grounded theory is more inductive in character, and content analysis more deductive.

In using content analysis, there are three procedures for identifying classes and categories. First, *common classes*, comprising categories in everyday thinking such as age, gender, boss, worker are identified. These common classes can be useful in linking or finding associations between the data and important demographic characteristics. Secondly, *special classes* are identified, comprising the kind of labels particular groups or communities use to distinguish amongst things, persons or events. This can include specialist types of language (including slang, the use of acronyms, specialist professional terms, etc.). Thirdly, *theoretical classes*, or those classes that arise in the process of analysing the data, are identified, providing the key linkages and patterns. As Flick (2009) points out, however, these categories are themselves often derived from theoretical models. So categories are brought to the empirical data, and not necessarily derived from them. Of course, they will be repeatedly evaluated against the data and modified if necessary.

Having identified categories within the text, the next step is the analysis itself. The key here is to reduce the volume of textual material. Using the work of Mayring (1983), Flick (2009) distinguishes three steps in the analysis process:

- *Summarizing content analysis*, where the material is paraphrased, with similar paraphrases bundled together and less relevant passages eliminated.
- *Explicating content analysis*, which clarifies ambiguous or contradictory passages by introducing context material into the analysis. This could include dictionary definitions of terms, statements from the text or outside the text (for example, contextual information, theoretical propositions) that illustrate the passages being analysed. Through this process a clarifying paraphrase is formulated and tested.
- *Structuring content analysis* seeks to identify types of formal structures in the materials. Hence, the analysis might extricate key features in the material and describe them in more detail. Alternatively, the material might be rated according to dimensions on a scale. So, in a passage dealing with, say, 'motivation', the concept could be given a rating scale from 'Highly motivated' to 'Completely demotivated'. The passage is then searched for examples of motivational feelings against the scale, resulting in a frequency count for each of the motivational levels.

Berg (2006) argues that content analysis can also be used with hypothesis testing, that is, a more experimental or quasi-experimental design. With hypothesis testing, he suggests going through the following stages:

- Make a rough hypothesis based upon observations from the data.
- Search the data to find cases that do not fit with the hypothesis.
- If negative cases are found, discard or reformulate the hypothesis to account for the negative cases (recall the process of analytical induction, above).

Hence, it is necessary to develop research questions in advance that are linked to previous research (Mayring, 1983 in Flick, 2009). It is because of this insistence on measurement and hypothesis testing that Locke (2001) places content analysis within the modernist, objectivist paradigm.

Content analysis is potentially a very important weapon in the researcher's armoury because it can be highly cost-effective. There may be no need to design and issue costly questionnaires – existing documentation such as company reports, memoranda or emails may provide the basis for the data (as in secondary data analysis, above). This, however, could also be construed as a disadvantage since the approach has to rely on 'old' data, rather than gathering fresh information. Another weakness is that it is incapable of exploring associations and causal relationships between variables. As Flick (2009) also points out, the very conceptual structures that content analysis imposes on the data may obscure some of the interpretations that may have emerged inductively from within it.

Thematic analysis

Thematic analysis is a method for identifying and analysing patterns (themes) within qualitative data (Braun and Clarke, 2006) and is a form of pattern recognition within the data (Fereday and Muir-Cochrane, 2006). A theme captures something important about the data in relation to the research question, and represents a level of *patterned* response or meaning within the data. According to Braun and Clarke (2006) an important question to address in the coding process is what counts as a pattern or theme and what 'size' a theme needs to be. In principle, there needs to be a number of instances of the theme across the data set, although the mere number of instances in themselves do not make the theme more or less important than other themes. It just means the theme can be identified. A theme becomes important when it captures something important in relation to the overall research question. Braun and Clarke (2006) also distinguish between inductive versus theoretical thematic analysis. An inductive approach means that the themes emerge from the data themselves – they are data driven. In contrast, a theoretical thematic analysis emerges from the researcher's theoretical stance and may provide a detailed analysis of some aspect of the data. Here, Fereday and Muir-Cochrane (2006) suggest the use of a template or codebook developed a priori based on the research question and theoretical framework.

THEMATIC
ANALYSIS

In terms of practical approach, Braun and Clarke (2006) identify six phases:

- Phase 1: Familiarize yourself with the data. Transcribe the data if necessary or at least read and re-read the data, noting down initial ideas.
- Phase 2: Generate initial codes. Code interesting features of the data systematically across the entire data set. If coding manually, do this by writing notes in the texts you

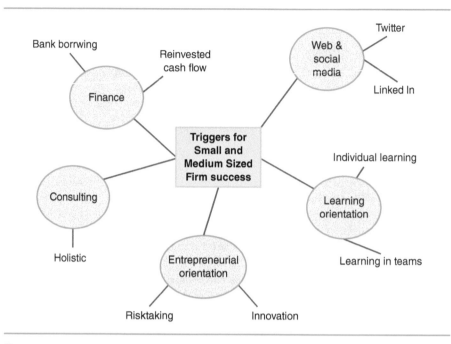

Figure 23.3 Development of a thematic map

THEMATIC
ANALYSIS
EXAMPLE

are analysing, by using highlighters to indicate potential patterns or by using 'post-it' notes to identify segments of data. Ensure that all data are collated to a code. Code extracts of the data inclusively (keep some of the surrounding data) so that the context is not lost. Individual extracts of data can be coded into as many different themes as they fit.

- Phase 3: Search for themes. Collate codes into potential themes, gathering together all data relevant to each theme. In this phase it is often useful to create visual representations of the themes in the form of thematic maps (see Figure 23.3). Hence, some codes may form main themes, while others constitute sub-themes. There may also be themes that do not initially fit into the thematic map and be temporarily labelled 'miscellaneous'.
- Phase 4: Review themes. Check if the themes selected are valid in relation to the coded extracts and the entire data set. At this stage it may become clear that some candidate themes are not actually themes because there is insufficient data to support them; in other cases, two themes might be integrated and renamed. Other themes might be broken down into separate themes.
- Phase 5: Define and name the themes. Refine each theme, generating clear definitions and names for each theme and identify the 'story' that each theme tells. Be clear about how each theme fits with the overall story. You should be able to describe the scope and content of each theme in no more than two sentences.
- Phase 6: Produce the report. Select vivid and compelling extracts relating back to the original research questions and the literature. The account must provide sufficient *evidence* of what have been identified as themes within the data.

Braun and Clarke (2006) argue that thematic analysis is relatively easy to conduct, but there are potential pitfalls. One of these is that the researcher merely paraphrases the data without actually developing an analytic narrative. Another is that the analysis itself might be weak or unconvincing. It is essential that the themes cohere around a central idea or concept.

Grounded theory

One of the most influential qualitative approaches is that of grounded theory, defined as a theory that is: 'discovered, developed and provisionally verified through systematic data collection and analysis of data pertaining to that phenomenon' (Strauss and Corbin, 1998: 23). Locke (2001) suggests that locating grounded theory in a particular research paradigm is difficult because it has been used in both modernist (objectivist) and interpretivist approaches. There is, however, a clear influence of symbolic interactionism, and this interpretivist paradigm's commitment to studying the social world and the rejection of a priori theorizing.

WHAT IS GROUNDED THEORY?

Grounded theory methods have been extensively used in education, evaluation research, nursing and organizational studies (Charmaz, 1995). Unlike the deductive approach, grounded theory does not begin with prior assumptions about hypotheses, research questions or what literature should underpin the study. This is not to say that grounded theorists embark on a study with no theoretical position. They will have a competent level of knowledge about the area. But, as Strauss and Corbin (1998) warn, grounded researchers should not be so steeped in the literature that their creative efforts become impeded or constrained. The research should commence with a defined purpose, but also with the realization that this purpose may become modified or even radically altered during the research process itself. Through data analysis new theoretical positions or understandings may emerge.

The grounded theory researcher works with his or her participants to actively construct the data, to get beyond static analysis to multiple layers of meaning. According to Charmaz (1995), these layers could include:

- The participant's stated explanations of her or his actions.
- The participant's unstated assumptions about these actions.
- The participant's intentions and motivation for engaging in the actions.
- The effects of the actions on others.
- The consequences of these actions for interpersonal relations and for further individual actions.

What about the data analysis process itself? Strauss and Corbin (1998) lay down a structured process and one that has become a highly influential way of analysing data comprising:

- Open coding: the disaggregation of the data into units.
- Axial coding: recognizing relationships between categories.
- Selective coding: the integration of categories to produce a theory.

These are pulled together into a framework that is called a conditional matrix, a 'complex web of interrelated conditions, action/interaction, and consequences pertaining to a particular phenomenon' (Strauss and Corbin, 1998: 181). These coding processes, however, are not necessarily completely distinct, and do not need to take place in sequence. In a single coding session, the researcher might move quickly from one coding method to another, particularly from open to axial coding. Another point to stress is that data collection and analysis should be an interwoven process with analysis, prompting the sampling of new data. Charmaz (1995) provides advice on the timing of the analysis, also suggesting that the data should be studied as they emerge, making it easier to identify respondents' implicit meanings and taken-for-granted assumptions. Hence, for the novice grounded researcher, it is best to transcribe your own tapes as this gets you into contact with the data at an early stage.

Before we begin to look at these coding categories in detail, a word of warning. As Dey (1999) discusses, not all advocates of grounded theory agree with Strauss and Corbin's approach. Glaser (1992), for example, accuses their later work of abandoning their earlier, influential ideas, suggesting that it has evolved into a quite different methodology (the coding paradigm, dealt with next). For Glaser, this smacks too much of rules and structure being imposed upon the data. However, despite these criticisms, the Strauss and Corbin approach is widely used and recognized as a valuable methodology. Given that the methodological advice coming from the grounded theory literature can be 'bewilderingly complex' (Partington, 2002: 138), an attempt is made here to supplement procedural descriptions with illustrative graphics. It must be stressed that this is just one interpretation of how grounded theory can be applied in practice.

Open coding

LOOKING AT
OPEN CODING

Open coding is defined as 'the naming and categorizing of phenomena through close examination of the data' (Strauss and Corbin, 1998: 62). Two analytical procedures are involved in the open coding process: the making of comparisons and the asking of questions, both of which help towards the labelling of phenomena in terms of concepts or categories (see Table 23.1). According to Strauss (1987), there are four essential guidelines to follow in the data analysis process:

- Ask the data a specific and consistent set of questions, keeping in mind the original objectives of the research study. The intention here is to uncover whether the data fit with these objectives. There may be occasions when new or unanticipated results emerge from the data, an outcome that is entirely valid.
- Analyse the data minutely, but also include as many categories, examples and incidents as possible.
- Frequently interrupt the coding to write a theoretical account. As the data are being coded, ideas or theoretical perspectives may arise. It is essential that these are noted immediately otherwise they may well be forgotten.
- Do not assume the analytical relevance of any traditional variable such as age, gender, social class, etc. until its relevance emerges from the data. This is particularly so if the impact of an expected variable does not emerge – this result must be accepted.

Open coding works through a process of making constant comparisons. Each time an instance of a category is found, it is compared with previous instances. If the new instance does not fit the original definition, then either the definition must be modified, or a new category created. Case Study 23.1 provides a practical example of how the process of asking questions and making comparisons can lead to the generation of concepts and categories.

Table 23.1   Open coding: definition of terms

Term	Definition
Concept	Conceptual labels placed on discrete happenings, events and other instances of phenomena
Category	A classification of concepts
Coding	The process of analysing data
Code notes	The products of coding
Open coding	The process of breaking down, examining, comparing, conceptualizing and categorizing data
Properties	Attributes or characteristics pertaining to a category
Dimensions	Location of properties along a continuum
Dimensionalization	The process of breaking a property down into its dimensions

Source: Adapted from Strauss and Corbin, 1998

CASE STUDY 23.1

Developing grounded theory – open coding

A researcher is asked to observe customer behaviour in a large department store. She positions herself in an unobtrusive way, where she can see customers entering and leaving the store, walking down the aisles, looking at merchandise and buying goods, etc. Although the store is very busy and the activity at first appears chaotic, some tentative patterns begin to emerge which she begins to label. Some customers, for example, seem content with examining goods (picking them up, looking at them, putting them down) but then just moving on. She asks herself: why are they doing this? This behaviour she labels *exploring*. Other customers approach counter staff or supervisors walking around and ask them questions. This she labels *questioning*. Still other customers approach the busy tills and seem content to stand in line to be served. The label attached to this is simply *queuing*.

UNDERSTANDING CUSTOMER BEHAVIOUR

Once at the till, they are, of course, *buying*. It is clear, however, that a minority of customers queue for a short time and grow impatient. They can be observed to put the merchandise down on a counter or shelf before leaving the store. This behaviour is labelled as *deserting*. One customer, however, is seen to be arguing with a supervisor. This behaviour is called *remonstrating*.

Later she notices that some customers not only pick up and look at goods they even rub them between their fingers and in some cases smell them! Hence under the category of exploring, she is able to identify three sub-categories: looking, feeling and smelling.

After the observation session our researcher begins the process of *categorizing* the data. In doing this, she is careful to choose categories that are more abstract in nature than the concepts they describe. Hence, she groups exploring and questioning to form the category *information seeking* while queuing and buying are grouped together as *intentional purchasing*.

Conduct a detailed observation of an event or phenomenon within a field setting. Analyse your data using open coding, providing your own set of descriptive labels.

Note that the labels given in Case Study 23.1 are original and specific to the researcher. This is important because if she had taken already existing and 'borrowed' categories, these can come with pre-existing meanings that can bias the research. Once categories are produced they still have to be developed so that they can be used in further data collection and analysis. Categories are developed in two ways: by their *properties* and by their *dimensions*. Using Case Study 23.1, we could take the category 'information seeking' and examine it for its properties and dimensions. Table 23.2 illustrates the results, showing that properties are the characteristics or attributes of a category. Dimensions represent the location of a property along a continuum. The development of properties and dimensions is crucially important because they are central in making relationships between categories and sub-categories and later between major categories. They thus provide the basis of the analytical processes of grounded theory.

Axial coding

LOOKING AT
AXIAL CODING

As we saw in the previous section, open coding disaggregates data so that categories can be located. **Axial coding** then takes these categories and tries to make connections between categories and sub-categories. Essentially, this means specifying:

- A *category* (phenomenon) in terms of the conditions that helped to give rise to it.
- The *context* in which it arises.
- The *actions* and *interactions* that stem from it.
- Its consequences.

We are also interested in what caused the phenomenon. Figure 23.4 provides a highly simplified illustration of the relationships between a phenomenon and its causes, context, actions and consequences. Note that Strauss and Corbin (1998), referring to the work of Dewey, caution that an initial condition rarely leads to an action/interaction and then a consequence in a direct manner.

> Rather, action/interaction may be taken in response to multiple conditions, some of which occurred in the past, some of which are happening in the present, and/or some of which are anticipated in the future. (Strauss and Corbin, 1998: 184)

Hence, in Figure 23.4, causal conditions may occur in a variety of different temporal states.

To illustrate the process of linking sub-categories to categories, let us take the example of our retail store in the previous case study. We have seen a customer remonstrating (phenomenon) with a supervisor. We observe that the reason (causal condition) for this is the fact that the queues for the tills were very long and that she could not get served. But the description of this phenomenon, 'remonstration', does

Table 23.2   The properties and dimensions of the category 'information seeking'

Category	Property	Dimensional	Range
Information-seeking	Questioning	Often	Never
	Looking	Up close	From a distance
	Smelling	Repeatedly	Once
	Feeling	Vigorously	Gently

Source: Adapted from Strauss and Corbin, 1998

CONTEXT

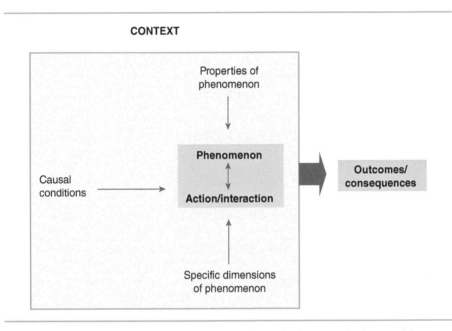

Figure 23.4   Making connections between categories and sub-categories by examining a phenomenon in terms of its properties, dimensions and causal conditions

little to fully describe the event. We need more detail. So we are also interested in the specific dimensions of the phenomenon, and discover that this was an angry remonstration (in terms of volume/language) that lasted 10 minutes (time) in the middle of the store (location). But we also need to know something about the properties of the causal condition (the queuing) and discover that the customer queued for eight minutes at a till that was shut seconds before she was about to be served. Next, we take a look at the context in which the phenomenon occurred, examining issues such as when, how and the type of cause. We discover that some tills are not operational due to staff shortages and that the till closure happened suddenly because the member of staff was due her lunchbreak.

Yet, there are also *intervening conditions*, or what could be called a 'broader structural context' (Strauss and Corbin, 1998: 103), which act either to constrain or facilitate the actions being taken (see Figure 23.5). For example, again using our illustration, we find that during the angry remonstration, the store manager happens

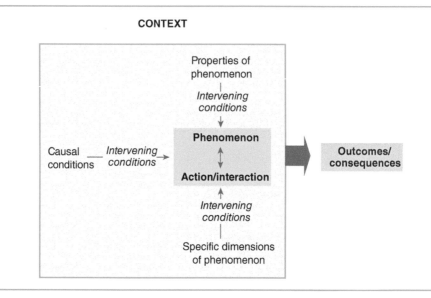

Figure 23.5 Making connections between categories and sub-categories: the impact of intervening conditions

to be passing and intervenes to help. She uses her cellphone to call for more staff and opens a till herself and serves the irate customer. But in general terms, intervening conditions within a context can include a wide range of conditions, including the influence of culture, time, economic status, hierarchical position in an organization, technological status, individual biography, etc. For example, the remonstration is a long one, not just because of the scale of the inconvenience, but because only the previous week the company that owns the store had announced record profits so the customer may be reasoning 'Why haven't they employed more staff?'

We can see from the above analysis that grounded theory is an action/interaction method of theory building which is concerned with the ways in which people manage and respond to phenomena, existing within a specific context or conditions. Recalling the discussion of symbolic interactionism in Chapter 2, people assign meaning to phenomena and then act upon these interpretations, these actions bringing forth fresh interpretations and actions amongst participants. But this action and interaction also has *consequences* that may be predictable or unanticipated. Indeed, the failure to take action also has its consequences. Yet, while axial coding can help us to identify relationships between categories, we still need to see how these categories or classes can be integrated to build theories. This is achieved through selective coding.

Selective coding

LOOKING AT SELECTIVE CODING

This is the process of selecting **core categories** from the data in order to form the grounded theory. In terms of processes, this is not too different to axial coding, the main difference being that it is completed at a much higher level of abstraction. Through axial coding you will have derived a set of phenomena or categories that

Table 23.3   Selective coding: definition of terms

Term	Definition
Story	A descriptive narrative about the central phenomenon of the study
Story line	The conceptualization of the story around the core category
Selective coding	The process of selecting the core category, systematically relating it to other categories, and validating these relationships
Core category	The central phenomenon around which all the other categories are integrated

Source: Adapted from Strauss and Corbin, 1998

have been defined in terms of their properties, dimensions, etc. Through selective coding, core categories are sought through which a 'story' can be told. The selective coding process involves a number of stages that illuminate the social processes going on unconsciously among a group of people comprising:

UNDERSTANDING
SELECTIVE
CODING

- Finding a story line formulated around core categories.
- Relating sub-categories to the core categories.
- Validating these relationships against the data.
- Filling in categories that need further refinement.

Table 23.3 provides a brief summary of some of these terms, after which we will discuss them in more detail.

One of the key features of grounded theory is *theoretical sampling*, which helps to make the emerging theory more generalizable. This is achieved by seeking to minimize and maximize the selected differences and similarities between core categories and the relationships between them across cases. Hence, finding strong similarities across cases (and minimum differences) helps to build confidence in the validity of the emerging theory. Attempting to find cases that contradict the theory may help to locate unexpected data and perhaps the emergence of new perspectives.

Identifying the story

The best way to start is to describe in a few short sentences the essence of the story to produce a general, descriptive overview. What are the most salient features? What are the main problems being scrutinized? It might be useful to return to the axial coding stage and find an abstract category that in some way summarizes the story. If such a category does not exist, then one will have to be formulated that encapsulates the categories in the study. If more than one category exists, it is necessary to make a choice between them so that only one core category is used. Taking our example of the observation in the retail store, the main story here could be construed as intentional shopping behaviour. Whether customers are asking questions, examining goods, leaving the store impatiently or patiently queuing, they behave, or attempt to behave, intentionally – that is, with a specific aim.

Relating sub-categories to the core categories

This involves relating subsidiary categories around the core category by means of the paradigm so that they fit and provide an analytical version of the story. This may mean writing or re-writing the story and rearranging categories until they achieve a better fit with the story. Within these conceptual categories there will be relationships and networks of patterns. Strauss and Corbin (1994) stress how important it is to identify these patterns because it is these that give the theory specificity. Hence, it becomes possible to say that under one set of conditions *this* happens, whereas under another set of conditions *that* happens. Case Study 23.2 takes our retailing research a little further.

CASE STUDY 23.2

Developing grounded theory – selective coding

THE SCIENCE OF
SHOPPING

Although the store is crowded and presents the appearance of chaos, in fact, thanks to the highly intentional behaviour of most customers, there are distinctive patterns of behaviour that become predictable. People do not simply rush into the store, grab the first item they see and then run out with it! They look around (touring) the isles, sometimes leaving this department, but returning later. Our researcher notices that those who examine merchandise closely tend to be with someone else rather than being alone – hence, exploratory behaviour is usually collaborative. Opinions are being shared (the 'second opinion'). People queue, because the alternative, pushing and shoving one's way to the counter, will lead to even more stress. Queuing is a time-consuming activity that is undertaken to save time. Customers who approach store staff for information are also attempting to save themselves time by gaining quicker access to information.

ACTIVITY 23.3

Returning to your data in Activity 23.2, take your open coding categories through the axial coding process, making connections between categories. Then, using selective coding, identify core categories and formulate a story line.

Validating these relationships against the data

Having found a story and related various categories to it, the relationships uncovered can be validated (grounding the theory) by returning to the data and asking whether the story fits for all those observed in the study. We may find, for example, that a minority of customers do not appear to behave intentionally at all. We noted in Case Study 23.1 that some customers spent some time queuing before losing patience and leaving the store. If their intention was to buy goods, they failed. Yet their behaviour may perhaps still be construed as intentional because leaving the store in this way has saved them time from not queuing. They valued their time more highly than the satisfaction to be gained from the purchased commodities. However, for instances that cannot be analysed as intentional, we need to fill in more detail. The researcher needs to trace back to the data to uncover the conditions that might be causing this variation.

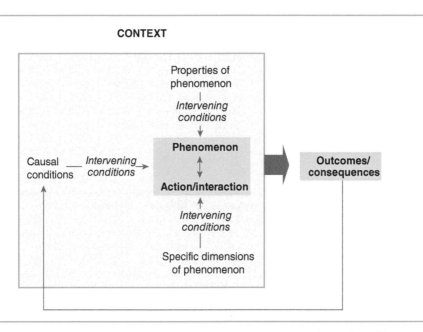

CONTEXT

Figure 23.6   The impact of outcomes and consequences on the original causal conditions

Filling in categories that need further refinement

This is necessary to give 'conceptual density' to the theory as well as developing more conceptual specificity. This filling in phase may continue even up to the process of writing up the project, since report writing itself may reveal gaps and inconsistencies that require attention. If this occurs, the researcher may have to return to the field to collect more data (for example, by interviewing some of the shoppers). This illustrates that the task of data collection and analysis is not necessarily sequential but can be an iterative process.

The grounded theory approach just described should be a dynamic one when *process* is built into the analysis. Process means showing the evolving nature of events by noting why and how action/interaction (in the form of events, doings or happenings) will change, stay the same or regress (Strauss and Corbin, 1998). In other words, it is a case of not only noticing changes in phenomena but also of explaining why they occur. As Strauss and Corbin (1998) concede, however, explanations may not always be obvious, even after additional data have been collected. They suggest, therefore, that a more deductive approach is adopted, in terms of a hypothesis, after which the researcher should return to the data to see if this hypothesis can be supported, modified or rejected.

But how and where do changes occur? There are three potential sources:

- Changes can occur in the causal conditions that led to the phenomenon.
- There may be a change in the intervening conditions.
- The outcomes or consequences of the action/interaction may in turn feed back into new causal conditions (see Figure 23.6).

Maintaining theoretical sensitivity

Strauss and Corbin (1998) argue that theoretical sensitivity, keeping an awareness of the subtleties of meaning in data, is an important element of grounded theory. Accordingly, they argue that theoretical sensitivity implies:

> the ability to give meaning to data, the capacity to understand, and capability to separate the pertinent from that which isn't. (Strauss and Corbin, 1998: 42)

Glaser (1992) links this sensitivity more overtly with theory building, arguing that it is the ability to generate concepts from the data and to relate them, according to normal models of theory. This sensitivity stems from a number of sources.

- The literature, which helps highlight issues and what might be important and unimportant.
- The professional experience of the researcher, showing what is important in the field of research chosen, and how things work, allowing events to be more clearly understood and interpreted.
- Personal experience, including experience in research, which can facilitate the making of comparisons.
- The analytical process itself, which can provide insights into the meaning of the data.

Theoretical sensitivity is a way of ensuring that the creativity involved in qualitative research is harnessed in such a way that the interests of science are not impeded. The process of scientific inquiry is further facilitated if the researcher is willing to 'step back from the data' and ask basic questions such as: do the data really fit the hypothesis? This is part of the process of maintaining a healthy scepticism and realizing that all elements of a study – hypotheses, concepts, questions, theories, etc. – are provisional. Strauss and Corbin (1998) advise that a sound approach is to alternate between collecting and analysing data. Through this approach, analysis can allow for further questions to emerge, for sample selection and data collection, and the verification of hypotheses as they are being developed.

Concluding grounded research

As we have seen, grounded theory research can involve a fairly continuous iteration between data collection and analysis and between the different levels of coding. So, when is the research completed? When is it time to stop? Glaser and Strauss (1967) suggest that this is when the level of 'theoretical saturation' is reached. By this they mean the non-emergence of new properties, classes, categories or relationships from the data. Knowing when this point is reached, of course, is a matter of experience and judgement. This decision is helped if the research has moved towards the clear identification of core categories (around which the main story line is woven) and peripheral categories of less central significance. Hence, once the analysis has been integrated around the core categories and an adequate theory has emerged, the research could be said to be complete. Note that Bryman (2007a) cautions that grounded theory may be effective in the generation of concepts, but he questions whether it actually produces theory itself.

Before finishing this section, it might be useful to look at grounded theory in relation to other research approaches. Locke (2001), for example, suggests that grounded theory has much in common with:

- Ethnography, in that data collection and theory building are woven together as the researcher progresses (although grounded theorists are less interested in the cultural aspects of contexts).
- Case studies, in that grounded theory may be incorporated into a case study as a means of handling and interpreting data.
- Action research (see Chapter 13), in that both seek to develop theoretical elements that are useful to practitioners within the research setting (although grounded theorists are less concerned with organizational transformation).

OTHER APPROACHES TO QUALITATIVE ANALYSIS

In a sense, having discussed two of the main analytical approaches, content analysis and grounded theory, we are left with the category of 'other' in which there are a considerable number of competing approaches. Three of the most significant, the use of narratives, conversational analysis and discourse analysis, are discussed, briefly, here.

Narrative analysis

One of the criticisms of content analysis, and particularly of grounded theory approaches, is that they lead to the fragmentation and decontextualization of data away from the social processes they are meant to represent. However, research that encourages the use of oral or life histories, or uses unstructured interviews, often elicits qualitative data in the form of narratives or stories that lead to more holistic data right from the start. Using narratives is an ideal way of capturing the lived experiences of participants and has been used extensively in settings such as research into medical illness, the study of traumatic events, in education, and studies in the life of organizations. Musson (1998), for example, shows how people's narratives can be used to explain the contradictions, confusions and complexities of working within a modern organization, and how this can illuminate how both individuals and their organizations function. The analysis of narrative data is also sensitive to the temporal sequence that people inject into the accounts of their lives or events that surround them (Bryman and Bell, 2007).

UNDER-
STANDING
NARRATIVE
ANALYSIS

While different approaches to the analysis of narratives have been put forward, all have a number of common characteristics. First, the text is viewed in the gestalt, that is, within the context and social situation in which it is created. Next comes the formal analysis of the text, including making distinctions between text that constitute narrative passages, and other forms of text. Where researchers generally differ is in their attitude to the status of the text itself. While some take the 'truth' of the narrative at face value, others see narratives as a special way of constructing events, that is, they are 'social constructions located within power structures and social milieux' (Punch, 2005: 223). In the context of research within organizational settings, narratives bring forth a variety of perspectives and viewpoints, some of which may contradict and contest each other. From a postmodern perspective, the analysis and interpretation of these narratives itself constitutes a narrative, which may be more or less compelling than other interpretations.

Conversational analysis

Conversational analysis is interested in the formal analysis of everyday conversations (Flick, 2009). Primarily, this includes the analysis of natural texts (often the results of transcribed tape recordings) and seeks to specify the formal principles and mechanisms with which participants express themselves in social interactions, or what Hutchby and Wooffitt (1998) term talk-in-interaction. Research in conversational analysis was originally limited to the study of everyday conversations such as telephone calls or family conversations, but has been extended to institutional-based conversations such as courtrooms, meetings and various kinds of interviews.

Conversational analysis is less concerned with the formal analysis of language *per se*, than with elements of social interaction such as 'turn taking' or 'opening up closings', interruptions and the distribution of speaking rights, often in relation to various aspects of an institution's functions (Have, 1999). Hence, conversational analysis is very much focused on the issue of context. Meaning or order in conversation can only be understood within the context of local practices and are embedded within concrete contexts. Through turn by turn analysis and the description of conversations, the researcher is able to sense how social order among participants is accomplished (Samra-Fredericks, 2004).

Discourse analysis

DISCOURSE
ANALYSIS

The focus of discourse analysis is on how both spoken and written language is used in social contexts. Attention is given to the structure and organization of language with an emphasis on how participants' versions of events are constructed. In contrast to content analysis, discourse analysis rejects the view that language is a transparent medium which merely reflects 'reality'. Analysis becomes focused on recognizing the regularities in language in terms of patterns and repertoires. These repertoires (constructs) do not emanate from the individual as such, but are embedded in culturally and socially constructed situations.

QUALITY IN QUALITATIVE ANALYSIS

QUALITY OF
RESEARCH

In Chapter 7 we explored how rigour can be enhanced at the design stage. Here we examine how quality can be improved at the data analysis and data presentation stages, looking once more at the themes of validity and reliability.

Validity

VALIDITY
THEORY

Validity refers to whether a researcher is observing, identifying or measuring what they claim they are (Mason, 2002). External validity refers to the degree to which findings can be generalized to other social or organizational settings. As was noted in Chapter 7, this is difficult to achieve in qualitative research due, in large part, to

Table 23.4   Techniques for demonstrating validity at the analysis and presentation stages

Type of technique	Technique
Analytic	Member checking for accuracy and interpretation
	Expert checking for interpretation
	Exploring rival explanations
	Writing memos (often done during coding process)
	Testing hypotheses in data analysis
	Analysing negative cases that contradict the analysis
	Performing a literature review to compare findings with those of previous studies
Presentation	Providing an audit trail between the analysis and the data so that others can check the connection between the two
	Providing evidence that supports interpretations
	Acknowledging the researcher perspective
	Providing thick descriptions

Source: Adapted from Whittemore et al. (2001)

the tendency to use case studies and small samples. Internal validity refers to whether there is compelling evidence that the researcher has achieved a strong link between their evidence and the theoretical ideas they develop from it. Table 23.4 summarizes a range of techniques through which the researchers can seek to enhance the internal validity of their results.

Member checking can involve getting respondents to review transcripts of their interviews both for accuracy and to see if there are any comments they would like to add. This can even include getting participants to comment on coding schemes. Expert checking, as the name implies, involves obtaining the collaboration of research or other experts in validating and approving the analysis. Does the expert, for example, using the same data, come to the same or similar conclusions? Are there rival explanations that have been overlooked? Writing memos both for themselves and for others to review, helps in the generation and checking of concepts and categories. As we saw earlier in this chapter, analytic induction makes use of hypotheses as part of the process. Deciding whether the weight of evidence supports or requires us to reject a hypothesis is a useful way of determining whether claims made for the data analysis are valid or not. Analysing negative or deviant cases can be important here, as they may require the hypothesis to be reformulated and more evidence collected, or the hypothesis to be reformulated so as to exclude the deviant case (as in analytical induction, above). Finally, performing a literature review allows for the findings of the research study to be compared and contrasted with what previous studies or experts have found.

Validity can be catered for at the data presentation stage through providing an audit trail from the analysis back to the concepts, constructs or data sets from which they were generated. In this way, other researchers can confirm that the analysis is based upon appropriate evidence. If, before this is done, the original researchers make explicit their own philosophical perspectives and intentions, then the task of validators is made much easier. The same goes for 'thick descriptions' through which we not only describe a phenomenon but the context in which it occurs. Providing context encourages more confidence that the interpretations that have been made are valid. For example, say you were researching public fear of crime. If your research highlighted periodic 'spikes' of concern amongst older residents in an area, you would want to provide both local context (reported burglaries) and national context (national press coverage of worries about crime rates) as possible mutually reinforcing environments.

ACTIVITY 23.4

Examine the list in Table 23.4. Which of these techniques would you find useful to implement to aid the validity of your own qualitative research?

Reliability

RELIABILITY
THEORY

External reliability is the extent to which the findings of a study can be replicated, frequently a challenge in qualitative research which often deals with unique social settings or cases. It is both for epistemological as well as practical reasons that some adherents of qualitative research regard external reliability as either unattainable, unnecessary, or both. Internal reliability is improved by the use of more than one observer in the field, or at the analysis stage when multiple researchers are used in the interpretation of the findings. This often starts with researchers sharing and comparing coding schemes to determine the extent of agreement and consistency. The use of computer-assisted programs for qualitative data analysis (see the following section) often help here. Also recall the discussion in Chapter 7 where some researchers reject this approach to rigour, arguing for criteria such as transferability, dependability, confirmability and credibility.

One element of qualitative analysis, conversational analysis, brings with it some different reliability issues. Since conversational analysis is often based on tapes and transcripts of conversations, in terms of reliability, it is fairly obvious that taped conversations will tend to present more reliable evidence than hastily written field notes. But as Peräkylä (2004) warns, video- or audio-recording of events may lose some important aspects of social interaction. These reliability problems include:

- Time: A single recording of events taking place in an organization may be either unenlightening or completely misleading if those events do not represent what typically happens most of the time. Hence, reliability will be improved with a more longitudinal research design, with multiple visits and recordings.
- 'Ambulatory events': That is, the movements of people that simply do not show up on video or audio recordings. One solution is the setting up of multiple cameras to catch these movements.
- Documentary realities: Some conversations (for example, professional people such as doctors or lawyers talking to their clients) may be influenced by the documents (such as forms) they are discussing. Researchers must have access to these documents and include them in the analysis process.

SOFTWARE FOR QUALITATIVE DATA ANALYSIS

Before the arrival of computer-assisted qualitative analysis programs, researchers had to perform a quite laborious process of writing marginal codes on field notes or transcripts, making photocopies of these documents and physically cutting chunks of text associated with a particular code and pasting them together. Over the last 20 years, or so, computer-assisted qualitative data analysis software (CAQDAS) has made this redundant. Typically, CAQDAS software allows the researcher to:

- Import transcripts or other computer-generated documents directly into the program.
- Work through the data, marking words, phrases or sections of text with codes.
- For each code, collect together all the chunks of text associated with that code.

It is important to note what CAQDAS programs do not do. They do not generate codes for you – this, obviously, is the task of the researcher. The researcher still also has to interpret the data. But CAQDAS software does cut out much of the drudgery of manipulating qualitative data. Yet in doing this, there can be drawbacks. Richards, for example, warns of the danger of 'coding fetishism' (2002: 269). Since computers can code so easily, the novice researcher can easily get 'hooked' on coding so that it becomes an end in itself. Coding, then, comes to drive out the need for interpretation. What is essential is that researchers move beyond the 'search-and-retrieve' functionality of CAQDAS programs. Certainly, such programs are very effective at doing this and it is an important function. But, as Richards (2002) points out, CAQDAS also provides you with the opportunity to retrieve all the data on a coded theme, to browse the data, and, if necessary, to recode it, or explore it against new dimensions. Hence, coding becomes an iterative, creative process, not something that is just done once and halted. The following case study provides an illustration of how one CAQDAS market leader, NVivo, was used in the analysis of qualitative data. Note that the intention here is not to provide you with a tutorial on how to use NVivo itself (there are many of these available on the Web) but to demonstrate the process of using a CAQDAS program in analysing raw data.

CHOOSING
A CAQDAS
PACKAGE

INTRODUCING
NVIVO

──── CASE STUDY 23.3 ────

Coding with NVivo

A study was undertaken which explored the kinds of criteria business leaders apply when choosing the people they employ as executive coaches. A literature review had identified the possibility that male and female executives might employ different criteria when making this choice. Thirty interviews were conducted, the tapes transcribed and the Word files imported into NVivo.

The first stage in the analysis process was the construction of *nodes*. A node in NVivo is used to represent a code, theme or idea about the data. Nodes can be selected in advance (for example on the basis of theoretical concepts arising from a literature search) or can arise when exploring the data itself (in vivo) or both. For this project, the nodes created from previous reading comprised a number of attributes that other research studies had revealed as potentially important: qualifications, experience, career development and coaching skills. These main codes are often referred to as parent nodes. Under coaching skills there were a number of sub-themes (child nodes) such as empathy, ability to set objectives and career development skills. However, on reading the text, several respondents (both men and women) mentioned that they had deliberately chosen female coaches. Hence, gender was added as a parent node.

An interactive and iterative process then took place, applying existing nodes to the data and creating new nodes from the data. For example, several respondents mentioned either a strong like or strong dislike for coaches who were experts in Neuro-linguistic programming techniques – NLP was therefore added as a node. Further exploration of the data then led to some nodes being modified or even eliminated. For example, the node 'career development' which came from the mentoring literature was not mentioned by these beneficiaries of coaching and was abandoned. As each node was created, a memo was written which described and explained the node and added some preliminary thoughts or ideas about the node and relationships within the data. These memos became part of the data analysis. A series of attributes (variables) were then added to each case node, including the gender of each respondent, their age and the industry sector they worked in.

The next stage in the process involved querying the data. Since it was suspected that male and female managers may have different attitudes towards the selection of coaches, a coding query was run on the attribute 'male' and then on 'female'. A more sophisticated query was then used which added a second attribute, age, making it possible to explore the data for the views of young and older women and then young and older men. Queries were then run on attitudes towards coaches with expertise in NLP. Two nodes had previously been created, 'Likes NLP' and 'Dislikes NLP'. The results of each query were then saved as nodes. Following this creative process of creating nodes and running (and saving) queries on the data, allowed for the testing out of ideas about the potential relationship between variables and for the development of at least provisional theories.

ACTIVITY 23.5

Explore some of the tutorials on NVivo at the following websites:

- http://www.qsrinternational.com/products_nvivo.aspx
- http://www.youtube.com/watch?v=K3wdeZUZGVY

Note that NVivo has progressed way beyond a program that just deals with text. You can now import websites as pdf documents and analyse the site text or add comments to website photographs. There is now also a facility for importing and analysing Twitter posts (see Figure 23.7).

TOP TIP 23.3

Should you use a CAQDAS program or not? The answer probably rests on the amount of qualitative data you are trying to analyse. All software programs come with a built-in overhead – the amount of time and effort you need to learn them to a sufficient level of proficiency. If, say, you have conducted 10 one-hour interviews, generating about 60 pages of transcripts, you could probably conduct a manual analysis, using the approach discussed in 'Elements of qualitative data analysis', above. If, however, you feel that the amount of data generated is substantial and fairly overwhelming, then by all means make use of NVivo or a similar program. Learning a CAQDAS program will also give you a useful research skill for the future.

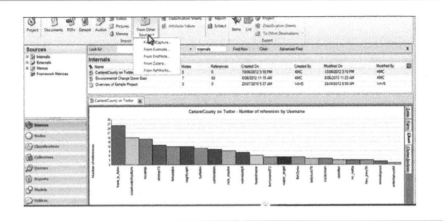

Figure 23.7   Twitter posts imported into NVivo 10

Source: QSR International website

━━━▶ **ON THE WEB 23.1** ◀━━━

Evaluate the wide range of software packages for qualitative analysis at the following websites:

http://caqdas.soc.surrey.ac.uk/index.htm

http://www.scolari.co.uk/

— Summary —

- Qualitative data can have a quality of 'undeniability' because they are rooted in the natural context of field settings.
- The main focus of qualitative analysis is to understand the ways in which people act and the accounts that people give for these actions.
- Approaches to qualitative data analysis include content analysis and grounded theory. Content analysis involves locating classes or categories within the data. These categories are usually derived from theoretical models. In contrast, grounded theory uses a process of open, axial and selective coding to develop categories and theories inductively from the data.
- Due to the lack of non-probability sampling methods, qualitative analysis is open to accusations of invalidity. However, claims for the validity of results can be strengthened, for example, by eliciting the views of research participants.
- The reliability of qualitative research can be strengthened by using multiple cases, or by supporting assertions using numerous examples, or by verifying the analysis using other researchers. Concepts such as credibility, authenticity, honesty and openness are also important in qualitative research.
- CAQDAS programs provide useful functionality for qualitative data coding and analysis. But before embarking on the process of learning a program, make sure that the quantity of data requiring analysis justifies the expenditure of time.

1. Strauss and Corbin (1998) point out that some qualitative researchers believe that data should 'speak for themselves', untainted by the analysis of the researcher. To what extent do you agree with this view?
2. The role of theory in qualitative research is emergent. Discuss.
3. To what extent is the reflexive voice of the researcher essential in qualitative accounts?
4. Some qualitative researchers consider that external reliability is either unattainable, unnecessary or both. Do you agree with this stance?

Bernard, H.R. and Ryan, G.W. (2010) *Analyzing Qualitative Data: A Systemic Approach*. Thousand Oaks, CA: Sage. Deals with the basics of coding and finding themes through to various approaches to data analysis such as narrative analysis, discourse analysis, grounded theory and content analysis.

Bazeley, P. and Jackson, K. (2013) *Qualitative Data Analysis with NVivo*, 2nd edn. London: Sage. Provides a step-by-step guide to using NVivo, plus a set of data files that the tutorials show you how to manipulate and analyse.

Flick, U. (2014) *An Introduction to Qualitative Research*, 5th edn. London: Sage. Deals with all the major theories and methods of qualitative research design, including some less well known approaches such as the use of personal narratives.

Symon, G. and Cassell, C. (2004) (eds) *Qualitative Methods and Analysis in Organizational Research*, 2nd edn. London: Sage. Presents a refreshing array of qualitative techniques that are dealt with only sparingly by many of the standard texts. Subjects include: life histories, critical incident techniques, qualitative research diaries and pictorial representation.

Etherington, K. (2004) *Becoming a Reflexive Researcher*. London: Jessica Kingsley. A book in which the author uses a range of personal narratives to show how reflexive research works in practice.

Locke, K. (2001) *Grounded Theory in Management Research*. London: Sage. Provides a detailed summary of the evolution of grounded theory, and illustrates how it can be applied in a management and organizational context.

Fielding, N. and Lee, R.M. (1998) *Computer Analysis and Qualitative Research*. London: Sage. A valuable introduction to some of the principles of using computers in qualitative research as well as a practical guide to managing data and coding categories.

Miles, M.B. and Huberman, A.M. (1994) *Qualitative Data Analysis*, 2nd edn. Thousand Oaks, CA: Sage. Still an outstanding source of many and varied qualitative analysis methods.

Atherton, A. and Elsmore, P. (2007) 'Structuring qualitative enquiry in management and organization research: A dialogue on the merits of using software for qualitative data analysis', *Qualitative Research in Organizations and Management: An International Journal*, 2(1): 62–77. Explores the cases for and against the use of computer-assisted qualitative data analysis software (CAQDAS) in qualitative organization and management research.

Mutch, M. (2006) 'The art and craft of rigorous analysis and authentic (re)presentation', *Qualitative Research Journal*, 6(1): 51–68. Demonstrates the application of semiotic analysis to analysing three transcripts at different levels of depth.

Goulding, C. (2005) 'Grounded theory, ethnography and phenomenology: A comparative analysis of three qualitative strategies for marketing research', *European Journal of Marketing*, 39(3/4): 294–308. Compares and contrasts three approaches to data collection and interpretation and highlights some of the strengths and weaknesses associated with each one.

SUMMARY OF WEB LINKS

http://www.qsrinternational.com/products_nvivo.aspx

http://www.youtube.com/watch?v=K3wdeZUZGVY

http://caqdas.soc.surrey.ac.uk/index.htm

http://www.scolari.co.uk/

24

WRITING UP THE RESEARCH

CHAPTER INTRODUCTION

Chapter outline

The report writing process 633

The report structure 637

Ethical and legal considerations 649

Developing a writing style and tone 652

Undertaking a review process 655

Keywords

Research report

Supervisor

Theses

Dissertations

Academic journals

Plagiarism

Intellectual property rights

Writing style

┌─ Chapter objectives ─┐

After reading this chapter you will be able to:

- Write a report that matches your original or evolving research objectives.
- Plan and resource the report writing process.
- Select from a number of different report formats.
- Present your findings in a written style, format and structure that is accessible to your intended audience.

You have planned your research project, adopted an appropriate research methodology, designed valid and reliable data gathering tools and collected and analysed the data. What could be easier than writing up the research report? Actually, it is not as easy as many would imagine. The most carefully planned and skilfully implemented research study will be doomed if you are incapable of presenting the findings in a manner that is engaging, coherent and accessible for your intended audience. As Murray (1994) warns, reports are too often written in a private language that excludes the very people who may have responsibility for actually implementing or assessing the research. One of the keys, therefore, is to keep it simple.

Timing is also important. Most people assume that reports are written at the end of a research project. This is not necessarily the case. Indeed, the more time you can devote to writing sections or chapters of the report during the research process itself, the better. This is because the process of writing is extremely valuable in clarifying your own thoughts, and in finding where gaps and inconsistencies may be emerging in the research. It is better to discover these problems well before the end of the research project so that they can be rectified.

OBJECTIVE
WRITING

Another concern is that of objectivity. It is likely that you are tackling a research project because you are interested in the subject, or have been asked to do it by a sponsor. Either way, even though at the start of the project you do not see yourself as an expert, it is probable that you have some interest or connection with the topic. The key here, then, is adopting and maintaining an objective 'distance' from the subject and not getting dragged into some sort of polemical argument. Failure to maintain an objective stance will not only cloud and obscure your writing, it may alienate your audience.

Report writing is (or should be) a creative process. Even using the same sets of data, two researchers will not produce reports that are identical. But report writing is also a skill and, like any skill, it must be learned through practice. It must also be based upon sound principles. Presented in this chapter, then, are some basic approaches to producing a research report that will hopefully complement rather than hinder the research effort that has preceded it. Note that the term 'report' is used here to mean actual reports produced in an organizational context, but many of the principles discussed apply equally to academic dissertations, theses and articles written for the academic literature. These are also discussed with reference to their own specific requirements.

THE REPORT WRITING PROCESS

You will recall that in Chapter 3 and, indeed, throughout this book, the importance of writing clear and unambiguous research objectives has been stressed. It would certainly be a pity if, at the final hour, these objectives were ignored and the report aimed at a completely different set of goals! Of course, it is possible that your objectives may have shifted or even radically changed during the research process itself. This is entirely acceptable, as long as you have clearly articulated what these new objectives are going to be. Even in the most heuristic research approach, the researcher sets off with an intended goal – even though this may become modified through the process of inquiry itself.

Planning the report

Some writers prefer to launch themselves immediately into the writing process, but it is usually prudent to start with at least a draft plan for the report, even if the plan may change during the writing itself. The plan can initially be sketched out on paper or typed straight into a word processed document. The plan might contain the main headings and sub-headings of the report, and references to where notes, files or data sets can be found for when the actual writing process starts. The report plan, for example, might comprise the following headings:

TIPS FOR
PLANNING
REPORTS

- Executive summary
- Introduction
- Background and aims
- Research methodology
- Findings
- Analysis and recommendations
- Conclusions
- Appendices

It is nearly always sensible to get this plan evaluated by a reviewer. This person might be your supervisor or tutor if you are undertaking an academic course of study, a peer or co-worker or even the report's organizational sponsor. In seeking this review, make it clear that you want critical feedback. Eliciting the views of managers or sponsors is always useful because it enables you to gain some assurance that the report meets with their interests and needs.

In some cases, the planning of the report may be assisted by terms of reference that describe the purposes of the report, its scope, type and readership. Sometimes these terms of reference may be given to you by whoever is commissioning you to carry out the research. Wainwright (1990) suggests that if you have not been given any terms of reference, you should write your own.

Knowing the purpose of the report

Before starting, as Turk and Kirkman (1989) warn, you must begin with a clear idea of what it is you want to achieve. This is not the same as your subject. By focusing on the aim of your report, you are considering what it is that the readers want to know, so that it is relevant, interesting and usable for them. Failure to think clearly about the needs, interests and motivations of the target audience is one of the most common reasons why reports fail to fulfil their potential. It often helps to think what it is you expect readers to actually do after they have read the report. For example, do you expect them to:

- Request a presentation.
- File the report.
- Pass the report on to another individual or committee.
- Send an email.
- Arrange a meeting.
- Sign a cheque.

— ACTIVITY 24.1 —

Examine each of the following words, and select one or more that describe the purpose of your report: describe, explain, instruct, specify, evaluate and recommend, provoke debate but does not seem to lead, persuade, concede and apologize, protest, reject.

Knowing your audience

ADAPTING TO
YOUR AUDIENCE

You also need to remember that the report may be read by a variety of people, each of whom has a different interest or motivation for reading it. If it is, say, a technical report, those with technical expertise in this field may be interested in issues of how and why. Senior managers in an organization, however, may have less time to read all the technical details, but want to get quickly to the issue of what is the purpose, what is the cost, and where are the resources? Writing for an academic audience will require a style of writing that includes a strong engagement with the academic literature. So you will need to think of how the report can be written in a way that is accessible to a diverse audience, at least some of whom will not want to read it in its entirety. Producing an executive summary at the beginning of the report can help here.

Turk and Kirkman (1989) suggest that, before you start, you ask yourself each of the following questions:

- Are all the readers alike?
- What do they already know about the subject?
- What do they need to know?
- What are their attitudes to the subject, to the writer, and to the writer's objectives?
- What are the psychological and physical contexts within which the report will be received?

Booth (1991) also suggests that the writer needs to decide whether the message to be delivered is going to be made explicit or implicit in the report. She argues that it is often better to make the argument implicit, and to lead the reader towards the appropriate conclusion.

Taking a report that you intend to write, now add a description of your audience using the bullet points above.

Getting started with the report

Even if it may seem logical to start writing with an Introduction, this is probably not the best place – indeed, it could be argued that it is easier to write this at the very end (when the whole 'story' of the project is clear). Most researchers find it easiest to begin with the literature review (if the report requires one). There are a number of reasons for this:

DOING A
LITERATURE
REVIEW

- The review will normally have been conducted at an early stage of the research and so can be attempted well before the final phases.
- The process of writing the literature review helps to articulate the objectives, focus and direction of the research.
- The literature review, of course, can always be updated and improved at a later stage, but writing a first draft early in the research can provide a solid theoretical and directional underpinning to the entire project. Where you start is obviously up to you. The only point to emphasize is that you should get started on the writing process as soon as possible!

Many researchers have difficulty in making the transition between reading books and articles and constructing a literature review. If they find the writing up stage challenging, they may indulge in 'displacement' activities which comprise endless reading but no writing! To avoid this, the best strategy is to:

- Read books, academic articles, conference papers, etc. Make notes and/or summaries.
- From the ideas generated by the literature (using notes/summaries), identify some main themes; type these into a document.
- Organize the themes into a logical structure; add sub-themes if possible.
- As themes are added, note the author/source; build up a number of authors/sources for each theme or sub-theme.
- Read more sources if necessary, make notes and summaries and add the source to existing themes or if necessary start a new theme.
- Once the structure is complete, flesh out each theme into an argument, supporting each argument with reference to the sources identified.

Making and using time

In writing a report, time is one of the most precious, but probably least available, commodities you have at your disposal. It is important, then, to use it wisely and to make as much time available to writing the report as possible. Good project management is the key. At the very start of the research process, you should have allocated a block of time (days, weeks or even months, depending on the scale of the project), for the report writing process. Within this elapsed time schedule, you should also have planned for the writing sessions you need in order to complete the report. If your research and data gathering efforts have overlapped into the report writing phase, then you need to evaluate whether you can complete the report in the planned time, or whether you need to negotiate an extension. What is vital here is that you take some control of decisions, and do not leave requests for extensions until the last minute.

As far as the report writing process is concerned, people tackle this in different ways. According to Saunders et al. (2012), most people can write about 2,000 words in a day, but this will depend on their experience, confidence and the complexity of the subject. Some people prefer to devote large blocks of time to writing and to keep going into the night until exhaustion overwhelms them. Others prefer to allocate discrete blocks, spread across a time period. What is important is that, whatever your preferred style, the time resource you allocate yourself is sufficient to get the job done. Whatever time you have planned for yourself, you obviously want to make the best use of it. In doing this you might want to:

- Find a place to work where distractions are minimized and where you can think clearly.
- Write at a time of day when you are physically and mentally fresh. Take regular breaks.
- Have access to all the resources you are going to need (a computer for word processing, keeping notes, files, data, and for data analysis, etc.).
- Set yourself challenging but realistic goals for each writing session. This might be a word count – in which case, you could keep a record of your production achievements.

Of course, the report writing process is made more complicated if it is a team effort. The general principles, however, are the same. Plan for the writing of the report and allocate roles and responsibilities. Set deadlines and meet or communicate regularly to see if all team members are on track. Since the timing of the report is now dependent on the speed of the slowest member, it is often prudent to have contingency plans in case the process is held up. For example, can another member of the team or additional staff resources be drafted in to write some more sections or to provide assistance?

➤ **TOP TIP 24.1** ◄

In preparing to write the report, consider how you are going to reward yourself as you write it. We all need incentives. For some people, merely keeping a word count of how they are progressing is enough. Others require more tangible incentives such as chocolate, or going out for a meal as key sections or chapters are completed!

Getting down to writing the report

Some people like to leave the report writing phase to a time when they have amassed all their data. This, however, can be a mistake partly because it is leaving the most vital phase right until the end. A better approach is to start the writing from day one. This will give you the satisfaction of achieving some 'output' and, even more importantly, will provide you with practice at writing skills. Writing up chapters or at least sections as you go along will both develop your writing style, and also allow you to elicit feedback from your supervisor.

GRAY ON KEEPING A RESEARCH DIARY

> ➤ **TOP TIP 24.2** ◄
>
> A useful tip is to keep a research diary to note ideas as they crop up, to keep notes of your meetings with your supervisor and to provide a reminder of which sources (books, academic articles) you have ordered and when.

Students often find structuring their report or thesis difficult, often because they find themselves immersed and drowning in detail. A useful approach is to reorganize material by creating mind maps, diagrams that illustrate how concepts and ideas relate to one another (see On the Web 24.1 below). Using mind maps can be particularly useful when trying to understand and describe the interrelationships between a large number of concepts or theoretical models. In dissertations or theses, then, mind maps can be particularly useful when structuring and writing up the literature stage.

> ➤ **ON THE WEB 24.1** ◄
>
> Take a look at the Inspiration software at the website:
>
> http://www.inspiration.com/productinfo/
>
> Download a trial copy and experiment mind mapping your study outline.

Using a supervisor

If you are studying for an academic qualification it is likely that you will have a tutor or supervisor to guide you, especially at the writing-up stage. Supervisors are a vital resource of knowledge, wisdom and experience, but are not always used well by students, partly because we find it hard to accept critical feedback. Yet such feedback is essential if the research output is to reach the necessary standard. When being given feedback, either face-to-face or through written comments, try to resist the temptation to be defensive and start justifying yourself. Any critique your supervisor offers is designed to help you and should be taken as such.

> ➤ **TOP TIP 24.3** ◄
>
> In order to gain the maximum benefit from your supervisor, make sure that you provide him or her with sections or chapters of written material well in advance of any meeting you may have booked. It is no good turning up for a supervision session with a rough draft your supervisor has had no time to read. You will also get more benefit if you provide your supervisor with 'good' rather than very rough drafts, as the feedback will be able to focus on 'polishing' the material, rather than concentrating on basics such as spelling, punctuation and structure.

GRAY ON WORKING WITH YOUR SUPERVISOR

THE REPORT STRUCTURE

The structure of the report will very much depend on what type of report you are producing and for whom. There are, essentially, two kinds of readers: those who commissioned or who are expecting the report, and those who are not expecting the report but who may, none the less, be interested in it. The commissioning group

Table 24.1   Example of heading hierarchy

Typographic style	Font description
HEADING 1	12 point font, capitals and bold
Heading 2	12 point font, lower case, bold
Heading 3	12 point font, lower case, bold italics
Heading 4	12 point, lower case

will want to know if this is the report they were waiting for and whether it contains the information they need. The second group will want to know if the report has any relevance to them, and whether it contains any new information. Therefore, for both groups, you need to give the audience information quickly and in an accessible way. It must compete for their limited time and attention. The kinds of criteria readers might apply in deciding whether they read the report or not might include:

- The title – does this sound relevant or interesting to me?
- Do the contents of the report actually match the title?
- How long is the report – what is my investment of time going to be and is it worthwhile?
- How well presented is the report – how confident am I in the abilities of the writer?

The structure of a report is made clear when some of the principals of typography are applied for heading structures. Many students simply use the same font type and size for all headings, but this can be confusing. Table 24.1 shows how typography (the size and style of fonts) can be used to illustrate to the reader where they are in the structure of the piece. These styles can be set up in Word quite easily by clicking on ⌈Format⌉ and then ⌈Styles and Formatting⌉. Click on the small downward arrow on the style you want to set up and click on ⌈Modify⌉ then ⌈Format⌉.

Writing organizational and technical reports

WRITING
TECHNICAL
REPORTS

A business report is taken to mean any report written for the purposes of general management or organization, whereas a technical report has, obviously, a more specifically technical focus. Of course, organizational research can often involve the need to understand and act upon technical issues. Some business and technical reports may be written for publication in an academic journal, and so will tend to follow the structure discussed later. Technical reports may be written for organizational purposes and be commissioned or sponsored by an individual or committee within the organization. When undertaking reports of this kind, both you and the sponsor need to be clear about:

- The objectives of the report.
- Access to resources needed to complete it.
- Timescales for delivery.
- The extent to which the report is purely descriptive or analytical. If the latter, are recommendations required?
- The importance, or otherwise, of theoretical underpinning. This, of course, is essential for academic journal articles but may be irrelevant for some kinds of technical report.
- The final intended audience for the report (which may not actually be the initial sponsor) and the style, tone and structure that the report should adopt.

In contrast to academic articles, business and technical reports tend to be much more utilitarian and 'to the point'. White (1997) suggests the following typical structure, but this should not be adhered to rigidly – select sections according to your needs.

AN ORGANI-
ZATIONAL
APPROACH

Cover: A well-designed cover can help to attract a reader's attention and give a positive impression about the report before it is even read. White (1997) recommends that a cover should include at least four elements: a descriptive title of the report; the names of the report's principle authors, investigators and editors, if applicable; publication number, if the organization requires a record of this; and the publication date.

Title page: This is the first page of the report and repeats some of the cover content. For example, it contains a descriptive title of the report, the author's name and the organization's name and address. This page can also include the name of the person who commissioned the report.

Abstract/executive summary: This is designed for busy people who do not usually have the time to read a report in its entirety, and may be between 200 and 500 words long. This summary, then, has to be both comprehensive in its coverage but also very succinct. It should present a short description of the project, plus findings and recommendations. Figures, illustrations and tables are not used.

Table of contents: White (1997) recommends that a table of contents should be used for reports that are over 10 pages long. The table of contents shows all main headings and even sub-headings. Since all headings should fully describe each section, the table of contents not only provides a guide to finding sections, it can actually help to describe what a document is about. Most word processing application programmes will generate a table of contents automatically, but only if you have formatted your report by allocating a style (for example, Heading 1, Heading 2, etc.) to your headings.

List of symbols, abbreviations, definitions: If your report contains complex terms, abbreviations or definitions, then it is helpful to provide an explanation at the beginning. Of course, you will still be required to explain each new term or abbreviation in the main body of your text as it occurs. For example, you will write 'Human Resource Management (HRM)' before alluding to HRM in the remainder of the report.

Introductory material: This might include any of the following:

- The nature of the problem being addressed.
- Why the research was undertaken.
- Any limitations on resources, materials or time in undertaking the research.
- The scope of the research (for example, did the study look at the problem from the perspective of individual employees, departments, sites or the entire organization?)
- An outline of previous work on this topic.

Report of work done: This will probably be the longest section and will, obviously, be determined by your subject, which might be:

- A new product or service. Readers may be interested in its potential uses, the risks involved, and its technical, financial and material requirements. They may also be interested in the life cycle of the product or service, its potential competitors and plans for its development.

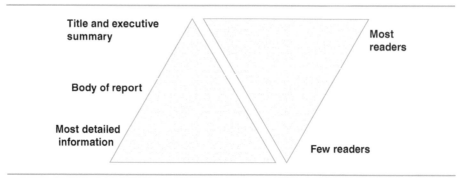

Figure 24.1   Pyramid of evidence model for report design

Source: Adapted from Turk and Kirkman, 1989

- Technical or managerial problems. Readers may be interested in the origins and nature of the problem, whether it is temporary or permanent, options for solving the problem, and which option is selected and why. They may also want to know how and when the recommendations are going to be implemented, and what the outcomes are likely to be.

One of the weaknesses of many reports is that the main findings are buried in the middle or end of the document. Hence, busy managers or supervisors will have to spend time delving for the nub of the argument. But this is not just an issue of time; it is also one of cognition and understanding. By presenting the important findings or arguments first, subsequent information can then be used to supplement and support them. Readers find it easier to process and assimilate detailed information if they are first given a general framework to work with. This is not to argue that there may not be reports where the argument proceeds like a detective story with the 'solution' arriving at the end, but most readers of business reports will be both irritated and confused by this approach and will want you to get to the point! Herbert (1990) offers a helpful suggestion here: imagine that you have been asked to appear on a serious radio programme to explain your report. Think of how you would have to quickly and succinctly explain what you have been investigating, how, why and with what results.

Turk and Kirkman (1989) suggest that reports should be written using a pyramid structure (see Figure 24.1). Since only the first few pages of the report will be read by most readers in an organization, this should contain an accurate summary of the main substance of the report (see *Abstract/executive summary*, above). The most detailed information, including appendices, will be included at the end of the document.

The main aim of the business report should be to put over the information needed, to those that require it, so that something can be done. It is not an exercise in writing down everything you have learned about the subject, no matter how interesting (to you) this may be. It is worth, however, just qualifying this last statement. It might be worthwhile noting problems encountered in undertaking the research, the false starts made and negative findings recorded, so that other researchers may learn from your experience. Managers who delve this far may also note some of the 'side issues' you were not able to pursue, so that further research might be commissioned. But, overall, try to maintain the focus of the report – keep to the point!

Results/findings: This section should not be a 'dumping ground' for all your research data. Most of the data sets will probably be presented in the appendices. The results section should contain summaries of the data that focus on the main findings of the research. For clarity, it helps if data can be presented in the form of tables or graphs. Note that the Results section should concentrate precisely on this and not discuss the findings. The Discussion section comes next.

ANALYSIS &
RESULTS

Discussion and analysis: This section is where you have an opportunity to draw inferences from the results (what do the data mean?), look at relationships between sets of data and also differences. What was unexpected? What were the causes and what are the likely effects. What do the results mean in terms of options for action? It must be stressed that the Discussion is not an opportunity merely to repeat the results, although reference may need to be made to the findings in drawing out the threads of the analysis. Remember, the Results tell you what has happened, the Discussion/Analysis section aims to understand how and why it happened.

Conclusions: Conclusion could be merely a number of remarks that 'round off' the report, or it could mean a 'logical outcome' of the report's arguments. The latter is probably preferable in most cases. A conclusion should not be used to repeat findings or facts – it should contain a series of statements that bring together, in a succinct format, what the study has discovered. Berry (2004) warns that Conclusions should not present new evidence, but should relate back to the original purpose and focus of the report.

Recommendations: These should flow logically from the evidence presented by the report, so that there should be no sudden surprises for the reader. This section should also focus completely on these recommendations and not contain other material such as data or discussion that has already been presented. Recommendations are usually presented in a concise format, so the use of a list is entirely appropriate. White (1997) advises that a recommendations section is only relevant if the author has been commissioned to make such recommendations.

Acknowledgements: Turk and Kirkman (1989) recommend limiting acknowledgements to those outside the organization that have provided you with help, and only if this assistance is beyond what one would normally expect from someone in their position. This section should not be used to flatter those who are acknowledged, but to provide the reader with a sense of where some of the information originated.

References: This will be used for citing all the books, journal articles, reports, websites and internal organizational documents used in the study. Only those sources that are actually referenced in the report should be cited, not all those that you read but did not necessarily use. If you want to refer to documents that you are not referencing but which readers might find useful, then place these in a Bibliography section. You might also want to indicate why these sources might be useful.

Appendix for tables, figures and graphs: Some of these tables and figures will probably appear in the main body of the report. Ensure that they are not gratuitous, that is, they should be there for a purpose. Also make sure that they are referred to and described in the body of the text (and not just dumped to stand on their own), and that they appear as close to this description as possible. The citation 'Table' should appear above the table to which it refers, while the citation 'Figure' should appear below the figure. This is the convention. More detailed data can be summarized in tables, figures and graphs in the appendix.

Other appendices: These should include any research instruments you have used, such as questionnaires, interview or observation schedules, and any accompanying documentation such as letters sent to survey participants. They might also include copies of emails or other communications generated during the process of the research (but remember not to breach confidentiality by revealing the names of research subjects without their permission). Whatever topic is covered in an appendix, it is important that there is a reference to the appendix and its purpose in the main body of the report.

Writing academic theses and dissertations

AN EXAMPLE
DISSERTATION

An academic thesis or dissertation is very different to an organizational or technical report in that it is usually more comprehensive and expansive. It seeks to marshal all the relevant information that relates to the topic or problem, and to support all data and arguments with sources of evidence, so that the way in which a case is built up can be judged (Halpenny, 2003). It also seeks to be original. According to Phillips and Pugh (2000), this could include:

- Carrying out empirical work that has not been done before.
- Using already known material but with a new interpretation.
- Replicating a study that has been done in another country or context.
- Bringing new evidence to bear on an old issue.

How a thesis or dissertation is structured will partly depend on the nature of the research itself, but it is sound advice to sketch out an intended outline at as early a stage as possible. Clearly, this tentative outline may change during the research or writing up process, but it does give the writer a sense of structure and direction (Teitelbaum, 1998). The usual convention for the layout is as follows:

- Title page (which should contain the title, the name of the author and qualifications, a statement of the degree for which the document is being presented, the names of the academic School or Department of the University or college and the date of submission).
- The Abstract (a summary – usually of not more than 300 words – of the content of the thesis).
- Contents page (a listing, giving precise headings for each section and their page numbers).
- Acknowledgements (thanking people and organizations that have assisted in the work).
- The main body of the thesis. This could comprise an Introduction, several chapters dealing with a review of the literature and comprising theoretical issues and arguments (recall Chapter 3), Research Methodology, plus Findings, Analysis and Conclusion and/or Recommendations.
- Appendices (if any).
- References (a complete listing of all works cited).

Table 24.2   Proportion of words in a typical piece of academic dissertation writing

Element	Proportion of words (approx.)	In an undergraduate thesis of 10,000 words		In a postgraduate thesis of 20,000 words	
		Words	Pages	Words	Pages
Introduction	5%	500	2	1,000	4
Literature review	30%	3,000	12	6,000	24
Design and methodology	15%	1,500	6	3,000	12
Findings	15%	1,500	6	3,000	12
Analysis and Discussion	30%	3,000	12	6,000	24
Conclusion	5%	500	2	1,000	4
Total	100%	10,000	40	20,000	80

As indicated above, we begin, naturally, with the title page – but this does not mean that the title is the starting point for writing. As Thomas (2013) comments, academic writing is a creative process and often any draft or provisional title will change by the time the writing is finished. What is important is that the title closely fits with what has been written. Similarly, the Introduction chapter (often just a few pages in length) will usually be written after the completion of the research and will often contain:

- A broad review, putting the work within a wider context.
- A coherent argument for the significance of the problem being considered.
- An outline of the thesis, showing how the problem was approached.

The final chapter may contain:

- A brief restatement of the problem, now seen from the perspective of what has been learned.
- A clear outline of what has been achieved.
- A discussion of the main recommendations for work in the future.

Between these chapters, of course, we have the all-important literature review. So, what is the balance in terms of size between all these chapters? Thomas (2013) offers a useful outline, as presented in Table 24.2.

➤ **TOP TIP 24.4** ◄

A very common mistake is that the literature review part of the dissertation reads like a 'laundry list of previous studies' (Rudestam and Newton, 2007: 46). Hence, every paragraph begins, 'Brown found that...', or 'Fletcher argues...'. Recall Figure 5.1 in Chapter 5 and the advice that you should gradually synthesize and focus your ideas, so that all material is linked to the central direction of the study. By the time the reader reaches the Methodology section, he or she should be saying to themselves: 'Yes, these are the questions I too am asking myself and this is what the study should focus on so that knowledge in the field can move forward.'

GRAY ON COMMON MISTAKES WHEN CONDUCTING A LITERATURE REVIEW

Writing for academic journals

HOW TO GET
PUBLISHED

You may undertake research with the specific intention of submitting the outcome for publication to an academic journal, or you may have written a thesis and want to see an edited version of it published. Berry (2004) warns that editors and publishers loath theses. This is because they are written in a cumbersome academic style where length is relatively unrestricted. For a professional reading public, the material will have to be completely reworked, with a succinct and taut prose.

Selecting the right journal

It is also not enough just to decide that you want to publish an article in a journal. The question is: which journal? All journals require contributors to adhere to a specific format. This is usually stated within the journal itself, and normally gives guidance on the structure of articles, writing style, reference system, length and so on. Obviously, this is the first place to look if your report is being written for publication. But you will also find it useful to go beyond this formal outline and in particular to look at:

- The types of articles that have been recently published. What kinds of subjects are of interest to the readers of this journal? Are the research approaches mainly quantitative, qualitative or a mixture of the two, and what epistemological traditions do they follow?
- The formality, or otherwise, of the academic style. In most journals, you should expect a very formal style to be adopted, using the past tense and the passive voice (for example, 'Fieldwork was undertaken using a structured observation schedule. It was then decided to ...').
- The depth and content of the academic underpinning. Review the reference section of a number of articles. How lengthy is the typical reference section? Is any particular research paradigm favoured?

As Berry (2004) notes, it is usually better to have details of your selected journal's format before writing the article rather than after. The following case study provides an example of what to look out for.

CASE STUDY 24.1

Typical structure for an academic journal article (abridged)

Aims and scope

The *International Journal of Human Resource Management* is the forum for HRM scholars and professionals worldwide. Concerned with the expanding role of strategic human resource management in a fast-changing global environment, the journal focuses on future trends in HRM, drawing on empirical research in the areas of strategic management, international business, organizational, personnel management and industrial relations.

The *International Journal of Human Resource Management* encourages strategically focused articles on a wide range of issues including employee participation, human resource flow, reward systems and high commitment work systems. The journal aims to address major issues arising from:

internationalization of market integration
increased competition

technological change

new concepts of line management

changing corporate climates

Notes for contributors

By submitting a manuscript, the authors agree that the exclusive rights to reproduce and distribute the article have been given to the Publishers, including reprints, photographic reproduction, microfilm, or any other reproduction of a similar nature, and translations. Submissions should be in English, typed in double spacing with wide margins, on one side only of the paper, preferably of A4 size. The title, but not the author's name, should appear on the first page of the manuscript. The publishers encourage submission on disk; however, please ensure that the typescript is exactly the same as the version of the article on disk. Articles should normally be between 7,000 and 8,000 words in length.

MORE JOURNAL
GUIDELINES

Source: Adapted and abridged from the *International Journal of Human Resource Management* (2008)

ACTIVITY 24.3

Locate at least two academic journals that cover issues within the subject field of your report or thesis. Looking at both the 'Notes for Contributors' and the kinds of articles published, are there any significant differences between the journals in terms of:

- Subject areas.
- Emphasis on approaches to research (qualitative/quantitative) and epistemology.
- Theoretical underpinning in the articles.
- Emphasis on original, empirical work as against descriptions of other people's research.

You will note from Case Study 24.1 that the journal editors have made it as transparent as possible as to what they are looking for. Note also that they want empirical research, not a reworking of past articles or reports. They also provide a list of the kinds of articles they are looking for.

You might want to select a journal that focuses on the subject of your report. On the other hand, you might argue that the journal has failed to publish anything on your subject and that your article would make a vital contribution. This may be so, but do check that the subject is one that is covered in the general rubric of subjects of interest. If you are in doubt about whether a journal might publish your work, you can send an abstract to the journal editor asking if the subject would be worthy of consideration.

Article submission and outcomes

These days most article submission is online, using the website Manuscript Central. Figure 24.2 illustrates the part of the Manuscript Central site used by the journal *Management Learning*, but most journals will have a site that looks something like this. If you have not registered for the site you will have to do so, creating your own

USING
SCHOLAR ONE

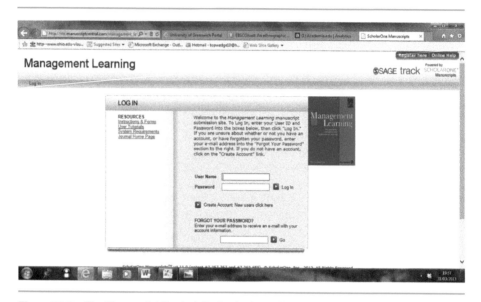

Figure 24.2   The Manuscript Central site for the journal *Management Learning*

login. Once logged in, you will see buttons to take you to either a 'Reviewer Center' (for academics peer reviewing the articles of others), or an 'Author Center'. To submit an article, go to the Author Center, where you will see **Click here to submit a new manuscript**. In doing this you will complete a number of boxes including the title, an abstract summarizing the article and some keywords. You also have an opportunity to submit a covering letter with any comments you want to make to the editor and reviewers (if it is sent out for review). This is not an opportunity to recapitulate the rationale, objectives and research methodology and results of the research. The editor will see these clearly from the actual article. The purpose of your letter is simply to offer the article for consideration and to thank the editor for his or her time. You then upload the file containing your article and submit it.

Once you have submitted an article to an academic journal the Manuscript Central website will send you an automated acknowledgement that the article has been received by the editor. You can then sit back for weeks, and probably months, before you hear whether it is to be published. This is because the article first of all has to be accepted by the editor as worthy of further consideration (many are rejected at this stage without ever being sent out for review), after which it will usually be sent to two or perhaps three peer reviewers. The review process is 'blind', that is, your name will not be divulged to the reviewers, who will work completely independently on their evaluations. The reviewers will recommend one of the following:

1. Publish with no revisions
2. Publish with minor revisions
3. Publish with major revisions
4. Reject

While 1 or 2 are obviously what all writers want to hear, response 3 still should be treated as a success because this means that the reviewers consider the article as interesting and relevant to the journal. It frequently happens that one reviewer likes the article and recommends publication and another rejects it. The editor then has to either make a casting decision, or may send the article out for further review. Not surprisingly all this takes time. You are entitled to make the occasional inquiry as to how the review process is going (just in case the busy editor has forgotten about you!), but it is best not to pester editors too much. They have a difficult and often thankless, unpaid task. If making revisions, help the reviewers by constructing a two column table, with the left hand column listing the reviewers' comments and recommendations and the right hand column listing what you have done and where the changes can be found. If there are recommendations you do not want to make, say so and explain your reasons.

Typical outline for an academic article

It would be wrong to be dogmatic about this, but presented below is a typical structure.

Title page: This includes the title itself, that should neatly summarize the main focus of the article. The title page should also include the name of the author and her/his institution, and acknowledgements (especially if the research has received external funding or assistance). The actual title itself should be short, and should specify exactly what the article is about. If the title is rather long, you could consider using the less significant element of it as a 'strap line'. For example:

> The influence of improved process control systems and resource allocation on widget production through the use of a case study.

This could read:

> Case study: widget production improvement – process control systems and resource allocation.

Abstract: The abstract provides a concise summary of the article (often between 150 and 200 words). The actual length of the abstract will usually be specified by the journal's Notes for Contributors. This is a very important section because it may be the only part of the article that some people read. Herbert (1990) suggests that the abstract should contain:

AN EXAMPLE
ABSTRACT

- The main hypothesis
- A synopsis of the methods used
- A summary of the major findings
- A brief mention of subjects and materials
- The conclusions based on the results
- Design procedures

In addition to the abstract, and perhaps adjacent to it, some journals ask for a list of keywords. In paper-based versions of the journal, these can provide readers with an indication of whether they want to read the article or not. For Web-based abstracting services, typing in one of these keywords will link another researcher to a list of articles containing this keyword, including your article.

Introduction: This explains the purpose of the study, the rationale for undertaking it and some background information. The Introduction also provides an opportunity to outline the main research questions and hypotheses (if any). If the research is based on findings in an organization, it is useful to provide the reader with some additional details on, say, the history of the organization, its size, products or services, mission, etc.

MORE
LITERATURE
REVIEW HELP

Literature review: After reading the literature review, the reader should understand why the study is being undertaken and how and why it is adding to the store of knowledge. A literature review written for an academic journal will usually be shorter than the kind of very comprehensive review that would be written for an academic thesis or dissertation. It should be self-evident after reading the literature review as to why the study's research questions (and hypotheses, if any) have been selected. Take care, however, not to merely label this section 'Literature review' even though this is what it is. Help and inspire the reader by choosing a title that reflects what the section is really about. If several themes or issues are being addressed, it may be necessary to write a number of literature sections, each with an appropriate heading.

Methodology: This is a key section and will be evaluated meticulously by reviewers and readers, and, of course, by anyone seeking to replicate the findings. The methodology should follow the principles outlined in many chapters in this book, including:

- A description of the research context: what kind of organization or setting, what were the original specifications for the study, what practical or ethical considerations were evident?
- The processes of sample selection: how was the sample selected? When was it selected: at the commencement of the study, or iteratively during it?
- A description of, and justification for, the sample: how many participants were there, what were their characteristics and how representative were they of the population?
- The research procedure, including the kinds of research methodology (experimental, survey, grounded study, etc.), research tools used and evidence for the validity, reliability and credibility of these tools.
- The duration, number and timing of the data gathering sessions: if used, how were interviewers or observers trained, what instructions were given to respondents?
- How were the data analysed?

Results: As the title suggests, this is the section in which you report on your findings. This may be in the form of descriptive text, tables and figures (recall Chapter 17) or through selected quotations. The key word here is 'selected'. Quotations should only be used where the comments themselves are revealing or interesting – they should not be used to carry the main burden of a description or argument. Quotations should also be used sparingly; try to avoid the phenomenon of 'death by quotation'.

Ensure that the results section is precisely this and not a discussion or commentary (which comes in the following section). The easiest way of differentiating between the two sections is that the Results should deal with what happened, while the Discussion section should deal with why (that is, the analysis). Make sure that you do not mix the two.

Discussion: The Discussion section, using the data (Results), presents answers to the original research questions and/or hypotheses. In doing this, it is particularly important to refer back to the literature review section, so that comparisons and contrasts can be drawn out between what your research found and what the literature suggested you might expect. In some cases you may be confirming the theoretical propositions from the literature, but within new (say, organizational) contexts. In other cases you may be finding relationships between variables that few studies have explored. Remember, all research does not have to be so original or unique that it puts you in line for a Nobel Prize. Nevertheless, unless it has something to add to knowledge, it is unlikely to be considered worthy of publication.

References: There are several types of referencing convention, one of the most widely used being the Harvard or author–date system, as used in this book.

Of course, what we have just discussed is quite a conventional format. Journals that take a more inductive, qualitative or ethnographic stance may discourage such a structured approach. The key, as has been suggested, is to look at these journals to see what approach they take.

A CLEARLY
STRUCTURED
ARTICLE

ETHICAL AND LEGAL CONSIDERATIONS

We have dealt with ethical issues in a number of previous chapters, but it is worth exploring some of them here in the context of writing up the research as well as looking at legal and copyright implications.

The ethics of report writing

Researchers have a responsibility for reporting their findings in a way that matches the data and which upholds the reputation of the researcher and the research community. However, as Table 24.3 shows, there is a spectrum of unethical behaviour in reporting research ranging from speculation to fabrication, the latter, of course, being the most serious. For example, it is important not to make interpretations that are inconsistent with the data or to make claims for the validity and generalizability of research that are exaggerated. Not only is it important that researchers do not make false claims (for example that a set of results are statistically significant, when they just failed to reach significance) they have a duty to speak out when clients or organizations in which they have conducted the research make such claims in public. Especially in cases where a research report is going to be presented to the organization in which the research was conducted, the limitations of the research must be clearly in evidence so that the organization is not misled. Polonsky (1998), for example, suggests that the research report should contain a section in which the potential problems and limitations of the research are explained. Academic supervisors could also append their comments regarding the limitations of the final report.

Table 24.3 Unethical reporting of results

Speculation	Expanding answers beyond what was required by the original research question.
Exaggeration	Making claims for the data that cannot be supported.
Neglect	Failing to acknowledge the limitations of the study and/or results.
Fabrication	Deleting data, modifying answers of respondents, faking results of analyses.
Plagiarism	Copying the work of others.

Source: Adapted from Blumberg et al., 2005

Avoiding plagiarism

ETHICS AND
PLAGIARISM

Plagiarism is becoming of increasing concern in the research community, partly because the growth of the Internet has made it easier. Plagiarism has many meanings, and is still the subject of much debate, but essentially refers to the submission of the words, ideas, images, or data of another person as one's own. Researchers can be confused about this, because they have to use the work of previous researchers to identify the kinds of questions that are worthy of research and the designs and methodologies needed to find the answers. According to Higher Education and Research in the UK (HERO) (2007), plagiarism takes several forms, including:

- Using published ideas as one's own.
- Representing images from books, journals or information published on the Web as one's own.
- Copying the work of another student or another person and presenting it as one's own.
- Collaborating inappropriately with another student when the assignment or report requires individual work.
- Resubmitting substantive excerpts of your own work from other assignments as a new piece of work.

Whether the plagiarism is unintentional or deliberate it still constitutes a serious offence, attracting sanctions depending on the institution, ranging from grading the paper at zero marks, or being dismissed from a course. Perpetrators of plagiarism are also now more likely to be caught, thanks largely to the heightened vigilance of academic institutions and the use of innovative computer software. So, how can it be avoided? HERO (2007) suggests that when reading, you keep a notebook handy so that you can note down the name of the author, date and place of publication, page numbers, etc. You can also minimize the risk of plagiarism by:

- Quoting directly from the source (but making sure, of course, that you cite the name of the author and date of publication).
- Paraphrasing the author's text but in your own words.
- Summarizing the text.

--------→ **TOP TIP 24.5** ←--------

Never be tempted to cut and paste passages from the Internet into your own work. This may appear at first sight to be a speedy way of accessing information, but it is plagiarism. If you do find a passage that is relevant, print out a 'hard' copy, read it through, and then paraphrase the content in your own words as you type your ideas into your assignment or dissertation.

Legal issues

Legal issues might arise through the process of conducting your research, and also at the report writing stage, for example, where you:

- Reveal your sources of information and use statements made by individuals – are they defamatory, libellous or in breach of sex discrimination laws?
- Present material – has it been published elsewhere and is it copyright? (See next section.)
- Make recommendations – do they infringe the law?

Common sense suggests that whenever you are in doubt about whether anything you have written contravenes a legal provision, you should consult a legal expert.

Intellectual property and copyright issues

Intellectual property (IP) refers to creations of the mind and includes: inventions, literary and artistic works, names, images, symbols and designs. The four main types of IP are:

- Patents for inventions – new and improved products and processes that are capable of industrial application.
- Trade marks for brand identity – of goods and services, allowing distinctions to be made between different traders.
- Designs for product appearance.
- Copyright for material including literary and artistic material, sound recordings, films, etc.

Copyright laws were first introduced in England in 1710 and now exist in most countries. While the precise nature of national copyright laws varies, the basic premise is that authors need to obtain permission before using another author's document, and must give the author appropriate acknowledgement. Take particular care when tempted to copy material from the Web. While websites are in the 'public domain', this does not mean that they are not protected by copyright laws. It is only safe to copy Web material when the author has abandoned copyright ownership, it is clear that the copyright has expired, or if it is a site owned by the government.

In many countries, what is written by a person while at work, automatically, in most circumstances, becomes the property of their employer. This may well apply to the research report itself.

→ ON THE WEB 24.2 ←

For more details on copyright laws see the following website:

http://whatiscopyright.org/

In particular take a look at the section of 'Fair Use'.

DEVELOPING A WRITING STYLE AND TONE

STYLISH
ACADEMIC
WRITING

It is difficult to exaggerate the importance of developing and using a fluent, concise and engaging writing style when writing up research. Put yourself, for a moment, in the place of someone who has to read your research, often having to wade through a long, detailed document containing complex arguments. A writing style that is laborious, repetitive, or simply ungrammatical, can not only make it hard for the reader to understand the work, but even make that person hostile to it.

ACTIVITY 24.4

Read through the dissertations or theses of previous students to recognize the different 'voices' used. Decide on the voice or style that is most appropriate to you. Write up a chapter or section of a chapter using this voice and ask your supervisor to comment on its style.

The appropriateness of a particular writing style can only be measured in the context of who the report is being written for. Hence, a style that is designed to inspire or enthuse will be very different from one that is meant to criticize or warn. Since the purpose of most reports is functional rather than imaginative, it has been suggested that this style of writing 'should be unobtrusive, an invisible medium, like a window pane through which the information can be clearly seen' (Turk and Kirkman, 1989: 90). Too many writers (particularly those writing scientific or technical documents) use leaden prose, and a stiff, formal style, failing to instill variety into their language.

One of the keys to good style is readability, a factor determined by:

- The writer, through the careful selection of material, by signposting, and by using a variety of emphases.
- The text, in terms of language (structures and vocabulary) and layout (e.g., headings).
- Readers, particularly their motivation and attitudes, and their overall interest in the report.

Presented next are a number of important areas where writing style can be improved.

Wordiness

Procter (2007) argues that one of the best ways of improving writing style is to be concise – that is, avoiding 'wordiness'. A wordy style not only adds unnecessary length to a proposal, thesis, or dissertation, but can give the writing a sense of pomposity. Table 24.4 presents some examples of wordiness and some more succinct alternatives.

Unbiased language

Sexist, racist and ageist language must also be avoided, of course, and reference made to particular genders, races or ages only when they are relevant to the subject of the report. Procter (2007) warns against what she calls the 'Man trap', that is, the

Table 24.4   Examples of wordiness and how to avoid it

Category	Wordy example	Succinct alternative
Doubling of words	Mutual agreement	Agreement
	Reconsider again	Reconsider
Intensifiers/qualifiers	Very Extremely	Either omit, or give specific
	To a certain extent	details of what you are trying to say
Formulaic phrases	At this moment in time	Now
	With regard to	About
	In view of the fact that	Because
Catch-all terms	Aspect	These words can sometimes
	Quality	be omitted
	Fact	
	Feature Problem	
	A surprising aspect of most coaching relationships is their friendly quality.	Most coaching relationships are surprisingly friendly
Padded verbs	To develop an understanding	To understand
	To have an expectation	To expect
	To formulate a plan	To plan

Source: Adapted from Procter, 2007

use of standard words that seem to assume that the subject is male. This can be avoided by using phrases such as 'him and her' or 'he or she' but this becomes clumsy. Better is to find a gender-neutral word. For example, rather than say: 'Every novelist has learned from those that came before him or her', you could say: 'Every artist has learned from previous artists'. Proctor also advises that feminine forms of words such as 'policewoman', 'women doctors' are becoming outdated, especially since there are neutral terms available such as 'police officer' and simply 'doctor'. In academic writing, titles such as Dr or Professor are rarely used. So, rather than refer to a source by saying 'Professor Brown argues', it is sufficient (and correct) to say, 'Brown (2008) argues ...'

Sentence construction

At a practical level, readability is aided by generating a balance between the use of long and short sentences. A report that contains just long, verbose sentences will be difficult to cognitively process and understand; conversely, a report based just on short, staccato sentences will appear disjointed and monotonous. Using sentences that vary in length will aid the reader's attention, concentration and, therefore, understanding. The readability of text can be measured by a variety of indices, one of the most common of which is the Flesch index.

ACTIVITY 24.5

You can measure the readability of the text you are producing using one of a number of alternative measuring indices. Microsoft Word, for example, can be used to give you both a Flesch Reading Ease score and a Flesch–Kincaid Grade Level score. For the Flesch readability score, text is rated on a 100-point scale. The higher the score, the easier the text is to understand. Most documents aim for a score of at least 60–70.

Perform a Flesch readability score on your own report. If this is not already set up in your program, go to the Help facility in Word and type in 'readability'. Follow the instructions to set up the readability statistics tool.

Vocabulary

The use of long, technical or unfamiliar words also affects readability. But, it is not the length in itself that is the problem. For example, the word 'organization' has many syllables, but would not cause the average reader any problems. As Turk and Kirkman (1989) warn, it is the combination of unfamiliarity with length that can inhibit readability. Unfamiliarity itself is linked to the frequency with which a word appears. Technical terms, in particular, will only be familiar to an audience that is also knowledgeable and competent in this field. So, in writing technical reports, you need to be particularly careful that either the terms you use are clearly explained, or that they are likely to be well known to your audience. Jargon can be useful because it can be used as a short and convenient way to name new ideas and concepts. Technical reports would be lost without it. But it must also be used with care since, if it is overused, or used in an attempt to give an air of importance, it can obscure the central message of the report.

Nominalization

Turk and Kirkman (1989) warn against the use of nominalization, that is, the habit of turning verbs into nouns. Take, for example, a perfectly good sentence:

> The survey collected data on customer attitudes, showing that ...

Nominalizing the verb in this sentence, 'collected', gives us the following nominalized sentence:

> Collection of the data through the survey revealed customer attitudes, which showed that ...

Nominalization reduces the effectiveness of the written style because it produces a passive sentence and also forces the writer to insert an additional verb, 'revealed'. While it is tempting to use passive forms of writing because they add a sense of detachment and perhaps spurious objectivity to the report, they also make it longer, more complex and lacking in dynamism.

Writing tone

The tone of a report relates to the general mood of the finished text. It is important, for example, not to betray personal feelings such as anger, frustration, jealousy, resentment or anxiety in the report, even if you are feeling these emotions. The overall tone of a report should reflect the nature of its message.

UNDERTAKING A REVIEW PROCESS

It is difficult to overstate the importance of a review process. After 'completing' the report, always regard this as merely the first draft. Leave the document for a few days (if this is possible) before you return to it, so that you will have forgotten the thoughts behind the report and will read what you actually said! You will almost certainly find not only typing and grammatical mistakes, but also gaps, inconsistencies and errors. Turk and Kirkman (1989) suggest first reading the draft without stopping, but noting problem passages or words so that you can return to them later. This top-level overview allows you to evaluate the general flow of information and ideas and to see if the structure 'hangs together'. In conducting this review, Potter (2006) also suggests that you take regular breaks so that you are always fresh and alert. If the report is for an important piece of assessment or intended for a very senior audience, then you will need to go through a number of iterations, ideally using a number of experienced and expert reviewers (see Top Tip 24.6 below).

In terms of content, Potter (2006) suggests that the review task should carefully check on:

- *Content*: Check that the main ideas are clear and of relevance for the reader.
- *Argument*: Check that the main line of argument is transparent, that alternative positions have been considered and that evidence and citations are provided to support arguments.
- *Organization*: Check that the headings describe the content beneath them and chapters and sections are in the right order. Ensure that there is progression from familiar to unfamiliar topics, and that different issues are dealt with in different paragraphs. Ensure that links are made between sections and topics.
- *Language*: Check that the style is appropriate to the intended audience and that meanings are clear.

Also ensure that tables and figures are described and numbered correctly and sources properly referenced.

➤ TOP TIP 24.6 ◄

If you are submitting a dissertation or thesis, or an important report, then it is useful getting two quite different kinds of people to act as reviewers. Subject matter experts can tell you whether the content is accurate and whether there are any important gaps. You should also elicit review help from someone totally unfamiliar with the subject area, who can read the work with a detached eye. Try to use the services of someone who is experienced and proficient at report writing and who has a good working knowledge of English grammar. Before submitting a final version of the thesis, you might also consider paying for the services of a professional proof reader.

Summary

- Understand the needs and interests of your intended audience and write for them.
- Plan the report writing process, allowing yourself sufficient time to write the report and resources to aid its completion.
- Different structures are required for case study reports, organizational and technical reports and academic dissertations and journal articles.
- A common structure for an organizational report is one that presents the substantive arguments and findings at the beginning, using the rest of the report to support them.
- Dissertations and theses usually contain an Abstract, an Introduction, several theoretical chapters, plus chapters on research Methodology, Findings, Analysis and a Conclusion and/or Recommendations.
- The precise structure of journal articles is determined by the journal in question, but such articles will usually contain, amongst other sections, a strong, theoretical underpinning.
- Some of the main ethical considerations to think about when writing up research include maintaining confidentiality and taking care not to breach copyright laws. Be particularly careful when copying material from the Web.
- Style and presentation are important for the impact of a research report and are improved through practice and redrafting. Expert reviewers are of value in this process.

REVIEW QUESTIONS

1. What displacement activities do you use for avoiding getting down to write your thesis, dissertation or report? Compare your list with those of a colleague and then coach each other on how to avoid them.
2. Should you write up the report during or at the end of the research process? Examine your own preferred approach and then write a list of counter-arguments.
3. If you are studying on a programme in an academic institution, what software programs does it use for testing students' work for plagiarism? Can you put your own work through the system to ensure you do not break any rules, even unintentionally?

FURTHER READING

Thomas, G. (2013) *How to do your Research Project: A Guide for Students of Education and Applied Social Sciences*, 2nd edn. London: Sage. Very readable and accessible, this book deals not only with academic writing but also offers help with the literature review.

THE DISSERTATION JOURNEY

Roberts, C.A. (2010) *The Dissertation Journey: A Practical and Comprehensive Guide to Planning, Writing and Defending your Dissertation*, 2nd edn. Thousand Oaks, CA: Corwin. Starts with personal motivation for undertaking a dissertation (do I have what it takes?), through to dealing with Institutional Review Boards, planning the dissertation, getting to grips with academic style, writing the Introduction and Methodology and defending the dissertation at a viva.

Rudestam, K.E. and Newton, R.R. (2007) *Surviving your Dissertation: A Comprehensive Guide to Content and Process*, 3rd edn. Newbury Park, CA: Sage. Provides practical guidance on selecting topics, and what the literature review, methods and results chapters should contain.

Berry, R. (2004) *The Research Project: How to Write it,* 5th edn. Oxford: Routledge. Covers themes such as choosing a topic, shaping and composing a project and avoiding common pitfalls. Includes an example of a well written paper along with notes and bibliography.

JOURNAL RESOURCES

Pratt, M.G. (2009) 'For the lack of a boilerplate: Tips on writing up (and reviewing) qualitative research', *Academy of Management Journal*, 52(5): 856–862. Notes the lack of accepted approach to writing up qualitative research and makes recommendations for achieving the greatest impact.

Smith, S. (2006) 'Encouraging the use of reflexivity in the writing up of qualitative research', *International Journal of Therapy & Rehabilitation*, 13(5): 209–215. The reasons why writers are reluctant to write about the self in published journals are explored. Two different approaches to qualitative writing up are discussed: the 'realist' and the 'confessional' approaches.

SUMMARY OF WEB LINKS

http://www.inspiration.com/productinfo/

http://whatiscopyright.org/

25

PREPARING FOR PRESENTATIONS AND VIVAS

CHAPTER INTRODUCTION

Chapter outline

Preparing the presentation	660	Creating interest in presentations	665
Structuring the presentation: beginning, middle and end	662	Delivering the presentation	666
Structuring the presentation – the density of ideas	663	Team presentations	668
		Preparing for and surviving vivas	670

Keywords

Presentation	PhD
Visual aids	Viva

┌─ **Chapter objectives** ─────────────────────────────

After reading this chapter you will be able to:

- Plan and structure a presentation.
- Deliver a presentation to meet the needs of your audience.
- Use visual aids effectively.
- Deliver a 'professional' presentation.
- Prepare for and pass a viva.

ORAL
EXAMINATION

In Chapter 24 we looked at writing and presenting through the written medium of the report or dissertation. In this chapter, we are going to explore two other common and important communication media – presentations and vivas. Vivas (or viva voces to give them their full title) are oral examinations usually taking place at the end of a programme such as a doctorate. However, they may also, occasionally, be used on masters or other programmes, so preparing for and conducting yourself well at a viva may be a skill you need to acquire.

In both business and academic environments presentations are also becoming increasingly popular, partly because they allow for two-way communication such as discussions and questioning. For some academic programmes, presentations are assessed instead of, or in addition to, the usual assignments or dissertations. One of the advantages of giving a presentation is that it is possible to gauge the reaction of members of the audience, and to adapt what you are saying to the situation (Billingham, 2003). So, for example, if you see doubt on the faces of your audience, you can inject more enthusiasm and commitment into your presentation. Presentations, of course, also have the advantage of allowing you to use visual aids to enhance both the clarity of your ideas and also their impact.

Many people quake when it comes to the notion of having to give a presentation, often because a lot depends on it. They fear presentations because it means having to stand up in front of other people (a feeling of exposure), with the attendant fears of 'drying up' and of facing the possibility of having to respond to difficult questions from the audience. These are just three fears, but everyone has individual dreads of their own. A survey in the USA found that public speaking is the greatest fear people face – even greater than a fear of snakes! (McCarthy and Hatcher, 2002). Presentations, however, can be both fulfilling and successful (even enjoyable) if you adopt the systematic approach presented in this chapter.

PREPARING THE PRESENTATION

Preparation and planning are key and include knowing about the needs of your audience and programme, knowing what you want to achieve in the presentation and defining your central message.

Knowing the audience

Knowing your audience means understanding what it is that they want to know, what they are interested in, whether they agree with or oppose your central arguments, and whether they are likely to find your subject matter useful. You also need to keep in mind the diversity of the audience – some of them might want knowledge while others want to be entertained. You also need to determine how much they already know about your subject, so that you can pitch the presentation at the right level of detail.

Knowing your programme

If your presentation is being given as part of an academic programme, then it is absolutely essential that you read and understand the module specifications, particularly when it comes to assessment criteria. Your course handbook or programme website will set out in some detail what these are. Check whether the presentation constitutes all or only a percentage of the total marks for the module. Typically, presentations make up a minority of the marks compared to assignments, but these marks might mean the difference between passing or failing the module, or between gaining a high or lower grade. Look at what content the presentation is required to cover in terms of subject matter. Is the presentation to be made by individuals or as part of a team? Is assessment going to be conducted by the academic in charge of the module, or does it also involve an element of peer assessment? If the latter, how is this to be done? For example, 20 per cent of the final presentation marks might be voted on by others in your class. Design your presentation with close reference to the assessment criteria.

Reconnoitring facilities

It is always a good idea to reconnoitre the environment in which you will be presenting. The reasons for doing this should be obvious. You might have planned for some group discussion work in the middle of your presentation, but on visiting the room, find that it is a 'raked' lecture theatre, making the movement of participants virtually impossible. Or you might find that the room is next to a busy main road and the acoustics are bad, requiring that you speak louder and with more energy or to arrange for the use of a microphone. Few elements sabotage a presentation more thoroughly than problems with audio-visual equipment. We have all seen presentations wrecked, for example, by the failure of a projector to work. It is sensible then, if possible, to visit the presentation room well in advance to ensure that all the equipment you need functions properly. Once you have done this, you will find that you will be more relaxed and confident – helping to calm your nerves.

PREPARING A VENUE

Dealing with nerves

Most people get nervous before an important presentation. However, good speakers know how to harvest these nerves to their own advantage. They acknowledge to themselves that having some nerves is important to improving performance. Then, they might go on to build their confidence by listing all their personal strengths as presenters and the qualities of the presentation itself. They think positive thoughts, not negative ones (see Table 25.1)

OVERCOMING NERVES

After this they might mentally move on to focus not on their nerves, but on the central message they are going to convey. In other words they focus on the task, not on themselves.

Table 25.1 From negative to positive thoughts

Negative thoughts	Positive thoughts
I will 'dry up'	I have practised this. I am fluent
I don't know enough	I am the expert in the room
Everyone will be looking at me	I will command their attention
I won't know the answers to their questions	I know most of the answers; I can always open issues up for discussion

— ACTIVITY 25.1 —

Think of some of the presentations you have given in the past. Now write down as many positive points as you can under the heading: 'Why I am a good presenter'.

———➤ TOP TIP 25.1 ◀———

Particularly if you have your presentation on a computer hard drive (rather than using the Cloud), also have it available on an external memory storage device. Also, email it to yourself so it can be accessed, if necessary, from the Internet. If you are presenting at an external institution never assume they have loaded your presentation for you and that it is 'ready to go'.

STRUCTURING THE PRESENTATION: BEGINNING, MIDDLE AND END

STRUCTURING A PRESENTATION

Having a sound structure allows you to be clearer in your mind as to what you are saying and gives your audience better access to your information. The basic structure of a good presentation is: a beginning; a middle; and an end. Each has its own internal structure.

The beginning of the presentation

Getting the presentation off to the best possible start is both vital and also challenging. In the first few moments you need to 'connect' with your audience, to get yourself relaxed and to relax them. Even if you are nervous (and even experienced speakers can be nervous on occasions), it is unwise to state this out loud as it will only make your audience nervous for you. If this feeling then transmits itself back to you, your nerves may only increase! The best approach is to greet your audience, introduce yourself (especially if there are people in the room who don't know you) and state the title of your presentation. It is also a good idea to tell the audience how long you will be speaking for, and whether they can ask their questions during the presentation or at the end. If you have handouts, make sure that these are distributed before you speak, or at the very end but not as you are speaking, otherwise you will find that people become distracted as they pass the paperwork around.

The middle of the presentation

In the middle of a presentation it is normal to find the audience drifting in and out of full concentration. They will be helped in maintaining focus if the middle phase of the presentation has a clear structure. Billingham (2003) suggests several approaches:

The inductive approach

Fact + Fact + Fact + Fact *therefore* Conclusion

Here, the audience has to build up their understanding of the facts before coming to their own conclusion (or at least validating in their own minds the conclusion they are presented with). This makes the presentation more interesting but also much harder work for participants.

The deductive approach

Conclusion *because* Fact + Fact + Fact + Fact

Here the conclusion or 'answer' is given right at the start and is then explained or supported by the facts that follow. This is easier for the audience to understand.

The discursive approach

With this approach, both sides of an argument are presented, with some kind of summary giving a recommendation as to which side is supported and why. In presenting the arguments, a choice needs to be made as to whether the case for the proposition is going to be presented first, or the case against.

Situation, options, and the way forward

This stands for: Situation which is explained; Options which are presented including arguments for and against each one; the Way forward is then presented and justified.

The end of the presentation

The end of the presentation is the final opportunity to make an impact. Here it is important not to either tail off into anticlimax, or repeat vast portions of your presentation. The focus here should be on emphasizing a small number of key points, and delivering this stage of the presentation with enthusiasm and energy. Flag to the audience that you have, indeed, reached the end by using signal words such as: 'So, in conclusion', 'Lastly', or 'In summary'.

STRUCTURING THE PRESENTATION – THE DENSITY OF IDEAS

The factor that sinks more presentations than any other, is the sheer volume of information bad presenters try to convey. Listeners are only capable of remembering two

Table 25.2   Typical structures for 10 and 20 minute presentations

Structure of a 10 minute presentation	Structure of a 20 minute presentation
Introduction	Introduction
Key point 1	Key point 1
Sub-theme 1	Sub-theme 1
Sub-theme 2	Sub-theme 2
Key point 2	Key point 2
Sub-theme 1	Sub-theme 1
Sub-theme 2	Sub-theme 2
Sub-theme 3	Key point 3
Conclusion	Sub-theme 1
	Sub-theme 2
	Key point 4
	Sub-theme 1
	Sub-theme 2
	Conclusion

Source: Adapted from McCarthy and Hatcher, 2002

or three key messages. So, you should be absolutely clear what your key messages are. McCarthy and Hatcher (2002) suggest that for a 10-minute presentation, two key points are acceptable, supported by some sub-themes (no more than 3 or 4 for each key point); for a 20 minute presentation, it is four key points plus sub-themes (see Table 25.2).

Presenting complex processes

It is often the case that you have to explain quite detailed processes to an audience. This might be to do with, say, the design of a research project, or a software system. If the system is complex and detailed there is plenty of opportunity to confuse and alienate your audience! Think of a presentation you have seen where a diagram is presented and you think: 'Wow! Too detailed! There's no way I'm going to understand this.' The best approach is to adopt the following process:

- Present a diagrammatic overview of the entire system; explain, in summary, the main components of the process, not the detail.
- Starting from a blank page, present the first stage of the system; ask for questions.
- Present the next stage of the system, linked to the first stage (in other words, you are building up the picture of the system in the diagram, step by step, back towards the overview); ask for questions.
- Present the next stage, etc., ask for questions.
- Use plenty of summaries.

By the end you will have a holistic diagram for which you will have explained each section in depth.

CREATING INTEREST IN PRESENTATIONS

Delivering a memorable presentation that has a real impact is helped if you make use of a number of approaches that add interest and a more personal touch.

Using personal stories

People often remember a speaker's presentation if they tell a personal story, especially if that story is original, amusing or shocking. Personal stories allow the audience to 'connect' with the speaker, seeing them as a real human being and not merely a presenter delivering a message. Personal stories work best, however, when they are short, and the audience can see a clear connection between the narrative and the main thread of the presentation. But using personal stories also has its risks. If the composition of the audience is diverse, some people from other cultures may not understand it, or may not like it. So, if possible, try to make your stories appealing to as wide a range of cultures as possible.

Using metaphors

A metaphor is a comparison that shows how two things are similar in one important way, although dissimilar in everything else. So, for example, we could say that having a problem getting someone to change their mind was like 'pulling teeth out'. The metaphor is powerful because it creates a strong visual image (in this case a dental one) that can arouse feelings such as curiosity, fascination or repulsion in the listener. Thinking up a metaphor to describe a situation, person or entity also allows the presenter to use a visual image of the metaphor helping the presentation to avoid a predominance of bullet point slides.

TOP TIP 25.2

If you can think of a metaphor that summarizes what you are trying to say, go to Google images and type in the metaphor's name. You should find a lot of choices for images. Import an image by right clicking your mouse and then [Copy] and [Paste] it into your presentation. But be careful not to infringe copyright laws.

ACTIVITY 25.2

Return to a presentation you have delivered recently. Explore the slides dominated by bullet points. Try to think of a metaphor or visual image for each slide; then search for this image in Google images.

Using visual aids

Visual aids have the capacity to enrich and enhance a presentation, but equally, when not used well, they have the capability to wreck it (see Table 25.3). Visual aids such as PowerPoint presentations or the use of flipcharts, whiteboards or

Table 25.3   Some of the 'deadly sins' when using visual aids: design

The sin	The consequence
Using fonts that are too small	Inability of audience to read the information
Using endless bullet point slides	Complete audience boredom
Making slides 'busy' and packed with text	Inability of audience to process the information
Using too many colours or inappropriate colours	Audience confusion
Using too many animation effects	Audience distraction or irritation

Table 25.4   Some of the 'deadly sins' when using visual aids: delivery

The sin	The consequence
Facing the screen when talking, not the audience	Lack of 'connection' with the audience; less interest in the presentation
Reading from notes	See above
Technical problems such as the equipment not working	Embarrassed speaker and embarrassed audience
Flat, monotone delivery	Audience falls asleep or 'switches off'

blackboards need careful planning and combining with the oral discourse. When done properly, visual aids help listeners to:

- Make better sense of the information.
- Recall key points.
- Enjoy the presentation.

In designing content you could make use of photos, pictures, charts, video clips and music.

The key is keeping the message simple, not making slides or other visual aids too cluttered, and using visual images rather than words. Avoid the temptation to use all of PowerPoint's tremendous range of font sizes, font types, colours, backgrounds and animation techniques. Keep it simple. In presenting data, for example, you can create graphics such as pie charts or histograms in Microsoft Excel and cut and paste them into your Word document (recall some of the graphics presented in Chapter 22).

DELIVERING THE PRESENTATION

Preparing good looking and visually pleasing visual aids is only half the battle. You also have to deliver the presentation in a way that engages and holds the attention of the audience, and which coordinates with the text and images you are presenting. Unfortunately, what wrecks most presentations is not the visual aids but the delivery. Table 25.4 summarizes some of the 'deadly sins' of presenting, which include facing the screen, not the audience, and reading verbatim from notes (again not looking at the audience).

Gaining attention

You must start by capturing the attention of your audience. According to McCarthy and Hatcher (2002) an audience decides in about the first 10 seconds of a presentation whether it is worth listening to. There are many ways of capturing attention. You could tell a 'scare' story that shows what will happen if the ideas you are about to present are not implemented. Or you could make a controversial statement about the topic. The key is to get the audience 'hooked in'.

➤ TOP TIP 25.3 ◄

Prepare, prepare, prepare. The more preparation you do, the more confident you will feel. Preparation means both planning and also practising delivery. When practising for delivery, it is best if you can go to where you will be giving your presentation so that you can get the 'feel' of the room. Make sure that you practise 'out loud', so that you can hear for yourself the words you use, the tone and pace of delivery. If possible, arrange for a friend or colleague to act as a critical friend so that you can elicit some feedback on your performance.

GRAY ON HOW TO PREPARE FOR PRESENTATIONS

Using body language

In many ways, you are the most important visual aid that you have (Billingham, 2003). An important feature of good presenting is the use of body language, particularly how you stand. Someone slumped in a chair, staring at their notes is unlikely to be perceived as confident and in control of their subject matter. However, if a presenter stands, they can make more effective use of their hands, and better use of their voice. They will appear to the audience as more confident, and so will become more confident. Standing also allows you to 'scan' the audience, seeking to gain occasional eye contact with everyone. You can move about, although do not be tempted to do this too much as it can become distracting.

Using your voice

Your voice is a vital tool in good presenting. You can use your vocal delivery to place an emphasis on key themes (helping your listeners to know where these key themes are). You can also alter the pace of delivery, slowing down for more detailed sections and even inserting a dramatic pause when a key point requires strong emphasis.

Handling questions from the audience

Presenters can sometimes be nervous about taking questions from the audience because they feel that if they cannot answer the questions they will appear ignorant or foolish. However, questions should be looked upon as an opportunity for you to repeat and reinforce some of your main points. Questions are usually asked because audience members have misunderstood an issue and just want more clarity. As someone asks a question, give them eye contact and then repeat the question so that all the audience have heard it. Avoid the feeling that it always has to be you

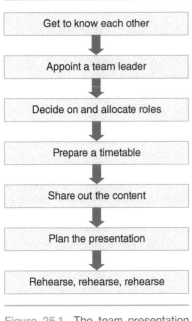

Figure 25.1 The team presentation preparation process

Source: Adapted from Billingham, 2003

who answers the question. Questions are sometimes an opportunity to 'throw the issue open' to the rest of the audience and to get a debate going. If you do not understand the question, then politely say so and ask for it to be repeated. If you do not know the answer, do not be tempted to invent a response, or to waffle – admit that you do not know the answer, then thank the person for their question.

TEAM PRESENTATIONS

You may have to present as part of a group. This brings both new challenges and opportunities. Figure 25.1 offers a summary of the processes involved.

Get to know each other

If you are all working under pressure (which may be because your presentation is going to be assessed as part of an accredited programme), you will need to get to know each other well so that collaboration is maximized. You do not want disagreements, jealousies or antagonisms to disrupt the work of the team. Try to organize a social event for you all to attend. Go for a coffee or have lunch together, so that group 'bonding' can begin.

Appoint a team leader

TEAM
PRESENTATIONS

Sometimes a group may decide not to appoint a leader, believing that they can manage the presentation process entirely by mutual agreement. This is naive because it allows no one to take responsibility for pulling the team together, sorting out problems and project managing the processes. Team leaders need to have a clear idea of the intended output and good interpersonal skills. When appointing a leader, other team members should be aware that they all still have responsibilities to the group and to the task in hand. It is not the leader's job to do all the work!

Decide on and allocate roles

These roles might include presentation design, implementation (using technology), and delivery. It is best to allocate these roles around the team based upon members' natural strengths or enthusiasm. It is the leader's role to ensure that once accepted, team members complete their tasks on time and to the necessary standard.

Prepare a timetable

A timetable should be prepared, working backwards from the date for the final presentation. This determines the amount of time the team has for preparing the presentation. Built into the timetable should be adequate time for practising delivering the presentation.

Share out the content

Share out the content based upon the known expertise of team members or at least motivation to talk about the subject. Not all team members may necessarily deliver, as some will have responsibility for the presentation's design and production. In situations where skills and knowledge are lacking, ensure that the person who takes on the 'not wanted' subject is given support by the team.

Plan the presentation

Try to ensure that listeners are treated to plenty of variety. So, follow a difficult section of subject matter (such as data and figures), with a lighter, less formal one. Ensure a lively speaker follows a slow, serious one. Structure the presentation so that its content is easy to understand.

Rehearse, rehearse, rehearse

It is impossible to overstress the importance of practising the presentation as much as possible. In team presentations you will need to determine where everyone stands and the 'batting order' for the speakers. It is important that when one team member is speaking, other members give them the respect of full attention. If team members do not do this, why should the audience? When practising aim for:

- A polished introduction.
- Smooth handovers.
- A slick and decisive summary/conclusion.

CASE STUDY 25.1

What happens when you don't rehearse and when you do

As part of an MSc module, the class was divided into four teams of five students, each team being required to give a 20-minute presentation, providing a solution to a case study problem. The team that achieved the lowest marks contained two dominant individuals who spent most of the time arguing about the structure and content of the presentation.

Although all teams had four weeks in which to prepare the presentations, this team did not meet at all during the first two weeks, and the arguments had a disastrous impact on progress. In the end, they did most of their content preparation the night before the presentation day and had only one 'dry run' practice on the day itself. The lack of preparation showed. There was no fluency between elements of the presentation, handovers between speakers were hesitant and the body language of all presenters was defensive and lacking in confidence.

In contrast, the winning team elected a leader at the soonest opportunity. Team roles were allocated quickly and meetings booked well in advance. All team members exchanged mobile phone numbers so that they could keep in regular contact, and communicated frequently using MSN. When one team member was seen to be struggling with his part of the subject matter, others offered to help him. The team spent quite a lot of time discussing the structure of their presentation before they researched the content. They also started their first of four practice sessions a week before the 'big day' and were slick and confident on the day itself. They looked relaxed and confident (because they were!) and even seemed to enjoy delivering the presentation.

Reflecting on presentations you have seen

Think back to one of the worst presentations you have seen. Make a list of all the factors that made you judge the presentation to be poor. Then recall a good presentation. Why was this better? What features of the good presentation are you able to repeat yourself?

PREPARING FOR AND SURVIVING VIVAS

A viva is an oral examination, usually taken as part of a postgraduate research degree. Vivas perform at least two important functions:

- They test the candidate's knowledge of their thesis to ensure that it is their own work.
- They provide the candidate with the opportunity to defend their ideas and, if necessary, add further detail and explanation.

PRESENTING AT THE VIVA

The viva normally takes place a number of weeks after the candidate's thesis has been submitted, and, typically, is attended by a person who chairs the meeting (to ensure that the academic institution's regulations are followed), an internal examiner from the candidate's institution and one or sometimes two external examiners. Two external examiners may be needed if the thesis covers a diverse range of themes or if one of the examiners is relatively inexperienced (for example, they have not examined a thesis before). Examiners must always be independent of the candidate and qualified in the subject area dealt with by the thesis. Some institutions also allow the candidate's supervisor to be present but in an observational capacity only – they are not part of the decision-making process. They might occasionally, however, be called upon to add points of clarification but only if the examiner seeks this.

The format for a viva meeting can vary widely. In some parts of continental Europe, for example, the viva is an open event, at which members of the public may not only attend, but also ask questions. The role of the examiners is to judge whether the dissertation is worthy of a pass. There are usually just six possible outcomes from the examination; the following are based upon the regulations at the University of Surrey:

- That the degree be awarded.
- That the degree be awarded, subject to minor corrections.
- That the degree be not awarded, but that the student be permitted to submit a revised thesis, by a specified date, with or without further research, and be examined with or without a further viva voce examination.
- That the degree be not awarded and with no recommendation regarding re-submission of the thesis.
- That the degree of Doctor of Philosophy be not awarded but that the Degree of Master of Philosophy be awarded, if appropriate, after specified minor corrections have been made to the thesis.
- That the degree of Doctor of Philosophy be not awarded, but the student be permitted to submit a revised thesis, for the Degree of Master of Philosophy, by a specified date, with or without further research and be examined with or without a further viva voce examination.

Obviously, most candidates hope that they will gain a pass with no amendments, but this happens on relatively few occasions. Probably the best outcome to hope for is a pass with minor corrections. The difference between 'major' and 'minor' corrections is partly one of semantics, and will depend on the judgement of the examiners as to which they choose. Minor corrections tend to include: minor errors of fact, typography, grammar, style, syntax and the layout of graphs and tables. Changes to the intellectual content or reasoning of a thesis would normally be regarded as major corrections. Whatever corrections are required, the candidate would normally be informed about them verbally at the end of the viva and subsequently in writing, as well as the date by which the corrections would have to be made.

Transferring from MPhil to PhD

In most UK higher education institutions, students first of all enrol on an MPhil programme and then, usually after two years' of study and having reached an appropriate level, upgrade or transfer onto a PhD. The MPhil stage involves the production of a 'transfer document' which has to be defended at a transfer meeting. It is therefore a very useful preparation for the viva itself. The report will, typically, contain an Introduction setting out the background and reasons for undertaking the study, one or more literature chapters and a methodology chapter, identifying a set of research questions and a plan for how the study is going to be conducted. The upgrade meeting is normally attended by two internal examiners but not by anyone from outside the university, but rules differ between higher education institutions. The examiners will be looking for evidence that the focus of the study is sound and that the literature search has identified a set of questions worthy and capable of being researched. Finally, of course, the Methodology chapter shows coherently how this is going to be done.

The kinds of outcomes reflect those of the PhD itself. These typically comprise:

- Transfer to PhD is permitted.
- Transfer is not permitted, but the candidate is permitted to submit a revised upgrade document during a prescribed timescale.
- Transfer is not permitted and the Degree of Master of Philosophy be awarded, if appropriate, after specified minor corrections have been made to the thesis.
- Transfer is not permitted and no award is to be made.

The kinds of weaknesses that examiners often identify at this stage include an expectation that merely describing the literature will be sufficient. For both the upgrade document as well as the final thesis, the literature needs to present a set of arguments that are then supported by the relevant literature.

→ TOP TIP 25.4 ←

Too often candidates present a long 'laundry list' of sources, expecting this will be enough to carry an argument. In this they are mistaken. Make sure that a clear set of research questions emerge. Once these questions are specified, the Methodology chapter needs to present a research design, capable of researching them. Reading the research literature on research design is therefore essential.

Table 25.5   Criteria for choosing an external examiner

Choose examiners who are ...	Avoid examiners who are ...
Highly respected in their field	Unknown in their field
Working in a research area related to your own	Working in a research area unrelated or only tangentially related to your own
Broadly sympathetic to your central arguments	Likely to be antipathetic or even hostile to your central arguments
Publishing research using broadly similar methodologies to your own	Publishing research using methodologies that contrast sharply with your own

Preparing for the viva

Selecting an examiner

PREPARING FOR YOUR VIVA

Probably several months before the viva (and even before you have actually completed your thesis) you should discuss the choice of examiners with your supervisor. It almost goes without saying that selecting an appropriate examiner is a key step in achieving success in the upcoming viva. Most examiners will want to be as professional, fair and objective as possible. But if you choose an examiner, for example, whom you know is from a theoretical position or research tradition unsympathetic or even hostile to your own, you may be asking for trouble. To use a stark example, if your thesis is based upon a constructivist philosophical position and a methodology that has used an ethnographic research design, but your examiner is from a 'hard science', objectivist, quantitative position, you may have some problems! Such an examiner may be both philosophically antipathetic to your approach, but also may simply have difficulty actually understanding your research design. This is partly because most academics become quite specialized and comfortable with a limited range of research approaches. So, choosing an examiner from a similar research tradition to yourself does not guarantee success – but it helps! Table 25.5 provides a brief summary of selection criteria.

--- **ACTIVITY 25.4** ---

Search for and read some of the academic articles written by one or more potential external examiners. Try to identify the kind of research tradition they belong to. Do their research studies favour a didactic, quantitative and experimental approach, or does their research tend to adopt an inductive, qualitative and interpretivist approach? Discuss the outcome of your investigation with your supervisor.

Becoming the 'master' of your own work

In the days or weeks leading up to the viva, ensure that you re-read your work so that you are as familiar with it as possible. This does not mean committing anything to memory. If an examiner wishes you to respond to an issue in a particular passage they will give you the page number and allow you some time to refresh your memory of the themes it contains. Clearly, however, it helps to be familiar and conversant with all your major themes and arguments.

Above all, ensure that you have identified any weaknesses – in a body of work up to 100,000 words long, there are bound to be some! Common limitations include:

- Key omissions in the literature chapters including omitting significant theories or sources.
- A failure to present a set of coherent and well formulated research questions.
- The lack of a coherent research design that is appropriate to the questions being asked.
- Problems in sample selection, including a reliance on convenience or volunteer samples, and a failure to acknowledge the limitations of these.
- Failure to acknowledge alternative interpretations of the data.
- Making exaggerated claims on the basis of limited data.

Like any skill, practice makes perfect. A sensible approach, then, is to use a 'mock' viva where either your supervisor, or another academic who is kind enough to help you, drafts a set of questions, poses them to you, and then provides you with feedback on your performance. Be warned, however, that it is unlikely that many, if any, of these questions will come up in the viva itself because, as Potter (2006) puts it, there is no such thing as a standard viva. The mock viva, though, will provide you with the opportunity to experience the pressure of thinking up answers when under pressure.

Publishing and referencing your own article(s)

It is not unusual, particularly for students working at doctoral level, to submit one or more articles to a peer reviewed academic journal. There are a number of good reasons for doing this. Firstly, the act of writing an academic article demands skills such as synthesis, evaluation and analysis, all of which are also needed for writing good theses and dissertations. Indeed, producing a piece of work of say, only 6,000 words in length can be harder than one of 60,000 precisely because the arguments need to be tight and focused. So, writing your own article is good practice for general academic writing. Secondly, if the article is published or only 'in print', that is, it has been accepted by a journal and will be published soon, you can make reference to it in your thesis, summarizing your main arguments and, of course, citing your own name and date of publication. Having a reference to your own published work in your dissertation can only impress an examiner, showing that you are capable of writing to a high academic standard.

Referencing the examiner

It might be thought rather ingratiating to make reference to one or more of the published works of the examiner but there are several good reasons for doing this, if at all possible. Firstly, if you do not think that making such a reference would be relevant to the arguments you are making, you have to ask yourself whether you have chosen the right examiner. Making reference, of course, will go some way towards massaging the ego of the examiner and so help him or her to see your work in a more positive light! However, you should not assume that any reference should be made without any hint of criticism. Examiners should expect (and many would wish) to have their theories evaluated critically, provided the criticism can be substantiated and justified. Many examiners like nothing more than an academic debate, and providing one, based upon evidence and a sustained argument, could give you an opportunity to show off your critical knowledge of the field. Of course, there is always the danger of going too far. Few examiners would appreciate having a convincing and complete refutation of their life's work!

During the viva

On the day of the viva, a number of processes will take place. Firstly, the external examiners will meet, probably for about an hour. While they may have had some provisional discussions about your work before the viva by telephone or email, it is possible that their discussion on the day of the viva is the first opportunity they have had to debate the quality of your work. You can rest assured, however, that in the vast majority of cases, examiners will have taken their responsibilities very seriously and read your dissertation with great care and thoroughness. All members of the viva panel, including your supervisor and the chairperson of the meeting will get together to agree the final format for the meeting, including its timing. Some examiners will give you the result of their deliberations right at the start of the viva, for example: 'Congratulations, we can tell you that you have passed but with some minor corrections. It is these that we would like to discuss with you'. But in most cases, the result will come right at the end.

There is no way of telling how long the viva will last. At a very minimum this could be as short as an hour (probably for those theses that are either excellent or very poor), to as much as 6 or 7 hours. Most, however, will take from 2 to 3 hours to complete. After your defence of your work is over (that is, the examiners have exhausted their stock of questions, or they are satisfied that they have covered the key areas they want answers to), your involvement in the viva comes to an end. You and your supervisor are asked to leave the room, so that the examiners can deliberate and come to a judgement on your work. This is, naturally, a nerve-wracking time for the candidate (and the supervisor!), not unlike waiting outside the delivery ward of a maternity hospital. The examiners can take as long as they like to come to a decision. Once this is reached, you and your supervisor will be called back into the room and told the outcome. Hopefully, it will be a positive one.

The likelihood of this will be increased by the way in which you conduct yourself and the quality of your arguments during the viva. You are not required to agree with everything the examiner says. Indeed, the examiner will be looking for a high level of original thinking and the ability to take and defend a position, even if the position is opposed to their own. A list of the kinds of questions often posed by examiners is presented in Table 25.6.

What are the 'killer features' that examiners are looking for in a successful thesis? Of course, there could be many, but some of the most common are:

Table 25.6 Examples of questions posed at a viva

What were your reasons for choosing this research topic?	How did you set about dealing with ethical issues?
What do you think is your original contribution to knowledge?	What do you think are the main weaknesses of your work?
What alternative research methodologies did you consider?	What are the major recent developments in your subject area?
How do your findings relate to the literature in your subject area?	What would you do differently if you were to conduct this study again?
What surprises emerged during your research?	How does your methodology fit with your research questions?
Have your opinions changed during the course of this research?	What do you see as the next steps in this research?

Source: Adapted from Rugg, G. and Petre, M. (2004) *The Unwritten Rules of PhD Research.* Reproduced with the kind permission of Open University Press. All rights reserved.

- Has the candidate picked up the key debates in the subject area? Are there any vital sources or debates that have been missed?
- Has the candidate identified the main gaps in the current literature on the research subject? Have these been clearly articulated?
- From these gaps, have a set of research questions been posed? Are they clearly formulated?
- Does the thesis contain helpful signposting to the reader? Is it easy to find one's way about the thesis? Is it always clear what the candidate is trying to achieve in each chapter and section?
- In presenting findings and discussion, does the candidate return to the original questions to answer them?

After the viva

If you have passed the viva and told you are to be awarded your doctorate or similar qualification, then congratulations. If, however, you have some amendments to do, you will be given a time period in which to complete them. First of all, ensure that you actually understand what the recommendations are asking for. If this is not the case, contact your supervisor who will then communicate with the examiners to shed light on the issue.

You may be tempted to rush off and make these changes as quickly as possible to 'get them over with'. It is suggested, however, that you make maximum use of the allowed time to make the changes. In doing this, construct a schedule or plan for completing the amendments.

➤ **TOP TIP 25.5** ◄

To help the examiner, you could construct a two column table, with the required changes itemized in the left-hand column and a description (with page numbers) of what you have changed or added in the right-hand column. This helps the examiner to identify your amendments quickly and efficiently once you have re-submitted.

CASE STUDY 25.2

Surviving the viva

Marion has spent five years on her research and is now about to face the examiner in her viva. She is obviously nervous, but has prepared herself as thoroughly as she could. Not only has she re-read her thesis several times, she has been through a mock viva with her supervisor, with some of her fellow PhD students in attendance. She also presented a short seminar paper at the doctoral students' monthly meeting. The examiner, whom she has never met, is a 'big name' in her field of study, and was recommended by her supervisor.

At the start, everything goes well. Marion finds herself understanding the questions and responding fluently. But suddenly the examiner stuns her with the comment: 'I just don't accept the central argument of your thesis'. He then goes on to elaborate on what he considers this central argument to be, and why it is fatally flawed. Marion feels five years' work ebbing away and her research life about to crumble in ruins. Fortunately, she does not respond immediately, but takes a sip of water, allowing her to collect her thoughts. She recalls the words of her supervisor: 'Whatever happens, don't get defensive. Be positive about your work'. Marion asks the examiner for further clarification of the point he is making. Drawing a deep breath, Marion then unfolds a calm and careful defence of her main ideas. The examiner begins to nod and smile. When Marion finishes her defence, the examiner thanks her and moves on to his next question.

Marion passes her viva. The experience teaches her that there are some examiners who like to 'rough' the candidate up a little, and to provoke a debate. They want to probe just how much the candidate knows and how far they are prepared to defend their position.

ACTIVITY 25.5

Talk to people you know who have been through the viva experience. Ask them how they prepared themselves for the viva, what surprised them and how they coped with any difficulties.

Summary

- If preparing a presentation that will be assessed, keep checking on the assessment criteria and follow them.
- Structure your presentation so that it has a clear beginning, middle and end, and keep to a limited number of key messages.
- Avoid 'death by bullet point'. Try to maximize the use of pictures, graphics and other visual images including the use of visual metaphors.
- In delivering the presentation consider yourself as your best visual aid. Stand confidently and face your audience, making eye contact. Speak clearly with variety in your tone and intonation.
- For team presentations, elect a leader and allocate roles based upon experience and commitment.
- In passing a viva, it helps if the external examiner understands and is not hostile to the research tradition which informs your research methodology.
- If possible, get at least one of your own articles published in the peer reviewed literature.
- Practice by undertaking a mock viva with your supervisor. Know your work thoroughly including its main weaknesses. Prepare to engage in a critical dialogue with the examiner. Remember, you know your research better than anyone in the room!

REVIEW QUESTIONS

1. Think of an effective presentation that you have attended which included the use of a personal story. What was it that made the story memorable or evocative for you? How can you make use of similar stories in your own presentations?
2. Imagine a world without PowerPoint. How would you now present?
3. For a viva, suggest at least three strategies you could use for minimizing the chances of being posed a question that you do not know the answer to.

PRESENTATION

FURTHER READING

Weissman, J. (2011) *Presentations in Action: 80 Memorable Presentation Lessons from the Masters*. Upper Sadle River, NJ: Pearson Education Inc. Presentation coach Jerry Weissman draws on over 20 years of helping top executives give better presentations. Includes telling more effective stories, using the 'elevator' pitch to get over a key idea and handling tough questions.

Potter, S. (ed.) (2006) *Doing Postgraduate Research*. London: Sage. See Chapter 11: 'The Examination Process and the Viva'. Provides a host of practical advice on preparing for and conducting yourself during the viva.

McCarthy, P. and Hatcher, C. (2002) *Presentation Skills: The Essential Guide for Students*. London: Sage. Practical and constructive advice for students that includes, but goes well beyond, how to use technology in making presentations.

JOURNAL RESOURCES

Omerovic, S., Tomazic, S., Milutinovic, M. and Milutinovic, V. (2010) 'Methodology for written and oral presentation of research results', *Journal of Professional Issues in Engineering Education & Practice*, 136(2): 112–117. Highlights an effective method for the organization of research results into written and oral forms.

Wellington, J. (2010) 'Supporting students' preparation for the viva: Their pre-conceptions and implications for practice', *Teaching in Higher Education*, 15(1): 71–84. Pre-viva students express their positive and negative thoughts about the viva process.

Carter, B. and Whittaker, K. (2009) 'Examining the British PhD viva: Opening new doors or scarring for life?', *Contemporary Nurse: A Journal for the Australian Nursing Profession*, 32(1/2): 169–178. Contends that the process of examining a PhD thesis is surrounded by different agendas, ideologies and practices.

Glossary of terms

Accretion measure   A type of unobtrusive measure that arises from the deposit of material (e.g. graffiti or litter) that can be analysed as having a significance.

Action research   Research that involves close collaboration between researchers and practitioners, and which usually aims to achieve measurable, practical benefits for the company, organization or community.

Analysis of variance (ANOVA)   A statistical test used to determine whether there are differences between two or amongst three or more groups on one or more variables. ANOVA is determined using the F-test.

Analytical survey   A survey design that uses a quasi-experimental approach that attempts to measure the impact of independent variables on dependent variables, while controlling for extraneous variables.

Anonymity   An assurance that data will not be traceable to participants in a research project.

A priori   A term indicating an idea is derived from theory rather than practice.

Areas of acceptance or rejection   For a one-tailed hypothesis test, the area of rejection is either the upper or lower tail of the distribution. For a two-tailed test both tails are used.

Association   The tendency of two events to occur together. When applied to variables it is more usual to refer to this as a correlation.

Audit trail   The presentation of material gathered within a naturalistic enquiry that allows other researchers to trace the original researcher's analysis and conclusions.

Axial coding   A type of coding that treats a category as an axis around which the researcher delineates relationships and specifies the dimensions of the category.

Bias   In general, any influence that distorts the results of a study. In statistics, a case of systematic error in a statistical result.

Case study   A research design focusing on one person or sample. Case studies provide limited information on a single issue, person or organization. There are dangers in generalizing from such limited samples, but results may be indicative of trends.

Categorical data   Data that include both nominal and ordinal data.

Cell   Area containing values in a table of data.

Census   The measurement of a complete population rather than a sample – particularly useful when researching organizations.

Chi-square distribution   Statistical test used with nominal data to determine if patterns or characteristics are common across populations.

Chi-square test   How well observed data fit an expected or theoretical distribution.

Closed question   A question where the possible answers are predetermined.

Cluster sampling   A sampling strategy involving successive sampling of units or clusters, progressing from larger units to smaller ones.

Coding   The process of transforming raw data into a standardized format for data analysis. In quantitative research this means attaching numerical values to categories; in qualitative research it means identifying recurrent words, concepts or themes.

Coding frame   A template of key coding instructions for each variable in a study (e.g. Agree = 1).

Confidence interval   This identifies a range of values that includes the true population value of a particular characteristic at a specified probability level (usually 95 per cent).

Confounding variable   A variable, other than the variable(s) under investigation, which may distort the results of experimental research, and so has to be controlled for.

Constant comparison method   A method of qualitative analysis that generates successively more abstract concepts and theories through the inductive process of comparing data with data, data with categories, categories with categories and categories with concepts.

Construct   The particular way in which an individual expresses meaning about a concept.

Constructivism   A perspective that assumes that people construct the realities in which they participate.

Construct validity   The extent to which an instrument measures a theoretical concept (construct) under investigation.

Content analysis   The examination of qualitative data by either qualitative or quantitative methods by systematically identifying special characteristics (classes or categories).

Content validity   An estimate of the extent to which a research tool takes items from the subject domain being addressed, including not only cognitive topics but also behaviours.

Contingency table   A display of frequencies for two or more variables.

Control group   As part of an experimental design, a group *not* given the intervention so that the effects of the intervention on the experimental group can be compared with it.

Convenience sampling   A non-probability sampling strategy that uses the most conveniently accessible people to participate in the study.

Conversational analysis   The formal analysis of everyday conversations, often based upon transcribed tape recordings.

Core category   The central category that is used in grounded theory to integrate all the categories identified.

Correlation   The extent of an association between and among interdependent variables such that when one variable changes, so does the other. Variables that are independent are not correlated.

Correlation coefficient (r)   A measure of the linear relationship between two numerical values made on the same set of variables. It ranges from –1 (a perfectly negative relationship) to +1 (a perfectly positive relationship), with 0 meaning no relationship. Linear relationships can be measured by Pearson's product moment correlation; changes in one variable causing changes in another in a fixed direction can be measured by Kendall's coefficient of rank correlation or Spearman's rank correlation coefficient.

Covert participant   Someone who participates in the activities of a research study without revealing his or her identity as a researcher.

Credibility   Seen by some supporters of qualitative approaches an more important than validity or reliability. Established through building confidence in the accuracy of data gathering and interpretation.

Criterion-related validity   Assessed through comparing the scores on an instrument with one or more external criteria such as a well-established existing test.

Critical inquiry   A process which questions currently held values and challenges conventional social structures.

Cross-sectional study   A study in which data are collected at one time only, usually for a large number of cases.

Data   Findings and results which, if meaningful, become information.

Data saturation   The point at which data collection can cease, because data have become repetitive with the emergence of no new themes or ideas.

Deduction   Drawing logical conclusions through the process of reasoning, working from the general to the specific.

Deductive approach   Experimental approach that uses a priori questions or hypotheses that the research will test.

Degrees of freedom (df)   The number of components in results that are free to vary. Measured by the number of categories minus 1.

Dependent variable   A variable that forms the focus of research, and depends on another (the independent or explanatory) variable.

Descriptive statistics   Statistical methods used to describe data collected from a specific sample (e.g. mean, mode, median, range, standard deviation).

Design   An approach to the collection of data that combines a validity of results with an economy of effort. Includes decisions on the case site, sample, data collection and analysis.

Deviation   The difference between the value of a variable and the mean of its distribution.

Discourse analysis   The study of how both spoken and written language is used in social contexts.

Emic   Specific language or cultural distinctions, meaningful to a cultural group (as opposed to etic, ideas meaningful to researchers). An insider's view of reality.

Empirical   Research methods in which data are collected.

Empirical data   The results of experiments or observations used to check the validity of assertions.

Episodic records   Archival records that are insufficiently complete to allow for the identification of trends.

Epistemology   A branch of philosophy that considers the criteria for determining what constitutes and what does not constitute valid knowledge.

Ethics   The study of standards of conduct and values, and in research, how these impact on both the researcher and research subjects.

Ethnography   A qualitative approach that seeks out the perspectives about the culture of individuals, groups or systems occurring in settings or 'fields'. Originally associated with anthropology and sociology.

Ethnomethodology   A research tradition that argues that people continually redefine themselves through their interactions with others.

Etic   Ideas meaningful to researchers (as opposed to emic, language and cultural distinctions meaningful to a cultural group). An outsider's view of reality.

Evaluation   The systematic collection of data about the characteristics of a programme, product, policy or service. Often performed to identify opportunities for change and improvement.

Expected frequencies   Frequencies that are observed in a contingency table if the null hypothesis is true.

Experimental group   In experimental research, the group of subjects who receive the experimental treatment, in contrast to the control group who do not.

Experimental research   A research methodology based upon cause-and-effect relationships between independent and dependent variables by means of the manipulation of independent variables, control and randomization.

External validity   The extent to which research results can be generalized to the population as a whole.

Extraneous variable   A variable that needs to be controlled for because it has the potential to adversely affect the results of a study.

Face validity   The extent to which a measuring instrument appears to be measuring what it claims to measure.

Field notes   Notes written when conducting interviews or observations in the field. They may include the researcher's personal comments or interpretations.

Fieldwork   The gathering of data at a research site.

Filter question   A question designed to exclude some respondents or direct them to later questions in a questionnaire.

Fisher's exact test   Used to test the null hypothesis that nominal characteristics are not associated. Usually used when the sample size is too small for the chi-square test.

Focus group   A group interview, usually framed around one issue.

Frequency count   Calculation of frequencies to determine how many items fit into a category (e.g. number of sales per product, members of a team, men and women in the workforce).

Gatekeepers   Individuals who have the power or influence to grant or refuse access to a field or research setting.

Generalizability   The extent to which the results of a study based upon evidence drawn from a sample can be applied to a population as a whole. Often referred to as external validity.

Goodness-of-fit   How well a given set of data fit a distribution. It may be measured by the chi-square statistic.

Grounded theory   An inductive approach to the analysis of qualitative data involving open, axial and selective coding.

Hermeneutics   An approach based on the interpretation of literary texts and human behaviour.

Heuristic inquiry   A process of open-ended inquiry that begins with a question that is usually focused on an issue that has posed a personal problem for the researcher.

Hypothesis   A statement that should be capable of measurement about the relation between two or more variables. Testing hypotheses, and especially the null hypothesis, is part of inferential statistics.

Ideographic   An approach that emphasizes that explanation of human behaviour is only possible through gaining access to participants' subjective interpretations or culture.

Independent variable   Used to explain or predict a result or outcome on the dependent variable.

Induction   The development of theory or inferences from observed or empirical reality. It is associated with naturalism and the 'grounded theory' approach to theory formation. It is the opposite of deduction.

Inductive approach   The establishment of facts on which theories or concepts are later built, moving from specifics to generalizations.

Inference   An assertion made on the basis of something else observed.

Inferential statistics   Used to draw inferences from a sample being studied to a larger population that the sample is drawn from.

Informed consent   The obtaining of voluntary participation in a research project based on a full understanding of the likely benefits and risks.

Instrument   A tool such as a questionnaire, survey or observation schedule used to gather data as part of a research project.

Inter-judge reliability   The extent to which two or more observers agree on what they have seen.

Internal validity   The extent to which changes in the dependent variable can be attributed to the independent variable, rather than to an extraneous variable.

Interpretivism   Interpretations of the world are culturally derived and historically situated. Interpretivist approaches include symbolic interactionism, phenomenology, hermeneutics and naturalistic inquiry.

Interval scale   A quantifiable, continuous scale that has an arbitrary zero point (for example, the Fahrenheit and Celsius temperature scales). Unlike ratio scales (where a score of 120 represents a figure twice as large as a score of 60), an IQ score of 120 (interval data) is not twice as large as one of 60.

Intervening variable   A hypothetical internal state that is used to explain relationships between observed variables.

Leading question   A question that suggests a possible answer, and hence promotes bias.

Likert scale   A scale in which items represent different sub-concepts of the measured object and responses are presented to indicate different degrees of agreement or disagreement with the item.

Linearity   An assumption that the relationship between variables is linear.

Literature review   The selection of documents (published and unpublished) on a topic, that contain information, ideas and evidence, and the evaluation of these documents in relation to a particular piece of research.

Longitudinal study   A research study that examines phenomena over a relatively long period of time.

Manipulation   Intentionally changing the value of an independent variable.

Mann-Whitney U test   See Wilcoxon signed-rank test.

Maturation   A threat to internal validity caused by changes in the value of the dependent variable that occurs without any intervention by the researcher.

Mean   The arithmetic average of observations. A measure of central tendency for interval or ratio data.

Measure of central tendency   Used in descriptive statistics, comprising measures of the mean, median and mode.

Measures of dispersion   Descriptive statistics that describe the spread of numerical data. They include measures of the range, standard deviation and percentiles.

Median A measure of central tendency where 50 per cent of observations are above it and 50 per cent below.

Method The systematic approach towards the collection of data so that information can be obtained.

Methodology The analysis of, and the broad philosophical and theoretical justification for, a particular method used in research, for example, action research.

Mode A measure of central tendency comprising the value of the observation that occurs most frequently.

Mortality A threat to the validity of the research caused by subjects prematurely withdrawing from the study.

Narratives The use of oral or life histories to capture personal lived experiences.

Naturalistic paradigm A paradigm that assumes that there are multiple interpretations of reality and that the goal of researchers is to work with people to understand how they construct their own reality within a social context.

Nominal scale Describes characteristics that have no numerical value (e.g. the name of organizations, products, departments, etc.). Sometimes referred to as a categorical scale.

Nomothetic Approaches that seek to construct a deductively tested set of general theories that explain and predict human behaviour. It is the opposite of ideographic.

Non-parametric tests Tests that do not make any assumption that the population is normally distributed (sometimes called distribution-free tests). These include all tests involving the ranking of data, including Kendall's rank correlation and Spearman's rho.

Non-probability sampling Techniques used to draw a sample in such a way that the findings will require judgement and interpretation before being applied to a population. Often necessary in practice.

Normal distribution Based on the assumption that the distribution of a population will be a smooth, bell-shaped curve that is symmetric around the mean and where the mean, median and mode are equal. Symbolized by the Greek letter mu (m).

Null hypothesis (H_0) A statement of the relationship between two variables which argues that no difference exists in the means, scores or other numerical values obtained for the two groups. These differences are statistically significant when the null hypothesis is rejected – suggesting that a difference does, in fact, exist.

Observed frequencies Frequency scores actually obtained through research – in contrast to expected frequencies (see above).

One-sample *t*-test See paired *t*-test.

One-tailed test The area of a normal distribution curve showing the region of rejection for the null hypothesis where the direction predicted by the hypothesis is known.

One-way ANOVA Used to test for differences for studies with one dependent variable with ratio or interval data. This test uses the *F*-statistic.

Ontology The study of the essence of phenomena and the nature of their existence.

Open question A question without fixed categories of answers.

Operational definition A concise statement that assigns meaning to a construct or variable by specifying the activities necessary to measure it.

Ordinal scale An ordering or ranking of values with no implication that the differences between the values are equal. Examples include: Strongly agree, Agree, Disagree and Strongly disagree; Frequently, Often, Sometimes, Never.

Outliers An observation that is numerically distant from the rest of the data.

Paired sample Two samples in which each member is paired with a member in the other sample (e.g. comparing the output of two groups of assembly-line workers). The paired *t*-test is used to measure whether any differences on the random variable (e.g. output) are significant.

Paired *t*-test or a one-sample *t*-test Compares the difference or changes in ratio or interval variables that is observed for two paired or matched groups. It can also be used for before and after measures on the same group.

Paradigm A perspective or world view based upon sets of values and philosophical assumptions, from which distinctive conceptualizations and explanations of phenomena are proposed.

Parameter The population value of a distribution such as the mean.

Parametric test Tests that assume that the data for a population are normally distributed. Examples include *t*-tests and the *F*-test. To be used for interval and ratio numerical data, but not ordinal data.

Participant observation Qualitative research, when a researcher both collects data and becomes involved in the site of the study.

Participatory action research   A research tradition in which people themselves act as participants to investigate their own reality.

Pearson product-moment   A statistical formula for calculating the correlation coefficient between two variables. Assumes that both variables are interval and that the relationship between them is linear.

Percentile   A number that indicates the percentage of a distribution that is above or below that number. A statement that a person scored on the 75th percentile indicates that 75 per cent of the others scored the same or below this.

Phenomenology   The search for how participants experience and give meaning to an event, concept or phenomenon.

Pilot survey   A small-scale survey carried out before a large-scale one to evaluate processes and research tools such as questionnaires.

Plausibility   An assessment of whether any truth claim is likely to be true, given the present state of knowledge. Associated with postmodern critiques.

Population   The totality of people, organizations, objects or occurrences from which a sample is drawn.

Positivism   A philosophical assumption that the purpose of theory is application, that the truth can be distinguished from untruth, and that the truth can be determined by either deduction or by empirical support.

Postal survey   A survey in which survey instruments such as questionnaires are distributed by post.

Postmodernism   A set of theories that argue that objective truth is unobtainable. All we have is 'truth claims' that are partial, partisan and incomplete.

Post-positivist   Sometimes referred to as anti-positivist, a research tradition that rejects the belief that human behaviour can be investigated through the use of the methods of scientific inquiry.

Post-test   A test that occurs after a treatment has been administered in an experimental study.

Predictive validity   The extent to which scores on an instrument can predict a subject's future behaviour in relation to the test's content (e.g. do scores on an engineering aptitude test predict the ability to perform engineering tasks?)

Pre-test   A test that occurs before a treatment has been administered in an experimental study.

Probability sampling Techniques used to ensure that a sample is representative of the population, so that findings can be generalized to that population.

Probe An interviewing technique in which the interviewer seeks clarification and elaboration of a respondent's answers.

Proposition A formal statement that relates two or more concepts.

Purposive sampling A non-probability sampling strategy in which participants are selected on the basis that they are considered to be typical of a wider population.

p-value The probability value that helps to determine the significance of a statistical test. A small p-value (typically ≤ 0.05) indicates strong evidence against the null hypothesis.

Qualitative methods Techniques by which qualitative data are collected and analysed.

Quantitative methods The systematic and mathematical techniques used to collect and analyse quantitative data.

Quasi-experimental design Approach using elements of experimental design such as the use of a control group, but without the ability to randomly select the sample.

Quota sampling A non-probability sampling strategy in which various strata are identified by the researcher who ensures that these strata are proportionately represented within the sample to improve its representativeness.

Random probability sampling The method of drawing a proportion of a population such that all *possible* samples have the same probability of being selected.

Range The difference between the largest observation and the smallest in a sample of a set of variables.

Rank The position of a member of a set in an order.

Ratio scales A measurement in which equal differences between points correspond to equal differences on the scale. Used for characteristics where there is an absolute zero point that does have some meaning, that is, an absence of the construct being measured (in contrast to interval scales where the zero is arbitrary) – for example, zero length on a ruler.

Reactivity The potential for the behaviour of research subjects to change due to the presence of the researcher.

Realism A research philosophy that presumes that a knowable, objective reality exists.

Reflexivity   The monitoring by a researcher of her or his impact on the research situation being investigated. A stance associated with postmodernism and anti-realism.

Reliability   The degree to which an instrument will produce similar results at a different period.

Representative sample   A sample in which individuals are included in proportion to the number of those in the population who are like them.

Research design   A strategic plan for a research project, setting out the broad structures and features of the research.

Research methodology   Approaches to systematic inquiry developed within a particular paradigm with associated epistemological assumptions (e.g. experimental research, survey research, grounded theory, action research).

Research question   A specific formulation of the issues that a research project will address, often describing general relationships between and among variables that are to be tested.

r-square   The square of the correlation between the response values and the predicted response values.

Sample   A set of objects, occurrences or individuals selected from a parent population for a research study.

Sampling error   The fluctuations in the value of a statistic from different samples drawn from the same population.

Sampling frame   A complete list of the people or entities in the entire population to be addressed by a research study, from which a random sample will be drawn.

Secondary data analysis   A reworking of data that have already been analysed to present interpretations, conclusions or knowledge additional to, or different from, those originally presented.

Significance level   The probability of rejecting a true null hypothesis. This should be chosen before a test is performed and is called the alpha value (a). Alpha values are usually kept small (0.05, 0.01 or 0.001), because it is important not to reject the null hypothesis when it is true (a Type I error), that is, there is no difference between the means of the groups being measured.

Skewed distribution   An asymmetrical distribution, positively skewed meaning the larger frequencies being concentrated towards the lower end of the variable, and negatively skewed, towards the higher end.

Snowball sampling   A non-probability sampling strategy through which the first group of participants is used to nominate the next cohort of participants.

Spearman's rank-order correlation (Spearman's)   Used to describe the relationship between two ordinal characteristics or one ordinal and one ratio/interval (rho) characteristic. Represented by the symbol r_s.

Standard distribution   The distribution that occurs when a normal random variable has a mean of zero and a standard deviation of one.

Standard deviation   A measure of the spread of data about the mean (average), symbolized by the Greek letter sigma (s), or the square root of the variance.

Statistical inference   A procedure using the laws of probability to generalize the findings from a sample to an entire population from which the sample was drawn.

Statistical significance   *See* Significance level.

Statistical validity   The extent to which a study has made use of the appropriate design and statistical methods.

Stratified random sampling   Drawing a sample from a specified stratum – for example, from a company's rural, out-of-town and town centre stores.

Subject error   A measure of the scores achieved on a test that is taken at two different time periods.

Subjects   A term most frequently used in positivist research to describe those who participate in a research study.

Survey   An investigation into one or more variables in a population that may involve the collection of both qualitative and quantitative data.

Symbolic interactionism   A school of sociology in which people are seen as developing a sense of identity through their interactions and communication with others.

Theoretical sampling   The selection of participants within a naturalistic inquiry, based on emerging findings during the progress of the study to ensure that key variables are adequately represented.

Theoretical sensitivity   Often used in grounded theory, involves maintaining an awareness of the subtleties of meaning in data.

Thick description   A detailed account of life 'inside' a field of study. Associated with humanistic ethnography but rejected by postmodern ethnography as just selective or partial descriptions.

Time sampling   An observational method in which data are collected at periodic intervals.

Time series   A set of measures on a single variable collected over time.

Traces   An unobtrusive measure in which physical evidence is collected to provide evidence about social behaviour.

Triangulation   The use of a variety of methods or data sources to examine a specific phenomenon either simultaneously or sequentially in order to improve the reliability of data.

_t_-test   A test used on the means of small samples to measure whether the samples have both been drawn from the same parent population.

Two-tailed test   The two areas of a normal distribution curve showing the regions of rejection for the null hypothesis where the direction predicted by the hypothesis is not known (hence the need for two tails).

Type I error   An error that occurs when the null hypothesis is rejected when it is true and a researcher concludes that a statistically significant relationship exists when it does not.

Type II error   An error that occurs when the null hypothesis is accepted when it is false and a researcher concludes that no significant relationship exists when it does.

Unit of analysis   The set of objects (individuals, organizations or events) on which the research is focused.

Unobtrusive measures   A non-reactive method of data collection using sources such as archives, documents or the Web.

Validity   The degree to which data in a research study are accurate and credible.

Variable   A characteristic that is measurable, such as income, attitude, colour, etc.

Variance   The differences measured in repeated trials of a procedure. The standard deviation squared – a measure of dispersion.

Verification   Drawing the implications from a set of empirical conclusions to theory.

Wilcoxon signed-rank test   A non-parametric test for comparing ordinal data from two dependent samples or interval/ratio data that is not normally distributed.

References

Abrams, L.S. (2010) 'Sampling "hard to reach" populations in qualitative research: The case of incarcerated youth', *Qualitative Social Work*, 9: 536–550.

Albaum, G., Wiley, J., Roster, C. and Smith, S.M. (2011) 'Visiting item non-responses in internet survey data collection', *International Journal of Market Research*, 53(5): 687–703.

Alcadipani, R. and Hodgson, D. (2009) 'By any means necessary? Ethnographic access, ethics and the critical researcher', *Tamara Journal*, 7(4): 127–146.

Alderson, P. and Morrow, V. (2006) 'Multidisciplinary research ethics review: Is it feasible?', *International Journal of Social Research Methodology*, 9(5): 405–417.

Alford, R.R. (1998) *The Craft of Inquiry: Theory, Methods, Evidence*. New York: Oxford University Press.

Allen, H. (1997) 'Reflexivity: A comment on feminist ethnography', *Journal of Research in Nursing*, 2(6): 455–467.

Alvesson, M. and Deetz, S. (2000) *Doing Critical Management Research*. London: Sage.

American Psychological Association (1992) *American Psychological Association Ethical Principles of Psychologists and Code of Conduct*. Available from: http://www.apa.org/ethics/code.html#materials. Accessed 23 November 2001.

Anderson, L. (1999) 'The open road to ethnography's future', *Journal of Contemporary Ethnography*, 28: 451–459.

Anderson, T. and Kanuka, H. (2003) *e-Research: Methods, Strategies, and Issues*. Boston, MA: Allyn & Bacon.

Arksey, H. and Knight, P. (1999) *Interviewing for Social Scientists*. London: Sage.

Asad, T. (1973) *Anthropology and the Colonial Encounter*. London: Macmillan.

Atkinson, P.A. (1990) *The Ethnographic Imagination: Textual Constructions of Reality*. London: Routledge.

Atkinson, P.A. (1992) *Understanding Ethnographic Texts*. Newbury Park, CA: Sage.

Atkinson, P.A. and Coffey, A. (2004) 'Analysing documentary realities', in D. Silverman (ed.), *Qualitative Research: Theory, Methods and Practice*, 2nd edn. London: Sage.

Atkinson, P. and Hammersley, M. (1994) 'Ethnography and participant observation', in P. Atkinson and M. Hammersley (eds), *Handbook of Qualitative Research*. Thousand Oaks, CA: Sage.

Atkinson, P. and Hammersley, M. (2004) 'Ethnography and participant observation', in N.K. Denzin and Y.S. Lincoln (eds), *Strategies of Qualitative Inquiry*, 2nd edn. Thousand Oaks, CA: Sage. pp. 134–164.

Avison, D., Baskerville, R. and Myers, M. (2001) 'Controlling action research projects', *Information Technology and People*, 14(1): 28–45.

Baake, K. (2007) 'Decision-making in a quasi-rational world: Teaching technical, narratological, and rhetorical discourse in report writing', *IEEE Transactions on Professional Communication*, 50(2): 163–171.

Badger, T.G. (2000) 'Action research, change and methodological rigour', *Journal of Nursing Management*, 8: 201–207.

Bailey, C.A. (2007) *A Guide to Field Research*, 2nd edn. Thousand Oaks, CA: Pine Forge Press.

Bailey, K.M. (1983) 'Competitiveness and anxiety in adult second language learning: Looking at and through the diary studies', in H. Seliger and M. Long (eds), *Classroom-Orientated Research in Second Language Acquisition*. Rowley, MA: Newbury House. pp. 67–103.

Bajpai, N. (2010) *Business Statistics*. New Delhi: Dorling Kindersley.

Bales, R.F. (1950) *Interaction Process Analysis: A Method for the Study of Small Groups*. London: University of Chicago Press.

Ballantine, J., Levy, M., Martin, A., Munro, I. and Powell, P. (2000) 'An ethical perspective on information systems evaluation', *International Journal of Agile Management Systems*, 2(3): 233–241.

Barbour, R.S. (1999) 'Are focus groups an appropriate tool for studying organizational change?', in J. Kitzinger and R.S. Barbour (eds), *Developing Focus Group Research: Politics, Theory and Practice*. London: Sage.

Barker, V. (2006) 'The politics of punishing: Building a state governance theory of American imprisonment variation', *Punishment & Society*, 8(5): 5–32.

Bartlett, J.E., Kotrlik, J.W. and Higgins, C.C. (2001) 'Organizational research: Determining appropriate sample size in survey research', *Information Technology, Learning and Performance Journal*, 19(1): 43–50.

Bartunek, J.M. and Myeong-Gu, S. (2002) 'Qualitative research can add new meanings to quantitative research', *Journal of Organizational Behavior*, 23(2): 237–242.

Basch, C.E. (1987) 'Focus group interviews: An underutilized research technique for improving theory and practice in health education', *Health Education Quarterly*, 14: 411–448.

Beaudin, C.I and Pelletier, L.R. (1996) 'Consumer-based research: Using focus groups as a method for evaluating quality of care', *Journal of Nursing Care Quality*, 10: 28–33.

Beed, T.W. and Stimson, R.J. (1985) (eds) *Survey Interviewing: Theory and Techniques*. North Sydney: George Allen & Unwin.

Begley, C.M. (1996) 'Using triangulation in nursing research', *Journal of Advanced Nursing*, 24: 122–128.

Bell, E. and Bryman, A. (2007) 'The ethics of management research: An exploratory content analysis', *British Journal of Management*, 18(1): 163–177.

Bennett, A. (2005) *Culture and Everyday Life*. London: Sage.

Berg, B.L. (2006) *Qualitative Research Methods for the Social Sciences*, 6th edn. Needham Heights, MA: Allyn & Bacon.

Berger, L. (2001) 'Inside out: Narrative autoethnography as a path toward rapport', *Qualitative Inquiry*, 7(4): 504–518.

Berry, K. (2011) 'The ethnographer's choice: Why ethnographers do ethnography', *Cultural Studies*, 11(2): 169–177.

Berry, R. (2004) *The Research Project: How To Write It*, 5th edn. London: Routledge.

Biemer, P.P. (2010) 'Total survey error: Design, implementation and evaluation', *Public Opinion Quarterly*, 74(5): 817–848.

Biernacki, P. and Waldorf, D. (1981) 'Snowballing sampling: Problems and techniques of chain referral sampling', *Sociological Methods & Research*, 10(2): 141–163.

Billingham, J. (2003) *Giving Presentations*. Oxford: OUP.

Bishop, L. (2007) 'A reflexive account of reusing qualitative data: Beyond primary/secondary dualism', *Sociological Research Online*, 12(3): 2.

Black, T.R. (1993) *Evaluating Social Science Research*. London: Sage.

Black, T.R. (1999) *Doing Quantitative Research*. London: Sage.

Blumberg, B., Cooper, D.R. and Schindler, P.S. (2005) *Business Research Methods*. Maidenhead: McGraw-Hill Education.

Blumer, H. (1969) *Symbolic Interactionism: Perspectives and Methods*. Englewood Cliffs, NJ: Prentice-Hall.

Blumstein, P. and Schwartz, P. (1983) *American Couples: Money, Work, Sex*. New York: William Morrow.

Boote, D.N. and Beile, P. (2005) 'Scholars before researchers: On the centrality of the dissertation literature review in research preparation', *Educational Researcher*, 34(6): 3–15.

Boote, J. and Mathews, A. (1999) '"Saying is one thing: doing is another": The role of observation in marketing research', *Qualitative Market Research: An International Journal*, 2(1): 15–21.

Booth, P.F. (1991) *Report Writing*, 2nd edn. Huntingdon: Elm Publications.

Bord Bia (2012) *Indonesia & Vietnam: An Ethnographic Study Exploring the Consumer Landscape and Opportunities for the Irish Dairy Industry*. Bord Bia: Dublin.

Bosk, C. (2004) 'The ethnographer and the IRB: Comments on Kevin D. Haggerty, "Ethics Creep: Governing Social Science Research in the Name of Ethics"', *Qualitative Sociology*, 27(4): 417–420.

Boslaugh, S. (2007) *Secondary Data Sources for Public Health*. Cambridge: Cambridge University Press.

Bourgois, P. and Schonberg, J. (2009) *Righteous Dopefiend*. Berkeley: University of California Press.

Bowling, A. (1997) *Research Methods in Health*. Buckingham: Open University Press.

Bradbury-Jones, C., Sambrook, S. and Irvine, F. (2009) 'The phenomenological focus group: An oxymoron?', *Journal of Advanced Nursing*, 65(3): 663–671.

Bramley, P. and Kitson, B. (1994) 'Evaluating training against business criteria', *Journal of European Industrial Training*, 18(1): 10–14.

Brannick, T. and Coghlan, D. (2007) 'Reflexivity in management and business research: What do we mean?', *The Irish Journal of Management*, 27(2): 143–160.

Braun, V. and Clarke, V. (2006) 'Using thematic analysis in psychology', *Qualitative Research in Psychology*, 3(2): 77–101.

Brennan, J. (1992) *Mixing Methods: Qualitative and Quantitative Research*. Aldershot: Ashgate.

Brennan, M. and Charbonneau, J. (2009) 'Improving mail survey response rates using chocolate and replacement questionnaires', *Public Opinion Quarterly*, 73(2): 368–378.

Brewer, J.D. (2000) *Ethnography*. Buckingham: Open University Press.

Brinkerhoff, R.O. (2006) *Telling Training's Story: Evaluation made Simple, Credible, and Effective*. San Francisco: Berrett-Koehler Publishers, Inc.

Brunt, L. (2001) 'Into the community', in P. Atkinson, A. Coffey, S. Delmont, J. Lofland and L. Lofland (eds), *Handbook of Ethnography*. London: Sage.

Bryman, A. (1988) *Quantity and Quality in Social Research*. London: Routledge.

Bryman, A. (1992) 'Quantitative and qualitative research: Further reflections on their integration', in J. Brannen (ed.), *Mixing Methods: Qualitative and Quantitative Research*. Aldershot: Avebury.

Bryman, A. (1999) 'The debate about quantitative and qualitative research', in A. Bryman and R.G. Burgess (eds), *Qualitative Research*. London: Sage. pp. 35–69.

Bryman, A. (2006) 'Integrating quantitative and qualitative research: How is it done?', *Qualitative Research*, 6: 97–113.

Bryman, A. (2007a) *Quantity and Quality in Social Research*. London: Taylor and Francis.

Bryman, A. (2007b) 'Barriers to integrating quantitative and qualitative research', *Journal of Mixed Methods Research*, 1(1): 8–22.

Bryman, A. and Bell, E. (2007) *Business Research Methods*, 2nd edn. Oxford: Oxford University Press.

Bulmer, M. (1984) *The Chicago School of Sociology: Institutionalization, Diversity, and the Rise of Sociological Research*. Chicago: University of Chicago Press.

Bunge, M. (1993) 'Realism and antirealism in social science', *Theory and Decision*, 35: 207–235.

Burgess, R.G. (1984) *In the Field: An Introduction to Field Research*. London: Routledge.

Campbell, C.P. (1997) 'Training course/program evaluation: Principles and practice', *Journal of European Industrial Training*, 22(8): 323–344.

Campbell, D.T. and Fiske, D. (1959) 'Convergent and discriminant validation by the multitrait-multimethod matrix', *Psychological Bulletin*, 56: 81–105.

Campbell, D.T. and Stanley, J.C. (1963) *Experimental and Quasi-experimental Designs for Research*. Chicago, IL: Rand McNally.

Cannell, C.F. (1985) 'Overview: Response bias and interviewer variability in surveys', in T.W. Beed and R.J. Stimson (eds), *Survey Interviewing: Theory and Techniques*. North Sydney: George Allen & Unwin.

Carrigan, M. and Kirkup, M. (2001) 'The ethical responsibility of marketers in retail observational research: Protecting stakeholders through the ethical "research covenant"', *International Review of Retail, Distribution and Consumer Research*, 11(4): 415–435.

Carroll, S. (1994) 'Questionnaire design affects response rate', *Marketing News*, 28(12): 25–27.

Cassell, J. (1982) 'Harms, benefits, wrongs and rights in fieldwork', in J.E. Sieber (ed.), *The Ethics of Social Research: Fieldwork, Regulation and Publication*. New York: Springer-Verlag.

Charmaz, K. (1995) 'Grounded theory', in J.A. Smith, R. Harré and L.V. Langenhove (eds), *Rethinking Methods in Psychology*. London: Sage.

Charmaz, K. (2013) *Constructing Grounded Theory*. 2nd edn. London: Sage.

Chenitz, W.C. and Swanson, J.M. (1986) *From Practice to Grounded Theory. Qualitative Research in Nursing*. Mass: Addison-Wesley.

Chia, R. (2002) 'The production of management knowledge: Philosophical underpinnings of research design', in D. Partington (ed.), *Essential Skills for Management Research*. London: Sage.

Clark, L. (2009) 'Focus group research with children and youth', *Journal for Specialists in Paediatric Nursing*, 14(2): 152–154.

Clarke, A. (1999) *Evaluation Research: An Introduction to Principles, Methods and Practice*. London: Sage.

Coffey, A. (1999) *The Ethnographic Self*. London: Sage.

Coghlan, D. (2001) 'Insider action research projects: Implications for practising managers', *Management Learning*, 32(1): 49–60.

Coghlan, D. and Brannick, T. (2010) *Doing Action Research in Your Own Organization*, 3rd edn. London: Sage.

Cohen, J.W. (1988) *Statistical Power Analysis for the Behavioural Sciences*, 2nd edn. Hillsdale, NJ: Lawrence Erlbaum Associates.

Cohen, L. and Manion, L. (2011) *Research Methods in Education*, 7th edn. London: Routledge.

Collins, K.M.T., Onwuegbuzie, A.J., and Jiao, Q.G. (2006) 'Prevalence of mixed methods sampling designs in social science research', *Evaluation and Research in Education*, 19(2), 83–101.

Cook, T.D. and Campbell, D.T. (1979) *Quasi-experimentation: Design and Analysis Issues for Field Settings*. Rand McNally: Chicago, Illinois.

Copas, A.J. and Farewell, V.T. (1998) 'Dealing with non-ignorable non-response by using an "enthusiasm-to-respond" variable', *Journal of the Royal Statistical Society*, 161(3): 385–396.

Cope, J. and Watts, G. (2000) 'Learning by doing: An exploration of experience, critical incidents and reflection in entrepreneurial learning', *International Journal of Entrepreneurial Behaviour & Research*, 6(3): 104–124.

Costa, A.L. and Kallick, B. (1993) 'Through the lens of a critical friend', *Educational Leadership*, 52(2): 49–51.

Coulon, A. (1995) *Ethnomethodology*. London: Sage.

Coyne, I.T. (1997) 'Sampling in qualitative research. Purposeful and theoretical sampling; merging or clear boundaries?', *Journal of Advanced Nursing*, 26: 623–630.

Cranny-Francis, A., Waring, W., Stavropoulos, P. and Kirkby, J. (2003) *Gender Studies: Terms and Debates*. Basingstoke: Palgrave Macmillan.

Cressey, P. (1932) *The Taxi-Dance Hall*. Chicago, IL: University of Chicago Press.

Creswell, J.W. (2009) *Research Design: Qualitative, Quantitative and Mixed Methods Approaches*, 3rd edn. Thousand Oaks, CA: Sage.

Creswell, J.W., Plano Clark, V., Gutmann, M. and Hanson, W. (2003) 'Advances in mixed methods design', in A. Tashakkori and C. Teddlie (eds), *Handbook of Mixed Methods in the Social and Behavioural Sciences*. Thousand Oaks, CA: Sage.

Crotty, M. (1998) *The Foundation of Social Research: Meaning and Perspectives in the Research Process*. London: Sage.

Crow, G., Wiles, R., Heath, S. and Charles, V. (2006) 'Research ethics and data quality: The implications of informed consent', *International Journal of Social Research Methodology*, 9(2): 83–95.

Czaja, R. and Blair, J. (2005) *Designing Surveys: A Guide to Decisions and Procedures*. Thousand Oaks, CA: Sage.

Darlington, Y. and Scott, D. (2002) *Qualitative Research in Practice: Stories from the Field*. Buckingham: Open University Press.

Dattalo, C. (2010) *Strategies to Approximate Random Sampling and Assignment*. New York: Oxford University Press.

Davies, D. and Dodd, J. (2002) 'Qualitative research and the question of rigor', *Qualitative Health Research*, 12(2): 279–289.

Davies, S. (2001) 'New techniques and technologies of surveillance in the workplace', Computer Security Research Centre, The London School of Economics. Available from: www.msf-itpa. org.uk/juneconf3.shtml. Accessed 17 November 2012.

de Laine, M. (2000) *Fieldwork, Participation and Practice*. London: Sage.

Delanty, G. (1997) *Social Science: Beyond Constructivism and Realism*, 2nd edn. Buckingham: Open University Press.

Dellinger, A.B. and Leech, N.L. (2007) 'Toward a unified framework in mixed methods research', *Journal of Mixed Methods Research*, 1(4): 309–332.

DeLorme, D.E., Zinkhan, G.M. and French, W. (2001) 'Ethics and the internet: Issues associated with qualitative research', *Journal of Business Ethics*, 33: 271–286.

Denzin, N.K. (1978) *Sociological Methods: A Sourcebook*, 2nd edn. New York: McGraw-Hill.

Denzin, N.K. (1989) *Sociological Methods*. New York: McGraw-Hill.

Denzin, N.K. (1990) 'The spaces of postmodernism: Reading Plummer on Blumer', *Symbolic Interactionism*, 13: 145–154.

Denzin, N.K. (1999) 'Interpretive ethnography for the next century', *Journal of Contemporary Ethnography*, 28(5): 510–519.

Denzin, N.K. and Lincoln, Y.S. (1994) *Handbook of Qualitative Research*. Thousand Oaks, CA: Sage.

De Vaus, D.A. (2002) *Surveys in Social Research*, 5th edn. London: George Allen & Unwin.

Dewey, J. (1933) *How We Think*. London: D.C. Heath & Co.

Dey, I. (1993) *Qualitative Data Analysis*. London: Routledge.

Dey, I. (1999) *Grounding Grounded Theory: Guidelines for Qualitative Inquiry*. London: Academic Press.

Diamantopoulos, A. and Schlegelmilch, B.B. (1997) *Taking the Fear out of Data Analysis*. London: Harcourt Brace.

Dickens, L. and Watkins, K. (1999) 'Action research: Rethinking Lewin', *Management Learning*, 30(2): 127–140.

Diener, E. and Crandall, R. (1978) *Ethics in Social and Behavioural Research*. Chicago, IL: University of Chicago Press.

Dillman, D.A. (2007) *Mail and Internet Surveys: The Tailored Design Method*, 2nd edn. Chichester: John Wiley.

Dochartaigh, N. (ed.) (2002) *The Internet Research Handbook: A Practical Guide for Students and Researchers in the Social Sciences*. London: Sage.

Dochartaigh, N.O. (2007) *Internet Research Skills: How To Do Your Literature Search and Find Research Information Online*. London: Sage.

Dooley, L.M. (2002) 'Case study research and theory building', *Advances in Developing Human Resources*, 4(3): 335–354.

Douglas, J.D. (1976) *Investigative Social Research: Individual and Team Field Research*. Beverly Hills, CA: Sage.

Duke, K. (2002) 'Getting beyond the 'official line': Reflections on dilemmas of access, knowledge and power in researching policy networks', *Journal of Social Policy*, 31(1): 39–59.

Dupuis, S.L. (1999) 'Naked truths: Towards a reflexive methodology in leisure research', *Leisure Sciences*, 21(1): 43–64.

Easterby-Smith, M. (1994) *Evaluating, Management Development, Training and Education*, 2nd edn. Aldershot: Gower.

Easterby-Smith, M., Thorpe, R. and Lowe, A. (2002) *Management Research: An Introduction*, 2nd edn. London: Sage.

Economic and Social Research Council (ESRC) (2004) *Research Ethics Framework*. Swindon: ESRC.

Eisenhardt, K.M. (1989) 'Building theories from case study research', *The Academy of Management Review*, 14(4): 532–550.

Eisner, E.W. (1991) *The Enlightened Eye: Qualitative Inquiry and the Enhancement of Educational Practice*. New York, NY: Macmillan Publishing Company.

Ekinci, Y. and Riley, M. (1999) 'Measuring hotel quality: Back to basics', *International Journal of Contemporary Hospitality*, 11(6): 287–293.

Eland-Goossensen, M.A., van de Goor, L.A.M., Vollemans, E.C., Hendriks, V.M. and Garretsen, H.F.L. (1997) 'Snowball sampling applied to opiate addicts outside the treatment system', *Addiction Research*, 5(4): 317–330.

Elger, A. and Smith, C. (1998) 'Exit, voice and "mandate": Management strategies and labour practices of Japanese firms in Britain', *British Journal of Industrial Relations*, 36(2): 185–207.

Ellen, R.F. (ed.) (1987) *Ethnographic Research: A Guide to General Conduct*. London: Academic Press.

Ellis, C. (1991) 'Sociological introspection and emotional experience', *Symbolic Interaction*, 14: 23–50.

Ellis, C. (1995) 'Emotional and ethical quagmires in returning to the field', *Journal of Contemporary Ethnography*, 24: 68–98.

Ellis, C. (2007) 'Telling secrets, revealing lives: Relational ethics in research with intimate others', *Qualitative Inquiry*, 13: 3–29.

Emerson, R.M., Fretz, R.I. and Shaw, L.L. (2001) 'Participant observation and fieldnotes', in P. Atkinson, A. Coffey, S. Delmont, J. Lofland and L. Lofland (eds), *Handbook of Ethnography*. London: Sage.

Erikson, K.T. (1967) 'A comment on disguised observation in sociology', *Social Problems*, 14: 366–373.

Fassin, D. (2006) 'The end of ethnography as collateral damage of ethical regulation?', *American Ethnologist*, 33(4): 522–524.

Faugier, J. (1996) *Looking for Business: A Descriptive Study of Drug Using Female Prostitutes, Their Clients and Their Health Care Needs*. Unpublished PhD thesis, Manchester University, Manchester.

Faugier, J. and Sargeant, M. (1997) 'Sampling hard to reach populations', *Journal of Advanced Nursing*, 26: 790–797.

Featherstone, M. (2000) 'Archiving cultures', *British Journal of Sociology*, 51(1): 161–184.

Ferdinand, J., Pearson, G., Rowe, M. and Worthington, F. (2007) 'A different kind of ethics', *Ethnography*, 8(4): 519–543.

Fereday, J. and Muir-Cochrane, E. (2006) 'Demonstrating rigor using thematic analysis: A hybrid approach of inductive and deductive coding and theme development', *International Journal of Qualitative Methods*, 5(1): 80–92.

Ferguson, S.D. (2000) *Researching the Public Opinion Environment: Theories and Methods*. Thousand Oaks, CA: Sage.

Fetterman, D.M. (2010) *Ethnography: Step-by-Step*, 3rd edn. Thousand Oaks, CA: Sage.

Fielding, J. and Gilbert, N. (2006) *Understanding Social Statistics*, 2nd edn. London: Sage.

Fielding, N. (2000) 'The shared fate of two innovations in qualitative methodology: The relationship of qualitative software and secondary analysis of archived qualitative data', *Forum: Qualitative Social Research*, 1(3). Available at: www.qualitative-research.net/index.php.

Fielding, N. (2004) 'Getting the most from archived qualitative data: Epistemological, practical and professional obstacles', *International Journal of Social Research Methodology*, 7(1): 97–104.

Fielding, N. and Fielding, J. (1986) *Linking Data: The Articulation of Qualitative and Quantitative Methods in Social Research*. London: Sage.

Fife-Schaw, C. (2000) 'Surveys and sampling issues', in G. Breakwell, S. Hammond and C. Fife-Schaw, *Research Methods in Psychology*, 2nd edn. London: Sage. pp. 88–104.

Fine, M. (1994) 'Working the hyphens: Reinventing self and other in qualitative research', in N.K. Denzin and Y.S. Lincoln (eds), *Handbook of Qualitative Research*. Thousand Oaks, CA: Sage. pp. 70–82.

Fink, A. (2002a) *How to Sample in Surveys*, 2nd edn. Thousand Oaks, CA: Sage.

Fink, A. (2002b) *The Survey Handbook*, 2nd edn. Thousand Oaks, CA: Sage.

Fink, A. (2003) *How to Manage, Analyze and Interpret Survey Data*. Thousand Oaks, CA: Sage.

Fink, A. (2005*) Conducting Research Literature Reviews*. Thousand Oaks, CA: Sage.

Fischer, E. and Parmentier, M.-A. (2010) 'Doing qualitative research with archival data: Making secondary data a primary resource', *Advances in Consumer Research: North American Conference Proceedings*, 37: 798–799.

Flanders, N.A. (1970) *Analyzing Teaching Behaviour*. London: Addison-Wesley.

Flick, U. (2009) *An Introduction to Qualitative Research*, 4th edn. London: Sage.

Foddy, W. (1993) *Constructing Questions for Interviews and Questionnaires: Theories and Practice in Social Research*. Cambridge: Cambridge University Press.

Freeman, T. (2006) '"Best practice" in focus group research: Making sense of different views', *Journal of Advanced Nursing*, 56(5): 491–497.

Freire, P. (2000) *Pedagogy of the Oppressed*. New York: Continuum.

Friedman, V.J. (2001) 'Action science: Creating communities of inquiry in communities of practice', in P. Reason and H. Bradbury (eds), *Handbook of Action Research: Participative Inquiry and Practice*. London: Sage.

Frith, U. (2003) *Autism: Explaining the Enigma*, 2nd edn. Oxford: Blackwell.

Frow, J. and Morris, M. (2003) *Australian Cultural Studies*. Chicago: University of Illinois.

Funder, M. (2005) 'Bias, intimacy and power in qualitative fieldwork strategies', *The Journal of Transdisciplinary Environmental Studies*, 4(1): 1–9.

Gaventa, J. and Cornwall, A. (2001) 'Power and knowledge', in P. Reason and H. Bradbury (eds), *Handbook of Action Research: Participative Inquiry and Practice*. London: Sage.

Gay, L.R. and Diehl, P.L. (1992) *Research Methods for Business and Management*. New York: Macmillan.

Gibbert, M., Ruigrok, W. and Wicki, B. (2008) 'Research notes and commentaries: What passes as a rigorous case study?', *Strategic Management Journal*, 29: 1465–1474.

Giddings, L.S. (2006) 'Mixed-methods research: Positivism dressed in drag?', *Journal of Research in Nursing*, 11: 195–203.

Gill, J. and Johnson, P. (2002) *Research Methods for Managers*, 3rd edn. London: Sage.

Gillham, B. (2007) *Developing a Questionnaire*, 2nd edn. London: Continuum.

Gladstone, B.M., Volpe, T. and Boydell, K.M. (2007) 'Issues encountered in a qualitative secondary analysis of help-seeking in the prodrome to psychosis', *Journal of Behavioural Health Services & Research*, 34(4): 431–442.

Glaser, B.G. (1992) *Basics of Grounded Theory Analysis.* Mill Valley, CA: Sociology Press.

Glaser, B.G. and Strauss, A. (1967) *The Discovery of Grounded Theory: Strategies for Qualitative Research.* Chicago, IL: Aldine.

Glaser, B. and Strauss, A.L. (1968): *The Discovery of Grounded Theory: Strategies for Qualitative Research.* Aldine de Gruyter, Chicago.

Glass, G.V. (1976) 'Primary, Secondary and Meta-Analysis of Research', *Educational Researcher*, 5(10): 3–8.

Goffman, E. (1961) *Asylums: Essays on the Social Situation of Mental Patients and Other Inmates.* Garden City, NY: Doubleday and Company.

Golafshani, N. (2003) 'Understanding reliability and validity in qualitative research', *The Qualitative Report*, 8(4): 597–607.

Gomm, R., Hammersley, M. and Foster, P. (2000) 'Case study and generalisation', in R. Gomm, M. Hammersley and P. Foster (eds), *Case Study Method: Key Issues, Key Texts.* London: Sage.

Goode, E. (1996) 'The ethics of deception in social research: A case study', *Qualitative Sociology*, 19(1): 11–33.

Gould, A. (2007) *A Brief Guide to the Harvard System.* Available at: http://www.gre.ac.uk/__data/assets/pdf_file/0019/232570/SS-Referencing-Rev5.pdf. Accessed 8 March 2013.

Gray, D., Griffin, C. and Nasta, T. (2000) *Training to Teach in Further and Adult Education.* Cheltenham: Stanley Thornes.

Gray, D.E., Iles, P. and Watson, S. (2011) 'Spanning the HRD academic-practitioner divide – bridging the gap through Mode 2 research', *Journal of European Industrial Training*, 35(3): 247–263.

Greene, J.C., Caracelli, V.J. and Graham, W.F. (1989) 'Toward a conceptual framework for mixed-method evaluation designs', *Educational Evaluation and Policy Analysis*, 11(3): 255–274.

Groenewald, T. (2004) 'A phenomenological research design illustrated', *International Journal of Qualitative Methods*, 3(1): Article 4. Available at: http://www.ualberta.ca/~iiqm/backissues/3_1/pdf/groenewald.pdf. Accessed 7 April 2013.

Grønhaug, K. and Olson, O. (1999) 'Action research and knowledge creation: Merits and challenges', *Qualitative Market Research: An International Journal*, 2(1): 6–14.

Guba, E.G. (1985) 'The content of emergent paradigm research', in Y.S. Lincoln (ed.), *Organizational Theory and Inquiry.* Newbury Park, CA: Sage.

Guba, E.G. (1990) *The Paradigm Dialog.* Newbury Park, CA: Sage.

Guba, E.G. and Lincoln, Y.S. (1994) 'Competing paradigms in qualitative research', in N.K. Denzin and Y.S. Lincoln (eds), *Handbook of Qualitative Research.* Thousand Oaks, CA: Sage.

Guillemin, M. and Gillam, L. (2004) 'Ethics, reflexivity, and "ethically important moments" in research', *Qualitative Inquiry*, 10: 261–280.

Gummesson, E. (2000) *Qualitative Methods in Management Research.* Thousand Oaks, CA: Sage.

Gurney, J.N. (2002) 'Female researchers in male-dominated settings', in M. Pogrebin (ed.), *Qualitative Approaches to Criminal Justice: Perspectives from the Field.* London: Sage.

Habermas, J. (1972) *Knowledge and Human Interests.* London: Heinemann.

Haggerty, K.D. (2004) 'Ethics creep: Governing social science research in the name of ethics', *Qualitative Sociology*, 27(4): 391–414.

Hakim, C. (2000) *Research Design: Successful Designs for Social and Economic Research*, 2nd edn. London: Routledge.

Halcomb, E.J., Gholizadeh, L., DiGiacomo, M., Phillips, J. and Davidson, P.M. (2007) 'Literature review: Considerations in undertaking focus group research with culturally and linguistically diverse groups', *Journal of Clinical Nursing*, 16(6): 1000–1011.

Hall, G. (2008) 'An ethnographic diary study', *ELT Journal*, 62(2): 113–122.

Hall, T. (2000) 'At home with the young homeless', *International Journal of Social Research Methodology*, 3(2): 121–133.

Hall, W.A. and Callery, P. (2001) 'Enhancing the rigor of grounded theory: Incorporating reflexivity and relationality', *Qualitative Health Research*, 11(2): 257–272.

Halpenny, F.G. (2003) 'The thesis and the book', in E. Harman and I. Montagnes (eds), *The Thesis and the Book*, 2nd edn. Toronto: University of Toronto Press.

Hammersley, M. (1990) *Reading Ethnographic Research: A Critical Guide*. London: Longman.

Hammersley, M. (1992) *What's Wrong with Ethnography?* London: Routledge.

Hammersley, M. (2010) 'Can we re-use qualitative data via secondary analysis? Notes on some terminological and substantive issues', *Sociological Research Online*, 15(1): 5.

Hammersley, M. and Atkinson, P. (2007) *Ethnography: Principles in Practice*, 3rd edn. London: Routledge.

Hampshire, A.J. (2000) 'What is action research and can it promote change in primary care?', *Journal of Evaluation in Clinical Practice*, 6(4): 337–343.

Hancock, D.R. and Flowers, C.P. (2001) 'Comparing social desirability responding on World Wide Web and paper-administered surveys', *Educational Technology Research and Development*, 49(1): 5–13.

Hanson, W., Plano Clark, V.L., Petska, K.S., Creswell, J.W. and Creswell, J.D. (2005) 'Mixed methods research designs in counseling psychology', *Journal of Counseling Psychology*, 52(2): 224–235.

Harrigan, J.I. (2008) 'Proxemics, kinesics and gaze', in J.I. Harrigan, R. Rosenthal and K.R. Scherer (eds), *The New Handbook of Methods in Nonverbal Behavior Research*. Oxford: Oxford University Press.

Hart, C. (1998) *Doing a Literature Review*. London: Sage.

Hart, C. (2001) *Doing a Literature Search*. London: Sage.

Hartley, J. (2001) 'Employee surveys: Strategic aid or hand-grenade for organisational and cultural change?', *The International Journal of Public Sector Management*, 14(3): 184–204.

Hartley, J. (2004) 'Case study research', in C. Cassell and G. Symon (eds), *Essential Guide to Qualitative Methods in Organizational Research*. London: Sage.

Have, P.T. (1999) *Doing Conversational Analysis: A Practical Guide*. London: Sage.

Hayter, M. (1999) 'Burnout and AIDS care-related factors in HIV community Clinical Nurse Specialists in the North of England', *Journal of Advanced Nursing*, 29: 984–993.

Heaton, J. (1998) 'Secondary analysis of qualitative data', *Social Research Update*, Autumn No. 22. University of Surrey.

Heaton, J. (2004) *Reworking Secondary Data*. London: Sage.

Heaton, J. (2008) 'Secondary analysis of qualitative data: An overview', *Historical Social Research*, 33: 33–45.

Hedrick, T.E., Bickman, L. and Rog, D.J. (1993) *Applied Research Design: A Practical Guide*. Newbury Park, CA: Sage.

Helgeson, J.G., Voss, K.E. and Terpening, W.D. (2002) 'Determinants of mail-survey response: Survey design factors and respondent factors', *Psychology & Marketing*, 19(3): 303–328.

Hellman, H. (1998) *Great Feuds in Science*. New York: John Wiley & Sons.

Herbert, M. (1990) *Planning a Research Project: A Guide for Practitioners and Trainees in the Helping Professions*. London: Cassell Educational.

Heron, J. and Reason, P. (2001) 'The practice of co-operative inquiry: Research "with" rather than "on" people', in P. Reason and H. Bradbury (eds), *Handbook of Action Research: Participative Inquiry and Practice*. London: Sage.

Herrera, C.D. (1999) 'Two arguments for "covert methods" in social research', *British Journal of Sociology*, 50(2): 331–343.

Heyl, B.S. (2001) 'Ethnographic interviewing', in P. Atkinson, A. Coffey, S. Delmont, J. Lofland and L. Lofland (eds), *Handbook of Ethnography*. London: Sage.

Higher Education and Research in the UK (HERO) (2007) Available at: www.hero.ac.uk.

Hinds, P.S., Vogel, R.J. and Clarke-Steffen, L. (1997) 'The possibilities and pitfalls of doing a secondary analysis of a qualitative data set', *Qualitative Health Research*, 7(3): 408–424.

Hoepfl, M.C. (1997) 'Choosing qualitative research: A primer for technology education researchers', *Journal of Technology Education*, 9(1): 47–61.

Hofferth, S.L. (2005) 'Secondary data analysis in family research', *Journal of Marriage and Family*, 67(4): 891–907.

Holliday, A. (2002) *Doing and Writing Qualitative Research*. London: Sage.

Holstein, J.A. and Gubrium, J.F. (1994) 'Phenomenology, ethnomethodology and interpretive practice', in N.K. Denzin and Y.S. Lincoln (eds), *Handbook of Qualitative Research*. Thousand Oaks, CA: Sage.

Holstein, J. and Gubrium, J.F. (1995) *The Active Interview*. Thousand Oaks, CA: Sage.

Holstein, J.A. and Gubrium, J.F. (2008) 'Interpretive practice and social action', in N.K. Denzin and Y.S. Lincoln (eds), *Strategies of Qualitative Inquiry*. Thousand Oaks, CA: Sage.

Homan, R. (1991) *The Ethics of Social Research*. Harlow: Longman.

House, E.R. (1980) *Evaluating with Validity*. Beverly Hills, CA: Sage.

Hudson, J.M. and Bruckman, A. (2004) '"Go away": Participant objections to being studied and the ethics of chatroom research', *The Information Society*, 20: 127–139.

Hughes, J. and Sharrock, W. (1997) *The Philosophy of Social Research*. London: Addison Wesley Longman.

Hugill, K. (2012) 'The 'auto/biographical' method and its potential to contribute to nursing research', *Nurse Researcher*, 20(2): 28–32.

Huisman, K. (2008) '"Does this mean you're not going to come visit me anymore?": An inquiry into an ethics of reciprocity and positionality in feminist ethnographic research', *Sociological Inquiry*, 78(3): 372–396.

Hunter, D., Bailey, A. and Taylor, B. (1994) *The Art of Facilitation*. Auckland: Tandem Press.

Husserl, E. (1983) *Ideas Pertaining to a Pure Phenomenology and to a Phenomenological Philosophy*. The Hague: Martinus Nijhoff Publishers.

Hutchby, I. and Wooffitt, R. (1998) *Conversational Analysis: Principles, Practices and Applications*. Cambridge: Polity Press.

Irvine, A. (2011) 'Duration, dominance and depth in telephone and face-to-face interviews: a comparative exploration', *International Journal of Qualitative Methods*, 10(3): 202–220.

Irwin, K. (2006) 'Into the dark heart of ethnography: The lived ethics and inequality of intimate field relationships', *Qualitative Sociology*, 29: 155–175.

Israel, M. and Hay, I. (2006) *Research Ethics for Social Scientists*. London: Sage.

Isaac, S. and Michael, W.B. (1995) *Handbook of Research and Evaluation*. San Diego: EdITS.

Jankowicz, A.D. (2004) *Business Research Projects for Students*, 4th edn. London: Cengage Learning.

Jarvis, P. (1995) *Adult and Continuing Education: Theory and Practice*. London: Routledge.

JISCmail (2008) *JISCmail Ethics Statement*. Available at: http://www.jiscmail.ac.uk/help/policy/ethics.htm. Accessed 3 January 2008.

Jobber, D. and O'Reilly, D. (1996) 'Industrial mail surveys: Techniques for inducing response', *Marketing and Intelligence*, 14(1): 29–34.

Johnson, P. and Harris, D. (2002) 'Qualitative and quantitative issues in research design', in D. Partington (ed.), *Essential Skills for Management Research*. London: Sage.

Johnson, R.B. and Onwuegbuzie, A.J. (2004) 'Mixed methods research: A research paradigm whose time has come', *Educational Researcher*, 33(7): 14–26.

Johnson, R.B., Onwuegbuzie, A.J. and Turner, L.A. (2007) 'Toward a definition of mixed methods research', *Journal of Mixed Methods Research*, 1(2): 112–133.

Jordan, S. and Yeomans, D. (1995) 'Critical ethnography: Problems in contemporary theory and practice', *British Journal of Sociology of Education*, 16(3): 389–408.

Jungermann, H., Hahn, P. and Ferger, R. (1981) 'Observation of interaction processes in practical training', *Journal of Occupational Psychology*, 54: 233–245.

Kabbani, R. (1986) *Europe's Myths of Orient*. Bloomington: Indiana University Press.

Kahan, J.P. (2001) 'Focus groups as a tool for policy analysis', *Analysis of Social Issues and Public Policy*, 1(1): 129–146.

Kaufman, R. and Keller, J.M. (1994) 'Levels of evaluation: Beyond Kirkpatrick', *Human Resource Development Quarterly*, 5(4): 371–380.

Keats, D.M. (2000) *Interviewing: A Practical Guide for Students and Professionals*. Buckingham: Open University Press.

Kelemen, M. and Rumens, N. (2012) 'Pragmatism and heterodoxy in organization research: Going beyond the quantitative/qualitative divide', *International Journal of Organizational Analysis*, 20(1): 5–12.

Kelly, G.A. (1955) *The Psychology of Personal Constructs*. New York: Norton.

Kemmis, S. (1993) 'Action research', in M. Hammersley (ed.), *Educational Research: Current Issues*. London: Paul Chapman/Open University.

Kemper, E.A., Stringfield, S. and Teddlie, C. (2003) 'Mixed methods sampling strategies in social science research', in A. Tashakkori and C. Teddlie (eds), *A Handbook of Mixed Methods Research in Social and Behavioral Research*. Thousand Oaks, CA: Sage.

Kenett, R.S. (2006) 'On the planning and design of sample surveys', *Journal of Applied Statistics*, 33(4): 405–415.

Kenyon, E. and Hawker, S. (1999) '"Once would be enough": Some reflections on the issue of safety for lone researchers', *International Journal of Social Research Methodology*, 2(4): 313–327.

Keppel, G., Saufley, W.H. and Tokunaga, H. (1992) *Introduction to Design and Analysis*, 2nd edn. New York: W.H. Freeman and Company.

Kerin, R.A. and Peterson, R.A. (1983) 'Scheduling telephone interviews', *Journal of Advertising Research*, 23(2): 41–47.

Kerlinger, F.N. and Lee, H.B. (2000) *Foundations of Behavioural Research*, 4th edn. Fort Worth, TX: Harcourt College Publishers.

Kettner, M. (1993) 'Scientific knowledge, discourse ethics and consensus formation in the public domain', in E. Winkler and J. Coombs (eds), *Applied Ethics*. Oxford: Blackwell.

Kidder, L.H. (1981) 'Qualitative research and quasi-experimental frameworks', in M.B. Brewer and B.E. Collins (eds), *Scientific Inquiry and the Social Sciences*. San Francisco, CA: Jossey-Bass.

King, H. (2012) *Indonesia and Vietnam: An Ethnographic Study Exploring the Consumer Landscape and Opportunities for the Irish Dairy Industry*. Bord Bia: Dublin.

Kinnunen, U., Mauro, S., Nätti, J. and Happonen, M. (2000) 'Organizational antecedents and outcomes of job insecurity: A longitudinal study in three organizations in Finland', *Journal of Organizational Behaviour*, 21: 442–459.

Kirkpatrick, D.L. (1959) 'Techniques for evaluating training programmes', *Journal of the American Society of Training Directors*, 13(3–9): 21–26.

Kirkpatrick, D. (2005) *Evaluating Training Programs: The Four Levels*, 3rd edn. Williston, VT: Berrett-Koehler Publishers, Inc.

Kirkup, M. and Carrigan, M. (2000) 'Video surveillance research in retailing; ethical issues', *International Journal of Retail and Distribution Management*, 28(11): 470–480.

Kitzinger, J. (1994) 'The methodology of Focus Groups: The importance of interaction between research participants', *Sociology of Health & Illness*, 16(1): 103–121.

Kitzinger, J. (1995) 'Qualitative research: Introducing focus groups', *British Medical Journal*, 311: 299–302.

Kitzinger, J. and Barbour, R.S. (1999) 'Introduction: The challenge and promise of focus groups', in J. Kitzinger and R.S. Barbour (eds), *Developing Focus Group Research: Politics, Theory and Practice*. London: Sage.

Klein, R.D. (1983) 'How to do what we want to do: Thoughts about feminist methodology', in G. Bowles and R.D. Klein (eds), *Theories of Women's Studies*. London: RKP. pp. 88–104.

Korac-Kakabadse, N., Kakabadse, A. and Kouzmin, A. (2002) 'Ethical considerations in management research: A "truth" seeker's guide', in D. Partington (ed.), *Essential Skills for Management Research*. London: Sage.

Kothari, C.R. (2004) *Research Methodology: Methods and Techniques*. New Delhi: New Age International Publishers.

Krahn, G.L., Hohn, M.F. and Kime, C. (1995) 'Incorporating qualitative approaches into clinical child psychology research', *Journal of Clinical Child Psychology*, 24(2): 204–213.

Krejcie, R. and Morgan, D. (1970) 'Determining sample size for research activities', *Educational and Psychological Measurement*, 30: 607–610.

Krueger, R.A. (1994) *Focus Groups: A Practical Guide for Applied Research*. Thousand Oaks, CA: Sage.

Krueger, R.A. (1998) *Developing Questions for Focus Groups*. London: Sage.

Krueger, R.A. and Casey, M.A. (2009) *Focus Groups: A Practical Guide for Applied Research*, 4th edn. Thousand Oaks, CA: Sage.

Kuhn, T.S. (1996) *The Structure of Scientific Revolutions*, 3rd edn. Chicago, IL: University of Chicago Press.

Kvale, S. (1996) *InterViews: An Introduction to Qualitative Research Interviewing*. Thousand Oaks: CA: Sage.

L'Angelle, D.D. (1996) 'An approach to program evaluation', in C.P. Campbell (ed.), *Education and Training for Work*. Lancaster, PA: Technomic Publishing.

Langer, J. (2001) *The Mirrored Window: Focus Groups from a Moderator's Point of View*. Ithaca: Paramount Market.

Lather, P. (1986) 'Research as praxis', *Harvard Educational Review*, 56: 257–277.

Lather, P. (1991) *Getting Smart: Feminist Research and Pedagogy with/in the Postmodern*. New York: Routledge.

Lathlean, J. (1994) 'Ethical dimensions of action research', in I. De Raeve (ed.), *Nursing Research: An Ethical and Legal Appraisal*. London: Bailliere Tindall. pp. 32–41.

Laurie, H. (1992) 'Multiple methods in the study of household resource allocation', in J. Brannen (ed.), *Mixing Methods: Qualitative and Quantitative Research*. Aldershot: Ashgate.

LeCompte, M.D. and Goetz, J.P. (1982) 'Problems of reliability and validity in ethnographic research', *Review of Educational Research*, 52(1): 31–60.

Lee, R.M. (1993) *Doing Research on Sensitive Topics*. London: Sage.

Lee, R.M. (2000) *Unobtrusive Measures in Social Research*. Buckingham: Open University Press.

Lempp, H. and Seale, C. (2004) 'The hidden curriculum in undergraduate medical education: Qualitative study of medical students' perceptions of teaching', *British Medical Journal*, 329: 770.

Lenette, C. and Boddy, J. (2013) 'Visual ethnography and refugee women: nuanced understandings of lived experiences'. *Qualitative Research Journal*, 13(1): 72–89.

Lewin, K. (1946) 'Action research and minority problems', *Journal of Social Issues*, 2(4): 34–36.

Lewis, J. (2003) 'Design issues', in J. Ritchie and J. Lewis, *Qualitative Research Practice*. London: Sage.

Lieberson, S. (2000) 'Small N's and big conclusions: An examination of the reasoning in comparative studies based on a small number of cases', in R. Gomm, M. Hammersley and P. Foster (eds), *Case Study Method: Key Issues, Key Texts*. London: Sage.

Lincoln, Y.S. (1985) 'The substance of the emergent paradigms: Implications for researchers', in Y.S. Lincoln (ed.), *Organizational Theory and Inquiry*. Newbury Park, CA: Sage.

Lincoln, Y.S. (2001) 'Engaging sympathies: Relationships between action research and social constructivism', in P. Reason and H. Bradbury (eds), *Handbook of Action Research: Participative Inquiry and Practice*. London: Sage.

Lincoln, Y.S. and Guba, E.G. (1989) 'Ethics: The failure of positivist science', *The Review of Higher Education*, 12(3): 221–240.

Lincoln, Y.S. and Guba, E.G. (1994) *Naturalistic Inquiry*, 2nd edn. Newbury Park, CA: Sage.

Lincoln, Y.S. and Guba, E.G. (2000) 'The only generalisation is: There is no generalisation', in R. Gomm, M. Hammersley and P. Foster (eds), *Case Study Method: Key Issues, Key Texts*. London: Sage.

Lincoln, Y.S. and Tierney, W.G. (2004) 'Qualitative research and institutional review boards', *Qualitative Inquiry*, 10(2): 219–234.

Lindlof, T.R. and Taylor, B.C. (2002) *Qualitative Communication Research Methods*, 2nd edn. Thousand Oaks, CA: Sage.

Locke, K. (2001) *Grounded Theory in Management Research*. London: Sage.

Locke, L.F., Spirduso, W.W. and Silverman, S.J. (2013) *Proposals that Work: A Guide for Planning Dissertations and Grant Proposals*, 6th edn. Thousand Oaks, CA: Sage.

Lofland, J. and Lofland, L.H. (1995) *Analyzing Social Situations*, 3rd edn. Belmont, CA: Wadsworth.

Lofland, J. and Lofland, L.H. (2006) *Analyzing Social Settings: A Guide to Qualitative Observation and Analysis*. Belmont, CA: Wadsworth Publishing.

Lozar Manfreda, K., Bosnjak, M., Berzelak, J., Hass, L. and Vehovar, V. (2008) 'Web surveys versus other survey modes: A meta-analysis comparing response rates', *International Journal of Market Research*, 50(1): 79–104.

MacIntosh, J. (1981) 'Focus groups in distance nursing education', *Journal of Advanced Nursing*, 18: 1981–1985.

Madill, A., Jordan, A. and Shirley, C. (2000) 'Objectivity and reliability in qualitative analysis: Realist, contextualist and radical constructionist epistemologies', *British Journal of Psychology*, 91: 1–20.

Mangione, T.W. (1995) *Mail Surveys: Improving the Quality*. Thousand Oaks, CA: Sage.

Market Research Society (2010) *Code of Conduct*. London: Market Research Society.

Martinko, M.J. and Gardner, W.L. (1990) 'Structured observation and managerial work: A replication and synthesis', *Journal of Management Studies*, 27(3): 329–357.

Mason, J. (2002) *Qualitative Researching*, 2nd edn. London: Sage.

Mauthner, N.S. and Doucet, A. (2003) 'Reflexive accounts and accounts of reflexivity in qualitative data analysis', *Sociology*, 37(3): 413–431.

Mauthner, N.S., Parry, O. and Backett-Milburn, K. (1998) 'The data are out there, or are they? Implications for archiving and revisiting qualitative data', *Sociology*, 32(4): 733–745.

Maxwell, J.A. (1996) *Qualitative Research Design: An Interactive Approach*. Thousand Oaks, CA: Sage.

Maxwell, J.A. (1997) 'Designing a qualitative study', in L. Bickman and D.J. Rog (eds), *Handbook of Applied Social Research Methods*. Thousand Oaks, CA: Sage. pp. 69–100.

Mayring, P. (1983) *Qualitative Inhaltsanalyse. Grundlagen und Techniken*, 7th edn. Weinheim: Deutscher Studien Verlag.

Mays, N. (1995) 'Qualitative research: Rigour and qualitative research', *British Medical Journal*, 311: 109–122.

Mays, N. and Pope, C. (1996) *Qualitative Research in Health Care*. London: BMJ.

McBurney, D.H. and White, T.L. (2009) *Research Methods*, 8th edn. Belmont, CA: Wadsworth.

McCarthy, P. and Hatcher, C. (2002) *Presentation Skills: The Essential Guide for Students*. London: Sage.

McKay, J. and Marshall, P. (2001) 'The dual imperatives of action research', *Information Technology and People*, 14(1): 46–59.

McKenna, H. and Hasson, F. (2002) 'A study of skill mix issues in midwifery: A multimethod approach', *Journal of Advanced Nursing*, 37(1): 52–61.

McKenzie, T.L. (2006) 'System for Observing Play and Recreation in Communities (SOPARC): Reliability and feasibility of measures', *Journal of Physical Activity & Health*, 3(1): 208–222.

McKie, L. and Ryan, L. (2012) 'Exploring trends and challenges in sociological research', *Sociology*, 46(1): 1–7.

McMillan, J. H. and Schumacher, S. (1997) *Research in Education: A Conceptual Framework*. New York: Longman.

McNamara, P. (2009) 'Feminist ethnography: Storytelling that makes a difference', *Qualitative Social Work*, 8(2): 161–177.

McNiff, J. (1988) *Action Research: Principles and Practice*. London: Routledge.

McNiff, J. and Whitehead, J. (2011) *All You Need To Know About Action Research*, 2nd edn. London: Sage.

McNiff, J., Lomax, P. and Whitehead, J. (1996) *You and Your Action Research Project*. London: Routledge.

McTaggart, R. (1997) 'Guiding principles for participatory action research', in R. McTaggart (ed.), *Participatory Action Research*. Albany, NY: State University of New York Press.

Merriam, S.B., Johnson-Bailey, J., Lee, M., Ntseane, G. and Muhamad, M. (2001) 'Power and positionality: Negotiating insider/outsider status within and across cultures', *International Journal of Lifelong Education*, 20(5): 405–416.

Meyer, P. (2000) 'Could net polling hasten demise of phone surveys?', *USA Today*, 31 October.

Mickelson, E. (2011) 'Autobiography and self-hood in the practice of adult learning', *Adult Education Quarterly*, 61(1): 3–21.

Miles, M.B. and Huberman, A.M. (1994) *Qualitative Data Analysis*, 2nd edn. Thousand Oaks, CA: Sage.

Miles, M.B., Huberman, A.M. and Saldana, J.M. (2013) *Qualitative Data Analysis: A Methods Sourcebook*, 3rd edn. Thousand Oaks, CA: Sage.

Milgram, S. (1974) *Obedience to Authority: An Experimental View*. New York: Harper Collins.

Miller, T., Birch, M., Mauthner, M. and Jessop, J. (2012) *Ethics in Qualitative Research*. London: Sage.

Mingers, J. (2000) 'What is it to be critical? Teaching a critical approach to management undergraduates', *Management Learning*, 31(2): 219–237.

Mintzberg, H. (1970) 'Structured observation as a method to study managerial work', *Journal of Management Studies*, 7(1): 87–104.

Moreno, J.D. (1999) 'Ethics of research design', *Accountability in Research*, 7: 175–182.

Morgan, D.L. (1997) *Focus Groups as Qualitative Research*, 2nd edn. Thousand Oaks, CA: Sage.

Morgan, D.L. (1998) 'Practical strategies for combining qualitative and quantitative methods: Applications to health research', *Qualitative Health Research*, 8: 362–376.

Morgan, D.L. and Krueger, R.A. (1993) 'When to use focus groups and why', in D.L. Morgan (ed.), *Successful Focus Groups*. London: Sage.

Morris, L.L., Fitz-Gibbon, C.T. and Freeman, M.E. (1987) *How to Communicate Evaluation Findings*. Newbury Park, CA: Sage.

Morse, J.M. (1991) 'Approaches to qualitative-quantitative methodological triangulation', *Nursing Research*, 40: 120–123.

Motulsky, H. (1995) *Intuitive Biostatistics*. Oxford University Press. Available at: http://www.graphpad.com/www/book/Choose.htm. Accessed 4 January 2001.

Moustakas, C. (1990) *Heuristic Research: Design, Methodology, and Applications*. Newbury Park, CA: Sage.

Moustakas, C.E. (1994) *Phenomenological Research Methods*. Thousand Oaks, CA: Sage.

Moye, R. (2006) *Addressing the Challenging Behaviour of Children With High Functioning Autism*. London: Jessica Kingsley.

Mulhall, A. (2003) 'In the field: Notes on observation in qualitative research', *Journal of Advanced Nursing*, 41(3): 306–313.

Mumford, E. (2001) 'Advice for an action researcher', *Information Technology and People*, 14(1): 12–27.

Murphy, E. and Dingwall, R. (2001) 'The ethics of ethnography', in P. Atkinson, A. Coffey, S. Delmont, J. Lofland and L. Lofland (eds), *Handbook of Ethnography*. London: Sage.

Murray, D.M. (1994) 'Write research to be read', in M. Langenbach, C. Vaughn and L. Aagaard (eds), *An Introduction to Educational Research*. Needham Heights, MA: Allyn and Bacon.

Musson, G. (1998) 'Life histories', in G. Symon and C. Cassell (eds), *Qualitative Methods and Analysis in Organisational Research*. London: Sage.

Napolitano, M., McCauley, L., Beltran, M. and Philips, J. (2002) 'The dynamic process of focus groups with migrant farmworkers: The Oregon experience', *Journal of Immigrant Health*, 4: 177–182.

National Institute of Health (2008) *Directives for Human Experimentation*. Available at: www.hhs.gov/ohrp/archive/nurcode.html

Neergaard, H. (2007) 'Sampling in entrepreneurial settings', in H. Neergaard and J.P. Ulhoi (eds), *Handbook of Qualitative Research Methods in Entrepreneurship Research*. Cheltenham: Edward Elgar Publishing Ltd.

Nicholson, N. (1994) 'Ethics in organizations: A framework for theory and research', *Journal of Business Ethics*, 13: 581–596.

Niiniluoto, I. (1999) *Critical Scientific Realism*. Oxford: Oxford University Press.

Oakley, A. (1981) 'Interviewing women: A contradiction in terms', in H. Roberts (ed), *Doing Feminist Research*. Routledge and Kegan Paul, London.

Oakley, A. (1999) 'Paradigm wars: Some thoughts on a personal and public trajectory', *International Journal of Social Research Methodology*, 2(3): 247–254.

OAS (Organization of American States) (2013) Department of International Law. Available at: http://www.oas.org/dil/data_protection_principles.htm. Accessed 11 March 2013.

O'Leary, Z. (2014) *The Essential Guide to Doing Research*. London: Sage.

Onwuegbuzie, A.J. and Leech, N.L. (2007) 'Sampling designs in qualitative research: Making the sampling process more public', *The Qualitative Report*, 12(2): 238–254.

Onwuegbuzie, A.J., Johnson, R.B. and Collins, K.M.T. (2009) 'Call for mixed analysis: A philosophical framework for combining qualitative and quantitative approaches', *International Journal of Multiple Research Approaches*, 3(2): 114–139.

Oppenheim, A.N. (1992) *Questionnaire Design, Interviewing and Attitude Measurement*, 2nd edn. London: Pinter.

Ortiz, S.M. (2004) 'Leaving the private world of wives of professional athletes: A male sociologist's reflections', *Journal of Contemporary Ethnography*, 33: 466–487.

Pallant, J. (2010) *SPSS Survival Manual*, 4th edn. Maidenhead: OUP/McGraw-Hill.

Park, P. (2001) 'Knowledge and participatory research', in P. Reason and H. Bradbury (eds), *Handbook of Action Research: Participative Inquiry and Practice*. London: Sage.

Partington, D. (2002) 'Grounded theory', in D. Partington (ed.), *Essential Skills for Management Research*. London: Sage.

Patton, M.Q. (1982) *Practical Evaluation*. Newbury Park, CA: Sage.

Patton, M.Q. (1990) *Qualitative Evaluation and Research Methods,* 2nd edn. Newbury Park, CA: Sage.

Patton, M.Q. (2002) *Qualitative Research and Evaluation Methods*, 3rd edn. Newbury Park, CA: Sage.

Pawson, R. and Tilley, N. (2001) 'Realistic evaluation bloodiness', *American Journal of Evaluation*, 22(3): 317–324.

Payne, G. and Williams, M. (2005) 'Generalization in qualitative research', *Sociology*, 39(2): 295–314.

Payne, S.L. (2000) 'Challenges for research ethics and moral knowledge construction in the applied social sciences', *Journal of Business Ethics*, 26: 307–318.

Peräkylä, A. (2004) 'Reliability and validity in research based on tapes and transcripts', in D. Silverman (ed.), *Qualitative Research: Theory, Methods and Practice*. London: Sage.

Perry, C. (1998) 'Processes of a case study methodology for postgraduate research marketing', *European Journal of Marketing*, 32(9/10): 785–802.

Pershing, J.A. and Pershing, J.L. (2001) 'Ineffective reaction evaluation', *Human Resource Development Quarterly*, 12(1): 73–90.

Phillips, E.M. and Pugh, D.S. (2000) *How to get a PhD: A Handbook for Students and Their Supervisors*, 3rd edn. Buckingham: Open University Press.

Pink, S. (2006) *The Future of Visual Anthropology: Engaging the Senses*. New York: Routledge.

Polkinghorne, D. (1983) *Methodology for the Human Sciences: Systems of Inquiry*. Albany, NY: State University of New York.

Polonsky, M.J. (1998) 'Incorporating ethics into business students' research projects: A process approach', *Journal of Business Ethics*, 17: 1227–1241.

Popper, K.R. (1968) *The Logic of Scientific Discovery*, 2nd edn. London: Hutchinson.

Possick, C. (2009) 'Reflexively positioning in a politically sensitive situation: Dealing with the threats of researching the West Bank settler experience', *Qualitative Inquiry*, 15: 859–875.

Potter, S. (2006) *Doing Postgraduate Research*. London: Sage.

Powell, R.A. and Single, H.M. (1996) 'Focus groups', *International Journal of Quality in Health Care*, 8(5): 499–504.

Procter, M. (2007) *Advice on Academic Writing*. Available at: http://www. utoronto.ca/writing/advise.html. Accessed 9 January 2008.

Punch, K.F. (2005) *Introduction to Social Research: Quantitative and Qualitative Approaches*, 2nd edn. London: Sage.

Punch, K.F. (2006) *Developing Effective Research Proposals*, 2nd edn. London: Sage.

Punch, S. (2002) 'Interviewing strategies with young people: The "Secret Box", stimulus material and task-based activities', *Children and Society*, 16: 45–56.

QAA (Quality Assurance Agency for Higher Education) (2000) *Code of Practice for the Assurance of Academic Quality and Standards in Higher Education, Section 7: Programme Approval, Monitoring and Review*. Gloucester: QAAHE.

Rabinovich, E. and Cheon, S. (2011) 'Expanding horizons and deepening understanding via the use of secondary data sources', *Journal of Business Logistics*, 32(4): 303–316.

Raimond, P. (1993) *Management Projects: Design, Research and Presentation*. London: Chapman & Hall.

Ray, N.M. and Tabor, S.W. (2003) 'Several issues affect e-research validity', *Marketing News*, 15 September.

Reason, P. (1981) 'Methodological approaches to social science'. In P. Reason and J. Rowan (eds), *Human Inquiry* (pp. 43–51). New York: Wiley.

Reason, P. (1994) *Participating in Human Inquiry*. London: Sage.

Reason, P. and Torbert, W.R. (2001) 'The action turn: toward a transformational social science', *Concepts and Transformations*, 6(1): 21–33.

Reay, D.G. (1994) *Evaluating Training*. London: Kogan Page.

Reed-Danahay, D. (1997) *Auto/Ethnography: Rewriting the Self and the Social*. Oxford: Berg Publishers.

Reeves, C.L. (2010) 'A difficult negotiation, fieldwork relations with gatekeepers', *Qualitative Research*, 10: 315–331.

Richards, L. (2002) 'Qualitative computing – a method revolution?', *International Journal of Social Research Methodology*, 5(3): 263–276.

Robson, C. (2002) *Real World Research*, 2nd edn. Oxford: Blackwell.

Rock, P. (2001) 'Symbolic interactionism and ethnography', in P. Atkinson, A. Coffey, S. Delmont, J. Lofland and L. Lofland (eds), *Handbook of Ethnography*. London: Sage.

Roldan, A.A. (2002) 'Writing ethnography. Malinowski's fieldnotes on Baloma', *Social Anthropology*, 10(3): 377–393.

Rorty, R. (1998). *Truth and Progress*. Cambridge: Cambridge University Press.

Roscoe, J.T. (1975) *Fundamental Research Statistics for the Behavioural Sciences*, 2nd edn. New York: Holt Rinehart & Winston.

Rossman, E.B. and Wilson, B.L. (1985) 'Combining quantitative and qualitative methods in a single large-scale evaluation study', *Evaluation Review*, 9(5): 627–643.

Roulston, K. (2010) *Reflective Interviewing: A Guide to Theory and Practice*. London: Sage.

Rowe, C. (1995) 'Incorporating competence into the long-term evaluation of training development', *Industrial and Commercial Training*, 27(2): 3–9.

Rowley, J. (2012) 'Conducting research interviews', *Management Research Review*, 35: 260–271.

Rubin, H.J. and Rubin, I. (2005) *Qualitative Interviewing: The Art of Hearing Data*, 2nd edn. Thousand Oaks, CA: Sage.

Ruby, J. (2007) 'Digital Oak Park: An experiment', *Critical Arts*, 2(2): 321–332.

Rudestam, K.E. and Newton, R.R. (2007) *Surviving your Dissertation: A Comprehensive Guide to Content and Process*, 3rd edn. Newbury Park, CA: Sage.

Rugg, G. and Petre, M. (2004) *The Unwritten Rules of PhD Research*. Buckingham: Open University Press.

Ryan, L. and Golden, A. (2006) '"Tick the Box Please": A reflexive approach to doing quantitative social research', *Sociology*, 40(6): 1191–1200.

Said, E. (1989) 'Representing the colonised: Anthropology's interlocutors', *Critical Inquiry*, 15: 205–225.

Samra-Fredericks, D. (2004) 'Conversational analysis', in G. Symon and C. Cassell (eds), *Qualitative Methods and Analysis in Organisational Research*. London: Sage.

Sandelowski, M. (1995) 'Sample size in qualitative research', *Research in Nursing & Health*, 18: 179–183.

Sandelowski, M. (2000) 'Combining qualitative and quantitive sampling, data collection, and analysis techniques in mixed-methods studies', *Research in Nursing & Health*, 23: 246–255.

Sapsford, R. (2006) *Survey Research*, 2nd edn. London: Sage.

Sarasvathy, S.D. (2004) 'The questions we ask and the questions we care about: Reformulating some problems in entrepreneurship research', *Journal of Business Venturing*, 19(5): 707–717.

Saunders, M.N.K. and Rojon, C. (2011) 'On the attributes of a critical literature review', *Coaching: An International Journal of Theory, Research and Practice*, 4(2): 156–162.

Saunders, M.N.K, Lewis, P. and Thornhill, A. (2012) *Research Methods for Business Students*, 6th edn. London: Prentice Hall.

Savaya, R., Monnickendam, M. and Waysman, M. 2000 'An assessment of the utilization of a computerized decision support system for youth probation officers', *Journal of Technology in Human Services*, 17(4): 1–14.

Sayre, S. (2001) *Qualitative Methods for Marketplace Research*. Thousand Oaks, CA: Sage.

Scheibelhofer, E. (2008) 'Combining narration-based interviews with topical interviews: Methodological reflections on research practices', *International Journal of Social Research Methodology*, 11(5): 403–416.

Scherer, M.J. and Lane, J.P. (1997) 'Assessing consumer profiles of "ideal" assistive technologies in ten categories: An integration of quantitative and qualitative methods', *Disability & Rehabilitation: An International Multidisciplinary Journal*, 19: 528–535.

Schneider, J.A. (2006a) 'Using multimethods ethnography to promote quality service and understand interactions among organizations', *Nonprofit Management & Leadership*, 16(4): 411–427.

Schneider, J.L. (2006b) 'Professional codes of ethics: Their role and implications for international research', *Journal of Contemporary Criminal Justice*, 22(2): 173–192.

Schofield, J.W. (2000) 'Increasing the generalisability of qualitative research', in R. Gomm, M. Hammersley and P. Foster (eds), *Case Study Method: Key Issues, Key Texts.* London: Sage.

Schratz, M. (1996) 'Collaborative, self-critical and reciprocal inquiry through memory work', in O. Zuber-Skerritt (ed.), *New Directions in Action Research.* London: Falmer Press.

Schumann, H. and Presser, S. (1981) *Questions and Answers in Attitude Surveys.* New York: Academic Press.

Schutt, R.K. (2007) *The Blackwell Encyclopaedia of Sociology, Volume III*, G. Ritzer (ed.). Oxford: Blackwell.

Scott, J. (1990) *A Matter of Record.* Cambridge: Polity.

Scriven, M. (1967) 'The methodology of evaluation', in R.W. Tyler, R.M. Gagne and M. Scriven (eds), *Perspectives of Curriculum Evaluation.* Chicago, IL: Rand McNally.

Scriven, M. (1973) 'Goal free evaluation', in E.R. House (ed.), *School Evaluation.* Berkeley, CA: McCutchan.

Seal, D.W., Bogart, L.M. and Ehrhardt, A.A. (1998) 'Small group dynamics: The utility of focus group discussions as a research method', *Group Dynamics: Theory, Research and Practice*, 2(4): 253–266.

Seale, C. (1999) *The Quality of Qualitative Research.* London: Sage.

Seidman, I. (2013) *Interviewing as Qualitative Research: A Guide for Researchers in Education and the Social Sciences*, 4th edn. New York: Teachers College Press.

Sekaran, U. and Bougie, R. (2013) *Research Methods for Business*, 6th edn. Chichester: John Wiley & Sons Ltd.

Shaffir, W. (1999) 'Doing ethnography: Reflections on finding your way', *Journal of Contemporary Ethnography*, 28: 676–686.

Short, D.C. (2006) 'Closing the gap between research and practice in HRD', *Human Resource Development Quarterly*, 17(3): 343–350.

Short, J.F. and Hughes, L.A. (2009) 'Urban ethnography and research integrity: Empirical and theoretical dimensions.' *Ethnography*, 10: 397–415.

Shulman, L.S. (1999) 'Professing educational scholarship', in E.C. Lagemann and L.S. Shulman (eds), *Issues in Educational Research: Problems and Possibilities.* San Francisco, CA: Jossey-Bass. pp. 159–165.

Silverman, D. (2000) *Doing Qualitative Research: A Practical Handbook.* London: Sage.

Sixsmith, J. and Murray, C.D. (2001) 'Ethical issues in the documentary data analysis of internet posts and archives', *Qualitative Health Research*, 11(3): 423–432.

Skrtic, T.M. (1985) 'Doing naturalistic research into educational organizations', in Y.S. Lincoln (ed.), *Organizational Theory and Inquiry.* Newbury Park, CA: Sage.

Slack, F. and Rowley, J. (2001) 'Observation: Perspectives on research methodologies for leisure managers', *Management Research News*, 24(1/2): 35–42.

Sleeman, P. (2002) 'Archives and statistics', in N. Dochartaigh (ed.), *The Internet Research Handbook: A Practical Guide for Students and Researchers in the Social Sciences.* London: Sage.

Smith, D. (1987) *The Everyday World as Problematic: A feminist sociology.* Toronto: University of Toronto Press.

Smith, E. (2006) *Using Secondary Data in Educational and Social Research.* Maidenhead: Open University Press.

Smith, M. (1995) 'Ethics in focus groups: A few concerns', *Qualitative Health Research*, 5: 478–486.

Snape, D. and Spencer, L. (2003) 'The foundations of qualitative research', in J. Ritchie and J. Lewis (eds), *Qualitative Research Practice.* London: Sage.

Springwood, C.F. and King, C.R. (2001) 'Unsettling engagements: On the ends of rapport in critical ethnography', *Qualitative Inquiry*, 7(1): 403–417.

Stacey, J. (1988) 'Can there be a feminist ethnography?', *Women's Studies International Forum*, 11(1): 21–27.

Stake, R.E. (1994) *The Art of Case Study Research*. Thousand Oaks, CA: Sage.

Stake, R.E. (2000) 'The case study method in social inquiry', in R. Gomm, M. Hammersley and P. Foster (eds), *Case Study Method: Key Issues, Key Texts*. London: Sage.

Stake, R.E. (2005) *Multiple Case Study Analysis*. New York: The Guilford Press.

Stanley, L. and Wise, S. (1993) *Breaking Out Again: Feminist Ontology and Epistemology*. London: Routledge.

Stewart, D.W., Shamdasani, P.N. and Rook, D.W. (2007) *Focus Groups: Theory and Practice*, 2nd edn. Thousand Oaks, CA: Sage.

Stoler, A. (2010) 'Archives and the art of governance', *Revista colombiana de antropologia*, 46(2): 465–496.

Strauss, A.L. (1987) *Qualitative Analysis for Social Scientist*. New York: Cambridge University Press.

Strauss, A.L. and Corbin, J. (1990) *Basics of Qualitative Research*. Thousand Oaks, CA: Sage.

Strauss, A.L. and Corbin, J. (1994) 'Grounded theory methodology: An overview', in N.K. Denzin and Y.S. Lincoln (eds), *Handbook of Qualitative Research*. London: Sage.

Strauss, A.L. and Corbin, J. (1998) *Basics of Qualitative Research*, 2nd edn. Thousand Oaks, CA: Sage.

Strickland, C.J. (1999) 'Conducting focus groups cross-culturally: Experiences with Pacific Northwest Indian people', *Public Health Nursing*, 16: 190–197.

Stringer, E.T. (2013) *Action Research*, 4th edn. Thousand Oaks, CA: Sage.

Sudman, S. (1998) 'Survey research and ethics', *Advances in Consumer Research*, 25: 69–71.

Sundin, O. and Johannisson, J. (2006) 'Pragmatism, neo-pragmatism and sociocultural theory: Communicative participation as a perspective in LIS', *Journal of Documentation*, 61(1): 23–43.

Swanson, R.A. (2001) 'Human resource development and its underlying theory', *Human Resource Development International*, 4(3:) 299–312.

Szabo, V. and Strang, V.R. (1997) 'Secondary analysis of qualitative data', *Advances in Nursing Science*, 20(2): 66–74.

Tabachnick, B.G. and Fidell, L.S. (2001) *Using Multivariate Statistics*, 4th edn. New York: Harper Collins.

Tashakkori, A. and Creswell, J.W. (2007) 'Editorial: The new era of mixed methods', *Journal of Mixed Methods Research*, 1: 3–7.

Tashakkori, A. and Teddlie, C. (1998) *Mixed Methodology: Combining Qualitative and Quantitative Approaches*. Thousand Oaks, CA. Sage.

Tashakkori, A. and Teddlie, C. (2009) (eds) *Handbook of Mixed Methods in Social and Behavioral Research*, 3rd edn. Thousand Oaks, CA: Sage.

Taylor, J.E., Dossick, C.S. and Garvin, M. (2011) 'Meeting the burden of proof with case-study research', *Journal of Construction Engineering and Management*, 137(4): 303–311.

Teddlie, C. and Yu, F. (2007) 'Mixed methods sampling: A typology with examples', *Journal of Mixed Methods Research*, 1(1): 77–100.

Teitelbaum, H. (1998) *How to Write a Thesis*, 4th edn. New York: Macmillan General Reference.

Tesch, R. (1994) 'The contribution of a qualitative method: Phenomenological research', in M. Langenbach, C. Vaughn and L. Aagaard (eds), *An Introduction to Educational Research*. Needham Heights, MA: Allyn and Bacon.

Thomas, G. (2013) *How to do your Research Project: A Guide for Students of Education and Applied Social Sciences*, 2nd edn. London: Sage.

Thompson, C. (1999) 'Qualitative research into nurse decision making: Factors for consideration in theoretical sampling', *Qualitative Health Research*, 9(6): 815–828.

Thorne, S. (1994) 'Secondary analysis in qualitative research: Issues and implications', in J.M. Morse (ed.), *Critical Issues in Qualitative Research Methods*. London: Sage.

Thorne, S. (1998) 'Ethical and representational issues in qualitative secondary analysis', *Qualitative Health Research*, 8: 547–555.

Tickle, L. (2001) 'Opening windows, closing doors: Ethical dilemmas in educational action research', *Journal of Philosophy of Education*, 35(3): 345–359.

Tight, M. (2010) 'The curious case of case study: A viewpoint', *International Journal of Research Methodology*, 13(4) 329–339.

Titmuss, R. (1970) *The Gift Relationship: From Human Blood to Social Policy*, London: Allen & Unwin.

Travers, M. (2001) *Qualitative Research Through Case Studies*. London: Sage.

Trost, J.E. (1986) 'Statistically nonrepresentative stratified sampling: A sampling technique for qualitative studies', *Qualitative Sociology*, 9(1): 54–57.

Turk, C. and Kirkman, J. (1989) *Effective Writing: Improving Scientific, Technical and Business Communication*, 2nd edn. London: E. & F.N. Spon.

Vazquez-Montilla, E., Reyes-Blanes, M.E., Hyun, E. and Brovelli, E. (2000) 'Practices for culturally responsive interviews and research with Hispanic families', *Multicultural Perspective*, 2(3): 3–7.

Vigderhous, G. (1981) 'Scheduling telephone interviews: A study of seasonal patterns', *Public Opinion Quarterly*, 45: 250–259.

Wainwright, G. (1990) *Report Writing*, 2nd edn. Shrewsbury: Management Update.

Wallerstein, N. (1999) 'Power between evaluator and community: Research relationships within New Mexico's healthier communities', *Social Science & Medicine*, 49(1): 39–53.

Warner, J.P., Wright, L., Blanchard, M. and King, M. (2003) 'The psychological health and quality of life of older lesbians and gay men: A snowball sampling pilot survey', *International Journal of Geriatric Psychiatry*, 18: 754–755.

Warr, P., Bird, M. and Rackman, N. (1970) *Evaluation of Management Training*. Aldershot: Gower.

Warr, P., Cook, J. and Wall, T. (1979) 'Scales for measurement of some work attitudes and aspects of psychological wellbeing', *Journal of Occupational Psychology*, 52: 129–148.

Warren, S. (2012) 'Having an eye for it: Aesthetics, ethnography and the senses', *Journal of Organizational Ethnography*, 1(1): 107–118.

Waterman, H. (1998) 'Embracing ambiguities and valuing ourselves: Issues of validity in action research', *Journal of Advanced Nursing*, 28(1): 101–105.

Waterson, J. (2000) 'Balancing research and action: Reflections on an action research project in a social services department', *Social Policy and Administration*, 34(4): 494–508.

Webb, C. (1993) 'Feminist research: Definitions, methodology, methods and evaluation', *Journal of Advanced Nursing*, 18: 416–423.

Webb, C. and Kevern, J. (2001) 'Focus groups as a research method: A critique of some aspects of their use in nursing research', *Journal of Advanced Nursing*, 33(6): 798–805.

Webb, E.J., Campbell, D.T., Schwartz, R.D. and Sechrest, L. (2000) *Unobtrusive Measures: Nonreactive Research in the Social Sciences*, revised edn. Thousand Oaks, CA: Sage.

Weber, R. (2003) 'The reflexive researcher', *MIS Quarterly*, 27(4): v–xiv.

Weiss, C.H. (1984) 'Increasing the likelihood of influencing decisions', in L. Rutman (ed.), *Evaluation Research Methods: A Basic Guide*, 2nd edn. Newbury Park, CA: Sage.

Welch, C. (2000) 'The archaeology of business networks: the use of archival records in case study research'. *Journal of Strategic Marketing*, 8: 197–208.

Wengraf, T. (2001) *Qualitative Research Interviewing: Biographic Narrative and Semi-Structured Methods*. London: Sage.

Westmarland, L. (2001) 'Blowing the whistle on police violence', *British Journal of Criminology*, 41: 523–535.

White, J.H. (1997) *From Research to Printout: Creating Effective Technical Documents*. New York: ASME Press.

Whittemore, R., Chase, S.K. and Mandle, C.L. (2001) 'Validity in qualitative research', *Qualitative Health Research*, 11(4): 522–537.

Whyte, W.F. (1943) *Street Corner Society*. Chicago: University of Chicago Press.

Whyte, W.F. (1991) 'Comparing PAR and action science', in W.F. Whyte (ed.), *Participatory Action Research*. Newbury Park, CA: Sage.

Wield, D. (2002) 'Planning and organising a research project', in S. Potter (ed.), *Doing Postgraduate Research*. London: Sage.

Williams, A. (1993) 'Diversity and agreement in feminist ethnography', *Sociology*, 27(4): 575–589.

Williams, D. (2002) 'Research proposals', in T. Greenfield (ed.), *Research Methods: Guidance for Postgraduates*. London: Arnold.

Williams, M. and May, T. (1996) *Introduction to the Philosophy of Social Research*. London: Routledge.

Willis, P. and Trondman, M. (2000) 'Manifesto for ethnography', *Ethnography*, 1(1): 5–16.

Wilson, K. and Roe, B. (1998) 'Interviewing older people by telephone following initial contact by postal survey', *Journal of Advanced Nursing*, 27: 575–581.

Winkler, A.C. and McCuen, J.R. (2007) *Writing the Research Paper: A Handbook*, 7th edn. Boston, MA: Heinle.

Winslow, W.W., Honein, G. and Elzubeir, M.A. (2002) 'Seeking Emirati women's voices: The use of focus groups with an Arab population', *Qualitative Health Research*, 12: 566–575.

Winter, R. (1996) 'Some principles and procedures for the conduct of action research', in O. Zuber-Skerritt (ed.), *New Directions in Action Research*. London: Falmer Press.

Wodarski, J.S., Feldman, R.A. and Pedi, S.J. (1975) 'Effects of different observational systems and time sequences upon non-participation observers' behavioral ratings', *Journal of Behavior Therapy and Experimental Psychiatry*, 6(4): 275–278.

Wolcott, H.F. (1994) *Transforming Qualitative Data: Description, Analysis and Interpretation*. Thousand Oaks, CA: Sage.

Yin, R.K. (2006) 'Mixed methods research: Are the methods genuinely integrated or merely parallel?', *Research in the Schools*, 13(1): 41–47.

Yin, R.K. (2009) *Case Study Research: Design and Methods*, 4th edn. Thousand Oaks, CA: Sage.

Yin, R.K. (2012) *Applications of Case Study Research*, 3rd edn. Thousand Oaks, CA: Sage.

Zaman, S. (2008) 'Native among the natives: Physician anthropologist doing hospital ethnography at home', *Journal of Contemporary Ethnography*, 37(2): 135–154.

Zimmerman, R., Restrepo, C.E., Culpen, A., Remington, W.E., Kling, A., Portelli, I. and Foltin, G.L. (2010) 'Risk communication for catastrophic events: results from focus groups', *Journal of Risk Research*, 13(7): 913–935.

Zubrzycki, G. (2011) 'History and the national sensorium: Making sense of polish mythology', *Qualitative Sociology*, 34: 21–57.

Name index

Abrams, L.S., 228
Alford, R.R., 130
Anderson, L., 441
Arksey, H., 354, 388, 389, 395
Asad, T., 459
Atkinson, P., 438, 442, 455, 456
Atkinson, P.A., 179, 463

Baake, K., 520
Badger, T.G., 343, 345
Bailey, C.A., 416–417, 443
Bajpai, N., 224
Ballantine, J., 304, 308, 322–323
Barbour, R.S., 494
Barker, V., 524
Bartlett, J.E., 231
Bartunek, J.M., 203–204
Basch, C.E., 470
Begley, C.M., 431
Beile, P., 53
Bell, E., 85–87, 180–181, 604, 605
Berg, B.L., 415, 418, 427, 444, 609
Berger, L., 444
Berry, R., 641, 644
Biemer, P.P., 256
Bishop, L., 526–527
Black, T.R., 131, 135, 147, 154, 238, 563
Blair, J., 240, 243, 246, 251, 364, 366
Blumberg, B., 130, 224
Blumer, H., 440
Blumstein, P., 202
Boote, D.N., 53
Booth, P.F., 634
Boslaugh, S., 528
Bourgois, P., 459
Bowling, A., 328
Bradbury-Jones, C., 493, 494
Bramley, P., 297, 298, 301
Brannick, T., 343
Braun, V., 609–610
Brennan, J., 192
Brewer, J.D., 430, 517
Brinkerhoff, R.O., 299–300
Bruckman, A., 87–89
Brunt, L., 448
Bryman, A., 21, 85–87, 180–181, 192, 193–194, 194, 199, 202, 281, 604, 605, 620
Burgess, R.G., 416, 417, 443, 444

Callery, P., 182
Campbell, C.P., 296, 311, 319
Campbell, D.T., 140, 141, 195
Cannell, C.F., 360
Carrigan, M., 505, 508, 510, 511
Carroll, S., 367
Casey, M.A., 473, 477, 478, 479, 482–483, 485–486, 489, 494
Cassell, J., 71, 432
Charmaz, K., 611
Cheon, S., 531
Chia, R., 20
Clark, L., 489
Clarke, A., 296, 305
Clarke, V., 609–610
Coffey, A., 179, 463, 606
Coghlan, D., 329, 338, 343
Cohen, L., 367, 585
Cohen, L. and Manion, L., 383
Collins, K.M.T., 225–226, 227, 228
Copas, A.J., 258
Copernicus, N., 22
Corbin, J., 175, 185, 602, 611, 614, 618, 619, 620
Cornwall, A., 329
Costa, A.L., 204
Coyne, I.T., 222
Crandall, R., 432
Cressey, P., 272
Creswell, J.W., 102, 117–118
Crotty, M., 19, 20, 21–22, 23
Czaja, R., 240, 243, 246, 251, 364, 366

Darlington, Y., 200
Dattalo, C., 215
Davies, D., 187
Davies, S., 504
de Laine, M., 418–419
De Vaus, D.A., 152, 238, 242, 365, 367, 373
Denzin, N.K., 184–185, 195, 441, 459
Dewey, J., 15, 18, 23–24, 28
Dey, I., 182, 183, 612
Diamantopoulos, A., 555, 575
Dickens, L., 328, 334
Diener, E., 432
Digwall, R., 69, 455
Dillman, D.A., 254, 258, 365, 367, 369, 370, 371–372
Dochartaigh, N.O., 108

Dodd, J., 187
Dooley, L.M., 280, 288
Doucet, A., 606
Douglas, J.D., 414
Duke, K., 442

Easterby-Smith, M., 19–20, 37, 301, 304,
    305, 309
Eisenhardt, K.M., 174, 266, 271, 276–277
Eisner, E.W., 168
Ekinci, Y., 356
Eland-Goossensen, M.A., 223
Ellis, C., 85, 455
Emerson, R.M., 448, 449
Erikson, K.T., 76

Farewell, V.T., 258
Fassin, D., 453
Faugier, J., 228, 229
Fereday, J., 609
Fetterman, D.M., 438
Fielding, J., 198
Fielding, N., 198, 526, 606
Fine, M., 452
Fink, A., 101, 112, 114, 146, 236, 584
Fischer, E., 517, 528
Fiske, D., 195
Flick, U., 42, 162, 170, 175, 177,
    608, 609
Flietas, J., 506
Flowers, C.P., 248
Foddy, W., 358–360
Freeman, T., 490
Freire, P., 166
Freud, S., 26
Friedman, V.J., 330–331
Funder, M., 447–448

Galilei, G., 22
Gardner, W.L., 426
Garfinkel, H., 165
Gaventa, J., 329
Gibbert, M., 280
Giddings, L.S, 199
Gill, J., 4, 45
Gillam, L., 85
Gillham, B., 353, 372, 373, 377
Gladstone, B.M., 526, 532, 533
Glaser, B., 166, 175, 185, 203, 222, 447,
    612, 620
Glass, G.V., 530–531
Goetz, J.P., 461, 463
Goffman, E., 440, 457
Gomm, R., 280
Goode, E., 76
Greene, J.C, 196
Groenewald, T., 30
Grønhaug, K., 342

Guba, E.G., 26, 174, 183, 186, 187, 280,
    342, 607
Guillemin, M., 85
Gummesson, E., 268, 331
Gurney, J.N., 443

Habermas, J., 322
Hakim, C., 518–519
Halcomb, E.J., 473, 474
Hall, T., 443, 445
Hall, W.A., 182
Hammersley, M., 430, 438, 442, 455,
    456, 526
Hampshire, A.J., 345
Hancock, D.R., 248
Hanson, W., 194
Harrigan, J.I., 429
Harris, D., 187
Hart, C., 100, 102, 104, 113
Hartley, J., 237
Hasson, F., 532
Hatcher, C., 664, 667
Hawker, S., 92
Heaton, J., 514, 525
Hedrick, T.E., 36, 131, 138
Heidegger, M., 493–494
Helgeson, J.G., 259–260
Heraclitus, 20
Herbert, M., 640
Heron, J., 331
Herrera, C.D., 432
Heyl, B.S., 452
Hinds, P.S., 532
Hofferth, S.L., 516, 527–528
Homan, R., 68
House, E.R., 316–317
Huberman, A.M., 194, 200, 204, 602
Hudson, J.M., 87–89
Hughes, J., 21
Hughes, L.A., 461–462
Huisman, K., 28, 458
Hunter, D., 474
Husserl, E., 493–494
Hutchby, I., 622

Irvine, A., 404
Irwin, K., 441, 457

James, W., 28
Jankowicz, A.D., 41
Jarvis, P., 47
Jobber, D., 259
Johnson, P., 4, 45, 187
Johnson, R.B., 195
Jordan, S., 438

Kabbani, R., 459
Kahan, J.P., 473, 475–476, 480

Kallick, B., 204
Kaufman, R., 296, 299
Keats, D.M., 400
Keller, J.M., 296, 299
Kelly, G.A., 313
Kenyon, E., 92
Kerlinger, F.N., 5, 6, 131, 134, 135,
    149–150, 246
Kevern, J., 493–494
Kidder, L.H., 271
Kinnunen, U., 203–204
Kirkman, J., 633, 634, 640, 654, 655
Kirkpatrick, D., 296
Kirkpatrick, D.L., 297, 301
Kirkup, M., 505, 508, 510, 511
Kitson, B., 297, 298, 301
Kitzinger, J., 470, 471, 490, 491–493
Knight, P., 354, 388, 389, 395
Krahn, G.L, 202–203
Kreuger, R.A, 470
Krueger, R.A., 473, 477, 478, 479, 482–483,
    485–486, 489, 490–491, 492, 494
Kuhn, T.S., 22
Kvale, S., 394, 451

Laczniak, G.R., 509
Lane, J.P., 227
Lathlean, J., 344
Laurie, H., 201
LeCompte, M.D., 461, 463
Lee, H.B., 5, 6, 131, 134, 135, 149–150, 246
Lee, R.M., 228, 499, 521
Leech, N.L., 172, 174, 227, 232
Lewin, K., 166, 328
Lieberson, S., 281
Lincoln, Y.S, 182, 328
Lincoln, Y.S., 26, 174, 181, 183, 186, 187, 280,
    342, 441, 607
Lindlof, T.R., 470
Locke, K., 609, 611, 621
Locke, L.F., 51–52, 57, 58
Lofland, J., 177
Lofland, L.H., 177

MacIntosh, J., 473
Madill, A., 26
Malinowski, B., 439–440, 462
Mangione, T.W., 246, 260–261
Manion, L., 367
Marshall, P., 328
Martinko, M.J., 426
Mason, J., 171, 180
Mauthner, N.S., 526, 605–606, 606
Maxwell, J.A., 36
Mayring, P., 608
Mays, N., 172
McBurney, D.H., 138, 141, 143, 150, 151, 256, 412
McCarthy, P., 664, 667

McCuen, J.R., 40, 49
McKay, J., 328
McKenna, H., 532
McKenzie, T.L., 426
McMillan, J. H., 182
McNiff, J., 329
McNiff, J., 332, 335, 342
McTaggart, R., 329, 334
Mead, G.H., 23–24, 440
Merriam, S.B., 445
Merton, R., 468
Miles, M.B., 162, 169, 174, 183, 194, 200,
    204, 602
Milgram, S., 71
Mingers, J., 118, 120
Mintzberg, H., 414, 422, 424–425
Moreno, J.D., 74
Morgan, D.L., 470, 473
Morris, L.L., 319
Motulsky, H., 572
Moustakas, C., 33
Muir-Cochrane, E., 609
Mulhall, A., 443
Mumford, E., 335, 338, 344
Murphy, E., 69, 453, 455
Murray, C.D., 506
Murray, D.M., 632
Musson, G., 621
Myeong-Gu, S., 203–204

Napolitano, M., 476, 478
Neergaard, H., 232
Neveril, T., 474

Oakley, A., 37, 457
O'Leary, Z., 56
Olson, O., 342
Onwuegbuzie, A.J., 23, 172, 174, 227, 232
Oppenheim, A.N., 152, 240, 317, 361, 364,
    373, 389, 392, 393, 560
O'Reilly, D., 259
Ortiz, S.M, 446–447

Pallant, J., 154, 543, 587, 592
Park, R., 451
Parmenides, 20
Parmentier, M.-A., 517, 528
Patton, M.Q., 215, 217, 219, 220, 274, 316,
    317–318, 319, 394, 397, 398, 443, 501
Payne, G., 183–184
Peirce, C., 28
Peräkylä, A., 624
Perry, C., 269
Phillips, E.M., 642
Polonsky, M.J., 90, 649
Popper, K.R., 22
Possick, C., 445
Potter, S., 655

Presser, S., 355
Procter, M., 652–653
Ptolemy of Alexandria, 22
Pugh, D.S., 642
Punch, K.F., 36, 50–51, 54, 58–59, 60, 163
Punch, S., 403

Rabinovich, R., 531
Raimond, P., 42
Reason, P., 331, 383
Reeves, C.L., 442, 444
Richards, L., 625
Riley, M., 356
Robson, C., 36, 152, 422, 554
Rock, P., 445–446
Roldan, A.A., 440, 462
Roscoe, J.T., 231
Rossman, E.B., 193
Roulston, K., 385
Rowe, C., 297
Rowley, J., 388–389, 395–396, 398, 399
Rubin, H.J., 451
Rubin, I., 451
Ruby, J., 452

Said, E., 459
Sapsford, R., 236
Sargeant, M., 228
Saunders, M.N.K, 36, 239, 245, 376, 377, 413, 555, 636
Savaya R., 228
Sayre, S., 490
Scheibelhofer, E., 387
Scherer, M.J., 227
Schlegelmilch, B.B, 555, 575
Schneider, J.A., 442, 462
Schneider, J.L., 83
Schofield, J.W., 280
Schonberg, J., 459
Schratz, M., 341
Schumacher, S., 182
Schumann, H., 355
Schutt, R.K., 514
Schutz, A., 165
Schwartz, P., 202
Scott, D., 200
Scott, J., 521–522
Scriven, M., 302, 308
Seal, D.W., 469
Shaffir, W., 456
Sharrock, W., 21
Short, D.C., 331
Short, J.F., 461, 461–462
Shulman, L.S., 98
Silverman, D., 179–180
Sixsmith, J., 506
Skrtic, T.M., 185
Sleeman, P., 498, 503

Smith, D., 459
Smith, E., 528
Snape, D., 161
Spencer, L., 161
Stacey, J., 457–458
Stake, R.E., 266, 274
Stanley, J.C., 140, 141
Stewart, D.W., 470, 471, 473, 476, 477, 489–490, 492
Stoler, A., 429
Strauss, A.L., 166, 175, 185, 203, 222, 447, 602, 611, 612, 614, 618, 619, 620
Stringer, E.T., 333, 338, 339
Sudman, S., 74, 75, 76

Taylor, B.C., 470
Teddlie, C., 215
Tesch, R., 24
Thomas, G., 643
Thorne, S., 526, 532–533
Tickle, L., 344
Tierney, W.G., 181
Tight, M., 266
Titmuss, R., 26
Travers, M., 272
Trondman, M., 438
Trost, J.E., 219
Turk, C., 633, 634, 640, 654, 655

Vazquez-Montilla, E., 400
Vigderhous, G., 404

Wainwright, G., 633
Wallerstein, N., 161
Warner, J.P., 229
Warr, P., 243, 262
Warren, S., 453
Waterman, H., 342
Waterson, J., 345–346
Watkins, K., 328, 334
Webb, C., 493–494
Webb, E.J., 195, 498, 501, 502
Weber, R., 607
Welch, C., 516, 517
Wengraf, T., 391, 395
Westmarland, L., 444
White, J.H., 63, 64, 65, 639, 641
White, T.L., 138, 141, 143, 150, 151, 256, 412
Whitehead, J., 329
Whyte, W.F., 331, 440
Wield, D., 130
Williams, A., 457
Williams, D., 65
Williams, M., 183–184
Willis, P., 438
Wilson, B.L., 193
Winkler, A.C., 40, 49
Winslow, W.W., 470, 476

Wodarski, J.S., 426
Wooffitt, R., 622

Yeomans, D., 438
Yin, R.K., 194, 266, 267, 268, 269, 270, 274, 276, 277, 279, 280, 281, 282, 288

Yu, F., 215

Zaman, S., 442
Zimbardo, P., 79–80
Zimmerman, R., 484
Zubrzycki, G., 524

Subject index

abstracting databases, 106
academic requirements, 42
academic sources, 521–522
Academy of Management, 77
access
　action research and, 343–344
　ethnography and, 442–443
　overview, 42–43
accreditation, 307
accuracy, 390, 400
action research
　ethics and, 343–345
　ethnography and, 459–460
　evaluations and, 309
　grounded theory and, 621
　limitations of, 345–346
　overview, 3, 31–32, 34, 328–332, **330, 332**
　process of, 332–338, *334*
　role of researchers and participants in, 161,
　　338–339, **339**
　validation and, 342–343
action science, 330–331
active listening skills, 396
affinity, 400
agency, 445
almanacs, 521–522
analytic generalization, 270
analytic induction, 603–604, *603*
analytical categories sampling, 311
analytical reporting, 288
analytical surveys, 31, 32, 236, 239–240
anonymity
　Internet and, 507
　interviews and, 403
　overview, 74
　privacy and, 79
　questionnaires and, 377
anthropology, 439–440, 459
applied research, 3, **3**
archives, 108, 498, 516–517
The Argonauts of the Western Pacific
　(Malinowski), 439–440
assessment tests, 313
association, 135
Asylums (Goffman), 440
attentive listening, 396
audience
　presentations and, 660–661, 666–668
　reports and, 286–287, 431–432, 634

audio recordings
　action research and, 340–341
　focus groups and, 483
　interviews and, 397, 604
audit trails, 185
authenticity, 186–187, 400
Avison, D., 335
axial coding, 614–616, *615, 616*

basic research, 3, **3**
bias
　ethnography and, 461
　interviews and, 389–390
　intra-judge reliability and, 155
　surveys and, 256
bibliographic databases, 103–106, **105**
bids, 63
Billingham, J., 663
Black, T.R., 562
Blumberg, B., 36
body language
　Internet and, 87
　interviews and, 382, 396, 400
　presentations and, 667
books, 106–107
brainstorming, 47
British Psychological Society, 77
British Sociological Association, 432–433
Bureau of Applied Social Research (USA), 468

case studies
　data analysis and, 282–286, *283*
　data collection and, 277–278, **278**
　grounded theory and, 621
　overview, 163, 266–267, 290–292
　purpose of, 267–268
　reliability and, 281–282
　reports and, 273–274, 286–290, **288,**
　　288, 289
　research design and, 268–274, *270,* **274**
　sampling and, 208
　types of, 274–277, *275, 277*
　validity and, 279–281
categorical data, 555–556, *555*
　See also nominal data; ordinal data
category questions, 362–363
census, 237
central tendency, 566–568
chatrooms, 87–89

chi-square distribution, 574–575, **575**
Chicago School of sociology, 440, 451, 457
children and young people, 488–489
chronologies, 286
classification questions, 358
closed circuit television (CCTV), 504–505,
 508–511
closed questions, 362–364, **365**
cluster sampling, 211–215, *214*
coding
 observation and, 422–424, **423**, *424*
 process of, 604–605
 quantitative data and, 559–560, **559**
 questionnaires and, 361
 surveys and, 245
colonialism, 459
communication, 344
complementarity, 197, **198**
complex time-series, 286
computer-assisted qualitative data analysis
 software (CAQDAS), 625–627, *627*
conceptual frameworks, 169, *169*
conference papers, 108
confidence, 230, **230**
confidence interval, 148
confidentiality
 Academy of Management and, 77
 action research and, 344
 interviews and, 383, 390–391
 privacy and, 79
 sampling and, 229
 surveys and, 262
confounding variables, 152
consistency, 390
constant comparison method, 203
construct validity, 153, 279
constructionism
 focus groups and, 490–493, **491**
 interviews and, 385
constructivism, 20, 23
content analysis, 607–609
content validity, 153
contingency tables, 574, **574**
control groups, 138, 310
controlled accretion measures, 501
controlled erosion measures, 502
convenience sampling, 223–224
converging evidence, 271
conversational analysis, 622
cooperative inquiry, 331
copyright laws, 651
Corporate Reports, 254–255
correlation analysis, 584–585, *585–586*, **586**
correlation coefficients, 154
covert observation
 ethics and, 76, 78–79, 414–415, 432, 433
 ethnography and, 443
 overview, 414–415

creative thinking, **46**
credibility, 185–186, 388–390, 430
Criminal Records Bureau (CRB), 488
criterion sampling, 221
criterion validity, 152
critical case sampling, 221
critical incidents, 315
critical inquiry, 27
critical literature review, 118–120, **119**
critical realism, 26
Cronback's alpha test, 154
cross-sectional studies, 35, 143–144
cultural studies, 166–167
culture, 77

data analysis
 case studies and, 282–286, *283*
 focus groups and, 483
 research proposals and, 60–61
 secondary data and, 525–527
 staff opinion surveys and, 254
 surveys and, 245
 See also qualitative data analysis;
  quantitative data analysis
data collection
 action research and, 336, *337*, 339–342
 case studies and, 277–278, **278**
 error and, 257–258
 evaluations and, 309–315
 research proposals and, 60
 surveys and, 244
 See also specific methods
Data Protection Act (1998), 79
data saturation, 277, 485
data triangulation, 185
deception, 73, 79–80
decision making evaluation, 307
Declaration of Helsinki, 71
deduction
 analytical surveys and, 236
 case studies and, 269, *269*
 literature review and, 99
 overview, 16–17, **17**, *18*
 presentations and, 663
 qualitative research and, 192
 quantitative research and, 128, 130, 192
degradation of data, 561, *561*
delivery and collection questionnaires, 246, 377
deontological perspective, 68–69, **69**
dependent variables
 analytical surveys and, 240
 identification of, 135–136, *136*
 literature review and, 6
 overview, 29
descriptive framework, 282
descriptive statistics
 data analysis and, 566–569, **567–568**,
  567, 569

descriptive statistics *cont.*
  nominal data and, 562–565, **562,**
    562–563, 565
  ordinal data and, 562–563
  overview, 136
  ratio data and, 563, **564,** *564,* 565–566, *566*
descriptive studies, 36, **57**
descriptive surveys, 236, 237–240
development, 197, **198**
developmental designs, 143–144
diaries. *See* research diaries
digital archives, 502–505
digital media, 452–453
digital recorders, 397–398
Digwall, R., 453
direct incentives, 259
direct participants, 310
directories, 521
discourse analysis, 622
dispersion, 568
dissertations
  literature search and, 107
  as secondary data, 521
  structure of, 642–644, **643**
documents, 502
  See also secondary data
Doomsday Book (1085), 236–237

EBSCO bibliographic database, 101–102
Economic and Social Data Service (ESDS),
    524–525, 526–527
Economic and Social Research Council
    (ESRC), 524
elimination, 136
Ellis, C., 453–454
email questionnaires, 370–371
emic approach, 438
empirical literature, 176
encyclopaedias, 107
epistemological reflexivity, 606
epistemology, 19–20, *19,* 34
equivalence, 154
ethics
  action research and, 343–345
  codes of conduct and, 432–433, 509
  codes of practice and, 69–73, 77, **78**
  covert observation and, 76, 78–79, 414–415,
    432, 433
  ethnography and, 453–454, 460
  evaluations and, 322–323, *324*
  focus groups and, 494
  focus of, 73
  hard to reach populations and, 228–229
  Internet and, 87–89, **89,** 506–508
  interviews and, 405–407, **407**
  monitoring technology and, 508–511
  non-participant observation and, 432–433
  organizations and, 83–84, 87, 90

ethics *cont.*
  overview, 68–69, 90–92, **91**
  perspectives on, 85–87
  practice and, 81–85
  principles of, 73–81
  qualitative research and, 180–181, **181**
  report writing and, 90, 649–651, **650**
  research proposals and, 61, 81–83
  secondary data and, 532–533
  surveys and, 262
  See also deception; harm; informed
    consent; privacy
ethnography
  criticism of, 459–460
  digital media and, 452–453
  ethics and, 453–454, 460
  feminist research and, 28, 452, 457–458
  field notes and, 416
  fieldwork and, 441–448
  grounded theory and, 621
  interviews and, 451–452
  methods for, 413
  origins of, 439–441
  overview, 164–165, 438–439
  vs. phenomenology, 24–25, **25**
  reports and, 463, **464**
  sampling and, 208
ethnomethodology, 165, 459
etic approach, 438
European Society for Opinion and Market
    Research (ESOMAR), 510
evaluations
  data collection and, 309–315
  ethics and, 322–323, *324*
  focus of, 297–304, *298,* **299,** *301–302,* **303**
  impact of, 319–322
  overview, 296
  reliability and, 317–318
  reports and, 318–319, *320–321*
  schools of, 304–309, *304,* **306**
  validity and, 316–317
event studies, 531
examiners, 672, **672,** 673–674
expansion, 197, **198**
experience, 44, *45*
experimental evaluations, 305
experimental groups, 138
experimental research
  overview, 29–30
  research design and, 129–138, *129,* **138,**
    142, **142**
explanatory studies, 36, **57**
exploratory studies, 36, **57**
external action research, 330
external validity (generalizability)
  case studies and, 276–277, 280–281
  ethnography and, 462–463
  focus groups and, 492

external validity (generalizability) *cont.*
  interviews and, 388
  non-participant observation and, 430
  qualitative research and, 181, 182–183
  quantitative research and, 152
extraneous variables, 135–136
extreme or deviant case sampling (outlier
    sampling), 218

face validity, 151
Facebook, 110
factorial designs, 144–145, *145*
feminist research
  action research and, 341
  ethnography and, 28, 452, 457–458
  overview, 27–28
  quantitative research and, 161
field notes
  ethnography and, 448–449, *450*
  focus groups and, 475–476, 482–483
  observation and, 416–418, *420–421*
  overview, 177
  transcription and, 604
filter questions, 361
Flanders interaction analysis (IA) system,
    422–424, **423**, *424*
focus groups
  epistemological perspectives and, 490–494, **491**
  ethics and, 494
  limitations of, 471, **471**
  overview, 250, 402, 468–469
  planning and organizing, 472–484, *472*, **475**,
    478, **479**, **481**
  research design and, 485–488, *485–488*, **486**
  special issues in, 488–490
  uses and benefits of, 469–470, **471**
focused interviews, 386
forums, 87–88
frequency distribution, 566–568, **567**
frequency polygon, 565–566, *566*

gatekeepers, 73
gender, 443
gender studies, 167–168
generativity, 98
Global Compact International Yearbook, 522
globalization, 2
goal-based evaluations, 306–307
goal-free evaluations, 308
good faith, 344
Google Groups, 110
Google Scholar, 48, 104
governments, 2
grey literature, 107, 111
grounded theory
  constant comparison method and, 203
  data analysis and, 611–621, **613**, **615**,
    615–616, **617**, *619*

grounded theory *cont.*
  overview, 166
  reliability and, 185
  validity and, 182
group interviews, 401–403, 468
guardians, 343

harm, 73, 74–75, 76, 85
Harvard system, 122, **122**
hermeneutics, 26
heuristic inquiry, 33
Higher Education and Research in the UK
    (HERO), 650
homogenous sampling, 219
hypotheses
  deduction and, 16–17
  inferential statistics and, 569–572, **571**, *572*
  research design and, 130, 134, 136–137
  research proposals and, 57–58

illuminative evaluations, 308
incentives, 259
incident sampling, 310
independent variables
  analytical surveys and, 240
  identification of, 135–136, *136*
  literature review and, 6
  overview, 29
Index to Theses, 107
indexing databases, 106
induction
  case studies and, 269, *269*
  descriptive surveys and, 236
  literature review and, 99
  overview, 16, 17–18, *18*
  presentations and, 663
  qualitative research and, 170, 192
  quantitative research and, 192
inferences, 17–18
inferential statistics, 136, 562, 569–572,
    571, *572*
informal conversational interviews, 386
informants, 309–310
informed consent
  ethnography and, 443
  forms for, 85, **86**
  Internet and, 506
  interviews and, *406*, 407
  overview, 73, 75–77
  privacy and, 78
  research proposals and, 60
  surveys and, 75, 76, 84, 262
initiation, 197, **198**
insider action research, 329, **330**
Institutional Review Boards (IRBs)
  ethnography and, 453
  qualitative research and, 181
  research proposals and, 81–83

Institutional Review Boards (IRBs) *cont.*
  sampling and, 222–223, 228
  secondary data and, 533
instruments
  reliability and, 154–155
  validity and, 150–153, *151*
intellectual property (IP), 651
intensity sampling, 218
inter-judge reliability, 155
inter-quartile range, 568
interaction, 492
internal reliability, 154
internal validity
  case studies and, 279–280
  ethnography and, 461
  non-participant observation and, 430
  qualitative research and, 182
  quantitative research and, 138, 152
*International Journal of Human Resource
    Management*, 644–645
Internet
  body language and, 87
  digital archives and, 502–504
  ethics and, 87–89, **89**, 506–508
  questionnaires and, 370–372
  sampling and, 87
  source materials and, 108–109
interpretive studies, 37, **57**
interpretivism, 20, 23–27, 490
  See also hermeneutics; naturalistic inquiry;
    phenomenology; realism; symbolic
    interactionism
interrupted time-series, 286
interval data, 557, **558**, 563, 565–566
intervening variables, 135, *136*
interventionist evaluations, 309
interviewer-administered questionnaires,
    249–252, 378
interviewer error, 261
interviewing skills
  conducting the interview, 393–397
  getting started, 391–393, *392*
  overview, 390–391, **401**
  recording and transcribing data, 397–398
  reports and, 398–399, *399*
interviews
  action research and, 340
  design of, 388–390
  document sheets and, *178*
  ethics and, 405–407, **407**
  ethnography and, 451–452
  vs. focus groups, 468
  overview, 177
  vs. questionnaires, 383–384, 384ebk, **384**
  transcription and, 604
  types of, 384–388
  uses of, 382–384, 382ebk
intra-judge reliability, 155

invalidity, 261–262, **261**
investigator triangulation, 185
ISI Web of Science, 106
item non-response, 260–261

JISCmail, 110, 507–508
joint interviews, 402
journal articles, 103–106, 521, 644–649, 673
judicial records, 520–521

kinesics, 429

language
  focus groups and, 489
  interviews and, 393–394
learning logs, 315
legal issues, 651
Likert scale, 363
LinkedIn, 43, 109–110
list questions, 362
listening, 396
literature reviews
  function of, 98–99
  overview, 6–7, 53–55
  position of, 118
  qualitative research and, 175–176
  references and, 120–122, **121, 122**
  research questions and, 54–55, *55*
  structure and content of, 117–118, 648
  See also critical literature review
literature search
  evaluation and, 112–116, **113, 114, 115**
  as journey, 99–100, *100*
  process of, 101–102, 111–112
  research design and, 130
  research logs and, 115–116
  research topics and, 46–47
  results from, 116–117
  source materials and, 102–112, **103**
longitudinal studies, 35, 144

management action science, 331
Management Learning (journal), 645, *646*
Management Report, 255
Mann-Whitney U test, 580–582
Manuscript Central, 645–646, *646*
Market Research Society (MRS), 509
Marxism, 27
mass media records, 521
maximum variation sampling, 218–219
mean, 148, 567–568
median, 568
memory, 482
memory work, 341
meta-analysis, 530–531
meta-ethics, 68
metaphors, 665
methodological literature, 176

methodological triangulation, 185
Microsoft Project, 50
missing data, 257–258, 549–550, 560–561, **561**
mixed methods research
    benefits of, 196–197, **198**
    criticism of, 198–199
    overview, 37, 190, 194–196, *195*, **196**
    research design and, 199–205, *200*
    sampling and, 225–228, **225**, *226*
    secondary data and, 531–532
mode, 568
moderators, 474–475, **475**, 479–480, **481**
monitoring technology, 505–506,
    508–511
MS Word, 551, 638
multi-stage sampling, 215
multicultural interviews, 400–401
multiculturalism, 452
multiple triangulation, 185

naïve realism, 26
narrative analysis, 166, 621–622
natural accretion measures, 499–501
natural erosion measures, 501–502
naturalistic inquiry, 26–27, 163–164, **164**
    See also specific paradigms
naturalistic observation. *See* non-participant
    observation
neo-Marxism, 161
neo-positivism, 385
networks, 43, *44*, 109–111
neutrality, 390
nominal data
    descriptive statistics and, 562–565, **562**,
        562–563, 565
    overview, 555, 556, **556**, *556*
non-directive interviews, 386
non-experimental research, **138**, 140, **140**
non-parametric tests, 572
non-participant observation
    data collection and, 416–426, **416**, *418*
    overview, 412–413
    process of, 426–429, **428**
    reliability and, 430–431
    reports and, 431–432
    unobtrusive data and, 428–429
    validity and, 430
non-probability sampling, 60, 215–224, **216**
non-response
    quantitative data and, 560–561, **561**, *561*
    surveys and, 257–258
    telephone interviews and, 404, **404**
non-verbal communication, 394
normal distribution, 569, *569*
note taking, 397
null hypothesis, 570
Nuremberg Code (1947), 69, **70**
NVivo, 625–626, *627*

objectivist epistemology, 20
objectivity, 161, 318
observation
    action research and, 340
    approaches to, 413–415
    evaluations and, 310–311
    interviews and, 396
    overview, 177, 412–413
    See also non-participant observation;
        participant observation
observer error, 155
observers, 310
official publications, 108
official statistics, 108, 522, **522–523**
one-tailed test, 571
online bookshops, 107
Online Public Access Catalogue (OPAC), 106
online questionnaires
    administration of, 377–378
    overview, 247–249, *248*
ontology, 19–20
open coding, 612–614, **613**, **615**
open questions, 249, 361–362, **365**
operational definitions, 135
opinion polls, 238–239
opinionnaires, 311, *312–313*
opportunistic sampling, 222–223
ordinal data
    descriptive statistics and, 562–563
    overview, 555, 556, **557**, *557*
Organization of American States (OAS), 79
organizational documents, 429, 517–519,
    638–642
organizational proposals, 63–65, *63*
organizations
    ethics and, 83–84, 87, 90
    globalization and, 2
    literature search and, 110–111
    research design and, 128
outcroppings, 428–429
outlier sampling (extreme or deviant case
    sampling), 218
overt observation, 414

paired *t*-tests, 575
paradigm crisis, 22
parameters, 148
parametric tests, 572
parents, 343
participant observation
    covert observation and, 433
    ethnography and, 448–449, *450*
    overview, 413–414
participants
    action research and, 339–342, **339**, 343
    communication with, 84–85
    covert observation and, 432
Participatory Action Research (PAR), 166, 329

pattern matching, 283–285, *283*
Pearson product-moment correlation, 588–590
people sampling, 310
personal documents, 517, *518*
personal reflexivity, 606
personal stories, 665
phenomenology
    focus groups and, 493–494
    interviews and, 382, 386
    overview, 24–25, **25**, 30–31, 165–166
    sampling and, 208
photographs, 178, 340–341
physical measures, 498–502
piloting
    focus groups and, 479
    questionnaires and, 372–374
plagiarism, 650
plausibility, 183–184, 430
political records, 520–521
politically important cases, 221
positivism, 20, 21–23, **25**
post-positivism, 23
post-test quantitative designs, 140–141, **140**,
        143, *144*
postal surveys
    administration of, 376–377, **377**
    error and, 257–258, **259**, 260–261
    overview, 246
postmodernism
    ethnography and, 452, 455
    overview, 20, 28
    quantitative research and, 161
power, 455
pragmatism, 28–29
pre-interview questionnaires, 391
pre-test quantitative designs, **140**, 141,
        143, *144*
pre-testing, 243–244
predictive validity, 153
presentations
    creating interest in, 665–666
    delivery of, 666–668
    density of ideas and, 663–664
    preparation of, 660–662, **662**
    structure of, 662–663, **664**
    team presentations, 668–669, *668*
primary data, 514
privacy, 73, 77, 78–79, 507
probes, 261, 395, 478
problem-centred interviews, 387–388
problem respondents, 399–400
procedural ethics, 85
professional associations, 110
professional reports, 519–520
progressive paradigms, 164, **164**
    See also specific paradigms
project planning, 50, *51*
proxemics, 429

psychoanalysis, 26
purposive sampling, 217–223

Q-sort methodology, 356–357
Qualidata, 524–525, 526–527
qualitative data analysis
    content analysis, 607–609
    conversational analysis, 622
    discourse analysis, 622
    elements of, 603–607, *608*
    grounded theory and, 611–621, **613**, **615**,
        615–616, **617**, *619*
    narrative analysis, 621–622
    overview, 174–175
    reliability and, 624
    research proposals and, 60–61
    software for, 625–627, *627*
    thematic analysis, 609–611, *610*
    validity and, 622–624, **623**
qualitative data collection
    overview, 177–180
    research proposals and, 60
    See also case studies; interviews; observation
qualitative research
    characteristics of, 161–162
    ethics and, 180–181, **181**
    vs. quantitative research, 190–194,
        191, *193*
    research methodologies and, **59**
    rigour in, 181–187, **183**
    secondary data and, 524–525, *528*
    types of data in, 172, **173**
qualitative research design
    approaches to, 168–175, *169*, **170**, *171*
    case studies and, 268–274, *270*, **274**
    focus groups and, 485–488, *485–488*, **486**
    overview, 160
    paradigms and strategies for, 162–168, **164**
    sampling and, 172–174, 208–209
Quality Assurance Agency for Higher
        Education (QAA), 307
quantifiable data, 555–556, *555*
    See also interval data; ratio data
quantitative data analysis
    categorizing data, 554–557, **555–558**,
        555–557
    data entry, layout and quality and, 558–561,
        559, **561**
    descriptive statistics and, 562–569, **562**,
        562–565, **564**, **567–568**
    inferential statistics and, 569–572, **571**, *572*
    research proposals and, 60–61
    statistical tests and, 572–598, **573**, **582**
quantitative research
    criticism of, 160–161, **161**
    vs. qualitative research, 190–194, **191**, *193*
    research methodologies and, **59**
    research proposals and, 60

quantitative research design
   experimental research and, 129–138, *129*,
      138, 142, **142**
   faulty designs, 140–141
   overview, 128
   quasi-experimental research and, 137–139,
      138, **142**, 143, *144*
   reliability and, 154–155
   sampling and, 145–150, *147*, 208
   sound designs, 141–145
   validity and, 150–153, *151*
quasi-experimental research
   overview, 29–30
   research design and, 137–139, **138**, **142**,
      143, *144*
questionnaires
   action research and, 340
   administration of, 376–378
   design of, 354–370, **357**, *359*, **360**, *364*, **365**,
      366, *368*, *370*
   Internet and, 370–372
   vs. interviews, 383–384, 384ebk, **384**
   interviews and, 382
   overview, 352–353
   piloting and, 372–374
   reliability and, 375–376
   research proposals and, 60
   types of, 245, *245*
   validity and, 375
questions
   focus groups and, 477–479, *478*, **479**
   interviews and, 395–396
quota sampling, 215–217
quotations, 398–399, *399*

race researchers, 161
random purposeful sampling, 220
random sampling
   overview, 60, 209–215, *211–214*
   quantitative research and, 147, 148–149, **148**
randomization, 136, 138
range, 568
ranking questions, 363
rapport
   ethnography and, 444
   interviews and, 392, 404
rapporteurs, 475–476
ratio data
   descriptive statistics and, 563, **564**, *564*,
      565–566, *566*
   overview, 557
rational thinking, **46**
reactivity, 178
real world, 3–5
realism
   focus groups and, 490–493, **491**
   overview, 25–26
reference sources, 107, 521

references
   literature review and, 120–122, **121**, **122**
   reports and, 641, 649
   research proposals and, 61
reflective reporting, 288
reflexivity
   data analysis and, 606–607
   ethnography and, 444–445, 455–456, 461
   overview, 162
   qualitative research and, 182
regression analysis, 590–598, *592*
relational ethics, 85
relevance trees, 47–48
reliability
   case studies and, 273, 274, 281–282
   ethnography and, 461
   evaluations and, 317–318
   interviews and, 389
   non-participant observation and, 430–431
   qualitative data analysis and, 624
   qualitative research and, 184–185
   quantitative research and, 154–155
   questionnaires and, 375–376
repertory grids, 313–315, *314*
reports
   case studies and, 273–274, 286–290, **288**,
      288, *289*
   ethics and, 90, 649–651, **650**
   ethnography and, 463, **464**
   evaluations and, 318–319, *320–321*
   interviews and, 398–399, *399*
   non-participant observation and, 430,
      431–432
   overview, 137, 632
   review process and, 655
   as secondary data, 519–520
   staff opinion surveys and, 254–255
   structure of, 637–649, **638**, *640*
   style and tone of, 652–655, **653**
   writing process and, 633–637
representative samples, 146–147
request for proposals (RFPs), 63
research
   importance of, 2–3
   real world and, 3–5, **4**
research design
   overview, 128
   selection of, **267**
   See also qualitative research design;
      quantitative research design
research diaries
   action research and, 340
   ethnography and, 449–450, *450*
   overview, 179–180
research logs, 115–116
research methodologies
   overview, 19, *19*
   qualitative and quantitative approaches, **59**

research methodologies *cont.*
  research process and, 34
  research proposals and, 58–61
  types of, 29–34
research methods
  importance of, 2
  literature review and, 99, **120**
  overview, *19*
research process, 4–7, *5, 7*, 34–35, *35*
research proposals
  ethics and, 61, 81–83
  final stages of, 64–65
  structure of, 50–62, **52**, **82**
research questions
  focus groups and, 472
  literature review and, 54–55, *55*
  literature search and, 101
  qualitative research design and, 170, **170**, *171*
  quantitative research design and, 129,
    130–134, **131, 132**
  research proposals and, 56–57
  surveys and, 241–242
  types of, **57**
research topics, 40–50
researchers
  action research and, 338–339, **339**
  qualitative research and, 175, 191
  quantitative research and, 175, 191
response rates, 258–260, **259**, *260*, 353
Romanticism, 385

safety, 92, **93**
sampling
  ethnography and, 442
  evaluations and, 310–311
  hard to reach populations and, 228–230
  Internet and, 87
  mixed methods research and, 225–228,
    225, *226*
  non-probability sampling, 60, 215–224, **216**
  qualitative research and, 172–174,
    208–209
  quantitative research and, 145–150,
    147, 208
  research proposals and, 59
  size and, 230–233, **230–231, 232**
  surveys and, 242–243
  See also random sampling
sampling error
  online questionnaires and, 247–248
  surveys and, 256–257
sampling frames
  focus groups and, 472–473
  quantitative research and, 146–147, *147*
  surveys and, 243
scale questions, 363–364
scientific realism, 26
search engines, 108

secondary data
  advantages and disadvantages of, 515–516
  analysis of, 525–527, 605–606
  ethics and, 532–533
  methodologies for, 530–531
  mixed methods research and, 531–532
  overview, 514
  qualitative research and, 524–525, *528*
  selection of, 527–528
  sources of, 516–524
  systems approach to, 528–530
selective coding, 616–617, **617**, 618
self-administered questionnaires
  administration of, 376–378
  vs. interviews, **384**
  types of, 246–249
self-criticism, 445
self-observation (reflection), 396
self-reflection, 445
self-reflexivity, 85
self-regulation, 85
semi-structured interviews
  overview, 382, 385–386, **387**
  questions and, 395–396
sensitive topics, 407, 489–490
sequencing questions, 364–366
sequential sampling, 221–222
significance level, 571
simple random sampling (SRS), 210, *211*
situational ethics, 85
skewed distribution, 569
Skype, 87, 405
small and medium-sized enterprises (SMEs), 2
snowball sampling, 223, 228
social anthropology, 459
social constructivism, 490
social media, 43
social networks, 109–111
Social Research Association, 77
socially desirable responses (SDRs), 246, 248
societal action science, 331
Spearman's rank-order correlation, 587
sponsors and sponsorship
  communication and, 84–85
  globalization and, 2
  networks and, 43, *44*
  non-participant observation and, 433
SPSS
  entering and modifying data in, 547
  Help facilities, 551
  interface of, 538–541, *539–542*, 548–549,
    548
  missing data and, 549–550
  MS Word and, 551
  naming and defining variables in, 543–547,
    543, **544**, *545–546*
  recoding data in, 550–551
stability, 154

staff opinion surveys, 252–255
stakeholders, 310
standard deviation, 568, 569
Statistical Package for the Social Sciences.
　　See SPSS
statistical validity, 153
stimulus material, 403
stratified purposeful sampling, 219, **220**
stratified random sampling, 210, *213*
Street Corner Society (Whyte), 440
Stringer, E.T., 335, 336
structured interviews, 249–250, 378, 382,
　　385, **387**
structured observation, 414, 422–426
subject error, 154
subjectivism, 20
summaries, 396
supervisors, 343, 637
SurveyMonkey, 371
surveys
　　error in, 256–262, **259**, *260*
　　ethics and, 75, 76, 84, 262
　　informed consent and, 75, 76, 84
　　methods for, 245–251, *245*
　　overview, 236–237
　　process of, 240–245, *241*
　　staff opinion surveys, 252–255
　　types of, *237*–240
　　See also analytical surveys; descriptive
　　　surveys
SWOT (Strengths, Weaknesses, Opportunities
　　and Threats) analysis, 48
symbolic interactionism
　　ethnography and, 440, 459
　　overview, 23–24
systematic sampling, 210, *212*
systems evaluations, 305–306, **306**

t-tests, 575
team presentations, 668–670, *668*
technical reports, 519–520, 638–642
teleological approach, 69, **69**
telephone interviews, 251, 378, 404–405, **405**
thematic analysis, 609–611, *610*
theoretical literature, 175–176
theoretical sampling, 222, 604, 617
theoretical sensitivity, 175, 620
theory
　　case studies and, 282
　　overview, 5–6, *19*, 21–29
　　See also deduction; induction
theses
　　as reference sources, 107
　　as secondary data, 521
　　structure of, 642–644
thick descriptions, 30
time management, 43–44, 50, *51*, 61, 635–636
time sampling, 310, 430

time-series analysis, 285–286
Total Quality Management (TQM) process,
　　301, *302*
total survey error (TSE), 256
transcription, 604
transcriptions, 398
triangulation
　　ethnography and, 462
　　mixed methods research and, 195,
　　　196–197, **198**
　　non-participant observation and,
　　　430–431
　　overview, 37
　　types of, 184–185
trustworthiness, 185, **186**
two-tailed test, 571
Type I error, 570–571, **571**
Type II error, 570–571, **571**
typical case sampling, 217–218

uncontrolled variables, 240
units of analysis
　　case studies and, 271, 275–276
　　ethnography and, 24
　　focus groups and, 483
　　phenomenology and, 24
　　qualitative research design and, 171
unobtrusive data
　　archives and, 108, 498, 516–517
　　digital archives and, 502–505
　　documents and, 502
　　ethics and, 506–508
　　non-participant observation and,
　　　428–429
　　overview, 178–179
　　physical measures, 498–502
unstructured interviews, **387**

validation, 307–308
validity
　　case studies and, 279–281
　　ethnography and, 461–462
　　evaluations and, 316–317
　　interviews and, 388–389
　　non-participant observation and, 430
　　qualitative data analysis and, 622–624, **623**
　　qualitative research and, 182–184, **183**
　　quantitative research and, 150–153, *151*
　　questionnaires and, 375
　　surveys and, 261–262, **261**
variables
　　case studies and, 283–285, *283*
　　experimental research and, 135–136, *136*
　　quasi-experimental research and, 137–138
　　See also dependent variables; independent
　　　variables
variance, 256, 568
video calls, 405

video recordings
    action research and, 340–341
    interviews and, 397
visual aids, 665–666, **666**
visual records, 521
viva voces, 660, 670–676, **672**, **675**

web-based questionnaires, 371, 373

web surveys, 258
Whitaker's Almanack, 522
Wikipedia, 109
Wilcoxon signed-ranks test, 575
wordiness, 652, **653**
work schedule, 61

yearbooks, 522